T0215748

Lecture Notes in Computer Science 9999

More information about this series at http://www.springer.com/series/7407

Petro Lutsyk · Jonas Oberhauser · Wolfgang J. Paul

A Pipelined Multi-Core Machine with Operating System Support

Hardware Implementation and Correctness Proof

Authors
Petro Lutsyk
Saarland University
Saarbrücken, Germany

Jonas Oberhauser
Saarland University
Saarbrücken, Germany

Wolfgang J. Paul
Saarland University
Saarbrücken, Germany

ISSN 0302-9743 ISSN 1611-3349 (electronic)
Lecture Notes in Computer Science
ISBN 978-3-030-43242-3 ISBN 978-3-030-43243-0 (eBook)
https://doi.org/10.1007/978-3-030-43243-0

LNCS Sublibrary: SL1 – Theoretical Computer Science and General Issues

This Springer imprint is published by the registered company Springer Nature Switzerland AG
The registered company address is: Gewerbestrasse 11, 6330 Cham, Switzerland

Preface

Building on previous work, we present at the gate level construction and correctness proof of a multi-core machine with pipelined processors and extensive operating system support. More precisely, the machine under consideration has the following features:

- MIPS instruction set architecture (ISA) for application and for system programming
- cache coherent memory system
- store buffers in front of the data caches
- interrupts and exceptions
- memory management units (MMUs)
- pipelined processors: the classical five-stage pipeline is extended by two pipeline stages for address translation
- local interrupt controller (ICs) supporting inter-processor interrupts (IPIs)
- I/O-interrupt controller and a disk

An overall correctness proof for such a machine poses several challenges, which are overcome with the following technical contributions:

- a new pipeline control which allows rollbacks of instructions from multiple pipeline stages while allowing to complete memory accesses that have already started
- a new induction scheme which permits to treat all rollbacks in such a pipeline in a uniformed way
- modeling of ISA by a nondeterministic transition system with guard conditions
- proof technology for exploiting software conditions in such a machine, which only have to hold if the ISA computation abstracted from the hardware computation obeys the guard conditions

February 2020

Petro Lutsyk
Jonas Oberhauser
Wolfgang J. Paul

Contents

Contents

1

Introductory Material

Building on results from [KMP14] we present at the gate level construction and correctness proof of a multi-core machine with pipelined processors and extensive operating system support. More precisely, the machine under consideration has the following features.

- MIPS instruction set architecture (ISA) for application and for system programming
- cache coherent memory system
- store buffers in front of the data caches
- interrupts and exceptions
- memory management units (MMUs)
- pipelined processors: the classical five-stage pipeline is extended by two pipeline stages for address translation
- local interrupt controller (ICs) supporting inter-processor interrupts (IPIs)
- I/O-interrupt controller and a disk

In a sense this text is self-contained; all terminology used throughout this book comes with an explanation. This includes in particular the notation for formulating the results from [KMP14] that we use without repeating the proofs. Section 1.1 contains a few short remarks about the possible relevance of this work. In Sect. 1.2 we give an overview of the book, where we outline in a single place the overall correctness theory for the hardware of multi-core processors. In section 1.3 we summarize some relevant mathematical notation.

Acknowledgment: the authors wish to thank Ernie Cohen, Alfred Hofmann, Holger Herrmanns, Kurt Mehlhorn and Raimund Seidel. Without their definitions, encouragement and support it would have been impossible to complete this work.

© Springer Nature Switzerland AG 2020
P. Lutsyk et al. (Eds.): A Pipelined Multi-Core Machine, LNCS 9999, pp. 1–28, 2020.
https://doi.org/10.1007/978-3-030-43243-0_1

1.1 So What?

In previous textbooks [KMP14, PBLS16] we have stressed that all classes of any kind of architecture (buildings, computer architecture, system architecture) should provide both prototype constructions and explanations for why these constructions work. We have also stressed that mathematical correctness proofs are an extremely fast and efficient way to provide these explanations. Moreover, such proofs have served in the past and can serve in the future as blueprints for formal verification work [LS09]. With this work there might be more benefits.

1.1.1 The Element of Chance in Multi-Core Programming

Documentation of ISA usually comes in two parts: a first part for user programs (*ISA-u*) and a larger and more complex second part for system programmers (*ISA-sp*). If one wishes to show the correctness of an *entire* processor, one obviously has to deal with the hardware implementing the complete ISA-sp too. The only published correctness proofs for the hardware of multi-core machines we are aware of are i) [KMP14] presenting detailed constructions and paper and pencil proofs for ISA-u and ii) [VCAD15] reporting about the formal verification of a multi-core machine with interrupts and exceptions. By adding MMUs, store buffers, IPIs and devices we end up here with a proof that the processor hardware implements a *complete ISA* which supports system programming in a reasonably comfortable way.

We quickly contrast this with the state of the art for commercial processors. There,

- ISA is complex and documented in a somewhat lengthy way.
- getting the implementation right is highly nontrivial and certainly done without a correctness proof for the entire processor.
- the errors which necessarily remain in the delivered products are documented in errata lists which are carefully updated and closely watched, in particular by developers of real time systems. Readers who find this hard to believe are encouraged to use 'processor errata list' in a search engine.

As there is no way of knowing that such an errata list is complete, and as all software is either — to a very small extent — written in ISA or compiled into ISA, *all programming of multi-core processors presently contains an element of chance.* The mathematical techniques provided in this text might be sufficient to remove this element of chance.

1.1.2 Standards and Verification in Classical Architecture versus System Architecture

When edifices like buildings or bridges collapse today — not 300 years back — we are really surprised. When our operating systems don't receive updates in regular short time intervals to prevent imminent collapse, we are really surprised too. The fundamental reason why edifices almost never collapse is amazingly simple:

- in order to erect an edifice at a particular location a permit is required.
- the permit can only be obtained if one presents a *complete proof* of the stability of the planned edifice at the intended location. We stress: proof in the 'naive' mathematical sense, not tests.
- the methodology to state the desired results and to produce the required proofs is well understood, *and* industry standards (for instance DIN 1053 in Germany for the construction of walls) require that this methodology be followed.
- there is also a well established profession of scientists who produce the desired proofs. They are the *exact* counter parts of verification engineers in computer science and are called *structural engineers*; in German: Statiker.
- as a side remark we add that in Germany even a master mason (a professional degree of the dual education system, *not* a university degree) is required to be able to check the corresponding calculations for simple buildings.

A quick comparison with computer system reveals:

- many systems (in particular real time systems) are required to conform to various safety standards and certification levels.
- standards only prescribe methods to be followed: in a nutshell the design and the tests procedures performed have to be documented at a level of detail which permits to track the source of mistakes in case things go wrong.
- even for basic components of computer systems like processors, compilers, and operating system kernels there is no consensus how correctness should be stated and certainly no standardized method for establishing that correctness.

As a computer scientist one is immediately tempted to state that the safety standards of classical architecture are impossible for us to reach, simply because 'computer systems are so much more complex than edifices'. A look at the field of structural engineering reveals that the reasons why edifices do not collapse are certainly far from simple. For the proof of stability of a simple house one has to establish among other things:

- the maximal wind pressure; dependent of i) the height of the building (wind speed is lower near the ground) ii) location (in Germany greatest on islands of the north sea) iii) the form of the roof. Not so trivial aerodynamics there, but reliable upper bounds are documented in tables. Derived from maximal observed wind speeds by D. Bernoulli's (1700–1782) law.
- the maximal snow load; dependent on i) geographical location ii) altitude above sea level; in Germany greatest in mountain villages of the Alps. iii) shape of the roof (snow falls off steep roofs). Precomputed in tables.
- choice of material for the roof construction. From this one gets i) the weight of the roof construction by a trivial calculation. ii) the structural stability of the beams (usually some quality of construction wood) under various kinds of pressure and tension along or orthogonal to the woods' fiber.
- the size of the beams for the roof construction. Hinges on i) Newtonian mechanics and Differential Calculus (Newton; Leibniz 1646–1716) for the calculation of centers of gravity and moments of force. ii) Elastomechanics, in particular

geometrical moments of inertia of the cross section of beams as discovered by Jakob Bernoulli (1654–1705). iii) The theory of Euler (1707–1783) about the buckling and folding of beams, pillars and walls depending on how they are attached to other walls and beams. Geometrical moments of inertia are tabulated for common shapes of construction wood (for rectangular cross sections — a trivial integral).

- choice of material for ceilings and walls. Again one obtains structural stabilities to calculate with.
- one proceeds to iterate from top to bottom for the ceilings and walls for each story of the house. Previous calculations give the weight of the stories above and the roof. The intended use of the building gives prescribed additional weights (traffic loads). Walls and pillars of each story have to sustain the pressure of the buildings structure from above, the traffic load without buckling or bending. Also no part of the building should be tipped over by the horizontal pressure of wind or the earth surrounding the walls of cellars.
- the foundations of the building (usually some variety of concrete) should be wide enough, such that the ground at the intended location of the edifice can absorb the pressure resulting from the building (including the foundation).

Teaching how to apply this method cookbook style takes about 200 pages [Kri15]. Teaching the underlying theories from physics takes another 500 pages [GHSW16, GHSW14]. Surprisingly enough this is quite comparable to the 300 pages of [KMP14] and the 600 pages of this text which we needed to establish with all explanations the correctness of a quite complex processor starting out from gates, registers, and drivers; and the order in which we presented the topics can of course — at least in theory — be turned both into a cookbook style methodology and into an industry standard for the development of correct processors. Although this is — as we pointed out before — a prerequisite for the development of really secure software of any kind, it may take time to happen. The first version of the aforementioned German industry standard DIN 1053 was established in 1937, that is 154 years after the death of Euler.

1.2 Overview

Some very basic mathematical notations are summarized at the end of this introductory chapter in section 1.3. Not surprisingly we touch concepts like set theory and boolean algebra, but due to the central role of memory, memory accesses (including read-modify-write) and memory embeddings in this text, we also choose to place the related basic definitions at this very exposed and easy to lookup place.

The processor designs and correctness proofs of this text are based on results of [KMP14]. They are also the largest designs for which correctness proofs have been attempted so far. As theories evolve and become more general, several things happen every now and then to their older parts:

- notation proves to be inadequate and needs to be generalized and/or simplified in order to deal with increased complexity in the larger theory. For this purpose we will follow ideas from computer aided design (CAD) systems for hierarchical designs, which allow the use of *local* and hence much shorter names for signals and hardware components. Syntax and semantics of the hardware design language that we use are developed in chapter 2. This is not completely trivial: along the same lines you could define the semantics of a sufficiently powerful subset of languages like VERILOG or VHDL.
- errors or gaps (hopefully few) in proofs are discovered and (hopefully) fixed.
- simpler new proofs are found.

As a consequence of these changes triggered by the new parts of the theory, also the old parts become streamlined. The purpose of chapters 3 through 6 is to summarize the results of [KMP14] in *streamlined* form. Hardware constructions and proofs are only repeated if they are modified or further developed in later portions of this text. Otherwise only specifications of hardware units resp. statements of lemmas are given, and the reader is referred to [KMP14] for constructions and proofs.

In Chap. 3 we present a library of building blocks for use in later designs: basic circuits, control automata, various designs of multi-port memory and (provably correct) control of tri-state buses. The greatest part of the library of these standard hardware components (schematics symbols and specifications) is copied without constructions and proofs from [KMP14]. Notable extensions (with constructions and proofs) are i) in section 3.3.6 a memory design supporting a 'compare and swap (CAS)' primitive and ii) in section 3.4.2 a particular form of latch, optimized to stabilize the inputs of cache memories in the case of rollbacks due to misspeculation. Control of tri-state buses is treated in a fairly detailed way in section 3.5. In particular we phrase correctness as: if request signals obey operating conditions until cycle $t - 1$ then data is correctly transmitted in cycle t[1]. This will permit to argue by induction at a subtle place of the correctness proof for a machine with inter-processor interrupts.

Chapter 4 contains the specification of basic MIPS ISA and the straightforward non-pipelined single-core processor construction from [KMP14]. We did, however, very slightly rearrange the material in several ways which speed up things later. i) CAS and move instructions are already included in the basic ISA. As a consequence the data paths of the implementation are extended by a few multiplexers and a special purpose register file, and the main memory has to be able to support CAS operations. If one postpones this until the treatment of exceptions, one has to revisit and embellish the existing correctness proof for the data paths with completely known arguments, and the repetition of known arguments costs time. ii) the main argument about the correctness of the shifters for loads and stores (used to shift words, half words and bytes to the appropriate portions of cache lines) is now formulated in

---

[1] Obviously data transmission trails requests here by one cycle. This is due to a pipeline stage in the bus control which prevents, that at the same clock edge one tri-state driver is enabled and a different driver is disabled. Section 3.5.1 gives a striking argument why this should be prevented.

the terms of the ISA memory $c.m$ resp. its double word addressable version $\ell(c.m)$ and not in terms of the (double word addressable) hardware memory $h.m$. Nothing is gained or lost by this here, but it permits later (as in [Krö01]) to argue about the correctness of pipelined implementations without referring to intermediate sequential reference implementations. iii) the partition of the data paths into pipeline stages (still without the pipeline registers) is also already introduced here, and the correctness lemmas for theses stages are formulated such that they can be used in literally identical form in the correctness proofs of pipelined and of sequential machines.

Also, starting at section 4.1.11 we begin to track software conditions (like alignment) with more formalism than in previous texts. The reason for this increased rigor comes from later chapters, where arguments about software conditions become much more subtle than one would expect.

In the comparatively short Chap. 5 we review the construction and correctness proofs of processors with a classical five-stage pipeline and a multi-port memory with a single cycle access time from [KMP14] and [MP00]. The previous texts have been streamlined in 5 places: i) like in Chap. 4 the special purpose register file is already included. As forwarding circuits from the general and special purpose register files are completely analogous, we can deal with both subjects at the same place. ii) the special purpose register file is now in stage 4 (the memory stage) as opposed to stage 5 in [MP00] and formally verified versions of that text. This saves a few gates in forwarding circuits. iii) as mentioned before correctness proofs are directly done with respect to ISA and not to the sequential reference implementation, which in our case would be the machine from Chap. 4. iv) a simpler proof is supplied for the crucial lemma that scheduling functions increase at full pipeline stages. v) self modifying code is allowed as in [MP00].

The construction and correctness proof of a cache coherent shared memory system (short: cache memory system, CMS) based on the MOESI protocol [SS86] is by far the longest and technically most involved part of [KMP14]. Fortunately it suffices to review in Chap. 6 the processor interface and the specification of this memory system. We proceed to replace in the *single-core* pipeline from Chap. 5 the multi-port RAM by a cache memory system with two caches: an instruction cache and a data cache (even in a single processor pipeline, these caches are better kept consistent). Then we present a streamlined correctness proof for the multi-core machine with pipelined processors from [KMP14]: i) correctness is shown directly relative to ISA, i.e., without reference to a sequential reference implementation. ii) also the new proof only uses the fact that the cache memory system in sequentially consistent and not the property of the implementation that reads and writes to the same address cannot end in the same cycle.

Software conditions are treated without any hand waving. The cache memory system we use has a ROM portion, which obviously cannot be updated by writes. Hence there is an operating condition opc for the CMS requiring that hardware writes must avoid the ROM portion; not just when the access ends but in *every* hardware cycle. The corresponding software condition in ISA is denoted by SC_{ROM}. The argument, that the software condition for ISA implies the operating condition for hardware is still straight forward, but now we explicitly state this in lemma 88 and give a detailed proof.

For readers familiar with [KMP14] the chapter contains a large exercise showing how one can extend the cache memory system such that it can handle several memory modes, in particular write-through mode. Section 6.5 contains the list of known typos and errata found in [KMP14] as well as their fixes.

In Chap. 7 we modify the pipeline control such that it can handle exceptions and interrupts, as well as rollbacks due to misspeculation. Although similar material is covered in [MP00, Krö01, BJK$^+$03], we choose to adjust specifications, constructions and proofs in several and sometimes major ways. The straight forward changes are: i) the list of possible interrupt and exception signals is modified to include misalignment signals computed in the processor core, page faults and general protection faults computed by memory management units (MMUs), as well as start up, 'init' (software reset), and external interrupts to be delivered by the local interrupt controllers (IC). With the exception of the misalignment signals for fetch and load/store, the new signals are still tied to zero, so this extension amounts *for the time being* to trivial bookkeeping. ii) The availability of misalignment signals adds a new case split to the pipeline correctness proof: usually it involves a case split on the content of the instruction register, but in case of a misaligned program counter no instruction is fetched at all, thus the instruction register is not even used iii) The 'exception return (eret)' instruction is implemented such that it drains the pipe. This permits to formulate the software condition for self modifying code as follows: between a write to a location and a fetch from this location an 'eret' instruction must be executed. As page fault handlers (in particular for pages with code) tend to end with an 'eret' instruction, this is a very natural condition.

Now for the major changes. iv) As in [BJK$^+$03] we have to deal with the additional complication that one has to wait until ongoing accesses to the cache memory system have finished before one can roll back a pipeline stage, but due to accesses by the MMUs this will later happen in more stages. Attempts to handle these extra difficulties in an ad-hoc way turned out to be extremely error prone, and we finally resorted to a systematic solution by the construction and analysis of a new and more general stall engine (section 7.4). If an instruction must be rolled back, which is currently accessing the cache memory system *and* this access has not finished, then rollback is performed in two phases: first it is marked 'pending' until the memory access has finished; then rollback is performed and the pipeline stages involved are marked 'not full'.

iv) the largest deviation from previous work concerns the overall induction scheme used from now on in the processor correctness proofs. As in [Krö01] we exploit that interrupts can be viewed as a special case of misspeculation (one speculates the absence of interrupts), and as in [Krö01] we could use speculation functions for the analysis. Indeed [Lut18] contains a correctness proof of a pipelined multi-core machine with interrupts — i.e. counter part of chapters 7, 9 and 11 of this text — along these lines. The reason we have chosen a different approach only becomes apparent if one treats several successively more complex machines in the same text (which is obviously desirable in a textbook or in a series of lectures). The core technical definition has to identify pipeline stages, for which correctness is not and *can not be* shown because the stage contains misspeculated data. Speculation functions identify the lowest pipeline stage which is interrupted in ISA but where this has not yet been discovered in hardware, thus essentially by stating the failure of a simulation relation involving both hardware and ISA. There is necessarily a mathematical theory relating the interplay of the ISA dependent speculation functions with the stall engine; and as machines and ISA evolve part of that theory has to be restated and proven anew. As always hand-waving is possible stating that proofs are along known lines, but this concerns extremely technical proofs. Instead we have opted for a *purely hardware dependent* definition of stages where we claim simulation of ISA instruction i in cycle t: the stages with instruction i will not be rolled back in cycles $\hat{t} \geq t$ and — for the purpose of showing that instructions below i eventually reach the stage where the interrupt signal is computed — all instructions below will eventually leave the pipe. Of course this is only meaningful if we also prove liveness.

v) this change of definitions does not go unnoticed in the proof, which is so far by induction on hardware cycles t. When we consider in cycle t a stage with an instruction i, that is not rolled back in hardware, we can obviously conclude, that instructions $j < i$ further down in the pipeline will also not be rolled back in hardware, but in the absence of speculation functions this does not allow anymore to conclude, that such instructions j are not interrupted in ISA: if one argues cycle by cycle this is only established when the interrupt signal of instruction j is computed, and this might only be in a future cycle $\hat{t} > t$. This problem is 'simply' remedied by a *change of the overall induction scheme*. We prove correctness by a double induction. The outer induction is on ISA instructions i. In the inner induction one shows correctness of simulation of instruction i for *all cycles* t[2]. In the situation described above one now has correct simulation of instructions j in future cycles; as they are not rolled back in hardware (otherwise i would be rolled back) their hardware interrupt signal will be off, and by induction hypothesis for $j < i$ (outer induction) instruction j is not interrupted in ISA. Admittedly one has to get used to this order of proof steps, but for the time being, i.e. for this chapter, it is *only* the order of proof steps. This will change in the next chapter, where for a short moment the new proof scheme skirts but does not meet disaster.

vi) a further sweeping change is in notation within the simulation relation. It is in the nature of pipelines, that register stages have ISA-visible as well as intermediate, invisible registers. Formally we track the progress of ISA instructions i through pipeline stages k during cycles t by scheduling functions/ghost registers I_k^t, where $I_k^t = i$ means that the visible registers of stage k contain relevant data for execution of instruction i. During the same cycle t the invisible registers of the same stage k contain intermediate data for the execution of instruction $i - 1$. For an outer induction on i it is more convenient to collect statements about the correct simulation of instruction i in a relation $t \sim i$ which gathers for stages k with $I_k^t = i$ the correctness statement of visible registers of stage k and the invisible registers of the stage $k - 1$ above.

---

[2] Note that this is a sort of 'flushing' [BD94]

This is the complete list of changes. With this long and technically involved chapter interrupt control clearly lives up to its reputation of being hard. On the other hand introducing a new stall engine permitting pending rollbacks is just the right thing to do. Changing the order of an induction scheme (together with an adjustment of notation to make this more comfortable) such that known arguments go through is not such a dramatic thing to do. And as future chapters will show: this does the job.

In chapter 8 the hardware of the machine is not changed at all, but an enriched *nondeterministic* ISA is defined, which allows to specify in a limited way what happens if software conditions about self modifying code are *not* satisfied. ISA configurations c get as a new component $c.ib$ an *instruction buffer*. Instruction buffer entries (a, I) of nondeterministically/speculatively chosen addresses a and instructions I, which are stored in memory at this address, can be prefetched into the instruction buffer at any time. Upon execution of an instruction with (delayed) program counter $dpc = a$ the instruction is not any more looked up in memory. Instead the instruction buffer is used as an associative memory: *if* an entry (a, I) is in the instruction buffer (there might be several), then one of them is chosen nondeterministically for execution. Instruction buffers are flushed when the mode of the machine changes, i.e. at interrupts and 'eret' instructions.

We don't blame the reader if he or she is surprised and suspicious about the use of nondeterminism and *guard conditions* like $(c.dpc, I) \in c.ib$ in a field as down to earth as computer architecture. But we choose to clarify here and now that this is about as far from abstract nonsense as one can get. i) in the end of the chapter we show that *if* software fulfills the old software condition about self modifying code, then we get the old ISA back. Such a result is called an *instruction buffer reduction theorem*. ii) if user programs run on a machine with an operating system, then the programmers of the operating system can only control software conditions of their own programs. If there is no specification whatsoever for what happens if user programs violate a software condition, then the operating system manufacturer has *no* information what happens in the next step of such a computation, and thus *no way to guarantee integrity of the operating system and the other user programs*. In contrast, we know with the instruction buffer model, that the user program will always execute *some* legal instruction or produce an illegal interrupt.

Technically there is quite a bit of action in this chapter. Obviously we have to choose a formalism to specify nondeterministic ISA for the current and all future machines in this text. Basically we use oracle inputs to specify nondeterminstic choices. More precisely we follow [Sch13] — the work which basically served as specification of the entire machine constructed in this text — and specify nondeterministic choices *and* ISA visible external inputs for step n of an ISA computation by the value $s(n) = (u, x_1, \ldots, x_n)$ of a *stepping function* where u specifies the unit (here processor or instruction buffer) making the step and $x_1, \ldots, x_n$ specify the parameters of the step which disambiguate nondeterministic choices. For processor steps (with $u = p$) one of these parameters $x_i = e$ specifies the ISA visible external input e. As in [KMP14] an ISA instruction is generated, when the memory stage of the pipeline is updated.

In the correctness proof we basically encounter four new techniques, three of which are not surprising at all. i) in order to reuse the old pipeline correctness proofs we have to couple global ISA steps n with local processor steps (section 8.2.3) ii) when we extract a stepping function from the hardware computation for a hardware cycle t, where an instruction is fetched from an address a and data is written to an address b, then we have to generate two ISA steps: an instruction buffer prefetch and a processor write. If addresses a and b are equal [3], we have to order the ISA steps by the sequentially consistent local order of the corresponding accesses in the CMS. iii) the ISA computation with the extracted stepping function has to obey the guard conditions. Thus once a committed (!) instruction i is fetched in hardware (and prefetched in the ISA instruction buffer), we have to argue that it stays there until the instruction reaches the memory stage. The instruction buffer won't be flushed by an interrupt because instruction i is committed. The instruction buffer is also not flushed by an 'eret' instruction in the pipe, because the pipe is drained behind 'eret' instructions. Thus a fetched instruction i behind an 'eret' instruction in the pipe is not possible.

iv) Please fasten seat belts. Clearly, we can only require software conditions to hold for ISA computations generated by stepping functions, where the guard conditions are satisfied. Checking for a software condition $SC(c^n)$ of ISA steps n the guard conditions $\gamma(c^m)$ of future steps $m > n$ makes no sense, thus software conditions for step n should already hold, if guard conditions for the present and past steps $m \leq n$ hold.

Now it looks like we can imply for each cycle t the operating condition opc^t of the cache memory system from the corresponding software condition SC_{ROM} in a straight forward way: consider a memory access by the fetch or memory stage in cycle t and corresponding ISA step n. We establish as above that the guard conditions hold until step n. Thus the software conditions hold until step n, the software does not write to the ROM region, by the simulation relation for ISA instruction n and (inner induction) cycle t we conclude the access belonging to instruction n does not violate the operating condition opc^t. All is fine for this access, *but* the function of the cache memory system will also cease to be specified if a concurrent access to a different port, which violates the operating condition, has started, say in a cycle $\hat{t} \leq t$ but not finished. Then the corresponding ISA step m is only generated later, i.e. we have $m > n$ and with an outer induction on ISA instructions n and m we have proven *nothing yet* about ISA instruction m.

Obviously in such a situation a different oder of the ISA steps would be highly desirable, and indeed we change the order of generating ISA instructions *in exactly this situation* where all would be lost anyway: if a write violating the operating conditions enters the input registers of the memory stage in cycle $\hat{t}$ we generate the corresponding ISA instruction m immediately. We infer guard and software conditions for step m and find from the coupling relation for instruction m and cycle $\hat{t}$ the very pleasant contradiction that the operating condition $opc^{\hat{t}}$ does hold for this ac-

---

[3] This does not happen in the CMS constructed in [KMP14] but it is allowed by the CMS specification we use.

cess. This shows, that this case split in the definition of the stepping function, which we called *emergency braking*, is never taken (lemma 169). From this point on the basic proof machinery of this text will not change.

Chapter 9 builds on results from [Sch14] and [Lut18]. It is devoted to various aspects of address translation and the related constructions and proof techniques. In a nutshell multilevel address translation (and the signaling of page faults) is achieved by pointer chasing through a graph of pages called page tables. Following a suggestion of E. Cohen we model this in ISA as a speculative and nondeterministic process of *walk creations* and *walk extensions*, where *walks* are either complete translations or incomplete paths. The new component in the ISA is a translation look aside buffer (TLB, a software controlled cache for translations), which models both the translations stored in the hardware TLB and the walks which the hardware MMUs are currently trying to extend. Obviously we have to construct hardware TLBs (based on an associative memory) as well as MMUs, and we have to analyze their interaction with cache ports. Rollbacks lead to aborted translation requests, which nevertheless have to complete their memory accesses; this is handled by control automata of the MMU and leads to some bookkeeping in the correctness proofs.

Address translation and page table walking only takes place in user mode. The pipeline is extended by two new stages, each with its own MMU: i) an 'instruction translate' stage IT for the translation of the instruction address and ii) an 'effective address translate translate' stage ET for the translation of the effective address. In system mode the new stages are just bypassed. We provide access of the memory management units to the cache memory system in a somewhat brute force way by providing each MMU with a separate cache[4].

Due to the extra stage above the instruction register, the instruction set has a second delay slot which in hardware is implemented with an additional 'delayed delayed PC' denoted by $ddpc$. As a consequence there is a new situation for rollback: if the decode stage ID discovers that an 'eret' instruction has been fetched, then stage IT has to be rolled back.

Although our MMUs are extremely simple and maintain at every time at most one one translation per virtual address, the user sees nondeterministic behavior, because the size of the hardware TLB is not revealed. Suppose i) a translation for page address a is present in the hardware TLB ii) the page tables defining this translation are subsequently updated such that they define a new translation, but the stale translation in the hardware TLB is not invalidated and expelled from the hardware TLB by an 'invlpg' instruction. iii) later virtual address a is used again. Then the user cannot predict the translation that the hardware will deliver. Although there was no 'invlpg' instruction, the stale translation may have been evicted from the TLB simply due to the limited size of this cache. Then the MMU will retranslate and the user gets the updated translation. If however the stale translation was not evicted, then the MMU will have a TLB hit and deliver the stale translation. If one of several walks can be

---

[4] Connecting the MMUs to the two existing caches is of course possible. But this requires arbitration between the pipeline and the MMUs, and we postponed arguing about the correctness of such a scheme to future work.

expected, then the choice of the walks w_I and w_E used for translation is yet another place where the nondeterministic ISA depends on its oracle inputs. Execution of an instruction in translated mode then depends on the guard condition that the walks used for translation currently reside in the ISA-TLB.

Overall proof technology is extended in three places, two of them obvious: i) the main induction hypothesis now also couples the hardware MMUs with the ISA TLB stating that walks present in the hardware TLBs and the walks being initialized or extended in the two MMUs are all contained in the ISA TLB (which has unlimited size). Whenever any of the hardware MMUs initializes or extends a walk, we make in ISA a TLB step, moving this walk into the ISA TLB. ii) we have to prove the guard conditions for walks. For this purpose in user mode walks w_I and w_E are sampled once they are delivered by the MMUs into the output registers of stages IT and ET. That they are in the ISA TLB follows from the main induction hypothesis. That they are not expelled from the ISA TLB until the instruction under consideration leaves the memory stage follows from the fact that instructions which perform this task are only legal in system mode and that a change from user to system mode cannot occur for committed instructions.

iii) there is a subtle new rule for the ordering of ISA steps for the same hardware cycle t. Suppose the stepping function creates a walk creation or extension steps n and a processor step with an interrupts m for the same cycle. Then the TLB step should be legal in ISA, because the hardware performs it. If we would step the processor in ISA first, then in ISA the mode would switch to system mode, where no TLB steps are performed. Thus in this situation the TLB has to be stepped first.

Note that for the time being we are down to a single software condition (no writes to the ROM portion of memory) *and* the operating system designer can enforce it, for instance by i) never translating/mapping user pages to the ROM portion of memory *and* ii) not giving user write permission to page tables so that the user cannot change translations.

Instruction buffers (as part of an extended ISA) and MMUs (in ISA and hardware) both belong to the machine's operating system support, and for well behaved user programs both should be invisible. For user programs this is for instance the case, if the user program does not modify itself and if the page fault handlers of the operating system end with an 'eret' instruction. This follows from the instruction buffer reduction theorem, and thus the reader should ask for a corresponding result for MMUs. Such results exist and are indeed of overwhelming importance: if page tables are properly set up, then *with help of the MMUs* the virtualization layer of the operating system simulates for each user u a virtual machine M_u *without MMUs*. In user mode user u then 'sees' his program run on his own virtual machine M_u. For construction and correctness proof of such a virtualization layer in textbook style see chapter 15 of [PBLS16]. For a mechanically verified version see [APST10].

Chapter 10 builds on work in [Lut14] and introduces store buffers. They are put in front of the data caches of each processor and buffer store requests in case the memory system is busy. Read requests now have to check for *store buffer hits*: pending writes to the same address as the read request. In case one or more such hits exist, data is *forwarded* from the store buffer; in case of several hits one obviously forwards from the latest such hit. Also data cache access now requires arbitration between read requests that cannot be answered by store buffer forwarding and write requests from the store buffer. In case of single-core machines one can show (with a nontrivial proof) that store buffers are invisible for the programmer and thus do not affect the ISA. But for multi-core machines, where they happen to destroy sequential consistency, they need to be visible in ISA. Therefore we make them already visible for single core ISA and extend ISA configurations c by a store buffer component $c.sb$.

The 'CAS' instructions as well as a new 'fence' instruction have the effect of flushing the store buffer. Store instructions write to the store buffer. Transmission of a write request from the head of the store buffer to the data cache is in ISA now a *store buffer step*.

The construction of hardware store buffers boils down to the construction of an optimized hardware queue (section 10.3). Very little happens in the overall structure of the processor correctness proof. The main induction hypothesis couples hardware store buffer and ISA store buffer in the almost obvious way stating that they are equal before each hardware cycle t and before any ISA step for cycle t is performed. In the induction steps one has however to argue about intermediate ISA configurations and match them with ghost store buffer components of the hardware. We illustrate this with the *stepping diagrams* introduced in section 10.5.3.

Also there is a new situation where the order of ISA steps generated for the same hardware cycle t becomes important. If a request is moved from the head of the store buffer to the cache by a store buffer step while its data are forwarded thereby stepping a load instruction of the processor core then — due to the pipelining — the hardware executes both instructions. This should be visible for the programmer. Therefore in ISA we have to step the processor load instruction (which uses the data from the store buffer) before the store buffer.

We conclude the chapter with a limited and easy enough to prove *store buffer reduction theorem*, stating that store buffers are invisible for ISA programs which obey some fairly natural software conditions.

In chapter 11 we arrive at the construction and hardware correctness proof of multi-core processors. Constructions and correctness proof are very much along the lines of chapter 9 of [KMP14]. However much less work is left to do. Clearly the technology used throughout this text for dealing with instruction sets, where several units are stepped in a nondeterministic way, stems from our previous work; but it has already been introduced in chapter 8 for the treatment of instruction buffers, and it has been reused in all chapters since.

Defining ISA of a multi-core machine with P processors is completely straight forward: configurations c now have *arrays* of units $c.x(q)$ with $x \in \{p, ib, tlb, sb\}$ and $q \in [0 : P-1]$ as well as a single shared memory $c.m$. Values of stepping functions $s(n) = (x(q), \ldots)$ define a step of unit x of processor q in step n. For the semantics of such a step one applies the old transition function for single core processors to the units $c^n.y(q)$ for processor q and the common shared memory $c^n.m$; other components are left unchanged. It is as simple as that.

Hardware construction is *now* equally straight forward: connect the $4P$ ports of the p processors – which were not easy to construct – to a cache memory system with $4P$ ports – which was not easy to construct either. End of construction.

Proof technology for several units connected to a common shared memory stays unchanged. In particular in each cycle t we step as before in ISA units, whose memory access ends in cycle t in the order defined by the sequentially consistent memory for the memory accesses generated by these steps.

The only extension of formalism in the correctness proof stems from the fact, that now more than one data access can end in a single cycle t, and at some point we have to introduce bookkeeping about the interleaving of the remaining accesses with these steps (section 11.4.7).

We conclude this chapter with the definition of a software discipline, which makes instruction buffers in the shared memory machine invisible: between a write of an instruction by processor p and a subsequent fetch of this instruction by processor q, the fetching processor q must perform an 'eret' instruction. This condition is easy enough to state and permits to prove an instruction buffer reduction theorem exactly along the liens of section 8.4. However it requires synchronization between processors, for which our machine still lacks adequate mechanisms. This is remedied in the next chapter.

Building on work in [Sch16] we provide processors with local interrupt controllers (*ICs*) in chapter 12. In ISA we model ICs as a simplified version of the advanced processor interrupt controllers (APICs) of the x86 architecture. ICs are memory mapped devices permitting to send and deliver inter-processor interrupts (IPIs), in particular interrupts, which start up a processor running or shut it down. Writing command registers and reading status registers of devices is done by store buffer or processor steps accessing the memory system. The broadcast of an IPI over the interrupt bus to other ICs and the signaling of the existence of such an interrupt to the processor by activation of the external interrupt event signal e are modeled in two separate ISA steps. A new software condition SC_{APIC} is introduced which essentially states, that once a command to deliver an IPI is issued (via the store buffer), that command cannot be withdrawn and no new command can be issued before the old command is executed.

The construction of hardware for interrupt controllers along the lines of their ISA specification succeeds without major difficulty. As interrupt bus we use the tri-state bus and its control which we carefully analyzed previously in section 3.5. The arbiter of that control is obviously needed in situations where several ICs simultaneously try to transmit interrupts. Surprises in the hardware construction, if any, arise in two places: i) after an interrupt request was received, the memory stage is first drained, before the hardware is allowed to activated the external event signal e. This is a technical consequence of the fact that external interrupts are of type *repeat* and therefore have to be sampled above the memory stage, where they can prevent the activation of memory request signals ii) external interrupts drain both in ISA and in hardware the local store buffers. The reason for this comes from software: for the purpose of synchronization one keeps at least a small portion of the shared memory (including the locks) sequentially consistent by brute force. This region is only accessed (e.g., by

'CAS' instructions) after the local store buffer is drained. In an analogous way one wishes to keep the external interrupts signals delivered to the processors sequentially consistent; as the software cannot prepare for the reception of an external interrupt, the corresponding flush of the local store buffer has to be performed automatically by the hardware. Based on ideas from [CS10] these mechanisms can be used in a nontrivial software discipline which permits to simulate by the full machines *as constructed here* with store buffers the same machines with store buffers removed and hence with sequentially consistent memory. For a specification of that discipline and a full proof see [Obe17].

Due to new units present the construction of the stepping function, in particular the order of ISA steps for the same hardware cycle, becomes more involved. A typical new case is a situation where an interrupt controller delivers an external interrupt to its local processor and in the same cycle receives a new IPI via the interrupt bus. In the correctness proof however, things get subtle when it comes to the control of the interrupt bus. Interrupt controllers request access to the interrupt bus if they store a request which is yet undelivered as indicated by an active local delivery status bit ds. This bit serves as request signal for the bus arbiter, and by the operating condition $opc\text{-}bc$ of the bus control it is required to stay active until access is granted to the bus. But writing to the APIC's command register *ICR*, which contains bit ds, might clear the bit and withdraw the request. Fortunately this is forbidden by the new software condition SC_{APIC}. Formally we proceed almost as we did with the operating condition opc for the cache memory system, but for technical reasons we can skip emergency braking. In the normal order of proof steps we can establish for every cycle t: if an IPI delivery step n is performed for cycle t, then all ISA instructions $m < n$ obey the guard conditions and hence the software conditions. From this we get the operating conditions of the bus control until cycle $t - 1$ which implies proper data transmission in cycle t.

Note that for practical purposes this chapter is essential: initialization of multicore processors usually proceeds in two steps: i) after reset, a single processor, the *boot processor*, is running and loads the operating system from the disk and sets up some data structures in shared memory. ii) the boot processor wakes up the remaining processors by a SIPI (start IPI) interrupt. Without devices and inter-processor interrupts in the ISA one obviously can neither program this routine nor prove its correctness.

In chapter 13 we incorporate the disk model from [PBLS16] both to ISA and hardware. These disks have two major parts: i) a page addressable proper disk memory (in this text called swap memory) ii) a set of I/O-ports that can be integrated into the entire memory system and thus become accessible by read and write commands of the processor resp. the store buffer. The ports in turn consist of i) a buffer of one page, i.e. 4K words ii) a command and status register and iii) a swap memory address register for addressing a page in swap memory. Disk reads copy the swap memory page addressed by the swap memory address register into the buffer. Disk writes copy the buffer into the swap memory page addressed by the swap memory address register. The disk signals the end of a disk read or disk write by changing the command and status register. While a disk read or disk write is in progress, the processor

processor side is only allowed to poll the command and status register. Also, it is not allowed to issue a disk read and disk write command at the same time. These conditions are formalized as a new operating condition $opc\text{-}d$ for disks. On the software side this leads to a corresponding software condition SC_{DISK}.

We hide the exact duration of disk reads and disk writes both in the hardware and ISA model. With nondeterminism this is easy enough to do: once a disk read or disk write is issued, hardware and ISA *can* perform (in any cycle or instruction) a *disk step* which performs the copy operation between buffer and swap memory and signals the end of the operation in the command and status register.

We provide a single disk which is accessible to all processors. Accesses addressing the disk bypass the caches. In hardware we provide for these accesses a new *device bus*, which is again arbitrated between the processors by the mechanism from section 3.5. Proofs only change in the most obvious way. There is a trivial simulation relation between hardware and ISA disks. The main induction hypothesis now includes guard conditions and operating conditions for the disk. There are new cases in the definition of stepping functions, for instance for hardware cycles t, where the processor polls the command and status register while the disk is busy, and this register is updated at the end of the cycle, because in the next cycle the disk is not busy any more. In this case the disk step is performed after the polling. The proof of the operating conditions for the disk follows the not completely trivial pattern that we know already from the APICs: i) show the guard conditions ii) conclude that software condition SC_{DISK} holds and finally iii) establish the operating condition $opc\text{-}d$ of the disk.

Note that with disks incorporated in the ISA model *and* a formal semantics of C with in-line assembly it is not terribly hard to argue formally about drivers, boot loading and page fault handling of operating system kernels. For details see chapter 15 of [PBLS16].

The disks as defined in chapter 13 produce interrupts signalling the end of disk read and disk write operations. In chapter 13 we still ignored these signals; thus processors could detect the completion of such operations only by polling the command and status register. This is remedied in the final chapter 14, where device interrupts are sampled by I/O APICs. This new kind of device i) samples interrupts from peripheral devices[5], ii) redirects such an interrupt by inter-processor interrupt (IPI) to a local APIC $apic(q)$ and iii) does not collect further interrupts from that device until it receives (also by IPI) and end of interrupt (EOI) message from $apic(q)$ signalling that processor q has serviced the interrupt.

Not surprisingly I/O APICs have much in common with local APICs, thus their specification and incorporation into ISA (including guard and software conditions) succeeds very much along known lines. In hardware they live on the device bus which is already present (and arbitrated) in the machine. Local APICs now request the interrupt bus i) for ordinary inter-processor interrupts but also ii) for EOI interrupts to the APC. A simple adjustment of the arbitration mechanism allows to guarantees that each local APIC eventually gets the interrupt bus for each kind of request. In

---

[5] here only the single disk

the correctness proof we only find the obvious extensions concerning i) simulation relation and guard condition for I/O APIC and ii) interleaving of I/O APIC steps with other ISA steps for the same hardware cycle.

1.3 Basics

This section mostly summarizes material from chapter 2 of [KMP14]. The definition of access based memory semantics has been moved forward (from section 8 of [KMP14]).

1.3.1 Sets, Cross Products and Sequences

We denote by

$$\mathbb{N} = \{0, 1, 2, \dots\}$$

the set of natural numbers *including zero*, by

$$\mathbb{Z} = \{\dots, -2, -1, 0, 1, 2, \dots\}$$

the set of integers, and by

$$\mathbb{B} = \{0, 1\}$$

the set of Boolean values. For $i, j \in \mathbb{N}$ intervals of integers are defined as

$$[i : j] = \{i, i+1, \dots, j\}$$

The cardinality of finite sets A is denoted by $\#A$. Thus

$$i \leq j \quad \rightarrow \quad \#[i : j] = j - i + 1$$

The *Cartesian Product* of two sets A and B is denoted by $A \times B$. It is defined as the set of pairs

$$A \times B = \{(a, b) \mid a \in A \text{ and } b \in B\}$$

Obviously

$$((1, 1), 1) \in (\mathbb{B} \times \mathbb{B}) \times \mathbb{B} \quad \text{and} \quad ((1, 1), 1) \notin \mathbb{B} \times (\mathbb{B} \times \mathbb{B})$$

Thus the Cartesian Product is clearly not associative. Relations between sets A and B are subsets

$$R \subseteq A \times B$$

and functions

$$f : A \rightarrow B$$

are relations $f \subseteq A \times B$ satisfying

$$(a, b) \in f \quad \text{and} \quad (a, b') \in f \rightarrow b = b'$$

For $(a,b) \in f$ one usually writes

$$f(a) = b$$

Thus the identity function id on $\mathbb{B}$ with $id(0) = 0$ and $id(1) = 1$ is formally the set

$$id = \{(0,0),(1,1)\} \subset \mathbb{B} \times \mathbb{B}$$

For functions $f : A \to B$ and set $\hat{A} \subseteq A$ the set

$$f(\hat{A}) = \{f(a) \mid a \in \hat{A}\} \subseteq B$$

is the set of all function values of f with arguments in $\hat{A}$. With $\hat{A} = A$ this gives us the *image* of f

$$im(f) = f(A)$$

The domain $dom(f)$ of a function $f : A \to B$ is the set of all elements $a \in A$ such that $f(a)$ is defined

$$dom(f) = \{a \in A \mid \exists b \in B. \ (a,b) \in f\}$$

The function is called *total* if $dom(f) = A$ and *partial* otherwise. *Sequences a* of *length n* with elements from A are formally defined as functions

$$a : [1 : n] \to A$$

and written as

$$a = (a_1, \ldots, a_n) \quad \text{or} \quad a = a_1 \ldots a_n \quad \text{or} \quad a = a[1 : n] \ .$$

Sequences of length n are also called *n-tuples*. Note that for $n = 2$ the completely common first notation for writing n-tuples is overloaded, because (a,b) stands *both* for the pair (a,b) as an element of some Cartesian product and for the sequence of length 2 (formally a set of two pairs)

$$\{(1,a),(2,b)\} \neq (a,b) \ .$$

In classical mathematics this is hardly ever noticed, because pairs and sequences of length 2 are obviously isomorphic. With correctness proofs for computer systems the situation is slightly more serious. In the process of *formal verification* such definitions and proofs are often formalized and entered into computer aided verification (CAV) systems, which in turn check that the formal proofs are complete. And because CAV systems distinguish very clearly tween pairs and sequences of length 2 we declare here and now:

- our only use of the notation (a,b) for pairs as elements of Cartesian products was in the definition of relations and functions.
- from now on (a,b) only stands for sequences of length 2.

Observe that the *set* of all elements of sequence a is exactly the image of a

$$set(a) = im(a) = \{\, a_i \mid i \in [1:n] \,\}$$

The length of sequence a is n

$$\#a = n$$

We allow ourselves to use the element symbol with lists with the obvious meaning

$$x \in a \quad \leftrightarrow \quad \exists i.\ x = a_i$$

and we use list comprehensions analogous to set comprehensions with the notation

$$(f(x) \mid x \in a)$$

defined by

$$(f(x) \mid x \in a)_i = f(a_i)$$

Note that unlike sets, sequences are ordered, and thus our list comprehension preserves order. For example

$$(x+1 \mid x \in (3,1,4,3)) = (4,2,5,4) \neq (2,4,5)$$

Multiple products $\times_{i=1}^{n} A_i$ of sets A_i are defined as the set of n-tuples with elements $a_i \in A_i$

$$\times_{i=1}^{n} A_i = \{\, (a_1,\ldots,a_n) \mid \forall i.\ a_i \in A_i \,\}$$

For $n = 2$ we again get overloaded notation, because $A \times B$ stands both for the Cartesian product of A and B and for the set of sequences of length 2

$$\{s \mid s : [1:2] \to A \cup B\ s_1 \in A,\ s_2 \in B\} \neq A \times B$$

As above we disambiguate for the future

- our only use of the notation $A \times B$ for the Cartesian products was in the definition of relations and functions.
- from now on $A \times B$ only stands for sets of sequences of length 2.

The set of all sequences of length n with elements from A is denoted by

$$A^n = \times_{i=1}^{n} A = \{a \mid a : [1:n] \to A\}$$

A^0 is defined to contain exactly the *empty sequence* ε.

$$A^0 = \{\varepsilon\}$$

The set of finite sequences of length greater than zero with elements from A is denoted by

$$A^+ = \bigcup_{n=1}^{\infty} A^n$$

the set of finite sequences of any length by

$$A^* = \bigcup_{n \in \mathbb{N}}^{\infty} A^n$$

Note that because of

$$A^1 = \{f : [1 : 1] \to A\} \neq A$$

we have

$$A \not\subseteq A^*$$

Single elements $a \in A$ can be casted to sequences $(a) \in A^1$ of length 1 by

$$dom((a)) = \{1\} , \ (a)(1) = a$$

Concatenation of sequences in A^+ is a function

$$\circ : A^+ \times A^+ \to A^+$$

defined by

$$(a[1 : n] \circ b[1 : m])_i = \begin{cases} a_i & i \leq n \\ b_{i-n} & i > n \end{cases}$$

In many circumstances it is obviously convenient to allow elements of A as operands of concatenation. Thus for

$$a \in A , b \in A^+$$

we extend

$$\circ : (A^+ \cup A) \times (A^+ \cup A) \to A^+$$

by simply casting a:

$$a \circ b = (a) \circ b , \ b \circ a = b \circ (a)$$

The empty sequence is defined as the neutral element of concatenation, i.e., for $a \in A^* \cup A$ we have

$$a \circ \varepsilon = \varepsilon \circ a = a$$

Thus we finally have

$$\circ : (A^* \cup A) \times (A^* \cup A) \to A^* \cup A$$

From our convention about the cross product notation it follows that we never use the notation A^2 for the Cartesian product $A \times A$. It always stands for the set of sequences of length 2 with elements form A. For $A = \mathbb{B}$ we get[6]

$$\mathbb{B}^2 = \{a \mid a : [1,2] \to \mathbb{B}\} = \{(0,0),(0,1),(1,0),(1,1)\}$$

resp.

---

[6] with pair notation for sequences of length 2

$$\mathbb{B}^2 = \{\, 00, 01, 10, 11 \,\}$$

In mathematics, finite or infinite sequences a of elements $a_i \in A$ are usually indexed starting from 1, i.e., they are written as

$$a = (a_1, \ldots, a_n) \quad \text{resp.} \quad a = (a_1, a_2, \ldots).$$

For computations or their sequences of inputs and outputs it is more convenient to start indexing with 0, i.e., to write

$$\left(c^0, c^1, \ldots \right).$$

In this way c^0 is the start configuration and c^i is the configuration reached after i steps. Finally, for finite bit strings b it is most convenient to number sequences from right to left starting with 0:

$$b = (b_{n-1}, \ldots, b_0) = b[n-1 : 0]$$

which formally amounts to

$$\mathbb{B}^n = \{\, b \mid b : [0 : n-1] \to \mathbb{B} \,\}$$

For finite subsequences of elements with indices from i to j we again borrow interval notation from computer aided design (CAD) system and write

$$a[i : j] = (a_i, \ldots, a_j)$$

but if finite bit strings are involved we write this as

$$a[j : i] = (a_j, \ldots, a_i)$$

The Hilbert epsilon operator picks an element εA from a set A. Applied to a singleton set it returns the unique element of the set.

$$\varepsilon \{x\} = x$$

For symbols $x \in \mathbb{B}$ and natural numbers $n \in \mathbb{N}^+$, a bit-string obtained by repeating x exactly n times is defined as

$$x^n = (\underbrace{x, \ldots, x}_{n \text{ times}})$$

For bit strings $x \in \mathbb{B}^n$ we abbreviate the high order and low order (approximately) half of the bits as

$$x_H = x[n-1 : \lfloor n/2 \rfloor]$$
$$x_L = x[\lceil n/2 \rceil - 1 : 0]$$

For bit strings x and y of equal length one defines

$$x \leq y \equiv \forall i.\, x_i \leq y_i$$

$x \wedge y$	and
$x \vee y$	or
$/x , \bar{x}$	not
$x \oplus y$	exclusive or, + modulo 2

Table 1. Logical connectives

1.3.2 Boolean Operators

In Boolean Algebra we use the connectives from Table 1. For logical connectives $\circ \in \{\wedge, \vee, \oplus\}$, bit-strings $a, b \in \mathbb{B}^n$, and a bit $c \in \mathbb{B}$, we borrow from vector calculus to define the corresponding bit wise operations:

$$/a[n-1:0] = (/a_{n-1}, \ldots, /a_0)$$
$$a[n-1:0] \circ b[n-1:0] = (a_{n-1} \circ b_{n-1}, \ldots, a_0 \circ b_0)$$
$$c \circ b[n-1:0] = (c \circ b_{n-1}, \ldots, c \circ b_0)$$

For records x with $t \in \mathbb{N}$ selectors $n_1, \ldots, n_t$ we denote as usual with $x.n_i$ the component of the record selected by n_i. For a subset $n_{s_1}, \ldots, n_{s_r}$ of the selectors we abbreviate the subrecord of record components selected by this subset as

$$x.(n_{s_1}, \ldots, n_{s_r}) = (x.n_{s_1}, \ldots, x.n_{s_r})$$

In a hardware configuration h with components $h.pc, h.dpc, \ldots$ we would for instance abbreviate

$$h.(dpc, pc) = (h.dpc, h.pc)$$

1.3.3 Binary and Two's Complement Numbers

For bit-strings

$$a = a[n-1:0] \in \mathbb{B}^n$$

we denote by

$$\langle a \rangle = \sum_{i=0}^{n-1} a_i \cdot 2^i$$

the interpretation of bit-string a as a *binary number*. String a is called the *binary representation* of length n of the natural number $\langle a \rangle$. The set of natural numbers representable as binary numbers of length n is denoted by

$$B_n = \{ \langle a \rangle \mid a \in \mathbb{B}^n \}$$

For $x \in B_n$ the binary representation of x of length n is denoted by

$$x_n = bin_n(x) = \varepsilon \{ a \in \mathbb{B}^n \mid \langle a \rangle = x \}$$

We denote by

$$[a] = -2^{n-1}a_{n-1} + \langle a[n-2:0] \rangle$$

the interpretation of bit-string a as a *two's complement number*. String a is called the *two's complement representation* of length n of the natural number $\langle a \rangle$. The set of natural numbers representable as two's complement numbers of length n is denoted by

$$T_n = \{ \langle a \rangle \mid a \in \mathbb{B}^n \}$$

For $x \in T_n$ the two's complement representation of x of length n is denoted by

$$twoc_n(x) = \varepsilon \{ a \in \mathbb{B}^n \mid [a] = x \}$$

The binary addition $+_n$ and subtraction $-_n$ of bit strings $a, b \in \mathbb{B}^n$ is defined by

$$a +_n b = bin_n(((\langle a \rangle + \langle b \rangle)) \bmod 2^n)$$
$$a -_n b = bin_n(((\langle a \rangle - \langle b \rangle)) \bmod 2^n)$$

A very easy computation shows that for the addition of n bit numbers whose last m bits are all zero it suffices to add the leading $n - m$ bits.

Lemma 1. *Let $a, b \in \mathbb{B}^n$ and let $a[m-1:0] = b[m-1:0] = 0^m$. Then*

$$a +_n b = (a[n-1:m] +_{n-m} b[n-1:m]) \circ 0^m$$

As arithmetic units process binary numbers as well as two's complement numbers, one would expect in their specification also a counter part of this definition for two's complement numbers. However, in manuals such a specification is usually absent; instead addition and subtraction of two's complement numbers are also specified by the binary addition and subtraction operations $+_n$ and $-_n$. In a nutshell this works because

$$\langle a \rangle \equiv [a] \bmod 2^n \quad \text{for} \quad a \in \mathbb{B}^n \quad \text{(lemma 2.14 of [KMP14])}$$

which immediately implies for $\circ \in \{+, -\}$:

$$\langle a \rangle \circ \langle b \rangle \equiv [a] \circ [b] \bmod 2^n$$

This is almost but not quite what one wants to know. Attempting to define two's complement operators $\circ_n'$ one observes that the exact result

$$S = [a] \circ [b]$$

might lie outside of the range T_n, just like $\langle a \rangle \circ \langle b \rangle$ might lie outside of B_n. For such situations one replaces S by a number $S \operatorname{tmod} 2^n$ which is congruent to S modulo 2^n and which lies in the representable range.

$$S \operatorname{tmod} 2^n = \varepsilon \{ x \mid x \in T_n \wedge S \equiv x \bmod 2^n \}$$

Observe that the set on the right hand side of the equation is a singleton set, because congruence modulo 2^n is an equivalence relation with T_n as a system of representatives. The definition of two's complement addition and subtraction operators $\circ_n'$ then becomes

$$a \circ_n' b = twoc_n(([a] \circ [b]) \bmod 2^n)$$

The desired result (lemma 5.1 of [KMP14]) is then simply formulated as follows.

Lemma 2.

$$a \circ_n b = a \circ_n' b$$

Proof. Let

$$s = a \circ_n b$$

Then

$$[s] \equiv \langle s \rangle \bmod 2^n$$
$$\equiv \langle a \rangle \circ \langle b \rangle \bmod 2^n$$
$$\equiv [a] \circ [b] \bmod 2^n$$

Trivially we have $[s] \in T_n$. Thus

$$[s] = ([a] \circ [b] \bmod 2^n) \qquad\qquad \square$$

1.3.4 Memory

The state of a byte addressable memory m with 32 address bits is modeled as a mapping

$$S : \mathbb{B}^{32} \rightarrow \mathbb{B}^8.$$

Such a memory will be used here in ISA specifications. For $x \in \mathbb{B}^{32}$ function value $m(x) \in \mathbb{B}^8$ models the current content of the memory at address x. The sequence $m_d(x)$ of d consecutive entries of memory S starting at address x is defined inductively as follows:

$$m_1(x) = m(x)$$
$$m_{d+1}(x) = m(x +_k d_k) \circ m_d(x)$$

For bit strings $s \in \mathbb{B}^{8k}$, whose length is a multiple of 8, and $i < k$ we identify byte i of s as

$$byte(i,s) = s[8(i+1) - 1 : 8i]$$

A trivial induction on d shows:

$$i < d \quad \rightarrow \quad byte(i, m_d(x)) = m(ax +_{32} i_{32}) \qquad\qquad (1)$$

The hardware memory systems we are going to construct will be addressable by cache lines which are 64 bits wide. The state resp. configuration of such a line addressable memory is thus modelled as a mapping

$$S : \mathbb{B}^{29} \rightarrow \mathbb{B}^{64}$$

The set of all such configurations is denoted by K_m.

Embedding

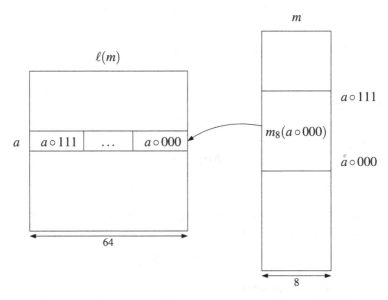

Fig. 1. Little endian embedding of byte-addressable memory into line-addressable memory

We define a conversion function ℓ which changes byte addressable memories

$$m : \mathbb{B}^{32} \to \mathbb{B}^8$$

to their line addressable version

$$\ell(m) : \mathbb{B}^{29} \to \mathbb{B}^{64}$$

For line addresses $a \in \mathbb{B}^{29}$ it is defined by

$$\ell(m)(a) = m_8(a \circ 000)$$

This is illustrated in Fig. 1. In processor correctness proofs it will serve as the simulation relation between the byte addressable ISA memory and the cache line addressable hardware memory system.

For the line addressable version of m we conclude the following.

Lemma 3.

$$i < 8 \quad \to \quad byte(i, \ell(m)(a)) = m(a \circ 000 +_{32} i_{32})$$

Proof.

$$byte(i, \ell(m)(a)) = byte(i, m_8(a \circ 000)) \quad \text{(definition)}$$
$$= m(a \circ 000 +_{32} i_{32}) \quad \text{(equation 1)} \qquad \square$$

135	107 106		43 42		11 10	3	2	1	0

a	data	cdata	bw	w	r	cas

Fig. 2. Format of memory accesses

For byte addresses $x \in \mathbb{B}^{32}$, resp. for line addresses

$$x.l = x[31:3]$$

and line offsets

$$x.o = x[2:0]$$

we then have

$$m(x) = byte(\langle x.o \rangle, \ell(m)(x.l))$$

Sequential Semantics

We define memory semantics for line addressable memory with the help of *accesses*. As illustrated in Fig. 2 accesses

$$acc \in \mathbb{B}^{136} = K_{acc}$$

have the following components:

- processor (line) address $acc.a = acc[135:107]$
- processor data $acc.data = acc[106:43]$ — the input data in case of a write or a compare-and-swap (CAS),
- comparison data $acc.cdata = acc[42:11]$ — the data for comparison in case of a CAS access,
- the byte-write signals $acc.bw = acc[10:3]$ for write and CAS accesses,
- write signal $acc.w = acc[2]$,
- read signal $acc.r = acc[1]$, and
- CAS signal $acc.cas = acc[0]$.

Thus we have

$$acc.a \in \mathbb{B}^{29} \ , \ acc.data \in \mathbb{B}^{64} \ , acc.cdata \in \mathbb{B}^{32} \ , \ acc.bw \in \mathbb{B}^{8}$$

$$x \in \{w, r, cas\} \rightarrow acc.x \in \mathbb{B}$$

At most one of the bits w, r or cas is allowed to be on.

$$acc.r + acc.w + acc.cas \leq 1$$

In case none of these bits is on, we call the access *void*.

$$void(acc) \equiv acc.r + acc.w + acc.cas = 0$$

For technical reasons, we also require the byte-write signals to be off in read accesses and to mask one of the words in case of CAS accesses:

$$acc.r \to acc.bw = 0^8$$
$$acc.cas \to acc.bw \in \{0^4 1^4, 1^4 0^4\}.$$

The set of all such accesses is denoted by K_{acc}. For CAS accesses and line addressable memory $m \in K_m$, we define the predicate $test(acc,m)$ which compares $acc.cdata$ with the upper or the lower word of the memory line $M(acc.a)$ addressed by the access, depending on the byte-write signal $acc.bw[0]$.

$$test(acc,m) \equiv acc.cdata = \begin{cases} m(acc.a)_L & acc.bw[0] = 1 \\ m(acc.a)_H & acc.bw[0] = 0 \end{cases}$$

For $n = 64$ and strings $x,y \in \mathbb{B}^n$ function $modify$ describes the replacement of bytes of x by the corresponding bytes of y under control of $byte$-$write$ signals $bw \in \mathbb{B}^8$.

$$byte(i, modify(x,y,bw)) = \begin{cases} byte(i,y) & bw[i] = 1 \\ byte(i,x) & bw[i] = 0 \end{cases}$$

Semantics of single accesses acc operating on a memory m is specified by a memory update function

$$\delta_M : K_m \times K_{acc} \to K_m$$

and the answers

$$dataout(m,acc) \in \mathbb{B}^{64}$$

of read and CAS accesses. Let

$$m' = \delta_M(m,acc)$$

Then memory is updated under control of signals bw, w and cas. The line addressed by $acc.a$ is updated in case of a write or in case of a CAS with positive outcome of the test. Only bytes $byte(i,m(acc.a))$ with active byte-write signal $acc.bw_i$ are updated by the corresponding bytes of $acc.data$.

$$m'(a) = \begin{cases} modify(m(a), acc.data, acc.bw) & acc.a = a \wedge (acc.w \vee \\ & acc.cas \wedge test(acc,m)) \\ m(a) & \text{otherwise} \end{cases}$$

The answers $dataout(m,acc)$ of read or CAS accesses are defined as follows.

$$acc.r \vee acc.cas \quad \to \quad dataout(m,acc) = m(acc.a)$$

We observe that certain components of the access are only relevant when certain control bits are active. For example, the compare data is irrelevant for a read access. Accesses that agree on all components that matter produce the same outputs and update memory in the same way. Formally we define an equivalence relation where accesses acc and $\widehat{acc}$ are considered equivalent, written

$$acc \equiv \widehat{acc}$$

iff all of the following are true:

- control bits are the same

$$x \in \{cas, w, r\} \;\rightarrow\; acc.x = \widehat{acc}.x$$

- if any control bits are raised, the address and byte-write signals are the same (in case of a read because they are all zero)

$$x \in \{cas, w, r\} \wedge acc.x \;\rightarrow\; acc.a = \widehat{acc}.a \wedge acc.bw = \widehat{acc}.bw$$

- if the accesses are a write or CAS access, then the data are the same

$$x \in \{cas, w\} \wedge acc.x \;\rightarrow\; acc.data = \widehat{acc}.data$$

- if the accesses are a CAS access, compare data is the same

$$acc.cas \;\rightarrow\; acc.cdata = \widehat{acc}.cdata$$

That accesses which are equivalent to each other behave the same way is stated in

Lemma 4.

$$acc \equiv \widehat{acc} \;\rightarrow\; \delta_M(m, acc) = \delta_M(m, \widehat{acc})$$
$$acc \equiv \widehat{acc} \wedge (acc.r \vee acc.cas) \;\rightarrow\; dataout(m, acc) = dataout(m, \widehat{acc})$$

Overloading notation we consider linear access sequences

$$lacc : \mathbb{N} \rightarrow K_{acc}$$

where access $lacc(i)$ is access number i of the sequence (counting from zero). Execution of the first n accesses of such a sequence is then inductively defined by

$$\Delta_M^0(m, lacc) = m$$
$$\Delta_M^{i+1}(m, lacc) = \delta_M(\Delta_M^i(m, lacc), lacc(i))$$

Readers familiar with [KMP14] will notice that accesses there had an extra component $acc.f \in \mathbb{B}$ whose activation signals so called *flush* accesses. These accesses necessarily have to be considered in the implementation of shared memory systems, but in the specification of such a system — and that is all we will rely on in this text — one can do without them.

On Hierarchical Hardware Design

Artefacts of computer science are almost always constructed in a hierarchical way. The standard building blocks of software are functions; their counter parts in hardware design are hardware units. The purpose of this section is to:

i) establish naming conventions for components and signals of hardware units in hierarchical designs in a basic hardware description language;
ii) identify a class of designs with well defined behaviour, which includes all designs in this book;
iii) to justify modular reasoning for all designs in this book.
iv) to enrich the basic description language with expressions and straight line programs for added comfort.

This is simple enough but not completely trivial. For the first part (Sect. 2.1) we have essentially to define the syntax of a minimal hardware description language.

For the second part (Sect. 2.2) we have to define the semantics of this language. As in circuit theory well defined behaviour will be deduced from the absence of cycles in certain graphs.

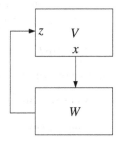

Fig. 3. Output x of unit V is used to compute in unit W input z of unit V

For the third part (Sect. 2.3) we have to address situations like in Fig. 3, where output x of subunit V is an input of a second subunit W, which in turn computes

© Springer Nature Switzerland AG 2020
P. Lutsyk et al. (Eds.): A Pipelined Multi-Core Machine, LNCS 9999, pp. 29–89, 2020.
https://doi.org/10.1007/978-3-030-43243-0_2

input z of subunit V. This is by no means an academic example. Take $V = ID$ as the instruction decode stage of a classical five-stage pipeline shown in figure 117, $x = rs$ as an address to the general purpose register file, $W = WB$ the write-back stage with the general purpose register file gpr and $z = A$ the register file content $A = gpr(rs)$ at address rs which is used in the ID stage to compute the next pc and dpc. In such situations one cannot simply use the specification of the values $||out(V)||$ of V as a function of the values $||in(V)||$ of the (i.e. all!) inputs $in(V)$ and possibly internal state c_V of V, because the value of input z is only computed later. Instead one has to use separate specifications of the outputs as a function of an appropriately defined *part* of the inputs.

In section 2.4 expressions and straight line programs are introduced as syntactic sugar. The usual semantics of expressions can be regained for most common designs, but not in examples like Fig. 3 where we only hope for expression semantics for the individual outputs of V but not for the entire vector of these outputs.

2.1 Syntax

2.1.1 Buses

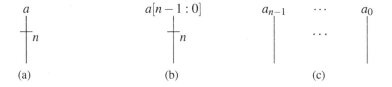

Fig. 4. Three ways to show a bus with specification $a(n)$ in hardware schematics

Hardware units communicate with their environment by input and output buses. A *bus declaration bd* consists always of name $bd.na$ followed by a possibly empty qualifier $bd.q$

$$bd = (bd.na \circ bd.q)$$

Depending on the qualifier they can have one of two formats:

- qualifier $bd.q = (n)$ with $n \in \mathbb{N}$. A bus specification of the form

$$bd = a(n)$$

  defines a *parallel* bus a and $n \in \mathbb{N}$ signals. Signal lines of the bus are indexed in little endian order as

$$a = a[n-1:0]$$

  and the set of these signals is

$$sig(bd) = \{a_{n-1}, \ldots, a_0\}$$

In schematics they are represented as in Fig. 4.

- empty qualifier $q = \varepsilon$. A bus specification of the form

$$bd = a$$

defines a *simple* bus with a single line a and we have

$$sig(bd) = \{a\}$$

In the theory of programming language a bus declaration bd would be viewed as the declaration of a variable $bd.na$ of type $bd.q$. Types of variable specify the range, i.e., the set of values the variable can assume. The set of possible signals on a bus depends only on the qualifier q and is defined as

$$\Sigma(q) = \begin{cases} \mathbb{B} & q = \varepsilon \\ \mathbb{B}^n & q = (n) \end{cases}$$

Observe, that the input signals of simple buses differs from the input signals of parallel buses of length 1.

$$\Sigma(\varepsilon) = \mathbb{B} \neq \mathbb{B}^1 = \Sigma((1))$$

It is tempting to forbid parallel buses of width 1 altogether, but for recursive constructions this would turn out to be inconvenient. We return to this topic in section 2.1.8. Hardware units will be defined inductively. We first specify *basic hardware units*; these are hardware units which have no subunits. We then proceed to define *composite hardware units*, which can have previously defined hardware units, in particular basic units, as subunits.

We denote by Na the set of names and by

$$Q = \{\varepsilon\} \cup \{(n) \mid n \in \mathbb{N}\}$$

the set of bus qualifiers. The set of bus declarations is then

$$BD = Na \circ Q$$

2.1.2 I/O Buses

All hardware units U are specified by a tuple with several components, which always include

- a sequence

$$ind(U) \in BD^*$$

of input bus declarations with distinct names

$$i \neq j \quad \rightarrow \quad ind(U)_i.na \neq ind(U)_j.na$$

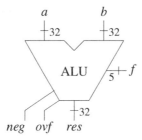

Fig. 5. ALU with three input buses a, b, f and three output buses neg, ovf and res.

- a sequence

$$outd(U) \in BD^*$$

of output bus declarations with distinct names

$$i \neq j \quad \rightarrow \quad outd(U)_i.na \neq outd(U)_j.na$$

We denote the lengths of these sequences by

$$ni(U) = \#ind(U) \quad \text{resp.} \quad no(U) = \#ind(U)$$

for the number of input and output buses, respectively.

The example of figure 5 shows a 32 bit ALU; it has operand buses a and b, a control bus f with five bits selecting the function to be performed with the operands, result output res as well as simple output buses neg and ovf indicating a negative result and an overflow resp. This would be declared as

$$ind(ALU) = (a(32), b(32), f(5))$$
$$outd(ALU) = (neg, ovf, res(32))$$

We thus have

$$ni(ALU) = 3$$
$$no(ALU) = 3$$

From sequences $ind(U)$ and $outd(U)$ we extract the *sets* of (names of) input and output buses

$$bus^{in}(U) = \{\, bd.na \mid bd \in ind(U) \,\}$$
$$bus^{out}(U) = \{\, bd.na \mid bs \in outd(U) \,\}$$

Together they form the IO buses of U

$$bus^{io}(U) = bus^{in}(U) \cup bus^{out}(U)$$

Input and output buses should have different names

$$bus^{in}(U) \cap bus^{out}(U) = \emptyset$$

The declaration of IO bus $a \in bus^{io}(U)$ in unit U is denoted by

$$bd_U(a) = \varepsilon \{ bd \in ind(U) \cup outd(U) \mid bd.na = a \}$$

and the qualifier of IO bus $a \in bus^{io}(U)$ in unit U is denoted by

$$q_U(a) = bd_U(a).q$$

The width of bus a in unit U is then

$$w_U(a) = \begin{cases} 1 & q_U(a) = \varepsilon \\ n & q_U(a) = (n) \end{cases}$$

The set of signals on this bus is collected into the set

$$sig_U(a) = sig(bd_U(a))$$

We denote the set of signals on the input and output buses of U by

$$sig^{in}(U) = \bigcup_{a \in bus^{in}(U)} sig_U(a)$$

$$sig^{out}(U) = \bigcup_{a \in bus^{out}(U)} sig_U(a)$$

The signals of all IO buses are collected into the set

$$pins(U) = sig^{in}(U) \cup sig^{out}(U)$$

So far the order of bus declarations did not matter. This changes when we try to define the sets of input and output values $\Sigma^{in}(U)$ and $\Sigma^{out}(U)$ for hardware unit U. Thus we extract from the bus declarations the ordered sequence of names input buses as

$$in(U) \in Na^{ni(U)}$$
$$in(U) = (bd.na \mid bd \in ind(U))$$

and the ordered sequence of names of output buses as

$$out(U) \in Na^{no(U)}$$
$$out(U) = (bd.na \mid bd \in outd(U))$$

Recall that $ind(U)$ is a sequence of buses, and this list comprehension keeps the order of this sequence intact. For the ALU in figure 5 we have

$$in(ALU) = (a,b,f), \quad out(ALU) = (neg,ovf,res)$$

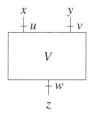

Fig. 6. Unit with 2 input buses x, y and a single output bus z

Note that $ind(U)$ and $outd(U)$ as well as $in(U)$ and $out(U)$ have been defined to be sequences even if there is only one such bus. Thus for the unit in figure 6 we have

$$ind(D) = (x(u),y(v))$$
$$outd(D) = (z(w))$$
$$in(D) = (x,y)$$
$$out(D) = (z)$$

The sets of input and output values for unit U are now defined as

$$\Sigma^{in}(U) = \times_{i=1}^{ni(U)}\Sigma(q_U(in(U)_i))$$
$$\Sigma^{out}(U) = \times_{i=1}^{nout(U)}\Sigma(q_U(out(U)_i))$$

For the ALU in figure 5 we have

$$\Sigma^{in}(ALU) = \mathbb{B}^{32} \times \mathbb{B}^{32} \times \mathbb{B}^{5}$$
$$\Sigma^{out}(ALU) = \mathbb{B} \times \mathbb{B} \times \mathbb{B}^{32}$$

For unit U in figure 6 we have

$$\Sigma^{in}(U) = \mathbb{B}^{u} \times \mathbb{B}^{v}$$
$$\Sigma^{out}(U) = \mathbb{B}^{w}$$

Observe that a bus $a(1)$ of length 1 is different from a single bit b, and takes on different values

$$\Sigma((1)) = \mathbb{B}^{1} \neq \mathbb{B} = \Sigma(\varepsilon)$$

Thus from the set of values of a bus we can infer the qualifier. We allow ourselves the notation

$$a \in \mathbb{B}^{n} \quad \text{to declare a bus} \quad a(n)$$

and
$$a \in \mathbb{B} \quad \text{to declare a bus} \quad a$$

For example, the ALU in fig. 5 could be declared as follows: an ALU has input buses

$$a \in \mathbb{B}^{32}, \quad b \in \mathbb{B}^{32}, \quad f \in \mathbb{B}^5$$

and output buses

$$res \in \mathbb{B}^{32}, \quad neg \in \mathbb{B}, \quad ovf \in \mathbb{B}$$

This is less compact, but is exactly the notation we used in [KMP14] and we will stick to this notation in future chapters. For the remainder of this chapter, however, we will usually use the more compact notation.

2.1.3 Basic Hardware Units

Hardware units will be defined inductively. We first specify *basic hardware units*; these are hardware units which have no subunits. We then proceed to define *composite hardware units*, which can have previously defined hardware units, in particular basic units, as subunits.

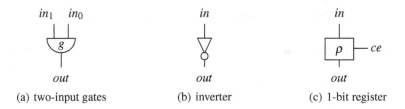

(a) two-input gates   (b) inverter   (c) 1-bit register

Fig. 7. Basic hardware units

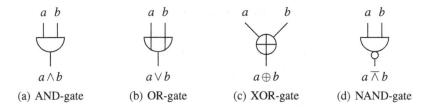

(a) AND-gate   (b) OR-gate   (c) XOR-gate   (d) NAND-gate

Fig. 8. Symbols for two-input hardware gates

We start with the basic hardware units shown in figure 7.

- two-input gates g with
$$g \in \{\wedge, \vee, \oplus, NAND\}$$
with two input buses
$$in \in \mathbb{B}^2$$
and one output bus
$$out \in \mathbb{B}$$
- inverters *inv* with input bus
$$in \in \mathbb{B}$$
and output bus
$$out \in \mathbb{B}$$
- edge triggered flip-flops ρ with two input buses, one input bit and a clock-enable bit
$$in, ce \in \mathbb{B}$$
and an output bit
$$out \in \mathbb{B}$$

We collect the basic units into the set of basic units

$$BU = \{\wedge, \vee, \oplus, NAND, inv, \rho\}$$

which correspond somewhat to basic types of programming languages.

2.1.4 Subunit Declarations

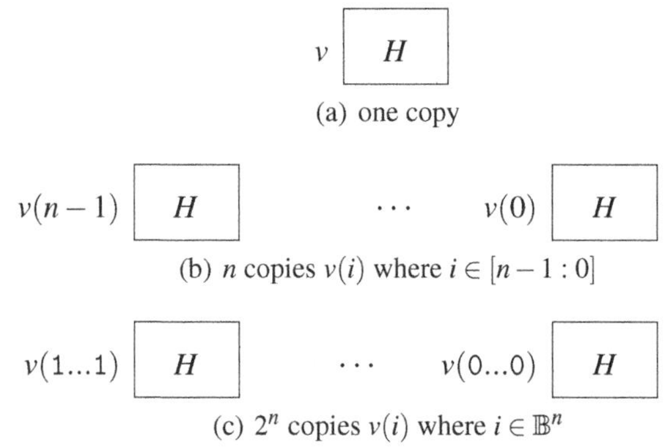
v
H
(a) one copy
v(n − 1)
H
...
v(0)
H
(b) n copies v(i) where i ∈ [n − 1 : 0]
v(1...1)
H
...
v(0...0)
H
(c) 2^n copies v(i) where i ∈ B^n

Fig. 9. Placing one copy or several copies of unit H

Suppose a hardware unit with name H has been defined, and we wish to place one or more instances of it in hardware unit U. Then this is specified by a *subunit declaration* which can have one of two forms, whose syntax is borrowed from variable declarations of programming languages:

- for names v a subunit declaration σ of the form

$$v : H$$

As shown in figure 9 this places a single subunit with *label*

$$\lambda = v$$

of type H into unit U.
- for sets I of indices of the form

$$I = [0 : n-1] \quad \text{or} \quad I = \mathbb{B}^n$$

a subunit declaration σ of the form

$$v : H(I)$$

As shown in figure 9 this places for each $i \in I$ a subunit with label

$$\lambda = v(i)$$

of type H into unit U. Index sets of the form $I = [n-1 : 0]$ are for instance used to construct registers from 1 bit registers ρ but also for arrays of caches or processor cores in a multi-core machine. Index sets of the form $I = \mathbb{B}^n$ turn out to be convenient for the construction of memories.

The hardware unit H placed by subunit declaration σ is called the *type* $t(\sigma)$ of the specification; the name of each copy is called $na(\sigma)$.

$$t(\sigma) = H \quad \leftrightarrow \quad \exists v, I. \ \sigma = v : H \ \vee \ \sigma = v : H(I)$$
$$na(\sigma) = v \quad \leftrightarrow \quad \exists H, I. \ \sigma = v : H \ \vee \ \sigma = v : H(I)$$

Thus

$$t(v : H) = t(v : H(I)) = H, \quad na(v : H) = na(v : H(I)) = v$$

The set $su(\sigma)$ of subunits λ generated by declaration σ is therefore defined as

$$su(\sigma) = \begin{cases} \{v\} & \exists H. \ \sigma = v : H \\ \{v(i) \mid i \in I\} & \exists H. \ \sigma = v : H(I) \end{cases}$$

Thus

$$su(v : H) = \{v\}, \quad su(v : H(I)) = \{v(i) \mid i \in I\}$$

2.1.5 Composite Hardware Units

Composite hardware units U are specified by a tuple with the following components

- declarations $ind(U)$ and $outd(U)$ as described above for the input and output buses.

- a set $sud(U)$ of subunit declarations using as types H previously defined hardware units. The names in subunit declarations should be distinct

$$\sigma, \sigma' \in sud(U) \wedge \sigma \neq \sigma' \quad \rightarrow \quad na(\sigma) \neq na(\sigma')$$

The *direct subunits* of U are then the subunits specified in the subunit declarations of U

$$su(U) = \bigcup_{\sigma \in sud(U)} su(\sigma)$$

and the type of each such a subunit is inherited from its specification

$$\lambda \in su(\sigma) \wedge \sigma \in sud(U) \quad \rightarrow \quad t_U(\lambda) = t(\sigma)$$

Unfolding definitions gives that a unit λ has type H if it comes from a specification of the form $v : H$ or $v : H(I)$

$$\lambda \in su(U) \wedge t_U(\lambda) = H \quad \leftrightarrow \quad \exists v, I, i.$$
$$\lambda = v \wedge v : H \in sud(U)$$
$$\vee \lambda = v(i) \wedge i \in I \wedge v : H(I) \in sud(U)$$

resp.

$$v \in su(U) \wedge t_U(v) = H \quad \leftrightarrow \quad v : H \in sud(U)$$
$$v(i) \in su(U) \wedge t_U(v(i)) = H \quad \leftrightarrow \quad i \in I \wedge v : H(I) \in sud(U)$$

From this we can define the set $sig(U)$ of *top level signals* visible in the specification of U as

- the signals on the inputs and output buses of U, i.e.

$$pins(U)$$

- for each subunit

$$\lambda \in su(U)$$

the pins of the type $t_U(\lambda)$ prefixed by λ

$$\{ \lambda.x \mid x \in pins(t_U(\lambda)) \}$$

Thus we set

$$sig(U) = pins(U) \cup \{ \lambda.x \mid \lambda \in su(U), x \in pins(t_U(\lambda)) \}$$

The output signals $sigsu^{out}(U)$ of the subunits of U are then

$$sigsu^{out}(U) = \{ \lambda.x \mid \lambda \in su(U), x \in sig^{out}(t_U(\lambda)) \}$$

- a *source* function

$$s_U \; : \; sig(U) \setminus (sig^{in}(U) \cup sigsu^{out}(U)) \; \rightarrow \; sig(U) \cup \{0,1\}$$

specifying for every signal x which is not an input of U or an output of a subunit the signal $s_U(x)$ which is driving it. Signals can be tied to constant values 0 or 1. If it is clear what unit is meant, we drop index U. We also abbreviate

$$s(x) = y \quad \text{with} \quad x = y$$

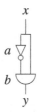

Fig. 10. Circuit with an inverter a and an AND-gate b

With hardware units whose only subunits are two input gates and inverters we can construct all circuits. As a simple example consider the unit U of figure 10 with bus declarations

$$ind(U) = (x), \quad outd = (y)$$

with subunits

$$a : inv$$
$$b : \wedge$$

and source function specified by

$$a.in = x$$
$$b.in1 = x$$
$$b.in2 = a.out$$
$$y = b.out$$

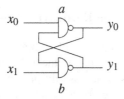

Fig. 11. Hardware unit with two NAND-gates a and b

We also can construct in this way unit V of figure 11 with bus declarations

$$ind(V) = (x(2)), \quad outd(V) = (y(2))$$

which is not a circuit due to the cycles of the paths through the network.

$$a \ : \ NAND$$
$$b \ : \ NAND$$
$$a.in1 = x_0$$
$$a.in2 = b.out$$
$$b.in1 = a.out$$
$$b.in2 = x_1$$
$$y_0 = a.out$$
$$y_1 = b.out$$

The nesting depth $nd(U)$ of units resp. types is defined in the obvious way.

$$nd(U) = \begin{cases} 0 & U \in BT \\ 1 + \max\{nd(t_U(\lambda)) \mid \lambda \in su(U)\} & \text{otherwise} \end{cases}$$

Streamlining Notation

For subunits λ with a single output bus x (this includes all basic units) we allow to abbreviate

$$\lambda.x = \lambda$$

independently of the name of the output bus x. Then the specification of the source function for the unit in figure 11 reduces to

$$a.in1 = x_0$$
$$a.in2 = b$$
$$b.in1 = a$$
$$b.in2 = x_1$$
$$y_0 = a$$
$$y_1 = b$$

2.1.6 Implicit Labels and Types in Hardware Schematics

Schematics are a classical used interface of computer aided design (CAD) systems for the construction of hardware. In hierarchical design systems the distinction between labels and types of units is necessarily present, because one cannot place a previously specified unit without referring to something like its type, and at least an internal name has to be generated by the system once a unit is placed.

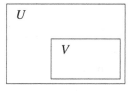

Fig. 12. If only a single direct subunit of type V is placed in U, we use V also as the label of the unit; there is no need to show it in schematics.

In the literature schematics also serve since ages to define or illustrate all kinds of hardware hardware constructions. This happens to work well enough even without reference to an underlying formal model of computation like the one we are developing here, but as a consequence the distinction between labels and types of units is less explicit. As a matter of fact, in the literature schematics with subunits as in figure 12 are almost *never* annotated by a label v *and* an explicit type for V at the same time. Thus one has somehow to infer if V stands — in our language — for a label, a type or both. Indeed V might stand for

1. a type as we have done it so far in the chapter. In texts about computer arithmetic one would find the carry chain incrementer of figure 28 but without the labels $ha(i)$ of the subunits of type HA for the half adders. Even for correctness proofs this is by no means catastrophic, as one could refer to the i'th half adder[1] as 'the unit connected to input bit a_i'.
2. a type *and* a label. This works perfectly if unit U contains only a single unit of type V
$$\#\{\lambda \in su(U)|t_U(\lambda) = V\} = 1$$
In this situation one can use $\lambda = V$ also as the label of this unit, i.e.
$$V : V \in sud(U)$$
There is no need to show the label of subunit V in hardware schematics outside the box for V because it would be identical with the type of the unit shown inside the box.
3. as a label. Then obviously the type $t_U(V)$ has to be specified by other means:
   - either in the accompanying text. An example is the general purpose register file gpr in figure 95 which is specified in the accompanying text as some form of 3 port RAM. In such situations the schematics are an illustration but not a complete a complete specification of a hardware unit.
   - by the use of a special symbol for V instead of a plain rectangle. The standard example in this text are n bit registers whose symbol is introduced in figure x. Returning to figure 95 we can infer from the symbol for the program counter pc in the schematics that subunit pc has as type a 32 bit register.

We will make freely use of methods 2) and 3) in order to keep our schematics uncluttered.

---

[1] in paper and pencil proofs !

2.1.7 Size Parameters

We often specify families of units $U(n,m,\ldots)$ with one or more parameters $n,m,\ldots$. Often these parameters are size parameters $n,m,\ldots \in \mathbb{N}$. In this situation functions $f(n,m,\ldots) \in \mathbb{N}$ can be used in the specification of index sets

$$I = [0 : f(n) - 1] \quad \text{or} \quad I = \mathbb{B}^{f(n)}$$

With size parameters a d bit register $reg(d)$ as shown in figure 13 a) can be constructed from d copies of flip-flop ρ with a common clock enable signal.

Fig. 13. Constructing a d-bit register $reg(d)$ from d copies of 1-bit register ρ with labels $R(i)$

Such a d-bit register has two input buses: a d-bit data input and a single bit clock-enable input

$$in \in \mathbb{B}^d, \quad ce \in \mathbb{B}$$

and a d-bit output bus

$$out \in \mathbb{B}^d$$

It uses subunits

$$R : \rho([0 : d - 1])$$

and the source function is specified by

$$R(i).in = in_i$$
$$R(i).ce = ce$$
$$out_i = R(i).out$$

resp. with streamlined notation

$$out_i = R(i)$$

For d bit registers one uses the symbol from Fig. 14.

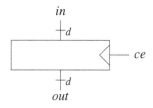

Fig. 14. Symbol for d-bit register $reg(d)$.

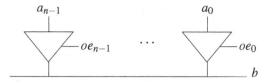

Fig. 15. Bus $\tau(n)$ with n tri-state drivers

With size parameter n we can also introduce as a new basic unit a one bit wide bus $\tau(n)$ driven by n tri-state drivers with input bit a_i and output enable signal oe_i represented as input buses

$$a, oe \in \mathbb{B}^n$$

and a single output bit

$$b \in \mathbb{B}$$

as shown in figure 15.

The set of basic units is extended to

$$BU = BU_{old} \cup \{ \tau(n) \mid n \in \mathbb{N} \}$$

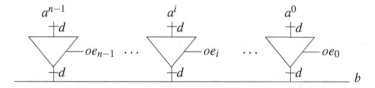

Fig. 16. Bus $\tau(d, n)$ has n tri-state drivers; each driver is d bits wide.

Tri-state buses $\tau(n, d)$ of width d as shown in figure 16 are constructed from d copies $T(i)$ of $\tau(n)$, one for each bit $i \in [d-1:0]$. Due to the constant shortage of letters and symbols we reuse names a and b for the input and output bus. Thus there are obviously $n \cdot d$ data inputs $a[n \cdot d - 1 : 0]$ that we group into subbuses

$$a^j[d-1:0:0] = a[(j+1) \cdot d - 1 : j \cdot d] \quad \text{for} \quad j \in [n-1:0]$$

i.e we rename

$$a_{j \cdot d + i} = a_i^j$$

We get input buses

$$a \in \mathbb{B}^{n \cdot d} , \ oe \in \mathbb{B}^n$$

and output bus

$$B \in \mathbb{B}^n$$

With subunit declaration

$$T : \tau(n)([0 : d - 1])$$

the source function is specified as

$$T(j).a_i = a_j^i$$
$$T(j).oe_i = oe_i$$
$$b_j = T(j).b$$

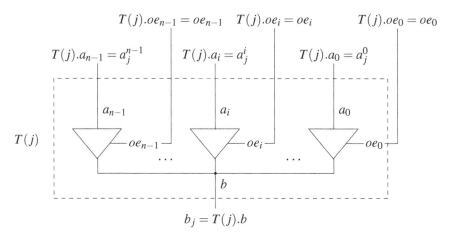

Fig. 17. Copy $T(j)$ of the basic tri-state bus τ handles bit j of each subbus a^i

The wiring of copy $T(j)$ of τ is illustrated in Fig. 17.

2.1.8 Recursive Constructions

By using in the specification of units $U(n)$ subunits $U(m)$ with size parameters $m < n$ one can obviously also specify recursive constructions.

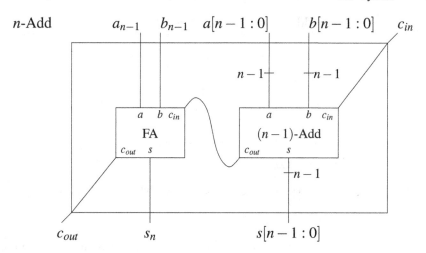

Fig. 18. Recursive construction of a carry chain adder

As an example figure 18 shows the construction of an n bit carry chain adder *n-Add* from a full adder *FA* and an $n-1$ bit adder $(n-1)$-*Add*. The natural way to specify the IO buses of the units involved is

- for the full adder *FA*

$$a, b, cin, s, cout \in \mathbb{B}$$

- for the n bit adder *n-Add*

$$a, b, s \in \mathbb{B}^n \,, \; cin, cout \in \mathbb{B}$$

and the specification of the units should be

- for the full adder

$$\langle cout, s \rangle = a + b + cin$$

- for the n bit adder

$$\langle cout \circ s \rangle = \langle a \rangle + \langle b \rangle + cin$$

which happens to be defined because in section 1.3.1 we allowed $cin \in \mathbb{B} \setminus \mathbb{B}^1$ as an operand of concatenation.

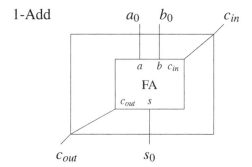

Fig. 19. 'Casting' a full adder with simple buses into a 1-bit adder with parallel buses of width 1

For the use in different recursive constructions we might also wish to say, that a full adder 'is' a 1 bit adder; but formally we shouldn't because the full adder has simple buses $a, b, s \in \mathbb{B}$ whereas a 1 bit adder has parallel buses $a, b, s \in \mathbb{B}^1$ of width 1. We can however construct a 1 bit adder from the full adder by the trivial construction in figure 18, which happens to work because in section 2.1.1 we allowed both simple buses and parallel buses of width 1.

2.1.9 Global Naming

For units U we have already defined the set $sig(U)$ of top level signals of U, i.e., the signals and direct subunits λ that are visible if we treat such subunits of U as black boxes, and the set $su(U)$ of labels of direct subunits of U. In a straight forward recursive way we proceed to define

- the set $Su(U)$ of *all* subunits of U, i.e., including the ones nested inside the direct subunits
- the set $Sig(U)$ of *all* signals in these units
- the source function $s_U(x)$ for all signals $x \in Sig(U)$
- the type $t_U(y)$ of the unit with label $y \in Su(U)$

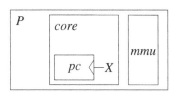

Fig. 20. Running example: processor P with subunits *core* and *mmu*. Subunit *core* has subunit *pc* of type $R(32)$ and is a nested subunit of P. Pin *ce* of $R(32)$ resp. signal $pc.ce \in sig(core)$ is driven by signal $x \in sig(core)$.

We refer to figure 20 as a running example. There a processor P has subunits of type *core* and *mmu*. We follow the convention of giving unique subunits of type V also label V and have

$$core, mmu \in su(P)$$

The core has subunit pc, which is a 32-bit register $R(32)$ with a clock enable pin ce.

$$pc : R(32) \in sud(core), \ ce \in pins(R(32))$$

In unit *core* this pin of subunit pc is signal $pc.ce$, and it is driven by signal $x \in sig(core)$

$$pc.ce \in sig(core), \ s_{core}(pc.ce) = x$$

Our goal are definitions of $Su(U)$, $Sig(U)$, $s_U(x)$, and $t_U(x)$ such that the program counter of the core is a subunit of P

$$core.pc \in Su(P)$$

its clock enable and signal x from subunit *core* are signals in P

$$core.pc.ce, \ core.x \in Sig(P)$$

the source function respects the source function of *core* by assigning $core.pc.ce = core.x$

$$s_P(core.pc.ce) = core.x$$

and which identifies $core.pc$ as a 32-bit register

$$t_P(core.pc) = R(32)$$

The definition of $Su(U)$ and $Sig(U)$ is by recursion. The set of all subunits $Su(U)$ consists of

- the set
$$su(U)$$
  of direct subunits of U
- for each direct subunit
$$\lambda \in su(U)$$
  the set of all subunits y of $type_U(\lambda)$ prefixed by λ.

Thus we define

$$Su(U) \ = \ su(U) \cup \{ \lambda.y \mid \lambda \in su(U), \ y \in Su(t_U(\lambda)) \}$$

Note that for units $U \in BT$ of basic type we have

$$Su(U) = su(U) = \emptyset$$

The *nesting depth* $nd_U(y)$ is the number of dots in the label y plus one. Formally for $\lambda \in su(U)$

$$nd_U(\lambda) = 1, \ nd_U(\lambda.y) = 1 + nd_{t_U(\lambda)}(y)$$

In the running example we have as promised

$$pc \in su(core) \cap Su(core), \ core.pc \in Su(P),$$

and the nesting depths of *core* and *core.pc* are

$$nd_P(core) = 1 \,, \ nd_P(core.pc) = 2$$

Global naming of signals in nested subunits is defined along the same lines. For composite designs the set $Sig(U)$ of signals consists of

- the set

$$pins(U)$$

  of input and output signals of U
- for each subunit $\lambda \in su(U)$ the set of all signals $x \in Sig(t_U(\lambda))$ of $t_U(\lambda)$ prefixed by λ.

$$\{\lambda.y \mid y \in Sig(t_U(\lambda))\}$$

Thus we define

$$Sig(U) = pins(U) \cup \{\lambda.y \mid y \in Sig(t_U(\lambda)), \ \lambda \in su(U)\}$$

In the running example we have

$$ce \in pins(pc), \ pc.ce \in sig(core) \cap Sig(core), \ core.pc.ce \in Sig(P)$$

Next we wish to extend the source functions s_U from the set $sig(U)$ to the set of signals $Sig(U)$ in nested units. A composite unit U is called *flat* if all its subunits are basic units. For flat units U we have

$$Sig(U) = sig(U)$$

and nothing needs to be done. Otherwise we can assume that the source functions s_H have already been extended to $Sig(H)$ for the types $H = t_U(\lambda)$ of the subunits $\lambda \in su(U)$ of U, and we define for global signals $x \in Sig(H)$ the source $s_U(\lambda.x)$ in U in the obvious way:

$$s_U(\lambda.x) = \lambda.s_H(x)$$

In the running example we have

$$s_{core}(pc.ce) = x, \ s_P(core.pc.ce) = core.x$$

Finally we extend the type $t_U(\lambda)$ of subunits $\lambda \in su(U)$ to nested subunits $y \in Su(U)$. The type of $\lambda.y$ in U is the type of y in $H = t_U(\lambda)$:

$$t_U(\lambda.y) = t_H(y)$$

As a sanity check we show

Lemma 5.
$$y.z \in Su(U) \quad\leftrightarrow\quad y \in Su(U) \wedge z \in Su(t_U(y))$$

Proof. We show that the statement holds for all units U by induction on the nesting depth $nd_U(y)$ of y.

- for subunits $\lambda \in su(U)$ of U we conclude directly from the definition of $Su(U)$:

$$\lambda.z \in Su(U) \leftrightarrow z \in Su(t_U(\lambda))$$

- for $\lambda.y$ with $\lambda \in su(U)$ we use the induction hypothesis for y in unit

$$H = t_U(\lambda)$$

and the definition of $t_U(\lambda.y)$ to conclude

$$\begin{aligned}
\lambda.y.z \in Su(U) &\leftrightarrow \lambda \in su(U) \wedge y.z \in Su(H) \\
&\leftrightarrow \lambda \in su(U) \wedge y \in Su(H) \wedge z \in Su(t_H(y)) \\
&\leftrightarrow \lambda.y \in Su(U) \wedge z \in Su(t_U(\lambda.y))
\end{aligned}$$

$\square$

2.1.10 Paths, Cycles and Depth

We review some basic graph theory. A *directed Graph* is a pair

$$G = (V, E)$$

where

- V is the set of nodes and
- $E \subseteq V \times V$ is the set of edges. An edge

$$(u, v) \in E$$

is illustrated as an arrow from u to v, and one calls u a *direct predecessor* of v and v a *direct successor* of u.

The nodes v without a direct predecessor are called the *sources* of G

$$src(G) = \{ v \in V \mid \nexists u.\ (u, v) \in E \}$$

A *path* in G is a sequence

$$p = p[0 : L]$$

of nodes

$$p_i \in V$$

with edges from nodes p_i to nodes p_{i+1} for $i < L$:

$$i < L \rightarrow (p_i, p_{i+1}) \in E$$

One says that p is a path *from* p_0 *to* p_L and L is called the *length* of the path. Clearly, paths p and q can be composed if the endpoint of p is the start point of q.

Lemma 6. *If $p[0:L]$ and $q[0:M]$ are paths in G and $p_L = q_0$, then $p[0:L] \circ q[1:M]$ is also a path in G.*

Path $p[0:L]$ is called a *cycle* if

$$p_0 = p_L \wedge L > 0$$

The graph G is called *finite* if V is finite.

Lemma 7. *In a finite cycle free graph $G = (V,E)$ every path has length at most #V.*

Proof. By the classical pigeonhole argument in a longer path p a node p_i would have to repeat at a later position p_j, $j > i$, and the portion

$$p[i:j]$$

of the original path p would constitute a cycle.   □

The depth $d_G(v)$ of a node v is the length of a longest path p from a source of G to v. For nodes on a cycle it obviously cannot exist. If it is clear which graph G is meant, we drop the subscript G.

Lemma 8. *In a finite cycle free graph every node v has a depth.*

Proof. If v is not a source follow from v repeatedly predecessors until you hit a source. By lemma 7 one eventually hits a source, and there are only finitely many paths p which can be obtained in this way. Thus the maximum of their lengths exists.
                              □

Lemma 9. *In a finite cycle free graph $G = (V,E)$ we have*

$$d_G(v) = \begin{cases} 0 & v \in src(G) \\ 1 + \max\{d_G(u) \mid (u,v) \in E\} & otherwise \end{cases}$$

Proof. For sources the claim immediately follows from the fact that there are only trivial paths to sources. Let now $v \in V \setminus src(G)$ be a non-source node. We show the equality by showing two inequalities:

- "$\geq$": Let u be the predecessor of v of greatest depth

$$L = d(u) = \max\{d(\hat{u}) \mid (\hat{u},v) \in E\}$$

with a longest path $p[0:L]$ to u from a source

$$p_0 \in src(G) \wedge p_L = u \wedge (u,v) \in E$$

Clearly $p \circ v$ is a path from a source to v of length $L + 1$, and thus

$$d(v) \geq L + 1 = 1 + d(u)$$

which proves the claim.

- "$\leq$": Let $p[0 : L+1]$ be a longest path from a source to v

$$p_0 \in src(G) \ \wedge \ p_{L+1} = v$$

Since p is a path p_L is a predecessor of v

$$(p_L, v) \in E$$

and thus subpath $p[0 : L]$ is a path from a source to a predecessor of v, which must thus have at least length L

$$d(p_L) \geq L$$

The claim follows

$$L+1 \ \leq \ d(p_L)+1 \ \leq \ 1 + \max\{d(u) \mid (u,v) \in E\}$$

$\square$

In order to define circuit evaluation in nested hardware units U we apply this to the following graph

$$G(U) = (N(U), E(U))$$

The nodes of the graph are the global signal names of U

$$N(U) = Sig(U)$$

For basic types which are not 1-bit registers $U \in BT \setminus \{\rho\}$ edges are created between all inputs $x \in in(U)$ and the output

$$E(U) = \{(x, out) \mid x \in in(U)\}$$

For 1-bit registers $U = \rho$, there are no edges

$$E(U) = \emptyset$$

For composite units edges in the set

$$E(U) = E_s(U) \cup E_b(U)$$

are generated in two cases:

- the source function s_U: we draw an edge from u to v if u is a source of v

$$E_s(U) = \{(u,v) \mid s_U(v) = u\}$$

Thus edges in $G(U)$ run opposite to the direction of the source function
- basic subunits y: we copy the edges from $E(t_U(y))$ (prefixed with $y.$)

$$E_b(U) = \{(y.x, y.z) \mid y \in Su(U), \ t_U(y) \in BT, \ (x,z) \in E(t_U(y))\}$$

From the examples from figures 10 and 11 one obtains the graphs from figures 21 and 22.

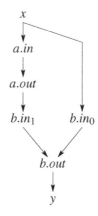

Fig. 21. The graph for Fig. 10 is cycle free

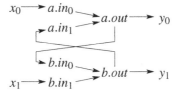

Fig. 22. The graph for the unit from Fig. 11 contains a cycle

For the definition of semantics in section 2.2.4 by circuit theory we require the graph $G(U)$ to be cycle free. This excludes the example of figure 11.[2] Obviously we can define now a *circuit* as a hardware unit whose only elementary subunits are gates and inverters.

Note that the sources of graph $G(U)$ are the input signals of U and the outputs of 1 bit registers:

Lemma 10.

$$src(G(U)) = sig^{in}(U) \cup \{ y.out \mid y \in Su(U),\ t_U(y) = \rho \}$$

For sequences $p[0:L]$ of signals and for subunits $\lambda \in su(U)$ we formally define the sequence

---

[2] The latter unit happens to be the classical construction of a 'set-clear flip-flop'. Its function can be explained in a more detailed physical circuit model with minimal and maximal bounds on the propagation delays of gates. For details see e.g. [Keller-Paul].

$$\lambda.p = (\lambda.p_0, \ldots, \lambda.p_L)$$

and show:

Lemma 11. *Let $\lambda \in su(U)$. Then $\lambda.p$ is a path in U iff p is a path in $t_U(\lambda)$.*

Proof. By bookkeeping: from

$$Sig(U) = pins(U) \cup \{\lambda.y \mid y \in Sig(t_U(\lambda)), \ \lambda \in su(U)\}$$

we conclude

$$\lambda.p_i \in Sig(U) \quad \leftrightarrow \quad p_i \in Sig(t_U(\lambda))$$

From

$$s_U(\lambda.x) = \lambda.s_{t_U(\lambda)}(x)$$

we get

$$p_i = s_{t_U(\lambda)}(p_{i+1}) \quad \leftrightarrow \quad \lambda.p_i = s_U(\lambda.p_{i+1})$$

Thus

$$(p_i, p_{i+1}) \in E_s(t_U(\lambda)) \quad \leftrightarrow \quad (\lambda.p_i, \lambda.p_{i+1}) \in E_s(U)$$

From

$$t_U(\lambda.y) = t_{t_U(\lambda)}(y)$$

we get with the definition of E_b

$$(p_i, p_{i+1}) \in E_b(t_U(\lambda))$$
$$\leftrightarrow \exists y \in Su(t_U(\lambda)), \ x, z. \ p_i = y.x \wedge p_{i+1} = y.z$$
$$\wedge \ t_{t_U(\lambda)}(y) \in BT \wedge (x,z) \in E(t_{t_U(\lambda)}(y))$$
$$\leftrightarrow \exists \lambda.y \in Su(U), \ x, z. \ \lambda.p_i = \lambda.y.x \wedge \lambda.p_{i+1} = \lambda.y.z$$
$$\wedge \ t_U(\lambda.y) \in BT \wedge (x,z) \in E(t_U(\lambda.y))$$
$$\leftrightarrow (\lambda.p_i, \lambda.p_{i+1}) \in E_b(U)$$

At this point the claim follows. $\qquad\qquad\square$

A signal $z \in Sig(U)$ will in general be relevant for the evaluation of signal $y \in Sig(U)$ if there is a path from z to y in graph $G(U)$, i.e., if z is a (not necessarily immediate) predecessor of y in $G(U)$. We collect the set of these signals into the set

$$pre_U(x) = \{z \in Sig(U) \mid \exists \text{ path from } z \text{ to } x \text{ in } G(U)\}$$

An input signal $q \in sig^{in}(U)$ will in general be relevant for the evaluation of a signal $y \in Sig(U)$ if there is a path from q to y in $G(U)$, and we collect the set of these input signals into the set

$$sig_U^{in}(x) = pre_U(x) \cap sig^{in}(U) = \{z \in sig^{in}(U) \mid \exists \text{ path from } z \text{ to } x \text{ in } G(U)\}$$

2.2 Semantics

2.2.1 Values of Input Signals

In classical switching theory circuits S with n inputs $a[n-1:0]$ and m outputs $b[m-1:0]$ have input values in $\mathbb{B}^n$, output values in $\mathbb{B}^m$ and compute switching functions

$$f : \mathbb{B}^n \to \mathbb{B}^m$$

Signals z in such a circuit compute functions

$$||z||_S : \mathbb{B}^n \to \mathbb{B}$$

which are defined by induction over the depth of the signals (which works because the underlying graphs are assumed to be cycle free). The induction obviously starts at the inputs a_i and for input values $x \in \mathbb{B}^n$ one defines

$$||a_i||_S(x) = x_i$$

Distinguishing signals z and the functions $||z||$ computed by them is formally clean but tedious. Overloading notation one can drop the double bars and reuse the signal names z for the computed functions

$$z_S : \mathbb{B}^n \to \mathbb{B}$$

Moreover, if it is clear what circuit is meant one can drop subscript S. The above definition of functions values computed by inputs then turns into

$$a_i(x) = x_i$$

In hardware units U inputs are partitioned into buses $b = in(U)_i$ with a single input signal $b \in sig^{in}(U)$ if b is a simple bus, i.e., $q_U(b) = \varepsilon$, or with n input signals $b_j \in sig^{in}(U)$ for $j \in [0:n-1]$ if b is a parallel bus with $q_U(b) = (n)$. Input values x for hardware units U are taken from the previously defined set

$$\Sigma^{in}(U) = \times_{i=1}^{ni(U)} \Sigma(q_U(in(U)_i))$$

We first define value $||in(U)||_U(x)$ for the entire sequence $in(U)$ of input buses as the identity on $\Sigma^{in}(U)$

$$||in(U)||(x) = x$$

From this we extract values $||b||_U$ for all buses $b \in bus^{in}(U)$ in the obvious way:

$$||in(U)_i||(x) = (||in(U)||(x))_i \quad \text{for} \quad i \in [1:ni(U)]$$

Thus in order to extract from x input value $||b||_U(x)$ of input bus $b \in bus^{in}(U)$ we have to refer to the index $ind(U,b)$ such that $in(U)_i = b$.

$$indx(U,b) = \varepsilon\{i \in [1:ni(U)] \ : \ in(U)_i = b\}$$

and get

Lemma 12. *For $b \in bus^{in}(U)$ holds*

$$||b||_U(x) = x_{indx(U,b)}$$

Proof. Using

$$b = in(U)_{indx(U,b)}$$

we obtain

$$\begin{aligned}||b||_U(x) &= ||in(U)_{indx(U,b)}||_U(x) \\ &= (||in(U)||_U(x))_{indx(U,b)} \\ &= x_{indx(U,b)}\end{aligned}$$

$\square$

Finally for parallel buses b, i.e. with $q_U(b) = (n)$ resp. width $w_U(b) = n$ we extract values $||b_j||(x)$ of components b_j in the obvious way by

$$||b_j||_U(x) = ||b||_U(x) \quad \text{for} \quad i \in [w_U(b) - 1 : 0]$$

resp.

$$||b_j||_U(x) = (x_{indx(U,b)})_j \quad \text{for} \quad i \in [w_U(b) - 1 : 0]$$

For the ALU in figure 5 we have

$$indx_{ALU}(a) = 1 \;,\; indx_{ALU}(b) = 2 \;,\; inx_{ALU}(f) = f$$

Thus for input value $x \in \Sigma^{in}(ALU)$ we get

$$||a||_{ALU}(x) = x_1 \;,\; ||b||_{ALU}(x) = x_2 \;,\; ||f||_{ALU}(x) = x_2$$

and for instance

$$||f_4||_{ALU}(x) = ((x)_3)_4$$

For output buses $b \in bus^{out}(U)$ we can also define the index $indx(U,b)$ of b in U as

$$indx(U,b) = \varepsilon \{ i \in [1 : no(U)] \mid out(U)_i = b \}$$

As names of input and output buses are disjoint this defines the index of IO buses $b \in bus^{io}(U)$ as

$$indx(U,b) = \begin{cases} \varepsilon \{ i \in [1 : ni(U)] \mid in(U)_i = b \} & b \in bus^{in}(U) \\ \varepsilon \{ i \in [1 : no(U)] \mid out(U)_i = b \} & b \in bus^{out}(U) \end{cases}$$

For later use we define for input values $x \in \Sigma^{in}(U)$ and simple or parallel input buses $b \in in(U)$ the value of the bus $x_U.b$ as

$$x_U.b = x_{indx(U,b)}$$

Trivial bookkeeping shows that $x_U.b$ has the intended meaning

Lemma 13. *For input values x and input buses b*

$$x \in \Sigma^{in}(U) \ \land \ b \in in(U)$$

we have for signals b

$$q_U(b) = \varepsilon \quad \rightarrow \quad ||b||_U(x) = x_U.b$$

and for signals b_i

$$q_U(b) = (n) \land i < n \quad \rightarrow \quad ||b_i||_U(x) = (x_U.b)_i$$

For signals $q \in sig^{in}(U)$ we define

$$x_U.q$$

as follows: if $q = b_i$ comes from a parallel bus, we take

$$x_U.q = x_U.(b_i) = (x_U.b)_i$$

If $q = b$ comes from a simple bus we already have

$$x_U.q = x_U.b$$

In contexts where it is clear which unit U is meant we drop the subindex U.

2.2.2 Configurations

A hardware unit U has *state* if it contains at least one 1-bit register, i.e., if it has a (possibly nested) subunit λ of type ρ, or is itself of type ρ

$$st(U) \quad \equiv \quad U = \rho \ \lor \ \exists \lambda \in Su(U). \ t_U(\lambda) = \rho$$

A subunit $z \in Su(U)$ of U has state, if the type of z in U has state

$$st_U(z) \equiv st(t_U(z))$$

The current state of such hardware units U is stored in *configurations h* taken from a set K_U. The set K_U of configurations for units U is defined inductively in a straight forward way. The only basic unit with state is the 1-bit register ρ. It can store a single bit, so its set of configurations is

$$K_\rho = \mathbb{B}$$

Now suppose unit H used as a direct subunit of U has state, i.e., we have

$$st(H)$$

and unit U has a subunit declaration σ of the form

$$v : H \quad \text{or} \quad v : H(I)$$

Then this contributes to the configurations

$$h \in K_U$$

a component $h.v$ of the following form:

- if $\sigma = v : H$, then component

$$h.v \in K_H$$

  is simply a configuration of H.
- if $\sigma = v : H(I)$, then

$$h.v : I \to K_H$$

  maps indices $i \in I$ to configurations

$$(h.v)(i) \in K_H$$

The configuration $h.(v(i))$ of subunit $v(i)$ is defined as the function value of $(h.v)(i)$

$$h.(v(i)) = (h.v)(i)$$

For nested subunits $\lambda.y$ of U with state, i.e.

$$\lambda.y \in Su(U) \wedge st(\lambda.y)$$

nested subcomponents of configurations h are defined by application of the above definition from left to right.

$$h.(\lambda.y) = \begin{cases} (h.v).y & \lambda = v \\ ((h.v)(i)).y & \lambda = v(i) \end{cases}$$

This recursion ends with basic nested subunits y of u with state, i.e. if

$$t_U(y) = \rho$$

Thus, configurations of units should be determined by the configurations of 1 bit registers present in the subunits of U.

Lemma 14. *Let U be any composite hardware unit and let $g, h \in K_U$ be configurations of U. If the subconfigurations $g.y$ and $h.y$ coincide on 1 bit registers*

$$\forall y \in Su(U). \, t_U(y) = \rho \to g.y = h.y$$

Then the configurations g and h are equal

$$g = h$$

Proof. The lemma is proven by induction on the nesting depth $nd(U)$

- $nd(U) = 1$. The only subunits λ of g and h with state are 1 bit registers ρ. For *lambda* $= v$ we get by hypothesis

$$g.v = h.v$$

For $\lambda = v(i)$ we get by hypothesis

$$(h.v)(i) = g.(v(i)) = h.(v(i)) = (h.v)(i)$$

As this holds for all i we get equality of the functions

$$g.v = h.v$$

As g and h agree on all components v we conclude

$$g = h$$

$nd(U) = d > 1$. For subunits $y = \lambda$ with nesting depth 0 we argue as above. For other subunits $\lambda.y$ let

$$V = t_U(\lambda) \quad \text{where} \quad nd(V) \leq d - 1$$

Thus we can use the induction hypothesis for configurations in K_V. If $\lambda = v$ we have by hypothesis

$$(g.v).y = g.(v.y) = h.(v.y) = (h.v).y$$

Thus $g.v$ and $h.v$ fulfil the hypothesis of the lemma and the induction hypothesis gives

$$g.v = h.v$$

For $\lambda = v(i)$ we get by hypothesis

$$((g.v)(i)).y = (g.(v(i))).y = (h.(v(i))).y = ((h.v)(i)).y$$

and we conclude with the induction hypothesis as in the base case successively

$$\forall i.(g.v)(i) = (h.v)(i) , \ g.v = h.v , \ h = v$$

□

For many designs U (in particular of registers and memories) configurations $h \in K_U$ happen to have only a single component $h.v$, usually for an arrys of subunits $h.v(i)$. Then h is a record with a single component $h.v$, and we allow to abbreviate

$$h = h.v \quad \text{and} \quad h(i) = h.v(i)$$

Examples

Let $h \in K_{reg(d)}$ be a configuration of the d bit register $reg(d)$ of figure 13. We have

$$K_\rho = \mathbb{B} \quad \text{and} \quad I = [0 : d - 1]$$

Thus $h.R$ is a mapping

$$h.R : [0 : d - 1] \to \mathbb{B}$$

which is of course equivalent to saying that $h.R$ is a bit sequence of length d, i.e.,

$$h.R \in \mathbb{B}^d$$

As $h.R$ is the only component of h we identify $h = h.R$ and get

$$K_{reg(d)} = \mathbb{B}^d$$

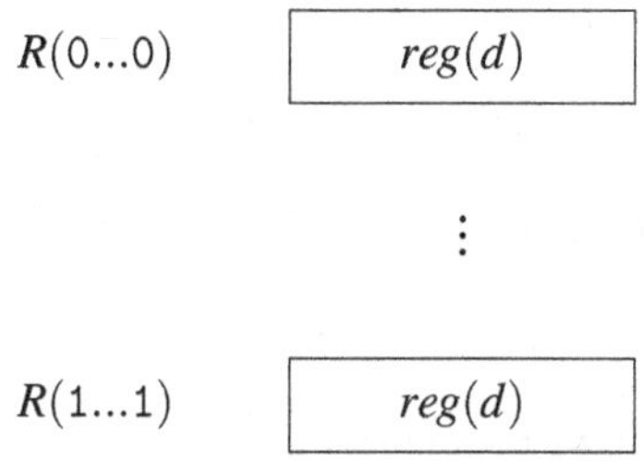

$R(0...0)$ $\boxed{reg(d)}$

$\vdots$

$R(1...1)$ $\boxed{reg(d)}$

Fig. 23. In constructions of a d-bit wide memory S with k address lines one stores data in 2^k copies of a d-bit register $reg(d)$, which are indexed with labels $R(i)$, $i \in \mathbb{B}^n$.

In constructions of a hardware memory S with k address lines and width d one places as a subunit an array R of 2^k such registers $reg(d)$ indexed by $I = \mathbb{B}^k$:

$$R : reg(d)\left(\right)$$

This is illustrated in figure 23. In this case we have for configurations $h \in K_S$

$$h.R : \mathbb{B}^k \to K_{R(d)}$$

i.e.,

$$h.R : \mathbb{B}^k \to \mathbb{B}^d$$

If R happens to be the only component of h we identify $h = h.R$ and get

$$h : \mathbb{B}^k \to \mathbb{B}^d$$

which — fortunately — is a classical memory configuration.

We can now define the value of signals which are outputs of 1-bit registers: the value of the output signal is simply the current configuration of the register. Recall that for 1-bit registers in U, i.e., subunits $r \in Su(U)$ with type $t_U(r) = \rho$, we abbreviated the output signal $r.out$ by r. We thus have

$$r \in Su(U) \wedge t_U(r) = \rho \quad \to \quad ||r||_U(h) = h.r$$

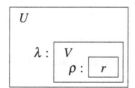

Fig. 24. Subunit r of direct subunit V of unit U

As illustrated in Fig. 24 let $\lambda \in su(U)$ be a direct subunit of U of type $V = t_U(\lambda)$ and let $r \in Su(V)$ be a subunit of V which is a register, i.e., with $t_V(r) = \rho$. Then $\lambda.r$ is also a subunit of U

$$\lambda.r \in Su(U)$$

Moreover $\lambda.r$ has in U also type ρ

$$t_U(\lambda.r) = t_V(r) = \rho$$

and the configurations of r in V and of $\lambda.r$ in U are by definition the same

$$h.(\lambda.r) = (h.\lambda).r$$

For the output signal of this unit we conclude

Lemma 15.
$$||\lambda.r||_U(h) = ||r||_V(h.\lambda)$$

Proof.
$$||\lambda.r||_U(h) = h.(\lambda.r) = (h.\lambda).r = ||r||_V(h.\lambda)$$

$\square$

2.2.3 Hardware Computations

Hardware units U are finite automata where

- states h are hardware configurations

$$h \in K_U$$

- the input alphabet is $\Sigma^{in}(U)$
- the output alphabet is $\Sigma^{out}(U)$

Semantics will then obviously defined by an output function

$$\eta_U : K_U \times \Sigma^{in}(U) \to \Sigma^{out}(U)$$

and a (hardware) state transition function

$$\delta_U : K_U \times \Sigma^{in}(U) \to K_U$$

Hardware computations are sequences

$$(h^t)$$

of *configurations in cycle t*; and if x^t is the input in cycle t, then output y^t in cycle t and the next state h^{t+1} are defined as

$$y^t = \eta_U(h^t, x^t) \quad \text{and} \quad h^{t+1} = \delta_U(h^t, x^t)$$

A reset signal is available as input for hardware units, i.e., we allow

$$reset \in in(U)$$

It is often convenient to number the cycle after *reset* with $t = 0$. Thus we choose

$$t \in \{-1\} \cup \mathbb{N} \quad \text{with start configuration} \quad h_s = h^{-1}$$

The reset signal is active in cycle $t = -1$ and inactive afterwards

$$reset^t = \begin{cases} 1 & t = -1 \\ 0 & t \geq 0 \end{cases}$$

In a start configuration $h_s = h^{-1}$ all 1-bit registers, i.e., subunits y of type ρ have binary but unknown value.

$$y \in Su(U) \wedge t_U(y) = \rho \rightarrow h^{-1}.y \in \mathbb{B}$$

We proceed to define transition function δ_H and output function η_H.

2.2.4 Circuit Evaluation

In general the value $||z||_U$ of a signal $z \in Sig(U)$ depends on the current configuration $h \in K_U$ and the current input value $x \in \Sigma^{in}(U)$. Thus we have

$$||z||_U : K_U \times \Sigma^{in}(U) \rightarrow \mathbb{B}$$

Function values $||z||_U(h,x)$ are defined by induction on the depth $d_{G(U)}(z)$ on signal z in graph $G(U)$. The base case is for signals $x \in src(U)$. For the sources of U we use the characterization of lemma 10, and obtain the following cases.

- for simple input buses $b \in bus^{in}(U)$ the value $||b||_U(x)$ of bus b with input $x \in \Sigma^{in}(U)$ was defined in section 2.2.1 as

$$||b||_U(x) = x_U.b$$

For parallel buses the value $||b_i||_U(x)$ of input signals b_i were defined as

$$||b_i||_U(x) = x_U.b_i \quad \text{for} \quad i \in [w_U(b) - 1 : 0]$$

We can thus define $||q||_U(h,x)$ for all input signals $q \in sig^{in}(U)$ by

$$||q||_U(h,x) = ||q||_U(x)$$

- for outputs r of 1-bit registers the current value $||r||_U(h)$ was defined in section 2.2.2 solely as a function of the current configuration h by the state $h.r$ of the register

$$t_U(r) = \rho \quad \rightarrow \quad ||r||_U(h) = h.r$$

We extend that definition to take both parameters by

$$||r||_U(h,x) = ||r||_U(h)$$

- the constant signals 0 and 1 have the obvious values independent of h and x

$$||0||_U(h,x) = 0, \; ||1||_U(h,x) = 1$$

For the remaining signals we distinguish the following cases:

- if z has in U a defined source signal $s_U(z)$, then the value is trivially taken from the source

$$z \in dom(s_U) \quad \rightarrow \quad ||z||_U(h,x) = ||s_U(z)||_U(h,x)$$

  This is obviously the only way to stay consistent with our abbreviation

$$z = s_U(z)$$

- inverters and gates z work as in switching theory. With the abbreviation $z.out = z$ we have for inverters

$$t_U(z) = inv \quad \rightarrow \quad ||z||_U(h,x) = /||z.in||_U(h,x)$$

  and for two-input gates $\circ \in \{\wedge, \vee, \oplus, NAND\}$

$$t_U(y) = \circ \quad \rightarrow \quad ||z||_U(h,x) = ||z.in_1||_U(h,x) \circ ||z.in_0||_U(h,x)$$

- for tri-state buses $\tau(n)$ with n inputs we require that at most one of the output enable signals is active

$$t_U(z) = \tau(n) \quad \rightarrow \quad \sum_{i=0}^{n-1} ||z.oe_i||_U(h,x) \leq 1$$

If an output enable signal oe_i is active, the input in_i of the corresponding driver is put on the bus. Otherwise we assume that the bus is pulled to value 1 by a pull up resistor

$$||z||_U(h,x) = \begin{cases} ||z.in_i||_U(h,x) & ||z.oe_i||_U(h,x) \\ 1 & \forall i. \; /||z.oe_i||_U(h,x) \end{cases}$$

If it is clear what unit is meant we can drop subscripts U, and if we abbreviate further

$$z^t = ||z||_U(h^t,x^t)$$

then the above definitions give for

- inputs $q \in sig^{in}(U)$
$$q^t = x^t.q$$

- outputs of 1 bit registers r with $t_U(r) = \rho$

$$r^t = h^t.r$$

- constants

$$0^t = 0, \ 1^t = 1$$

- signals $z \in dom(s)$ with source $s(z)$

$$z^t = s(z)^t$$

- inverters and gates z

$$t_U(z) = inv \quad \rightarrow \quad z^t = /z.in^t$$

$$t_U(z) = \circ \quad \rightarrow \quad z^t = z.in_1^t \circ z.in_0^t$$

- tri-state buses z

$$t_U(z) = \tau(n) \ \wedge \ 1 \geq \sum_i z.oe_i^t \quad \rightarrow \quad z^t = \begin{cases} z.in_i^t & z.oe_i^t = 1 \\ 1 & \text{otherwise} \end{cases}$$

As an additional requirement for the proper operation of tri-state buses we require: if different drivers drive the bus in cycles s and t, then there must be an intermediate cycle u when all drivers are disabled.

$$z.oe_i^s \ \wedge \ z.oe_j^t \ \wedge \ s < t \ \wedge \ i \neq j \quad \rightarrow \quad \exists u \in (s:t). \ \forall k. \ /z.oe_k^u$$

If you happen to be a hardware designer and feel like ignoring this rule, please consult section 3.5.1 first. This is not a joking matter.

2.2.5 Values of Buses and Outputs of Units

We have already defined functions $||z||_U$ for all *single* signals $z \in Sig(U)$. We extend this definition to internal buses and output buses b of U, i.e.,

$$b \in bus^{int}(U) \cup bus^{out}(U)$$

in a straight forward way. For subunits $\lambda \in su(U)$ of type $V = t_U(\lambda)$ we collect the sequence of input buses

$$\lambda.b, \ b \in bus^{in}(V)$$

into the sequence $in_U(\lambda)$ setting

$$in_U(\lambda) = (\lambda.b \mid b \in in(t_U(\lambda)))$$

Analogously we define a sequence of output buses by

$$out_U(\lambda) = (\lambda.b \mid b \in out(t_U(\lambda)))$$

If the ALU from figure 5 is placed with label λ into a unit U we have

$$in_U(\lambda) = (\lambda.a, \lambda.b, \lambda.f)$$
$$out_U(\lambda) = (\lambda.neg, \lambda.ovf, \lambda.res)$$

If unit V from figure 6 is placed as subunit λ we get

$$in_U(\lambda) = (\lambda.x, \lambda.y)$$
$$out_U(\lambda) = (\lambda.z)$$

Note that some of these buses are parallel buses that define multiple signals. This is obviously defined by qualifier

$$q_U(\lambda.b) = q_{l_U(\lambda)}(b)$$

With this we can treat the IO buses of direct subunits as buses with bus declaration

$$bd_U(\lambda.b).na = \lambda.b, \; bd_U(\lambda.b).q = q_U(\lambda.b)$$

We evaluate parallel buses b (including both the IO buses of U and the IO buses of direct subunits) with qualifier $q_U(b) = (n)$ by evaluating each individual signal in the bus

$$||b||_U(h,x) = (||b_{n-1}||_U(h,x), \ldots, ||b_0||_U(h,x))$$

The value of an n-bit bus is a bit string of length n.

$$||b||_U(h,x) \in \mathbb{B}^n$$

For simple buses b with qualifier $q_U(b) = \varepsilon$ we can use the same notation, because b is already a signal, and we have

$$||b||_U(h,x) \in \mathbb{B}$$

We evaluate sequences S of buses by evaluating each individual bus

$$||S||_U(h,x) = (||b||_U(h,x) \mid b \in S)$$

In the above example we obtain for the ALU with label λ

$$||in_U(\lambda)||_U(h,x) = (||\lambda.a||_U(h,x), ||\lambda.b||_U(h,x), ||\lambda.f||_U(h,x))$$

Returning to the interpretation of hardware units as finite state machines, we finally define the output $\eta(h,x)$ of unit U with configuration h and input x as

$$\eta(h,x) = ||out(U)||_U(h,x)$$

2.2.6 Updating Configurations

With signals

$$||z||_U(h,x)$$

we have in particular defined the input and clock enable signals

$$||r.in||_U(h,x) \quad \text{and} \quad ||r.ce||_U(h,x)$$

of all 1-bit registers r in U, i.e., of all nested subunits with $t_U(r) = \rho$. Such units are updated with the usual register semantics: if the clock enable signal is active, the current input is saved in the next state; otherwise the state stays the same. For the next state resp. configuration $\delta_U(h,x)$ we get

$$\delta_U(h,x).r = \begin{cases} ||r.in||_U(h,x) & ||r.ce||_U(h,x) \\ h.r & \text{otherwise} \end{cases}$$

By lemma 14 this already determines the entire next configuration $\delta_U(h,x)$. With abbreviations

$$z^t = ||z||_U(h^t,x^t)$$

we have in particular defined the input and clock enable signals

$$z^t = r.in^t \quad \text{and} \quad z^t = r.ce^t$$

of all 1 bit registers r and the above definition for the next state resp. configuration

$$h^{t+1} = \delta_U(h^t,x^t)$$

turns into

$$h^{t+1}.r = \begin{cases} r.in^t & r.ce^t = 1 \\ h^t.r & \text{otherwise} \end{cases}$$

With

$$r^t = r.out^t = h^t.r$$

we obtain

$$r^{t+1} = \begin{cases} r.in^t & r.ce^t = 1 \\ r^t & \text{otherwise} \end{cases}$$

2.2.7 Streamlining Notation

For signals x and y we have already abbreviated

$$s(x) = y \quad \text{to} \quad x = y$$

and for subunits λ with a single output bus x

$$\lambda.x \quad \text{to} \quad \lambda$$

We use three more abbreviations.

Abridged Subunit Specifications

For *nested subunits v.w* of a unit U we abbreviate

$$v.w \quad \text{to} \quad w$$

if w is not a direct subunit of U nor of other subunits u of U other than v.

$$(u \in su(U) \wedge u \neq v) \rightarrow (u \neq w \wedge w \notin Su(t_U(u)))$$

In the running example from figure 20 we allow to abbreviate

$$core.pc \quad \text{to} \quad pc$$

We carry over this abbreviation if unit U is placed into another unit as subunit z, i.e., we abbreviate

$$z.v.w \quad \text{to} \quad z.w$$

In multi-core machine MC with many such processors $p(i)$, i.e., with declaration

$$p : P(I)$$

we cannot abbreviate $p(i).core.pc$ to pc because

$$\forall j. \; pc \in Su(t_{MC}(p(j)))$$

We can however abbreviate

$$p(i).core.pc \quad \text{to} \quad p(i).pc$$

Implicit t Notation

Although signals and configurations z^t are time dependent, we often deal with predicates between them, which hold for all t. Trivial examples are *identities between signals* which might be defined or provable by say boolean algebra without any reference to t. Less trivial examples are *invariants*, which are stated for all t but might (subsequently, i.e. later) require proofs by induction involving t and $t+1$. In predicates which hold for all t we very often abbreviate

$$z^t = z$$

and call this *implicit t notation*. In this notation the semantics of inverters y simply becomes

$$y = /y.in$$

For $\circ$-gates y we get

$$y = y.in_1 \circ y.in_0$$

For basic tri-state buses y (with pull up resistor) we get under the operating conditions

$$y = \begin{cases} y.in_i & y.oe_i = 1 \\ 1 & \sum y.oe_i = 0 \end{cases}$$

and for d bit wide tri-state buses y

$$y = \begin{cases} y.in^{(i)} & y.oe_i = 1 \\ 1^d & \sum y.ou_i = 0 \end{cases}$$

Primed Notation

In induction steps or in definitions by induction over time, we usually deal with successive cycle t and $t + 1$ for all t. Following temporal logic [Lamport] we abbreviate in these situations

$$z^t = z \quad \text{and} \quad z^{t+1} = z'$$

The definition of semantics of nested hardware units then simplifies for 1-bit registers r to

$$r' = \begin{cases} r.in & r.ce = 1 \\ r & r.ce = 0 \end{cases}$$

For n-bit registers $R(n)$ we get analogously

$$R' = \begin{cases} R.in & R.ce = 1 \\ R & R.ce = 0 \end{cases}$$

Primed notation for tuples of components and signals

For components and signals $x_1, \ldots, x_n$ we also abbreviate

$$(x_1, \ldots, x_n)^t = (x_1^t, \ldots, x_n^t)$$

With implicit t notation, this becomes

$$(x_1, \ldots, x_n) = (x_1^t, \ldots, x_n^t) \quad \text{and} \quad (x_1, \ldots, x_n)' = (x_1^{t+1}, \ldots, x_n^{t+1})$$

For example, in a processor with program counters pc and dpc, we would write

$$(pc, dpc) \quad \text{for} \quad (pc^t, dpc^t)$$

and similarly

$$(pc, dpc)' \quad \text{for} \quad (pc^{t+1}, dpc^{t+1})$$

2.3 Modular Reasoning

The semantics defined so far hinges on very detailed mechanisms: the update of 1-bit registers ρ, the wiring structure of *global* signals $y \in Sig(U)$ in nested subunits and the functions computed by gates, inverters and buses. The formalism involved, in particular the global naming of nested subunits and their signals, is a bit on the heavy side, but *in certain situations* less won't do. Imagine a multi-core machine with a cache memory system with caches $ca(i)$, each with a control automaton $ca(i).con$ controlling the cache coherence protocol and storing state in a register $ca(i).con.st$. If we wish to argue, say as in [KMP14], about the correctness of the implementation of such a protocol, we have to be able to speak simultaneously about the states $ca(i).con.st^t$ and $ca(j).con.st^t$ of different caches i and j during cycle t.

Using streamlined notation we can abbreviate to $ca(i).st^t$ and $ca(j).st^t$ and we can even further abbreviate

$$st(i)^t = ca(i).st^t$$

But in order to abbreviate, one has to start with something general enough to abbreviate from. So introducing global names for units and signals does not appear to be redundant. On the other hand while arguing about the working and correctness of a unit U one obviously wishes to argue *as often as possible* about the (direct) subunits $\lambda \in su(U)$ of U alone. For example, one would like to prove the correctness of an arithmetic unit (AU) using the correctness of the adder as a unit, rather than the exact wiring and gates of the adder. To enable this we define a big-step semantics of units which encapsulates the implementation.

In full notation the big step semantics of a unit λ of type V is defined by

- value

$$||q||_V(h,x)$$

  of output signals $q \in sig^{out}(V)$ as a function of configurations $h_V \in K_V$ for V and of inputs $x \in \Sigma_V^{in}$.
- next configuration

$$h' = \delta_V(h_V, x)$$

  as a function δ_V of full inputs $x \in \Sigma^{in}(U)$ and configurations $h_V \in K_V$

If these functions are *defined and known* for all types V of direct subunits of U, then we would like to be able to compute signals $||z||_U$ and next configuration δ_U arguing only about the wiring in unit U and the big step semantics of the subunits. But before we can do that we have of course to be able to check in a hierarchical way whether signals in U are well defined, i.e., the graph $G(U)$ is cycle-free. It turns out that the latter problem can be solved with very little extra knowledge about information flow in the subunit types V, which we will encapsulate in graphs $G'(V)$.

2.3.1 Tracking Paths

For hardware units U we define the directed bipartite graph

$$G'(U) = (N'(U), E'(U))$$

The nodes of $G'(U)$ are the IO signals of U and edges are between input and output signals

$$N'(U) = pins(U), \quad E'(U) \subseteq sig^{in}(U) \times sig^{out}(U)$$

There is an edge in $E'(U)$ from input bus a to output bus b if there is a path from a to b in $G(U)$

$$(a,b) \in E'(U) \quad \leftrightarrow \quad \exists \quad \text{path from} \quad a \quad \text{to} \quad b \quad \text{in} \quad G(U)$$

We conclude

Lemma 16.
$$(u,x) \in E'(U) \quad \leftrightarrow \quad u \in sig_U^{in}(x)$$

The graphs $G'(U)$ can be constructed inductively — i.e., using only graphs $G'(V)$ of direct subunits of type V, without needing to know the full graphs $G(V)$ — in a straight forward way. For basic units $U \in BT$ graph $G'(U)$ has simply edges from all inputs $a \in sig^{in}(U)$ to the single output $b \in sig^{out}(U)$. Now assume that graphs $G'(V)$ are known for the types

$$V = t_U(\lambda), \ \lambda \in su(U)$$

Then we can construct $G'(U)$ by studying instead of the full graph $G(U)$ the much simpler graph

$$G''(U) = (N''(U), E''(U))$$

that we obtain if we replace in $G(U)$ subgraphs generated by subunits λ by graphs $G'(t_U(\lambda))$. Formally the nodes of $G''(U)$ are the *top level* signals of U

$$N''(U) = sig(U)$$

Edges in $E''(U)$ come from the source function s_U of unit U and from the edges in graphs $G'(t_U(\lambda))$ of the subunits λ of U

$$E''(U) = \{ (y,z) \in sig(U) \mid y = s_U(z) \} \cup \bigcup_{\lambda \in su(U)} \{ (\lambda.a, \lambda.b) \mid (a,b) \in E'(t_U(\lambda)) \}$$

We can now easily show

Lemma 17. *There is a path from x to y in $G(U)$ if and only if there is a path from x to y in $G''(U)$.*

Proof. By case distinction on whether U is a basic unit or not. For basic types graphs $G(U)$ and $G''(U)$ are identical and there is nothing to show.

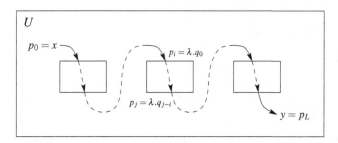

Fig. 25. Path in $G(U)$ entering and leaving direct subunit λ at nodes $p_i = \lambda.q_0$ and $p_j = \lambda.q_{j-i}$

For composite units U first assume the existence of a path $p[0:L]$ from x to y in $G(U)$ as illustrated in figure 25. Identify in this path traversals of direct subunits λ. Formally with

$$V = t_U(\lambda),\ nd(V) < d$$

this are segments

$$p[i:j] = \lambda.q[0:j-i] \quad \text{with} \quad q_0 \in sig^{in}(V),\ q_{j-i} \in sig^{out}(V)$$

By lemma 11 we conclude that q is a path in $G(V)$. By definition of $G'(V)$ there is an edge from q_0 to q_{j-i} in $E'(V)$. As illustrated in figure 26 replacing in p segments $p[i:j]$ by edges (p_i, p_j), i.e., throwing away intermediate nodes, gives therefore a path from $x = p_0$ to $y = p_L$ in $G''(U)$.

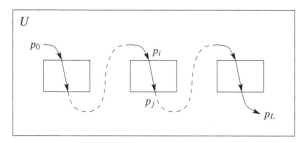

Fig. 26. In graph $G''(U)$ path segments $p[i:j]$ traversing unit λ are replaced by edges

For the other direction assume the existence of a path $p[0:L]$ from x to y in $G''(U)$. Identify in this path edges

$$(p_i, p_{i+1}) = (\lambda.a, \lambda.b) \quad \text{with} \quad t_U(\lambda) = V \wedge (a,b) \in E''(V)$$

For each such edge (a,b) there is by definition a path $q[0:M]$ from a to b in $G(V)$. By lemma 11 we conclude that $\lambda.q$ is a path in $G(U)$. Replace in p edge $(\lambda.a, \lambda.b)$ by the corresponding path $\lambda.q$. The resulting path is a path from y to z in $G(U)$ (formally by repeated application of lemma 6). □

Trivial consequences are

Lemma 18.

- $(u,x) \in E'(U) \quad \leftrightarrow \quad \exists\, path\ from\ u\ to\ x\ in \quad G''(U)$
- *Graph $G(U)$ is cycle free if and only if $G'(U)$ and all graphs $G'(t_U(y))$ with $y \in Su(U)$ are cycle free*

The first part of the lemma gives an inductive construction of graphs $G'(U)$. The second part gives an inductive method to decide well-definedness of semantics of nested hardware units. It remains to deal with circuit evaluation.

2.3.2 Evaluating Circuits

Here things get more technical than one would expect; therefore we explain the issues involved first with some examples.

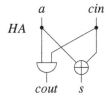

Fig. 27. Half adder HA

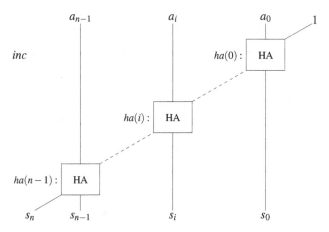

Fig. 28. Standard construction of an incrementer inc. The half adders are direct subunits of inc, here with labels $ha(i)$.

Suppose we use the half adder HA from figure 27 with specification

$$\langle cout, s \rangle = a + cin$$

to construct an n-bit incrementer inc. As illustrated in figure 28 the usual way would be to place n copies of the half adder with labels $ha(i)$ as direct subunits inc and wired in the usual way. The resulting unit is a circuit with inputs $a[n-1:0]$ and outputs $s[n:0]$. Abbreviating

$$cout_i = ha(i).cout$$

one would show by induction on i

$$\langle cout_i \circ s[i:0]\rangle = \langle a[i-1:0]\rangle + 1$$

and get for unit *inc* the specification

$$\langle s[n:0]\rangle = \langle a[n-1:0]\rangle + 1$$

which is in a natural way consistent with the bus structure. There should be no problem to use unit *inc* as a subcircuit of other units very much like a gate, and we will show shortly how this can be done in a quite general theory of subcircuit evaluation.

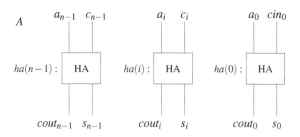

Fig. 29. Half adder array A with n half adders as direct subunits but without internal wiring

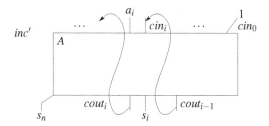

Fig. 30. Incrementer inc' is constructed by completing the wiring of the half adders outside of array A

But before let us play devil's advocate and construct an incrementer inc' in two steps: i) place the half adders into a half adder array A as shown in figure 29 and then ii) place a single instance of this array as a direct subunit of inc' with label A (i.e., following the naming convention for such situations) and complete the wiring of unit inc' *outside* the half adder array as shown in figure 30. Due to the edges $(A.cin_{i+1}, A.cout_i)$ the path of the carry chain now leaves and reenters unit A several times. The specification of A is obviously

$$\langle cout_i, s_i\rangle = a_i + cin_i \quad \text{for} \quad i \in [n-1:0]$$

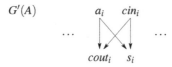

$$G'(A) \qquad a_i \quad cin_i$$
$$\cdots \qquad \qquad \cdots$$
$$cout_i \quad s_i$$

Fig. 31. Graph $G'(A)$ of the half adder array

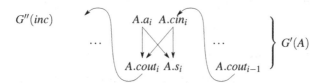

Fig. 32. Graph $G''(inc')$ of incrementer inc'

Clearly, the resulting circuit is completely equivalent to the previous construction, and our general theory of well-definedness even suggests an evaluation order: construct graphs $G'(A)$ and $G''(inc')$ as shown in figures 31 and 32 evaluate signals *in the order of their depth in* $G''(inc')$.

In the example the inputs of subunit A are $A.cin[n-1:0[$ and $A[n-1:0]$; its outputs are $A.s[n-1:0]$ and $A.cout[n-1:0]$. When we determine in inc' the functions computed by outputs $A.s_i$ and $A.cout_i$ of subunit A in the order of their depth in $G''(inc')$ we obtain with little effort

$$A.s_i = (\langle a[i:0]\rangle + 1 \bmod 2^i)$$
$$A.cout_i \equiv (\langle a[i:0]\rangle + 1 = 2^{i+1})$$

Trying to return to the full notation of section 2.2 we observe however, that for $i < n-1$ the obvious arguments x in $||A.si||_{inc'}(x)$ and $||A.cout_i||_{inc'}(x)$ only have $i+1 < n$ bits, i.e.

$$x \in \mathbb{B}^{i+1}, \ \mathbb{B}^{i+1} \neq \mathbb{B}^n = \Sigma^{in}(inc')$$

This does not fit the prescribed format for signals s in subunit A requiring

$$||s||_{inc'}(h,x) \quad \text{with} \quad x \in \Sigma^{in}(inc')$$

This formal difficulty is easily remedied. For

$$I \subset sig^{in}(U) \quad \text{and} \quad x \in \Sigma^{in}(U)$$

we define a *restricted* version

$$x|_I \in \Sigma^{in}(U)$$

of x by forcing input bits outside of I to zero. Recall that at the end of section 2.2.1 we defined for input signals $q \in sig^{in}(U)$ and input values $x \in \Sigma^{in}(U)$ the bit $x.q$ of x determining the value $||q||_U(x)$, i.e. with

$$||q||_U(x) = x.q$$

For such input signals q we now simply define

$$(x|_I).q = (x.q \land q \in I) = \begin{cases} x.q & q \in I \\ 0 & q \notin I \end{cases}$$

In order to compute $||s||_U(h,x)$ in cases, when the relevant but not all bits of x are known, we simply force input bits outside of $I = sig_U^{in}(s)$ to zero, i.e. we define it in the form

$$||s||_U(h,x) = t(h,x|_I) \quad \text{with} \quad x \in \Sigma^{in}(U)$$

In the above examples we have

$$sig_{inc'}^{in}(s_i) = set(a[i:0])$$

and

$$x|_{set(a[i:0])} = 0^{n-i-1} \circ x[i:0]$$

In general a trivial induction on the depth $d_{G(U)}(s)$ of signals $s \in Sig(U)$ shows that predecessors of s are evaluated correctly with $x|_{sig_U^{in}(s)}$

Lemma 19. *Suppose*

- $s \in Sig(U)$ *is a signal of* U
- $h \in K_U$ *is a configuration of* U
- $x \in \Sigma^{in}(U)$ *is an input value for* U *and*
- $r \in pre_U(s)$ *is a predecessor of* s *in* U.

Then

$$||r||_U(h,x) = ||r||_U(h,x|_{sig_U^{in}(s)})$$

This is illustrated in figure 33.

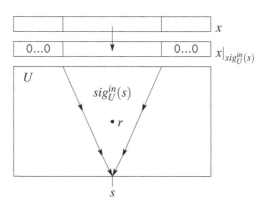

Fig. 33. For predecessors r of s the value of $||r||_U(h,x)$ does not change if we set input signals which are not predecessors of s to zero

We now can show in complete generality how to evaluate circuits of nested hardware units in a hierarchical way. We have to compute signals

$$||s||_U(h,x) \quad \text{for} \quad s \in sig(U),\ h \in K_U,\ x \in \Sigma^{in}(U)$$

The order of evaluation of these (top level) signals $s \in sig(U)$ is by their depth $d_{G''(U)}(r)$ in graph $G''(U)$.

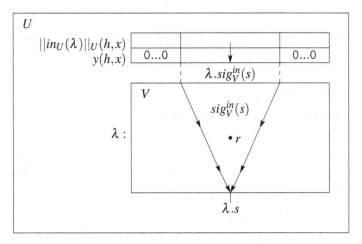

Fig. 34. For predecessors r of s in V the value of $||\lambda.r||_V(h,x)$ is computed only from the portion $y(h,x)$ of $||in_U(\lambda)||_U(h,x)$ belonging to the predecessors of s in V

When it comes to evaluation of a signal $\lambda.s$ of a direct subunit λ of U with type

$$V = t_U(\lambda)$$

as shown in figure 34, we know from lemma 19 that it suffices to consider for subunit λ input $||in_U(\lambda)||_U(h,x)$ restricted to $sig_V^{in}(s)$. We abbreviate this input as

$$y(h,x) = ||in_U(\lambda)||_U(h,x)\big|_{sig_V^{in}(s)}$$

Unfolding definitions this gives for $q \in sig^{in}(V)$:

$$y(h,x).q = \begin{cases} ||\lambda.q||_U(h,x) & q \in sig_V^{in}(s) \\ 0 & \text{otherwise} \end{cases}$$

By construction of graphs $G'(U)$ we have

$$q \in sig_V^{in}(s) \rightarrow d_{G'(U)}(\lambda.q) < d_{G'(U)}(\lambda.s)$$

so this is well defined. We now use the rules of circuit evaluation for nested hardware units to show

Lemma 20. *For all predecessors $r \in prev(s)$ of s in V holds*

$$||\lambda.r||_U(h,x) = ||r||_V(h.\lambda, y(h,x))$$

Proof. By induction on the depth $d_V(r)$. If $d_V(r) = 0$, then r is either an input signal of V, i.e., $r \in sig^{in}(V) \cap prev(s)$, or r is the output of a 1 bit register in V.

- if r is an input signal of V

$$||r||_V(y(h,x)) = y(h,x).r = ||\lambda.r||_U(h,x)$$

- if r is (the output of) a 1 bit register in V we use lemma 15 need to show

$$||\lambda.r||_U(h,x) = ||\lambda.r||_U(h) = ||r||_V(h.\lambda) = ||r||_V(h.\lambda, y(h,x))$$

which is exactly lemma 15.

For the induction step we only consider $\circ$-gates r, i.e.,

$$r \in Su(V),\ t_V(r) = \circ$$

The argument for inverters and buses is completely analogous. Using the rules of circuit evaluation and the induction hypothesis for signals $r.in1$, $r.in2$ we obtain

$$\begin{aligned}
||\lambda.r||_U(h,x) &= ||\lambda.r.in1||_U(h,x) \circ ||\lambda.r.in2||_U(h,x) \\
&= ||r.in1||_V(h.\lambda, y(h,x)) \circ ||r.in2||_V(h.\lambda, y(h,x)) \\
&= ||r||_V(h.\lambda, y(h,x))
\end{aligned}$$

$\square$

For $s = r$ this allows to compute the desired value $||\lambda.s||_U(h,x)$ in unit U from the specification $||s||_V(h.\lambda, y)$ of output s in V with input $y(h,x)$

$$||\lambda.s||_U(h,x) = ||s||_V(h.\lambda, y(h,x))$$

2.3.3 The Easy Common Case

That paths leave and reenter the same subunit is rare in real designs. In fact in the vast majority of real designs it does not happen for any of the subunits. In the construction of graphs $G''(U)$ one can in this situation replace for each subunit λ of type $V = t_U(\lambda)$ graphs $G'(V)$ by the complete bipartite graphs

$$\begin{aligned}
H(V) &= (N(H(V)), E(H(V))) \\
N(H(V)) &= sig^{in}(V) \cup sig^{out}(V) \\
E(H(V)) &= sig^{in}(V) \times sig^{out}(V)
\end{aligned}$$

If no path in $G(U)$ leaves and reenters the same direct subunit $\lambda \in su(U)$, the graph $G''(U)$ constructed from these subgraphs $H(t_U(\lambda))$ is cycle free.

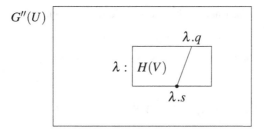

Fig. 35. In graphs $H(V)$ any pair of input signals $q \in sig^{in}(V)$ and $s \in sig^{out}(U)$ is connected by an edge.

As illustrated in figure 35 for any input and output signals

$$q \in sig^{in}(V), \ s \in sig^{out}(V)$$

of V we have in graph $G''(U)$ the edge

$$(\lambda.q, \lambda.s) \in G''(U)$$

and therefore

$$d_{G''(U)}(\lambda.r) < d_{G''(U)}(\lambda.s)$$

This has the very desirable consequence that when we try do define values $||\lambda.r||_U(h,x)$ for any output signals $r \in sig^{out}(V)$, the values $||\lambda.q||_U(h,x)$ are already defined for *all* inputs signals $q \in sig^{in}(V)$.

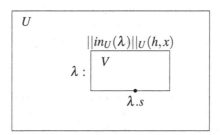

Fig. 36. If graphs $H(V)$ can be used in the construction of graphs $G''(U)''$, then we can assume the entire input input value $||in_U(\lambda)||_U(h,x)$ to be available when we try to evaluate any output $\lambda.s$ of subunit λ.

As illustrated in figure 36, the entire input $||in_U(\lambda)||_U(h,x)$ of subunit λ is known when we try to evaluate the circuits in subunit λ. There is no need for a restriction of the inputs to the bits that are already known, and instead of lemma 20 we can use

Lemma 21. *For any signal $r \in Sig(V)$*

$$||\lambda.r||_U(h,x) = ||r||_V(h.\lambda, ||in_U(\lambda)||_U(h,x))$$

Proof. Exactly along the lines of the proof of lemma 20 without the need to worry about restricted inputs.   □

As a corollary we get the following very intuitive result.

Lemma 22.

$$||out_U(\lambda)||_U(h,x) = ||out(V)||_V(h.\lambda, ||in_U(\lambda)||_U(h,x))$$

Observe that the last two lemmas also hold in the general case considered in section 2.3.2. But there they can not always be used to compute the value of signals, because sometimes only portions of the input values of subunits are known.

2.3.4 Cycles of Buses Between Units

In section 2.3.2 we were able to show, how to do modular reasoning for all units U. The paths inside a subunit V were summarized by the graphs $G'(V)$. The prize of this generality was that we had to argue about every single output signal $s \in sig^{out}(V)$ and its relevant inputs $sig_V^{in}(s)$; for circuit evaluation we had to argue in lemma 20 about restricted inputs

$$y(h,x) = (||in_U(\lambda)||_U(h,x))|_{sig_V^{in}(s)}$$

Working with restricted input values for single output signals is cumbersome and can be avoided if one stays away from designs like the incrementer inc'.

In contrast we made in section 2.3.3 no assumption whatsoever about internal paths of subunits V. Formally this was reflected in graphs $H(V)$ which showed *possible* — not necessarily *present* — paths from any input signal q to any output signal s of V. Freedom of cycles in the resulting graphs $G''(U)$ is a sufficient criterion for the well definedness of signal values. Fortunately it happens to work for the vast majority of practical designs, and in lemma 22 we could argue *in the usual way* about the value of all inputs

$$||in_U(\lambda)||_U(h,x)$$

We will find however very natural and practical examples where the usual way does not work. Fortunately, in these designs we will not need to study how single output signals of V depend on the values of single input signals. It will suffice to study how the values $||b||_V$ of output *buses* $b \in bus^{out}(V)$ depend on the values $||a||_V$ of certain input *buses* $a \in bus^{in}(V)$ relevant for b. For output buses b of U we proceed to define the set $bus_U^{in}(b)$ of relevant input buses for b.

The relevant input signals for all signals y of an output bus

$$b \in bus^{out}(U)$$

are collected into the set

$$sig_U^{in}(b) = \bigcup \{ sig_U^{in}(q) \mid q \in sig_U(b) \}$$

and the predecessors of signals of bus b are

$$pre_U(b) = \bigcup\{pre_U(q) \mid q \in sig_U(b)\}$$

An input bus $a \in bus^{in}(U)$ is relevant for output bus b if its signals intersect the relevant input signals for bus b; the set of these buses is collected into the set

$$bus_U^{in}(b) = \{a \in bus^{in}(U) \mid sig_U(a) \cap sig_U^{in}(b) \neq \emptyset\}$$

Obviously we have

$$sig_U^{in}(b) \subseteq \bigcup\{sig_U(a) \mid a \in bus_U^{in}(b)\}$$

We require the sets $sig_U^{in}(b)$ to be compatible with the bus structure, i.e., that they consist *exactly* of the signals on the relevant input buses $a \in bus_U^{in}(b)$ for b:

$$sig_U^{in}(b) = \bigcup\{sig_U(a) \mid a \in bus_U^{in}(b)\}$$

This can always be achieved by splitting buses, but designers usually partition pins into buses such that this condition is fulfilled.

Instead of graphs $G'(V)$, which model all existing paths, and graphs $H(V)$ which model all possible paths (not just those actually present), we now model dependencies between buses by graphs $F(V)$. As before graphs $F(V)$ are bipartite graphs between the input and output signals of V

$$F(V) = (N(F(V)), E(F(V)))$$
$$N(F(V)) = sig^{in}(V) \cup sig^{out}(V)$$
$$E(F(V)) \subseteq sig^{in}(V) \times sig^{out}(V)$$

An edge from a signal q of an input bus a of V

$$q \in sig_V(a), \ a \in bus^{in}(V)$$

and a signal s of an output bus b of V

$$s \in sig_V(b), \ b \in bus^{out}(V)$$

is present iff a is a relevant input bus for b

$$(q,s) \in E(F(V)) \quad \leftrightarrow \quad a \in bus_V^{in}(b)$$

Thus, for the edge (q,s) to be present, it suffices that there is some path from some signal q of a to some signal s of b. A path from q to s does not have to be present. If we construct now graph $G''(U)$ with $F(V)$ instead of $G'(V)$ resp. $H(V)$ we find for any signals q and s as above: if a is a relevant input bus for b, then q has in $G''(U)$ a smaller depth than s

$$a \in bus_V^{in}(b) \quad \rightarrow \quad d_{G''(U)}(q) < d_{G''(U)}(s)$$

Thus if we evaluate circuit signals in the order of depth in these graphs $G''(U)$ and we come for any such s to the definition of $||\lambda.s||_U$ in U we can assume that the values $||\lambda.q||_U$ are already defined for all signals q on input buses b relevant for a. I.e., we can assume that

$$||\lambda.a||_U(h,x) \quad \text{for} \quad a \in bus_V^{in}(b)$$

is defined. Input values $||in_U(\lambda)||_U(h,x)$ now have to be restricted at the bus levels, which for practical purposes is much less tedious than at the signal level. For subsets of input buses of V

$$B \subseteq bus^{in}(V)$$

and input values x of V

$$x \in \Sigma^{in}(V)$$

the restriction $x|_B$ of x to the buses in B is obtained by setting the signals on all buses not in B to zero.

$$(x|_B)_V.b = \begin{cases} x_V.b & b \in B \\ 0^{w_V(b)} & b \notin B \end{cases}$$

For the computation of $||\lambda.b||_U$ we have to restrict input $||in_U(\lambda)||_U$ to the set $bus_V^{in}(b)$ of relevant input buses for b, i.e., we have to consider

$$(||in_U(\lambda)||_U(h,x))|_{bus_V^{in}(b)}$$

For output buses $b \in bus^{out}(V)$ we define the set $prev(b)$ of predecessor signals of b in the obvious ways as the set of predecessors of the signals of bus b

$$prev(b) = \bigcup_{s \in sig_V(b)} prev(s)$$

and lemma 20 now becomes

Lemma 23. *For all predecessors $r \in prev(b)$ of bus b in V holds*

$$||\lambda.r||_U(h,x) = ||r||_V(h.\lambda, (||in_U(\lambda)||_U(h,x))|_{bus_V^{in}(b)})$$

For the evaluation of output buses b of V this gives the reasonably intuitive result

Lemma 24.

$$||\lambda.b||_U(h,x) = ||b||_V(h.\lambda, (||in_U(\lambda)||_U(h,x))|_{bus_V^{in}(b)})$$

In schematics we will not draw the graphs $F(V)$ in the usual way, because for $a \in bus_V^{in}(b)$ we would have to draw a complete bipartite graph between the signals of the buses a and b. As shown in figure x we will instead compress such a complete bipartite graph simply by a double arrow from a to b.

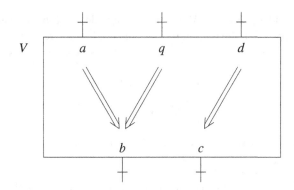

Fig. 37. In schematics $a \in bus_V^{in}(b)$ is visualized as a double arrow from a to b. Here $bus_V^{in}(b) = \{a, q\}$, $bus_V^{in}(c) = \{d\}$.

2.3.5 Updating Configurations

This can be postponed until all circuit signals are evaluated, thus no restricted inputs need to be considered. For any direct subunit λ of U with state and of type

$$t_U(\lambda) = V$$

we compute component $\delta_U(h, x).\lambda$ — in the obvious way — by updating $h.\lambda$ with the transition function δ_V for V and the input $||in_U(\lambda)||_U(h, x)$, i.e., by

$$\delta_V(h.\lambda, ||in_U(\lambda)||_U(h, x))$$

That this reproduces the small steps semantics is stated in the following result.

Lemma 25.

$$\lambda \in su(U) \wedge V = t_U(\lambda) \wedge st(\lambda) \quad \rightarrow \quad \delta_U(h, x).\lambda = \delta_V(h.\lambda, ||in_U(\lambda)||_U(h, x))$$

Proof. There is a fairly obvious case split by the nesting depth of unit V. For nesting depth $nd(V) \geq 1$ we consider subunits $\lambda.y$ of V type ρ and study their next state $(\delta_U(h, x).\lambda).y$. With lemma 22 we conclude

$$
\begin{aligned}
&(\delta_U(h, x).\lambda).y \\
&= \delta_U(h, x).(\lambda.y) \\
&= \begin{cases} ||\lambda.y.in||_U(h, x) & ||\lambda.y.ce||_U(h, x) = 1 \\ h.(\lambda.y) & \text{otherwise} \end{cases} \\
&= \begin{cases} ||y.in||_V(h.\lambda, ||in_U(\lambda)||_U(h, x)) & ||y.ce||_V(h.\lambda, ||in_U(\lambda)||_U(h, x)) = 1 \\ (h.\lambda).y & \text{otherwise} \end{cases} \\
&= \delta_V(h.\lambda, ||in_U(\lambda)||_U(h, x)).y
\end{aligned}
$$

Thus $\delta_U(h,x).\lambda$ and $\delta_V(h.\lambda||, in(V)||_U(h,x))$ coincide on 1 bit registers, and by lemma 14 this implies that the configurations are equal. In the remaining case unit V has state and it has nesting depth 0, i.e., it is already a single 1 bit register

$$t_U(\lambda) = V = \rho$$

Replacing in the above computation $\lambda.y$ by λ we get

$$\delta_U(h,x).\lambda = \begin{cases} ||\lambda.in||_U(h,x) & ||\lambda.ce||_U(h,x) = 1 \\ h.\lambda & \text{otherwise} \end{cases}$$

$$= \begin{cases} ||in||_\rho(h.\lambda, ||in_U(\lambda)||_U(h,x)) & ||ce||_\rho(h.\lambda, ||in_U(\lambda)||_U(h,x)) = 1 \\ h.\lambda & \text{otherwise} \end{cases}$$

$$= \delta_\rho(h.\lambda, ||in_U(\lambda)||_U(h,x))$$

and are done.   □

2.4 Expressions and Assignments as Syntactic Sugar

In classical switching theory the semantics of boolean expressions and circuits is defined independently. There is a straight forward translation of boolean expressions into circuits, i.e., gates interconnected by wires. That the translation is correct, i.e., preserves semantics is a completely trivial exercise. Because it is easier to write down expressions than to specify interconnections between single gates, this can save much work, and thus we would like to use formulae as an efficient means to specify source functions of hardware units too. For technical reasons however we deviate from the order known in switching theory. Instead

- we define the syntax of formulae and assignments as parts of hardware units
- we immediately specify how units with the new constructs are transformed into the units defined so far, i.e., we treat the new constructs as syntactic sugar, which i) implicitly place further subunits λ and ii) specify (portions of) the source function
- we finally show that signals defined by formulae have the expected behavior *if* the transformed nested hardware unit is cycle free.

2.4.1 Syntax

Obviously we have to argue by induction on the structure of formulae, and we need to talk about hardware units which are gradually augmented by subunits and partial wiring/source functions. Thus we define *partial hardware units* as hardware units where the source function is allowed to be partial. We say that partial hardware unit U' *extends* partial hardware unit U (and write $U \subseteq U'$) if all direct subunits of U' are subunits of U and the source functions s_U and $s_{U'}$ coincide on the domain of s_U.

$$U \subseteq U' \quad \leftrightarrow \quad su(U) \subseteq su(U') \wedge s_U = s_{U'}|_{dom(s_U)}$$

We allow bus names as arguments of expressions. In a partial hardware U the visible buses $B(U)$ are the input buses of U and the output buses of the direct subunits of U

$$B(U) = bus^{in}(U) \cup \{ \lambda.b \mid \lambda \in su(U),\ b \in bus^{out}(t_U(\lambda)) \}$$

We define sets $E(B,F)$ of expressions relative to

- a set B of buses b with a defined qualifier $q(b)$. Initially we take

$$B = B(U) \quad \text{and} \quad q(b) = w_U(b)$$

- a set F of circuits with single output buses that has already been defined. As elementary circuits are obviously defined, the set F certainly includes the inverter and gates. In units $f \in F$ with single output buses we reuse f as the name of the output bus, and abbreviate the qualifier of this bus as

$$q(f) = q_f(f)$$

The width $w(e)$ of expressions will be derived in the usual way from the qualifiers

$$w(e) = \begin{cases} n & q(e) = (n) \\ 1 & q(e) = \varepsilon \end{cases}$$

The expressions $e \in E(B,F)$ and the qualifiers $q(e)$ of their result are then defined by the obvious inductive rules.

- buses $b \in B$ are expressions

$$b \in B \to b \in E(B,F)$$

By assumption their qualifier $q(b)$ is already defined.
- it is allowed to pick subbuses (possibly of width 1) from expressions

$$e \in E(B,F) \wedge w(e) - 1 \geq j \geq i \geq 0 \to e[j:i] \in E(B,F) \wedge q(e[j:i]) = (j-i+1)$$

We use $e[i]$ as a shorthand for $e[i:i]$. Note that $e[i]$ has as output a parallel bus of width 1.
- it is allowed to concatenate expressions

$$e_1, e_2 \in E(B,F) \to e_1 \circ e_2 \in E(B,f) \wedge q(e_1 \circ e_2) = (w(e_1) + w(e_2))$$

- it is allowed to form expressions by composition of functions f computed by circuits in F. Overloading notation we will use the unit names $f \in F$ as function names. Recall that the sequence of input buses of f is denoted as

$$in(f) = in(f)[1 : ni(f)]$$

and that the width of the i'th input bus $in(f)_i$ is denoted by $w_f(in(f)_i)$. For function composition we only require that width of the i'th argument e_i matches the width of this bus.

$$\forall i \in [1 : ni(f)].\ e_i \in E(B,F) \wedge w(e_i) = w_f(in(f)_i)$$

Then we get a new expressions with qualifier $q(f)$ by substituting expressions e_i as arguments in f

$$f(e_1,\ldots,e_{ni(f)}) \in E(B,f) \wedge q(f(e_1,\ldots,e_{ni(f)})) = q(f)$$

- constants 0 and 1 are expressions

$$0,1 \in E(B,F) \wedge q(0) = q(1) = \varepsilon$$

As we have predefined hardware units for the boolean connectives we can in particular write down all formulae of boolean algebra. As usual we allow infix notation

$$e\ f\ e' = f(e,e')$$

for gates $f \in \{\wedge,\ \vee,\ \oplus,\ \ldots\}$, and use the shorthand

$$\neg e = inv(e)$$

for the inverter.

Expressions are used in straight line programs S of the form

$$b^1\ =\ e^1$$

$$\ldots$$

$$b^s\ =\ e^s$$

An assignment of the form $b^i = e^i$ will connect the single bus $b(e^i)$, which sometimes is the single output bus of an implicitly placed unit $\lambda(e^i)$ for e^i, with a bus b^i. Multiple assignments to the same bus make no sense in hardware, thus we request

$$i \neq j \quad \rightarrow \quad b^i \neq b^j$$

Each bus b^i is either

- an output bus of U or an input bus to a subunit of U. Then the width of e^i is *required* match the type of the bus

$$b^i \in bus^{out}(U) \cup \{\lambda.a \mid a \in bus^{in}(t_U(\lambda)),\ \lambda \in su(U)\} \quad \rightarrow \quad w_U(b^i) = w(e^i)$$

- a newly introduced synonym for the single output bus of implicitly placed subunit $\lambda(e_i)$. Then the width of b^i is *defined* to be the width of e^i

$$b^i \notin bus^{out}(U) \cup \{\lambda.a \mid a \in bus^{in}(t_U(\lambda)),\ \lambda \in su(U)\} \quad \rightarrow \quad w(b^i) = w(e^i)$$

In either case b_i can be used as an input bus in subsequent expressions e^j with $j > i$. Thus we allow

$$e^1 \in E(B(U),F)$$

$$e^{i+1} \in E(B(U) \cup \{b^1,\ \ldots,\ b^i\},F)$$

2.4.2 Implementation

Buses a and b can be simple or parallel. In the following constructions we will sometimes connect a bus a to a source bus b with matching width

$$w(a) = w(b)$$

but possibly different qualifiers $q(a)$ and $q(b)$. In these situations

$$a = b$$

is a shorthand for

$$q(a) = (n) \wedge i < n \rightarrow a_i = \begin{cases} b_i & q(b) = (n) \\ b & i = 0 \wedge q(b) = \varepsilon \end{cases} \tag{2}$$

$$q(a) = \varepsilon \rightarrow a = \begin{cases} b_0 & q(b) = (1) \\ b & q(b) = \varepsilon \end{cases} \tag{3}$$

Now assignments $b^i = e^i$ of straight line programs are implemented in a completely straight forward way. First expression e^i is implemented. For every subexpression e of e^i a bus $b(e)$ computing e and possibly a unit $\lambda(e)$ is defined by induction

- In case e is an input bus we obviously can take $b(e) = e$

$$e \in B(U) \cup \quad \rightarrow \quad b(e) = e$$

- If $e = b^j$ with $j < i$ is the left hand side of a previous assignment $b^j = e^j$ of the straight line program we take $b(e)$ as the bus $b(e^j)$ of the right hand side of the assignment.

$$e = b^j \rightarrow b(e) = e^j$$

- in case $e = e'[j : i]$ picks a subbus of e' we use the unit V of figure 38

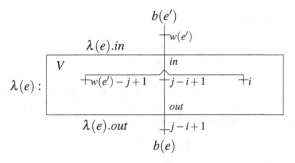

Fig. 38. Unit V outputs bits $[j : i]$ of its input bus

It has inputs and outputs

$$in \in \mathbb{B}^{w(e')} \ , \ out \in \mathbb{B}^{j-i+1}$$

and the obvious source function

$$s(out[k]) = in_{k+i} \quad \text{for} \quad 0 \le k \le j - i$$

This unit is placed as

$$\lambda(e) : V$$

We connect

$$\lambda(e).in_i = b(e')_i$$

and define

$$b(e) = \lambda(e).out$$

- in case $e = e_1 \circ e_2$ is a concatenation we use the unit V of figure 39

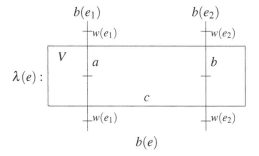

Fig. 39. Unit V outputs the concatenation $a \circ b$ of its input buses

Unit V has parallel input buses output buses

$$a \in \mathbb{B}^{w(e_1)} \ , \ b \in \mathbb{B}^{w(e_2)} \ , \ c \in \mathbb{B}^{w(e_1)+w(e_2)}$$

With

$$m = w(e_2)$$

it has the trivial source function

$$s(c_i) = \begin{cases} b_i & i < m \\ a_{i-m} & i \ge m \end{cases}$$

Note that the input buses $b(e_i)$ are both allowed to be parallel or simple buses, but with the abbreviation from the beginning of this subsection we can specify the connections of the IO buses of subunit λ as

$$\lambda(e).a = b(e_1)$$
$$\lambda(e).b = b(e_2)$$
$$b(e) = \lambda(e).c$$

- if $e = f(e_1, \ldots, e_n)$ we place an instance $\lambda(e)$ of circuit f

$$\lambda(e) : f$$

Each input bus $\dot{in}(f)_k$ is connected to the bus $b(e_k)$ of expression e_k

$$k \leq ni(f) \rightarrow in(f)_k = b(e_k)$$

We define $b(e)$ to be the single output bus of $\lambda(e)$, which with our shorthand for units with a single output bus can be abbreviated as

$$b(e) = \lambda(e)$$

This is illustrated in figure 40.

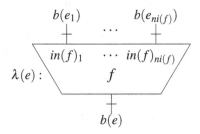

Fig. 40. Unit f computes $f(||b(e_1)||, \ldots, ||b(e_{ni(f)})||)$

- if $e \in \mathbb{B}$ is a bit we trivially connect bus $b(e)$ to the corresponding input signal $e \in sig^{in}(U)$ of unit U.

$$e \in \mathbb{B} \rightarrow b(e) = e$$

Assignment $b^i = e^i$ is then obviously implemented by

$$b^i = b(e_i)$$

which either connects $b(e_i)$ to an existing bus

$$b^i \in bus^{out}(U) \cup \{ \lambda.a \mid a \in bus^{in}(t_U(\lambda)), \ \lambda \in su(U) \}$$

or introduces a synonym for $b(e_i)$.

2.4.3 Semantics

For an incomplete hardware unit U and a straight line program S, let $X(U,S)$ be the hardware unit obtained by implementing straight line program S starting with unit U. In the spirit that the semantics of a programming language can be defined by its compiler, we define the (big steps or small steps) semantics of (U,S) as the semantics of its implementation $X(U,S)$. In particular the semantics is well defined if graph $G(X(U,S))$ is cycle free. At first sight this obviously looks extremely brute force, because "expressions and assignments are so much simpler than general hardware units". This view however ignores the fact that the circuits implementing these expressions are hooked to subunits λ of U and that cycles in $G(X(U,S))$ can arise from paths through these subunits. Returning to the incrementer design inc' of figure 30 we can produce 'essentially the same' design by i) starting with an incomplete design inc'' containing only half adder array A and an empty source function and then ii) completing the design with the straight line program

$$A.a = a$$
$$A.cin = A.cout[n-1:0] \circ 1$$
$$s = A.cout_n \circ A.s$$

As this was the example motivating the treatment of the general case for modular reasoning in section 2.3 we cannot expect a simpler general semantics of incomplete units U completed by straight line programs S. Analogous to section 2.3.3 there is fortunately a simple sufficient criterion permitting to work with classical expression semantics:

- for every expression e implemented in

$$X = X(U,S)$$

by subunit $\lambda(e)$ of type
$$V = t_X(\lambda(e))$$

use in the construction of $G''(X)$ for subunit $\lambda(e)$ the complete bipartite graph

$$H(V)$$

instead of $G'(X)$.
- test if the resulting graph $G''(X)$ is cycle free.

If this is the case and we compute as usual signal values by induction on the depth of signals in $G''(X)$ and we come to the evaluation of output signals

$$\lambda(e).s \quad \text{with} \quad s \in sig^{out}(V)$$

of subunit $\lambda(e)$ then we know for all input signals

$$\lambda(e).q \quad \text{with} \quad q \in sig^{in}(V)$$

of this subunit, that
$$d_{G''(X)}(\lambda(e).q) < d_{G''(X)}(\lambda(e).s)$$

Thus we can assume that the *entire* value

$$||in_X(\lambda(e))||_X(h,x)$$

is already defined, and we obtain the obvious formulae for the output buses

$$||\lambda(e)||_X(h,x) = ||b(e)||_X(h,x)$$

Lemma 26.

1. *if $e = a$ is a bus, then*

$$||b(e)||_X(h,x) = ||a||_X(h,x)$$

2. *if $e = e'[i : j]$ picks a subbus of the output bus of e' then*

$$||b(e)||_X(h,x) = (||b(e')||_X(h,x))[j : i]$$

3. *if $e = e_1 \circ e_2$ concatenates two expressions, then*

$$||b(e)||_X(h,x) = ||b(e_1)||_X(h,x) \circ ||b(e_2)||_X(h,x)$$

4. *if $e = f(e_1, \ldots, e_{ni(f)})$ evaluates circuit f with arguments e_i, then*

$$||b(e)||_X(h,x) = ||out(f)||_f(h.\lambda(e), (\, || \, b(e_1)||_X(h,x), \ldots, ||b(e_{ni(f)})||_X(h,x)))$$

5. *if $e \in \mathbb{B}$ is a bit, then*
$$||b(e)||_X(h,x) = e$$

Proof. All parts except part 4 deal only with implicitly defined subunits $\lambda(e)$ of a type V without gates, buses and registers. These units just connect output signals s with input or constant signals q by

$$s_V(s) = q$$

and the lemma follows by applying the small steps semantics for the source function

$$||\lambda(e).s_V(s)||_X(h,x) = ||\lambda(e).q||_X(h,x)$$

to each output signal s of unit V. Part 4 follows from lemma 22

$$||b(e)||_X(h,x) = ||out_X(\lambda(e))||_X(h,x)$$
$$= ||out(f)||_f(h.\lambda(e), ||in_X(\lambda(e))||_X(h,x))$$

$\square$

3

Hardware Library

We specify a library of building blocks for use in later designs. Section 3.1 deals with some basic and arithmetic circuits. Control automata are very briefly treated in section 3.2. In section 3.3 we present various designs of multi-port memory. Ways to control registers (by *set*/*clear* signals or as latches) are the theme in section 3.4. Finally in section 3.5 we explain the operating for tri-state buses from section section 2.1.7 and present a bus control which guarantees these conditions.

3.1 Circuit Library

3.1.1 Basic Circuits

Using vector notation for boolean operations introduced in section 1.3.1 we list (mostly very simple) basic circuits that will explicitly be used later in this text. Constructions and proofs are only provided for those circuits that are not already treated in sect. 3.2 of [KMP14]. The construction of 'find last one' circuits is a trivial variation of 'find first one' circuits. The construction of half decoders with logarithmic depth is new.

Multiplexers

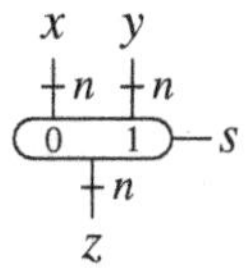

Fig. 41. n-bit multiplexer

For $x, y, z \in \mathbb{B}^n$ and $s \in \mathbb{B}$ in Fig. 41:

© Springer Nature Switzerland AG 2020
P. Lutsyk et al. (Eds.): A Pipelined Multi-Core Machine, LNCS 9999, pp. 91–135, 2020.
https://doi.org/10.1007/978-3-030-43243-0_3

$$z = \begin{cases} x & /s \\ y & s. \end{cases}$$

Vector Inverters

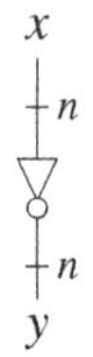

Fig. 42. *n*-bit inverter

For $x, y \in \mathbb{B}^n$ in Fig. 42:

$$y = /x.$$

Vector Gates

Fig. 43. Vector gates for *n*-bit wide inputs

For $x, y, z, u \in \mathbb{B}^n$ and $v \in \mathbb{B}$ in Fig. 43:

$$z = x \circ y$$
$$u = v \circ y.$$

Modifiers

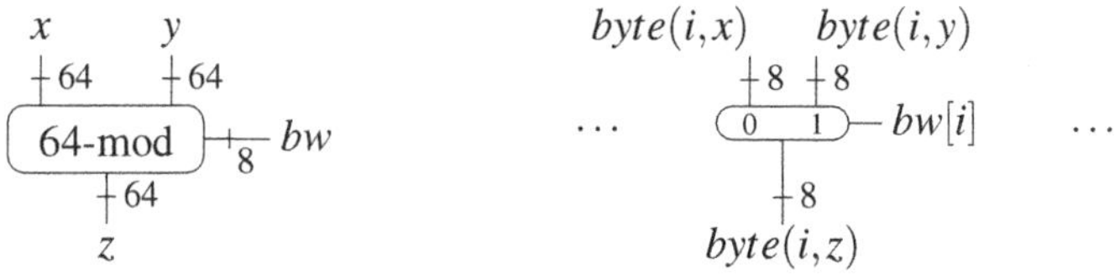

Fig. 44. *n*-bit modifier circuit

Recall that for $n = 64$, strings $x, y \in \mathbb{B}^n$ function *modify* describes the replacement of bytes of x by the corresponding bytes of y under control of *byte-write* signals $bw \in \mathbb{B}^8$.

$$byte(i, modify(x, y, bw)) = \begin{cases} byte(i, y) & bw[i] \\ byte(i, x) & /bw[i] \end{cases}$$

For $x, y, z \in \mathbb{B}^{64}$ and $bw \in \mathbb{B}^8$ one constructs a modifier circuit from 8-MUXes working in parallel as shown in Fig. 44.

n-○-tree

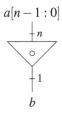

Fig. 45. *n*-○-tree of gates for $○ \in \{\wedge, \vee, \oplus\}$

For $a \in \mathbb{B}^n$, $b \in \mathbb{B}$, and $○ \in \{\wedge, \vee, \oplus\}$ in Fig. 45:

$$b = ○_{i=0}^{n-1} a[i].$$

(n, K)-∨-trees

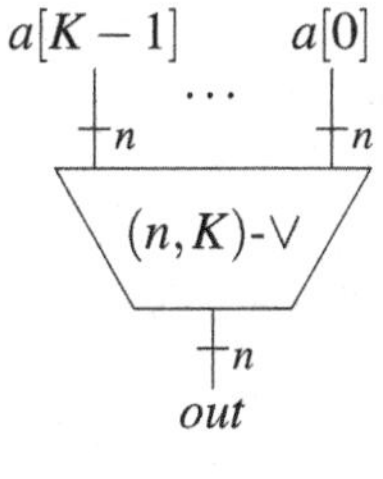

Fig. 46. (n, K)-∨-tree of gates

For $i \in [0 : K-1]$ and $out, a[i] \in \mathbb{B}^n$ in Fig. 46:

$$out[j] = \bigvee_{i=0}^{K-1} a[i][j].$$

Consists of K copies of an *n*-∨-tree working in parallel.

Zero Tester

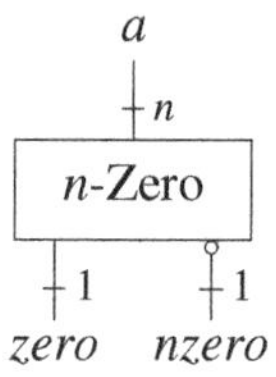

Fig. 47. n-bit zero tester

For $a \in \mathbb{B}^n$ and $zero, nzeoro \in \mathbb{B}$ in Fig. 47:

$$zero \equiv a = 0^n$$
$$nzero \equiv /zero.$$

Equality Tester

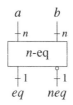

Fig. 48. n-bit equality tester

For $a, b \in \mathbb{B}^n$ and $eq, neq \in \mathbb{B}$ in Fig. 48:

$$eq \equiv a = b$$
$$neq \equiv /eq.$$

Decoder

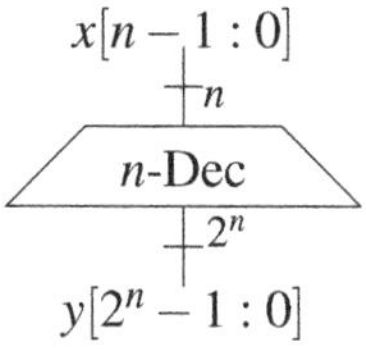

$$x[n-1:0]$$

n-Dec

$$y[2^n - 1 : 0]$$

Fig. 49. n-bit decoder. Used with $k = \lceil n/2 \rceil$.

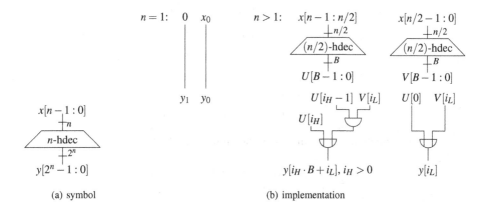

(a) symbol

(b) implementation

Fig. 50. n-bit half decoder

For $x \in \mathbb{B}^n$ and $y \in \mathbb{B}^{2^n}$ in Fig. 49:

$$y_i = 1 \equiv \langle x \rangle = i.$$

Half Decoder

For $x \in \mathbb{B}^n$ and $y \in \mathbb{B}^{2^n}$ in Fig. 50.

$$y = 0^{2^n - \langle x \rangle} 1^{\langle x \rangle}$$

resp.

$$y_i \equiv i < \langle x \rangle.$$

The construction presented in [KMP14] has depth linear in n. Half decoders with depth logarithmic in n can be constructed in the following way. For simplicity assume n to be a power of two and split $x \in \mathbb{B}^n$ into an upper and lower half.

$$x_L = x[n/2 - 1 : 0]$$
$$x_H = x[n - 1 : n/2]$$
$$\langle x \rangle = \langle x_H \rangle \cdot 2^{n/2} + \langle x_L \rangle$$

Recursively feed these two strings into $n/2$-half decoders with outputs U and V as shown in Fig. 50. For output y_i of the n-half decoder represent indices $i \in [0 : 2^{n-1}]$ as two digit numbers with base

$$B = 2^{n/2}.$$

Thus

$$i = i_H \cdot B + i_L$$
$$i_H = \lfloor i/B \rfloor$$
$$i_L = (i \bmod B).$$

Then

$$i < \langle x \rangle \leftrightarrow i_H < \langle x_H \rangle \vee i_H \leq \langle x_H \rangle \wedge i_L < \langle x_H \rangle$$
$$\leftrightarrow i_H < \langle x_H \rangle \vee i_H - 1 < \langle x_H \rangle \wedge i_L < \langle x_H \rangle$$

and we can compute the new outputs as shown in Fig. 50 by

$$y_i = \begin{cases} U(i_H) \vee U(i_H - 1) \wedge V(i_L) & i_H \geq 1 \\ U(i_H) \vee V(i_L) & i_H = 0. \end{cases}$$

Encoder

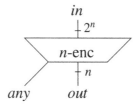

Fig. 51. Symbol of *n*-bit encoder.

The *n*-bit encoder in fig. 51 is essentially the inverse of the decoder: given a bit string $in \in \mathbb{B}^{2^n}$ with exactly a single raised bit, it computes the binary number $out \in \mathbb{B}^n$ representing the index of that bit

$$in = 0^{2^n - i - 1} 1 0^i \quad \rightarrow \quad \langle out \rangle = i$$

This is illustrated in fig. 52.

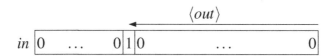

Fig. 52. Specification of encoder: find the position of the only raised bit.

Furthermore, the circuit uses output $any \in \mathbb{B}$ to indicate that there are any raised bits in the input. Using the notation for membership of sequences introduced on page

19 in section 1.3.1 whether there is a 1 somewhere in *in* can be expressed succinctly as $1 \in in$. Thus our specification for the *any* output is

$$any \equiv 1 \in in$$

A simple construction detects whether the raised bit is in the upper or lower half of the input and encodes both halves of the input recursively with subunits λ_H and λ_L, selecting the half which has the raised bit to compute the lower n bits of *out*. As illustrated in fig. 53 resp. fig. 54, the correct result is obtained by prepending a 1 (in case the bit is in the upper half of the input) or a 0 (in case the bit is in the lower half of the input).

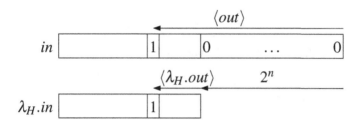

Fig. 53. Recursive case of $(n+1)$-bit encoder in case the raised bit is in the upper half. We have $\langle out \rangle = 2^n + \langle \lambda_H.out \rangle = \langle 1 \circ \lambda_H.out \rangle$

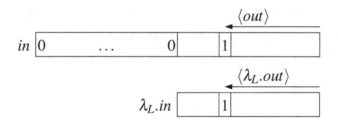

Fig. 54. Recursive case of $(n+1)$-bit encoder in case the raised bit is in the lower half. We have $\langle out \rangle = \langle \lambda_L.out \rangle = \langle 0 \circ \lambda_H.out \rangle$

The optimized construction in fig. 55 does exactly this; however, it uses the fact that it outputs 0^n in case the input is 0^{2^n} to do the selection of the half with the raised bit with a parallel $\vee$-gate rather than a multiplexer. The resulting construction has delay $O(n)$ and cost $O(2^n)$. This sounds like much, but note that the number of bits of the input is 2^n; thus delay is logarithmic and cost is linear in the number of bits of the input.

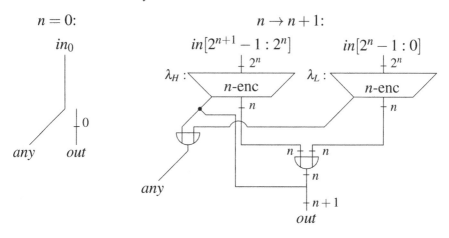

Fig. 55. Implementation of n-bit encoder.

We first show that the *any* bus is correct.

Lemma 27.
$$any \equiv 1 \in in$$

Proof. By induction on n. The base case is trivial. For the inductive step $n \to n+1$ the claim follows from the induction hypothesis

$$
\begin{aligned}
any &\equiv \lambda_H.any \lor \lambda_L.any \\
&\equiv 1 \in \lambda_H.in \lor 1 \in \lambda_L.in &&\text{IH} \\
&\equiv 1 \in in[2^{n+1} - 1 : 2^n] \lor 1 \in in[2^n - 1 : 0] \\
&\equiv 1 \in in
\end{aligned}
$$

$\square$

We then show that the output is indeed zero if the input is zero

Lemma 28.
$$/any \quad \to \quad out = 0_n$$

Proof. By induction on n. The base case is trivial. For the inductive step $n \to n+1$ assume that we do not have any raised bit in the input

$$/any$$

and hence by construction both subunits also have no raised input bits

$$/\lambda_H.any \land /\lambda_L.any$$

Thus by the induction hypothesis both subunits produce zeros

$$\lambda_H.out = \lambda_L.out = 0_n$$

The claim follows by construction

$$
\begin{aligned}
out &= \lambda_H.any \circ (\lambda_H.out \lor \lambda_L.out) \\
&= 0 \circ (0_n \lor 0_n) \\
&= 0_{n+1}
\end{aligned}
$$

$\square$

We can now show the correctness of the *out* output in case the input includes exactly one raised bit.

Lemma 29.

$$in = 0^{2^n-i-1}10^i \quad \rightarrow \quad \langle out \rangle = i$$

Proof. The proof is by induction on n. The base case is trivial. In the inductive step $n \rightarrow n+1$ we distinguish as in figs. 53 and 54 whether the raised bit is in the upper or lower half.

- $i \geq 2^n$: Let $i = 2^n + j$. We have by construction for the input of λ_H

$$\lambda_H.in = 0^{2^{n+1}-i-1}10^{i-2^n} = 0^{2^n-j-1}10^j$$

and for λ_L

$$\lambda_L.in = 0^{2^n}$$

With lemma 27 we conclude immediately

$$\lambda_H.any = 1, \ \lambda_L.any = 0$$

From lemma 28 we obtain

$$\lambda_L.out = 0_n$$

and from the induction hypothesis

$$\langle \lambda_H.out \rangle = j$$

The claim follows

$$
\begin{aligned}
\langle out \rangle &= \langle \lambda_H.any \circ (\lambda_H.out \lor \lambda_L.out) \rangle \\
&= \lambda_H.any \cdot 2^n + \langle \lambda_H.out \lor 0_n \rangle \\
&= 2^n + \langle \lambda_H.out \rangle \\
&= 2^n + j = i
\end{aligned}
$$

- $i < 2^n$: We have by construction for the input of λ_H

$$\lambda_H.in = 0^{2^n}$$

and for λ_L

$$\lambda_L.in = 0^{2^n-i-1}10^i$$

With lemma 27 we conclude immediately

$$\lambda_H.any = 0$$

From lemma 28 we obtain

$$\lambda_H.out = 0_n$$

and from the induction hypothesis

$$\langle \lambda_L.out \rangle = i$$

The claim follows

$$
\begin{aligned}
\langle out \rangle &= \langle \lambda_H.any \circ (\lambda_H.out \vee \lambda_L.out) \rangle \\
&= \lambda_H.any \cdot 2^n + \langle 0_n \vee \lambda_L.out \rangle \\
&= 0 + \langle \lambda_L.out \rangle \\
&= i
\end{aligned}
$$

$\square$

Parallel Prefix

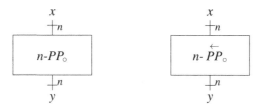

Fig. 56. n-bit parallel prefix (on the left) and reversed parallel prefix (on the right)

For $x, y \in \mathbb{B}^n$ in Fig. 56 and associative function $\circ : \mathbb{B} \times \mathbb{B} \to \mathbb{B}$

$$y_0 = x_0, \ y_{i+1} = x_{i+1} \circ y_i$$

The well known construction presented in [KMP14] has cost $O(n)$ and delay $O(\log n)$.

Reverse Parallel Prefix

For $x, y \in \mathbb{B}^n$ in Fig. 56 and associative function $\circ : \mathbb{B} \times \mathbb{B} \to \mathbb{B}$

$$y_{n-1} = x_{n-1}, \; y_{i-1} = x_i \circ y_{i-1}$$

Constructed in an analogous way. Alternatively one could also flip inputs, compute parallel prefix and then flip the outputs again. But flipping n lines in a basically planar technology like chips or printed circuit boards costs area $O(n^2)$. Thus one tries to avoid it.

Find First and Last One

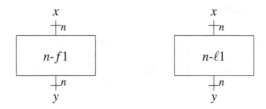

Fig. 57. n-bit find-first-one and find-last-one circuits

Define functions

$$f1, \ell1 : \mathbb{B}^n \to \mathbb{B}^n$$

which find the first and last one[1] by

$$f1(x) = u$$
$$u_i \equiv i = \min \{ j \mid x_j = 1 \}$$
$$\ell1(x) = v$$
$$v_i \equiv i = \max \{ j \mid x_j = 1 \}$$

Construct an n-f1-circuit in Fig. 57 from a parallel prefix OR circuit and then generate

$$u_0 = y_0$$
$$u_{i+1} = x_{i+1} \wedge /y_i$$

Construct an n-$\ell1$-circuit in Fig. 57 from a reverse parallel prefix circuit in an analogous way.

---

[1] from the right

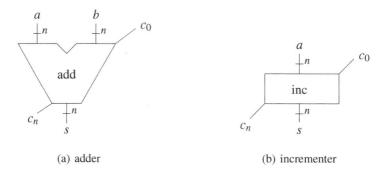

(a) adder   (b) incrementer

Fig. 58. Symbols for n-bit adder and incrementer

3.1.2 Arithmetic Circuits

We list here only specifications of circuits used later in processor constructions. Due to new notation, pins a of units X are renamed: basically from Xa to $X.a$. Constructions and correctness proofs can be found in chapter 5 of [KMP14]. Readers who are not familiar with this material are strongly encouraged to read up on it.

Adder

An n bit adder as shown in Fig. 58(a) has the following pins.

- operands $a, b \in \mathbb{B}^n$
- carry in and carry out $c_0, c_n \in \mathbb{B}$
- sum bits $s \in \mathbb{B}^n$

Output signals satisfy

$$\langle a \rangle + \langle b \rangle + c_0 = \langle c_n \circ s \rangle.$$

Incrementer

An n bit incrementer as shown in Fig. 58(b) has the following pins.

- operand $a \in \mathbb{B}^n$
- carry in and carry out $c_0, c_n \in \mathbb{B}$
- sum bits $s \in \mathbb{B}^n$

Output signals satisfy

$$\langle a \rangle + c_0 = \langle c_n \circ s \rangle.$$

Arithmetic Unit

An n bit arithmetic unit as shown in Fig. 59 has the following pins.

- operands $a, b \in \mathbb{B}^n$
- control input $u \in \mathbb{B}$ distinguishing between unsigned (binary) and signed (two's complement) numbers

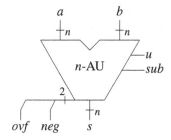

Fig. 59. Arithmetic unit

- control input $sub \in \mathbb{B}$ indicating whether input b should be subtracted from or added to a
- sum bits $s \in \mathbb{B}^n$
- overflow bit $ovf \in \mathbb{B}$
- negative bit $neg \in \mathbb{B}$

We define the exact result $S \in \mathbb{Z}$ of an arithmetic unit as

$$S = \begin{cases} [a] + [b] & (u, sub) = (0,0) \\ [a] - [b] & (u, sub) = (0,1) \\ \langle a \rangle + \langle b \rangle & (u, sub) = (1,0) \\ \langle a \rangle - \langle b \rangle & (u, sub) = (1,1) \end{cases}$$

The sum bits s then satisfy

$$[s] = (S \operatorname{tmod} 2^n) \quad \text{if} \quad u = 0$$
$$\langle s \rangle = (S \bmod 2^n) \quad \text{if} \quad u = 1$$

Overflow and negative bits are defined by

$$ovf = \begin{cases} S \notin T_n & u = 0 \\ 0 & u = 1 \end{cases}$$
$$neg \equiv S < 0$$

ALU

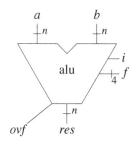

Fig. 60. Symbol of an n bit ALU

An n bit arithmetic logic unit (ALU) as shown in fig. 60 has the following pins.

- operands $a, b \in \mathbb{B}^n$
- function bits $f \in \mathbb{B}^4$ and $i \in \mathbb{B}$
- result $res \in \mathbb{B}^n$
- overflow bit $ovf \in \mathbb{B}$

Outputs are computed according to Table 2

$f[3:0]$	i	$res[31:0]$	ovf
0000	*	$a +_n b$	$[a] + [b] \notin T_n$
0001	*	$a +_n b$	0
0010	*	$a -_n b$	$[a] - [b] \notin T_n$
0011	*	$a -_n b$	0
0100	*	$a \wedge b$	0
0101	*	$a \vee b$	0
0110	*	$a \oplus b$	0
0111	0	$\overline{a \vee b}$	0
0111	1	$b[n/2 - 1 : 0]0^{n/2}$	0
1010	*	$0^{n-1}([a] < [b] \ ? \ 1 : 0)$	0
1011	*	$0^{n-1}(\langle a \rangle < \langle b \rangle \ ? \ 1 : 0)$	0

Table 2. Specification of ALU operations

Cyclic Shifter

For shift operands $a \in \mathbb{B}^n$ and shift distances $i \in [0 : n - 1]$ the results of cyclic left shift slc, cyclic right shift srl are defined by

$$slc(a, i) = a[n - i - 1 : 0]a[n - 1 : n - i]$$
$$src(a, i) = a[i - 1 : 0]a[n - 1 : i]$$

These shifts are related by

$$src(a,i) = slc(a,n-i)$$

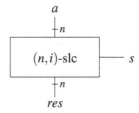

Fig. 61. Symbol of an (n,i)-cyclic left shifter

A cyclic (n,i)-shifter as shown in fig. 61 has the following pins.

- shift operand $b \in \mathbb{B}^n$
- select signal $s \in \mathbb{B}$
- result $res \in \mathbb{B}^n$

The result bits satisfy

$$res = \begin{cases} slc(a,i) & s = 1 \\ a & \text{otherwise} \end{cases}$$

Shift Unit

For shift operands $a \in \mathbb{B}^n$ and shift distances $i \in [0 : n-1]$ the results of logical left shift *sll*, logical right shift *srl* and arithmetic right shift *sra* of operand a by distance i are defined by

$$sll(a,i) = a[n-i-1:0]0^i$$
$$srl(a,i) = 0^i a[n-1:i]$$
$$sra(a,i) = a_{n-1}^i a[n-1:i] \ .$$

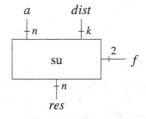

Fig. 62. Symbol of an n-shift unit

$f[1:0]$	res
00	$sll(b,\langle dist\rangle)$
10	$srl(b,\langle dist\rangle)$
11	$sra(b,\langle dist\rangle)$

Table 3. Specification of shift unit operations

For $n = 2^k$ an n bit arithmetic shift unit su as shown in Fig. 62 has the following pins.

- shift operand $a \in \mathbb{B}^n$
- (binary coded) shift distance $dist \in \mathbb{B}^k$
- function bits $f \in \mathbb{B}^2$
- result $res \in \mathbb{B}^n$

Outputs are computed according to Table 3

3.1.3 Branch Condition Evaluation Unit

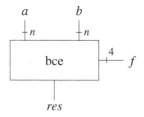

Fig. 63. Symbol of a branch condition evaluation unit

An n bit branch condition evaluation unit bce as shown in fig. 63 has the following pins.

- operands $a, b \in \mathbb{B}^n$
- function bits $f \in \mathbb{B}^4$
- result $res \in \mathbb{B}$

Outputs are computed according to table 4

3.2 Control Automata

Control automata (also called *finite state transducers*) are finite automata which produce an output in every step. Formally, a finite state transducer M is defined by a 6-tuple $(Z, z_0, I, O, \delta_A, \eta)$, where Z is a finite set of states, $I \subseteq \mathbb{B}^\sigma$ is a finite set of *input symbols*, $z_0 \in Z$ is called the *initial state*, $O \subseteq \mathbb{B}^\gamma$ is a finite set of *output symbols*,

$f[3:0]$	res
0010	$[a] < 0$
0011	$[a] \geq 0$
100*	$a = b$
101*	$a \neq b$
110*	$[a] \leq 0$
111*	$[a] > 0$

Table 4. Specification of branch condition evaluation

$$\delta_A : Z \times I \to Z$$

is the *transition function*, and

$$\eta : Z \times I \to O$$

is the *output function*.

Such an automaton performs steps according to the following rules:

- the automaton is started in state z_0,
- if the automaton is in state z and reads input symbol *in*, then it outputs symbol $\eta(z, in)$ and goes to state $\delta_A(z, in)$.

If the output function does not depend on the input, i.e., if it can be written as

$$\eta : Z \to O \, ,$$

the automaton is called a *Moore automaton*. Otherwise, it is called a *Mealy automaton*.

Fig. 64. Two control states z and z' with transition i...

Automata are often visualized in graphical form. Then state z is drawn as a circle with z written inside. A state transition

$$z' = \delta_A(z, i)$$

is visualized by an arrow from state z to state z' with label i as shown in Fig. 64. Initial states are sometimes drawn as a double circle.

In this text we will specify control automata usually in graphical form. For their implementation and proofs, that the implementation is correct, we refer the reader to section 3.6 of [KMP14]

3.3 Random Access Memory (RAM)

To a large part this is summary of results from Section 4 of [KMP14]. In addition we construct

- the line addressable bw-R-RW-RAM, specified by the access based memory semantics from Section 1.3.4. Compared to the multi bank RAMs from [KMP14] it also supports compare and swap (cas) operations. This type of RAM *does* implicitly occur in [KMP14]: draw in figure 143 a box around boxes *m* and *mask4cas* and you have it. But the overall theory is cleaner if one constructs it here.
- the two ported R-W SPR-RAM implementing the special purpose register file of pipelined machines. This is an very simple variant of the corresponding basic SPR-RAM in [KMP14].

For use in section 4.2 we will determine for some of the RAMs the graphs $F(V)$ from section 2.3.4, which visualize the dependency of output buses from input buses.

3.3.1 Basic Design

Numerous variants of random access memory (RAM) are used in a all sorts of places. It is therefore important to understand i) how to design basic RAM from the building blocks introduced so far and how to generate variants of the basic design. Any variant of RAM is characterized — among other things — by two parameters: The number k of address bits and the width n of data stored in the RAM.

The symbol of a basic (n,k)-RAM S (a unit with type (n,k)-RAM and label S) is shown in Fig. 65(a). It has the following pins:

- address input $a \in \mathbb{B}^k$
- data input $in \in \mathbb{B}^n$
- write signal (input) $w \in \mathbb{B}$
- data output $out \in \mathbb{B}^n$

The state of RAM S as a subunit in hardware configurations h is specified as a mapping

$$h.S : \mathbb{B}^k \to \mathbb{B}^n$$

where for all addresses a function value $h.S(a)$ specifies the current memory content S at address a. The data output out is the current memory content at address a. Initial content is binary but unknown. In case the write signal is active, the memory content at address a is replaced by the data input, and the content at any other addresses x stays the same. The latter property is kind of essential for memory.

$$S^0(x) \in \mathbb{B}^n$$
$$out = S(a)$$
$$S'(x) = \begin{cases} in & w \wedge x = a \\ S(x) & \text{otherwise} \end{cases}$$

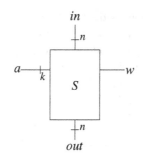

(a) symbol

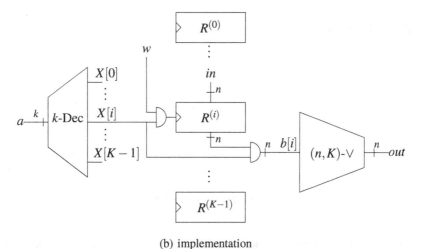

(b) implementation

Fig. 65. (n,a)-RAM

A construction of a basic (n,k)-RAM S from registers and circuits is shown in fig. 65(b). Data are stored in an array R of d bit registers indexed by $\mathbb{B}^k$

$$R : reg(d)(\mathbb{B}^k)$$

In the figure registers have been numbered from $i = 0$ to $2^k - 1 = K - 1$ by

$$R(x) = R^{(\langle x \rangle)} \quad \text{resp.} \quad R^{(i)} = R(bin_k(i))$$

The memory content at address x is stored in register $R(x)$. As shown in section 2.2.2 we get

$$h.S.R : \mathbb{B}^k \to \mathbb{B}^d$$

As no other subunits of the memory construction have state we identify $h.S = h.S.R$ and have as required

$$h.S : \mathbb{B}^k \to \mathbb{B}^d$$

The k-decoder at the left hand side decodes binary addresses into unary signals $X[i]$ indicating that the current address a addresses register $R^{(i)}$. Register $R^{(i)}$ is updated with the data input in if it is addressed (as indicated by $X[i]$) and the write signal w is active. For the computation of the data output, register contents $R^{(i)}$ are masked (with a vector operation) by bits $X^{(i)}$. ORing the masked register outputs $b[i]$ together with a (n, K)-OR tree then gives the desired output out. For the few missing details of the correctness proof see Section 4.1 of [KMP14].

The only paths from input buses a, in, w to the output bus out, that do not hit registers, are from a to via the address decoder and the or tree to out. Thus we have

$$bus^{in}_{RAM}(out) = \{a\}$$

3.3.2 Read Only Memory (ROM)

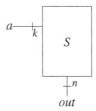

Fig. 66. Read only memory

An (n, k)-ROM is a memory without data input and write signal as shown in fig. 66. Initial content S^0 is known and stays the same for all cycles t.

$$out = S(a) = S^0(a)$$

Realized by replacing in the basic design each register $R^{(i)}$ by the constant with the intended memory content $S^0(bin_n(i))$. Note that the resulting 'RAM' is really a circuit computing the boolean function

$$S^0 : \mathbb{B}^k \to \mathbb{B}^n$$

and that any boolean function

$$f : \mathbb{B}^k \to \mathbb{B}$$

can be computed by a $(1, k)$-ROM with $S^0 = f$. By looking at the construction of the decoder in [KMP14], one obtains that the number of gates involved in this construction is $O(2^k)$, which is less than the up to $O(k \cdot 2^k)$ gates needed if f is computed by a disjunctive normal form. Trivially we have

$$bus^{in}_{ROM}(out) = \{a\}$$

3.3.3 R-W-RAM

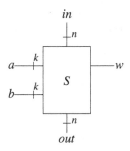

Fig. 67. Symbol of R-W-RAM

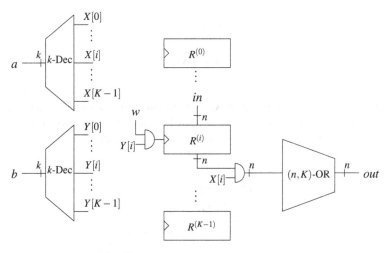

Fig. 68. Implementation of R-W-RAM

For the construction of queues we will need 2-port (n,k)-R-W-RAMs. This are RAMs S as shown in Fig. 67 with a read port addressed by pins a and a write port addressed by bins b. The specifications is as follows:

$$out = S(a)$$

$$S'(x) = \begin{cases} in & x = b \wedge w \\ S(x) & \text{otherwise.} \end{cases}$$

Such RAMs can be constructed by an easy modification of the basic RAM design as shown in Fig. 68. An extra decoder for the write address b produces signals $Y[i]$ for registers $R^{(i)}$. Registers are clocked under control of the decoded address b.

$$R^{(i)}.ce = w \wedge Y[i]$$

All paths from the second address decoder for b end in registers. Thus we still have

$$bus^{in}_{\text{R-W-RAM}}(out) = \{a\}$$

3.3.4 R-RW-RAM

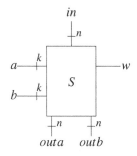

Fig. 69. R-RW-RAM...

An (n,k)-R-RW-RAM is a two port RAM with two addresses a and b and two data outputs *outa* and *outb* as shown in fig. 69, where address a controls only reads to output *outa*, whereas address b controls both reads to output *outb* and writes.

$$outa = S(a)$$
$$outb = S(b)$$
$$S'(x) = \begin{cases} in & w \wedge a = x \\ S(x) & \text{otherwise} \end{cases}$$

Constructed from R-W-RAM. An additional (d, K) OR tree produces the new output *outb* by ORing together the masked register outputs $Y[i] \wedge R^{(i)}$

$$outb = \bigvee_{i=0}^{K-1} Y[i] \wedge R^{(i)}$$

We use it as a building block in several designs. The address decoder for b now has paths via the OR tree for b to *outb*. Thus

$$bus^{in}_{\text{R-RW-RAM}}(outa) = \{a\} \;,\; bus^{in}_{\text{R-RW-RAM}}(outb) = \{b\} \;.$$

3.3.5 Two port ROM

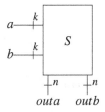

Fig. 70. Two port ROM...

Constructed from a ROM in the same way. Its symbol is shown in Fig. 70.

$$bus^{in}_{\text{Two port ROM}}(outa) = \{a\} \,, \ bus^{in}_{\text{two port ROM}}(outb) = \{b\} \,.$$

3.3.6 bw-R-RW-RAM

This is two ported line addressable memory producing answers and updates in a single cycle. The RAM considered here has two ports: read port a and a general port b. As shown in Fig. 71(a) it has the following pins.

- address inputs $a, b \in \mathbb{B}^{29}$
- data input $in \in \mathbb{B}^{64}$
- comparison data input $cdata \in \mathbb{B}^{32}$
- data output $outa, outb \in \mathbb{B}^{64}$
- byte-write signals $bw \in \mathbb{B}^8$
- cas signal $cas \in \mathbb{B}$

Output is generated in the usual way:

$$outa = S(a), \ outb = S(b)$$

Updates are specified by the transition function δ_M for line addressable memory.

$$S' = \delta_M(S, dacc)$$

where (data) access $dacc$ corresponds to input data

$$dacc.a = b$$
$$dacc.data = in$$
$$dacc.cdata = cdata$$
$$dacc.cas = cas$$
$$dacc.bw \neq 0^8 \rightarrow dacc.cas \lor dacc.w$$

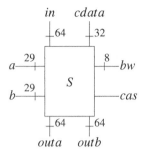

(a) symbol

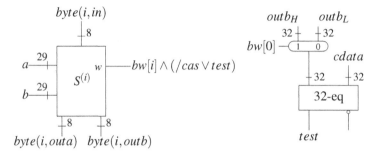

(b) implementation

Fig. 71. bw-R-RW-RAM...

Note, that if we have for (instruction) access *iacc*

$$iacc.a = a$$
$$iacc.r = 1$$

and the data access is a read

$$dacc.r = 1$$

then we have

$$outa = dataout(S, iacc)$$
$$outb = dataout(S, dacc)$$

As shown in fig. 71(b) one constructs such a RAM by 8 banks of $(8, 29)$-R-RW-RAMs placed in parallel. Write signals $S^{(i)}.w$ are generated in a straight forward way. We have

$$bus^{in}_{\text{bw-R-RW-RAM}}(outa) = \{a\} \, , \ bus^{in}_{\text{bw-R-RW-RAM}}(outb) = \{b\} \, .$$

3.3.7 bw-R-RW-RAM-ROM

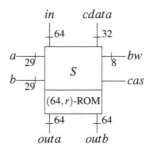

Fig. 72. Symbol of bw-R-RW-RAM-ROM

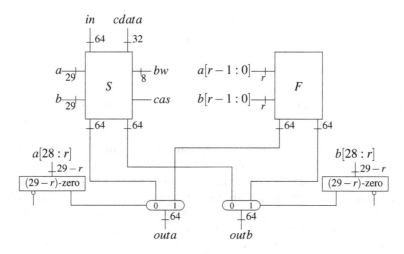

Fig. 73. Implementation of bw-R-RW-RAM-ROM

In a bw-R-RW-RAM/ROM S as shown in fig. 72 the lowest 2^r lines are replaced by an $(64, r)$-ROM F. Formally a line address y selects the ROM, if its leading $29 - r$ bits are all zero.

$$romsel(y) \equiv y[28 : r] = 0^{29-r}$$

We impose the operating condition that these lines are not written

$$dacc.w \lor dacc.cas \to /romsel(dacc.a)$$

For addresses selecting the ROM we then can guarantee known (and unchangeable) memory contents

$$romsel(y) \rightarrow S(y) = F(y[r-1:0])$$

Constructed from a bw-R-RW-RAM S and a two port ROM F as shown in Fig. 73. We have

$$bus_{\text{bw-R-RW-RAM-ROM}}^{in}(outa) = \{a\} \; , \; bus_{\text{bw-R-RW-RAM-ROM}}^{in}(outb) = \{b\} \; .$$

This is visualized in figure 74.

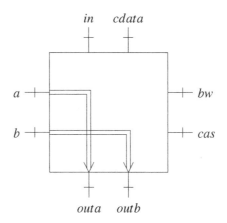

Fig. 74. Illustration of graph F(bw-R-RW-RAM-ROM)

We will use such a RAM in basic sequential and pipelined processor designs. Constructions and correctness proofs of processors and pipelines are *much* simpler when all memory accesses are performed in a single cycle, but with a single cycle implementation we necessarily have paths leaving and reentering the memories M of the machine. According to section 2.3.4 we will establish the well-definedness of the entire design by arguing about the graphs $F(M)$ which relate the output buses y of units V with their relevant input buses $bus_M^{in}(x)$. Thus if m is a bw-R-RW-RAM-ROM declared as

$$m : \text{bw-R-RW-RAM-ROM}$$

and a path leaves m at output $m.outa$ it can reenter m at any input bus other than $m.a$ without closing a cycle in m.

3.3.8 GPR-RAM

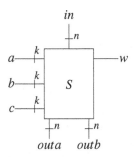

Fig. 75. (n,k)-GPR-RAM

As shown in fig. 75 it has three addresses $a,b,$ and c. Compared with a two port RAM there is now a third address c controlling which register is updated by writes.

$$outa = S(a)$$
$$outb = S(b)$$
$$S'(x) = \begin{cases} in & w \wedge c = x \\ S(x) & \text{otherwise} \end{cases}$$

A third address decoder with outputs $Z[i]$ decodes c. Registers are clocked under control of the decoded address c.

$$R^{(i)}.ce = w \wedge Z[i]$$

Such a RAM is used as general purpose register file of processors with $k = 5$ and $n = 32$. In the sequential processor designs of section 4.2 we will find paths leaving this hardware unit via outputs *outa* and *outb* and reentering the unit via inputs *in* and c. According to section 2.3.4 we will establish the well-definedness of the entire design by arguing about the graphs $F(\text{GPR-RAM})$ which relate the output buses b of units V with their relevant input buses $bus_V^{in}(b)$. For the GPR-RAM the only paths from inputs to outputs, that do not hit registers, go i) from a via the decoder for a and the OR tree for a to *outa*. ii) from b via the decoder for b and the OR tree for b to *outb*. Thus

$$bus_{\text{GPR-RAM}}^{in}(outa) = \{a\} , \ bus_{\text{GPR-RAM}}^{in}(outb) = \{b\}$$

This is illustrated in figure 76.

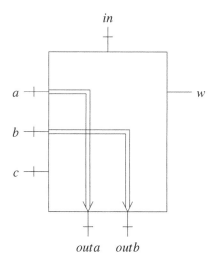

Fig. 76. Illustration of graph F(GPR-RAM)

Thus, if gpr is a GPR-RAM declared as

$$gpr : \text{GPR-RAM}$$

then paths leaving this unit via outputs $gpr.outa, gpr.outb$ can reenter it via inputs in, c, and w without closing a cycle.

3.3.9 SPR-RAM

An (n,k)-SPR RAM as shown in Fig. 77 (a) is used here for the realization of special purpose register files and in the construction of device ports. It behaves both as an (n,k)-RAM and as a set of $K = 2^k$ many n-bit registers. It has the following inputs and outputs:

- data input $in \in \mathbb{B}^n$,
- address input $a \in \mathbb{B}^k$,
- data output $out \in \mathbb{B}^n$,
- a write signal $w \in \mathbb{B}$,
- for each $i \in [0 : K - 1]$ an individual n-bit data input $din[i] \in \mathbb{B}^n$ for register $R^{(i)}$,
- for each $i \in [0 : K - 1]$ an individual n-bit data output $dout[i] \in \mathbb{B}^n$ for register $R^{(i)}$, and
- for each $i \in [0 : K - 1]$ an individual clock enable signal $ce[i] \in \mathbb{B}$ for register $R^{(i)}$.

Ordinary data output is generated as usual, and the individual data outputs are simply the outputs of the internal registers:

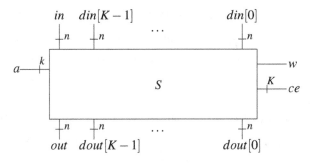

(a) symbol

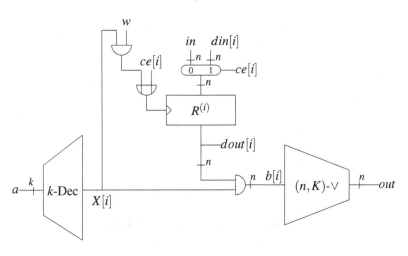

(b) implementation

Fig. 77. (n,k)-SPR-RAM

$$out = S(a)$$
$$dout[i] = S(bin_k(i)) .$$

Registers $R^{(i)}$ are updated either with *in* for regular writes or with $din[i]$ if the individual clock enables are activated. Individual writes take precedence over ordinary writes:

$$S'(x) = \begin{cases} din[\langle x \rangle] & ce[\langle x \rangle] = 1 \\ in & ce[\langle x \rangle] = 0 \wedge x = a \wedge w = 1 \\ S(x) & \text{otherwise} . \end{cases}$$

A single address decoder with outputs $X[i]$ and a single OR-tree suffices. fig. 77(b) shows the construction satisfying

$$R^{(i)}.ce = ce[i] \vee X[i] \wedge w$$

$$R^{(i)}.in = \begin{cases} din[i] & ce[i] = 1 \\ in & \text{otherwise} . \end{cases}$$

We have

$$bus^{in}_{\text{SPR-RAM}}(out) = \{a\} \quad \text{and} \quad \forall i. \ bus^{in}_{\text{SPR-RAM}}(dout[i]) = \emptyset$$

This is illustrated in figure 78.

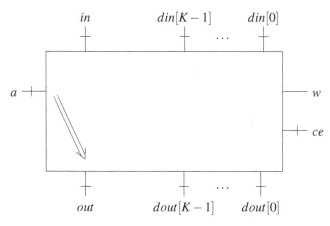

Fig. 78. Illustration of graph F(SPR-RAM)

Thus if spr is a GPR-RAM declared as

$$spr : \text{SPR-RAM}$$

then paths leaving this unit via outputs $spr.out$ can reenter it via all inputs other than $spr.a$ without closing a cycle. Paths leaving spr via an individual output $dout[i]$ can reenter spr at any input without closing a cycle.

3.3.10 R-RW-SPR RAM

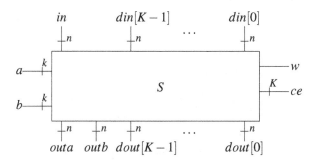

Fig. 79. R-RW-SPR-RAM

For pipelined designs an additional read port a has to be added. As shown in fig. 79 we update the list of pins to

- address inputs $a, b \in \mathbb{B}^k$,
- data output $outa, outb \in \mathbb{B}^n$,

and specify the data outputs as

$$outa = S(a), \ outb = S(b)$$

Obvious modification of the single port design as in the construction of R-W-RAM. Add a second address decoder for the b port producing output $Y[i]$, which in turn control the clock enable signals of the registers:

$$R^{(i)}.ce = ce[i] \vee Y[i] \wedge w.$$

We have

$$bus^{in}_{\text{R-RW-SPR-RAM}}(outa) = \{a\} \ , \ bus^{in}_{\text{R-RW-SPR-RAM}}(outa) = \{a\}$$
$$\forall i. \ bus^{in}_{\text{R-RW-SPR-RAM}}(dout[i]) = \emptyset$$

This is illustrated in figure 80.

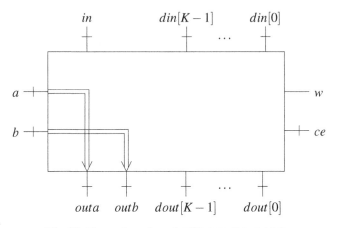

Fig. 80. Illustration of graph F(R-RW-SPR-RAM)

3.4 Register Control

We construct a few new building blocks.

3.4.1 Set-Clear Flip-Flop

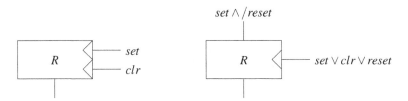

Fig. 81. Symbol and implementation of a set-clear flip-flop

Set-clear flip-flops are 1 bit registers R with two control inputs

$$set, clear \in \mathbb{B}$$

which define the next state of the register. Symbol and implementation are shown in figure 81. In this implementation the register is cleared at *reset* and *set* takes precedence over *clear*. Thus it obeys

$$R' = \begin{cases} 1 & /reset \wedge set \\ 0 & reset \vee clr \wedge /set \\ R & \text{otherwise} \end{cases}$$

These flip-flops will for instance be used in the standardized bus control of tri-state buses in section 3.5.2.

3.4.2 Stabilizer Latch

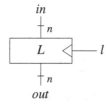

Fig. 82. Symbol of a stabilizer latch L

As shown in Fig. 82 an n-stabilizer latch L has data input $in \in \mathbb{B}^n$, data output $out \in \mathbb{B}^n$ and a control input $l \in \mathbb{B}$. Such latches are capable of storing data $L \in \mathbb{B}^n$. Depending on the control input one says such a latch is *transparent* (if $l = 0$) or *latched* (if $l = 1$).

$$out = \begin{cases} in & l = 0 \\ L & l = 1 \end{cases}$$

While the unit is latched state, it maintains the same output:

$$L' = \begin{cases} in & l = 0 \\ L & l = 1. \end{cases}$$

A straight forward implementation with the help of a register R that is always clocked ($R.ce = 1$) is shown in Fig. 83.

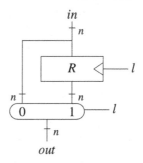

Fig. 83. Implementation of a latch

3.5 Control of Tri-State Buses

3.5.1 Justifying the Operating Conditions

For tri-state buses, more precisely subunits z of type $t_U(z) = \tau(n)$ we required in section 2.2.4 that at most one driver at a time is enabled, and in this case the result (also denoted by z) of the unit was defined to be the input $z.in$ of the enabled driver.

$$t_U(z) = \tau(n) \;\wedge\; 1 \ge \sum_i z.oe_i^t \quad \rightarrow \quad z^t = \begin{cases} z.in_i^t & z.oe_i^t = 1 \\ 1 & \text{otherwise} \end{cases}$$

As operating condition we extract

$$\sum_i z.oe_i^t \le 1 \tag{4}$$

As an additional operating condition for the proper operation of tri-state buses we required: if different drivers drive the bus in cycles s and t, then there must be an intermediate cycle u when all drivers are disabled.

$$z.oe_i^s \;\wedge\; z.oe_j^t \;\wedge\; s < t \;\wedge\; i \ne j \quad \rightarrow \quad \exists u \in (s:t).\; \forall k.\; /z.oe_k^u \tag{5}$$

The latter rule was introduced, because the simple and intuitive first rule above for controlling tri-state buses turns out to be catastrophically incomplete. For later reference we summarize the conditions from equations 4 and 5 as the operating condition $opc\text{-}b^t$ for buses, stating that the operating conditions are satisfied in all cycles $u < t$

$$opc\text{-}b^t \equiv \forall u < t.\; \Big(\sum_i z.oe_i^u \le 1\Big)$$

$$\wedge\, \forall u \le t, s < u.\; z.oe_i^s \;\wedge\; z.oe_j^u \;\wedge\; i \ne j \quad \rightarrow \quad \exists v \in (s:u).\; \forall k.\; /z.oe_k^v$$

The reason things go wrong without the second condition is, that the well known and beloved digital hardware model is only an abstraction of physical hardware. All physical hardware components have minimal and maximal propagation delays. Physical registers also have setup and hold times; drivers have minimal and maximal enable and disable times. Indeed, that digital hardware *without drivers and with a long enough cycle time* simulate physical circuits is a theorem (Lemma 3.5. of [KMP14]).

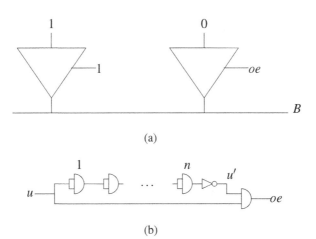

Fig. 84. Short circuit on a bus, which is not visible in the digital model

With drivers the game changes. Consider Fig. 84(a). Two drivers connected to the same bus have different input signals. If both of them would be enabled, then the left driver would try to pull bus B to 1 and the right driver would try to pull it to 0. The noble name for this phenomenon is *bus contention*, but in the physical world the much more profane name *short circuit* would describe it equally well. If we tie on the other hand the output enable signal *oe* of the right driver to zero, the sum of the output enable signals is 1, the right driver is always disabled and all is fine. In the digital model all *stays* fine if we control the right driver with an output enable signal, which (in boolean algebra) is equivalent to zero, like

$$oe = u \wedge u', \ u' = /u$$

for some signal u.

The trouble is that in the physical world such signals are not constant at all. Typically, maximal propagation delays are about 3 times larger than minimal propagation delays. Thus let us assume that in some unit of time the minimal propagation delay of gates and is 1 and that the maximal propagation delay is 3. For times a and b we say that an event like a signal falling or rising happens at (a,b), if it happens at the earliest at time a and at the latest at time b. Now consider fig. 84(b), where input signal u is first sent through a 'delay line' consisting of n AND gates and then inverted to produce signal u'.

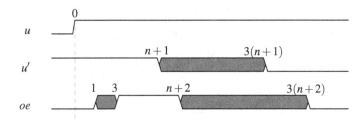

Fig. 85. Timing diagram for a pulse generator

The detailed timing diagram in fig. 85 shows what happens if we raise signal u at time 0 after it has been low long enough. Signal u' falls after $n+1$ gate delays, thus at time $((n+1),3(n+1))$. Signal *oe* rises after 1 gate delay at time $(1,3)$. It falls one gate delay after u' falls, i.e. at time $((n+2),3(n+2))$. Thus signal *oe* which is zero in the digital model, reacts to a raising edge of u with a *pulse* of length at least $(n-1)$. During this time we have a short circuit on the bus. At time $3(n+2)$ we can lower signal u again without effect on the pulse we have created. Thus if we make u a clock signal with a cycle time of

$$\tau = 6(n+2)$$

we will have a guaranteed periodical short circuit for almost 1/6 of the time. Physical circuits are delicate structures and tend to go up in smoke in such situations [2].

3.5.2 Controlling Tri-State Buses

Motivated by this example we standardize bus control. As auxiliary hardware component we use the set-clear flip-flops R from section 3.4.1.
Using an array oe of n such set-clear flip-flops of type scf

$$oe : scf(n)$$

we control a tri-state bus B with n drivers with data width d

$$B : \tau(n,d)$$

via output-enable set and clear signals

$$oeset, oeclear \in \mathbb{B}^n$$

of the set-clear flip-flops:

$$B.oe(i) = oe(i) \quad oe(i).set = oeset_i \ , \ oe(i).clear = oeclear_i$$

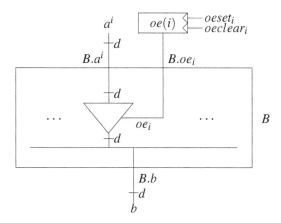

Fig. 86. Controlling an n,d tri-state bus B with set-clear flip-flops oe_i for every input bus a^i

With data inputs

$$a^i[d-1:0]$$

---

[2] A slightly more involved construction in section 3.5.4 of [KMP14], which triggers a second short circuit with the falling edge of the clock, produces short circuits for almost 1/3 of the time.

for $i \in [0:n-1]$ this results in the construction illustrated in fig. 86.

We demand for all drivers that their output enable flip-flop $oe(i)$ is only set when the bus is idle

$$oeset_i \rightarrow \bigvee_j oe_j = 0 \qquad (6)$$

The latter rule prevents that different drivers on the bus are turned on and off at the same clock edge. Thus it implies equation 5 , i.e. the second part of $opc\text{-}b$.

That with long enough cycle time this additional *digital* design rule prevents short circuits of any kind *in the physical model* is shown in Lemma 3.9 of [KMP14]. For technical reasons this design is not useful to us as a stand-alone unit, but we will shortly build a unit incorporating this control scheme.

3.5.3 Arbitration

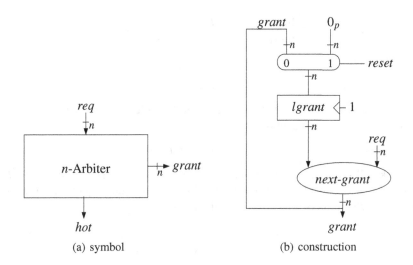

Fig. 87. Arbiter n-Arbiter for a bus driven by n tri-state drivers

In situations where multiple participants try to access a resource, but only one participant at a time is allowed, one has to arbitrate between simultaneous access requests. Here we present a simple arbiter. Symbol and construction of the arbiter for $n \in \mathbb{N}$ participants are depicted in fig. 87. The interface is straightforward:

- input $req \in \mathbb{B}^n$ — request signals. The request of participant number k is $req[k]$
- output $grant \in \mathbb{B}^n$ — grant signal to the participants. While $grant[k]$ is raised, participant number k has access to the resource. Obviously at most one such grant signal at a time should be raised by the arbiter.

In order to access the resource, participant k first activates its request signal $req[k]$. It must maintain this request until the arbiter grants the request the by raising $grant[k]$.

$$req[k] \wedge /grant[k] \rightarrow req[k]' \tag{7}$$

We will construct the arbiter such that a participant, which has access and keeps its request signal up, will keep access. Thus, in order to ensure fairness request signals should eventually be lowered.

$$grant[k]^t \rightarrow \exists u > t./req[k]^u \tag{8}$$

For later reference we summarize the conditions specified by equations 7 and 8 as operating conditions $opc\text{-}a^t$ for arbiters.

$$opc\text{-}a^t \equiv (req[k]^t \wedge /grant[k]^t \rightarrow req[k]^{t+1}) \wedge (grant[k]^t \rightarrow \exists u > t./req[k]^u)$$

In order to provide fairness, we use a round-robin scheme. When access was last given to participant ℓ and some request is active, we will give access in the next cycle to

$$x = \begin{cases} \min\{m \geq \ell \mid req[m]\} & \text{if it exists} \\ \min\{m \mid req[m]\} & \text{o.w.} \end{cases} \tag{9}$$

This is implemented by use of a register

$$lgrant : \text{reg}(n)$$

recording the last grant. Requests from consumers with high numbers $m \geq k$ (where k is the last grant) are computed by

$$hreq = req \wedge \text{PP}_\vee(lgrant)$$

which masks all requests coming from consumers with numbers $m < k$ but not k itself. The requests considered for the next grant are either the requests from consumers with high numbers if any exist, or all requests

$$creq = \begin{cases} hreq & hreq \neq 0_n \\ req & \text{o.w.} \end{cases}$$

and of these requests the request coming from the unit with the lowest index is chosen

$$grant = \text{f1}(creq)$$

The resulting grant signals are again stored in the $cgrant$ register. The register is also initialized as all zeros on reset

$$lgrant.in = \begin{cases} 0_n & reset \\ grant & \text{o.w.} \end{cases}$$

The register is always updated

$$lgrant.ce = 1$$

The obvious correctness statement is

Lemma 30.

- *At most one grant signal is active at a time*

$$\sum_i grant[i] \le 1$$

- *A participant that receives a grant has a request*

$$grant[k] \;\rightarrow\; req[k]$$

- *Assume the operating conditions opc-a^t for arbiters always hold.*

$$\forall t.opc\text{-}a^t.$$

Then all requests are eventually granted

$$req[k]^t \;\rightarrow\; \exists r \ge t.\, grant[k]^r$$

Proof. Vector *grant* is the output of a first one circuit, thus at most one signal $grant[i]$ is active. This shows the first part. The second part follows because we have for all i

$$grant[i] \le creq[i] \le req[i] = 1$$

For the third part assume $req[k]^t$. If the request is immediately granted with $grant[k]^t$ we are done. Otherwise a participant $\ell \ne k$ gets access at cycle t, i.e. we have

$$req[k]^t \wedge grant[\ell]^t$$

By equation 8 participant ℓ lowers its request at a later cycle u. In the first such cycle the request of k is still on by equation 7, and we have

$$\lgrant[\ell]^u \wedge /req[\ell]^u \wedge req[k]^u$$

By construction the arbiter will grant access to a participant x as defined in equation 9. If $x = k$ we are done. Otherwise we consider the number of bits we have to go cyclically to the right from k to reach ℓ. This distance is

$$\begin{cases} \ell - k & k < \ell \\ n - k + \ell & k \ge \ell \end{cases} \;=\; (\ell - k \bmod n)$$

As $x \ne k$ it must have a smaller cyclic distance to k than ℓ

$$(x - k \bmod n) < (\ell - k \bmod n)$$

An easy induction on s now gives:

$$req[k]^t \wedge grant[\ell]^t \wedge (\ell - k \bmod n) = s \rightarrow \exists v \ge t.grant[k]^v$$

$\square$

3.5.4 Combined Arbiter and Tri-State Bus

We combine arbiter and tri-state bus into a single unit, the (n,d)-controlled bus. This unit attaches n participants to a d-bit wide tri-state bus and completely handles the control of this bus. For the sake of simplicity we construct this unit specifically for use with APICs in chapter 12 and chapter 13, where access rights are granted for a single cycle. The design of a more general controlled bus, which can handle multi-cycle accesses[3], will be treated as an exercise.

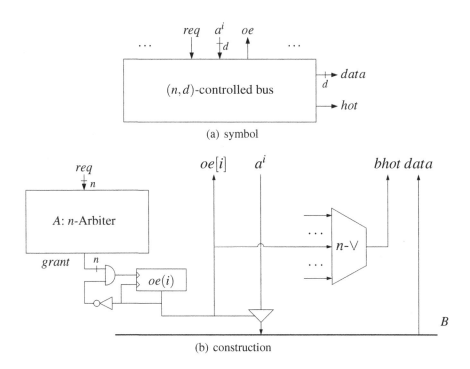

(a) symbol

(b) construction

Fig. 88. Controlled tri-state bus (n,d)-controlled bus for n consumers and data width d

As illustrated in fig. 88 this controlled bus is connected to participant $i \in [0 : n-1]$ through the following input and output buses

- input $req[i] \in \mathbb{B}$ signaling a request of the consumer
- input $a^i \in \mathbb{B}^d$ consisting of the data to be broadcast by the consumer
- output $oe[i] \in \mathbb{B}$ signaling that the consumer is currently broadcasting the data

Furthermore, it has two outputs that are used by the consumers to listen to broadcasts:

- $bhot \in \mathbb{B}$ signaling that some consumer is currently broadcasting

---

[3] whose end then needs to be signalled

- $data \in \mathbb{B}$ consisting of the data which is currently broadcast in case *bhot* is raised. This data is meaningless if *bhot* is low and must be ignored by all units listening on the tri-state bus.

In the construction we are using the bus control of section 3.5.2 together with the arbiter from section 3.5.3. Thus we use a tri-state bus

$$B : \tau(n,d)$$

which is connected to the data inputs of the consumers and an array of set-clear flip-flops

$$oe : scf(n)$$

which control the output enable inputs of the tri-state bus. Thus

$$B.oe(i) = oe(i), \quad B.a^i = a^i$$

The set and clear inputs of these registers are controlled by the bus arbiter

$$A : n\text{-Arbiter}$$

We pass the requests of the participants to this arbiter

$$A.req[i] = req[i]$$

to compute which consumer should be granted access next. The output enable register for that consumer is set as soon as the arbiter gives the grant to that consumer, and cleared in the next cycle

$$oe(i).set = A.grant[i] \wedge /oe(i)$$
$$oe(i).clr = oe(i)$$

The output enable signal from the set-clear flip-flop is placed on output bus $oe[i]$

$$oe[i] = oe(i)$$

The data output is the data on the tri-state bus

$$data = B$$

and the bus is hot if any consumer is broadcasting

$$bhot = \bigvee_i oe[i]$$

This completes the construction of the (n,d)-controlled bus. The operating conditions for the controlled bus have two parts. Request i stay active until their output i is enabled.

$$req[i] \wedge /oe[i] \rightarrow req[i]' \tag{10}$$

Once output i is enabled, request i is turned off.

$$oe[i] \to /req[i]' \tag{11}$$

We collect both of these conditions for all cycles $u < t$ in a predicate $opc\text{-}cb^t$ defined by

$$opc\text{-}cb^t = \forall u < t. \ (req[i]^u \wedge /oe[i]^u \ \to \ req[i]^{u+1})$$
$$\wedge (oe[i]^u \ \to \ /req[i]^{u+1})$$

The obvious correctness statement is

Lemma 31. *Assume the operating conditions $opc\text{-}cb^t$ for the controlled bus are fulfilled. Then*

- *output enable signals are only granted to a participant that requests the bus*

$$oe[i]^t \ \to \ req[i]^t$$

- *the operating conditions $opc\text{-}b^t$ for the tri-state bus are fulfilled*
- *if a participant has an output enable signal, it is also driving the data on the bus*

$$oe[i]^t \ \to \ data^t = (a^i)^t$$

Proof. We show the claims separately. The first claim is shown by case split on the cycle t. After reset we have

$$oe[i]^0 = 0$$

and the first claim vacuously holds. For later cycles assume

$$oe[i]'$$

By construction we have

$$/oe[i] \wedge A.grant[i]$$

and by part 2 of lemma 30

$$req[i]$$

By the operating condition we conclude from $/oe[i]$ and $req[i]$:

$$req[i]'$$

which is the first claim.

For the second claim, we have to show the operating conditions for tri-state buses.

$$\forall u < t. \ (\sum_i z.oe_i^u \le 1)$$
$$\wedge \forall u \le t, s < u. \ z.oe_i^s \wedge z.oe_j^u \wedge i \ne j \quad \to \quad \exists v \in (s : u). \ \forall k. \ /z.oe_k^v$$

We show the first operating condition, i.e., eq. (4), by case split on u. After reset we have

$$\sum oe[i]^0 = \sum 0 = 0$$

For later cycles we have by lemma 30 part 1

$$\sum oe[i]' = \sum /oe[i] \wedge grant[i] \leq \sum grant[i] \leq 1$$

For the second operating condition, i.e., equation 5 it suffices to show for all $u < t$ (!) equation 6, i.e.

$$u < t \wedge oe(i).set^u \quad \rightarrow \quad \forall j. /oe(j)^u$$

Again we show this by case split on u. For cycle 0 there is nothing to show. For cycles $u > 0$ assume

$$oe[j]'$$

By construction and part 2 of lemma 30 we get

$$/oe[j] \wedge grant[j] \leq grant[j] \leq req[j]$$

By the operating condition for controlled buses in equation 10 the request is not taken away and bit j and by construction of the arbiter bit j of register $lgrant$ is turned on we get

$$req[j]' \wedge lgrant[j]'$$

Again by construction of the arbiter participant j keeps the grant

$$grant[j]'$$

By part 1 of lemma 30 no other participant gets the grant

$$i \neq j \rightarrow /grant[i]$$

Using also $oe[j]'$ we conclude for all i that not output enable bit can be on

$$\forall i. /oe(j).set'$$

This proves equation 5 and the completes the proof of the second part of the lemma. For the third claim assume that participant i has an output enable signal

$$oe[i]$$

We already know that we are satisfying the operating conditions of the tri-state bus (this was part two of the lemma). Thus the tri-state bus behaves as specified and we have

$$data = B = B.a^i = a^i$$

which is the claim.   □

Liveness is shown in the following lemma.

Lemma 32. *If the operating conditions always hold*

$$\forall t.\ opc\text{-}cb^t$$

then after activation of request i output i is eventually enabled

$$\forall t.\ req[i]^t \quad \rightarrow \quad \exists u \geq t.\ oe[i]^u$$

Proof. By construction output enable follows grant with at most 1 cycle delay

$$grant[i] \rightarrow oe[i] \vee oe[i]'$$

By operating condition equation 11 for the controlled bus requests are turned off after output enable. Thus requests are taken away at most 2 cycles after grant is active

$$grant[i]^t \rightarrow /req[i]^{t+1} \vee /req[i]^{t+2}$$

This is the operating condition from equation 8 of the arbiter. In cycle 0 output enables are off, and for cycles $t > 0$ we have shown in the proof of lemma 31 that $oe[j]'$ implies both $req[j]'$ and $A.grant[j]'$. Thus

$$oe[j] \rightarrow req[j] \wedge A.grant[j]$$

Thus

$$req[i] \wedge /A.grant[i] \rightarrow /oe[i]$$

which implies by the operating condition for controlled buses (equation 10), that the request stays on

$$req[i]'$$

This also gives the operating condition from equation 7 of the arbiter. Thus we know by part 3 of lemma 30 that requests will eventually be granted

$$req[i]^t \rightarrow \exists r > t. \quad grant[i]^r$$

Because output enable follows grant with at most 1 cycle delay we get

$$oe[i]^r \vee oe[i]^{r+1}$$

Thus a request is eventually followed by output enable and the lemma is proven.   □

3.6 Exercises

1. Implement (without using tri-state buses) a unit that is functionally equivalent to a tri-state bus. Hint: use a tree of multiplexers.

2. Design a more advanced (n,d)-controlled bus which can handle multi-cycle requests. For such a request, as illustrated in fig. 89, the output enable register needs to be cleared in the same cycle as the request signal, i.e., it must hold

$$oe[i] \rightarrow (oe[i])' = (req[i])'$$

To guarantee this, the clear input of the register needs to be set in the last cycle in which the request bit is raised. Obviously this can not be inferred using only the inputs of the unit as it is designed, so add a new input

$$end^i \in \mathbb{B}$$

indicating the end of a request, i.e., the last cycle in which the request bit is still raised. Use this signal to control the output enable register.

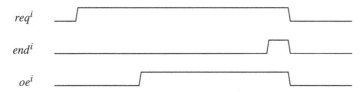

req^i

end^i

oe^i

Fig. 89. Timing diagram for an improved arbiter.

3. We claimed without proof that an n-bit encoder has cost $O(2^n)$. Prove this claim. Hint: prove

$$\sum_{i=0}^{n} 2^i(n-i) = \sum_{i=0}^{n}(2^i - 1)$$

4. The n-bit encoder presented above works as an encoder only if the input has exactly one raised bit. We want to construct an n-bit min-encoder which returns the encoding of the first 1, i.e., with specification

$$1 \in in \quad \rightarrow \quad \langle out \rangle = \min\{i \mid in[i] = 1\}$$

   a) Construct the circuit by using a find-first-one circuit
   b) Construct the circuit without using a find-first-one circuit. Hint: follow the construction of the n-bit encoder, but use multiplexers.
   c) Compare the detailed cost and delay of your two constructions

4

Basic Processor Design

This is a fairly detailed summary and extension of results from chapter 5 of [KMP14]. We go into considerable level of detail here, because i) the MIPS ISA is part of the formulation of every processor correctness theorem in this book and ii) *all* processor designs will be derived in one way or the other from the basic design. Understanding of future chapters will be greatly facilitated if readers have these specifications, constructions, and arguments really at their fingertips.

The special purpose register file, move instructions and cas instructions are already included in the basic design, because constructions and correctness proofs require no additional concepts. Changes in notation are marginal. Besides renaming of pins of units we only write the simulation relation between byte addressable ISA memory $c.m$ and line addressable hardware memory $h.m$ as

$$h.m = \ell(c.m)$$

instead of

$$h.m \sim c.m$$

The introduction of instruction access $iacc(c)$ and data access $dacc(c)$ of ISA configurations have been moved forward from chapter 9 of [KMP14], and the crucial result relating the update of byte addressable ISA memory $c.m$ with the update of its line addressable version $\ell(c.m)$ by data access $dacc(c)$ (Lemma 7.5 of [KMP14]) is now formulated and proven in terms of ISA configurations c alone.

Although the machine considered here is sequential, we partition its circuits already into stages, which will reappear in almost identical form in all later designs of pipelined machines. The introduction of the concepts of circuits stage correctness and the use of signals for instruction execution has been moved forward from the pipelining chapter (chapter 7) of [KMP14]. As a sanity check we derive the correctness of the *sequential* design from the correctness of the *circuit stages*.

Most of the following is taken verbatim from [KMP14] and [PBLS16].

© Springer Nature Switzerland AG 2020
P. Lutsyk et al. (Eds.): A Pipelined Multi-Core Machine, LNCS 9999, pp. 137–181, 2020.
https://doi.org/10.1007/978-3-030-43243-0_4

Table 5. J-type instructions

opcode	Mnemonic	Assembler-Syntax	Effect
Jumps			
000 010	j	j *iindex*	pc = bin_{32}(pc+4_{32})[31:28]iindex00
000 011	jal	jal *iindex*	R31 = pc + 4_{32},
			pc = bin_{32}(pc+4_{32})[31:28]iindex00

4.1 MIPS ISA

4.1.1 Instruction Tables

For the purpose of reference we include the full instruction tables from [Sch13]. In contrast to [KMP14] we will already support move and cas instructions in our basic processor designs. The treatment of the following instructions is deferred to later chapters: i) eret and sysc (chapter 7), ii) mfence (chapter 10) and iii) TLB instructions (chapter 9).

Recall that for numbers $y \in \mathbb{B}^n$ we abbreviate the binary representation of y with n bits as $y_n = bin_n(y)$ and for memories $m : \mathbb{B}^{32} \to \mathbb{B}^8$, addresses $a \in \mathbb{B}^{32}$, and numbers d of bytes, we denote the content of d consecutive memory bytes starting at address a by $m_d(a)$. In the tables we use the following shorthand:

$$\begin{aligned} m &= c.m_{d(c)}(ea(c)) \\ &= c.m_{d(c)}(c.gpr(rs(c)) +_{32} sxtimm(c)), \end{aligned}$$

where $d(c)$ denotes the access width.

Table 6. I-type instructions

opcode	rt	Mnemonic	Assembler-Syntax	Effect	Access Width
Data Transfer					
100 100		lbu	lbu *rt rs imm*	rt = 0^{24}m	1
100 101		lhu	lhu *rt rs imm*	rt = 0^{16}m	2
100 000		lb	lb *rt rs imm*	rt = sxt(m)	1
100 001		lh	lh *rt rs imm*	rt = sxt(m)	2
100 011		lw	lw *rt rs imm*	rt = m	4
101 000		sb	sb *rt rs imm*	m = rt[7:0]	1
101 001		sh	sh *rt rs imm*	m = rt[15:0]	2
101 011		sw	sw *rt rs imm*	m = rt	4
Arithmetic, Logical Operation, Comparison					
001 000		addi	addi *rt rs imm*	rt = rs + sxt(imm)	
001 001		addiu	addiu *rt rs imm*	rt = rs + sxt(imm)	
001 010		slti	slti *rt rs imm*	rt = (rs < sxt(imm) ? 1_{32} : 0_{32})	
001 011		sltiu	sltiu *rt rs imm*	rt = (rs < sxt(imm) ? 1_{32} : 0_{32})	
001 100		andi	andi *rt rs imm*	rt = rs $\wedge$ zxt(imm)	
001 101		ori	ori *rt rs imm*	rt = rs $\vee$ zxt(imm)	
001 110		xori	xori *rt rs imm*	rt = rs $\oplus$ zxt(imm)	
001 111		lui	lui *rt imm*	rt = imm0^{16}	
Branch					
000 001	00000	bltz	bltz *rs imm*	pc = pc + (rs < 0 ? imm00 : 4_{32})	
000 001	00001	bgez	bgez *rs imm*	pc = pc + (rs $\geq$ 0 ? imm00 : 4_{32})	
000 100		beq	beq *rs rt imm*	pc = pc + (rs = rt ? imm00 : 4_{32})	
000 101		bne	bne *rs rt imm*	pc = pc + (rs $\neq$ rt ? imm00 : 4_{32})	
000 110	00000	blez	blez *rs imm*	pc = pc + (rs $\leq$ 0 ? imm00 : 4_{32})	
000 111	00000	bgtz	bgtz *rs imm*	pc = pc + (rs > 0 ? imm00 : 4_{32})	

Table 7. R-type instructions

opcode	fun	rs	Mnemonic	Assembler-Syntax	Effect
Shift Operations					
000 000	000 000		sll	sll *rd rt sa*	rd = sll(rt,sa)
000 000	000 010		srl	srl *rd rt sa*	rd = srl(rt,sa)
000 000	000 011		sra	sra *rd rt sa*	rd = sra(rt,sa)
000 000	000 100		sllv	sllv *rd rt rs*	rd = sll(rt,rs)
000 000	000 110		srlv	srlv *rd rt rs*	rd = srl(rt,rs)
000 000	000 111		srav	srav *rd rt rs*	rd = sra(rt,rs)
Arithmetic, Logical Operations					
000 000	100 000		add	add *rd rs rt*	rd = rs + rt
000 000	100 001		addu	addu *rd rs rt*	rd = rs + rt
000 000	100 010		sub	sub *rd rs rt*	rd = rs − rt
000 000	100 011		subu	subu *rd rs rt*	rd = rs − rt
000 000	100 100		and	and *rd rs rt*	rd = rs $\wedge$ rt
000 000	100 101		or	or *rd rs rt*	rd = rs $\vee$ rt
000 000	100 110		xor	xor *rd rs rt*	rd = rs $\oplus$ rt
000 000	100 111		nor	nor *rd rs rt*	rd = $\overline{\text{rs} \vee \text{rt}}$
Comparison Operations					
000 000	101 010		slt	slt *rd rs rt*	rd = (rs < rt ? 1_{32} : 0_{32})
000 000	101 011		sltu	sltu *rd rs rt*	rd = (rs < rt ? 1_{32} : 0_{32})
Jumps, System Call					
000 000	001 000		jr	jr *rs*	pc = rs
000 000	001 001		jalr	jalr *rd rs*	rd = pc + 4_{32}, pc = rs
000 000	001 100		sysc	sysc	System Call
Synchronizing Memory Operation					
000 000	111111		cas	cas *rd rt rd cdata*	rd'=m
					m'= (rd=cdata? rt: m)
Coprocessor Instructions					
opcode	fun		Mnemonic	Assembler-Syntax	Effect
010 000	011 000	10000	eret	eret	Exception Return
010 000		00100	movg2s	movg2s *rd rt*	spr[rd] := gpr[rt]
010 000		00000	movs2g	movs2g *rd rt*	gpr[rd] := spr[rt]
TLB Instructions					
000 000	111 101		flusht	flusht	flushes TLB translations
000 000	111 100		invlpg	invlpg *rs rt*	flushes TLB translations
					for addr. *rt* from ASID *rs*
Store Buffer Instruction					
000 000	111 110		mfence	mfence	flushes the SB

4.1.2 Configuration and Instruction Fields

A basic *MIPS configuration* c has four user visible data structures (fig. 90):

- $c.pc \in \mathbb{B}^{32}$ – the program counter (PC).
- $c.gpr : \mathbb{B}^5 \to \mathbb{B}^{32}$ – the general purpose register (GPR) file consisting of 32 registers, each 32 bits wide. Register 0^5 is tied to 0^{32}. Writing to it will have no effect.

$$c.gpr(0^5) = 0^{32}.$$

- $c.m : \mathbb{B}^{32} \to \mathbb{B}^8$ – the processor memory. It is byte addressable; addresses have 32 bits.
- $c.spr : \mathbb{B}^5 \to \mathbb{B}^{32}$– the special purpose register (SPR) file.

Program counter and general purpose registers belong to the central processing unit (CPU).

Let K be the set of all basic MIPS configurations. A mathematical definition of the ISA will be given by a function

$$\delta_{isa} : K \to K ,$$

where

$$c' = \delta_{isa}(c)$$

is the configuration reached from configuration c, if the next instruction is executed. An ISA computation is a sequence (c^i) of ISA configurations with $i \in \mathbb{N}$ satisfying

$$c^0.pc = 0^{32}$$
$$c^{i+1} = \delta_{isa}(c^i) ,$$

i.e., initially the program counter points to address 0^{32} and in each step one instruction is executed. In the remainder of this section we specify the ISA simply by specifying function δ_{isa}, i.e., by specifying $c' = \delta_{isa}(c)$ for all configurations c.

The current instruction $I(c)$ to be executed in configuration c is defined by the 4 bytes in memory addressed by the current program counter:

$$I(c) = c.m_4(c.pc) .$$

Note that our memory can not provide values for two adjacent memory lines with a single memory access. In order to be able to fetch an instruction with a single memory access, we require for the time being that instructions are *aligned* at and fetched from 4 byte boundaries:

$$c.pc[1 : 0] = 00 .$$

Later designs will raise a misalignment interrupt when a processor attempts to fetch from a misaligned address, and will thus no longer need this condition.

The six high order bits of the current instruction are called the op-code:

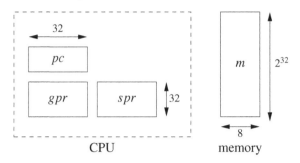

Fig. 90. Visible data structures of MIPS ISA

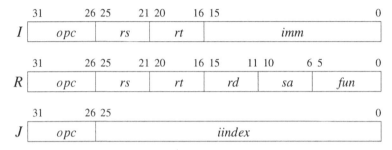

Fig. 91. Types and fields of MIPS instructions

$$opc(c) = I(c)[31:26] \ .$$

There are three instruction types: R-, J-, and I-type. The current instruction type is determined by the following predicates:

$$rtype(c) \equiv opc(c) = 0{*}0^4$$
$$jtype(c) \equiv opc(c) = 0^4 1{*}$$
$$itype(c) = \overline{rtype(c) \vee jtype(c)} \ .$$

To distinguish among the R-type instructions between coprocessor instructions and processor instructions, we define[1]

$$proc(c) \equiv rtype(c) \wedge opc(c)[4] = 1,$$
$$coproc(c) \equiv rtype(c) \wedge opc(c)[4] = 0.$$

Depending on the instruction type, the bits of the current instruction are subdivided as shown in fig. 91. Register addresses are specified in the following fields of the current instruction:

---

[1] This definition is missing in [PBLS16], which leads to an error when a coprocessor instruction happens to have the same function field as a normal R-type instruction.

$$rs(c) = I(c)[25:21]$$
$$rt(c) = I(c)[20:16]$$
$$rd(c) = I(c)[15:11] \, .$$

For R-type instructions, ALU-functions to be applied to the register operands can be specified in the function field:

$$fun(c) = I(c)[5:0] \, .$$

Three kinds of immediate constants are specified: the shift amount sa in R-type instructions, the immediate constant imm in I-type instructions, and an instruction index $iindex$ in J-type (like jump) operations:

$$sa(c) = I(c)[10:6]$$
$$imm(c) = I(c)[15:0]$$
$$iindex(c) = I(c)[25:0] \, .$$

The immediate constant imm has 16 bits. In order to apply ALU functions to it, the constant can be extended with 16 high order bits in two ways: zero extension and sign extension:

$$zxtimm(c) = 0^{16} imm(c)$$
$$sxtimm(c) = imm(c)[15]^{16} imm(c)$$
$$= I(c)[15]^{16} imm(c) \, .$$

4.1.3 Instruction Decoding

For every mnemonic mn of a MIPS instruction from the tables above, we define a predicate $mn(c)$ which is true if instruction mn is to be executed in configuration c. For instance,

$$lw(c) \equiv opc(c) = 100011$$
$$bltz(c) \equiv opc(c) = 0^5 1 \wedge rt(c) = 0^5$$
$$add(c) \equiv rtype(c) \wedge proc(c) \wedge fun(c) = 10^5 \, .$$

The remaining predicates directly associated to the mnemonics of the assembly language are derived in the same way from the tables. We group the basic instruction set into 5 groups and define for each group a predicate that holds, if an instruction from that group is to be executed:

- ALU-operations of I-type are recognized by the leading three bits of the opcode, resp. $opc(c)[5:4]$; ALU-operations of R-type (which are processor instructions) - by the two leading bits of the function code, resp. $I(c)[5:4]$:

$$alur(c) \equiv proc(c) \wedge fun(c)[5:4] = 10$$
$$alui(c) \equiv itype(c) \wedge opc(c)[5:3] = 001$$
$$alu(c) = alur(c) \vee alui(c) \, .$$

- Shift unit operations are processor instructions of R-type and are recognized by the three leading bits of the function code. If bit $fun(c)[2]$ of the function code is on, the shift distance is taken from register specified by $rs(c)$[2]:

$$su(c) \equiv proc(c) \wedge fun(c)[5:3] = 000$$
$$suv(c) = su(c) \wedge fun(c)[2]$$

- Loads and stores are of I-type and are recognized by the three leading bits of the opcode. Memory operations are, loads, stores and cas. Loads and cas read from memory. Stores and cas (potentially) write to memory. Thus cas is both reading and (potentially) writing.

$$l(c) \equiv opc(c)[5:3] = 100$$
$$s(c) \equiv opc(c)[5:3] = 101$$
$$ls(c) = l(c) \vee s(c)$$
$$mop(c) = ls(c) \vee cas(c)$$
$$read(c) = l(c) \vee cas(c)$$
$$write(c) = s(c) \vee cas(c)$$

- Branches are of I-Type and are recognized by the three leading bits of the op-code:

$$b(c) \equiv itype(c) \wedge opc(c)[5:3] = 000$$
$$\equiv itype(c) \wedge I(c)[31:29] = 000 .$$

- Jumps are defined in a brute force way:

$$jump(c) = jr(c) \vee jalr(c) \vee j(c) \vee jal(c)$$
$$jb(c) = jump(c) \vee b(c) .$$

- moves are from gpr to spr or vice versa.

$$mov(c) \rightarrow movg2s(c) \vee movs2g(c) .$$

4.1.4 Reading out Data from Register Files

Addressing the general purpose register file $c.gpr$ with $rs(c)$ and $rt(c)$ and the special register file $c.spr$ with $rs(c)$ we obtain shorthands for register file contents:

$$A(c) = c.gpr(rs(c))$$
$$B(c) = c.gpr(rt(c))$$
$$S(c) = c.spr(rs(c))$$

---

[2] Mnemonics with suffix v as "variable"; one would expect instead for the other shifts a suffix i as "immediate".

4.1.5 Moves

Instruction $movg2s$ writes $B(c)$ into the special purpose register file at address $rd(c)$. Instruction $movs2g$ writes $S(c)$ into the general purpose register file at address $rd(c)$. The memory and other register file contents are not changed. The pc is incremented by 4.

$$mov(c) \rightarrow$$

$$c'.gpr(x) = \begin{cases} S(c) & x = rd(c) \wedge movs2g(c) \wedge x \neq 0^5 \\ c.gpr(x) & \text{otherwise} \end{cases}$$

$$c'.spr(x) = \begin{cases} B(c) & x = rd(c) \wedge movg2s(c) \\ c.gpr(x) & \text{otherwise} \end{cases}$$

$$c'.m = c.m$$

$$c'.pc = c.pc +_{32} 4_{32}.$$

4.1.6 ALU-operations

ALU operations are defined with the help of table 2. It defines functions $res(a,b,f,i)$ and $ovf(a,b,f,i)$. As we do not treat interrupts yet, we use only the first of these functions here. We observe that in all ALU operation of the ISA the left operand is always

$$alu.a(c) = A(c).$$

For R-type operations the right operand is the register specified by the rt field of R-type instructions. For I-type instructions it is the sign extended immediate operand if $opc(c)[2] = I(c)[28] = 0$ or zero extended immediate operand if $opc(c)[2] = 1$. Thus, we define immediate fill bit $ifill(c)$, extended immediate constant $xtimm(c)$, and right operand $alu.b(c)$ in the following way:

$$ifill(c) = \begin{cases} imm(c)[15] & opc(c)[2] = 0 \\ 0 & opc(c)[2] = 1 \end{cases}$$

$$xtimm(c) = \begin{cases} sxtimm(c) & opc(c)[2] = 0 \\ zxtimm(c) & opc(c)[2] = 1 \end{cases}$$

$$= ifill(c)^{16} imm(c)$$

$$alu.b(c) = \begin{cases} B(c) & rtype(c) \\ xtimm(c) & \text{otherwise}. \end{cases}$$

Comparing Table 2 with the tables for I-type and R-type instructions we see that bits $af[2:0]$ of the ALU control can be taken from the low order fields of the opcode for I-type instructions and from the low order bits of the function field for R-type instructions:

$$alu.f(c)[2:0] = \begin{cases} fun(c)[2:0] & rtype(c) \\ opc(c)[2:0] & \text{otherwise} \end{cases}$$

For bit $alu.f[3]$ things are more complicated. For R-type instructions it can be taken from the function code. For I-type instructions it must only be forced to 1 for the two comparison operations, which can be recognized by $opc(c)[2:1] = 01$:

$$alu.f(c)[3] \equiv \begin{cases} fun(c)[3] & rtype(c) \\ opc(c)[2:1] = 01 & \text{otherwise} \end{cases}$$

The i-input of the ALU distinguishes for $af[3:0] = 0111$ between the lui-instruction of I-type for $i = 0$ and the nor-instruction of R-type for $i = 1$. Thus, we set it to $itype(c)$

$$alu.i(c) = itype(c).$$

The result of the ALU computed with these inputs is denoted by

$$alu.res(c) = alu.res(alu.a(c), alu.b(c), alu.f(c), itype(c)) .$$

Depending on the instruction type, the destination register $rdes$ is specified by the rd field or the rt field:

$$rdes(c) = \begin{cases} rd(c) & rtype(c) \\ rt(c) & \text{otherwise} . \end{cases}$$

A summary of all ALU operations is then

$$alu(c) \rightarrow$$

$$c'.gpr(x) = \begin{cases} alu.res(c) & x = rdes(c) \wedge x \neq 0^5 \\ c.gpr(x) & \text{otherwise} \end{cases}$$

$$c'.spr = c.spr$$
$$c'.m = c.m$$
$$c'.pc = c.pc +_{32} 4_{32} .$$

4.1.7 Shift Unit Operations

Results of shift unit operations is defined with the help of table 3 as a function $res(b, dist, f)$. They come in two flavors: i) for $fun(c)[2] = 0$ the shift distance $su.dist(c)$ is an immediate operand specified by the sa field of the instruction. For $fun(c)[2] = 1$ the shift distance is specified by the last bits of the register specified by the rs field:

$$su.dist(c) = \begin{cases} sa(c) & fun(c)[2] = 0 \\ c.gpr(rs(c))[4:0] & fun(c)[2] = 1 . \end{cases}$$

The left operand that is shifted is always the register specified by the rt-field:

$$su.b(c) = c.gpr(rt(c)) .$$

and the control bits $su.f[1:0]$ are taken from the low order bits of the function field:

$$su.f(c) = fun(c)[1:0] .$$

The result of the shift unit computed with these inputs is denoted by

$$su.res(c) = su.res(su.b(c), su.dist(c), su.f(c)) .$$

For shift operations the destination register is always specified by the rd field. Thus, the shift unit operations can be summarized as

$$su(c) \rightarrow$$

$$c'.gpr(x) = \begin{cases} su.res(c) & x = rd(c) \wedge x \neq 0^5 \\ c.gpr(x) & \text{otherwise} \end{cases}$$

$$c'.spr = c.spr$$

$$c'.m = c.m$$

$$c'.pc = c.pc +_{32} 4_{32} .$$

4.1.8 Branch and Jump

A branch condition evaluation unit was specified in Table 4. It computes a function $res(a,b,bf)$. We use this function with the following parameters:

$$bce.a(c) = c.gpr(rs(c))$$
$$bce.b(c) = c.gpr(rt(c))$$
$$bce.f(c) = opc(c)[2:0] \circ rt(c)[0]$$

and define the result of a branch condition evaluation as

$$bce.res(c) = bce.res(bce.a(c), bce.b(c), bce.f(c)) .$$

The next program counter $c'.pc$ is usually computed as $c.pc +_{32} 4_{32}$. This order is only changed in jump instructions or in branch instructions, where the branch is taken, i.e., the branch condition evaluates to 1. We define

$$jbtaken(c) = jump(c) \vee b(c) \wedge bce.res(c) .$$

In case of a jump or a branch taken, there are three possible jump targets.

Branch Instructions

Branch instructions involve a *relative* branch. The PC is incremented by a branch distance:

$$b(c) \wedge bres(c) \rightarrow$$
$$bdist(c) = imm(c)[15]^{14}imm(c)00$$
$$btarget(c) = c.pc +_{32} bdist(c) .$$

Note that the branch distance is a kind of a sign extended immediate constant, but due to the alignment requirement the low order bits of the jump distance must be 00. Thus, one uses the 16 bits of the immediate constant for bits $[17 : 2]$ of the jump distance. Sign extension is used for the remaining bits. Thus, backward jumps are realized with negative $[imm(c)]$.

R-type Jumps $jr(c)$ and $jalr(c)$

The branch target is specified by the *rs* field of the instruction:

$$jr(c) \vee jalr(c) \rightarrow btarget(c) = c.gpr(rs(c)) .$$

J-type Jumps $j(c)$ and $jal(c)$

The branch target is computed in a rather peculiar way: i) the PC is incremented by 4, ii) *then* bits $[27 : 2]$ are replaced by the *iindex* field of the instruction:

$$j(c) \vee jal(c) \rightarrow btarget(c) = (c.pc +_{32} 4_{32})[31 : 28]iindex(c)00 .$$

Now we can define the next PC computation for *all* instructions as

$$btarget(c) = \begin{cases} c.pc +_{32} bdist(c) & b(c) \wedge bres(c) \\ c.gpr(rs(c)) & jr(c) \vee jalr(c) \\ (c.pc +_{32} 4_{32})[31 : 28]iindex(c)00 & \text{otherwise} \end{cases}$$

$$c'.pc = next\,pc(c) = \begin{cases} btarget(c) & jbtaken(c) \\ c.pc +_{32} 4_{32} & \text{otherwise} . \end{cases}$$

Jump and Link $jal(c)$ and $jalr(c)$

Jump and link instructions are used to implement calls of procedures. Besides setting the PC to the branch target, they prepare the so called *link address*

$$linkad(c) = c.pc +_{32} 4_{32}$$

and save it in a register. For the R-type instruction *jalr*, this register is specified by the *rd* field. J-type instruction *jal* does not have an *rs* field, and the link address is stored in register 31 $(= \langle 1^5 \rangle)$. Branch and jump instructions do not change the memory.

Therefore, for the update of registers in branch and jump instructions, we have:

$$jb(c) \rightarrow$$

$$c'.gpr(x) = \begin{cases} linkad(c) & jalr(c) \wedge x = rd(c) \wedge x \neq 0^5 \vee jal(c) \wedge x = 1^5 \\ c.gpr(x) & \text{otherwise} \end{cases}$$

$$c'.spr = c.spr$$

$$c'.m = c.m .$$

4.1.9 Memory Operations

Load and store operations access a certain number $d(c) \in \{1,2,4\}$ of bytes of memory starting at a so called *effective address* $ea(c)$. Letters b,h, and w in the mnemonics define the width: b stands for $d = 1$ resp. a byte access; h stands for $d = 2$ resp. a half word access, and w stands for $d = 4$ resp. a word access. Inspection of the instruction tables gives

$$d(c) = \begin{cases} 1 & opc(c)[0] = 0 \\ 2 & opc(c)[1:0] = 01 \\ 4 & opc(c)[1:0] = 11 \vee cas(c) . \end{cases}$$

Addressing is always relative to $A(c)$. Except for cas operations (which have R-type) the offset is specified by the immediate field:

$$ea(c) = \begin{cases} A(c) & cas(c) \\ A(c) +_{32} sxtimm(c) & \text{otherwise} \end{cases}$$

Note that the immediate constant is sign extended. Thus, negative offsets can be realized in the same way as negative branch distances. In the absence of misalignment interrupts addresses are for the time being required to be *aligned*. If we interpret them as binary numbers they have to be divisible by the width $d(c)$:

$$d(c) \mid \langle ea(c) \rangle$$

or equivalently

$$mop(c) \wedge d(c) = 2 \rightarrow ea(c)[0] = 0 \quad , \quad mop(c) \wedge d(c) = 4 \rightarrow ea(c)[1:0] = 00 .$$

Stores

A store instruction takes the low order $d(c)$ bytes of $B(c)$ and stores them as $m_{d(c)}(ea(c))$. The PC is incremented by 4 (but we have already defined that on page 148). Other memory bytes and register values are not changed:

$$s(c) \rightarrow$$

$$c'.m(x) = \begin{cases} byte(i, B(c)) & x = ea(c) +_{32} i_{32} \wedge i < d(c) \\ c.m(x) & \text{otherwise} \end{cases}$$

$$c'.gpr = c.gpr$$

Loads

Loads, like stores, access $d(c)$ bytes of memory starting at address $ea(c)$. The result is stored in the low order $d(c)$ bytes of the destination register, which is specified by the *rt* field of the instruction. This leaves $32 - 8 \cdot d(c)$ bits of the destination register to be filled by some bit $fill(c)$. For unsigned loads (with a suffix "u" in the mnemonics) the fill bit is zero; otherwise it is sign extended by the leading bit of $c.m_{d(c)}(ea(c))$. In this way a load result $lres(c) \in \mathbb{B}^{32}$ is computed and the general purpose register specified by the *rt* field is updated. Other registers and the memory are left unchanged:

$$u(c) = opc(c)[2]$$

$$fill(c) = \begin{cases} 0 & u(c) \\ c.m_{d(c)}(ea(c))[8 \cdot d(c) - 1] & \text{otherwise} \end{cases}$$

$$lres(c) = fill(c)^{32 - 8 \cdot d(c)} \circ c.m_{d(c)}(ea(c))$$

$$l(c) \rightarrow$$

$$c'.gpr(x) = \begin{cases} lres(c) & x = rt(c) \wedge x \neq 0_5 \\ c.gpr(x) & \text{otherwise} \end{cases}$$

$$c'.m = c.m \,.$$

Compare and Swap (CAS)

Recall that cas operations have R-type, thus no immediate constant is available and the effective address is just $ea(c) = A(c)$. A load word operation with destination $gpr(rd)$ is performed. The content of register 10 of special purpose register file

$$cdata(c) = c.spr(10_5)$$

is compared with the memory word addressed by the effective address

$$castest(c) \equiv cdata(c) = c.m_4(ea(c)).$$

If the test is positive, the memory content is replaced by $B(c)$.

$$cas(c) \rightarrow$$

$$c'.gpr(x) = \begin{cases} c.m_4(ea(c)) & x = rd(c) \wedge x \neq 0^5 \\ c.gpr(x) & \text{otherwise} \end{cases}$$

$$c'.m(x) = \begin{cases} byte(i, B(c)) & x = ea(c) +_{32} i_{32} \wedge i < 4 \wedge castest(c) \\ c.m(x) & \text{otherwise} \end{cases}$$

$$c'.spr = c.spr$$

4.1.10 ISA Summary

We collect all previous definitions of destination registers for the general purpose register file and the special purpose register file into

$$Xad(c) = \begin{cases} 1^5 & jal(c) \\ rd(c) & rtype(c) \\ rt(c) & \text{otherwise} . \end{cases}$$

Also we collect the data $gprin$ to be written into the general purpose register file. For technical reasons, we define on the way an intermediate result C that collects the possible GPR input from arithmetic, shift, and jump instructions:

$$C(c) = \begin{cases} S(c) & movs2g(c) \\ B(c) & movg2s(c) \\ su.res(c) & su(c) \\ linkad(c) & jal(c) \vee jalr(c) \\ alu.res(c) & \text{otherwise} \end{cases}$$

$$gpr.in(c) = \begin{cases} lres(c) & l(c) \vee cas(c) \\ C(c) & \text{otherwise} . \end{cases}$$

Finally, we collect in a general purpose register write signal all situations when some general purpose register is updated:

$$gprw(c) = alu(c) \vee su(c) \vee l(c) \vee cas(c) \vee jal(c) \vee jalr(c)$$

and analogously for the special purpose register

$$sprw(c) = movg2s(c)$$

Now we can summarize the MIPS ISA in four rules concerning the updates of PC, general purpose registers, special purpose registers and memory:

$$c'.pc = \begin{cases} btarget(c) & jbtaken(c) \\ c.pc +_{32} 4_{32} & \text{otherwise} \end{cases}$$

$$c'.gpr(x) = \begin{cases} gpr.in(c) & x = Xad(c) \wedge x \neq 0^5 \wedge gprw(c) \\ c.gpr(x) & \text{otherwise} \end{cases}$$

$$c'.spr(x) = \begin{cases} C(c) & x = Xad(c) \wedge movg2s(c) \\ c.gpr(x) & \text{otherwise} \end{cases}$$

$$c'.m(x) = \begin{cases} byte(i, B(c)) & x = ea(c) +_{32} i_{32} \wedge i < d(c) \wedge \\ & (s(c) \vee cas(c) \wedge castest(c)) \\ c.m(x) & \text{otherwise} . \end{cases}$$

4.1.11 Software Conditions

In the absence of misalignment interrupts we have already required that instruction fetch and memory operations are aligned. We call this software condition SC_{align}

$$SC_{align}(c) \leftrightarrow 4|\langle ia(c)\rangle \wedge (mop(c) \rightarrow d(c)|\langle ea(c)\rangle)$$

Most of ISA memory will be implemented by some kind of RAM, which happens to have unknown content after power up. The program counter points initially to address 0^{32} and starts fetching instructions from some initial program, for instance a boot loader. This program will reside in ROM occupying the low order 2^{r+3} byte addresses of the memory system for some r. Because write operations to ROM have no effect, we simply forbid store or cas operations to that region. We call this software condition SC_{ROM}

$$SC_{ROM}(c) \leftrightarrow (write(c) \rightarrow \langle ea(c)\rangle > 2^{r+3})$$

4.2 A Sequential Processor Design

4.2.1 Hardware Configurations and Simulation Relation

With the exception of memory, hardware components $h.X$ of the basic sequential processor design are the obvious counter parts of ISA components $c.X$.

- register $h.pc \in \mathbb{B}^{32}$. The program counter.
- GPR-RAM $h.gpr : \mathbb{B}^5 \rightarrow \mathbb{B}^{32}$. The general purpose register file.
- R-RW-SPR-RAM $h.gpr : \mathbb{B}^5 \rightarrow \mathbb{B}^{32}$. The special purpose register file.
- bw-R-RW-RAM/ROM $h.m : \mathbb{B}^{29} \rightarrow \mathbb{B}^{64}$. The line addressable hardware memory.

The basic processor design implements one ISA instruction per hardware cycle and maintains a simulation relation $sim(h, c)$ where

- components other than memory are equal:

$$X \neq m \rightarrow h.X = c.X$$

- hardware memory is the line addressable version of ISA memory:

$$h.m = \ell(c.m)$$

The intended correctness theorem for the processor is then:

Lemma 33.

- *There is an initial configuration c^0 satisfying*

$$sim(h^0, c^0)$$

- *If for the ISA computation (c^i) with that initial configuration, the software conditions are maintained, then hardware simulates ISA*

$$(\forall i. \, SC_{align}(c^i) \wedge SC_{ROM}(c^i)) \rightarrow \forall t > 0. \, sim(h^t, c^t)$$

The straightforward way to guarantee these software conditions is for the program to be contained in the ROM region and to read registers only after they are written. Only once we introduce disks in chapter 13 will it be possible to load additional code that can be guaranteed to maintain the software conditions into the memory outside the ROM region from persistent storage. For details about this process in a machine with much simpler hardware, in particular about how to load an operating system with a boot loader in ROM, see chapter 15 of [PBLS16].

Using the auxiliary circuits one can translate the ISA summary from section 4.1.10 into hardware in a mechanical and almost completely straightforward way. The only technical issues arise for memory operations due to the fact that the byte addressable ISA memory is embedded in the line addressable hardware memory. We summarize results from [KMP14] about this embedding.

4.2.2 Memory Embedding

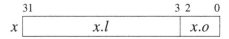

Fig. 92. Line address $x.l$ and offset $x.o$ of a byte address x

As illustrated in fig. 92, we divide byte addresses $x \in \mathbb{B}^{32}$ into *line address* $x.l \in \mathbb{B}^{29}$ and *offset* $x.o \in \mathbb{B}^3$ as

$$x.l = x[31 : 3]$$
$$x.o = x[2 : 0] \, .$$

We are interested in locating the single bytes of sequences $m_d(x)$ in the line addressable memory $\ell(m)$. Access widths are powers of two and cover at most 8 bytes:

$$d \in \{2^k \mid k \in [0:3]\} \, .$$

A pair (x,d) is *aligned* if the access width d divides the line offset of x interpreted as a binary number

$$aligned(x,d) \equiv d|\langle x.o \rangle$$

For such pairs address arithmetic does not produce carries to the line address (lemma 6.3 of [KMP14]).

Lemma 34. *For aligned(x,d) and $i < d$:*

1. $\langle x.o \rangle + i \leq 7$,
2. $\langle x.o +_3 i_3 \rangle = \langle x.o \rangle + i$,
3. $x +_{32} i_{32} = x.l \circ (x.o +_3 i_3)$.

Single bytes $m(x)$ are found in $\ell(m)$ at byte $x.o$ in line $x.l$ (lemma 6.5 of [KMP14]). This is illustrated in Fig. 93.

Fig. 93. Locating $m(x)$ in $\ell(m)$

Lemma 35.

$$byte(\langle x.o \rangle, \ell(m)(x.l)) = m(x)$$

For aligned pairs (x,d) the bytes of $m_d(x)$ occupy in $\ell(m)$ consecutive bytes in the single line $x.l$ (lemma 6.6 of [KMP14], also shown in section 1.3.4). This is illustrated in figure 94.

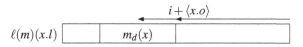

Fig. 94. Locating byte i of $m_d(x)$ in $\ell(m)$

Lemma 36. *For aligned(x,d) and $i < d$:*

$$byte(i, m_d(x)) = byte(\langle x.o \rangle + i, \ell(m)(x.l))$$

Word accesses with aligned pairs (a,d) cover the upper or lower half of line $x.l$ depending on address bit $a[2]$ (lemma 6.7 of [KMP14]).

Lemma 37. *For $x[1:0] = 00$:*

$$m_4(x) = \begin{cases} \ell(m)(x.l)_L & x[2] = 0 \\ \ell(m)(x.l)_H & x[2] = 1 \end{cases}$$

4.2.3 Overview of the Hardware

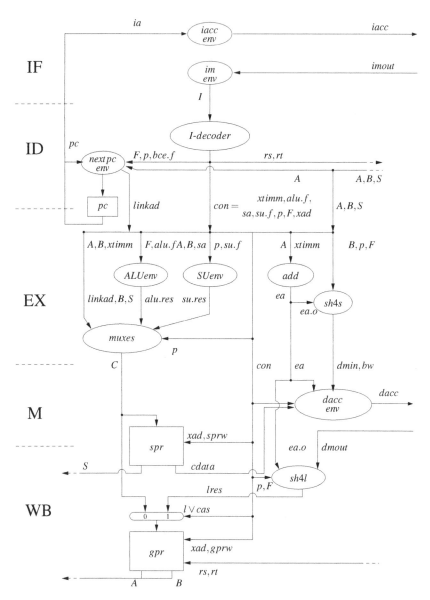

Fig. 95. Stages of a simple MIPS core

An overview of the basic processor core, which is already arranged in pipeline, stages
is shown in fig. 95. The core is connected via buses *iacc*, *imout*, *dacc* and *dmout*

to a bw-R-RW-ROM-RAM m which serves here as main memory. Details will be explained subsequently.

4.2.4 Initialization and Instruction Fetch

Figure 96 shows how the program counter is initialized and how instructions are fetched from port a of the memory.

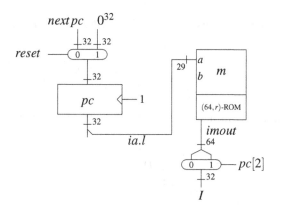

Fig. 96. PC initialization and the instruction port environment

Using that *reset* is on in cycle -1 and off afterwards, one concludes

$$h^0.pc = 0^{32} = c^0.pc.$$

The initial ISA configuration is constructed from the initial state of the hardware by

$$X \in \{gpr, spr\} \rightarrow c^0.X = h^0.X$$
$$c^0.m(x) = byte(\langle x.o \rangle, h^0.m(x.l))$$

With lemma 35 one concludes

$$sim(h^0, c^0).$$

From now on assume as an induction hypothesis $sim(h, c)$ as well as $SC_{align}(c)$ and $SC_{ROM}(c)$ and let

$$h' = \delta_H(h), \quad c' = \delta_{isa}(c).$$

Hardware is constructed such that $sim(h', c')$ can be shown for the induction step of lemma 33.

We rephrase the specification ISA instruction $I(c)$ in terms of instruction accesses $iacc(c)$ to the line addressable version $\ell(c.m)$ of ISA memory.

$$iacc(c).a = c.pc.l$$
$$iacc(c).r = 1$$
$$imout(c) = \ell(c.m)(iacc.a)$$

By the software condition the program counter is word-aligned

$$ia(c)[1:0] = 00$$

and with lemma 37 about memory embedding we conclude

$$I(c) = c.m_4(c.pc) = \begin{cases} imout(c)_L & c.pc[2] = 0 \\ imout(c)_H & c.pc[2] = 1. \end{cases}$$

In hardware we denote the instruction memory address and the instruction data output resp. as

$$ia(h) = h.pc.l = h.m.a$$
$$imout(h) = h.m.outa.$$

The instruction access in hardware $iacc(h)$ is defined to match the corresponding access in ISA:

$$iacc(h).a = ia(h)$$
$$iacc(h).r = 1$$

and therefore

$$iacc(h) = iacc(c).$$

From the induction hypothesis and the specification of hardware components, we conclude that instructions are fetched correctly.

Lemma 38.

$$imout(h) = imout(c)$$
$$I(h) = I(c)$$

4.2.5 Straight Forward Constructions

The major part of the processor hardware is now obtained by translating the ISA in the most straight forward way.

Instruction Decoder

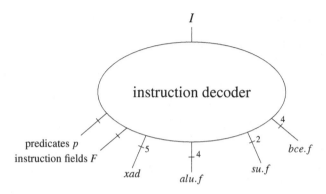

Fig. 97. Instruction decoder

The instruction decoder belongs to the instruction decode stage. As shown in fig. 97 it computes the hardware version of functions $f(c)$ that only depend on the current instruction $I(c)$, i.e., which can be written as

$$f(c) = \hat{f}(I(c)) .$$

$$rtype(c) \equiv opc(c) = 0*0^4$$
$$\equiv I(c)[31:26] = 0*0^4$$

or

$$rd(c) = I(c)[15:11]$$

This trivial transformation gives a straightforward way to construct circuits for all predicates $p(c)$ from the ISA specification that depend only on the current instruction:

- Compute $\hat{p}(I)$ by a Boolean formula; a disjunctive normal form will always work, but usually a single monomial suffices. In the above example

$$r\hat{t}ype(I) = /I[31] \wedge /I[29] \wedge /I[28] \wedge /I[27] \wedge /I[26] .$$

- in the hardware connect a circuit for $\hat{f}$ to signal $I(h)$. Because instructions are fetched correctly (lemma 38) the output $p(h)$ of this circuit satisfies

$$p(h) = \hat{p}(I(h)) = \hat{p}(I(c)) = p(c)$$

Thus, the instruction decoder produces correct instruction predicates. All instruction fields F have the form

$$F(c) = I(c)[m:n] \, .$$

For the hardware version we take exactly the same bits from $I(h)$ and get with lemma 38

$$F(h) = I(h)[m:n] = I(c)[m:n] = F(c)$$

Thus instruction fields are computed correctly.

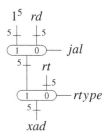

Fig. 98. x address computation

The output $Xad(h)$ in fig. 98 computes the address of the destination register of for the general purpose register file or the special purpose register file. Because predicates and instruction fields are computed correctly we get:

$$Xad(h) = \begin{cases} 1^5 & jal(h) \\ rd(h) & rtype(h) \\ rt(h) & \text{otherwise} \end{cases}$$
$$= \begin{cases} 1^5 & jal(c) \\ rd(c) & rtype(c) \\ rt(c) & \text{otherwise} \end{cases}$$
$$= Xad(c) \, .$$

The fill bit $ifill(c)$ is a predicate and $imm(c)$ is a field of the instruction. Thus, we can compute the extended immediate constant in hardware as

$$xtimm(h) = ifill(h)^{16} imm(h) = ifill(c)^{16} imm(c) = xtimm(c) \, .$$

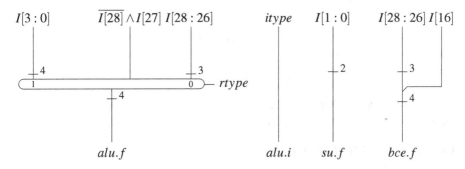

Fig. 99. Computation of function fields for ALU, SU, and BCE

Figure 99 shows the computation of the function fields $alu.f$, $alu.i$, $su.f$, and $bce.f$ for the ALU, the shift unit, and the branch condition evaluation unit. That the computed hardware signals equal the ISA signals is shown along the same lines. We summarize for the instruction decoder.

Lemma 39 (Instruction Decoder). *For all outputs X of the instruction decoder holds:*

$$X(h) = X(c)$$

Reading from Register Files

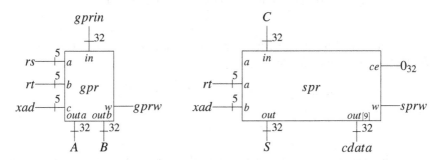

Fig. 100. General purpose register file

Register files $h.gpr$ and $h.spr$ of the hardware are shown in fig. 100. The a and b addresses of the gpr are connected to $rs(h)$ and $rt(h)$; the a address of the special purpose register file is connected to $rs(c)$. From the correctness of the signals rs and rd as well as the induction hypothesis we get

$$A(h) = gpr.outa(h)$$
$$= h.gpr(rs(h))$$
$$= c.gpr(rs(c))$$
$$= A(c)$$

That signals $B(h)$ and $S(h)$ are computed correctly is shown in the same way. Thus we conclude that the outputs of register files are computed correctly.

Lemma 40 (Register File Outputs).

$$X \in \{A, B, S\} \to X(h) = X(c)$$

BCE-Unit, ALU and Shifter

The wiring of the branch condition evaluation unit *BCE* is shown in fig. 101.

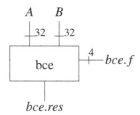

Fig. 101. The branch condition evaluation unit and its operands

Using the correctness of register outputs (lemma 40) and of the instruction decoder (lemma 39) one concludes

$$bce.res(h) = bce.res(A(h), B(h), bce.f(h))$$
$$= bce.res(A(c)), B(c), bce.f(c))$$
$$= bce.res(c) .$$

Thus the results of unit *BCE* are computed correctly. That the results of units *ALU* and *SU* shown in figures 102 and 103 are computed correctly is shown along the same lines.

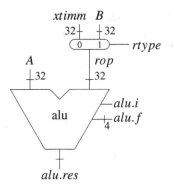

Fig. 102. ALU environment

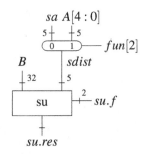

Fig. 103. Shift unit environment

Thus we have

Lemma 41 (BCE, ALU and SU result).

$$X \in \{bce, alu, su\} \rightarrow X.res(h) = X.res(c)$$

Incremented PC and Link Address

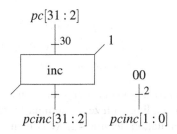

Fig. 104. Incrementing an aligned PC with a 30-incrementer

The computation of an incremented PC as needed for the next PC environment as well as for the link instructions is shown in fig. 104. The binary representation of 4 ends with 2 zeros. The same holds by alignment for the *pc*. By lemma 1 a 30 bit incremeter therefore suffices for this computation. With the induction hypothesis for the pc we get

Lemma 42.
$$linkad(c) = pcinc(c) = pcinc(h) = linkad(h)$$

Next PC Computation

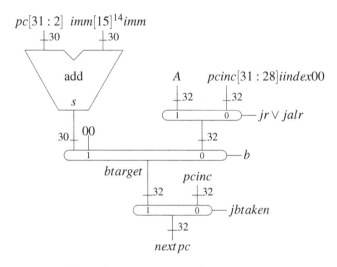

Fig. 105. Next PC computation

The circuit computing the next PC input, which was left open in fig. 96 when we treated the instruction fetch, is shown in fig. 105. Immediate constant *imm* and predicates *jr, jalr, jump, b* are correctly computed in the instruction decoder (lemma 39). We compute *jbtaken* in the obvious way and conclude with the correctness of the bce result (lemma 41):

$$jbtaken(h) = jump(h) \vee b(h) \wedge bce.res(h)$$
$$= jump(c) \vee b(c) \wedge bce.res(c)$$
$$= jbtaken(c) .$$

Using correctness of the instruction decoder, induction hypothesis for the pc, simplified addition for numbers ending with zeros (lemma 1), register outputs (lemma 40) and incremented pc computation (lemma 42) we conclude successively

$$imm(h)[15]^{14}imm(h)00 = bdist(c)$$
$$add.s(h)00 = c.pc +_{32} bdist(c)$$
$$btarget(h) = btarget(c)$$
$$nectpc(h) = nextpc(c).$$

Exploiting for $h = h'$ and $t \geq 0$

$$reset(h) = 0$$

and by the semantics of register updates we conclude

$$h'.pc = nextpc(c) = c'.pc$$

We summarize:

Lemma 43 (next PC).

$$nextpc(h) = nextpc(c)$$
$$h'.pc = c'.pc.$$

This finishes the induction step for the pc.

Collecting Results

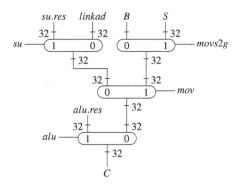

Fig. 106. Collecting results into signal C

fig. 106 shows a small multiplexer-tree collecting results *linkad, S, alu.res, su.res* into an intermediate result C. Using correctness of the decoder (lemma 39), the incremented pc computation (lemma 42), register outputs (lemma 40), and unit results (lemma 41) one concludes that the intermediate result C is computed correctly:

Lemma 44 (C result).

$$C(h) = C(c)$$

Effective Address

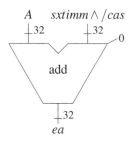

Fig. 107. Effective address computation

The effective address computation is shown in fig. 107. Using the correctness of the instruction decoder (lemma 39) and of register outputs (lemma 40) one concludes the correctness of the effective address computation:

Lemma 45 (effective address).

$$ea(h) = ea(c)$$

4.2.6 Data Accesses

Data Accesses of ISA

As a guideline for the construction of environments $sh4s$ and $sh4l$ with their shifters supporting the memory operations of the ISA, we rephrase these operations in terms of data accesses $dacc(c)$ to the line addressable version $\ell(c.m)$ of ISA memory. In a completely straight forward way one specifies

$$dacc(c).a = ea(c).l$$
$$dacc(c).cdata = cdata(c)$$
$$dacc(c).r = l(c)$$
$$dacc(c).w = s(c)$$
$$dacc(c).cas = cas(c)$$

For the construction of the data memory input $dmin(c)$ of store or cas operations one shifts the register $B(c)$ whose low order $d(c) \le 4$ bytes are to be stored by $\langle ea(c)[1 : 0]\rangle$ bytes to the left and the makes two copies of the result F; which copy is used will be determined by the byte-write signals.

$$F(c) = slc(B(c), \langle ea(c)[1 : 0]\rangle)$$
$$dmin(c) = F(c) \circ F(c)$$

For $i < d(c)$ we locate the bytes of B to be stored in the data memory input by

$$
\begin{aligned}
byte(i, B(c)) &= byte(i + \langle ea(c)[1:0] \rangle, F(c)) \\
&= byte(i + \langle 0 \circ ea(c)[1:0] \rangle, dmin(c)) \\
&= byte(i + \langle 1 \circ ea(c)[1:0] \rangle, dmin(c)) \\
&= byte(i + \langle ea(c)[2:0] \rangle, dmin(c)) \\
&= byte(i + \langle ea(c).o \rangle, dmin(c))
\end{aligned}
$$

For the byte-write signals bw — and also for byte-read signals br to be used later for store buffer forwarding — one constructs first a 4 bit wide mask $mmask$ for memory operations with $d(c)$ many ones at the right end. This mask is shifted left by $\langle ea(c) \rangle$. Two copies of the result $f(c)$ are produced. The left copy is used in the byte-write and byte-read signals if $ea(c)[2]$ is on, otherwise the right copy.

$$
\begin{aligned}
mmask(c) &= mop(c) \wedge (0^{4-d(c)} 1^{d(c)}) \\
f(c) &= slc(mmask(c), \langle ea(c)[1:0] \rangle) \\
bw(c) &= (s(c) \vee cas(c)) \wedge ((ea[2] \wedge f(c)) \circ (/ea[2] \wedge f(c))) \\
br(c) &= l(c) \wedge ((ea[2] \wedge f(c)) \circ (/ea[2] \wedge f(c)))
\end{aligned}
$$

Using the definitions above, we specify the missing components of $dacc(c)$:

$$
\begin{aligned}
dacc(c).data &= dmin(c) \\
dacc(c).bw &= bw(c).
\end{aligned}
$$

For $aligned(ea(c), d(c))$ and $i < d(c)$ we locate the byte-write and byte-read signals of the bytes to be stored in $bw[7:0]$ respectively $br[7:0]$ by

$$
\begin{aligned}
f(c)[j] = 1 &\leftrightarrow mop(c) \wedge \exists i < d(c).\ j = \langle ea(c)[1:0] \rangle + i \\
bw(c)[j] = 1 &\leftrightarrow (s(c) \vee cas(c)) \wedge \exists i < d(c).\ j = \langle ea(c)[2:0] \rangle + i \\
br(c)[j] = 1 &\leftrightarrow (l(c)) \wedge \exists i < d(c).\ j = \langle ea(c)[2:0] \rangle + i
\end{aligned}
\tag{12}
$$

Note that byte-read signals are not generated for cas instructions, because these instructions will not use store buffer forwarding.

For later reference we summarize

Lemma 46.

$$
\begin{aligned}
byte(i, B(c)) &= byte(i + \langle ea(c).o \rangle, dmin(c)) \\
SC_{align}(c) \rightarrow bw(c)[j] = 1 &\leftrightarrow (s(c) \vee cas(c)) \wedge \exists i < d(c).\ j = \langle ea(c)[2:0] \rangle + i
\end{aligned}
$$

We prove the crucial result that the line addressable version $\ell(c'.m)$ of the next ISA computation is obtained by applying the data access $dacc(c)$ defined in this way to $\ell(c.m)$ (which is what the hardware memory $h.m$ is specified to do).

Lemma 47.

$$
SC_{align}(c) \rightarrow \ell(c'.m) = \delta_M(\ell(c.m), dacc(c))
$$

Proof. Abbreviating the right hand side

$$M' = \delta_M(\ell(c.m), dacc(c))$$

and applying the definition of memory semantics δ_M we get

$$M'(a) = \begin{cases} modify(\ell(c.m)(a), dmin(c), bw(c)) & a = dacc(c).a \\ & \wedge (dacc(c).w \vee dacc(c).cas \\ & \wedge test(dacc(c), \ell(c.m))) \\ \ell(c.m)(a) & \text{otherwise .} \end{cases}$$

For cas accesses $(dacc(c).cas = 1)$ we have by lemma 37 with SC_{align}:

$$test(dacc(c), \ell(c.m)) \equiv dacc(c).cdata = \begin{cases} \ell(c.m)(dacc(c).a)_L & /dacc(c).bw[0] \\ \ell(c.m)(dacc(c).a)_H & dacc(c).bw[0] \end{cases}$$

$$\equiv cdata(c) = \begin{cases} \ell(c.m)(ea(c).l)_L & /ea(c)[2] \\ \ell(c.m)(ea(c).l)_H & ea(c)[2] \end{cases}$$

$$\equiv cdata(c) = c.m_4(ea(c))$$

$$\equiv castest(c)$$

Thus

$$M'(a) = \begin{cases} modify(\ell(c.m)(a), dmin(c), bw(c)) & a = ea(c).l \wedge (s(c) \vee cas(c) \\ & \wedge castest(c)) \qquad\qquad (13) \\ \ell(c.m)(a) & \text{otherwise .} \end{cases}$$

With $x \in \mathbb{B}^{32}$, $a = x.l \in DR$, $j = \langle x.o \rangle \in B_3$, and the definition of function *modify*, we rewrite (13) as

$$byte(\langle x.o \rangle, M'(x.l)) = byte(j, M'(a))$$

$$= \begin{cases} byte(j, dmin(c)) & bw(c)[j] \wedge a = ea(c).l \wedge (s(c) \vee cas(c) \\ & \wedge castest(c)) \\ byte(j, \ell(c.m)(a)) & \text{otherwise} \end{cases}$$

$$= \begin{cases} byte(i, B(c)) & j = \langle ea(c).o \rangle + i \wedge i < d(c) \\ & \wedge a = ea(c).l \wedge (s(c) \vee cas(c) \\ & \wedge castest(c)) \qquad\qquad \text{(lemma 46)} \\ c.m(x) & \text{otherwise} \qquad\quad \text{(lemma 35)} \end{cases}$$

$$= c'.m(x) .$$

A second application of lemma 35 gives

$$M' = \ell(c'.m)$$

□

Shift for Store Environment and Hardware Memory

The construction of this environment is now completely straight forward. The data memory input is generated by the hardware in fig. 108.

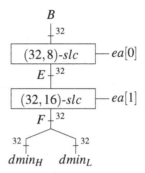

Fig. 108. Shifter for store operations in the sh4s-environment

The initial memory mask is generated as

$$mmask(h)[3:0] = ls(h) \land (I(h)[27]^2 I(h)[26] 1) \lor cas(h)^4$$

Byte-write and byte-read signals are then generated by the hardware from fig. 109

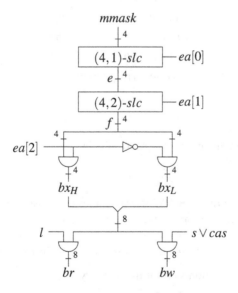

Fig. 109. Computation of byte-write signals $bw[7:0]$ in the sh4s-environment

Easy calculations show successively

$$X \in \{F, dmin, mmask, f, bw, br\} \to X(h) = X(c)$$

Memory Stage

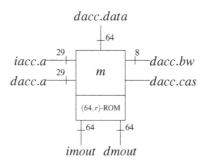

dacc.data

$$iacc.a \xrightarrow{29} \quad \xrightarrow{8} dacc.bw$$

m

dacc.cas

(64, r)-ROM

imout dmout

Fig. 110. Wiring of the hardware memory

The complete wiring of the hardware memory $h.m$ is shown in fig. 110, using the data memory access $dacc(h)$ of the hardware defined by

$$dacc(h).a = ea(h).l$$
$$dacc(h).data = dmin(h)$$
$$dacc(h).cdata = cdata(h)$$
$$dacc(h).bw = bw(h)$$
$$dacc(h).w = s(h)$$
$$dacc(h).r = l(h)$$
$$dacc(h).cas = cas(h)$$

with which we can summarize previous results by

$$dacc(h) = dacc(c)$$

From the specification of bw-R-RW-ROM-memories, the software condition, the induction hypothesis for memory and lemma 47 we get

$$h'.m = \delta_M(h.m, dacc(h)) = \delta_M(\ell(c'.m), dacc(c)) = \ell(c'.m)$$

This completes the induction step for the memory.

Shifter for Load

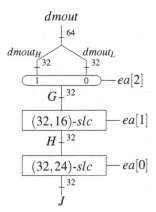

Fig. 111. Shifter for load operations in the sh4l-environment

For later use in pipeline stage correctness proofs we define

$$dmout(c) = \ell(c.m)(dacc(c).a)$$

and conclude with the specification of memory and the induction hypothesis:

Lemma 48.

$$dmout(h) = dmout(c)$$

A shifter construction supporting load operations is shown in Fig. 111. Assume $l(c) \vee cas(c)$ holds, i.e., a read from memory is executed. By the software condition, the memory address is aligned

$$aligned(ea(c), d(c))$$

We can use Lemma 36 to locate for $i < d(c)$ the bytes to be loaded in $\ell(c.m) = h.m$ and subsequently — using memory semantics — in $dmout(h)$. Then we simply track the effect of the two shifters taking into account that a 24-bit left shift is the same as an 8-bit right shift:

$$
\begin{aligned}
& byte(i, c.m_{d(c)}(ea(c))) \\
& = byte(\langle ea(c).o \rangle + i, \ell(c.m)(ea(c).l)) \quad \text{(lemma 36)} \\
& = byte(\langle ea(h).o \rangle + i, dmout(c))) \\
& = byte(\langle ea(h).o \rangle + i, dmout(h)) \quad \text{(lemma 48)} \\
& = byte(\langle ea(h)[1:0] \rangle + i, G(h)) \\
& = byte(i, J(h)) . \quad \text{(hardware construction)}
\end{aligned}
$$

Hence, we can conclude the following lemma.

Lemma 49 (shift for load).

$$J(h)[8d(c) - 1 : 0] = c.m_{d(c)}(ea(c))$$

By setting

$$fill(h) = J(h)[7] \wedge lb(h) \vee J(h)[15] \wedge lh(h)$$

we conclude

$$s(c) \wedge d(c) \neq 4 \rightarrow fill(h) = fill(c) .$$

We generate a load mask $lmask \in \mathbb{B}^{32}$ by repeating each bit of the 4 bit memory mask 8 times

$$lmask(h) = mmask[3]^8 \circ mmask[2]^8 \circ mmask[1]^8 \circ mmask[0]^8$$

In case of load operations ($l(c)$ holds) it satisfies

$$lmask(h) = 0^{32-8 \cdot d(c)} 1^{8 \cdot d(c)} .$$

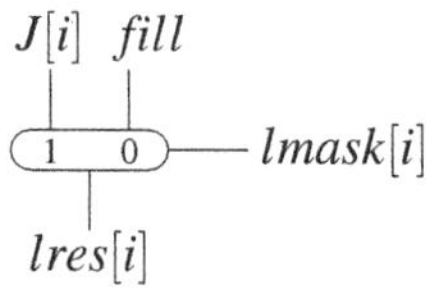

Fig. 112. Fill bit computation for loads

As shown in fig. 112 we insert the fill bit at positions i where the corresponding mask bit $lmask[i]$ is zero:

$$lres(h)[i] = \begin{cases} fill(h) & lmask(h)[i] = 0 \\ J(h)[i] & lmask(h)[i] = 1 . \end{cases}$$

With lemma 49 we conclude that the load result is correct.

Lemma 50.

$$lres(h) = fill(c)^{32-8 \cdot d(c)} c.m_{d(c)}(ea(c)) = lres(c)$$

Writing to the Register Files

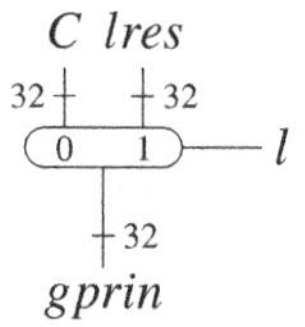

Fig. 113. Computing the data input of the general purpose register file

fig. 113 shows the last multiplexer connecting the data inputs of the register files with intermediate result C and the load result $lres$ coming from the sh4l-environment. Using correctness of the instruction decoder (lemma 39) , the intermediate result (lemma 44) and the load result we conclude, that the register input is computed correctly.

Using Lemmas 44 and 50 we conclude

$$gprin(h) = gprin(c)$$

Using decoder correctness (lemma 39), RAM semantics and the induction hypothesis for register files, we complete the induction step for the register files:

$$h'.gpr(x) = \begin{cases} gprin(h) & gprw(h) \wedge x = Xad(h) \wedge x \neq 0^5 \\ h.gpr(x) & \text{otherwise} \end{cases}$$

$$= \begin{cases} gprin(c) & gprw(c) \wedge x = Xad(c) \wedge x \neq 0^5 \\ c.gpr(x) & \text{otherwise} \end{cases}$$

$$= c'.gpr(x) .$$

and

$$h'.spr(x) = \begin{cases} C(h) & movg2s(h) \wedge x = Xad(h) \\ h.spr(x) & \text{otherwise} \end{cases}$$

$$= \begin{cases} C(c) & movg2s(c) \wedge x = Xad(c) \\ c.spr(x) & \text{otherwise} \end{cases}$$

$$= c'.spr(x) .$$

This completes the induction step of lemma 33 and hence the correctness proof of the entire (simple) processor.

4.2.7 Absence of Cycles

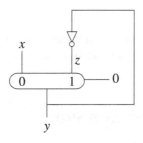

Fig. 114. A circuit forbidden in our model but with well defined behaviour

In order to obtain well defined semantics we required in section 2.1.10 the graphs $G(U)$ of hardware units U to be cycle free. If U is the sequential processor design under consideration, we just have established that all signals $x \in Sig(U)$ are well defined, by showing that they match their counter part in ISA. Indeed we have established an order between these signals: $x < y$ if the correctness of x is shown before the correctness of y. It is tempting to conclude: if in $G(U)$ a path from x to y is present, then we must have $x < y$, otherwise 'the correctness proof for y would not have worked out'. The example in Fig. 114 shows that this is wrong. In spite of the cycle one would not hesitate to establish (outside of our definitions, which forbid the example) $x = y$ and $z = /x$, because the right input of the multiplexer is always ignored. In order to make sure that our design lies within the limits of our model, we therefore should prove:

Lemma 51. $G(U)$ *is cycle free*

Proof. All subunits of U are cycle free. This is established by checking their constructions. We have in U three subunits M such that paths leave and reenter M: the memories m, gpr, spr. For these subunits we replace in $G''(U)$ graphs $G(t_U(M))$ by graphs $F(t_U(M))$ showing the dependencies of output buses from their relevant input buses. This only adds edges. All other subunits V behave like big gates, and we replace $G(t_U(V))$ by the complete bipartite graphs $H(t_U(V))$. This also only adds edges. If the resulting graph is cycle free, then by lemma 18 graph $G(U)$ is also cycle free and the overall design is well defined according to our definitions. Now reconsider fig. 95. Easy bookkeeping establishes that the paths leaving and reentering memories M do not close cycles:

- m (not shown in the figure). The relevant paths leaves via $m.outa = imout$ (which includes the fetched instruction). They reenter via the components of $dacc$, but not via $m.a$. At the end of section 3.3.7 we have shown that this cannot close a cycle in m.
- gpr. The relevant paths leave via $gpr.outa = A$ and $gpr.outb = B$. They reenter via $gpr.in = gprin$, but not via $gpr.a$ and $gpr.b$. At the end of section 3.3.8 we have shown that this cannot close a cycle in gpr.
- spr. The relevant paths leave via $spr.out = A$. They reenter via $spr.in = C$, but not via $spr.a$. At the end of section 3.3.9 we have shown that this cannot close a cycle in spr.

$\square$

In pipelined designs there will be additional registers in the data paths. These registers break cycles in the present design. Thus the corresponding argument for pipelined machines will be easier.

4.3 Repackaging the Induction Step

As before we assume for the induction step as a general hypothesis $sim(h,c)$ and $SC_{align}(c)$ and $SC_{ROM}(c)$.

4.3.1 Numbers and Correctness of Circuit Stages

One commonly refers to pipeline stages k *both* by names like $IF, ID, \ldots$ and by numbers, say

$$k \in [1:5]$$

Even in a mathematical treatment we can have the best of both worlds by simply using names and numbers a synonyms as defined in table 8 .

k	pipeline stage
1	IF
2	ID
3	EX
4	M
5	WB

Table 8. Numbering of pipeline stages in a basic pipeline

For the pipeline stages k of the basic machine we denote by $cir(k)$ the circuits belonging to pipeline stage k, as seen in fig. 95. With the synonyms not only have identities like

$$cir(1) = cir(IF) \, , \, cir(2) = cir(ID) \, , \, \ldots$$

but we can also do arithmetic on the names of pipeline stages like

$$IF + 1 = 1 + 1 = 2 = ID$$

which is a very convenient way to say, that ID is the next pipeline stage after IF. We wish to extract from the proof of section 4.2 lemmas, which state the correctness of the circuit stages

$$cir(k)$$

in isolation. The correctness statement for $cir(k)$ should have the following form:

Lemma 52. *If the inputs signals for $cir(k)$ are correct for ISA configuration c*

$$\forall X \in in(cir(k)). \, X(h) = X(c)$$

then the output signals are correct for configuration c

$$\forall Y \in out(cir(k)). \, Y(h) = Y(c)$$

We group the output signals of circuit stage ID into output buses in the following way:

- *decoder_out*: the sequence of all decoder outputs

- *i2ex*: the signals going from the instruction decoder to the execute stage but to no other pipeline stages.

$$i2ex = (xtimm, alu.f, su.f, itype, sa, mmask)$$

- *con*: this is a part of *decoder_out* consisting of the predicates p and the register address Xad, which are also used further down in the pipe stages.

The circuit stages with their inputs and outputs are summarized in table 9. Observe that circuit stage $cir(M)$ consists presently just of wires.

k	$in(cir(k))$	$out(cir(k))$
IF	ia, imout	iacc, I
ID	I, A, B, S, pc	nextpc, linkad, decoder_out
EX	i2ex, con, linkad, A, B, S	C, con, ea, dmin, bw, br
M	C, con, ea, dmin, bw, br, cdata, dmout	dacc, C, ea.o, con
WB	C, ea.o, con	gprin, con

Table 9. groups $cir(k)$ of circuits with their input and output signals

For later reference we observe

$$bus^{in}_{cir(ID)}(decoder\_out) = \{I\}$$

Extracting for each circuit $cir(k)$ the proof of lemma 52 for k from the correctness proof of section 4.2 is obviously a completely trivial exercise. It is not even book-keeping, just paste and glue: when you reach in the big proof the portion dealing with circuit U, throw away everything proven so far and replace it by the hypothesis of the lemma. Then take everything in the big proof until you have reached the statement of the lemma.

Completely analogously we extract correctness lemmas for each register and register file $R \in \{pc, gpr, spr\}$ which states the correctness of the register content *after* the step in case the inputs were correct

Lemma 53. *If the content of $R \in \{pc, gpr, spr\}$ is correct for ISA configuration c*

$$h.R = c.R$$

and its inputs signals are correct for ISA configuration c

$$\forall X \in in(R). X(h) = X(c)$$

then the register content is correct after the step for the ISA configuration c'

$$h'.R = c'.R$$

and for the memory we have

Lemma 54. *If the content of the memory is correct for ISA configuration c*

$$h.m = \ell(c.m)$$

and the data access is correct for ISA configuration c

$$dacc(h) = dacc(c)$$

then the memory is correct after the step for the ISA configuration c'

$$h'.m = \ell(c'.m)$$

Conversely, as a sanity check, we would also like to show processor correctness by proving the above lemmas and then concluding from the induction hypothesis successively the statements of $sim(h,c)$. However, there are loops between the circuit stages. For example, input A of the instruction decoder is computed using output rs of the instruction decoder (which passes through gpr). With our current formulation of the circuit correctness lemma, which only states the correctness of *all* outputs if *all* inputs are already proven correct, this will cause problems: we cannot prove that the A input is correct before we have proof that the rs output is correct, but we can not use our lemma to prove that the rs output is correct before we have proof that the A input is correct. The following naive proof therefore fails in the fourth equation.

Lemma 55. *Assume lemma 52 for all circuits stages cir(k) of table 9. Then sim(h', c')*
holds.

Proof.

$$ia(h) = ia(c) \quad (sim)$$
$$imout(h) = imout(c) \quad (sim)$$
$$I(h) = I(c) \quad (cir(IF))$$
$$decoder\_out(h) = decoder\_out(c) \quad (cir(ID))\text{\textit{f}}$$
$$X \in \{A, B, S\} \to X(h) = X(c) \quad (sim)$$
$$X \in \{nextpc, linkad\} \to X(h) = X(c) \quad (cir(ID))$$
$$h'.pc = c'.pc \quad (pc)$$
$$X \in \{C, ea, dmin, con\} \to X(h) = X(c) \quad (cir(EX))$$
$$cdata(h) = cdata(c) \quad (sim)$$
$$dmout(h) = dmin(c) \quad (sim)$$
$$h'.spr = c'.spr \quad (spr)$$
$$h'.m = \ell(c'.m) \quad (m)$$
$$gprin(h) = gprin(c) \quad (cir(WB))$$
$$h'.gpr = c'.gpr \quad (gpr)$$

$\square$

Note that lemma 52 for $cir(ID)$ cannot be applied to conclude the correctness of the decoder output until we have the correctness of A, B, and S, which are also inputs of $cir(ID)$ even though they are not relevant to the value of the decoder output. Fortunately we know already from section 2.3 how to deal with this situation. Recall that we denote the set of all relevant input buses of $decoder.out$ by

$$bus^{in}_{cir(k)}(decoder\_out)$$

which does not include A, B, or S

$$A,\ B,\ S \notin bus^{in}_{cir(k)}(decoder\_out)$$

We will strengthen lemma 52 so that we can obtain the correctness of each individual output using *only* the correctness of the relevant inputs of that output, rather than of all inputs.

Lemma 56. *Let Y be an output of $cir(k)$ such that all relevant inputs of Y are correct for ISA configuration c*

$$\forall X \in bus^{in}_{cir(k)}(Y).\ \ X(h) = X(c)$$

then the output signal is correct for configuration c

$$Y(h) = Y(c)$$

The proof of this, again, is simply copy and paste, since input signals which are not wired to the outputs never occur in the correctness proof of that output. With this version of the lemma, the proof above is correct and goes through.

4.3.2 Use of Signals for Instruction Execution

It turns out that we can weaken the hypothesis of lemma 55 and still push the proof through. Certain signals X from table 9 are only used by certain instructions. Signal S is for instance only used by $movs2g$ instructions and signal B is not used in $alui$ instructions. For ISA configurations c and signals X we therefore define in table 10 predicates[3]

$$used[X](c)$$

which hold *at least* for all signals which are used for execution of instruction $I(c)$. For these signals we will guarantee correctness, and if we can guarantee correctness more often without extra cost, this will not hurt.

The key observation is that if a signal other than the data access is used, all its relevant input signals are also used.

---

[3] Note that in [KMP14] we used the slightly different notation $used(X,c)$ for $used[X](c)$; the new notation is chosen for the sake of uniformity with other signals $Y(c)$.

X	$used[X](c)$
ia, iacc, imout, I, decoder_out, con, linkad, nextpc, pc, dacc	1
A	$alur(c) \vee su(c) \wedge fun(c)[2] \vee cas(c)$ $\vee jr(c) \vee jalr(c) \vee itype(c) \wedge /lui(c)$
B	$movg2s(c) \vee write(c) \vee beq(c) \vee bne(c) \vee su(c) \vee alur(c)$
S	$movs2g(c)$
C	$sprw(c) \vee gprw(c) \wedge /(l(c) \vee cas(c))$
ea, bw, br	$mop(c)$
cdata, dmin	$write(c)$
dmout	$read(c)$
gprin	$gprw(c)$

Table 10. Signals X used in the instructions executed in ISA configuration c.

Lemma 57. *Suppose output signal $Y \neq dacc$ of $cir(k)$ is used in configuration c*

$$Y \in out(cir(k)) \wedge used[Y](c) \wedge Y \neq dacc$$

Then all relevant input signals of Y are also used

$$\forall X \in bus^{in}_{cir(k)}(Y). \ used[X](c)$$

Proof. Bookkeeping exercise. □

For the data access, we only obtain that inputs computing components of the data access that are relevant are used. For example, *dacc.data* is only relevant for write and CAS accesses, in which case we have $write(c)$ and thus *dmin* is used. Thus we can not prove that the data access is the same in hardware and ISA by looking only at the correctness of relevant input signals. Luckily this is not necessary as we only need equivalence of accesses (as defined in section 1.3.4), which we are able to prove based only on relevant input signals.

A more fine-grained version of lemma 56 is then:

Lemma 58. *Suppose for output signal Y of $cir(k)$ all relevant inputs which are used in configuration c are correct*

$$\forall X \in bus^{in}_{cir(k)}(Y). \ used[X](c) \quad \rightarrow \quad X(h) = X(c)$$

Then Y is correct if it is used

$$used[Y](c) \quad \rightarrow \quad \begin{cases} Y(h) = Y(c) & Y \neq dacc \\ Y(h) \equiv Y(c) & Y = dacc \end{cases}$$

Proof. We distinguish between the data access and all other signals.

- $Y \neq dacc$: By assumption Y is used and we have with lemma 57 that all of its relevant inputs are also used

$$\forall X \in bus^{in}_{cir(k)}(Y). \ used[X](c)$$

By assumption all used relevant inputs are correct, thus all relevant inputs are correct. Relevant inputs of circuit stages are never the data access, thus

$$\forall X \in bus^{in}_{cir(k)}(Y). \ X(h) = X(c)$$

The claim is now lemma 56.
- $Y = dacc$: In this case we need to prove only that the relevant components are equal. We only show the proof for $dacc(h).data$, the other proofs are completely analogous. We need to show

$$x \in \{w, cas\} \wedge dacc(h).x \quad \rightarrow \quad dacc(h).data = dacc(c).data$$

Control signals s and cas are decoder outputs and always used, thus

$$dacc(h).(w, cas) = (s(h), cas(h)) = (s(c), cas(c))$$

We conclude from $dacc(h).x$ with $x \in \{w, cas\}$ that at least one of them is raised, and we conclude successively

$$s(c) \vee cas(c), \quad write(c), \quad used[dmin](c)$$

Since $dmin$ is also a relevant input we have by assumption

$$dmin(h) = dmin(c)$$

and the claim follows

$$dacc(h).data = dmin(h) = dmin(c) = dacc(c).data$$

$\square$

Completely analogously we can obtain

Lemma 59. *If the content of $R \in \{pc, gpr, spr\}$ is correct for ISA configuration c*

$$h.R = c.R$$

and its used inputs signals are correct for ISA configuration c

$$\forall X \in in(R). \ used[X](c) \quad \rightarrow \quad X(h) = X(c)$$

then the register content is correct after the step for the ISA configuration c'

$$h'.R = c'.R$$

and for the memory

Lemma 60. *If the content of the memory is correct for ISA configuration c*

$$h.m = \ell(c.m)$$

and the data access is correct for ISA configuration c

$$dacc(h) \equiv dacc(c)$$

then the memory is correct after the step for the ISA configuration c′

$$h'.m = \ell(c'.m)$$

With these lemmas we can again prove the correctness of the basic sequential processor and obtain first the induction step

Lemma 61.
$$sim(h', c')$$

and then the overall correctness theorem (lemma 33) follows.

Pipeline stage correctness lemmas, which rely only on inputs that are used, will later allow to build faster pipelined machines: there is no need to stall a pipeline stage k in order to wait for the forwarding of an input, that is not used by the instruction currently in stage k.

5

Pipelining

We review the construction and correctness proofs of processors with a classical five-stage pipeline and a multi-port memory with a single cycle access time from [KMP14] and [MP00]. The previous texts have been streamlined in 5 places.

- Like in chapter 4 the special purpose register file is already included. As forwarding circuits from the general and special purpose register files are completely analogous, we can deal with both subjects at the same place.
- The special purpose register file is now in stage 4 (the memory stage) as opposed to stage 5 in [MP00] and formally verified versions of that text. This saves a few forwarding circuits.
- Correctness proofs are directly done with respect to ISA and not to the sequential reference implementation, which in our case would be the machine from chapter 4. As we have already constructed the sequential reference machine and established its correctness, not much is gained (or lost) by this *yet*.
- A simpler proof is supplied for the crucial lemma that scheduling functions increase at full pipeline stages.
- Self modifying code is allowed.

We maintain the approach of the previous texts to successively construct three more and more powerful machines and incrementally prove their correctness. As this chapter is mostly a survey of previous work, it was tempting (and of course possible) to construct the most powerful of these machines with all hardware features included right away. But the resulting correctness proof would be quite massive, compared to the 3 reasonably easy steps of the incremental proof.

The reason we repeat these proofs in such detail is, that *all* subsequent processor correctness proofs of this text build on them.

© Springer Nature Switzerland AG 2020
P. Lutsyk et al. (Eds.): A Pipelined Multi-Core Machine, LNCS 9999, pp. 183–215, 2020.
https://doi.org/10.1007/978-3-030-43243-0_5

5.1 General Concepts

5.1.1 ISA, Circuit Stages and Software Conditions

We use delay slots and model them formally by a delayed PC dpc. Thus ISA configurations get a new component

$$c.dpc \in \mathbb{B}^{32}$$

PC and delayed PC are initialized as

$$c^0.pc = 4_{32}, \; c^0.dpc = 0_{32}$$

For the time being the delayed PC simply stores the previous PC

$$\delta(c).dpc = nextdpc(c) = c.pc.$$

We thus have for $t \geq 0$

$$c^{t+1}.dpc = c^t.pc$$

With interrupts and *eret* (exception return) instructions this is going to change. Instructions are fetched from the address in the delayed PC

$$I(c) = c.m_4(c.dpc)$$

and the instruction access changes accordingly to

$$iacc(c).a = c.dpc.l$$
$$iacc(c).r = 1$$

Other parts of the definition of ISA are so far not affected. For a proof that this is equivalent to conventional delayed branch semantics see theorem 4.1 in [MP00].

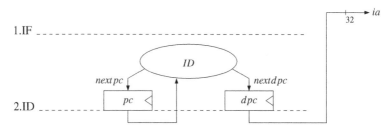

Fig. 115. Instruction address computation

The non pipelined implementation of the new ISA stays almost the same. There are two obvious changes shown in Fig. 115. The first concerns the use of dpc instead of pc as the instruction address ia.

$$ia = dpc$$

The second concerns the input to the dpc, which comes out of the circuit stage ID. Analogous to the $nextpc$ signal providing the input to the pc register from the circuit stage, we add a $nextdpc$ output to the nextpc environment and thus to circuit stage ID

$$nextdpc = pc \,, \; nextdpc(32) \in out(cir(ID))$$

The new component and signal are always used

$$used[nextdpc](c) = used[dpc](c) = 1.$$

With this change of definition the counter parts of circuit stage correctness lemma 58 and register correctness lemma 59 is obtained exactly as before.

Lemma 62. *Suppose for output signal* $Y \in out(cir(k))$ *of* $cir(k)$ *all relevant inputs which are used in configuration c are correct*

$$\forall X \in bus^{in}_{cir(k)}(Y). \; used[X](c) \quad \rightarrow \quad X(h) = X(c)$$

Then Y *is correct if it is used*

$$used[Y](c) \quad \rightarrow \quad \begin{cases} Y(h) = Y(c) & Y \neq dacc \\ Y(h) \equiv Y(c) & Y = dacc \end{cases}$$

Lemma 63. *If the content of* $R \in \{ pc, \, dpc, \, gpr, \, spr \}$ *is correct for ISA configuration c*

$$h.R = c.R$$

and its used input signals are correct for ISA configuration c

$$\forall X \in in(R). \; used[X](c) \quad \rightarrow \quad X(h) = X(c)$$

then the register content is correct after the step for the ISA configuration c'

$$h'.R = c'.R$$

In the absence of interrupts we have to keep the software condition SC_{align} from section 4.1.11

$$4|\langle ia(c) \rangle \wedge (mop(c) \rightarrow d(c)|\langle ea(c) \rangle)$$

Due to the existence of ROM we also have to keep software condition SC_{ROM} from section 4.1.11 which forbids writes to the address range of ROM:

$$write(c) \rightarrow \langle ea(c) \rangle \geq 2^{r+3}$$

As we intend to cover hardware for operating system support, we sooner or later *have to* deal with self modifying code. The reason is paging. Even if neither the user program nor the operating system are self modifying, their combination definitely is:

after a page fault during instruction fetch, the handler swaps in the missing page and the user program subsequently reads from the locations modified by the handler. We therefore allow self modifying code already in the first pipelined designs and restrict its use — for now — by a very simple software condition: when an in instruction $I(c^i)$ (possibly) writes a line, the next 3 instructions are not allowed to fetch from it. We call this software condition $SC_{selfmod}$ and we state it as a function of the entire ISA computation (c^i)

$$SC_{selfmod}((c^i)) \leftrightarrow \forall i.\ write(c^i) \wedge j \in \{i+1,\ i+2,\ i+3\} \rightarrow ia(c^j).l \neq ea(c^i).l$$

This latter condition will later be modified such that the pipeline depth is not exhibited to the programmer. With interrupts, violation of the first condition will simply trigger an interrupt. Thus the first condition will be dropped altogether.

5.1.2 Cost Effectiveness of Pipelining

The basic sequential processor construction will be augmented by four pieces of hardware.

- a hardware delayed PC and some surrounding circuits. This is obviously due to the change of ISA.
- pipeline registers. They are supposed to cut the cycle time of the hardware roughly to 1/5.
- a stall engine. This engine will have for every pipeline stage k a full bit $full_k$, which is on if the stage is currently processing an instruction. A stage, whose full bit is off in cycle t, does not process meaningful data in this cycle. This is called a *pipeline bubble*.
- forwarding circuits

That pipelining *might* be a good idea can quantitatively argued 'on the back of an envelope' in the following way. Imagine a compiled benchmark program completes on a sequential machine with cost C and cycle time τ after T instructions. The speed in which the benchmark is processed can then be defined as

$$S = 1/(T \cdot \tau)$$

and the cost effectiveness, i.e. the speed gained per invested unit of hardware as

$$E = S/C = 1/(T \cdot \tau \cdot C)$$

On a pipelined machine the extra hardware mentioned above might increase hardware cost by 20 % to say
$$C' = 1.2 \cdot C$$

Pipeline bubbles or noops (instructions with no effect other than increasing the program counter) inserted by the compiler might also increase the number of instructions executed by 20 % to say

$$T' = 1.2 \cdot T$$

If we are lucky cycle time might get down to

$$\tau' = \tau/5$$

and in this situation cost effectiveness goes up to

$$E' = 1/(T' \cdot \tau' \cdot C') = 5 \cdot E/(1.2 \cdot 1.2) = 3.47 \cdot E$$

which looks like a spectacularly good thing to do. But the extra hardware we add might have a cycle time which is higher than the ideal $\tau/5$ obtained if we could by splitting the original circuitry in an ideal way and obtain pipeline stages with exactly this (local) cycle time. Indeed the forwarding circuits described in sec. 5.3 do increase cycle time in a serious way. Imagine we are unlucky, and the cycle time goes only down to

$$\tau'' = 2 \cdot \tau' = 2 \cdot \tau/5$$

The cost effectiveness still increases to

$$E'' = E'/2 = 1.74 \cdot E$$

If you manage to improve the cost effectiveness of a machine by this much in a company, you are by all means a hero. But it is not quite as spectacular as in the first scenario.

The exact increase in effectiveness is of course in no way a matter of luck. Concrete designs have costs and cycle times, which can be measured. If we settle for a gate level model of cost and cycle time, it is not overly hard to derive them from our designs and gain some extra orientation [MP00]. For more precise information however, one *has* to consider layouts on chips or printed circuit boards. A striking example is Booth recoding, which saves only a few gate delays, but in a planar technology cycle time goes down by a constant factor, because the length of the longest wire is roughly cut in half [PS98].

5.1.3 Notation

Hardware configurations are denoted by h. In previous texts we used notation to distinguish between configurations h_π of the pipelined hardware and configurations h_σ of the sequential reference implementation. Although we do not plan to use the latter any more here, the subscript π and σ allow the use of some very concise shorthands in situations where we consider hardware signals or components and their counter parts in ISA simultaneously. Obviously this is the case during correctness proofs. Thus, for registers, memories, or signals R of ISA and instruction indices i we abbreviate

$$R_\sigma^i = \begin{cases} c^i.R & R \text{ is a register or memory} \\ R(c^i) & \text{otherwise} \end{cases}$$

For registers, memories or signals R of the hardware and hardware cycles t we abbreviate

$$R_\pi^t = \begin{cases} h^t.R & R \text{ is a register or memory} \\ R(h^t) & \text{otherwise} \end{cases}$$

Wherever possible we use the primed notation introduced in section 2.2.7 and abbreviate

$$R_\pi = R_\pi^t, \; R_\pi' = R_\pi^{t+1}$$

if it is clear which cycles t and $t+1$ are meant. During induction on the number of hardware cycles this is typically in the case during the induction step. For components or signals occurring only in hardware we can obviously drop the subscript π.

For tuples of components and signals $R_1, \ldots, R_n$ of ISA and ISA steps i we abbreviate further

$$(R_1, \ldots, R_n)_\sigma^i = (R_{1\sigma}^i, \ldots, R_{n\sigma}^i)$$

and for tuples of components and signals $R_1, \ldots, R_n$ of hardware and hardware cycles t we abbreviate

$$(R_1, \ldots, R_n)_\pi^t = (R_{1\pi}^t, \ldots, R_{n\pi}^t)$$

As before we use primed notation where applicable, and would write for example in the case of program counters pc and dpc

$$(pc, dpc)_\pi \text{ for } (pc_\pi^t, dpc_\pi^t) \quad \text{and} \quad (pc, dpc)_\pi' \text{ for } (pc_\pi^{t+1}, dpc_\pi^{t+1})$$

5.2 Basic Pipelined Processor

5.2.1 Pipeline Registers

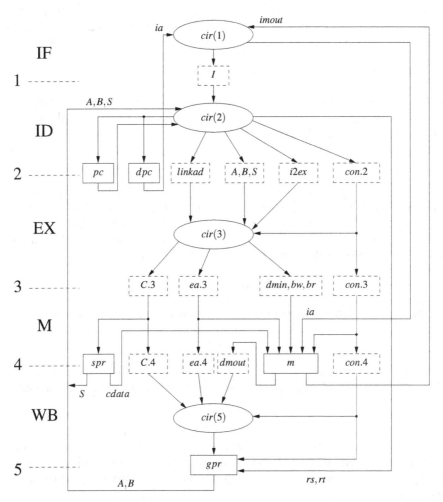

Fig. 116. Arranging the sequential MIPS design into pipeline stages

Registers or memories $h.R$ of the hardware which are direct counter parts of the ISA are called visible registers because the ISA programmer can directly refer to them.

$$vis(R) \equiv R \in \{ pc, dpc, m, spr, gpr \}$$

For signals

$$X \in \mathbb{B}^n \quad \text{resp.} \quad X \in \mathbb{B}$$

of the sequential hardware crossing the border from pipeline stage k to pipeline stage $k+1$ we insert in the pipelined hardware the *invisible registers X.k* with

$$h.X.k \in \mathbb{B}^n \quad \text{resp.} \quad h.X.k \in \mathbb{B}$$

at the bottom of stage k as shown in Fig. 116. Thus $X.k$ is the invisible (to the ISA programmer) register for ISA signal X at the bottom of circuit stage k. Using the synonyms from table 8 we can also write the index k as a name, e.g., for $EX = 3$

$$X.EX = X.3$$

with the interpretation that $X.EX$ is an invisible register in the execute register stage.

In ISA we will also allow to talk about signals $X.k$, but there it will only serve as a synonym for the original signal:

$$X.k(c) = X(c)$$

Note that visible registers R correspond to components $c.R$ of an ISA configuration c, whereas invisible registers $X.k$ correspond to signals $X.k(c) = X(c)$. Looking now at hardware cycle t in the sequential processor which is coupled with ISA configuration c^i in the sequential correctness proof, we observe that the values to be clocked into the visible registers are the values of the *next* ISA configuration

$$R.in^t = \delta(c^i).R = c^{i+1}.R$$

but the values of signal X are the values of the signal for the *current* configuration

$$X_\pi^t = X(c^i)$$

In the pipelined processor, this value is clocked into an invisible register, and we observe that for invisible registers we clock in the value of the same configuration

$$X.k.in^t = X^t = X(c^i)$$

This index shift between the visible registers — corresponding to components in step $i+1$, i.e., *after* step i is done — and invisible registers — corresponding to signals *in* step i — will be central in our coupling relation between the pipelined processor and the ISA.

For pipeline stages k we define register stage $reg(k)$ as the set of registers and memories at the bottom of stage k. For invisible registers this are the signals $X.k$. A visible register or memory R is included in register stage $reg(k)$, if it is updated in stage k. As 'bottom of' and 'updated in' are obviously not formally defined, we define $reg(k)$ simply by table 11.

k	$reg(k)$
1	I.1
2	pc, dpc, A.2, B.2, i2ex.2, con.2
3	C.3, ea.3, dmin.3, bw.3, br.3, con.3
4	m, spr, C.4, dmout.4, ea[2:0].4, con.4
5	gpr

Table 11. Definition of register stages $reg(k)$.

This arrangement of the hardware constructed so far into stages is shown in fig. 116 resp. in more abstract form in fig. 117.

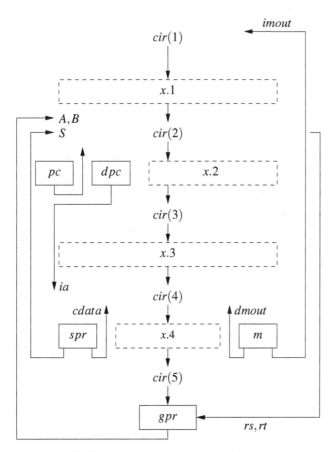

Fig. 117. Simplified view of register and circuit stages

Invisible registers in register stage $reg(k)$ are updated under control of signals ue_k coming from a so called *stall engine*.

$$X.k.ce = ue_k$$

Subsequently several successively more powerful stall engines will be defined. For invisible registers $X.k$ that appear in only one register stage k, we abbreviate

$$X_\pi \text{ for } X.k_\pi$$

5.2.2 Trivial Stall Engine

We start out with an extremely rudimentary stall engine, which only keeps track of the pipe fill after reset. It has five bits $full[4:0] \in \mathbb{B}^5$. Pipe stage 0 is always full. Stages 1 to four are initially empty. Stage k is full in cycle $t+1$ iff stage $k-1$ was full in cycle $t-1$. Register stages are updated when the stage above has meaningful data

$$
\begin{aligned}
full_0 &= 1 \\
full[1:4]^0 &= 0^4 \\
full_k^{t+1} &= full_{k-1}^t \\
ue_k &= full_{k-1}
\end{aligned}
$$

Observe that a stage is full iff it was updated in the previous cycle

$$full_k^{t+1} = ue_k^t$$

or in primed notation

$$full_k' = ue_k$$

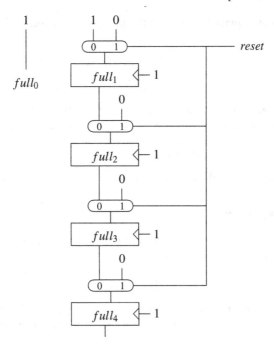

Fig. 118. Tracking full register stages with a basic stall engine

Hardware for this engine consists of four 1-bit registers connected in straightforward fashion as shown in fig. 118. As illustrated in fig. 119 pipeline registers $X.k$ of register stage $reg(k)$ are updated, if stage $k-1$, which provides inputs for circuit stage $cir(k)$, is full.

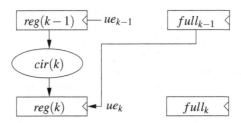

Fig. 119. Updating register stage k under control of full bit $full_{k-1}$

The write signals $spr.w$ of the special purpose register file $spr \in reg(4)$ is only activated if stage 3 is full and the (meaningful) control bits $con.3$ of stage 3 require a write to spr.

$$spr.w_\pi = full_3 \wedge sprw.3$$

Byte-write and cas signals bw, cas for the memory are generated in a completely analogous way

$$bw_\pi = full_3 \wedge bw.3$$
$$cas_\pi = full_3 \wedge cas.3$$

The write signal $gpr.w$ of the general purpose register file $gpr \in reg(5)$ is only activated if stage 4 is full and the control bits of stage 4 require a write to gpr

$$gpr.w_\pi = full_4 \wedge gprw.4$$

and this completes already the construction of the basic pipelined processor.

5.2.3 Scheduling Functions

The progress of ISA instructions i through the pipeline stages k is monitored by scheduling functions $I(k,t)$ where

$$I(k,t) = i$$

roughly means that in circuit stage $cir(k)$ we are in cycle t before execution of ISA instruction i. Initially we are in all stages before execution of instruction 0, thus

$$I(k,0) = 0$$

The index of the instruction at stage k changes with the update enable signal ue_k for that stage:

$$k = 1 : I(k,t+1) = \begin{cases} I(k,t)+1 & ue_k^t \\ I(k,t) & \text{otherwise} \end{cases}$$

$$k \geq 2 : I(k,t+1) = \begin{cases} I(k-1,t) & ue_k^t \\ I(k,t) & \text{otherwise} \end{cases}$$

One can think of the scheduling function $I(k,t) \in \mathbb{N}$ as the content I_k^t of so called *ghost* registers $I_k \in reg(k)$ capable of storing natural numbers of arbitrary size, and which extend the hardware *only* in the correctness proof. Except for initialization with zeros these ghost registers would be 'wired' as shown in fig. 120.

(a) stage $k = 1$ (b) stages $k > 1$

Fig. 120. Ghost pipe for scheduling functions

Indeed, we can extend hardware configurations h by ghost components

$$h.R \in \mathbb{N}$$

which in turn can connect to ghost signals X with

$$X(h) \in \mathbb{N} \cup \mathbb{B}$$

Register semantics stays literally the same:

$$h^{t+1}.R = \begin{cases} R.in(h^t) & R.ce(h^t) \\ h^t.R & \text{otherwise} \end{cases}$$

With ghost components defined in this way, we can make use of the usual abbreviations for hardware and rewrite the definition of scheduling functions

$$I(k,t) = h^t.I_k = I_k^t$$

as

$$I_k^0 = 0$$
$$I_k.ce = ue_k$$
$$I_k.in = \begin{cases} I_k + 1 & k = 1 \\ I_{k-1} & k > 1 \end{cases}$$

and regain the definition of the scheduling functions from register semantics. In primed notation

$$I_k' = \begin{cases} I_k & /ue_k \\ I_k + 1 & k = 1 \wedge ue_1 \\ I_{k-1} & k > 1 \wedge ue_k \end{cases}$$

We define a pipeline to be *well-formed* if the scheduling function increases at full stages:

$$wf(t) \equiv \forall k > 1. \quad I(k-1,t) = I(k,t) + full_{k-1}^t$$

which can be rewritten in implicit t notation as a ghost hardware predicate

$$wf \equiv \forall k < 1. \quad I_{k-1} = I_k + full_{k-1}.$$

In a well-formed pipeline a stage handles after an update always the next instruction.

Lemma 64.

$$wf \rightarrow I_k' = I_k + ue_k$$

Proof. For circuit stage $k = 1$ this follows directly from the definition. For circuit stages $k > 1$ we have by definition and wf

$$I'_k = \begin{cases} I_{k-1} & ue_k \\ I_k & /ue_k \end{cases}$$

$$= \begin{cases} I_k + full_{k-1} & ue_k \\ I_k & /ue_k \end{cases}$$

$$= \begin{cases} I_k + 1 & ue_k \\ I_k & /ue_k \end{cases}$$

$$= I_k + ue_k$$

$\square$

Lemma 65. *The pipeline is always well formed*

$$\forall t. \ wf^t$$

resp. in implicit t notation for invariants

$$wf$$

Proof. Using primed notation we show wf^t for all t by induction on t. The original pipe is obviously well formed, i.e. we have wf^0. In the induction step we have to conclude from wf

$$I'_{k-1} = I'_k + full'_{k-1}$$

We rewrite with lemma 64 and the observation that stages are full after they were updated:

$$I_{k-1} + ue_{k-1} = I_k + ue_k + ue_{k-1}$$

and after dropping ue_{k-1} on both sides and unfolding the definition of ue_k we obtain

$$I_{k-1} = I_k + full_{k-1}$$

which is exactly well-formedness for cycle t. $\square$

For $k' > k$ well-formedness implies that the scheduling functions in stages k and k' differ at most by $k' - k$.

$$I_k = I - k' + \sum_{i=k'+1}^{k} full_i \leq I_{k'} + k - k'$$

5.2.4 Delayed PC

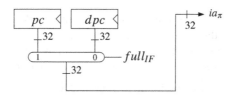

Fig. 121. New instruction address computation

The delayed hardware PC

$$dpc_\pi \in \mathbb{B}^{32}$$

is wired as shown in fig. 121. Recall that with the indices of table 8 the next dpc computation is now in circuit stage $ID = 2$, which is full if full bit $full_{ID-1} = full_{IF}$ is set. The multiplexer computing the new instruction address ia is controlled by signal $full_{IF}$ of the stall engine, i.e., we have

$$ia_\pi = \begin{cases} dpc_\pi & /full_{IF} \\ pc_\pi & full_{IF} \end{cases}$$

Note that in ISA we always use the delayed program counter for the instruction address, so it may seem strange at first glance that the hardware sometimes uses the delayed pc and sometimes uses the regular pc. However there is a very simple reason for this. In order for the hardware to correctly simulate the ISA, the instruction address used in circuit IF has to correspond to the delayed program counter of the ISA instruction that is currently being processed in that circuit stage. That instruction is the instruction of ISA step I_{IF}. Due to well-formedness, we have with the indices of table 8

$$I_{IF} = I_{ID} + full_{IF} \tag{14}$$

and we conclude: if register stage IF has meaningful data (i.e., $full_{IF} = 1$), we need to use the delayed program counter of the ISA step *after* the instruction in the decode stage; by definition of the ISA, this is the program counter of the instruction in the decode stage. If the stage does not have meaningful data, then the instructions in the decode stage and in the fetch stage are the same and have the same dpc. We conclude

Lemma 66.

$$ia_\sigma^{I_{IF}} = \begin{cases} dpc_\sigma^{I_{ID}} & /full_{IF} \\ pc_\sigma^{I_{ID}} & full_{IF} \end{cases}$$

In a sense, the multiplexer is a simple forwarding circuit which forwards the changes made by the instruction in ISA step I_{ID} to the dpc.

5.2.5 Correctness Statement and Additional Software Condition

Processor correctness for the basic pipelined processor is formulated by stating simulation relations for each pipeline stage k separately. If $I_k = i$ and register or register file R belongs to register stage $reg(k)$, then R_π^t of the pipelined computation equals its counter parts R_σ^i in the sequential computation if R is visible. If R is not visible it corresponds to R_σ^{i-1}, but only if the intermediate data in R are meaningful in cycle t, i.e. if $full_k^t$ holds, and if R is used. For the hardware memory it is the line addressable version of $m_\sigma^{I_M^t}$ of the instruction in the memory stage.

For the statement of the start of the induction we rename the trivial simulation relation $sim(h,c)$ of the previous chapter into $sim_{old}(h,c)$ and extend it as

$$sim(h,c) = sim_{old}(h,c) \wedge c.dpc = h.dpc$$

Lemma 67. *There exists an ISA configuration c^0 satisfying*

$$sim(h^0, c^0)$$

Furthermore, if the ISA computation (c^i) with initial state c^0 satisfies the software conditions stated so far and an additional software condition $SC_{gprdelay}$ to be stated shortly, i.e.,

$$SC_{selfmod}((c^i)) \wedge SC_{gprdelay}((c^i)) \wedge \forall i.\ SC_{ROM}(c^i) \wedge SC_{align}(c^i)$$

then in all cycles t, for all register stages k and all memories or register files $R \in reg(k)$ holds:

$$R_\pi^t = \begin{cases} R_\sigma^{I_k^t} & vis(R) \\ R_\sigma^{I_k^t - 1} & /vis(R) \wedge full_k^t \wedge used[R]^{I_k^t - 1} \end{cases}$$

For the memory holds

$$m_\pi^t = \ell(m_\sigma^{I_M^t})$$

In implicit t notation notation this becomes

$$R_\pi = \begin{cases} R_\sigma^{I_k} & vis(R) \\ R_\sigma^{I_k - 1} & /vis(R) \wedge full_k \wedge used[R]^{I_k - 1} \end{cases}$$

and

$$m_\pi = \ell(m_\sigma^{I_M})$$

We call this the *coupling relation* between hardware and ISA. Before we prove lemma 67 we (try to) provide some extra intuition for the formulation of the coupling relation and formulate some more software conditions.

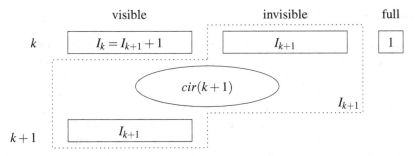

Fig. 122. Circuit stage $k+1$, if full, is handling the instruction of ISA step I_{k+1}. To do so, it uses previously computed signals from the invisible registers in register stage k, which belong to the same ISA step I_{k+1}, as well as visible registers from register stage $k+1$, which are also coupled to the ISA step I_{k+1}.

5.2.6 Intuition

Some intuitive reason for the index shift for invisible registers has been explained before: visible registers correspond to components of the ISA configuration, and thus the value written into the register is the value of the component *after* the step; invisible registers correspond to signals of the ISA step, and thus the value written into the register is the value of the signal *during* the step. We show more ways to visualize this index shift and to understand better the way the scheduling function couples the pipeline to the ISA computation. From well-formedness we obtain for full register stages k

$$I_k = I_{k+1} + 1$$

and thus the instruction $I_k - 1$, that we couple with for invisible registers in stage k, is the instruction we couple the visible registers with in stage $k+1$

$$I_k - 1 = I_{k+1}$$

In other words, visible registers in stage $k+1$ and invisible registers in a full stage k are coupled with ISA step I_{k+1}; visible registers R in stage $k+1$ with the components of the ISA configuration

$$R \in reg(k+1) \wedge vis(R) \rightarrow R_\pi = R_\sigma^{I_{k+1}} = c^{I_{k+1}}.R$$

and invisible registers in a full stage k with the signals in that cycle

$$X \in reg(k) \wedge \neg vis(X) \rightarrow X_\pi = X_\sigma^{I_{k+1}} = X(c^{I_{k+1}})$$

We can thus say that in case register stage k is full, circuit stage $k+1$, which is between register stages k and $k+1$, computes ISA step I_{k+1}. This gives rise to the powerful visualization in fig. 122.

5.2.7 Software Conditions

Without an additional software condition, lemma 67 cannot possibly be shown. On an abstract level, this is obviously true because for the computation of the instruction of ISA step I_{k+1} in circuit stage $k+1$ we sometimes use visible registers of register stages below $k+1$ which are not coupled with ISA step $k+1$ and thus do not have the correct value. For a more concrete example, consider an instruction $j = I_{ID}$ in the ID circuit (i.e., writing into register stage 2) which reads general purpose register x, and another instruction $i = I_{WB} < j$ in the write-back circuit which writes register x. In this case, instruction j will in the hardware read data from the hardware gpr, which is coupled with ISA step $i < j$, where instruction i has not yet modified the register. Note that in this case we have due to well-formedness at most three instructions between i and j

$$j = I_{ID} \leq I_{EX} + 1 \leq I_M + 2 \leq I_{WB} + 3 = i + 3.$$

Thus we require: if an instruction i writes to general purpose register x, then the next three instructions do not read from it. For the special purpose register file there is an analogous condition, but as the special register file is further up in the pipeline, it concerns only 2 instructions. Writing of a register x of a register file in ISA configuration c is formalized as

$$writesgpr(x,c) \equiv gprw(c) \wedge xad(c) = x$$
$$writesspr(x,c) \equiv sprw(c) \wedge xad(c) = x$$

Reading register x is defined as

$$readsgpr(x,c) \equiv used[A](c) \wedge rs(c) = x \vee used[B](c) \wedge rt(c) = x$$
$$readsspr(x,c) \equiv used[S](c) \wedge rs(c) = x$$

The additional software condition $SC_{gprdelay}((c^i))$ is then

$$\forall i, j. (writesgpr(x,c^i) \wedge j \in [i+1 : i+3] \rightarrow /readsgpr(x,c^j))$$
$$\wedge (writesspr(x,c^i) \wedge j \in [i+1 : i+2] \rightarrow /readsspr(x,c^j))$$

5.2.8 Correctness Proof

Proof. Lemma 67 is shown by induction on hardware cycles t. For $t = 0$ we set

$$gpr_\sigma^0 = gpr_\pi^0$$
$$spr_\sigma^0 = spr_\pi^0$$
$$m_\sigma^0(a) = byte(\langle a.o \rangle, m_\pi^0(a.l))$$

For the induction step from t to $t+1$ we use the primed notation from section 2.2.7. Because the proof is somewhat lengthy we summarize here the structure of the proof. We first distinguish whether 'something happens' at all, i.e., whether we have ue_k. If nothing happens ($ue_k = 0$) the proof is as trivial as it should be, but in case the register stage is updated ($ue_k = 1$), we show first with lemma 68 that all inputs that are used by the circuit stage k are correct. For inputs which come from invisible registers this proof is the same for all pipeline stages, but for inputs which do not come from invisible registers (such as the instruction word in stage $k = IF$, which comes from memory) we need to do a proof by case distinction on k. After this case distinction we conclude from the correctness of all used inputs using the circuit stage correctness lemmas that also all used outputs of the circuit stage are correct, including the outputs clocked into register stage k. At this point the proof is basically over.

We now split cases on ue_k. If

$$ue_k = 0$$

we successively infer

$$/full_{k-1}, \; /full'_k, \; I'_k = I_k$$

Thus we have nothing to prove for invisible registers in $reg(k)$. For visible registers or register files R we use the induction hypothesis and get

$$R'_\pi = R_\pi = R^{I_k}_\sigma = R^{I'_k}_\sigma$$

For the memory we get from

$$ue_M = 0$$

in the same way

$$m'_\pi = m_\pi = \ell(m^{I_k}_\sigma) = \ell(m^{I'_k}_\sigma)$$

So nothing happens in the hardware, in the ISA or in the proof and we are done for stages which are not updated. It remains to consider stages k which are updated. So let

$$ue_k = 1 \quad \text{and} \quad I_k = i$$

We successively infer — using well-formedness:

$$full_{k-1}, \; full'_k, \; I'_k = I_{k-1} = I_k + 1 = i + 1$$

We now show that all used inputs to the circuit stage are correct.

Lemma 68.

1. For $k > 1$ all invisible registers $Q \in reg(k - 1)$ that are used in instruction i are correct

$$used[Q]^i_\sigma \rightarrow Q_\pi = Q^i_\sigma$$

2. All used inputs to circuit stage k, that are used in instruction i are correct

$$\forall X \in in(cir(k)). \; used[X]^i \quad \rightarrow \quad X_\pi = X^i_\sigma$$

Proof. We show the two parts of the lemma separately.

1. Let $k > 1$ and let $Q \in reg(k-1)$ be an invisible register used by instruction $I_{k-1} - 1 = i$, i.e. with

$$used[Q]^i = used[Q]^{I_{k-1}-1}$$

By the coupling relation we get

$$Q_\pi = Q_\sigma^{I_{k-1}-1} = Q_\sigma^i$$

which is the claim.

2. As shown in fig. 117 inputs to a circuit stage come from two sources: either directly from the invisible registers above, or from below from other sources, such as the memory system or visible registers. For the invisible registers, the claim is exactly part one of the lemma with $Q := X$. For the remaining inputs let $X \notin reg(k-1)$ be an input to circuit stage k which does not come from the register stage above. For such inputs the proof is by case distinction on k. Only stages fetch, decode, and memory have such inputs.

   • $k = IF = 1$: In this case we have

   $$i = I_k = I_{IF}$$

   The first input that we have to consider is the instruction address. Using well-formedness and the coupling relation for stage $k := ID = 2$ and $R := pc, dpc$ we obtain

   $$
   \begin{aligned}
   ia_\pi &= \begin{cases} dpc_\pi & /full_{IF} \\ pc_\pi & full_{IF} \end{cases} \\
   &= \begin{cases} dpc_\sigma^{I_{ID}} & /full_{IF} \\ pc_\sigma^{I_{ID}} & full_{IF} \end{cases} & \text{IH} \\
   &= \begin{cases} dpc_\sigma^{I_{ID}} & /full_{IF} \\ dpc_\sigma^{I_{ID}+1} & full_{IF} \end{cases} & \text{dpc semantics} \\
   &= dpc_\sigma^{I_{IF}} & \text{E (14)} \\
   &= ia_\sigma^{I_{IF}}
   \end{aligned}
   $$

   The second input we have to consider is the instruction memory output $imout$. Using the circuit correctness lemma (lemma 62 for $k := IF$ and $Y := iacc$), and the fact that the instruction address is simulated correctly, we obtain that the instruction access is simulated correctly

   $$iacc_\pi = iacc_\sigma^{I_{IF}}$$

   By the specification of memory and the coupling relation for the memory we have

   $$imout_\pi = m_\pi(iacc_\pi.a) = \ell(m_\sigma^{I_M})(iacc_\pi.a) = \ell(m_\sigma^{I_M})(iacc_\sigma^{I_{IF}}.a)$$

Due to well-formedness, there are at most three instructions between I_M and I_{IF}

$$I_{IF} \leq I_{ID} + 1 \leq I_{EX} + 2 \leq I_M + 3$$

Due to the software condition $SC_{selfmod}$ for I_M, I_{EX}, I_{ID} as the writing instruction and I_{IF} as the fetching instruction, we obtain that those instructions do not modify the instruction address of ISA step I_{IF}

$$j \in \{ I_M, I_{EX}, I_{ID} \} \wedge write^j_\sigma \wedge j < I_{IF} \quad \rightarrow \quad ia^i_\sigma.l \neq ea^j_\sigma.l$$

Since the line address of the instruction access is the instruction address

$$iacc^{I_{IF}}_\sigma.a = iacc^i_\sigma.a = ia^i_\sigma.l$$

we conclude with the memory semantics that none of the instructions between the memory stage and the fetch stage actually change the line that is being fetched

$$\ell(m^{I_M}_\sigma)(iacc^{I_{IF}}_\sigma.a) = \ell(m^{I_{IF}}_\sigma)(iacc^{I_{IF}}_\sigma.a) = imout^{I_{IF}}_\sigma$$

which concludes the proof of part two for stage IF

$$imout_\pi = \ell(m^{I_M}_\sigma)(iacc^{I_{IF}}_\sigma.a) = imout^{I_{IF}}_\sigma$$

• $k = ID = 2$: In this case we have

$$i = I_k = I_{ID}$$

The only additional inputs are A, B, and S from the gpr and spr. Note first that I is always used and thus by part one of the lemma with $Q := I$

$$I_\pi = I^{I_{ID}}_\sigma$$

As observed in section 4.3.1 this already determines the value of the decoder outputs.

$$bus^{in}_{cir(ID)}(decoder\_out) = \{ I \}$$

Thus we obtain with the circuit correctness lemma (lemma 62 for $k := ID$ and $Y := rt$, rs)

$$rt_\pi = rt^{I_{ID}}_\sigma \wedge rs_\pi = rs^{I_{ID}}_\sigma$$

By the induction hypothesis, the gpr content is that of ISA step I_{WB} and the spr content is that of ISA step I_M. Due to well-formedness, the number of instructions since these ISA steps is at most 3 resp. 2

$$I_{ID} \leq I_{IF} + 1 \leq I_M + 2 \leq I_{WB} + 3$$

and we obtain with the software condition for the gpr and spr ($SC_{gprdelay}$) that none of the instructions in the intermediate stages modify a register used by the instruction in step I_{ID}

$$j \in \{I_{WB}, I_M, I_{EX}\} \wedge writesgpr(x, c^j) \quad \rightarrow \quad /readsgpr(x, c^i)$$
$$j \in \{I_M, I_{EX}\} \wedge writesspr(x, c^j) \quad \rightarrow \quad /readsspr(x, c^i)$$

Using the coupling relation and the semantics of the MIPS ISA, we obtain that in case a register is read by instruction $i = I_{ID}$, then the value of that register is the same in ISA steps I_M (resp. I_{WB}) and I_{ID}

$$readsgpr(i, x) \quad \rightarrow \quad gpr_\pi(x) = gpr_\sigma^{I_{WB}}(x) = gpr_\sigma^{I_{ID}}(x) \qquad (15)$$
$$readsspr(i, x) \quad \rightarrow \quad spr_\pi(x) = spr_\sigma^{I_M}(x) = spr_\sigma^{I_{ID}}(x) \qquad (16)$$

We can now show that inputs A, B, S have the correct value, if they are used. Assume first that A is used

$$used[A]_\sigma^i$$

and thus the instruction reads gpr register rs_σ^i

$$readsgpr(i, rs_\sigma^i)$$

We obtain with eq. (15) that the A input is simulated correctly

$$A_\pi = gpr_\pi(rs_\pi) = gpr_\pi(rs_\sigma^i) = gpr_\sigma^i(rs_\sigma^i) = A_\sigma^i$$

If B is used the equality

$$B_\pi = B_\sigma^i$$

is shown in the same way. Assume finally that S is used

$$used[S]_\sigma^i$$

and thus the instruction reads spr register rs_σ^i

$$readsspr(i, rs_\sigma^i)$$

Thus we obtain with eq. (16) that the S input is simulated correctly

$$S_\pi = spr_\pi(rs_\pi) = spr_\pi(rs_\sigma^i) = spr_\sigma^i(rs_\sigma^i) = S_\sigma^i$$

This concludes the proof of part two for stage ID.

- $k = M = 4$: In this case we have

$$i = I_k = I_M$$

For the memory stage, we have to argue about the compare data $cdata$ and the data memory output $dmout$. For the compare data, we have by the coupling relation that the spr is coupled with instruction i

$$cdata_\pi = spr_\pi(cdata) = spr_\sigma^{I_M}(cdata) = spr_\sigma^i(cdata) = cdata_\sigma^i$$

To show the claim for the data memory output assume it is used and we conclude successively

$$used[dmout]_\sigma^i, \quad read_\sigma^i, \quad r_\sigma^i \vee cas_\sigma^i, \quad dacc_\sigma^i.r \vee dacc_\sigma^i.cas$$

We obtain with the circuit correctness lemma (lemma 62 for $k := M$ and $Y := dacc$)

$$dacc_\pi \equiv dacc_\sigma^i$$

Since the data access is reading and the data access is by SC_{align} aligned, both ISA and hardware produce the same output

$$dmout_\pi = dataout(m_\pi, dacc_\pi) = dataout(m_\sigma^i, dacc_\sigma^i) = imout_\sigma^i$$

$\square$

With this lemma we have that all inputs of the circuit stages, that are used, are the same in hardware and ISA

$$\forall X \in in(cir(k)). \ used[X]_\sigma^i \quad \rightarrow \quad X_\pi = X_\sigma^i$$

and we conclude with circuit correctness lemma (lemma 62) that all outputs of the circuit stages that are used (except for the data access) are the same

$$\forall Y \in out(cir(k)). \ used[Y]_\sigma^i \wedge Y \neq dacc \quad \rightarrow \quad Y_\pi = Y_\sigma^i$$

Note that instruction

$$i = I_k$$

is by lemma 64 and the assumption $ue_k = 1$ the instruction right before I_k'

$$I_k' = I_k + ue_k = I_k + 1 = i + 1 \quad \text{and} \quad i = I_k' - 1$$

Showing that register contents of stage k are updated in a way that maintains the simulation relation is now trivial. For invisible registers X, that are used, we obtain immediately from the circuit correctness

$$X_\pi' = X.in_\pi = X_\sigma^i = X_\sigma^{I_k'-1}$$

The visible registers and register files take their inputs from these signals, except for the write signals, which are ANDed with the update enable signal. Since the update enable signal is raised, we obtain for visible register or register file $R \in reg(k)$

$$\forall Z \in in(R). \ used[Z]_\sigma^i \quad \rightarrow \quad Z_\pi = Z_\sigma^i$$

and conclude with register correctness lemma (lemma 63)

$$R_\pi' = R_\sigma^{i+1} = R_\sigma^{I_k'}$$

This leaves only the memory for $k = M$. By lemma 62 the data access is correct

$$dacc_\pi \equiv dacc_\sigma^i$$

and we obtain that the memory is updated in the same way by lemma 60 (which uses SC_{ROM} and SC_{align})

$$m_\pi' = m_\sigma^{i+1} = m_\sigma^{I_k'}$$

$\square$

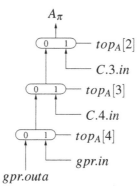

Fig. 123. Forwarding circuit for A

5.3 Forwarding

5.3.1 Forwarding Circuits

The idea of forwarding is very simple. Instead of fetching the A, B and S operands from the register files alone, one uses also results which will be written to the register file, but which are still in the pipeline. In other words, rather than using a software condition to show that

$$gpr^{J_M}(rs^{I_{ID}}) = gpr^{J_{ID}}(rs^{I_{ID}})$$

we use hardware to precompute $gpr^{I_{ID}}(rs^{I_{ID}})$ based on the data of instructions in the pipeline.

Detecting such data is reasonably straight forward. Consider the A operand. For $k \in [2:4]$ we say that there is a hit for this operand in stage k if i) the instruction in the decode stage uses A, ii) the registers in stage $reg(k)$ to that circuit stage have meaningful data, and iii) the instruction in the invisible registers of that stage writes to the gpr at address rs and which is different from 0. We reformulate the used predicate of A, B, S as a function of the instruction register as

$$\widehat{used}[X](I(c^i)) = used[X](c^i)$$

and define the hit signals as

$$hit_A[k] \equiv \widehat{used}[A](I.IF) \wedge full_k \wedge gprw.k \wedge rs = xad.k \wedge rs \neq 0^5$$
$$hit_B[k] \equiv \widehat{used}[B](I.IF) \wedge full_k \wedge gprw.k \wedge rt = xad.k \wedge rt \neq 0^5$$
$$hit_S[k] \equiv \widehat{used}[S](I.IF) \wedge full_k \wedge sprw.k \wedge rs = xad.k$$

In case there are several hits for an operand in the pipeline, we are interested in the most recent one, i.e. the topmost hit in the pipe.

$$top_X[k] = hit_X[k] \wedge \bigwedge_{j<k} /hit_X[j] \quad \text{for} \quad X \in \{A, B, S\}$$

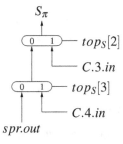

Fig. 124. Forwarding circuit for S

In the pipelined hardware we now compute the A operand with the 3 stage forwarding circuit from Fig. 123 as

$$A_\pi = \begin{cases} C.3.in & top_A[2] \\ C.4.in & top_A[3] \\ gpr.in & top_A[4] \\ gpr.outa & \text{otherwise} \end{cases}$$

The B óperand is computed in a completely analogous way using signals $top_B[k]$ and $gpr.outb$. For the S operand the two stage forwarding circuit from Fig. 124 suffices:

$$S_\pi = \begin{cases} C.3.in & top_S[2] \\ C.4.in & top_S[3] \\ spr.out & \text{otherwise} \end{cases}$$

In the simple forwarding circuits above priorities between hits are resolved by the arrangement of the multiplexers. The delay of such forwarding circuits grows linearly with the number of pipeline stages. For deep pipelines this is obviously not desirable. Using a tree of multiplexers with properly controlled select signals one gets forwarding circuits whose delay grows only logarithmically with the number of stages covered. Nevertheless in all cases the forwarding circuits have a tendency to increase the cycle time of the processor. For the machine constructed here we have for instance now quite a long path i) through the ALU ii) the forwarding circuit for A iii) the branch condition evaluation unit and then iv) the nextpc computation.

5.3.2 Correctness

Forwarding resolves a very large portion of the situations forbidden by software condition $SC_{gprdelay}$. Only load or cas operations remain problematic. There we can only forward A after the lookup in memory has been performed, i.e. when we have $top_A[4]$ resp. $top_B[4]$. The remaining situations still have to be forbidden. So we formulate software condition $SC_{loaddelay}$. If an instruction performs a load or cas operation to general purpose register x, then the two next instructions do not read register $gpr(x)$.

$$SC_{loaddelay}((c^i)) \leftrightarrow \forall i, j. \, writesgpr(x, c^i) \wedge read(c^i) \wedge j \in [i+1:i+2]$$
$$\rightarrow /readsgpr(x, c^j)$$

A counter part of lemma 67 can now be shown with the weaker software condition $SC_{loaddelay}$ instead of $SC_{gprdelay}$.

Lemma 69. *There exists an ISA configuration c^0 satisfying*

$$sim(h^0, c^0)$$

Furthermore, if the ISA computation (c^i) with initial state c^0 satisfies the software conditions $SC_{loaddelay}$, $SC_{selfmod}$, SC_{ROM}, and SC_{align}, i.e.,

$$SC_{selfmod}((c^i)) \wedge SC_{loaddelay}((c^i)) \wedge \forall i. \, SC_{ROM}(c^i) \wedge SC_{align}(c^i)$$

then in all cycles t, for all register stages k and all memories or register files $R \in reg(k)$ holds:

$$R_\pi^t = \begin{cases} R_\sigma^{I_k^t} & vis(R) \\ R_\sigma^{I_k^t - 1} & /vis(R) \wedge full_k^t \wedge used[R]^{I_k^t - 1} \end{cases}$$

For the memory holds

$$m_\pi^t = \ell(m_\sigma^{I_M^t})$$

The only new argument in the proof concerns the correctness of operands A, B, and S. Also, we have to do now the induction step for stage ID after the induction step for the stages below, because we need to use the correctness of the forwarded values. In the induction step for stage ID one now has to show

Lemma 70.

$$X \in \{A, B, S\} \wedge ue_{ID} \wedge i = I_{ID} \wedge used[X]_\sigma^i \rightarrow X_\pi = X_\sigma^i$$

Proof. We elaborate the proof for the A operand and split cases on the hit signals.

- $top_A[k]^t$. Let

$$j = I_{k+1}$$

From $hit_A[k]$ and the induction hypothesis for stages IF and k we conclude

$$1 = \widehat{used}[A](I.IF) = \widehat{used}[A](I_\sigma^{I_{ID}}) = used[A](c^i)$$

and

$$gprw(c^j) \wedge rs(c^i) = xad(c^j)$$

By well-formedness of the pipeline we know

$$j \geq i - k + 1 \, ,$$

and by software condition $SC_{loaddelay}$ we know that if $k \in [2:3]$, the instruction j cannot be a load or cas, i.e. not a memory read

$$k \in [2:3] \quad \rightarrow \quad /read_\sigma^j$$

By the induction step for stage k we get

$$C.k + 1.in = gprin_\sigma^j$$

If $k = 4$ we always have

$$gprin_\pi = gprin_\sigma^j$$

Hence

$$A_\pi = gprin_\sigma^j = gpr_\sigma^{j+1}(rs(c^i))$$

For full stages $\hat{k}$ between stages 1 and k we know with the induction hypothesis from the absence of hit signal $hit_A[\hat{k}]$ that instruction $\hat{j} = I_{\hat{k}}$ does not write register $gpr(rs^i)$, and we conclude the proof with

$$gpr_\sigma^{j+1}(rs(c^i)) = gpr_\sigma^i(rs(c^i))$$

- $/hit_A[k]$ for all $k \in [2:4]$. This case is analogous to the proof with software condition $SC_{gprdelay}$ for $j := I_{WB}$. The forwarding circuit forwards $gpr.outa$ and we argue as in a machine without forwarding circuits

$$A_\pi = gpr.outa = gpr_\sigma^j(rs(c^i)) = gpr_\sigma^i(rs(c^i))$$

$\square$

5.4 Stalling

5.4.1 Stall Engine with Hazard Signals

We get rid of software condition $SC_{loaddelay}$ with the help of a more complex stall engine. The engine receives now from circuit stages k hazard signals haz_k which become active if correct data for the update of register stage register stage $reg(k)$ *cannot* be provided. Such stall engines were introduced in [MP00]. The stall engine we use here was first presented in [Krö01]. The signals involved are now

- full signals $h.full_k \in \mathbb{B}$ for $k \in [0:4]$. As before these 1 bit registers keep track of pipeline stages with meaningful content.
- update enable signals $ue_k \in \mathbb{B}$ for $k \in [1:5]$. They trigger the update of register stage $reg(k)$ once input data are ready.
- stall signals $stall_k \in \mathbb{B}$ indicate that stage k should presently not be clocked for $k \in [1:6]$; the stall signal for stage 6 is only introduced to make definitions more uniform,

- hazard signal $haz_k \in \mathbb{B}$ generated for circuit stage k for $k \in [1:5]$ indicating that input data for circuit stage $cir(k)$ is not available, and thus the data of circuit stage k must not be clocked into the registers of register stage k

Register stage 0 is always full and register stages 1 to 4 are initially empty. Register stage $reg(6)$ does not exist, and thus it is never stalled.

$$full_0 = 1$$
$$full[1:4]^0 = 0^4$$
$$stall_6 = 0$$

The working of the stall engine is now specified with three equations:

$$stall_k = full_{k-1} \wedge (haz_k \vee stall_{k+1})$$
$$ue_k = full_{k-1} \wedge /stall_k$$
$$full'_k = ue_k \vee stall_{k+1}$$

Observe that a stage with a hazard signal is never updated.

Lemma 71.

$$haz_k \quad \rightarrow \quad /ue_k$$

Proof. By case distinction on $full_{k-1}$

- $full_{k-1}$: We conclude successively

$$stall_k, /ue_k$$

- $/full_{k-1}$: We conclude immediately

$$/ue_k$$

$\square$

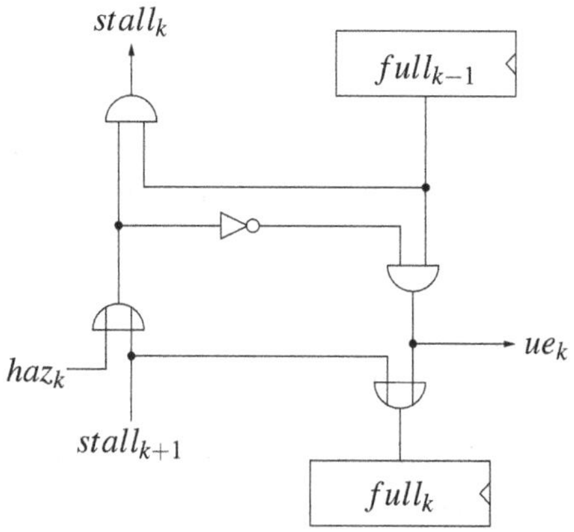

Fig. 125. Stall engine data paths

Hardware schematics for this stall engine are shown in fig. 125. The definitions of scheduling functions and of well-formedness stay the same. The proof that the pipeline is always well formed becomes slightly more complex.

Lemma 72.

$$wf \to I'_k = I_k + ue_k$$

Proof. For circuit stage $k = 1$ this follows directly from the definition. For circuit stages $k > 1$ we have by definition and wf

$$I'_k = \begin{cases} I_{k-1} & ue_k \\ I_k & /ue_k \end{cases}$$

$$= \begin{cases} I_k + full_{k-1} & ue_k \\ I_k & /ue_k \end{cases}$$

Since

$$ue_k \to full_{k-1}$$

this is the same as

$$I'_k = \begin{cases} I_k + 1 & ue_k \\ I_k & /ue_k \end{cases}$$

$$= I_k + ue_k. \qquad \square$$

As before we prove that the pipeline is always well formed (lemma 7.14 from [KMP14]).

Lemma 73.

$$\forall t. \ wf^t$$

Proof. By induction on t. The original pipe is obviously well formed, i.e. we have wf^0. In the induction step we use primed notation and have to conclude from wf:

$$I'_{k-1} = I'_k + full'_{k-1}.$$

We rewrite with lemma 72 and the definition of $full'$ and obtain

$$I_{k-1} + ue_{k-1} = I_k + ue_k + (stall_k \vee ue_{k-1}).$$

We distinguish two cases:

- $stall_k = 1$. We successively conclude

$$/ue_k, \ full_{k-1}, \ stall_{k-1}, \ /ue_{k-1}$$

  and the claim reduces to

$$I_{k-1} = I_k + 1$$

  which is exactly well-formedness in cycle t.

- $stall_k = 0$. Then the claim reduces to

$$I_{k-1} + ue_{k-1} = I_k + full_{k-1} + ue_{k-1}$$

which follows from well-formedness in cycle t. □

We proceed to define a hazard signal haz_2 which stalls the ID stage when the instruction in that stage uses a register operand that cannot be delivered correctly by the forwarding circuits. This is only the case if we need to forward the result of a read operations which have not yet reached the memory stage

$$haz_A = \bigvee_{k=2}^{3} top_A[k] \wedge read.k$$

$$haz_B = \bigvee_{k=2}^{3} top_B[k] \wedge read.k$$

$$haz_{ID} = haz_A \vee haz_B$$

The remaining hazard signals are tied to zero.

$$k \neq 2 \to haz_k = 0$$

5.4.2 Correctness and Liveness

Lemma 74. *There exists an ISA configuration c^0 satisfying*

$$sim(h^0, c^0)$$

Furthermore, if the ISA computation (c^i) with initial state c^0 satisfies the software conditions $SC_{selfmod}$, SC_{ROM}, and SC_{align}, i.e.,

$$SC_{selfmod}((c^i)) \wedge SC_{loaddelay}((c^i)) \wedge \forall i.\ SC_{ROM}(c^i) \wedge SC_{align}(c^i)$$

then in all cycles t, for all register stages k and all memories or register files $R \in reg(k)$ holds:

$$R_\pi^t = \begin{cases} R_\sigma^{I_k^t} & vis(R) \\ R_\sigma^{I_k^t-1} & /vis(R) \wedge full_k^t \wedge used[R]^{I_k^t-1} \end{cases}$$

For the memory holds

$$m_\pi^t = \ell(m_\sigma^{I_M^t})$$

Proof. The previous correctness proof works except for a single place in lemma 70, namely the line in which we concluded from software condition $SC_{loaddelay}$ that the instruction with the top hit

$$top_A[k] \wedge j = I_{k+1}$$

could not be a read

$$k \in [2:3] \to /read_\sigma^j$$

Instead from ue_{ID} and the construction of the stall engine we obtain successively

$$/haz_{ID}, /haz_A, /haz_B$$

and by definition of the haz_A signal and the fact that k is the top-hit the claim follows

$$k \in [2:3] \to /read_\sigma^j$$

$\square$

A small argument is required to show *liveness*, i.e. that pipeline stages cannot be stalled forever by hazard signals. Because the lower stages produce no hazard signals, stages 3 and below are never stalled:

$$k \geq 3 \to /stall_k$$

Easy bookkeeping now shows that stage 2 can at most be stalled for at most 2 successive cycles (lemma 7.18 of [KMP14]).

Lemma 75.
$$full_1^t \wedge haz_2^t \wedge haz_2^{t+1} \to /haz_2^{t+2}$$

Proof. One successively concludes

$$/ue_2^t, /ue_2^{t+1}, /full_2^{t+1}, /full_2^{t+2}, /ue_3^{t+1}, /full_3^{t+2}$$

With the full bits off no hit signal can be active in cycle $t+2$.

$$X \in \{A,B\} \wedge k \in [2:3] \to /hit_X[k]^{t+2}$$

and consequently also no top hit signal

$$X \in \{A,B\} \wedge k \in [2:3] \to /top_X[k]^{t+2}$$

and one successively concludes

$$/haz_A^{t+2}, /haz_B^{t+2}, /haz_2^{t+2}$$

$\square$

5.4.3 Proof Summary

In future chapters the basic pipelined machine studied here will evolve into much more powerful and complex machines. Obviously this will affect the correctness proof; in particular new arguments will be needed for each new unit added to the machine (like cache memory system, MMU,...). Fortunately we never have to redo the entire proof in this process. In each chapter large parts of the proof will stay unchanged, and new arguments will mostly focus on the new units just introduced.

For later reference we therefore conclude from now on *each* section containing a proof of the main induction hypothesis with a summary of proof. This permits later to point clearly to the portions which stay the same and to the portions of the new proof, where the action is. The current proof hinges almost entirely on the pipeline stage correctness lemmas (lemma 62) , which state that correct input signals that are used produce correct output signals, that are used. Inputs for circuits stages $cir(k)$ come from four sources:

- invisible pipeline registers. Their correctness follows directly from the main induction hypothesis for invisible registers, and this is never going to change.
- visible registers and register files from the register stage $reg(k)$ at the bottom of $cir(k)$. Their correctness follows directly from the main induction hypothesis for visible registers, and again this is not going to change.
- signals coming from lower stages $q > k$. Their correctness is shown either by arguing that the ISA instructions between I_q and I_k did not change the signal or by arguing about forwarding circuits. This includes the correctness of the instruction address computation, because the multiplexer between pc_π and dpc_π is a forwarding circuit for dpc_σ
- signals form other units. So far this is only the memory. Matching the hardware and ISA accesses of memory together with the coupling of hardware and ISA memory gave almost immediately the correctness of memory outputs and of the updated memory.

5.5 Final Remark: Getting Rid of Software Conditions

Software conditions appear in the sequential processor due to implementation details (such as the usage of a line-addressable memory rather than a byte-addressable memory), and in the pipelined processor as a result of data not being processed in a single cycle so that dependencies across instructions are violated. Software conditions are used to bridge the gap between the simple sequential instruction set architecture, and the real behavior of the machine.

Note that so far we have proven nothing about our processors for programs that violate these software conditions. This is fine in a machine with a single user, because even though there is no guarantee about how the processor would behave for a program that violates the software conditions, that behavior affects only that single user.

Since we are creating here a machine with multi-user operating system support, software conditions become very dangerous. Imagine that one user installs malicious software that violates the software condition. With our current theorems, we do not guarantee *anything* about the behavior of the machine, not even for the operating system or other users. In particular we cannot guarantee that the software condition violation will not give full control over the machine to the malicious user, allowing him to take over banking software and to wire enormous amounts of money to his account in the Cayman Islands.

To prevent this from happening, we will in the future have to *eliminate all software conditions* from our theorems, *at least for the user programs*. We have already seen three ways to eliminate software conditions:

1. Add forwarding hardware to provide results ahead of time,
2. Add stalling hardware in case results can not be provided,
3. Make the behavior of the machine explicit and/or change the instruction set architecture (e.g., by introducing delayed branch semantics/dpc)

Similar techniques will also allow us to get rid of the software condition for misalignment (by introducing a misalignment interrupt) and for self modifying code (by making the behavior explicit) without much effort. But the software condition about not writing to the ROM region will remain. This brings us to a fourth, more subtle way to get rid of software conditions: to program the operating system in such a way that users can not violate them. This is not always possible; for example, the operating system can not prevent the user program from using the result of a load before the load reaches the memory stage (but stalling hardware can). But with the addition of memory virtualization in chapter 9, the operating system can force the physical address space of the user programs to be disjoint from the ROM region, and thus users can never access the ROM region.

6

Cache Memory Systems

The construction and correctness proof of a cache coherent shared memory system (short: cache memory system, CMS) based on the MOESI protocol [SS86] is by far the longest and technically most involved part of [KMP14]. Although we will later treat such a system as a black box, i.e. we build exclusively on the *specification* of such a system, we give in section 6.1 an overview of this construction and the process leading to its memory abstraction. Fortunately, in spite of the complexity of the construction, cache memory systems happen to have at the processor side an extremely clean interface and specification, that we present in section 6.2. As a first application we show in section 6.3 how to replace in the *single* core pipelines from chapter 5 the multi-port RAM with a cache memory system with two caches: an instruction cache and a data cache. Note that even in a single processor pipeline, these caches are better kept consistent[1]. We use cache memory systems from now on in all machines that we construct including of course the multi-core machines in later chapters. In contrast to [KMP14] the correctness proofs presented here will not use the implementation detail that reads and writes to the same address of the cache memory system cannot end in the same cycle; we rely *only* on the sequential consistency of the cache memory system.

For readers who are familiar with the construction and correctness proof of cache memory systems in [KMP14] we present in section 6.4 a large exercise: we extend the cache memory system such that it supports several memory modes. As suggested by a remark in [SS86] we allow the same cache line to have different modes in different caches. In section 6.5 we fix a few (minor) errors of chapter 8 of [KMP14].

---

[1] In [MP00] and subsequent formal verification work [BJK+03, DHP05], cached data was held exclusively in one of the two caches.

© Springer Nature Switzerland AG 2020
P. Lutsyk et al. (Eds.): A Pipelined Multi-Core Machine, LNCS 9999, pp. 217–242, 2020.
https://doi.org/10.1007/978-3-030-43243-0_6

6.1 Reviewing A Concrete Example

In section 6.1.1 we review at a very high level the construction of the cache memory system *cms* constructed in [KMP14] using the language introduced in chapter 2^2. Translating the existing complex design into our formal model turns out to be as straight forward as it should be. Even the very few details of the design revealed until that point permit to define in section 6.1.2, how a memory abstraction $m(h)$ is gained from the hardware configuration $h.cms$ of the cache memory system in a two stage process. The reader can treat this as background material: in the sequel the cache memory system will be used as a black box, and no details of this section other than the existence of the memory abstraction $m(h)$ will be used.

6.1.1 Construction

The construction in [KMP14] hinges on a decomposition of byte addresses $a \in \mathbb{B}^{29}$ into subsequences

$$a = a.t \circ a.c$$

where

- $a.t \in \mathbb{B}^\tau$ is the tag
- $a.c \in \mathbb{B}^\ell$ is the *cache line* address (used for the physical addressing of cache RAMs storing 2^ℓ cache lines, not to be confused with line address $a.l \in \mathbb{B}^{29}$)

of line address a and

$$29 = \tau + \ell$$

A cache memory system with $C \in \mathbb{N}$ caches has the following subunits:

- array of direct mapped caches $ca(i)$ with $i \in [0 : C - 1]$ with data paths for data RAM (figure 135 of [KMP14]), tag RAM (figure 136 of [KMP14]) and state RAM (figure 137 of [KMP14]). Nested subunits $ca(i).v$ and their configurations $h.ca(i).v$ in these data paths include
  - data RAM with ℓ line addresses

$$ca(i).data : \mathbb{B}^\ell \to \mathbb{B}^{32}$$

  - tag RAM for tags of length τ

$$ca(i).tag : \mathbb{B}^\ell \to \mathbb{B}^\tau$$

  - state RAM

$$ca(i).s : \mathbb{B}^\ell \to \mathbb{B}^5$$

where the 5 states of the MOESI protocol are coded in unary

$$M = 10000 , \; O = 01000 , \; E = 00100 , \; S = 00010 , \; I = 00001$$

---

[2] In [KMP14] we used the notation *h.ms* for the cache memory system. Some renaming became necessary, because with devices we will later be forced to extend memory systems with I/O-ports. For the memory abstraction of memory systems comprising cache memory system and ports we will reserve (as in [PBLS16]) the notation *ms(h)*.

- master control automaton with 10 unary coded states (figure 138 of [KMP14])

$$ca(i).M \in \mathbb{B}^{10}$$

- slave control automaton with 7 unary coded states (figure 139 of [KMP14])

$$ca(i).S \in \mathbb{B}^{7}$$

- main memory mm with with a ROM portion and state

$$mm : \mathbb{B}^{29} \rightarrow \mathbb{B}^{64}$$

- memory bus b (page 238 of [KMP14]). Formally we split this bus it into four subunits
  - data bus $b.data$. This is a $(C+1, 64)$ controlled tri-state bus $b.data$ as constructed in section 3.5.2 for exchange of cache lines $\in \mathbb{B}^{64}$ between the C caches and the main memory.
  - address $b.ad$. This is a $(C, 29)$ controlled tri-state bus used by the C caches to specify line addresses $\in \mathbb{B}^{29}$ for exchange between the main memory and a cache.
  - main memory protocol bus $b.mmprot$. This is a $(C, 3)$ controlled tri-state bus with protocol signals $mmreq, mmw, mmack$ used by the caches for the control of main memory.
  - 5 bit wide cache coherence protocol bus $b.prot$ between the caches with signals CA, im, bc, ch, di of the MOESI protocol. As subunits it has i) a 5 bit wide *open collector bus*[3] with C input buses, each 5 bits wide. ii) some inverters for the computation of the logical OR of the driver outputs by de Morgan's law (figure 134).
  - bus arbiter arb with C individual grant signals for each cache (figure 140)

$$arb.grant \in \mathbb{B}^{C}$$

Because this is the only arbiter in the cache memory system we can abbreviate

$$arb.grant = grant$$

For further details see [KMP14] .

6.1.2 Memory Abstraction

From the hardware configuration $h.cms$ of the cache memory system we gain a memory abstraction

$$m(h) : \mathbb{B}^{29} \rightarrow \mathbb{B}^{64}$$

in two steps. First we abstract from the tags of the individual caches $h.ca(i)$ or short $ca(i)$ with the help of so called *abstract caches*. In contrast to the physical cache RAMs with their ℓ address lines abstract caches are line addressable just like the main memory. Thus abstract caches aca have two components

---

[3] Constructed from a new basic unit, the 1 bit wide open collector bus computing the logical AND of the outputs of all enabled drivers and 1 if all drivers are disabled

- state memory $aca.s : \mathbb{B}^{29} \to \{M,O,E,S,I\}$ mapping each line address to a state of the MOESI protocol.
- data memory $aca.data : \mathbb{B}^{29} \to \mathbb{B}^{64}$. For line addresses a, $aca.data(a)$ is the data of the cache at line address a. It is meaningless if $s(a) = I^4$.

In a hardware cache configurations ca of direct mapped caches we have a *hardware hit* at line address a if the tag $ca.tag(a.c)$ stored at cache line address $a.c$ matches the tag $a.t$ of a and if the state $ca.s(a.c)$ stored at that cache line address is valid.

$$hhit(ca,a) \equiv h.ca.tag(a.c) = a.t \wedge h.ca.s(a.c) \neq I$$

From hardware cache configuration ca we abstract $aca(ca)$ in the following way. In case of a hit $hhit(ca,a)$ at line address a state and data are copied from the hardware cache.

$$hhit(ca,a) \to aca(ca).s(a) = ca.s(a.c) \ \wedge \ aca(ca).data(a) = ca.data(a.c)$$

Otherwise the abstract state is invalid and the data does not matter

$$/hhit(ca,a) \to aca(ca).s(a) = I$$

From the hardware configuration $h.cms$ of the cache memory system we can now gain from each hardware cache configuration $h.cms.ca(i)$ or short $h.ca(i)$ an abstract cache $aca(h,i)$ as

$$aca(h,i) = aca(h.ca(i))$$

The point of cache coherence protocols like MOESI is to guarantee that cache lines a which are valid in different caches i and j have the same data

$$aca(h,i).s(a) \neq I \wedge aca(h,j).s(a) \neq I \to aca(h,i).data(a) = aca(h.j).data(a)$$

From this one immediately obtains a well defined memory abstraction $m(h)$ of the entire cache memory. If cache line a is valid in any cache i, take $m(h)(a)$ from the data of such a cache; it does not matter which one. Otherwise take it from the main memory

$$m(h)(a) = \begin{cases} aca(h,i).data(a) & aca(i,h).s(a) \neq I \\ h.mm(a) & \text{otherwise} \end{cases}$$

6.2 Specification

For the user of a cache memory system it does not matter how caches, main memory, and ROM are interconnected. What matters are

- the signals at the processor interface of a cache as well as the protocol used with them. The processor interface of cache i will also be called *port i*.

---

[4] In the MOESI protocol I stands for 'invalid'

- the (line addressable) memory abstraction

$$m(h) : \mathbb{B}^{29} \rightarrow \mathbb{B}^{64}$$

provided by the cache memory system and
- the (sequentially consistent) answers given by the system at various ports in response to the accesses generated at the processor interfaces. While the hardware processes these accesses in parallel, there will be a sequential order (constructed from the hardware computation) in which the answers to accesses appear at the interfaces.

6.2.1 Signals of the Processor Interface

$p \rightarrow ca$:

Signals from a processor to one of its caches $ca(i)$:

- $ca(i).preq \in \mathbb{B}$ – processor request signal,
- $ca(i).pacc \in K_{acc}$ – processor access coming into the cache,

$ca \rightarrow p$:

Signals from cache to processor:

- $ca(i).mbusy \in \mathbb{B}$ – memory system is busy (generated by a control automaton of the cache),
- $ca(i).pdout \in \mathbb{B}^{64}$ – data output to processor.

Note that nothing has changed for the interface of the processor except for signals *preq* going to the cache and *mbusy* coming from the cache, which are necessary to define timings.

6.2.2 Protocol

We need to define a protocol for interaction between a processor and its caches (data and instruction cache). If one looks inside the construction of cache memory systems one has to distinguish between *external accesses* as generated at the processor side and *internal accesses*. Internal accesses are i) the counter parts of external accesses and ii) flush accesses freeing cache lines prior to loading a new line in response of an external access. Thus, internal processing of an access may start many cycles after it was issued externally at the processor interface. Fortunately, internal and external end cycles of external accesses coincide and it suffices here to consider only external accesses and their external start and end times.

Communication between processor and its cache is done under the following rules:

- The processor starts a request by activating *preq*,

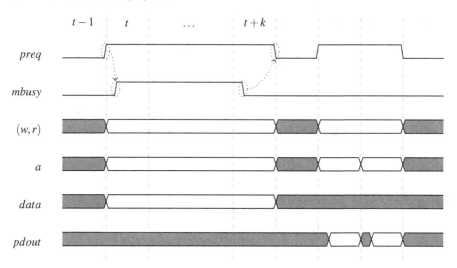

Fig. 126. The timing diagram for a k-cycle write access followed by two consecutive 1-cycle read accesses

- The cache in the same cycle acknowledges the request by raising (Mealy[5]) signal *mbusy* (unless a one-cycle access is performed),
- The cache finishes and lowers *mbusy*, and
- The processor disables *preq* in the next cycle (or starts a new memory request by leaving *preq* activated).

The timing diagram for a k-cycle (write) cache access is shown on the left side of fig. 126. Cycle t is the first cycle of an external access iff

$$\neg mbusy^{t-1} \wedge preq^t .$$

Cycle $t' \geq t$ is the last cycle of an external access iff

$$\neg mbusy^{t'} \wedge preq^{t'} .$$

Observe that 1-cycle accesses are desirable and will indeed be possible (in case of local reads, including negative CAS hits). Then signal *mbusy* is not raised at all and the processor can immediately start a new request in cycle $t + 1$. The timing diagram for two consecutive 1-cycle read accesses is shown on the right side of fig. 126.

6.2.3 Operating Conditions for the CMS

For proper functioning of the CMS two operation conditions have to be imposed.

---

[5] Recall that a Mealy output of the control automaton is a function of the input and the current state.

Stable Accesses and Request Signals:

Once the processor request signal is raised, inputs from the processor must be stable until the cache takes away the *mbusy* signal. In primed notation:

$$ca(i).preq \wedge ca(i).mbusy \wedge X \in \{\, pacc, preq \,\} \rightarrow ca(i).X' = ca(i).X \ .$$

No Write to ROM Region

We use a main memory behaving as ROM for addresses $0^{29-r}b^r$, where $b \in \mathbb{B}^r$ for some small r. As a result, any write performed to this memory region has no effect. Yet, in the sequential memory semantics given in section 1.3.4, we consider the whole memory to be writable. To resolve that problem we added in [KMP14] the operating condition that the processors never issue write and CAS requests to addresses smaller than or equal to $0^{29-r}1^r$.

$$ca(i).preq \wedge ca(i).pacc.a[28:r] = 0^{29-r} \rightarrow ca(i).pacc.bw = 0^8$$

That the latter operating condition is satisfied until cycle t is expressed by

$$opc^t \equiv \forall u < t.\ ca(i).preq^u \wedge ca(i).pacc^u.a[28:r] = 0^{29-r}$$
$$\rightarrow ca(i).pacc^u.bw = 0^8$$

6.2.4 External Access Sequence

For caches $ca(i)$ and components X of their interfaces we abbreviate

$$X(i) = ca(i).X$$

For numbers $k \in \mathbb{N}$ we define a sequence $acc(i,k)$ of external accesses issued at cache port i in order of their end times. Obviously an access ends at port i in cycle t if that cycle is the last cycle of an access. In implicit t notation:

$$end(i) \equiv preq(i) \wedge /mbusy(i)$$

The end time $e(i,k)$ of access k at port i (if it exists) is defined as

$$e(i,0) = \min \{\, t \mid end(i)^t \,\}$$
$$e(i,k+1) = \min \{\, t \mid t > e(i,k) \wedge end(i)^t \,\}$$

and $acc(i,k)$ is defined as the processor access to port i ending at time $e(i,k)$.

$$acc(i,k) = pacc(i)^{e(i,k)}$$

We remind readers familiar with [KMP14] that flushes are absent in the external access sequences we are defining here.

Note that sequence $acc(i,k)$ can be finite in case there are only finitely many memory requests at port i. We define the set of local accesses that actually occur in the hardware computation by

$$A = \{ (i,k) \mid e(i,k) \text{ exists} \}$$

We will use this definition to define sequential consistency in section 6.2.5.

We state without proof that e exactly characterizes the end times of accesses.

Lemma 76.
$$end(i)^t \equiv \exists k. \ e(i,k) = t$$

This lemma is used implicitly in the proofs of lemmas 9.12 and 9.13 of [KMP14].

6.2.5 Sequential Consistency

The cache memory system is *sequentially consistent* if for every multi-port access sequence

$$acc : A \to K_{acc}$$

operating on the cache memory system according to the protocol there exists a linear access sequence

$$lacc : \mathbb{N} \to K_{acc}$$

operating on a single memory, which 'gives the same answers' and respects the orders of the local access sequences at each port. Formally we assign to each actually occurring index

$$(i,k) \in A$$

of the multi-port sequence a sequential index $seq(i,k) \in \mathbb{N}$ of the linear sequence with an injective[6] function

$$seq : A \to \mathbb{N}$$

The linear access sequence (for function seq) is then simply defined by

$$lacc(seq(i,k)) = acc(i,k)$$

If the inverse of some index n does not exist[7], we fill the sequence with void accesses:

$$n \notin im(seq) \quad \to \quad lacc(n).(r,w,cas) = (0,0,0)$$

---

[6] In the literature, sequential consistency often requires bijectivity. In our case this would lead to complications as the set of actual accesses A may be finite, whereas the codomain $\mathbb{N}$ of seq obviously is not. Luckily we will not need that seq is a full bijection, although we will need some additional guarantees on seq that will be introduced shortly.

[7] With the additional requirements on seq that we will introduce shortly, this is only the case if A is finite, in which case indices $[0 : \#A)$ will be defined as above and indices $[\#A : \infty)$ will be filled up with void accesses.

'Giving the same answer' is now formalized in a straight forward way: one starts with the original memory abstraction $m(h^0)$ after power up. As usual the ROM portion is known and everything else is determined by the state of the main memory after power up. After n steps of the linear access sequence one obtains a memory configuration

$$\Delta_M^n(m(h^0), lacc)$$

If access $acc(i,k)$ is a read or cas access, then the answer $pdout(i)$ observed at port i at the end of the access should be the same as the content of memory $\Delta_M^{seq(i,k)}(m(h^0), lacc)$ at address $acc(i,k).a$.

$$acc(i,k).(r, cas) \neq 00 \wedge e(i,k) = t \to pdout(i)^t = \Delta_M^{seq(i,k)}(m(h^0), lacc)(acc(i,k).a)$$

Respecting the local access order is also easily formalized as follows

$$k \leq k' \to seq(i,k) \leq seq(i,k').$$

Some remarks are in order. i) although the underlying hardware of a cache memory system is usually deterministic (at least as long as signals do not cross clock domains), sequential consistency is a nondeterministic computational model. It hides the order seq stemming from the implementation details of the system from the user. As usual this comes at the expense that applications of the system now have to work for *all* orders seq. ii) in a correctness proof for such a cache memory system one has to construct the order seq from the implementation. iii) the above properties alone are too weak for our purposes. We also need the crucial property that accesses in the sequential order seq are ordered by their end cycle in hardware. To understand why this is necessary, consider our simple pipelined machine, which fetches a few cycles before the instruction reaches the memory and performs its memory access. If we can not guarantee that the end cycles in hardware are respected by the global order seq, the fetched value might come from a sequential memory configuration in the far future, possibly by which time the address to be fetched has been overwritten by another store operation which in the sequential ISA computation comes long after the fetch.

6.2.6 Ordering External Accesses by their End Cycle

In each hardware cycle t, the set E of indices of external accesses ending in that hardware cycle is

$$E^t = \{(i,k) \mid e(i,k) = t\}$$

Then $\#E^t$ is the number of such accesses ending in that cycle, and the number NE of external accesses completed *before* a hardware cycle can be kept in ghost register NE which is initialized to zero and incremented by $\#E$ in each cycle

$$NE^0 = 0$$
$$NE' = NE + \#E$$

We require for the sequential order *seq* used to specify the behavior of the cache memory system that it respects the order of hardware cycles, i.e., exactly the accesses ending in a hardware cycle appear in the sequential order in cycles $[NE : NE + \#E - 1]$

$$seq(E) = [NE : NE + \#E - 1] \tag{17}$$

Since the number of accesses in E is by definition of NE' equal to the number of elements in the interval $[NE : NE')$, we get that *seq* (restricted to E) must be a bijection between E and the interval $[NE : NE')$.

For $x \in [1 : \#E^t]$ we identify the x-th access in the current cycle with

$$n_x^t = NE^t + x - 1$$

Note that this access is indeed in the current cycle

$$n_x^t \in [NE^t : NE^t + \#E^t - 1]$$

and from eq. (17) we obtain the port and local access index

$$(i_x, k_x)$$

which is linearized as access n_x

$$seq(i_x, k_x) = n_x$$

The main correctness results about cache memory systems from [KMP14] can then be expressed on a cycle by cycle basis in the following lemmas, which in [KMP14] have the implicit assumption that the operating conditions are met, i.e., that all accesses up to cycle t do not write into the ROM region. Because arguing about operating conditions will become somewhat tricky in the future, we prefer to make the assumption explicit.

Lemma 77. *Assume opc^t. The memory abstraction $m(h)$ is obtained by executing in the linear access sequence lacc all accesses that ended before that cycle.*

$$m(h^t) = \Delta_M^{NE^t}(m(h^0), lacc) \quad resp. \quad m(h) = \Delta_M^{NE}(m(h^0), lacc)$$

This is almost lemma 8.65 of [KMP14]

Lemma 78. *Assume opc^{t+1}. Let $x \in [1 : \#E^t]$ be the index of access n_x ending in cycle t*

$$e(i_x, k_x) = t$$

If this access produces an answer, then that answer is sequentially consistent.

$$acc(i_x, k_x).(r, cas) \neq 00 \rightarrow pdout(i_x)^t = \Delta_M^{n_x}(m(h^0), lacc)(acc(i_x, k_x).a)$$

This is almost lemma 8.67 of [KMP14]. The differences at first glance seem only to affect notation, but the access sequences *acc* and *lacc* of the lemmas in [KMP14] also contain the flush accesses internally generated by the cache memory system. The lemmas above are then obtained by observing that flush accesses do not change the memory abstraction.

We state without proof that no two accesses end in the same cycle at the same port. In [KMP14] this is obvious from the construction, but as the construction is missing here we restate this as a property of the abstract specification.

Lemma 79.

$$x,y \in [1:\#E^t] \wedge x \neq y \quad \rightarrow \quad i_x \neq i_y$$

6.2.7 Liveness

Lemma 80. *The request signal at port i is turned on, the cache memory system eventually ceases to be busy.*

$$preq(i)^t \rightarrow \exists u \geq t : /mbusy(i)^u$$

Without request signal, the cache memory system is not busy

$$/preq(i) \rightarrow /mbusy(i)$$

This is lemma 8.68 from [KMP14].

6.3 Using a Cache Memory System in a Single Pipeline

Pipelined single core processors with cache memory systems have an instruction cache and a data cache which need to be kept coherent. We use in the pipelined processor construction in place of hardware memory $h.m$ the cache memory system $h.cms$ from chap. 8 of [KMP14] with two caches. Port $i = 0$ is for the instruction cache and port $i = 1$ for the data cache.

6.3.1 Connecting Interfaces

As long as no interrupts are involved the integration of a cache memory system into a classical five-stage pipeline is straight forward. The signals of a cache memory system are connected in a fairly obvious way (see sect. 9.3.3 of [KMP14]). The instruction cache

$$ica = h.ca(0)$$

is connected as follows:

$$ica.pacc = iacc$$
$$ica.preq = 1$$
$$imout = ica.pdout$$
$$haz_{IF} = ica.mbusy.$$

For the data cache

$$dca = h.ca(1)$$

we connect:

$$dca.pacc = dacc$$
$$dca.preq = mop.EX \wedge full_{EX}$$
$$dmout = dca.pdout$$
$$haz_M = dca.mbusy.$$

6.3.2 Stability of Inputs of Accesses

That the inputs to the caches remain stable during accesses is stated in

Lemma 81.

- *For the instruction cache:*

$$ica.mbusy \quad \rightarrow \quad ia_\pi = ia'_\pi$$

- *For the data cache:*

$$dca.preq \wedge dca.mbusy \quad \rightarrow \quad /ue_{M-1}$$

Proof. This is almost Lemma 9.11 of [KMP14] for a single processor machine with two caches with ports $q = 0$ and $q = 1$. The only thing that has changed is that for the data cache we have added the guarantee that the memory stage which includes the special purpose register is not updated during the memory access ($/ue_M$), which is now necessary as we take the compare data directly from the special purpose register. We only show this new guarantee. From $dca.mbusy$ we conclude successively

$$haz_M, /ue_M$$

which is the claim. □

In machines with interrupts we will have to invest considerable effort to adapt this lemma.

6.3.3 Relating Update Enable Signals and Ends of Accesses

Ending external accesses to the caches correspond exactly to update enable signals of stages *IF* and *M*. This is stated in the following two lemmas.

Lemma 82.

1. An active update enable signal in stage IF signals the end of read accesses to the instruction cache.

$$ue^t_{IF} \quad \rightarrow \quad \exists k. \ e(0,k) = t \wedge acc(0,k).r$$

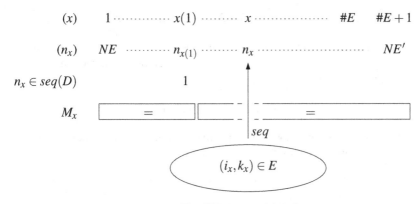

Fig. 127. Sequential Order

2. An active update enable signal in stage 4 together with an active processor request signals the end of an external access.

$$ue_M^t \wedge dca.preq^t \quad \rightarrow \quad \exists k. \ e(1,k) = t$$

Lemma 83. *When a read, write or CAS access ends in cycle t, then the corresponding stage is updated unless it is stalled from the stage below.*

1. For the instruction cache:

$$e(0,k) = t \wedge /stall_{ID}^t \quad \rightarrow \quad ue_{IF}^t$$

2. For the data cache:

$$e(1,k) = t \quad \rightarrow \quad ue_M^t$$

These are Lemmas 9.12 and 9.13 from [KMP14] for the case $q = 0$. The proofs are obtained from the general proofs by dropping the subscript q. In contrast to [KMP14] the external accesses and their end times considered here — from the outside of the memory system — are never flushing. So this has not to be restated in the formulation of the lemmas.

6.3.4 Software Conditions and Main Induction Hypothesis

As software conditions we use exactly $SC_{selfmod}$, SC_{ROM}, and SC_{align} from section 5.1.1. All memory accesses must be aligned

$$4|\langle ia(c)\rangle \wedge (mop(c) \rightarrow d(c)|\langle ea(c)\rangle)$$

Writes to the ROM portion of memory are forbidden

$$write(c) \rightarrow \langle ea(c)\rangle \geq 2^{r+3}$$

and if an instructions writes a line, the next 3 instructions are not allowed to fetch from this line:

$$write(c^i) \wedge j \in \{j+1, j+2, j+3\} \rightarrow ia(c^j).l \neq ea(c^i).l$$

From the well-formedness of the pipeline we concluded in section 5.2.8 that the instructions before I_{IF}, which have not yet updated the memory, do not write to the line of the instruction address.

$$i = I_{IF} \wedge j \in \{I_M, I_{EX}, I_{ID}\} \rightarrow ia^i_\sigma \neq ea^j_\sigma.l$$

With the cache memory system as we have specified it[8] a new situation could arise: If the data cache is written in the cycle of the fetch, i.e. if

$$d = 1 \quad \text{and} \quad full_M$$

then the write access might occur in the sequential order *before* the fetch access. In this case the fetch will be from $m^{I_M+1}_\sigma$ instead of I_M. Actually this makes life easier, because less instructions in the pipe have not yet updated the memory. Formally, because of $full_M$ we have

$$I_M + 1 \in \{I_{EX}, I_{ID}\} \subset \{I_M, I_{EX}, I_{ID}\}$$

and no new software condition will be required. As far as registers and register files are concerned the correctness statement stays completely the same. For the memory we now have to relate the ISA memory m_σ to the memory abstraction $m(h)$. In order to be able to apply lemmas 77 and 78, we also now need to establish that the operating condition is satisfied.

For the start of the induction we redefine the trivial simulation relation $sim(h,c)$ from the previous chapter

$$sim(h,c) \leftrightarrow (\forall X \neq m. \ h.X = c.X) \wedge m(h) = \ell(c.m)$$

---

[8] not the construction in [KMP14]

Lemma 84. *There exists an initial configuration c^0 satisfying*

$$sim(h^0, c^0)$$

Furthermore, if for the computation (c^i) with initial configuration c^0 the software conditions hold

$$SC_{selfmod}((c^i)) \wedge \forall i.\ SC_{ROM}(c^i) \wedge SC_{align}(c^i)$$

then in all cycles:

- *For registers or register files $R \in reg(k)$:*

$$R_\pi = \begin{cases} R_\sigma^{l_k} & vis(R) \\ R_\sigma^{l_k-1} & /vis(R) \wedge full_k \wedge used[R]_\sigma^{l_k-1} \end{cases}$$

- *For memory:*

$$m(h) = \ell(m_\sigma^{l_M})$$

- *The operating condition is satisfied until the current cycle:*

$$opc$$

For

$$x \in [1 : \#E^t]$$

we define the memory M_x^t before access n_x^t by applying the first n_x^t accesses of *lacc*, i.e., $lacc[0 : n_x^t - 1]$ to the original memory abstraction $m(h^0)$.

$$M_x^t = \Delta_M^{n_x^t}(m(h^0), lacc)$$

The last memory $M_{\#E^t}^t$ defined this way is the memory before the last access $n_{\#E^t}^t$ of the current cycle. As we also need to argue about the memory after the last access, we define also

$$M_{\#E^t+1}^t = \Delta_M^{n_{\#E^t}^t+1}(m(h^0), lacc)$$

We switch to implicit t notation. By the above case split we have now defined M_x for

$$x \in [1 : \#E + 1]$$

Dealing with this case split in the proofs would be tedious, but both cases can be treated uniformly with the following lemma.

Lemma 85.

$$M_x = \Delta_M^{NE+x-1}(m(h^0), lacc)$$

Thus M_x and M_{x+1} are the memory system abstractions before and after access $lacc(n_x)$. In particular we have by lemma 77 with $t := t + 1$:

Lemma 86. *Assume opc'.*

$$M_1 = \Delta_M^{NE}(m(h^0), lacc) = m(h)$$
$$M_{\#E+1} = \Delta_M^{NE'}(m(h^0), lacc) = m(h')$$

This is illustrated in the top two lines of fig. 127.

6.3.5 External Accesses to the Data Cache Ending in the Current Cycle

As the machine under consideration has only two caches, at most two external accesses can end in each cycle, i.e., we have

$$\#E \leq 2.$$

We denote the set of external accesses in E to the data cache $h.ca(1)$ by

$$D = \{(1,k) \mid (1,k) \in E\}$$

and its cardinality by

$$d = \#D \leq 1$$

In case such an access exists, we denote its index as

$$xd = \varepsilon\{x \mid n_x \in seq(D)\}$$

Because accesses in $E \setminus D$ are reads from the instruction cache, they do not change the memory abstraction and we get by an easy induction on x:

Lemma 87. *For $x \in [1 : \#E + 1]$:*

$$M_x = \begin{cases} M_1 & d = 0 \lor x \in [1 : xd] \\ \delta_M(M_1, lacc(n_{xd})) & d = 1 \land x \in [xd + 1 : \#E + 1] \end{cases}$$

This is illustrated in the bottom lines of Fig. 127.

6.3.6 Induction Step

We first establish *opc'*.

Lemma 88.

$$opc'$$

Proof. From the induction hypothesis we know that all accesses before the current cycle obey the operating condition. For the accesses in the current cycle, only the access at the data port is interesting as the access at the instruction port by definition has no byte-write signals

$$ica.pacc.bw = 0_8$$

For the data cache assume that there is a processor request with an access that addresses the ROM region

$$dca.preq \wedge dca.pacc.a[28:r] = 0^{29-r}$$

We conclude from the induction hypothesis that data access in hardware and in ISA are the same as the data cache access

$$dacc_\sigma^{I_M} \equiv dacc_\pi = dca.pacc$$

Thus the effective address is in the ROM region

$$\langle ea_\sigma^{I_M} \rangle < 2^{r+3}$$

By contraposition of the software condition SC_{ROM} the instruction is not a write

$$/write_\sigma^{I_M}$$

Thus by definition the byte-write signals in ISA are off

$$dacc_\sigma^{I_M}.bw = bw_\sigma^{I_M} = write_\sigma^{I_M} \wedge \ldots = 0_8$$

Because there is a request, one of the access signals is on

$$dca.pacc.(r, w, cas) \neq (0, 0, 0)$$

and thus equivalence of the accesses implies that they have the same byte-write signals, and the claim follows

$$dca.pacc.bw = dacc_\sigma^{I_M}.bw = 0_8$$

$\square$

For the induction step of the main induction hypothesis (lemma 84) we have to adjust the proof for processors with one-cycle memory, which was summarized in section 5.4.3 in the following three places:

- stage M: update of the cache memory system,
- stage M: result of loads, and
- stage IF: instruction fetch.

For stage M we split cases as usual on ue_M.

- $ue_M = 0$. Nothing happens. Formally, by lemma 83 no external access to the data cache ends in the current cycle. We have

$$d = 0 \quad \text{and} \quad I'_M = I_M$$

Hence

$$m(h') = M_{\#E+1} \qquad \text{L 86}$$
$$= M_1 \qquad \text{L 87}$$
$$= m(h) \qquad \text{L 86}$$
$$= \ell(m_\sigma^{I_M}) \qquad \text{IH}$$
$$= \ell(m_\sigma^{I'_M})$$

- $ue_M = 1$. A new instruction is clocked into register stage M. We have

$$full_{EX} \quad \text{and} \quad I_{EX} = I_M + 1 = I'_M.$$

Because the control bits are always used, we get from the induction hypothesis

$$X \in \{l, s, cas, mop\} \quad \rightarrow \quad X.EX = X_\sigma^{I_{EX}-1} = X_\sigma^{I_M}$$

We split sub-cases on $mop.EX$.

- $mop.EX^t = mop_\sigma^{I_M} = 0$. Then the data cache is not accessed and the ISA memory stays the same

$$/dca.preq \quad \text{and} \quad m_\sigma^{I'_M} = m_\sigma^{I_M+1} = m_\sigma^{I_M}$$

Because accesses to caches end when signal $preq$ is active and signal $mbusy$ is off, no access to the data cache ends in the current cycle. We have

$$d = 0$$

and conclude as above

$$m(h') = \ell(m_\sigma^{I_M}) = \ell(m_\sigma^{I'_M})$$

- $mop.EX = mop_\sigma^{I_M} = 1$. Then the data cache is accessed

$$dca.preq$$

We have by assumption
$$SC_{align}(c^{I_M})$$

which allows to apply lemma 47. Thus

$$\ell(m_\sigma^{I_M+1}) = \delta_M(\ell(m_\sigma^{I_M}), dacc_\sigma^{I_M})$$

By Lemma 82 some access

$$acc(1, k_x) = lacc(n_x)$$

ends at the data cache in the current cycle. Thus

$$d = 1 \quad \text{and} \quad x = xd$$

By the circuit stage correctness (lemma 62) the access currently ending is equivalent to the data access of ISA configuration c^{I_M}.

$$lacc(n_{xd}) = dacc_\pi \equiv dacc_\sigma^{I_M}$$

We finish the proof that the cache memory system is correctly updated by

$$
\begin{aligned}
m(h') &= M_{\#E+1} & \text{L 86} \\
&= \delta_M(M_1, lacc(n_{xd})) & \text{L 87} \\
&= \delta_M(m(h), lacc(n_{xd})) & \text{L 86} \\
&= \delta_M(\ell(m_\sigma^{I_M}), dacc_\sigma^{I_M}) & \text{IH} \\
&= \ell(m_\sigma^{I'_M}) & \text{L 47}
\end{aligned}
$$

In case a load or CAS operation is performed we argue about hardware signal $dca.pdout$ and ISA signal $dmout$:

$$
\begin{aligned}
dca.pdout &= \Delta_M^{n_{xd}}(m(h^0), lacc)(acc(1, k_{xd}.a)) & \text{L 78} \\
&= M_{xd}(lacc(n_{xd}).a) & \text{Defn.} \\
&= M_1(lacc(n_{xd}).a) & \text{L 87} \\
&= \ell(m_\sigma^{I_M})(dacc_\sigma^{I_M}.a) & \text{IH} \\
&= dmout_\sigma^{I_M} & \text{Defn.}
\end{aligned}
$$

For stage $IF = 1$ we consider cycles with $ue_{IF} = 1$, which implies

$$stall_{ID} = 0.$$

By lemma 82 we know that a read access

$$acc(0, k_x) = lacc(n_x)$$

to the instruction cache ends in the current cycle. The usual argument shows

$$lacc(n_x) = iacc_\pi = iacc_\sigma^{I_{IF}}.$$

Now it almost looks like we can finish the proof in a straight forward way, but this is not the case. A complication arises if a writing or CAS access

$$lacc(n_{xd}) \equiv dacc_\sigma^{I_M}$$

is also ending in the current cycle and we have

$$xd < x.$$

In this case we will use the software condition $SC_{selfmod}$ to show that the data access does not modify the instruction which is being fetched. Arguing about hardware signal $ica.pdout$ and ISA signal $imout_\sigma$ we obtain:

$$ica.pdout = \Delta_M^{n_x}(m(h^0), lacc)(acc(0, k_x).a) \qquad \text{L 78}$$

$$= M_x(lacc(n_x).a) \qquad \text{Defn.}$$

$$= \begin{cases} \delta_M(M_1, lacc(n_{xd}))(lacc(n_x).a) & d = 1 \wedge x > xd \\ M_1(lacc(n_x).a) & \text{otherwise} \end{cases} \qquad \text{L 87}$$

$$= \begin{cases} \delta_M(\ell(m_\sigma^{I_M}), dacc_\sigma^{I_M})(iacc_\sigma^{I_{IF}}.a) & d = 1 \wedge x > xd \\ \ell(m_\sigma^{I_M})(iacc_\sigma^{I_{IF}}.a) & \text{otherwise} \end{cases} \qquad \text{IH}$$

$$= \begin{cases} \ell(m_\sigma^{I_M+1})(iacc_\sigma^{I_{IF}}.a) & d = 1 \wedge x > xd \\ \ell(m_\sigma^{I_M})(iacc_\sigma^{I_{IF}}.a) & \text{otherwise} \end{cases} \qquad \text{L 47}$$

$$= \ell(m_\sigma^{I_{IF}})(iacc_\sigma^{I_{IF}}.a) \qquad \text{SC}$$

$$= imout_\sigma^{I_{IF}} \qquad \text{Defn.}$$

6.3.7 Proof Summary

The main induction hypothesis now includes the proof obligation that the operating conditions are satisfied.

In order to be able to apply the pipeline stage correctness lemmas (lemma 62), we show as before the correctness of inputs signals of these stages. Inputs for circuits stages $cir(k)$ still come from four sources:

- invisible pipeline registers, whose correctness follows from the main induction hypothesis for invisible registers,
- visible registers and register files from $reg(k)$, whose correctness follows from the main induction hypothesis for visible registers.
- signals coming from lower stages $q > k$. Their correctness is shown either by arguing that the ISA instructions between I_q and I_k did not change the signal (like the software condition on self modifying code) or by arguing about forwarding circuits, which have not changed.
- signals from the memory.

With a cache memory system we had to use lemmas 77 and 78 for the effect of memory updates and the results of reads. In order to apply the lemmas we had to

- show that inputs during memory requests are stable, hereby guaranteeing the operating conditions of the cache memory system (section 6.3.2).
- identifying external hardware accesses of the cache memory system with the help update enable signals ue_{IF} and ue_M (section 6.3.3).
- use circuit stage correctness to couple these accesses with the ISA accesses.
- use the software condition SC_{ROM} to establish the operating condition for the CMS in a straightforward way (section 6.3.6).

6.4 Exercises

1. Show that by appropriately restricting seq, we obtain a bijective function. Hints:

a) Show that the set of actual accesses is the union of all sets of ending accesses

$$A = \bigcup_t E^t$$

b) Show that

$$seq : A \rightarrow \bigcup_t [NE^t : NE^{t+1})$$

is a bijection

2. In a series of exercises show how to provide different memory modes in a multi-core machine. Throughout the exercises we refer to the shared memory construction of [KMP14]. The memory mode used so far is called *write-back mode*. We wish to provide a second memory mode called *write-through* where writes always update a cache line *and* the main memory.

   The same line can be accessed at different ports with different modes. The mode, in which a line was accessed last is *not* maintained in the cache state of lines. Accesses *acc* are provided with a new component $acc.wt \in \mathbb{B}$ indicating that the access is performed in write-through mode. This bit has only an effect for writes. We use a new special purpose register $wt = spr(x)$ for some x. The last bit of this register indicates if writes should be performed in write-back mode, i.e. we set both in hardware and ISA

   $$wt(h) = h.spr(x)[0] \quad , wt(h) = c.spr(x)[0]$$

   We will implement write or cas+ in write-through modes in two steps: i) as already implemented and ending in state M followed by ii) an internal copy back access cb, which is only performed in state M and turns it to state E.

   a) Modify the protocol tables (sec. 8.3.2 of [KMP14]) in the following way: add a new column cb for the copy back operation. Also replace in the table for master transitions columns *write* and *cas+* by $(write, /wt)$, $(write, wt)$, $(cas+, /wt)$ and $(cas+, wt)$. Hints:
      - in *wt* mode activate Ca also in the case of write resp. cas hits. This reserves the bus for the final write operation to main memory.
      - activate in *wt* mode a master control signal *wt*. We do not use it in the tables. It is used later to keep control automata in sync. You need to specify this activation in columns $(write, wt)$ and $(cas+, wt)$.
   b) Translating tables to switching functions (sec. 8.3.3 of [KMP14]).
      i. which of the circuits C1, C2, C3 depend on signal *wt*?
      ii. redraw figure 132 of [KMP14].
   c) adjust the algebraic specification of the atomic protocol (sec. 8.3.4 of [KMP14]).
      Hints:
      - writes in write-through mode are not local.
      - activating Ca for write hits does not cause problems: there will be no owner and thus no cache intervention. The master knows that a load from memory is not necessary.

- the copy back to memory in write-through mode is similar to a flush.

d) Cache protocol automata (sec. 8.4.3 of [KMP14])

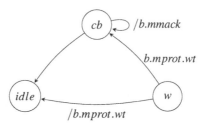

Fig. 128. Augmented master automaton

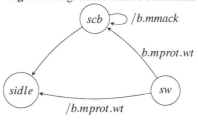

Fig. 129. Augmented slave automaton

We augment master and slave automata as shown in figs. 128 and 129. In state *cb* (copy back) the master will update the memory after a write in write-through mode. The corresponding slave state *scb* serves only to keep the automata in sync. Note that master protocol signal *mprot.wt* is used here by the slaves to trigger the transition to state *scb*.

Adjust the definitions of transition (2), (3), (4) and (5). Hints:

- (2) and (3): in write-through mode writes are not local.
- (4) and (5): after a write miss in write-through mode there is no need to flush, because the line is not cached.

e) Specify the control signals generated at the new states. In particular
   i. set the output enable bits of drivers to bus *bdata* in state *w*.
   ii. update caches states in the last cycle of *cb* resp. *scb*.
   iii. turn signal *mbusy* off during the last cycle of *cb*.
   iv. do not forget to disable drivers again.
   v. so far state after a write or cas+ is updated to M or O in state *w*. Maintain this in *wt* mode and update again to E resp. S in state *cb*. This permits to treat the copy back in the correctness proof as an internal access, i.e. very much like a flush.

f) In what part of the correctness proof do we use that we have kept the slave automata in sync with the states *scb*?

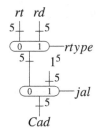

Fig. 130. Computation of the C-address

6.5 Errata

Known errata in [KMP14].

Nine Shades of RAM

1) p.91, typo in the name of the address input, should be

$$Sout(h) = h.S(Sa(h))$$

A Basic Sequential MIPS Machine

2) p.145, figure 99: the figure is wrong. The correct figure is Fig. 130.
3) p.146, figure 100: typo in the name of the fields of the BCE unit, should be

$$bf[3:1] \quad \text{and} \quad bf[0].$$

Pipelining

4) p.164: typo in the text, should be
   ...into 5 circuit stages $cir(i)$ with $i \in [1:5]$, such that...
5) p.167: typo in the text, should be
   For $k \in [1:5]$ circuit stage $cir(k)$ is input for register stage k and...
6) p.189: typos in the proof, should be

$$gprin_\pi^t = lres_\pi^t$$
$$= lres_\sigma^i$$
$$= gprin_\sigma^i$$

and

$$gprin_\pi^t = C.4_\pi^t$$
$$= C_\sigma^i$$
$$= gprin_\sigma^i$$

in the cases of resp. load and not-store instructions.
7) p.198, figure 123: the figure is wrong, the multiplexer is missing. The correct figure is Fig. 131.

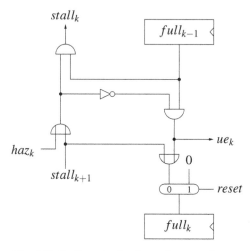

Fig. 131. Stall engine hardware for stage k

Caches and Shared Memory

8) p.214, proof of Lemma 8.1: typo in the first line, should be

$$hhit(h.ca,a) \equiv h.ca.s(a.c) \neq I \wedge h.ca.tag(a.c) = a.t$$

9) p.218: definition of the outputs of the fully associative cache, should be

$$h.ca.data(b) \quad \text{and} \quad h.ca.s(b)$$

10) p.223: typo in the notation, should be

$$aca(i).X^t = aca(h^t.ca(i)).X$$

11) p.232: typo in the definition of semantics of the global access, should be

$$\vdots$$
$$\forall j : sprot(j) = C2(aca(j).s(a), mprot)$$
$$\vdots$$

12) p.246, figure 137, comment:
   For *souta* there is a multiplexer forcing the state of the abstract cache to invalid in case of $/phit$. For the slave state *soutb* the corresponding mux is not present. The reason is, that the slave only participates in the protocol (and the output of circuit C2 is only used) if $bhit = 1$.
13) p.254, figure 140: the figure is wrong, the multiplexer is missing. The correct figure is Fig. 132.

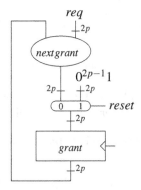

Fig. 132. The bus arbiter

14) p.262, lemma 8.16: one case is not covered in the proof. When considering $G(i)^{t-1}$ we should neither be in state $w(i)^{t-1}$ (which is present) nor take transition (9) (which is missing). However, the statement of the lemma still holds, while the proof is easily fixable by adding the missing case.

15) p.286, lemma 8.51: typo in the proof, should be

$$q = \max\{t' \mid wait(i)^{t'} \wedge t' < t\}$$

16) p.290, lemma 8.56: typo in the formulation, in the second line it should be

$$\neg acc(i,k).f$$

17) p.291, lemma 8.57: typo in the formulation, should be

$$X \in \{s, tag, data\}$$

18) p.294, lemma 8.58: typo in the formulation, should be

$$X \in \{s, tag, data\}$$

19) p.298, lemma 8.62: the proof uses $\neg acc(i,k).f$

In the proof of lemma 8.64 (one step) the application of lemmas 8.58 (stable slaves) and the data transfer lemma 8.35 (m1) does not work out. Splitting cases on *localw* in the three lemmas concerned fixes this problem.

20) Lemma 8.35 (m1) ignores the multiplexer at the s input of circuit $C2$ forwarding the next state

$$M = aca(j).s^{t+1}(badin(j)^t)$$

in case of a local write. Thus the correct statement is

$sprotout(j)^{t+1}$

$$= \begin{cases} C2(M, mprotin(j)^t) & localw(j)^t \wedge ca(j).pa^t = badin(j)^t \\ C2(soutb(j)^t, mprotin(j)^t) & \text{otherwise} \end{cases}$$

$$= \begin{cases} C2(aca(j).s^{t+1}(badin(j)^t), mprotin(j)^t) & localw(j)^t \wedge ca(j).pa^t = badin(j)^t \\ C2(aca(j).s^t(badin(j)^t), mprotin(j)^t) & \text{otherwise} \end{cases}$$

21) Lemma 8.58 (stable slaves) must hold for one more cycle in the absence of local writes

$$q(j) \in \begin{cases} [s(i,k)+2:t] & localw(j)^{s(i,k)+1} \wedge ca(j).pa^{s(i,k)+1} = a \\ [s(i,k)+1:t] & \text{otherwise} \end{cases}$$

In cycle $s(i,k)+1$ only local writes to address a can end. If no such write ends, one concludes with lemma 8.57 (unchanged cache lines)

$$aca(j).X^{s(i,k)+1}(a) = aca(j).X^{s(i,k)+2}(a)$$

22) In the proof of lemma 8.64 (one step) one uses in the case $w(i)^{e(i,k)}$ first the data transfer lemma 8.35 with $t = s(i,k)+1$ and then lemma 8.58 literally to conclude

$sprotout(j)^{s(i,k)+2}$

$$= \begin{cases} C2(aca(j).s^{s(i,k)+2}(a), mprotin(j)^{s(i,k)+1}).(ch, di) & localw(j)^{s(i,k)+1} \wedge \\ & ca(j).pa^{s(i,k)+1} = a \\ C2(aca(j).s^{s(i,k)+1}(a), mprotin(j)^{s(i,k)+1}).(ch, di) & \text{otherwise} \end{cases}$$

$$= C2(aca(j).s^{e(i,k)}(a), mprotout(i)^{e(i,k)}).(ch, di)$$

A Multi-core Processor

23) p.329: typo in the definition of the instruction cache interface, should be

$$Iin_\pi = \begin{cases} ica.pdout[63:32] & ima_\pi[2] = 1 \\ ica.pdout[31:0] & ima_\pi[2] = 0 \end{cases}$$

24) p.329: typo in the definition of the data cache interface, should be

$$dmout_\pi = dca.pdout$$

25) p.330: missing lines in the proof of lemma 9.11:

$$ue_3^{q,t} = full_2^{q,t} \wedge \neg(haz_3^{q,t} \vee stall_4^{q,t})$$
$$= full_2^{q,t} \wedge \neg(0 \vee 1)$$
$$= 0.$$

26) p.340: index i is incorrect, should be i_y

7

Interrupt Mechanism

We basically use the interrupt mechanism from [PBLS16] and [MP00]. In the specification we adjust things in several ways:

- Besides *reset* there are now two kinds of external interrupt signals
  - i) *sipi* and *init*. In multi-core machines these inter-processor interrupts will serve to start and to stop processors from running. As long as we are dealing with single core machines we simply tie them to zero.
  - ii) a single external interrupt signal $e \in \mathbb{B}$. In multi-core machines this signal will be generated by an advanced programmable interrupt controller (APIC). It gets priority 3 and is enabled by bit 0 of the status register.
- there are two kinds of misalignment interrupts:
  - i) *malf*: misaligned instruction address (*ia*) during fetch, and
  - ii) *malls*: misaligned effective address (*ea*) during load/store.
- overflow is not maskable. As instructions *add*, *addi*, and *sub* create overflow interrupts and their 'unsigned' counterparts do not; there is no need to mask twice.
- we distinguish between page faults and general protection faults. Until we treat address translation we tie the corresponding interrupt event signals to zero.
- We take advantage of the fact that the new *eret* (exception return) instruction drains the pipe to reformulate the software condition for self modifying code in a way which does not expose the concrete depth of the pipeline.

Because misaligned memory accesses are now signaled by interrupts, there is no need any more to forbid them via a software condition. In correctness proofs, even for the sequential implementation of section 7.2 this comes at the price of extra bookkeeping, because with a misaligned instruction fetch, signal $I(c)$ and the control signals derived from it all have no meaning; hence the proof has in this case to work without referring to such signals. This is easily handled by redefining when signal $I(c)$ is used.

The pipelining and forwarding of signals of section 7.5 follows in a fairly straight forward way the lines of [MP00]. But when it comes to rolling back interrupted instructions things get involved. As in [Krö01] we treat interrupts as a special case of

© Springer Nature Switzerland AG 2020
P. Lutsyk et al. (Eds.): A Pipelined Multi-Core Machine, LNCS 9999, pp. 243–330, 2020.
https://doi.org/10.1007/978-3-030-43243-0_7

misspeculation (we speculate that no interrupts occur and roll back instructions in the pipeline in case we discover that we were wrong), and as in [Bey05] and [BJK$^+$03] we stabilize the inputs to the cache memory system in case an instruction is rolled back while a memory access is still in progress. But in later constructions we will have rollback due to interrupts *and* due to 'ordinary' speculative execution. For this purpose we present already in section 7.4 a new stall engine which allows to trigger rollbacks in any pipeline stage and simultaneously stabilizes accesses to the cache memory system during such rollbacks.

In the implementation of rollbacks we change the implementation of [Krö01] in a small but crucial way: a rollback request generated by an instruction say i rolls back only instructions *behind* instruction i and not instruction i itself. The correctness statement of the machines is then in section 7.6 simply restricted to instructions in the pipeline, which are *committed*, i.e., which will not be rolled back in the future.

The main technical effort of this chapter goes into the derivation of basic properties of the new stall engine in section 7.4 and into the liveness theory of committed instructions in section 7.8. The other proofs of this chapter follow the established lines.

7.1 Specification

7.1.1 Special Purpose Registers Revisited

The machines specified and constructed before have already a special purpose register file $c.spr$, and data can be transported between this file and the general purpose register by means of move instructions. So far however, only the *cas* instruction made use of this file by taking the 'compare data' $cdata(c)$ from register $c.spr(10_5)$. The interrupt mechanism to be introduced in this chapter makes use of quite a few more special purpose registers. In table 12 we introduce shorthands for the first 11 registers of the special purpose register file; except for *pto* and *eddpc*, which are used for address translation, the interrupt mechanism and the cas instruction together make use of all of them. Thus we abbreviate

$$c.sr = c.spr(0_5)$$

$$\vdots$$

$$c.cdata = c.spr(10_5)$$

The mode register $c.mode \in \mathbb{B}^{32}$ distinguishes between *system mode*, where

$$c.mode[0] = 0$$

and *user mode*, where

$$c.mode[0] = 1$$

We abbreviate

Table 12. Special purpose registers

$\langle a \rangle$	synonym for $spr(a)$	name
0	sr	status register
1	esr	exception status register
2	eca	exception cause
3	epc	exception pc
4	$edpc$	exception dpc
5	$eddpc$	exception $ddpc$
6	$edata$	exception data
7	pto	page table origin
8	$mode$	mode register
9	$emode$	exception mode register
10	$cdata$	compare data

$$mode(c) = c.mode[0]$$

Clearing bit $spr[0]$ of the status register will mask external interrupts. After reset the machine should be in system mode, the external interrupts should be masked, and the lowest bit of the exception cause register should be set.

$$mode(c^0) = 0$$
$$c^0.sr[0] = 0$$
$$c^0.eca[0] = 1$$

The purpose of the other special purpose registers will be explained shortly.

7.1.2 Types of Interrupts

Interrupts are triggered by interrupt event signals; they change the control flow of programs. Here we consider event signals $ev[1 : 12]$ from Table 13. We classify interrupts in three ways:

- internal or external. The first four interrupts are generated outside of CPU and memory system. We rename

$$reset = ev[0] \,, \; sipi = ev[1] \,, \; init = ev[2] \,, \; e = ev[3]$$

The other interrupts are generated within CPU and memory system, and we call them *internal interrupts*. Their activation depends only on the current ISA configuration c. More internal interrupt signals must be introduced for machines with floating point units (see [MP00]). In multi-core processors one tends to additionally implement inter-processor interrupts.
- maskability. Only e is maskable. When an interrupt is masked, the processor will not react to it if the corresponding event signal is raised.

Table 13. Interrupts handled by our design

index j	synonym for $ev[j]$	name	maskable	resume
0	*reset*	reset	no	abort
1	*sipi*	start processor running	no	
2	*init*	stop processor from running	no	abort
3	*e*	external event signal	yes	repeat
4	*malf*	misalignment on fetch	no	abort
5	*pff*	page fault on fetch	no	repeat
6	*gff*	general-protection fault on fetch	no	abort
7	*ill*	illegal instruction	no	abort
8	*sysc*	system call	no	cont.
9	*ovf*	arithmetic overflow	no	cont.
10	*malls*	misalignment on load/store	no	abort
11	*pfls*	page fault on load/store	no	repeat
12	*gfls*	general-protection fault on load/store	no	abort

- resume type: whether and where execution of a program should be resumed after handling of an interrupt. In many cases, when interrupts signal error conditions the program is simply aborted. If page faults are handled transparently one obviously wants to repeat the interrupted instruction after the missing page has been swapped into memory. For the external interrupts one also repeats the interrupted instruction for slightly less obvious reasons: interrupts will be handled according to their priority with small numbers signaling high priority. If an external interrupt occurs simultaneously with an internal interrupt and we would resume execution behind the interrupted instruction, then the internal interrupt (with the lower priority) would be lost. In the remaining cases one wishes to continue execution of the program behind the interrupted instruction. Clearly this should be the case for system calls, i.e., interrupts generated by the *sysc* instruction, but also for overflows.

For the time being we have neither devices generating external interrupts nor memory management units generating page faults and general protection faults. Therefore we will temporarily tie the corresponding event signals to zero.

7.1.3 MIPS ISA with Interrupts

Recall that the transition function δ_{isa} for MIPS ISA defined so far computes a new MIPS configuration c' from an old configuration c

$$c' = \delta_{isa}(c)$$

We rename this transition function to δ_{isa}^{old} and the configuration computed by it to c^*

$$c^* = \delta_{isa}^{old}(c)$$

Then we define the new transition function

$$c' = \delta_{isa}(c, e)$$

which takes as inputs the old configuration c and the external event signal e.

We proceed to define a predicate $jisr(c, e)$ which indicates that a jump to the interrupt service routine is to be performed, and a predicate $eret(c)$ which indicates a return from the interrupt service routine. If these signals are inactive, the machine behaves as it did before

$$/jisr(c, e) \wedge /eret(c) \rightarrow c' = c^*$$

For the computation of the $jisr$ predicate we unify notation for external and internal interrupts and define vectors $mev(c, e)[12 : 0]$ and $mca(c, e)[12 : 0]$ of masked event and masked cause signals. In the MIPS ISA, the external interrupt $e = ev[3]$ is enabled by setting bit 0 of the status register sr, and masked by clearing it

$$ien(c) = c.sr[0] = c.spr[0][0]$$

No other event signal is ever directly masked. The masked event signals $mev(c, e)[i]$ are therefore defined as

$$mev(c, e)[i] = \begin{cases} ien(c) \wedge e & i = 3 \\ ev(c, e)[i] & \text{otherwise} \end{cases}$$

We handle interrupts with small indices with higher priority than interrupts with high indices. In the masked cause vector $mca[0 : 12]$ we keep from the active masked event signals only the one with the highest priority, i.e., with the lowest index.

$$mca(c, e)[i] = mev(c, e)[i] \wedge / \bigvee_{j < i} mev(c, e)[j].$$

Thus low priority interrupts are masked by high priority interrupts; moreover e is masked if the interrupt enable signal $ien(c)$ is low. We jump to the interrupt service routine if any of the masked cause or event bits is on:

$$jisr(c, e) = \bigvee_i mca(c, e)[i] = \bigvee_i mev(c, e)[i].$$

In cases this signal is active we define the interrupt level $il(c, e)$ as the smallest index of an active masked cause bit.

$$il(c, e) = \min\{i \mid mca(c, e)[i]\}$$

Note that there is in fact at most one such signal

Lemma 89.

$$mca(c, e)[i] \equiv i = il(c, e)$$

We will exploit this in the hardware construction. Execution of the interrupted instruction continues if the highest priority interrupt has type continue.

$$cont(c, e) \equiv il(c, e) \in \{8, 9\}$$

Thus the interrupt level gives the index of the interrupt that should receive service.

With an active $jisr(c, e)$ signal many things happen at the transition to the next state c':

- we jump to the start addresses $sisr$ and $sisr +_{32} 4_{32}$ of the interrupt service routine. We fix $sisr$ to 0_{32}, i.e., to the first address in the ROM.

$$c'.dpc = 0_{32}$$
$$c'.pc = 4_{32}$$

- the maskable interrupt event signal e is masked.

$$c'.sr = 0_{32}$$

The purpose of this mechanism is to make the first instructions of the interrupt handler (which save the exception registers $epc, \ldots, emode$ of the context) not interruptible by external interrupts. Of course, the interrupt service routine should also be programmed in such a way that its execution does not produce internal interrupts.

- the old value $c.sr$ of the status register is saved into the exception status register $c.esr$.

$$c'.esr = c.sr$$

Thus it can be restored later. This does not work if the interrupted instruction writes the status register ($movs2g$) and the resume type is continue. But only system calls and arithmetic instructions have resume type continue, and they do not write the special purpose register file.

- in the exception registers epc and $edpc$ we save something similar to the link address of a function call. It is the pair of addresses where program execution will resume after the handling of the interrupt, if it is not aborted. In ISA (and the hardware) we only distinguish if the resume type is $continue$ or not. In case of continue we resume after the interrupt in configuration c^*, i.e., after execution of the current instruction. In all other cases we prepare for repetition of the interrupted instruction by saving the current pc and dpc. No harm is done by this, if the handler/operating system decides to abort execution.

$$c'.(edpc, epc) = \begin{cases} c^*.(dpc, pc) & cont(c, e) \\ c.(dpc, pc) & \text{otherwise.} \end{cases}$$

- in the exception data register $edata$, we save the effective address $ea(c)$. After a page fault on load/store this provides the effective address, which generated the interrupt to the page fault handler.

$$c'.edata = ea(c)$$

- we save the masked cause bits into the exception cause register so that the interrupt level of the interrupt can be computed by software

$$c'.eca = 0^{19} \circ mca(c, e)$$

- we back-up the current machine mode into the exception mode register.

$$c'.emode = c.mode$$

- finally, we switch to system mode.

$$c'.mode = 0_{32}$$

- in case of continue interrupts we need to finish the interrupted instruction. We collect the special purpose registers that are updated at *jisr* into set

$$J = \{\, sr, esr, eca, epc, edpc, edata, mode, emode \,\}$$

Then we define
  - for the general purpose register file and the memory:

$$c'.(gpr, m) = \begin{cases} c^*.(gpr, m) & cont(c, e) \\ c.(gpr, m) & \text{otherwise.} \end{cases}$$

  - for special purpose registers $spr(x) \notin J$:

$$spr(x) \notin J \rightarrow c'.spr(x) = c.spr(x)$$

No harm is done by this simple specification, because instructions generating continue interrupts do not update the special purpose register file.

This completes the definition of what happens on activation of the $jisr(c, e)$ signal.

During a return from exception, i.e., if predicate $eret(c)$ is active but predicate $jisr(c, e)$ is not, also several things happen simultaneously:

- pc and dpc are restored resp. from the exception pc and exception dpc.

$$c'.(dpc, pc) = c.(edpc, epc)$$

- the status register is restored from the exception status register.

$$c'.sr = c.esr$$

- the mode register is restored from the exception mode register.

$$c'.mode = c.emode$$

7.1.4 Specification of Most Internal Interrupt Event Signals

Except for the fault event signals, which obviously depend on the not yet defined mechanism of address translation, we already can specify when internal event signals are to be activated.

- illegal instruction. By inspection of the tables in Sect. 4.1 we define a predicate $undefined(c)$ which is true if the current instruction $I(c)$ is not defined in the tables. Moreover we forbid in user mode i) the access of the special purpose registers by move instructions, except for *movg2s* instructions with the target register number 9 $(c.cdata)$[1], as well as ii) the execution of the *eret* instruction. Moreover we forbid in any mode explicit moves to the mode register. Thus *mode* can only be changed by interrupts and *eret*.

$$
\begin{aligned}
ill(c) \equiv\ & undefined(c) \vee \\
& mode(c) \wedge eret(c) \vee \\
& mode(c) \wedge move(c) \wedge /(movg2s(c) \wedge rd(c) = 8_5) \vee \\
& movg2s(c) \wedge rd(c) = 7_5
\end{aligned}
$$

- misalignment. Misalignment occurs during fetch if the low order bits of the instruction address are not both zero. It occurs during during memory operations if the effective address $ea(c)$ interpreted as a binary number is not a multiple of the access width $d(c)$.

$$
\begin{aligned}
malf(c) &\equiv ia(c)[1:0] \neq 00 \\
malls(c) &\equiv mop(c) \wedge d(c) \nmid \langle ea(c) \rangle
\end{aligned}
$$

- system call. This event signal is simply identical with the predicate decoding a system call instruction.

$$
sysc(c) \equiv opc(c) = 0^6 \wedge fun(c) = 001100
$$

- arithmetic overflow. This signal is taken from the overflow output of the ALU specification if the ALU is used.

$$
ovf(c) \equiv alu(c) \wedge alu.ovf(alu.a(c), alu.b(c), alu.f(c), itype(c))
$$

- page faults and general protection faults. For the time being we tie the corresponding event signals to zero.

Except for the generation of the fault signals this already completes the formal specification of the interrupt mechanism.

7.1.5 Instruction and Data Accesses Revisited

Due to misalignment on fetch an instruction access can now be void, and we redefine its read component as

$$
iacc(c).r = /malf(c)
$$

Note that we still perform a read in case of an external event. The reason for this is that *iacc* and *dacc* are only defined for the proof, and in hardware we do perform the read even in case of an external event, which in a pipelined machine we will only sample after the fetch access is completed.

---

[1] This move to the special purpose register is allowed in user mode in order to let unprivileged users set the compare data for the *cas* instruction appropriately.

This is different for data accesses, which thus need to consider the external event and can become void due to any interrupt which is not of type continue; note that this includes misalignment on load/store. We redefine the read, write and cas components of these accesses as

$$dacc(c,e).(r,w,cas) = \begin{cases} (0,0,0) & jisr(c,e) \wedge /cont(c,e) \\ (l(c),s(c),cas(c)) & \text{o.w.} \end{cases}$$

We observe that in the definition of $dacc$ and in the definition of c' in case of an interrupt, we execute the normal instruction iff there is no interrupt which is not of type continue. We capture that in a predicate

$$exec(c,e) \equiv /(jisr(c,e) \wedge /cont(c,e)).$$

The definition of $dacc$ can then be rewritten as

$$dacc(c,e).(r,w,cas) = \begin{cases} (l(c),s(c),cas(c)) & exec(c,e) \\ (0,0,0) & \text{o.w.} \end{cases}$$

Lemma 47 relating the data access of ISA with the memory update stays almost the same, except for the inclusion of the external event:

Lemma 90.
$$\ell(c'.m) = \delta_M(\ell(c.m),dacc(c,e))$$

In the proof interrupts which are not of type continue now have to be treated as an additional case.

7.2 Sequential Implementation

As in section 4.2, a non pipelined implementation with a 1 cycle memory can be gained from the ISA specification in a completely straight forward way. The existing construction is modified in three places: i) the computation of pc and dpc, ii) collecting interrupt causes, computing the $jisr$ signal and disabling the update of memory and register files in case of interrupts which are not of type continue, iii) wiring the individual inputs, outputs and clock enables of the special purpose register file as well as the special clock enables.

7.2.1 PC Environment

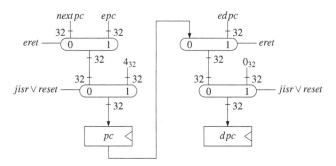

Fig. 133. Program Counters hardware

The pc environment for the two program counters pc and dpc is adapted as shown in Fig. 133. In a 1 cycle implementation these registers are always clocked.

7.2.2 Cause Processing Environment

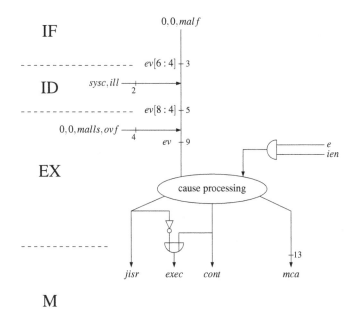

Fig. 134. Cause Processing hardware

Hardware for the collection of interrupt causes as well as the computation of the *jisr* and *cont* signal is shown in fig. 134. At the places of the page fault and general protection fault interrupts we have inserted four signals which are tied to zero.

Note that we placed the cause processing circuit above the memory stage (presently in stage $cir(EX)$). Thus we sample the external event signal e and can compute the *cont* signal above the memory stage. In the pipelined machine this permits to turn off memory operations in case of non masked external interrupts (which are of type *repeat*) *before* the access has started. Recall that once an access to the cache memory system has started, inputs at the port are required to stay constant until the access has finished. Thus we cannot simply sample e in the memory stage and abort ongoing accesses if the signal should become active after the access has started.

To efficiently compute the masked cause vector *mca* in the cause processing environment, we use the masked event vector $mev[12:0]$ which ignores masking of low-priority interrupts by high-priority interrupts

$$mev[j] = \begin{cases} e \wedge ien & j = 3 \\ ev[j] & j \neq 3 \end{cases}$$

and compute the masked cause vector by a 'find first one' circuit (numbering the signals from 0 to 12)

$$mca = 13\text{-}f1(mev)$$

Recall that the interrupt level equals an index iff the masked cause bit is raised at that index (lemma 89). Thus the interrupt level is 8 or 9 iff masked cause bits 8 or 9 are raised. This allows us to restate the definition of *cont* as follows

$$cont(c,e) \quad = \quad il(c,e) \in \{6,7\} \quad = \quad \bigvee_{j \in \{8,9\}} mca(c,e)[j]$$

According to this rephrased definition we compute

$$cont = \bigvee_{j \in \{8,9\}} mca[j]$$

$$jisr = \bigvee_{j \geq 1} mca[j]$$

$$exec = /(jisr \wedge /cont)$$

7.2.3 Accesses and Write Signals

We update the computation of signals for updating memory and the register files to

$$iacc.r = /malf$$

$$dacc.(r,w,cas) = (l \wedge exec, \ s \wedge exec, \ cas \wedge exec)$$

$$gpr.w = gprw \wedge exec$$

$$spr.w = sprw \wedge exec$$

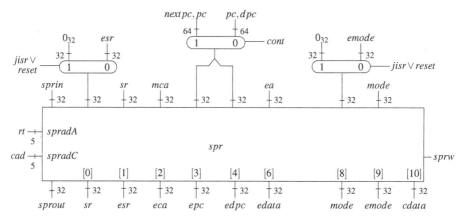

Fig. 135. Special Purpose Register file hardware

7.2.4 Special Purpose Register File

Wiring of the individual inputs of the special purpose register file follows in a straight forward way from the specification and is shown in fig. 135. Hardware signals $sr, \ldots,$ $cdata$ are defined analogous to table 12 on page 245 as

$$sr = spr.dout[0] = spr(0_5)$$

$$\vdots$$

$$cdata = spr.dout[10] = spr(10_5)$$

As individual inputs for $edpc$ and epc one uses pc and $nextpc$ in case of a continue interrupt. In all other cases one uses dpc and pc.

The individual clock enable signals $spr.ce[j]$ of the special purpose register file are generated under control of signals $jisr$ and $eret$ in a fairly obvious way.

$$spr.ce[j] = \begin{cases} jisr \vee reset \vee eret & j \in \{0,8\} \\ jisr \vee reset & j \in \{1,2,3,4,6,9\} \\ 0 & \text{otherwise} \end{cases}$$

7.2.5 Software Conditions and Correctness

Without a pipeline, self modifying code is not a problem. And with misalignment interrupts in place there is no more need to forbid misaligned memory accesses by a software condition. Thus, for the sequential implementation we are left with the single software condition SC_{ROM}, that writes do not go to the ROM portion of memory.

$$SC_{ROM}(c) \leftrightarrow write(c) \rightarrow \langle ea(c) \rangle + d(c) \geq 2^{r+3}$$

Due to the existence of the external inputs $e, reset$ in hardware and e in ISA, we have to consider the sequence of these signals. Because we assume $reset^{-1} = 1$ and $reset^t = 0$ for $t \geq 0$, we can define the resulting hardware and ISA computations (h^t) and (c^t) based only on a sequence of external interrupts (e^t) as

$$h^{t+1} = \begin{cases} \delta_H(h^t, (e^t, 1)) & t = -1 \\ \delta_H(h^t, (e^t, 0)) & t \geq 0 \end{cases}$$

$$c^{t+1} = \delta_{isa}(c^t, e^t)$$

Analogous to section 4.2 the correctness theorem we are aiming at is

Lemma 91. *There is an initial configuration c^0 satisfying*

$$sim(h^0, c^0)$$

Furthermore, if the computation (c^i) with initial configuration c^0 and external event sequence (e^i) satisfies the single software condition

$$\forall i.\ SC_{ROM}(c^i)$$

then for all $t > 0$

$$sim(h^t, c^t)$$

At first glance the previous correctness proof seems to generalize in a completely trivial way. At the start of the induction $(t = 0)$ a tiny extra proof effort is required, because one has to guarantee that registers sr, mca, and $mode$ are properly initialized after $reset$. This is the case, because the construction from fig. 135 guarantees for the individual inputs of these registers

$$reset \rightarrow spr.din[0][0] = 0\ \wedge$$
$$spr.din[2][0] = 1\ \wedge$$
$$spr.din[8][0] = 0$$

For the remainder of the correctness proof and in particular during any induction step on hardware cycles t with $t > 0$ we can assume the reset signal to be off. For the induction step we presented in section 4.2 two proofs, and somewhat unexpectedly the first proof happens to fall completely apart. There we argued for *all* hardware signals X:

$$sim(h, c) \rightarrow X(h) = X(c)$$

But in case of a misaligned fetch this already wrong for the instruction:

$$sim(h, c) \wedge malf(c) \nrightarrow I(h) = I(c)$$

So now we are obviously forced to argue that in this case no harm is done because the instruction fetched is not used anyway. A similar situation arises for the load result in case of a misaligned read from memory. In contrast the second correctness proof — the one hinging on the pipeline stage correctness lemmas — happens to generalize if we reformulate them in the appropriate way. The following fixes are necessary:

U	$in(U)$	$out(U)$
$cir(IF)$	ia, imout	iacc, I, ev[6:4]
$cir(ID)$	I, A, B, S, pcs, mode, epcs, ev[6:4]	nextpcs, linkad, decoder.out, ev[8:4]
$cir(EX)$	i2ex, con, linkad, A, B, S, ev[8:4], ien, e	C, dmin, ea, bw, br, con, mca, jisr, cont, exec
$cir(M)$	C, con, ea, dmin, bw, br, cdata, dmout, mca, jisr, exec	dacc, C, ea.o, con, exec
$cir(WB)$	C, ea.o, con	gprin, con

Table 14. groups U of circuits with their input and output signals

- Individual outputs of the special purpose register file become inputs of circuits stages higher up in the pipeline, and this in turn will require extra forwarding circuits (or other measures) in the pipelined implementation. This results in a new list of input and output signals for the circuit stages shown in table 14.
- The cause processing circuit is now part of circuit stage $cir(EX)$, which now has an external input e. Thus several signals X of ISA or of hardware now depend on e or $(e, reset)$, and therefore we have to write them as $X(c, e)$ resp. $X(h, (e, reset))$. Since in hardware and the correctness proof *reset* is zero most of the time, we define a shorthand

$$X(h, e) = X(h, (e, 0))$$

- In the presence of interrupts some signals are not used. With a misalignment on fetch instruction (register) I and all functions derived from it are not used. With a repeat interrupt the memory output and the input to the general purpose register file are not used. With *malls* the byte-write and byte-read signals bw and br are not used; $dmin$ is not used in the intuitive sense either, but as the hardware will compute it correctly we can define it as used anyway. This results in the new definition of *used* signals shown in table 15 . In the presence of page faults and general protection faults even more bookkeeping of this kind will become necessary in later chapters.
- For the sake of uniform notation when we generalize over ISA signals X we write $X(c, e)$ even if e is not used in the definition of all signals that X ranges over, with the obvious meaning

$$X(c, e) = X(c)$$

For example, let Z be some set of signals including signal ia

$$Z = \{\ldots, ia, \ldots\}$$

Even though e is not used by signal ia we write

$$\forall X \in Z. \ X(c, e) = X(h, e)$$

In more specialized contexts we continue to drop the e if it is not used, so we will still write

$$ia(c)$$

X	$used[X](c,e)$
ev[4], ien, mca, jisr, mode, cont, exec, ia, iacc, pcs, nextpc	1
imout, I, decoder.out, con, linkad, ev[8:5]	$/malf(c)$
emode, epcs	$/malf(c) \wedge eret(c)$
A	$/malf(c) \wedge (alur(c) \vee su(c) \wedge fun(c)[2] \vee cas(c)$ $\vee jr(c) \vee jalr(c) \vee itype(c) \wedge /lui(c))$
B	$/malf(c) \wedge (movg2s(c) \vee write(c) \vee beq(c) \vee bne(c)$ $\vee su(c) \vee alur(c))$
S	$/malf(c) \wedge movs2g(c)$
C	$/malf(c) \wedge sprw(c) \vee gprw(c) \wedge /read(c)$
ea	$/malf(c) \wedge mop(c)$
bw, br	$/malf(c) \wedge /malls(c) \wedge mop(c)$
dmin, dacc	$/malf(c) \wedge write(c)$
dmout	$exec(c,e) \wedge read(c)$
gprin	$exec(c,e) \wedge gprw(c)$

Table 15. Signals X used in the instructions executed in ISA configuration c.

With these augmented definitions we first regain the circuit stage correctness lemmas

Lemma 92. *Suppose for output signal Y of $cir(k)$ all relevant inputs of the non-pipelined processor with delayed pc and interrupts which are used in configuration c are correct*

$$\forall X \in bus_{cir(k)}^{in}(Y). \; used[X](c,e) \quad \rightarrow \quad X(h,e) = X(c,e)$$

Then Y is correct if it is used

$$used[Y](c,e) \quad \rightarrow \quad \begin{cases} Y(h,e) = Y(c,e) & Y \neq dacc \\ Y(h,e) \equiv Y(c,e) & Y = dacc \end{cases}$$

We then regain the register stage correctness lemmas

Lemma 93. *If the content of $R \in \{pc, dpc, gpr, spr\}$ is correct for ISA configuration c*

$$h.R = c.R$$

and its input signals, which are used are correct for ISA configuration c

$$\forall X \in in(R). \; used[X](c,e) \quad \rightarrow \quad X(h,e) = X(c,e)$$

then the register content is correct after the step for the ISA configuration c'

$$h'.R = c'.R$$

Finally we regain the memory correctness lemma (proven with lemma 90)

Lemma 94. *If the content of the memory is correct for ISA configuration c*

$$h.m = \ell(c.m)$$

and the data access is correct for ISA configuration c

$$dacc(h,e) \equiv dacc(c,e)$$

then the memory is correct after the step for the ISA configuration c'

$$h'.m = \ell(c'.m)$$

The induction step of the processor correctness proof then proceeds along the lines of the proof of lemma 55. Data memory output is meaningless in case of an interrupt which is not of type continue. Thus lemma 48 becomes

Lemma 95.

$$exec(c,e) \wedge read(c,e) \to dmout(h,e) = dmout(c,e)$$

Note that the data memory output is only used in case of a read which is executed

$$used[dmout](c,e) = exec(c,e) \wedge read(c,e).$$

Thus the above lemma can be restated as

Lemma 96.
$$used[dmout](c,e) \to dmout(h,e) = dmout(c,e)$$

7.3 Pipelining a Processor With Interrupts

Pipelining interrupts adds considerable complexity to the design and correctness proof of the system. Recall that in the basic pipelined processor, the program counter is updated on ue_{ID}, i.e., when an instruction in the ID circuit stage is clocked down. This was the earliest point in the pipeline where the next pc was available; this forced us to introduce a delayed pc to compensate the fact that an instruction could pass the IF stage without updating the pc. In the processor with interrupts, the next pc depends on the presence and type of interrupts. The presence of interrupts can be known as late as the execute stage, when the external event is sampled; the return type of the highest priority interrupt is not known before the memory stage, where the cause processing environment resides. In other words, the next program counter is not always fully available until the memory stage. While one could move the program counters down in the pipeline into the memory register stage, this would introduce two additional delay slots for a five-stage pipeline, and four additional delay slots for the seven-stage pipeline that we will use when we introduce address translation.

Such a huge number of delay slots is unacceptable, since they often have to be filled with NOPs and thus slow down program execution.

Instead, we continue to write the program counter when an instruction leaves the *ID* stage; as a consequence we sometimes temporarily write wrong values into the program counter registers. In the memory stage we then compute the correct next pc and compare. If we happened to write the correct value — which we always do in the absence of interrupts — everything is fine. If we wrote an incorrect value due to an interrupt, we cover our tracks by rolling back instructions that used the incorrect program counter, i.e., the instructions behind the instruction that wrote the incorrect pc.

To implement this, we add in section 7.4 nontrivial rollback support to our stall engine. A naive hardware implementation of a rollback would simply clear full bits. Unfortunately with a cache memory system in place this does not work: accesses to the CMS, that have already started, have to be completed, and the corresponding memory requests have to be kept stable. Therefore we split roll backs in up to two phases: i) in case a memory access has to be completed a *rollback pending* bit *rbp* is activated. ii) a full bit is cleared only when its rollback pending bit is off. The results of memory operations, which have been completed in this way, can of course be discarded.

Rollbacks will also be used for the implementation of *eret* instructions, which like interrupts change the *dpc* and thus may cause the next instruction to fetch from an incorrect address.

In the correctness proof, we now have to deal with the fact that 1) visible pc registers sometimes have incorrect values, and 2) invisible registers of instructions that were fetched using an incorrect pc are also incorrect. Following [Krö01] we treat this as *misspeculation*: when writing the program counters in circuit stage *ID*, we speculate that the instruction is not interrupted (for the sake of simplicity, we will speculate this even in case we already have detected misalignment interrupts). When the misspeculation is detected in the memory stage, i.e., we compute $jisr = 1$, we trigger rollback. In the pipeline correctness statement, we then track instructions that misspeculated, and do not guarantee anything for visible or invisible registers coupled with instructions after the misspeculating instruction.

7.4 Stalling, Rollback and Pipe Drain

As mentioned before, following [Krö01] we treat the discovery of a regular interrupt as a case of (implicit) *misspeculation*: we speculated that the instruction would not be interrupted by fetching the following instructions and starting their executions, and this turned out to be wrong. However, we slightly deviate from the course of action taken in [Krö01]: instead of rolling back the interrupted instruction i and recomputing the next program counters when instruction i is again in circuit stage *ID*, we only roll back the instructions $i' > i$ *behind i* and correct the program counters when instruction i is clocked into register stage *M*. As in [Krö01] the rollback mechanism will be triggered by misspeculation signals

$$misspec_n$$

indicating that instructions in circuit stage $cir(n-1)$ and all stages above should be rolled back.

In the processor correctness proof one should not attempt to prove anything about stages containing misspeculated data. In [Krö01] such stages are tracked by a *speculation function* Σ. Here we track instead – with a predicate $c(i)^t$ – for any cycle t the ISA instructions i in the pipeline which will not be rolled back in the future. We call such ISA instructions i *committed* in cycle t and only prove correctness for hardware stages containing committed instructions. The liveness proof in section 7.9 will show that all instructions are eventually committed.

Recall that we introduce a new stall engine with pending rollbacks because

- memory accesses can take more than one cycle.
- accesses that have already started at the discovery of a regular interrupt have to be completed and
- while these accesses complete, the input data for theses accesses have to be stable.

Presently this concerns only the instruction cache. In [Bey05] and [BJK$^+$03] the stabilization of input data for accesses to this cache was already handled by introduction of a *stabilizer circuit* which latches the program counters of such accesses. In spite of the fact that the stabilizer increases hardware cost and possibly cycle time we will use it in this chapter, because it simplifies here both the hardware and the correctness proof. In the machine with address translation of chapter 9 the stabilizer is not needed because the latching is already done by a register in the memory management unit (MMU) for the instruction memory.

This is not the end of the problems. With a full pipeline stage 1 we fetch in the pipelined machine with pc instead of dpc as in the sequential reference machine. The proof that this works hinges on the fact that

$$dpc_\sigma^{i+1} = pc_\sigma^i \tag{18}$$

i.e., that dpc holds indeed the delayed pc. In a machine without interrupts and exception returns this is always true. But at *jisr* of *eret* both pc and dpc are updated simultaneously in the ISA, which of course violates eq. (18). Consequently, after *jisr* or at *eret* we have to fetch in the pipelined machine from dpc. After *jisr* we get this for free because the instruction in stage 1 is rolled back resulting in $full_1 = 0$ and $ima = dpc$, but for *eret* something needs to be done.

In the formally verified machine from [Bey05] and [BJK$^+$03] this problem was handled by fetching for *eret* instructions directly form the *edpc* in the special purpose register file (fig. 4.8 in [Bey05]). In contrast upon decoding an *eret* instruction in circuit stage $cir(ID)$ by signal $eret(ID)$ we will do here two things:

- we will roll back the instruction above the decode stage. Presently this affects only circuit stage 1. It will not clear full bits and has only the side effect of completing ongoing (and misspeculated) instruction cache accesses using data from the stabilizer. In chapter 9 the corresponding rollback is more serious: there will be a new *instruction translate* stage *IT* above the instruction fetch state. Thus upon detection of *eret* — then in circuit stage $cir(3)$ — a full rollback of instructions in circuit stage $cir(2)$ and above will have to be implemented.

- we will drain the pipe *behind eret* instructions. This is achieved by activating haz_1 as long as the instruction is in any stage of the pipe. As page fault handlers end with the *eret* instruction this has the desirable side effect that any writes executed before the *eret* will have been executed before the first instruction of the user is executed, which simplifies the software condition for self modifying code: rather than counting instructions and thus exposing the pipeline depth, we will simply require in section 7.6.1 that between writing to an address and fetching from that address, the software has to execute an *eret* instruction. It will also allow us to show that the instruction following *eret* is fetched with $full_1 = 0$.

7.4.1 Stall Engine and Scheduling Functions with Rollbacks and Stabilized Full Bits

Full bit $full[0]$ is always raised and the other full bits are all zero after reset.

$$full[0] = 1$$
$$full[1:4]^0 = 0^4$$

For stages k we introduce misspeculation signals $misspec_k$ indicating that signals in *circuit* stage k and above might be misspeculated. As outlined above there will be two possible causes of misspeculation:

- an interrupt. It is signaled by $jisr \in cir(M) = cir(4)$. The interrupted instruction in the invisible registers of $reg(3)$ is not rolled back. Rollback starts with the instruction currently in circuit stage $cir(3)$. Thus this will affect signal

$$misspec_3$$

- an *eret* instruction in the decode stage. It is signaled by the instruction decoder output $eret(ID)$ in circuit stage $cir(ID) = cir(2)$. Rollback affects only the instruction currently in circuit stage $cir(1)$. Thus this will affect signal

$$misspec_1$$

All other misspeculation signals will be set to 0 in this pipeline

$$k \notin \{1,3\} \rightarrow misspec_k = 0$$

Active misspeculation signals $misspec_k$ activate rollback request signals rbr_j for all circuit stages $j \le k$

$$rbr_6 = 0$$
$$rbr_j = rbr_{j+1} \lor misspec_j \quad \text{for} \quad j < 5.$$

For memory where all accesses take a single cycle the new stall engine would be

$$stall_5 = haz_5$$
$$stall_k = full_{k-1} \wedge (stall_{k+1} \vee haz_k)$$
$$ue_k = full_{k-1} \wedge /stall_k \wedge /rbr_k$$
$$full'_k = (stall_{k+1} \vee ue_k) \wedge /rbr_{k+1}.$$

For memory — or later MMUs — with multi-cycle accesses we cannot always rollback immediately. A *rollback hazard* for circuit stage k is signaled by $rhaz_k$. This signal is active if a memory access — or later an access to a memory management unit — is in progress in circuit stage k. In the absence of rollback requests it is ignored. Presently we have no MMUs, stage 4 is never rolled back, and we simply set

$$rhaz_k = \begin{cases} ica.mbusy & k = 1 \\ 0 & \text{otherwise} \end{cases}$$

In general we require the *operating condition* that the rollback hazard $rhaz_k$ for circuit stage k is only on if the register stage $reg(k-1)$ above is full and if the cause of the rollback hazard would also generate an ordinary hazard.

$$rhaz_k \rightarrow full_{k-1} \wedge haz_k$$

i.e., a circuit stage that is to be rolled back can never be clocked down or updated from above.

If a rollback request rbr_{k+1} for circuit stage $k+1$ cannot be executed immediately due to a rollback hazard, we set for the register stage $reg(k)$ *above* a rollback pending bit rbp_k which stays on as long as the hazard persists. The instruction in circuit stage $k+1$ currently resides in the invisible registers of register stage k, and is only rolled back in the absence of a rollback hazard for the circuit stage $cir(k+1)$ below.

$$rbp'_k = (rbr_{k+1} \vee rbp_k) \wedge rhaz_{k+1}$$
$$rollback_k = (rbr_{k+1} \vee rbp_k) \wedge /rhaz_{k+1}$$

After reset, there are not pending rollbacks

$$rbp_k^0 = 0$$

Requested rollbacks for circuit stage k or pending rollbacks of the register stage $reg(k-1)$ feeding this circuit stage prevent the update of register stage $reg(k)$ *below*. Thus the new update enable signals are

$$ue_k = full_{k-1} \wedge /stall_k \wedge /rbr_k \wedge /rbp_{k-1}$$

Observe that an instruction which is rolled back is never clocked into the next register stage

$$ue_k \rightarrow /rollback_{k-1}$$

but the rollback engine allows us to clock a new instruction into a stage which is rolled back

$$ue_k \nrightarrow /rollback_k$$

This can not happen yet in our five-stage pipeline, but after the introduction of MMUs a pending rollback request in one of the lower stages can be executed and in the same cycle a new instruction can be clocked into that register stage.

In the absence of a rollback hazard we allow a stage to be rolled back even if the hazard signals for the stage are active. Consequently we clear the full bits of a rolled back register stage even if it is stalled and redefine

$$full_k' = stall_{k+1} \wedge /rollback_k \vee ue_k$$

We summarize the new definitions. Let K be the maximal stage number in the machine under consideration. Presently, we have $K = 5$.

$$
\begin{aligned}
stall_{K+1} &= 0 \\
rbr_{K+1} &= 0 \\
stall_k &= full_{k-1} \wedge (stall_{k+1} \vee haz_k) \\
rbr_k &= rbr_{k+1} \vee misspec_k \\
rollback_k &= (rbr_{k+1} \vee rbp_k) \wedge /rhaz_{k+1} \\
rbp_k' &= (rbr_{k+1} \vee rbp_k) \wedge rhaz_{k+1} \\
ue_k &= full_{k-1} \wedge /stall_k \wedge /rbr_k \wedge /rbp_{k-1} \\
full_k' &= stall_{k+1} \wedge /rollback_k \vee ue_k
\end{aligned}
$$

Operating condition:

$$rhaz_k \quad \rightarrow \quad full_{k-1} \wedge haz_k \tag{19}$$

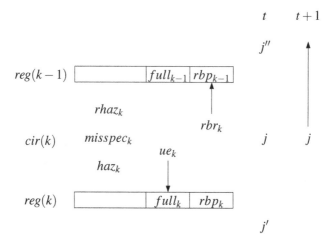

Fig. 136. Illustration of the rollback mechanism in cycle t. In case k is the lowest stage with a rollback request and $j = I_k$, then execution is rolled back to the state before execution of instruction j.

These definitions are illustrated in fig. 136. Signals $misspec_k, haz_k, ue_k, rbr_k$ and $rhaz_k$ all belong to circuit stage k. Bits $full_{k-1}$ and rbp_{k-1} belong to register stage $reg(k-1)$, which contains the signals $X(c^j)$ of instruction $j = I_k$. Signal $rhaz_k$ influences the computation of the rollback pending bit rbp_{k-1} in the register stage $reg(k-1)$. Activation of ue_k sets the full bit $full_k$ of the register stage $reg(k)$ *below*.

Scheduling functions are redefined in the following way:

- I_k is already rolled back by the corresponding rollback *request* signals rbr_k.
- the corresponding full bits $full_k$ are only cleared by the rollback signals $rollback_k$ after memory accesses in the circuit stage below have completed.

We previously had lemmas which stated that the scheduling function increases at full stages. Because I_k is rolled back before the full bits are cleared, the lemma is no longer directly true. Instead, we introduce *real full bits* or true full bits, which are full bits that are not pending a rollback, i.e., which are not going to be cleared

$$rfull_k \; = \; full_k \wedge /rbp_k$$

We will later show that the scheduling function increases at really full stages.

Observe that the expression $rbr_{k+1} \vee rbp_k$ occurs several times in the definitions above. Both signals indicate that a rollback should be executed as soon as possible in stage k. We introduce the shorthand

$$rbs_k \; = \; rbr_{k+1} \vee rbp_k$$

for *rollback signal*.

With these definitions the definition of update enable can be rephrased as

$$ue_k = full_{k-1} \wedge /stall_k \wedge /rbr_k \wedge /rbp_{k-1}$$
$$= full_{k-1} \wedge /rbp_{k-1} \wedge /stall_k \wedge /rbr_k$$
$$= rfull_{k-1} \wedge /stall_k \wedge /rbr_k \tag{20}$$

and similarly one can simplify the definitions of rollback and pending rollback signals

$$rollback_k = rbs_k \wedge /rhaz_{k+1} \tag{21}$$
$$rbp'_k = rbs_k \wedge rhaz_{k+1} \tag{22}$$

We number these simplified definitions for future reference.

We denote the largest stage number with an active rollback request in cycle t by

$$R^t = \max\left\{ k \mid rbr^t_k \right\}$$

This, of course, can be rewritten as a ghost signal

$$R = \max\left\{ k \mid rbr_k \right\}$$

Note that this is only a definition when some stage has a rollback request. When there is a rollback request, stage R must have a misspeculation signal.

Lemma 97.

$$rbr_k \quad \rightarrow \quad misspec_R$$

Proof. By definition of R we have

$$rbr_R \wedge /rbr_{R+1}$$

and the claim follows by definition of rbr_R

$$misspec_R$$

$\square$

If $k = R$ and $j = I_k$ is the index of the instruction whose values are computed by circuit stage $cir(k)$, then after the rollback triggered by rbr_k circuit stage $cir(k)$ and all stages above are rolled back.

After the rollback request, circuit stage $cir(k)$ and all stages above must eventually recompute the values belonging to the instruction j which was rolled back. Scheduling functions must indicate that we are before execution of instruction j. Therefore in the next cycle the scheduling functions of stage k and all stages above are set to j. Guided by this intuition we define

$$\forall k : I^0_k = 0$$

$$I'_k = \begin{cases} I_1 + 1 & k = 1 \wedge ue_1 \\ I_{k-1} & k > 1 \wedge ue_k \\ I_R & rbr_k \\ I_k & \text{otherwise.} \end{cases}$$

This is well defined because

$$rbr_k \to /ue_k$$

Full bits $full_k$ can now be on in two situations:

- $rbp_k = 0$, i.e., without the corresponding rollback pending. This is a *real full bit*, as we know it.
- $rbp_k = 1$, i.e., with the corresponding rollback pending, This is a *stabilized full bit*, which is only kept on in order to stabilize request signals of ongoing requests in the circuit stage below.

In forwarding circuits we will only use data from stages with true full bits.

7.4.2 Properties of the New Stall Engine

After a register stage is updated, it does not have a pending rollback.

Lemma 98.

$$ue_k \to /rbp'_k$$

Proof. We conclude successively from ue_k

$$full_{k-1} \wedge /stall_k, /haz_k, /rhaz_k, /rbp'_k$$

$\square$

A rollback signal either immediately causes a rollback or creates a pending rollback, and this is the only way to cause rollbacks and pending rollbacks.

Lemma 99.

$$rollback_k \vee rbp'_k = rbs_k$$

Proof. Follows from the simplified definition of *rollback* and *rbp'* (eqs. (21) and (22)) and simple boolean logic

$$
\begin{aligned}
rollback_k \vee rbp'_k &= rbs_k \wedge /rhaz_{k+1} \vee rbs_k \wedge rhaz_{k+1} \\
&= rbs_k
\end{aligned}
$$

$\square$

The real full bit in the next cycle can be defined analogously to the full bit. While a full bit is killed by *rollback*, the real full bit is killed by *rbs*.

Lemma 100.

$$rfull'_k = stall_{k+1} \wedge /rbs_k \vee ue_k$$

Proof. Using simple boolean logic we obtain

$$
\begin{aligned}
rfull'_k &= full'_k \wedge /rbp'_k \\
&= (stall_{k+1} \wedge /rollback_k \vee ue_k) \wedge /rbp'_k \\
&= stall_{k+1} \wedge /rollback_k \wedge /rbp'_k \vee ue_k \wedge /rbp'_k \\
&= stall_{k+1} \wedge /(rollback_k \vee rbp'_k) \vee ue_k \wedge /rbp'_k
\end{aligned}
$$

The claim now follows with lemmas 98 and 99

$$
rfull'_k = stall_{k+1} \wedge /rbs_k \vee ue_k
$$

$\square$

We now observe a few simple properties:

Lemma 101. *After a rollback request for circuit stage $k > 1$ the register stage above is not really full*

$$
rbr_k \rightarrow /rfull'_{k-1}
$$

Proof. From rbr_k we conclude successively

$$
rbs_{k-1}, \ rbr_{k-1}, \ /ue_{k-1}
$$

and the claim follows from lemma 100. $\square$

Lemma 102. *If circuit stage k is stalled, then the register stage above is not updated.*

$$
stall_k \rightarrow /ue_{k-1}
$$

Proof. By case split on $full_{k-2}$.

$/full_{k-2}$: then $/ue_{k-1}$ follows immediately.
$full_{k-2}$: then $stall_{k-1}$ and hence $/ue_{k-1}$.

$\square$

Lemma 103. *If circuit stage k has a hazard, then will not clock down*

$$
haz_k \rightarrow /ue_k
$$

Proof. By case split on $full_{k-1}$

- $/full_{k-1}$: then $/ue_k$ follows immediately.
- $full_{k-1}$: then $stall_k$ and hence $/ue_k$.

$\square$

We show that scheduling functions increase at real full bits.

Lemma 104.

$$
I_{k-1} = I_k + rfull_{k-1}
$$

To do that we now define the pipeline to be well-formed if the scheduling function differs at real full stages:

$$wf \equiv \forall k > 1. \quad I_{k-1} = I_k + rfull_{k-1}$$

In a well-formed pipeline, as long as the instruction in stage k does not have a rollback request, the scheduling function in stage k is increased on update enable.

Lemma 105.

$$wf \wedge /rbr_k \quad \rightarrow \quad I'_k = I_k + ue_k$$

Proof. For circuit stage $k = 1$ this follows directly from the definition. For circuit stages $k > 1$ we have by definition of I'_k and wf

$$I'_k = \begin{cases} I_{k-1} & ue_k \\ I_k & /ue_k \end{cases}$$

$$= \begin{cases} I_k + rfull_{k-1} & ue_k \\ I_k & /ue_k. \end{cases}$$

Since by the simplified definition of ue_k (eq. (20))

$$ue_k \rightarrow rfull_{k-1}$$

this is the same as

$$I'_k = \begin{cases} I_k + 1 & ue_k \\ I_k & /ue_k. \end{cases}$$

$$= I_k + ue_k.$$

$\square$

The same is true if the instruction in stage $k + 1$ does not have a rollback request.

Lemma 106.

$$wf \wedge /rbr_{k+1} \quad \rightarrow \quad I'_k = I_k + ue_k$$

Proof. We distinguish two cases.

rbr_k: In this case from $/rbr_{k+1}$ we conclude

$$R = k$$

and by definition

$$I'_k = I_R = I_k.$$

The claim now follows from

$$ue_k = 0.$$

$/rbr_k$: The claim is lemma 105.

$\square$

We now prove that well-formedness is an invariant.

Lemma 107.
$$wf \rightarrow wf'$$

Proof. We have to show for $k > 0$

$$I'_{k-1} = I'_k + rfull'_{k-1} \tag{23}$$

We distinguish two cases.

rbr_k: In this case also rbr_{k-1} and

$$I'_{k-1} = I'_k = I_R,$$

and we also obtain from lemma 101

$$/rfull'_{k-1}$$

and the claim follows.

$/rbr_k$: We rewrite with lemmas 105 and 106 in the claim (eq. (23)) to obtain

$$I_{k-1} + ue_{k-1} = I_k + ue_k + rfull'_{k-1}$$

From well-formedness we can rewrite I_{k-1} as $I_k + rfull_{k-1}$ and obtain

$$I_k + rfull_{k-1} + ue_{k-1} = I_k + ue_k + rfull'_{k-1}$$

We drop I_k at both sides

$$rfull_{k-1} + ue_{k-1} = ue_k + rfull'_{k-1}$$

We rewrite the claim with lemma 100 to

$$rfull_{k-1} + ue_{k-1} = ue_k + (stall_k \wedge /rbs_{k-1} \vee ue_{k-1})$$

From lemma 102 we know that $stall_k$ and ue_{k-1} can never be on at the same time and we can thus replace $\vee$ by $+$

$$rfull_{k-1} + ue_{k-1} = ue_k + (stall_k \wedge /rbs_{k-1} + ue_{k-1})$$

We drop ue_{k-1} on both sides

$$rfull_{k-1} = ue_k + stall_k \wedge /rbs_{k-1}$$

We now distinguish whether the circuit stage was stalled or not.

$stall_k$: By definition of ue_k we obtain $/ue_k$ and the claim reduces to

$$rfull_{k-1} = /rbs_{k-1}$$

From $stall_k$ we obtain $full_{k-1}$ and in the absence of a rollback request the claim follows from the definition of $rfull$ and the definition of rbs_{k-1}

$$\begin{aligned}
rfull_{k-1} &= full_{k-1} \wedge /rbp_{k-1} \\
&= /rbp_{k-1} \\
&= /rbp_{k-1} \wedge /rbr_k \\
&= /rbs_{k-1}
\end{aligned}$$

$/stall_k$: In this case the claim reduces to

$$rfull_{k-1} = ue_k$$

which in the absence of stall and rollback requests follows from the simplified definition of ue_k (eq. (20))

$$rfull_{k-1} = rfull_{k-1} \wedge /stall_k \wedge /rbr_k = ue_k$$

□

This also completes the proof of lemma 104. A simple induction gives for $k < \hat{k}$:

$$I_k = I_{\hat{k}} + \sum_{j=\hat{k}-1}^{k} rfull_j$$

A consequence about the monotonicity of the scheduling functions in k is stated in

Lemma 108. *Let $k < \hat{k}$:*

- $$I_{\hat{k}} \leq I_k$$
- $$(\exists j \in [k : \hat{k}).rfull_j) \rightarrow I_{\hat{k}} < I_k$$

The first part can be generalized to the case $k = \hat{k}$, since in that case scheduling functions are obviously equal

Lemma 109.

$$k \leq \hat{k} \quad \rightarrow \quad I_{\hat{k}} \leq I_k$$

We can deduce a similar lemma in the opposite direction

Lemma 110.

$$I_k \leq I_{\hat{k}} \wedge rfull_{\hat{k}-1} \quad \rightarrow \quad \hat{k} \leq k$$

Applying this twice yields

Lemma 111.

$$I_k = I_{\hat{k}} \wedge rfull_{\hat{k}-1} \wedge rfull_{k-1} \quad \rightarrow \quad \hat{k} = k$$

Since scheduling functions differ by at most one, every instruction between the scheduling functions of two stages can be found in a stage between the two stages.

Lemma 112.

$$I_k \leq i < I_{\hat{k}} \quad \rightarrow \quad \exists m.\ I_m = i \wedge rfull_{m-1} \wedge k \geq m > \hat{k}$$

Proof. Let m be the earliest stage with instruction at most i

$$m = \min\{m \mid I_m \leq i\}$$

Since k is such a stage, m exists and is at most k

$$k \geq m \tag{24}$$

By contraposition of lemma 109 with $k := m$ we obtain from $I_m \leq i < I_{\hat{k}}$

$$m > \hat{k} \tag{25}$$

By definition of m and the fact that there are stages above m we have

$$I_{m-1} > i$$

and thus

$$I_{m-1} \neq I_m$$

From well-formedness we obtain

$$I_{m-1} = I_m + rfull_{m-1} \neq I_m$$

and thus

$$rfull_{m-1} = 1 \tag{26}$$

From $I_m \leq i$ and $I_{m-1} = I_m + 1 > i$ we conclude

$$I_m = i \tag{27}$$

The claim is now the combination of eqs. (24) to (27). □

The next two lemmas concern the conservation of true full bits.

Lemma 113. *A stage that is updated has afterwards a true full bit.*

$$ue_k \rightarrow rfull'_k$$

Proof. Follows from lemma 100. □

Lemma 114. *In stages k which are not clocked into the next stage and have no roll-back request, true full bits are preserved. Moreover such stages are not overwritten.*

$$/rbr_{k+1} \wedge /ue_{k+1} \wedge rfull_k \quad \rightarrow \quad rfull'_k \wedge /ue_k$$

Proof. From $rfull_k$ and $/rbr_{k+1}$ we obtain successively

$$full_k \wedge /rbp_k, \ /rbs_k$$

and from $/ue_{k+1}$, $rfull_k$, and $/rbr_{k+1}$ we obtain with the simplified definition of ue_{k+1} (eq. (20))

$$stall_{k+1}$$

With lemma 100 we obtain the first claim

$$rfull'_k = stall_{k+1} \wedge /rbs_k \vee \ldots = 1$$

and lemma 102 is the second claim. $\qquad\square$

We show that in the pipeline instructions cannot appear out of the blue.

Lemma 115. *Suppose instruction i is in cycle t + 1 in a stage k + 1 > 2 with a true full bit above, i.e.*

$$k > 1 \wedge i = I'_{k+1} \wedge rfull'_k$$

Then — depending on ue_k — this instruction was in the previous cycle in stage $k + 1$ or k and this stage had a true full bit.

$$/ue_{k+1} \wedge /ue_k \wedge rfull_k \wedge i = I_{k+1}$$
$$\vee \ ue_k \wedge rfull_{k-1} \wedge i = I_k$$

Proof. We first handle the case

$$ue_k$$

which with the simplified definition of ue_k (eq. (20)) and the definition of I'_k imme-diately implies

$$rfull_{k-1} \wedge I'_k = I_{k-1}$$

Thus

$$I'_k = I_{k-1} \quad \text{and} \quad rfull'_k = 1 = rfull_{k-1}$$

and with two applications of lemma 104 the claim follows

$$i = I'_{k+1} \stackrel{\text{L 104}}{=} I'_k - rfull'_k = I_{k-1} - rfull_{k-1} \stackrel{\text{L 104}}{=} I_k$$

Now assume

$$/ue_k$$

From lemma 100 and $rfull'_k$ we conclude successively

$$
\begin{array}{ll}
stall_{k+1} \wedge /rbs_k, & \text{L 100} \\
full_k, & \text{from } stall_{k+1} \\
/rbp_k, & \text{from } /rbs_k \\
rfull_k, & \text{from } full_k, /rbp_k \\
/rbr_{k+1}, & \text{from } /rbs_k \\
/ue_{k+1} & \text{from } stall_{k+1} \text{ and eq. (20)}
\end{array}
$$

From $/ue_k$ we conclude with the definition of I'_k

$$
I'_k = \begin{cases} I_R & rbr_k \\ I_k & \text{otherwise} \end{cases}
$$
$$
= I_k
$$

because

$$
rbr_k \wedge /rbr_{k+1} \to k = R
$$

We thus have

$$
I'_k = I_k \quad \text{and} \quad rfull'_k = 1 = rfull_k
$$

and with two applications of lemma 104 the claim follows

$$
i = I'_{k+1} \stackrel{\text{L 104}}{=} I'_k - rfull'_k = I_k - rfull_k \stackrel{\text{L 104}}{=} I_{k+1}
$$

$\square$

The following lemma shows, that instructions with true full bits are not overwritten.

Lemma 116. *If a stage other than the bottom stage with a true full bit is updated, then the stage below it is updated.*

$$
k < K-1 \wedge rfull_k \wedge ue_k \to ue_{k+1}
$$

Proof. From ue_k we get successively

$$
full_{k-1}, /stall_k, /stall_{k+1}
$$

and also

$$
/rbr_k, /rbr_{k+1}
$$

and the claim follows from the simplified definition of ue_{k+1} (eq. (20)).

$\square$

7.4.3 Liveness and Correctness in the Presence of Rollback

In previous chapters, it was easy to show that the processor was live: scheduling functions I_k were monotonically increasing, and it sufficed to show that each individual stage eventually generates an update enable signal. With the new stall engine, instructions can be rolled back, and liveness is a bit harder to show.

Furthermore, in the presence of misspeculation, the old pipeline invariant which couples registers in each stage to an abstract ISA computation will no longer work: sometimes, speculating instructions will write wrong values into registers, breaking the invariant.

We introduce a technology that deals with both problems with one clean definition: instead of looking at all instructions in the pipeline, we will only look at instructions that will not be rolled back in the future. Note that during a rollback request, instruction I_R and all instructions behind it are rolled back. We thus say an instruction i is *committed* in cycle t when it is not rolled back in any cycle $u \geq t$ and write

$$c(i)^t = \forall u \geq t, k.\ rbr_k^u \to I_{R^u}^u > i$$

Another way to look at committed instructions, which will often be much more useful for us due to its compact representation, is to say that an instruction is committed if it is not rolled back in the current cycle and stays committed in the next cycle.

Lemma 117.

$$c(i) \equiv (\forall k.\ rbr_k \to I_R > i) \wedge c(i)'$$

Proof. We add the missing indices and the claim follows by definition of $c(i)$

$$\begin{aligned}
c(i)^t &\equiv (\forall k.\ rbr_k^t \to I_R^t > i) \wedge c(i)^{t+1} \\
&\equiv (\forall k.\ rbr_k^t \to I_R^t > i) \wedge (\forall u \geq t+1, k.\ rbr_k^u \to I_R^u > i) \\
&\equiv \forall u \geq t, k.\ rbr_k^u \to I_R^u > i
\end{aligned}$$

$\square$

We construct a simple "induction scheme" for showing that an instruction i is committed when it satisfies some property $P(i)^t$: show that it can not be rolled back in the current cycle, and that the property still holds in the next cycle.

Lemma 118. *If a property $P(i)$ implies that instruction i is not rolled back in the current cycle, and property $P(i)$ still holds in the next cycle*

$$\forall t.\ P(i)^t \quad \to \quad (\forall k.\ rbr_k^t \to I_{R^t}^t > i) \wedge P(i)^{t+1}$$

then every instruction that satisfies P is committed

$$\forall u.\ P(i)^u \to c(i)^u$$

Proof. Let u be a cycle in which $P(i)$ holds

$$P(i)^u$$

and by repeated application of the assumption, $P(i)$ holds forever

$$\forall v \geq u.\ P(i)^v$$

Thus by assumption also the instruction is never rolled back

$$\forall v \geq u.\ (\forall k.\ rbr_k^v \rightarrow I_R^v > i)$$

and the claim holds by definition of $c(i)$.   □

Note that in the statement of the lemma, there are two cycle indices, and we cannot use primed notation. However the conclusion of the lemma uses exactly one cycle index, and the assumption of the lemma uses exactly one cycle index. As a result, when applying the lemma to prove a statement of the form

$$P(i) \quad \rightarrow \quad c(i)$$

we only have to prove the statement

$$P(i) \quad \rightarrow \quad (\forall k.\ rbr_k \rightarrow I_R > i) \wedge P(i)'$$

and the cycle indices disappear.

Note that instructions $i > I_1$ which have not yet entered the pipeline and are thus not physically rolled back during a rollback still count as not committed for this definition, as we have

$$I_R \leq I_1 < i$$

This is by design and will make the proof slightly simpler. For example, we can easily show that when an instruction is committed, all earlier instructions must also be committed; with a definition that considered only physical rollbacks, instruction i would be considered committed (provided it will not be physically rolled back in a future cycle) even though instruction I_1 is being rolled back and hence is not committed yet.

Lemma 119.

$$c(i) \wedge i \geq j \quad \rightarrow \quad c(j)$$

Proof. With lemma 118 and $P(j) := c(i) \wedge i \geq j$ the claim reduces to

$$c(i) \wedge i \geq j \quad \rightarrow \quad (\forall k.\ rbr_k \rightarrow I_R > j) \wedge c(i)' \wedge i \geq j$$

Assume thus that i is committed and $i \geq j$ and with lemma 117 we obtain

$$rbr_k \quad \rightarrow \quad I_R > i \geq j$$

and

$$c(i)'$$

and the claim follows.   □

If an instruction is committed in some cycle t, it will indeed never be rolled back.

Lemma 120.

$$c(I_k^u)^t \wedge u \geq t \quad \rightarrow \quad /rbr_k^u$$

Proof. Assume for the sake of contradiction that instruction I_k^u is rolled back

$$rbr_k^u.$$

We conclude from the definition of $c(I_k^u)^t$ that the rolled back instruction must be after I_k^u

$$I_R^u > I_k^u$$

But because R is defined to be the lowest (largest) stage with a rollback request we have

$$R \geq k$$

and we obtain a contradiction with lemma 109.   □

With implicit t notation we obtain a simpler version of this lemma for a single cycle.

Lemma 121.

$$c(I_k) \quad \rightarrow \quad /rbr_k$$

Proof. By introducing the implicit t the claim becomes

$$c(I_k^t)^t \quad \rightarrow \quad /rbr_k^t$$

which is solved by lemma 120 with $u := t$.   □

When an instruction is in the pipeline in the next cycle (in any stage l), instructions before it must not have been rolled back in the current cycle.

Lemma 122.

$$j < I_l' \rightarrow (\forall k. \ rbr_k \rightarrow I_R > j)$$

Proof. By lemma 109 the instruction in stage $l \geq 1$ is not a later instruction than that in stage 1

$$I_1' \geq I_l' > j$$

Assume now that there was a rollback request in stage k

$$rbr_k$$

By definition of rbr this means that there was also a rollback request in all higher stages, including stage 1

$$rbr_1$$

and hence by definition of I_1' in case of a rollback request the claim follows

$$I_R = I_1' > j$$

□

Instructions that left the pipeline are never rolled back, and thus the scheduling function for the last stage K of the pipeline is monotonic.

Lemma 123.

$$I_K \leq I'_K$$

Thus if the current lowest instruction is still in the pipeline in a future cycle, it must still be the lowest instruction.

Lemma 124.

$$t \leq u \wedge I^t_K = I^u_k \quad \rightarrow \quad I^t_K = I^u_K$$

Proof. By repeated application of lemma 123, the lowest instruction in the pipeline in cycle $u \geq t$ is no earlier than I^t_K

$$I^t_K \leq I^u_K$$

and with lemma 109 and $k \leq K$ we obtain that it is also no later than the instruction in stage k, which is also I^t_K

$$I^t_K = I^u_k \geq I^u_K \geq I^t_K$$

and the claim follows. $\qquad\square$

Therefore if the lowest instruction in the pipeline is in some (possibly) future cycle still in the pipeline, all stages below it must be empty.

Lemma 125.

$$t \leq u \wedge I^t_K = I^u_k \quad \rightarrow \quad \forall l > k. \ /rfull^u_{l-1}$$

Proof. By lemma 124 the lowest instruction in the pipeline is unchanged and also equal to I^u_k

$$I^u_k = I^t_K = I^u_K$$

and the claim follows by repeated application of lemma 104 $\qquad\square$

Instructions that left the pipeline are committed.

Lemma 126.

$$i < I_K \quad \rightarrow \quad c(i)$$

Proof. By lemma 118 with $P(i) := i < I_K$ it suffices to show that instructions that left the pipeline are not rolled back and stay outside the pipeline

$$i < I_K \quad \rightarrow \quad (\forall k. \ rbr_k \rightarrow I_R > i) \wedge i < I'_K$$

Assume thus that instruction i left the pipeline

$$i < I_K$$

The first claim follows with lemma 109 since the rolled back stage is within the pipeline ($R \leq K$)

$$I_R \geq I_K > i$$

The second claim follows with lemma 123

$$I'_K \geq I_K > i$$

□

The instruction in stage K is committed (at the latest) on update enable

Lemma 127.

$$ue_K \quad \rightarrow \quad c(I_K)$$

Proof. From ue_K we infer

$$rfull_{K-1}, \, /rbr_K$$

With lemma 117 the claim reduces to

$$(\forall k. \, rbr_k \rightarrow I_R > I_K) \wedge c(I_K)'$$

and we show the two claims separately.

$rbr_k \rightarrow I_R > I_K$: The rolled back stage is in the pipeline

$$R \leq K$$

and has by definition a rollback request

$$rbr_R$$

With $/rbr_K$ we obtain successively

$$R \neq K, \, R < K$$

and the claim is lemma 108 with $k := R$, $\hat{k} := K$, $j := K - 1$.
$c(I_K)'$: From lemma 105 we have

$$I'_K \, = \, I_K + ue_K \, = \, I_K + 1 \, > \, I_K$$

and the claim is lemma 126 (for the next cycle).

□

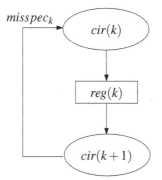

Fig. 137. No self rollback

In all machines we will build, a misspeculation signal $misspec_k$ for circuit stage $cir(k)$ will always be computed in the next circuit stage $cir(k+1)$ in the pipe and only if register stage $reg(k)$ has a real full bit. This is illustrated in figure 137. Thus an instruction in circuit stage $cir(k+1)$ which discovers a misspeculation only triggers rollback requests rbr_l with $l \leq k$, i.e., for instructions behind it in the pipeline and *never for itself*. We formalize this property of the pipeline by the *no self rollback* predicate

$$nsr \equiv \forall k.(misspec_k \rightarrow rfull_k \wedge k \neq K).$$

In particular the lowest instruction in the pipeline is never rolled back; this makes liveness proofs considerably easier.

True full bits mark the border between instructions in the pipeline. In the absence of self-rollback, if there is a rollback request in some stage l (and thus the lowest stage R which is rolled back is defined) but not in stage k, then stage k is not rolled back.

Lemma 128.

$$nsr \wedge rbr_l \wedge /rbr_k \quad \rightarrow \quad I_R > I_k$$

Proof. Stage l has a rollback request. By definition of R and rbr, all stages above R have a rollback request. Since stage k has no rollback request we have

$$R < k$$

By lemma 97 we have a misspeculation in stage R

$$misspec_R$$

From nsr we conclude that stage R must be truly full

$$rfull_R$$

and the claim is lemma 108. $\qquad \square$

Because the lowest instruction is never rolled back, the lowest instruction is committed. We capture this in the following lemma, which we will reuse in all machines we will construct in the future.

Lemma 129.

$$nsr \wedge i \leq I_K \quad \rightarrow \quad c(i)$$

Proof. We prove the claim by lemma 118 with $P(i) := nsr \wedge i \leq I_K$. Assume thus

$$nsr \wedge i \leq I_K$$

and we have to prove

- nsr': this is trivial as nsr always holds.

- $i \leq I'_K$: follows immediately with lemma 123

$$i \leq I_K \leq I'_K$$

- $\forall k.\ rbr_k \rightarrow I_R > i$: We show

$$I_R > I_K \geq i$$

with lemma 128, for which we only need to show

$$/rbr_K.$$

This follows because the contraposition of *nsr* implies $/misspec_K$ and hence $/rbr_K$.

□

A committed instruction is never rolled back. Thus once it passes a stage, it is never seen in that stage again.

Lemma 130.

$$c(i) \wedge i < I_k \quad \rightarrow \quad i < I'_k$$

Proof. We distinguish whether there is a rollback request.

rbr_k: The claim follows from the definition of I'_k and lemma 117

$$I'_k = I_R > i$$

$/rbr_k$: By lemma 105 the claim follows

$$I'_k = I_k + ue_k \geq I_k > i$$

□

While a committed instruction is not clocked down, it stays in its current stage and maintains its real full bit.

Lemma 131.

$$c(I_k) \wedge /ue_k \quad \rightarrow \quad I_k = I'_k \wedge c(I'_k)' \wedge (rfull_{k-1} \rightarrow rfull'_{k-1})$$

Proof. With lemma 121 we obtain that the instruction is not rolled back

$$/rbr_k$$

and since by assumption it is not clocked down, the first part of the claim is the definition of I_k

$$I'_k = I_k$$

The second part of the claim follows with lemma 117

$$c(I_k)'$$

For the third part we conclude successively from $rfull_{k-1}$, $/ue_k$, and $/rbr_k$

$stall_k$,	from eq. (20)
$/rbp_{k-1}$,	from $rfull_{k-1}$
$/rbs_{k-1}$,	from $/rbr_k$, $/rbp_{k-1}$
$rfull'_{k-1}$	from L 100

$\square$

By repeated application of the last two lemmas we obtain almost immediately that the committed instruction only moves down

Lemma 132.

$$c(I_k^t)^t \wedge rfull_{k-1}^t \wedge u \geq t \wedge I_l^u = I_k^t \quad \rightarrow \quad l \geq k$$

Proof. Let $v \in [t : u]$ be the first cycle which updates stage k or equal to u if such a cycle does not exist

$$(v = u \vee ue_k^v) \wedge \forall w \in [t : v). \ /ue_k^w$$

By repeated application of lemma 131 we have

$$I_k^t = I_k^v \wedge c(I_k^v)^v \wedge rfull_{k-1}^v$$

If $v = u$ we thus have

$$I_k^u = I_l^u \wedge rfull_{k-1}^u$$

and the claim is lemma 110 with $\hat{k} := k$, $k := l$.

If $v < u$ we have ue_k^v and thus $/rbr_k^v$. With lemma 105 we get

$$I_k^{v+1} = I_k^v + ue_k^v = I_k^v + 1 > I_k^v = I_k^t$$

By repeated application of lemma 130 the instruction $i := I_k^t$ is never again seen in stage k

$$I_k^u > I_k^t = I_l^u$$

and the claim is the contraposition of lemma 108 with $\hat{k} := k$, $k := l$. $\square$

7.4.4 Pipelining Signals

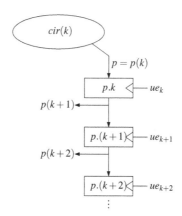

Fig. 138. Pipelining of signals p starting from stage $k = stage(p)$.

Since committed instructions only move downwards, for any pipelined signal p which is first computed in circuit stage $stage(p)$ and then simply carried down through the pipeline as shown in fig. 138

$$p.k.in = \begin{cases} p & k = stage(p) \\ p.(k-1) & \text{o.w.,} \end{cases}$$

the value of p never changes for the committed instruction. We wish to show this, and introduce some shorthands to make this simpler. Such pipelined signals are used in multiple circuit stages. In circuit stage $stage(p)$ the signal is computed in the circuit, in later circuit stages the signal comes from the register of the register stage above. We use the shorthand

$$p(k) = \begin{cases} p & k = stage(p) \\ p.(k-1) & \text{o.w.} \end{cases}$$

for the value of p in circuit stage k. With this shorthand, one can restate the definition of the input of $p.k$ in the obvious way: we clock into pipelined register $p.k$ the value of signal p in stage k

$$p.k.in = p(k) \tag{28}$$

We show that as a committed instruction moves through the circuit stages, that value does not change.

Lemma 133. *If the instruction in circuit stage $k > stage(p)$ has been committed*

$$c(I_k^t)^t \wedge rfull_{k-1}^t \wedge k > stage(p)$$

the value of pipelined signal p does not change as that instruction moves through the pipeline

$$\forall u \geq t, \ l. \ I_k^t = I_l^u \wedge rfull_{l-1}^u \quad \rightarrow \quad p(k)^t = p(l)^u$$

Proof. By induction on u, starting from t. In the base case $u = t$ and hence

$$rfull_{l-1}^t \wedge I_k^t = I_l^t$$

and from lemma 111 we obtain

$$l = k$$

The claim follows.

In the induction step $u \rightarrow u+1$ we assume that the instruction is in cycle $u+1$ in stage l

$$I_k^t = I_l^{u+1} \wedge rfull_{l-1}^{u+1}$$

By lemma 132 with $u := u+1$ we obtain that the instruction moved down and is thus not in stage 1

$$l \geq k > stage(p) \geq 1$$

and by lemma 115 with $k := l-1$ and $i := I_k^t = I_l^{u+1}$ we know that the instruction did not appear out of the blue, but rather either came from the same stage or from above. We distinguish between these two cases.

$/ue_l^u \wedge /ue_{l-1}^u \wedge rfull_{l-1}^u \wedge I_k^t = I_l^u$: By the induction hypothesis with $l := l$, definition of $p(l)$, and $/ue_{l-1}^u$ the claim follows

$$p(k)^t \overset{\text{IH}}{=} p(l)^u = p.(l-1)^u = p.(l-1)^{u+1} = p(l)^{u+1}$$

$ue_{l-1}^u \wedge rfull_{l-2}^u \wedge I_k^t = I_{l-1}^u$: From the induction hypothesis with $l := l-1$ we obtain thus by definition and eq. (28) and ue_{l-1}^u the claim follows

$$p(k)^t \overset{\text{IH}}{=} p(l-1)^u \overset{\text{E 28}}{=} p.(l-1).in^u = p.(l-1)^{u+1} = p(l)^{u+1}$$

$\square$

7.4.5 Sampling the External Interrupt Signal

This is more tricky than meets the eye. Without interrupts *reset* was the only external event signal. It occurred only in hardware and had no counter part in ISA. The reason was that *reset* is only active in cycle $t = -1$, where it serves to compute the initial hardware configuration h^0 such that it simulates the initial ISA configuration c^0. For cycles $t \geq 0$ the reset signal *reset^t* is always off, and for the set K_{isa} of ISA configurations we could define the next ISA configuration δ_{isa} as a function

$$\delta_{isa} : K_{isa} \rightarrow K_{isa}$$

In contrast the external *hardware* interrupt event signal e^t is allowed to change during a computation, and thus an *ISA version* e_σ^i of that signal has to be an argument of the ISA transition function

$$\delta_{isa} : K_{isa} \times \mathbb{B} \to K_{isa} \quad , \quad \delta_{isa}(c^i, e_\sigma^i) = c^{i+1}.$$

Given that we are sampling hardware signal e in stage

$$stage(e) = EX = M - 1$$

i.e., the stage above the memory stage, we consider the cycle t_i when instruction i is committed and leaves stage $M - 1$

$$t_i = \varepsilon \left\{ t \mid c(I_{M-1}^t)^t \wedge I_{M-1}^t = i \wedge ue_{M-1}^t \right\}$$

The value of hardware signal e sampled in this cycle is a natural candidate to be used in ISA for instruction i:

$$e_\sigma^i = e^{t_i}$$

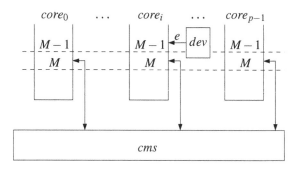

Fig. 139. Wiring in a multi-core machine with CMS and devices

Actually t_i is the last cycle when we can sample e, because in cycle t_i writing memory accesses for instruction i are clocked into register stage $reg(M - 1)$ and cannot be stopped by an event signal which becomes active in a later cycle. Unfortunately there is a catch. As illustrated in fig. 139 external event signals come from devices[2]. Thus while signal e is external to the processor core, it is really an internal signal of the system consisting of core, memory system and device. If we wish to provide a full ISA model for this system, we must in ISA somehow step core, the memory system and devices in parallel to the hardware computation. As we also aim at multi-core machines we will have to interleave in this process the ISA steps of the cores. Basically we will interleave for each cycle t instructions in the sequentially consistent order in which their accesses to the data caches complete. Thus an instruction i on a core *has* to be stepped for cycle t in ISA when

---

[2] whatever a device is

$$I_M^t = i \wedge ue_M^t$$

and our hardware will do this with the value of e sampled earlier in cycle t_i. In ISA this will correspond to

$$\delta_{isa}(c^i, e_\sigma^i) = \delta_{isa}(c^i, e^{t_i})$$

For devices we try to make things simple. If a device changes state in cycle t this should immediately become visible in ISA. Thus consider a situation, when the device producing e changes state in cycle $t - 1 \geq t_i$ such that afterwards e is changed

$$e^t \neq e^{t_i}$$

For the update of cycle t this should be visible in ISA. Thus in ISA we would wish to compute

$$\delta_{isa}(c^i, e^t)$$

which is not what the hardware does. We will be saved by the fact that signal e is produced by an *advanced programmable interrupt controller* (APIC), a device that we will construct in chapter 12 and whose behavior we can control. In particular the APIC will deliver for any instruction i hardware signal e in such a way, that it does not change between cycle t_i when it is sampled and the cycle when instruction i leaves the memory stage. In particular we will guarantee

$$I_M^t = i \wedge ue_M^t \rightarrow e^t = e^{t_i}$$

So because memory accesses cannot be stopped once they are started we kind of have to speculate on value e^t by sampling already e^{t_i}, and the APIC will ensure that this speculation is always correct.

Technically the APIC will achieve this by two measures

- Signal e is only activated when the memory stage is empty. The APIC can enforce this by activation of a hazard signal haz_{M-1} for the stage above M.
- Signal e is only turned off, when the APIC observes $jisr \wedge mca[3]$, i.e. that the external interrupt was delivered.

7.5 Pipelining and Forwarding

7.5.1 Data Paths

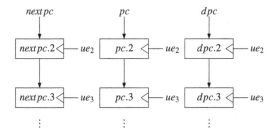

Fig. 140. Program Counters pipeline

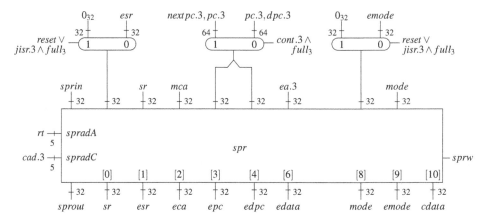

Fig. 141. Special Purpose Register file hardware

Recall that the instruction register resides in register stage $reg(1)$, the program counters reside in register stage $reg(2)$ and the general purpose register file resides in register stage $reg(5)$. In contrast to [MP00, Krö01, BJK$^+$03, DHP05] we have placed the special purpose register file in register stage $reg(4)$. Copies $X.k$ of the following signals X need to be pipelined through various stages:

- *con*, *xad*, C: as in [KMP14];
- *pc*, *dpc* and *nextpc*: For these signals X we define

$$stage(X) = 2$$

and pipeline them down in the way described in section 7.4.3

So, with every instruction we pipeline the *pc*, *dpc* and *nextpc* belonging to this instruction in the invisible registers $X.k$. This is illustrated in Fig. 140.

For the inputs of the special purpose register file one now has to use pipelined versions of most sequential signals, as shown in Fig. 141.

As memory we use a cache memory system with two ports: with the instruction cache *ica* at port 0 and the data cache *dca* at port 1.

7.5.2 Forwarding Data

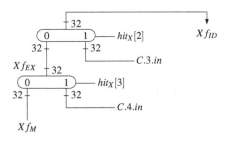

Fig. 142. 2-stage forwarding circuit for $X \in \{epc, edpc\}$

Forwarding of signals A, B and S stays almost as before, but now we forward only from stages with true full bits. Thus we redefine the corresponding hit signals as

$$hit_A[k] \equiv \widehat{used}[A](I.1) \wedge rfull_k \wedge gprw.k \wedge rs = xad.k \wedge rs \neq 0^5$$
$$hit_B[k] \equiv \widehat{used}[B](I.1) \wedge rfull_k \wedge gprw.k \wedge rt = xad.k \wedge rt \neq 0^5$$
$$hit_S[k] \equiv \widehat{used}[S](I.1) \wedge rfull_k \wedge sprw.k \wedge rs = xad.k$$

An (uninterrupted) *eret* instruction updates visible registers in the following stages:

- stage 2 (*ID*): *pc* and *dpc* are updated resp. by *epc* and *edpc*;
- stage 4 (*M*): *sr* and *mode* are updated resp. by *esr* and *emode*.

For the update of stage 2 we forward the result of move instructions which update *epc* and *edpc* using the two stage forwarding circuit from Fig. 142, which takes for $X \in \{epc, edpc\}$ either the value stored in the special purpose register file

$$X f_M = \begin{cases} spr.dout[3] & X = epc \\ spr.dout[4] & X = edpc \end{cases}$$

or the most recent value to be written by a move instruction by computing successively more up-to-date values $X f_k$ corresponding to the value of X for the instructions in stages $k \in [ID : EX]$

$$X f_k = \begin{cases} X f_{k+1} & /hit_X[k] \\ C.(k+1).in & hit_X[k] \end{cases}$$

where hit signals are computed as

$$hit_{epc}[k] = rfull_k \wedge sprw.k \wedge xad.k = 3_5$$
$$hit_{edpc}[k] = rfull_k \wedge sprw.k \wedge xad.k = 4_5.$$

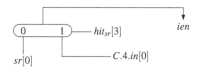

Fig. 143. 1-stage forwarding circuit for the interrupt enable bit

The output of the topmost multiplexer is the signal Xf_{ID}, which is fed into pc resp. dpc, in case of forwarding for $eret$. Thus for $X \in \{epc, edpc\}$ we replace in Fig. 133 inputs X by the outputs of their forwarding circuits. Finally we also have to forward data written to the status register from the memory stage to cause processing circuit in the stage above. Thus we define

$$hit_{sr}[k] = rfull_k \wedge sprw.k \wedge xad.k = 0_5$$

and then compute the new interrupt enable signal as

$$ien = \begin{cases} C.4.in[0] & hit_{sr}[3] \\ sr[0] & \text{otherwise.} \end{cases}$$

This is illustrated in fig. 143.

7.5.3 Connecting the new Rollback Engine

As mentioned before, we need to roll back the instruction in circuit stage 1 when an eret instruction is detected in the decode stage

$$misspec_1 = full_1 \wedge eret(2)$$

and the instruction in circuit stages 3 and above have to be rolled back when a jisr is detected in the memory stage (i.e., after cause processing)

$$misspec_3 = full_3 \wedge jisr.3$$

Note that this definition seems to violate the no-self-rollback requirement from section 7.4.3 which requires true full bits, but we show that these stages never have a pending rollback and thus are truly full whenever they are full.

Lemma 134.

$$\forall k \geq M-1. \; /rbp_k \wedge rfull_k = full_k$$

Proof. The second part immediately follows from the first part

$$/rbp_k \rightarrow rfull_k = /rbp_k \wedge full_k = full_k$$

so we only show the first part. The proof is by induction on the implicit t. Originally all of the rollback pending bits are zero

$$/rbp_k^0$$

In the induction step we have that all lower misspeculations are off by construction

$$\forall \hat{k} > M-1. \ /misspec_{\hat{k}}$$

and thus there is no rollback request

$$/rbr_{k+1}$$

By the induction hypothesis there is also no pending rollback

$$/rbp_k$$

and by definition of rbp' there is no pending rollback in the next cycle either, which is the claim

$$/rbp_k'$$

$\square$

Stage $1 = IF$ can not be rolled back while it is accessing memory

$$rhaz_1 = mbusy(IP)$$

We wish to drain the pipe when an *eret* instruction is discovered anywhere in the pipe above register stage $reg(4)$. Thus we define

$$drain = \bigvee_{k=2}^{4} rfull_{k-1} \wedge eret(k)$$
$$haz_1 = mbusy(IP) \vee drain$$

With the new hit signals the remaining hazard signals are computed as before:

$$haz_2 = haz_A \vee haz_B$$
$$haz_3 = 0$$
$$haz_4 = mbusy(DP)$$
$$haz_5 = 0$$

Because $full_0 = 1$ the operating condition for the new stall engine (eq. (19)) is trivially fulfilled

Lemma 135.

$$rhaz_k \rightarrow full_{k-1} \wedge haz_k$$

That the pipe is indeed drained behind an eret instruction is stated in

Lemma 136. *For $k \in [2:3]$, if an eret instruction is in the invisible registers in register stage $reg(k)$, then the register stages behind it are empty.*

$$rfull_k \wedge eret.k \wedge j \in [1:k-1] \quad \rightarrow \quad /rfull_j$$

Proof. We prove the lemma by induction on t for configurations h^t of the hardware computation. For $t = 0$ the pipe is empty and there is nothing to show. For the induction step, where we consider

$$h = h^t \quad \text{and} \quad h' = h^{t+1}$$

assume we have an eret in the pipeline in some stage k

$$rfull'_k \wedge eret.k'$$

We consider some stage j above k

$$j \in [1 : k-1]$$

and have to show that it is not really full

$$/rfull'_j$$

Assume for the sake of contradiction that it is

$$rfull'_j$$

With lemma 115 we obtain that the instruction must have been there and not moved down, or must have come from above

$$/ue_{j+1} \wedge /ue_j \wedge rfull_j \vee ue_j \wedge rfull_{j-1} \tag{29}$$

We distinguish whether the eret was just clocked into register stage k or not

ue_k: In this case we conclude successively

$$rfull_{k-1} \wedge eret(k), \, drain, \, haz_1, \, /ue_1$$

We distinguishing between $k = 2$ and $k > 2$
$k > 2$: In this case we obtain from $eret(k)$

$$eret.(k-1)$$

and by the induction hypothesis for $k - 1 \geq 2$ we obtain

$$j \in [1 : k-2] \; \rightarrow \; /rfull_j$$

or equivalently

$$j \in [2 : k-1] \; \rightarrow \; /rfull_{j-1}$$

With eq. (29) we conclude by contraposition of these implications

$$/ue_{j+1} \wedge /ue_j \wedge j \notin [1 : k-2] \vee ue_j \wedge j \notin [2 : k-1]$$

and from $j \in [1 : k-1]$ we conclude

$$/ue_{j+1} \wedge /ue_j \wedge j = k-1 \vee ue_j \wedge j = 1$$

which contradicts ue_k and $/ue_1$.

$k = 2$: In this case $j = 1 = k - 1$ and from eq. (29) we conclude directly

$$/ue_{j+1} \wedge /ue_j \wedge j = k - 1 \ \vee \ ue_j \wedge j = 1$$

which contradicts ue_k and $/ue_1$.

$/ue_k$: In this case we conclude with lemma 100 from $rfull'_k$ successively

$stall_{k+1} \ \wedge \ /rbs_k,$	L 100
$full_k,$	from $stall_{k+1}$
$/rbp_k,$	from $/rbs_k$
$rfull_k,$	from $full_k$ and $/rbp_k$
$eret.k,$	from $eret.k'$ and $/ue_k$
$rfull_k \wedge eret(k+1),$	from $eret.k$
$drain,$	from $rfull_k \wedge eret(k+1)$ with $k \in [2:3]$
$haz_1,$	from $drain$
$/ue_1$	from haz_1

By the induction hypothesis for k we have with $j := j$

$$/rfull_j$$

and for $j \neq 1$ with $j := j - 1$

$$j \neq 1 \rightarrow /rfull_{j-1}$$

With eq. (29) we conclude

$$ue_j \ \wedge \ j = 1$$

which contradicts $/ue_1$.

$\square$

Together with lemma 104 we conclude

Lemma 137. *When an eret instruction is in the invisible registers of register stage* $reg(k)$ *with* $k \in [1:3]$, *then pipe stages above are synchronized to the same ISA instruction.*

$$eret.k \wedge rfull_k \quad \rightarrow \quad \forall i \in [1:k]. \ I_k = I_i$$

Pipe drain behind an instruction will become somewhat more complex when we add address translation.

As promised, our machine has no self rollback.

Lemma 138.

nsr

Proof. We unfold the definition of *nsr* and add cycle indices

$$misspec_k^t \quad \rightarrow \quad rbr_k^t \wedge k \neq K$$

By definition $misspec_k$ can only be active with the corresponding full bit, and only in stages above K. Thus we have

$$full_k^t \wedge k \neq K$$

The only roll back hazard signal which can become active is $rhaz_1$. Hence

$$/rhaz_{k+1}^{t-1}$$

The claim follows by definition of rbp and $rfull$

$$/rbp_k^t, \ rfull_k^t.$$

$\square$

7.5.4 Program Counter Environment

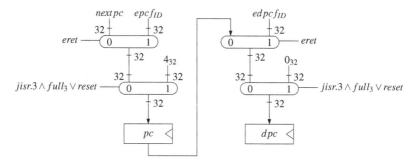

Fig. 144. Program Counters pipelined hardware

Interrupt causes are now collected in a pipeline by introducing invisible pipeline registers at the borders of pipeline stages in fig. 134, almost completely analogous to how the basic pipelined machine was constructed. There is, however, one key place where we need to be careful, and that is the program counter environment, which uses the *jisr* signal. Here we need to use the pipelined *jisr* signal from the memory stage, rather than the execute stage. Furthermore, we must use that signal only in case that stage is full. As depicted in fig. 144, we thus have

$$pc.in = \begin{cases} 4_{32} & jisr.3 \wedge full_3 \vee reset \\ epc & eret \\ nextpc & \text{otherwise} \end{cases}$$

$$dpc.in = \begin{cases} 0_{32} & jisr.3 \wedge full_3 \vee reset \\ edpc & eret \\ pc & \text{otherwise.} \end{cases}$$

7.5.5 Write and Clock Enable Signals

Write signals for general and special purpose register files are generated as.

$$sprw(4) = ue_4 \wedge sprw(4) \wedge exec(4)$$
$$gprw(5) = ue_5 \wedge gprw(5) \wedge exec(5)$$

Clock enable signals for pc and dpc are generated as

$$pc.ce = dpc.ce = ue_{ID} \vee (jisr.3 \wedge full_3)$$

where ue_{ID} is generated by the new stall engine. The individual clock enable signals $spr.ce[j]$ of the special purpose register file are generated under control of signals $reset$, $jisr.3$, and $eret.3$ in a fairly obvious way. In order to initialize sr, $mode$, and eca, the special purpose registers are also clocked at $reset$.

$$spr.ce[j] = reset \vee ue_4 \wedge \begin{cases} jisr.3 \vee eret.3 & j \in \{0,8\} \\ jisr.3 & j \in \{1,2,3,4,6,9\} \\ 0 & \text{otherwise} \end{cases}$$

7.5.6 Connecting the Cache Memory System

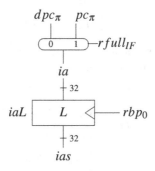

Fig. 145. Latch iaL stabilizing the instruction memory address

The caches are connected almost exactly like before, except for three places:

1. We select between pc and dpc using real full bits. This is shown in fig. 145
2. Now during a pending rollback for stage 1 we stabilize the address input $iacc.a$ to the instruction cache ica in a brute force way by a latch iaL as indicated in Fig. 145. Thus

$$iaL.in = ia$$
$$iaL.out = ias$$
$$iaL.l = rbp_0$$
$$iacc.a = ias.l$$

3. We update the computation of the processor request for the data cache to

$$dca.preq \; = \; full_3 \wedge mop.3 \wedge exec.3$$

In contrast, we keep the instruction cache request signals always turned on.

$$ica.preq = 1$$

Thus in case of a misalignment on fetch we perform a redundant access to the instruction cache.

7.5.7 Stability of the Instruction Memory Address

We can immediately show the operating conditions of the cache memory system that accesses are stable.

For the data cache nothing changes as all data comes from registers which are not updated during the memory request, but for the instruction cache obviously the address computation now depends on the latch. Thus we only show the proof of stability of the instruction address. Recall that the old instruction memory address computed by the mux under the program counters is

$$ia_\pi = \begin{cases} pc_\pi & full_{IF} \\ dpc_\pi & /full_{IF} \end{cases}$$

The stabilized instruction memory address ias was computed by the latch iaL with input ia_π and latch input rbp_0 as shown in fig. 145. From the specification of latches we get

$$ias = \begin{cases} ia_\pi & /rbp_0 \\ iaL & rbp_0 \end{cases}$$

$$iaL' = \begin{cases} ia_\pi & /rbp_0 \\ iaL & rbp_0 \end{cases}$$

The stability of this input during accesses to the instruction cache is stated in the following lemma, which is the counter part of lemma 9.11, part 1 of [KMP14].

Lemma 139.
$$mbusy(IP) \to iacc.a = iacc.a'$$

Proof. We split cases first on rbp_0, and then on rbr_1.

- rbp_0:
  The stabilized input in the current cycle comes from the latch, which is not updated
  $$iacc.a = ias.l = iaL.l = iaL'.l$$

From
$$mbusy(IP) \wedge rbp_0$$
we get successively
$$rhaz_1, \ rbp_0'$$
and thus the stabilized input comes from the latch in the next cycle too, and the claim follows
$$iacc.a' = ias'.l = iaL'.l = iacc.a$$

- $/rbp_0 \wedge rbr_1$: With $mbusy(IP)$ we get successively
$$rhaz_1, \ rbp_0'$$
and thus the latch is transparent in the current cycle and latched in the next cycle, and the claim follows
$$iacc.a' = ias'.l = iaL'.l = ia_\pi.l = ias.l = iacc.a$$

- $/rbp_0 \wedge /rbr_1$: We conclude that there was no rollback request or misspeculation in the lower stages
$$/rbr_2, \ /rbr_3, \ /misspec_3$$
and thus no interrupt in the memory stage
$$/(jisr.3 \wedge full_3)$$
and thus the program counters are clocked analogously to a machine without interrupts
$$pc.ce = dpc.ce = ue_{ID}$$
There is also no misspeculation in circuit stage 1
$$/misspec_1$$
and thus no *eret* instruction in the decoder
$$/(eret(2) \wedge full_1)$$
Thus by the multiplexers of the pc environment, the program counters are updated precisely in the same manner as in a machine without interrupts
$$pc.in = nextpc, \quad \text{and} \quad dpc.in = pc$$
and thus by precisely the old argument for the instruction address we obtain from $mbusy(IP)$
$$ia_\pi = id_\pi'$$
Since there is neither a pending rollback nor a rollback request we obtain
$$/rbp_0'$$
and thus the latch is transparent in both cycles and the claim follows
$$iacc.a = ias.l = ia_\pi.l = id_\pi'.l = ias'.l = iacc.a'$$

$\square$

7.6 Stating Processor Correctness

7.6.1 Software Condition for Self Modifying Code

Due to the fact that *eret* instructions drain the pipe, we can now replace software condition $SC_{selfmod}$ with a new condition SC_{eret} which does not expose the pipeline depth. We maintain the requirement that software does not write to the ROM portion of memory:

$$write(c) \rightarrow \langle ea(c) \rangle \geq 2^{r+3}$$

And we require: if in ISA step g we write to a cache line $ea(c^g)$ and in a later cycle i fetch an instruction from this line, then in the mean time — i.e., in an ISA step h with $g < h < i$ — the pipe must have been drained by an *eret* instruction.

$$SC_{eret}((c^i)) \leftrightarrow \forall g, i.\ g < i \wedge write(c^g) \wedge ea(c^g).l = ia(c^i).l$$
$$\rightarrow \exists h.\ g < h < i \wedge eret(c^h))$$

7.6.2 A New Induction Hypothesis

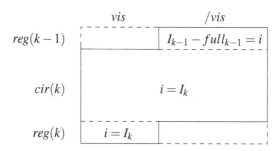

Fig. 146. Data for instruction $i = I(k,t)$ can occur in $cir(k)$, the visible registers of $reg(k)$ and the invisible registers of $reg(k-1)$.

Due to the possibility of misspeculated data in the pipeline we have to carefully weaken the main induction hypothesis, which states so far for $R \in reg(k)$ and $i = I_k^t$:

$$R_\pi^t = \begin{cases} R_\sigma^i & vis(R) \\ R_\sigma^{i-1} & /vis(R) \wedge full_k^t \wedge used[R]^{i-1} \end{cases}$$

Before we do this consider Fig. 146 and observe that data belonging to instruction $i = I_k^t$ are found in the following places

- in the visible registers of stage $reg(k)$ as stated in the main induction hypothesis.
- in the invisible registers of stage of register stage $k-1$ in case that stage is full, because

$$I_{k-1}^t - 1 = I_k^t + full_k^t - 1 = i$$

- in circuit stage $cir(k)$ when register stage k is updated as argued in the induction step.

Viewing $i = I_k^t$ as the index of the instruction in *circuit* stage k, we can expect data for instruction i in $cir(k)$, the visible registers of $reg(k)$ and the invisible registers of $reg(k-1)$. This intuition will help us to reformulate the main induction hypothesis.

We begin by reformulating the main induction hypothesis in terms of data of instruction i, rather than stage k. We obtain for visible registers

$$R \in reg(k) \land vis(R) \quad \rightarrow \quad R_\pi^t = R_\sigma^i$$

and for invisible registers

$$R \in reg(k-1) \land /vis(R) \land full_{k-1}^t \land used[R]^i \quad \rightarrow \quad R_\pi^t = R_\sigma^i$$

Obviously at least two things need to be changed: 1) only real full bits should be considered, and 2) we want to prove nothing about data which will not reach the memory stage, e.g., because it will be rolled back.

For 1) we adjust the main induction hypothesis and formalize it as a coupling relation between hardware and ISA. We say pipeline in cycle t simulates instruction i when visible registers in stages k and invisible used registers in really full stages $k-1$ corresponding to instruction $i = I_k^t$ correctly simulate ISA signals in cycle t

$$t \sim_p i \equiv \forall k, R. \ I_k^t = i \land (R \in reg(k) \land vis(R)$$
$$\lor \ R \in reg(k-1) \land /vis(R) \land rfull_{k-1}^t \land used[R]^i)$$
$$\rightarrow \quad R_\pi^t = R_\sigma^i$$

Similarly we define a simulation relation for the memory, and we require in addition that the operating condition holds

$$t \sim_m i \equiv (i = I_M^t \rightarrow m(h^t) = \ell(m_\sigma^i) \land opc^t)$$

For 2) one is tempted to simply use predicate $c(i)^t$ of committed instructions, which states that instruction i will never be rolled back. This is insufficient: imagine that an instruction i receives incorrect data because of a misspeculating instruction $j < i$ lower in the pipeline. Intuitively, this is fine if instruction j eventually creates a rollback request. Thus if the program counter of instruction i is incorrect due to instruction j with an interrupt, i.e., we have $jisr_\sigma^j$, we would like to rely on the fact that instruction j will later (i.e., in a future hardware cycle) cause a rollback request when it leaves the memory stage.

But if the processor is not live — i.e., some instructions can get stuck in the pipeline — this may never happen: instruction j might get stuck and never trigger the rollback. In this case, instruction i will never be rolled back and predicate $c(i)$ will hold, even though the data for instruction i is incorrect. To make the correctness proof go through, we would need to first prove the liveness of the processor, a property that itself depends on correctness in subtle ways: for example, the memory must only be live if it is used correctly, e.g., only one access bit (read/write/cas) is set in the memory stage. While these circular dependencies can be resolved in a brute force manner (by proving correctness partially, and then proving liveness, and then proving correctness), we use a simple trick to avoid the brute force argument: we add an assumption that all instructions *before* instruction i are *live* in cycle t, i.e., when they enter a stage they will eventually leave it. Formally, we define liveness by

$$live(j)^t \equiv \forall u \geq t, k. \; rfull_{k-1}^u \wedge I_k^u = j \quad \rightarrow \quad \exists v \geq u. \; I_k^v = j \wedge ue_k^v$$

and abbreviate that all instructions before i are live by

$$lb(i)^t \equiv \forall j < i. \; live(j)^t$$

Note that this does not imply that the instruction i itself is live, nor that instructions before i will never be rolled back. Note also that an instruction which never enters the pipeline is vacuously live, which for most of our purposes will be fine — as we mostly argue about instructions which are currently in the pipeline.

The reformulated main induction hypothesis now states the following:

Lemma 140. *There is an initial configuration c^0 satisfying*

$$sim(h^0, c^0)$$

Furthermore, if the computation (c^i) with initial configuration c^0 and external event sequence (e_σ^i) sampled from hardware satisfies the software conditions SC_{ROM} and SC_{eret}

$$SC_{eret}((c^i)) \wedge \forall i. \; SC_{ROM}(c^i)$$

then for all i and t such that instructions before i are live, and instruction i is committed in cycle t

$$lb(i)^t \wedge c(i)^t$$

the pipeline and memory in cycle t simulate instruction i

$$t \sim_p i \wedge t \sim_m i$$

7.7 Properties of Liveness

This section establishes

- properties of liveness needed to show processor correctness (section 7.7.1).
- those parts of the liveness proof which do not hinge on processor correctness (section 7.7.2).

Once processor correctness is shown (section 7.8) the liveness proof will then be completed in section 7.9.

7.7.1 Properties needed for Correctness

If all instructions before instruction i are live, so are all instructions before earlier instructions.

Lemma 141.
$$lb(i) \quad \rightarrow \quad \forall j < i. \; lb(j)$$

Proof. Let $g < j$ be an instruction before j for which we have to show that it is live. Clearly g is also before i

$$g < j < i$$

and the claim follows from $lb(i)$

$$live(g)$$

$\square$

Instructions that are live remain live, and hence if all instructions before an instruction are live they remain live also.

Lemma 142.
$$live(j) \quad \rightarrow \quad live(j)'$$

Proof. We make cycle index t explicit and unfold the definitions. Assume thus that in cycles $u \geq t$ the instruction will eventually leave stage k

$$\forall u \geq t, k. \; rfull_{k-1}^u \wedge I_k^u = j \quad \rightarrow \quad \exists v \geq u. \; I_k^v = j \wedge ue_k^v$$

and we have to show that in all cycles $u \geq t+1$ the same holds

$$\forall u \geq t+1, k. \; rfull_{k-1}^u \wedge I_k^u = j \quad \rightarrow \quad \exists v \geq u. \; I_k^v = j \wedge ue_k^v$$

This follows immediately by the assumption as $u \geq t+1 \geq t$. $\square$

Lemma 143.
$$lb(i) \quad \rightarrow \quad lb(i)'$$

Proof. We unfold the definition of lb

$$(\forall j < i. \; live(j)) \quad \rightarrow \quad (\forall j < i. \; live(j)')$$

and the claim follows immediately with lemma 142. $\square$

When an instruction in any stage is live, it will eventually leave all lower stages.

Lemma 144.

$$live(I_k^t)^t \wedge rfull_{k-1}^t \quad \rightarrow \quad \forall l \geq k. \; \exists u \geq t. \; I_l^u = I_k^t \wedge ue_l^u$$

Proof. The proof is by induction on l starting from k. The base case $l = k$ follows immediately from the definition of liveness with $u := t$ and $k := l$. In the induction step $l \rightarrow l + 1$, we have by the induction hypothesis a cycle $u \geq t$ in which the instruction leaves stage l

$$I_l^u = I_k^t \wedge ue_l^u$$

and conclude with lemma 100 that it is in stage $l + 1$ in the next cycle

$$I_{l+1}^{u+1} = I_k^t \wedge rfull_l^{u+1}$$

By definition of liveness with $u := u + 1$ and $k := l + 1$ there is a cycle

$$v \geq u + 1 \geq t$$

in which the instruction leaves stage $l + 1$

$$I_{l+1}^v = I_k^t \wedge ue_{l+1}^v$$

and the claim follows for $u := v$.   □

Instructions before the lowest instruction, i.e., which left the pipe, are live.

Lemma 145.
$$lb(I_K^t)^t$$

Proof. Let $j < I_K^t$ be some instruction before the one in the lowest stage, and we have to show that it is live. For that assume that in some (possibly) future cycle u the instruction is in stage k

$$rfull_{k-1}^u \wedge I_k^u = j$$

By lemma 109, the instruction in the lowest stage is not after the instruction in stage $k \leq K$

$$I_k^u \geq I_K^u$$

but by repeated application of lemma 123 we obtain that the lowest instruction in the future is not before I_K^t and thus after j

$$I_K^u \geq I_K^t > j = I_k^u$$

which is a contradiction.   □

We now combine the two technologies of liveness and committed instructions in a key lemma: live instructions will reach every stage and not roll back any committed later instructions. Thus we can "fast forward" to cycles in which an instruction which in the pipeline is below a committed instruction might raise a misspeculation signal, and obtain that it will not. Since in our pipeline misspeculations are raised by interrupted instructions and *eret* instructions, we can use this key lemma to show that instructions in the pipeline below a committed instruction are neither interrupted nor *eret* instructions.

Lemma 146. *If the instruction in stage k is live and a later instruction i is committed*

$$rfull_{k-1}^t \wedge live(I_k^t)^t \wedge c(i)^t \wedge i > I_k^t$$

then for each lower stage l there is a (possibly) future cycle u in which the instruction is in that stage and does not raise a misspeculation signal

$$\forall l \geq k.\ \exists u \geq t.\ I_l^u = I_k^t \wedge rfull_{l-1}^u \wedge /misspec_{l-1}^u$$

Proof. By lemma 144 the instruction will leave that stage in cycle $u \geq t$

$$I_l^u = I_k^t \wedge ue_l^u$$

and by the simplified definition of *ue* (eq. (20)) it must be in the stage to leave it

$$rfull_{l-1}^u$$

From well-formedness we conclude that the instruction in circuit stage $l - 1$ is no later than instruction i

$$I_{l-1}^u = I_l^u + 1 = I_k^t + 1 \leq i$$

and by lemma 119 we conclude that that instruction is also committed in cycle t

$$c(I_{l-1}^u)^t$$

With lemma 120 with $k := l-1$ we obtain that the instruction has no rollback request in cycle u

$$/rbr_{l-1}^u$$

By definition of *rbr* there is also no misspeculation signal

$$/misspec_{l-1}^u$$

which proves the claim.   □

If a committed instruction is live in the next cycle, it must have been live in the current cycle.

Lemma 147.
$$c(i) \wedge live(i)' \quad \rightarrow \quad live(i)$$

Proof. We add the cycle indices, changing the goal to the following

$$c(i)^t \wedge live(i)^{t+1} \quad \rightarrow \quad live(i)^t$$

By definition of liveness, it suffices to show that in all cycles $u \geq t$, instruction i will leave any stage it is in. By assumption, this is true for all $u \geq t+1$, and it remains to be shown only for $t = u$. Assume thus that instruction i is in some stage k in cycle t

$$rfull_{k-1}^t \wedge I_k^t = i$$

and we have to show that the instruction eventually leaves the stage

$$\exists v \geq t. \ I_k^v = i \wedge ue_k^v$$

By lemma 120 with $u := t$ the instruction is not rolled back

$$/rbr_k^t$$

We split cases on ue_k^t:

- $/ue_k^t$: in this case we have

$$I_k^{t+1} = I_k^t = i$$

  and the claim follows from $live(i)^{t+1}$.
- ue_k^t: the claim immediately follows with $v := t$.

□

If instructions before i are going to be live and instruction i is committed, instructions before i are already live.

Lemma 148.

$$c(i) \wedge lb(i)' \quad \rightarrow \quad lb(i)$$

Proof. With lemma 119 we obtain that instructions j before i are committed

$$j < i \quad \rightarrow \quad c(j)$$

and by assumption instruction j before i is going to be live

$$j < i \quad \rightarrow \quad live(j)'$$

Thus by lemma 147 instruction j before i is already live

$$j < i \quad \rightarrow \quad live(j)$$

which is the claim.

□

7.7.2 Towards the Liveness Proof

To show that all instructions enter the pipeline eventually, it suffices to show two things: 1) that the lowest instruction in the pipeline is always live and committed, and 2) that rollback hazards are eventually turned off.

Lemma 149. *If the lowest instruction is always live and committed*

$$\forall t. \ live(I_K^t)^t \wedge c(I_K^t)^t$$

and all rollback hazards are resolved eventually

$$\forall t, k. \ full_{k-1}^t \quad \rightarrow \quad \exists u \geq t. \ /rhaz_k^u$$

then all instructions are eventually in the pipeline and live

$$\forall i. \ \exists k, t. \ rfull_{k-1}^t \wedge I_k^t = i \wedge live(i)^t$$

Proof. By induction on i. In the base case we have

$$i = 0 = I_1^0 = I_K^0 \wedge rfull_0^0 = 1$$

and the claim follows with $t := 0$ as by assumption that instruction is live

$$live(I_K^0)^0$$

In the induction step $i \to i+1$ we have as induction hypothesis that instruction i is in some stage k in some cycle t and live

$$i = I_k^t \wedge rfull_{k-1}^t \wedge live(i)^t$$

By lemma 144 with $l := K$ it also leaves the pipeline in some possibly future cycle $u \geq t$

$$I_K^u = i \wedge ue_K^u$$

and we conclude that the lowest instruction in the cycle after that is $i+1$

$$I_K^{u+1} = i+1$$

We now split cases on whether some stage k is really full or all stages are empty.

- $\exists k. \ rfull_{k-1}^{u+1}$: Let without loss of generality k be the lowest full stage

$$\forall l > k. \ /rfull_{k-1}^{u+1}$$

and thus by repeated application of lemma 104 we obtain

$$I_k^{u+1} = I_K^{u+1} = i+1$$

The claim now follows with $t := u+1$ as by assumption that instruction $i+1 = I_K^{u+1}$ is live

$$live(I_K^{u+1})^{u+1}$$

- $\forall k. \ /rfull_{k-1}^{u+1}$: by repeated application of lemma 104 we obtain that the instruction is in the fetch stage

$$I_1^{u+1} = I_K^{u+1} = i+1$$

and by assumption is committed from cycle $u+1$ on

$$c(i+1)^{u+1}$$

The first stage is full (but not necessarily real full)

$$full_0^{u+1} = 1$$

and we can split cases on rbp_0^{u+1}. In case $/rbp_0^{u+1}$ we are done immediately as we have then $rfull_0^{u+1}$ and by assumption instruction $i+1 = I_K^{u+1}$ is live.

In case rbp_0^{u+1} we know that by assumption in some (possibly) future cycle v the rollback hazard in the first stage is turned off

$$/rhaz_1^v$$

Without loss of generality let v be the first such cycle

$$\forall w \in [u+1 : v). \; rhaz_1^w$$

By repeated application of the definition of rbp_0 we obtain that the rollback is pending until cycle v

$$\forall w \in [u+1 : v]. \; rbp_0^w$$

By the operating condition of the rollback engine (eq. (19)) we have not only a rollback hazard, but also a stalling hazard until v

$$\forall w \in [u+1 : v). \; haz_1^w$$

and thus by lemma 103 no update enable

$$\forall w \in [u+1 : v). \; /ue_1^w$$

By repeated application of lemma 131 we obtain that the instruction is still in the instruction fetch stage in cycle v

$$I_1^v = I_1^{u+1} = i+1$$

We conclude with $/rhaz_1^v$ and $full_0^{v+1}$ successively

$$/rbp_0^{v+1}, \; rfull_0^{v+1}$$

and also from rbp_0^v we conclude with the regular definition of ue_1 that stage 1 is not updated and instruction $i+1$ stays in that stage

$$/ue_1^v, \; I_1^{v+1} = I_1^v = i+1$$

By lemma 124, that instruction $I_1^{v+1} = i+1 = I_K^{u+1}$ is still the lowest instruction in the pipeline

$$i+1 = I_K^{u+1} = I_K^{v+1}$$

and the claim follows with $t := v+1$ by assumption

$$live(I_K^{v+1})^{v+1}$$

$\square$

To show that the lowest instruction is always live, for a machine with no self-rollback, it suffices to show that hazard signals of the lowest (not necessarily real) full stage eventually get turned off. This is because all lower full stages are not really full, and thus must have a pending rollback. Since a rollback hazard implies a hazard, the pending rollback is resolved and the full bit cleared once the hazard signal turns off. Thus one by one, all lower full bits are cleared, and eventually the lowest instruction is in the lowest stage with a full bit, and is not stalled from below. At that point it can only be stalled by its own hazard signal, which by assumption eventually turns off. We will now turn this intuition into a liveness theorem stating that if in a machine without self-rollback the lowest hazard signal is eventually turned off, the lowest instruction is always live.

We first show the following simple lemma.

Lemma 150. *If in full stages a rollback hazard is eventually turned off in circuit stage $k+1$*

$$full_k^t \quad \to \quad \exists u \geq t. \ /rhaz_{k+1}^u$$

stage k which is not really full will eventually be empty or clocked from above

$$/rfull_k^t \quad \to \quad \exists u \geq t. \ /full_k^u \vee ue_k^u$$

Proof. We distinguish whether that stage is full. If the stage is not full we are done with $u := t$. In the remaining case assume $full_k^t$. By definition of $rfull_k$ we obtain that there must be a pending rollback

$$rbp_k^t$$

We obtain by assumption a (possibly) future cycle $u \geq t$ in which there is no rollback hazard signal

$$/rhaz_{k+1}^u$$

Let u without loss of generality be the first cycle since t without a rollback hazard

$$\forall v \in [t:u). \ rhaz_{k+1}^v$$

We show that for all such cycles v and also for cycle u, stage k remains full with a pending rollback by induction on v. For the base case $v = t$ we already have the claim; for the induction step $v \to v+1$ with $v \in [t:u)$ we have

$$full_k^v, \ rbp_k^v, \ rhaz_{k+1}^v$$

and from the operating condition of the rollback engine (eq. (19))

$$haz_{k+1}^v$$

and thus successively from the definitions of the stall engine

$$stall_{k+1}^v, \ /rollback_k^v, \ full_k^{v+1}, \ rbp_k^{v+1}$$

Thus in cycle u the stage is still full and has a pending rollback

$$full_k^u \wedge rbp_k^u$$

and since there is no rollback hazard, the stage is rolled back

$$rollback_k^u$$

and we have by definition of $full_k$

$$full_k^{u+1} = stall_{k+1}^u \wedge /rollback_k^t \vee ue_k^u = ue_k^u$$

We now split cases on ue_k^u.

- ue_k^u: this is the claim with $u := u$.
- $/ue_k^u$: we obtain

$$/full_k^{u+1}$$

which is the claim with $u := u + 1$.

$\square$

We can now prove the key liveness theorem.

Lemma 151. *If in full stages all rollback hazards are eventually turned off*

$$\forall t, k. \ full_{k-1}^t \quad \rightarrow \quad \exists u \geq t. \ /rhaz_k^u$$

and in the really full stage containing the lowest instruction the hazard is eventually turned off

$$\forall t, k. \ rfull_{k-1}^t \wedge I_k^t = I_K^t \quad \rightarrow \quad \exists u \geq t. \ /haz_k^u$$

then the lowest instruction is always live and committed

$$\forall t. \ live(I_K^t)^t \wedge c(I_K^t)^t$$

Proof. By lemma 129 with $i := I_K^t$ we have

$$c(I_K^t)^t \tag{30}$$

which is the second part of the claim.

For the first part of the claim, we unfold the definition of *live*. Let in cycle $u \geq t$ the instruction be in stage k

$$rfull_{k-1}^u \wedge I_k^u = I_K^t$$

and we have to show that the instruction leaves the stage eventually

$$\exists z \geq u. \ I_k^z = I_K^t \wedge ue_k^z$$

By lemma 124 the instruction is still the lowest instruction in cycle u

$$I_K^u = I_K^t = I_k^u$$

which is thus by lemma 129 committed

$$c(I_k^u)^u$$

At this point the proof distinguishes between the lowest stage $k = K$, which is never stalled from below, and upper stages $k < K$. We only show the proof for the upper stages, which is slightly more involved.

By contraposition of lemma 108 we obtain that stage $k < K$ is not really full

$$/rfull_k^u$$

By lemma 150 we obtain a cycle $w \geq u$ in which the stage below is either empty or clocked

$$/full_k^v \lor ue_k^v \tag{31}$$

Without loss of generality that is the first such cycle

$$\forall w \in [u : v). \ full_k^w \land /ue_k^w$$

By repeated application of lemma 131 we conclude that the instruction stays in the stage and stays committed

$$I_k^v = I_k^u = I_K^u \land rfull_{k-1}^v \land c(I_k^v)^v$$

By lemma 124 with $t := u, u := v$ the instruction is still the lowest instruction in the pipeline

$$I_k^v = I_K^u = I_K^v$$

The proof now splits between the two branches of the disjunction in eq. (31).

- $/full_k^v$: By assumption and $rfull_{k-1}^v$ there is a cycle $x \geq v$ in which stage k has no hazard signal

$$/haz_k^x$$

Let without loss of generality x be the first such cycle

$$\forall y \in [v : x). \ haz_k^y$$

and thus by lemma 103 there is no update enable in any of these cycles

$$\forall y \in [v : x). \ /ue_k^y$$

By repeated application of lemma 131 we conclude that the instruction stays in the stage

$$I_k^x = I_k^v = I_K^u \land rfull_{k-1}^x \land c(I_k^x)^x$$

By repeated application of the definitions of $stall_{k+1}$ and $full_k$ we obtain that circuit stage $k + 1$ is not stalled and stage k remains empty

$$\forall y \in [v : x)./stall_{k+1}^y, \ /full_k^{y+1}$$

Thus in cycle x stage k is not stalled from below and not from a hazard (which is off)

$$/stall_{k+1}^x, \ /haz_k^x$$

With lemma 121 we obtain that there is no rollback request

$$/rbr_k^x$$

and we conclude successively with the definition of $stall_k$ and the simplified definition of ue_k (eq. (20))

$$/stall_k^x, \ ue_k^x$$

The claim follows for $z := x$

$$I_k^x = I_k^u = I_K^t \ \wedge \ ue_k^x$$

- ue_k^v: in this case we are done, as instruction I_k^u leaves stage k in cycle $z := v$

$$I_k^v = I_k^u = I_K^t \ \wedge \ ue_k^v$$

$\square$

7.8 Proving Processor Correctness

7.8.1 Induction Scheme

For the proof of lemma 140 we have to to show for all t and i

$$lb(i)^t \wedge c(i)^t \quad \rightarrow \quad t \sim_p i \wedge t \sim_m i \qquad (32)$$

In previous machines, it sufficed to show this in a series of lemmas by induction on t and a case split on stages k in the induction step. With rollbacks however the following difficulty arises.

Imagine we wish to show in the induction step that an instruction i which is in stage 1 in cycle $t + 1$ is correctly simulated. From $c(i)^{t+1}$ we can conclude that instruction i will not be rolled back in *hardware*. Thus the ISA instructions $j < i$ which are below i in the pipeline will not signal interrupts $jisr_\pi^u$ in the cycle $u \geq t$ when they reach stage $M - 1 = 3$. Unfortunately for an instruction j currently in stage 2 this cycle $u < t$ lies in the *future*. Thus with the induction scheme used so far we simply have no induction hypothesis which would allow us to conclude $/jisr_\sigma^j$ and thus to conclude that instruction i is not rolled back in ISA.

The good news is that we need induction hypotheses for future cycles $u > t$ only for instructions $j < i$, i.e. before i. We therefore simply change the order in which we prove the main induction hypothesis and proceed by *nested induction*.

- The outer induction is a complete induction on i. When we conclude from $i - 1$ to i this gives us as an induction hypothesis that lemma 140 holds for all instructions $j < i$ and for *all* cycles u

$$\forall j < i, u. \ lb(j)^u \wedge c(j)^u \quad \rightarrow \quad u \sim_p j \wedge u \sim_m j \qquad (33)$$

- The inner induction is on t. When we conclude from (i, t) to $(i, t + 1)$ we can use (32) and (33) both as induction hypotheses. In particular we can use (33) for $j < i$ and $u > t$.

Base case for t = 0 and all i

We first observe that the base case $t = 0$ with $reset^{t-1} = 1$ of the inner induction can be shown for all i directly without reference to any induction hypothesis: we need to prove for all instructions i

$$0 \sim_p i \wedge 0 \sim_p i$$

Since by definition $I_M^0 = 0$, and opc^0 holds trivially, this simplifies to

$$0 \sim_p i \wedge m(h^0) = \ell(m_\sigma^0)$$

The right conjunct follows immediately from the construction of c^0. For the left conjunct we unfold the definition of $\sim_p$ and obtain

$$\forall k, R. \; I_k^0 = i \wedge (R \in reg(k) \wedge vis(R)$$
$$\vee \; R \in reg(k-1) \wedge /vis(R) \wedge rfull_{k-1}^0 \wedge used[R]^i)$$
$$\rightarrow \quad R_\pi^0 = R_\sigma^i$$

By definition $I_k^0 = 0$ thus we actually only need to argue about $i = 0$

$$\forall k, R. \; (R \in reg(k) \wedge vis(R)$$
$$\vee \; R \in reg(k-1) \wedge /vis(R) \wedge rfull_{k-1}^0 \wedge used[R]^0)$$
$$\rightarrow \quad R_\pi^0 = R_\sigma^0$$

and this claim follows immediately from the definition of c^0 and from the way we initialize visible registers after reset.

Induction step of the inner induction for all i

For the base case $i = 0$ of the outer induction we now would have to show (32) by induction on t for all t. The induction step $(0,t) \rightarrow (0,t+1)$ of this proof happens to by extremely similar to the induction step $(i,t) \rightarrow (i,t+1)$ of the inner induction. The reason is that the outer induction hypothesis for $j < i$ is only needed for instructions *below* instruction i in the pipeline, which for instruction $i = 0$ simply don't exist. Formally we will do both proofs in parallel and only point out the places where the proofs differ.

Induction hypothesis of former instructions for future cycles

In general the induction step $t \rightarrow t+1$ with $reset^t = 0$ follows the argument in section 6.3. We focus here only on the new arguments required in the induction step. The induction hypothesis for t states that hardware in the previous cycle simulated instruction i

$$lb(i)^t \wedge c(i)^t \quad \rightarrow \quad t \sim_p i \wedge t \sim_m i \tag{34}$$

We have to show for cycle $t+1$

$$lb(i)^{t+1} \wedge c(i)^{t+1} \quad \rightarrow \quad t+1 \sim_p i \wedge t+1 \sim_m i$$

Let thus in what follows instruction i be some instruction such that all instructions before i are live and instruction i is committed in cycle $t+1$

$$lb(i)^{t+1} \wedge c(i)^{t+1}$$

and k be some stage in which instruction i is in cycle $t+1$

$$i = I_k^{t+1}$$

We will now massage the induction hypothesis for i (eq. (33)) to obtain a more useful hypothesis. By lemma 119 and $c(i)^{t+1}$, each earlier instruction j is also committed in cycle $t+1$

$$j < i \quad \rightarrow \quad c(j)^{t+1}$$

and by lemma 122, instruction j was not rolled back in the current cycle

$$j < i \quad \rightarrow \quad \forall k. \; rbr_k^t \quad \rightarrow \quad I_R^t > j$$

By lemma 117 we obtain that instruction j was committed in cycle t

$$j < i \quad \rightarrow \quad c(j)^t$$

By repeated application of lemma 117 we obtain also that instruction j is committed in all (possibly) future cycles $u \geq t$

$$j < i \wedge u \geq t \quad \rightarrow \quad c(j)^u \tag{35}$$

With lemma 141 and $lb(i)^{t+1}$ we obtain that all instructions before instructions before i are live

$$j < i \quad \rightarrow \quad lb(j)^{t+1}$$

By lemma 148 with $c(j)^t$ we obtain that they were already live in cycle t

$$j < i \quad \rightarrow \quad lb(j)^t$$

and by repeated application of lemma 143 they will continue to be live in all (possibly) future cycles $u \geq t$

$$j < i \wedge u \geq t \quad \rightarrow \quad lb(j)^u$$

Plugging this and eq. (35) into the induction hypothesis for i (eq. (33)) we obtain that all earlier instructions j are simulated correctly in all cycles $u \geq t$

$$\forall j < i, \; u \geq t. \; u \sim_p j \wedge u \sim_m j \tag{36}$$

We call this the *induction hypothesis for previous instructions and all cycles*.

In the following sections we show the proof of the induction step using implicit t notation.

7.8.2 Induction Step of the Inner Induction

Operating conditions opc' are established as before (section 6.3.6). The structure of large portions of the remainder of the correctness proof is still as in section 5.2.8: we first prove the correctness of the memory update, then of the pipeline stages.

However, before we split cases on ue_k in the pipeline correctness proof, we need a new case split on rbr_k. Recall that we have to show in the induction step of the inner induction

$$lb(i)^{t+1} \wedge c(i)^{t+1} \rightarrow t+1 \sim_p i \wedge t+1 \sim_m i$$

The instruction i under consideration is by hypothesis committed in cycle $t+1$ but not necessarily in cycle t, because it may have been rolled back — for the last time — in the previous cycle. Thus for stages k with

$$I_k^{t+1} = k$$

we have to split cases on rbr_k^t. In case there is a rollback, we need to show that visible registers are updated correctly by the instruction that caused the rollback request. In the case without rollback, the proof uses the known arguments, but due to the new inductions scheme (nested induction) we have to adjust notation in some places.

7.8.3 Correctness of Memory Update

We have to show that in case committed instruction i where all previous instructions are live is in the memory stage in the next cycle, then the memory is correct in the next cycle and the operating conditions are maintained

$$lb(i)' \wedge c(i)' \wedge i = I_M' \rightarrow m(h') = \ell(m_\sigma^{I_M'}) \wedge opc'$$

By construction, stage M is never rolled back

$$rbr_M = rbr_K \vee misspec_M = rbr_{K+1} \vee misspec_M \vee misspec_K = 0 \vee 0 \vee 0 = 0$$

Since the instruction i is committed in the next cycle and not rolled back in the current cycle, it is also committed in the current cycle

$$c(i)$$

By lemma 148 instructions before i are already live in the current cycle

$$lb(i)$$

and we can apply the induction hypothesis for the current cycle (eq. (34)).

With the induction hypothesis we obtain that in case i is in the memory stage in the current cycle, the memory is correct in the current cycle

$$i = I_M \rightarrow m(h) = \ell(m_\sigma^{I_M})$$

For instructions j before i we have the same by eq. (36) with $u := t$

$$i > j = I_M \;\rightarrow\; m(h) = \ell(m_\sigma^{I_M})$$

We combine both to

$$i \geq I_M \;\rightarrow\; m(h) = \ell(m_\sigma^{I_M}) \tag{37}$$

Since the scheduling function in the absence of rollback only increases, we have

$$i = I'_M \geq I_M$$

and we conclude immediately that the memory is correct in the current cycle and the operating conditions were satisfied so far

$$m(h) = \ell(m_\sigma^{I_M}) \wedge opc$$

Since the instruction i is committed and previous instructions are live, with eq. (34) we obtain that instruction i is simulated by hardware; in particular, all registers used to compute the data access are correct. Using circuit stage correctness we conclude like before that the data access is correct

$$dacc_\sigma^i \equiv dacc_\pi$$

At this point one can prove completely analogous to before (lemma 88) that the operating conditions are satisfied

Lemma 152.

$$opc'$$

For the instruction access we can no longer prove that it is correct, as there might be an interrupted instruction between the instruction fetch stage and the memory stage that will modify program counters and hence the instruction address. Luckily that does not matter as the instruction fetch access in hardware is a read

$$iacc_\pi.(r,w,cas) = (1,0,0)$$

which does not update memory, and for the memory updates the address of this read does not matter.

Thus completely analogously to before — and exploiting as before that operating conditions opc' have already been established — we conclude

$$m(h') = \ell(m_\sigma^{I'_M})$$

7.8.4 Pipeline Correctness with Rollback Request

Assume that there is a rollback request in stage k

$$rbr_k$$

and thus by definition of I'_k, instruction i is the instruction which is rolled back

$$i = I'_k = I_R$$

from a stage possibly below k

$$R \geq k$$

Because the instruction is committed in the next cycle, this is the last cycle in which the rollback request is active

$$/rbr'_k$$

We have by lemma 97 there is a misspeculation in stage R

$$misspec_R$$

By contraposition of lemma 101, after rollback stage $k - 1$ can only be truly full if $k = 1$

$$rfull'_{k-1} \rightarrow k = 1$$

and stage $k - 1$ does not have any invisible registers. Thus the claim for invisible registers is vacuously true, and we only need to worry about the visible registers.

By construction, a misspeculation only occurs in case of an eret in stage ID or a jisr from stage M, and we distinguish between these two cases.

- $R = 1$: By definition of $misspec_1$ we just discovered an eret instruction in the decoder

$$eret(2) \wedge full_1$$

Clearly k must be stage 1

$$k \leq R = 1$$

and since there are no visible registers in register stage 1, we are done.
- $R = 3$: By definition of $misspec_3$ we just discovered an interrupt in the memory stage

$$jisr.3 \wedge full_3$$

The only visible registers in a stage $k \leq 3$ are the program counters, and we have to show that these will be correct in the next cycle, i.e.,

$$pc'_\pi = pc^i_\sigma \quad \text{and} \quad dpc'_\pi = dpc^i_\sigma$$

From lemma 138 we obtain that stage $R = 3$ was really full

$$rfull_3$$

and we conclude with well-formedness

$$i = I_R = I_3 = I_4 + 1 > I_4$$

Thus $i = 0$ is impossible, we are not in the base case of the outer induction and can thus apply the induction hypothesis for previous instructions and all cycles (eq. (36)) with $j := I_4$ and the present implicit cycle t. We obtain that the pipeline in the current cycle simulates instruction I_4, and thus

$$jisr.3 = jisr_\sigma^{I_4}$$

The claims follow since both hardware and ISA are now at the beginning of the interrupt service routine.

$$(pc, dpc)_\pi' = (4_{32}, 0_{32}) = (pc, dpc)_\sigma^{I_4+1} = (pc, dpc)_\sigma^i$$

Note that we did not refer to future cycles and thus the old induction scheme still would have worked here.

7.8.5 Pipeline Correctness without Rollback Request

Assume that there is no rollback request in stage k

$$/rbr_k$$

We have no self-rollback by lemma 138

$$nsr$$

Thus in the absence of rollback (of stage k, not necessarily of higher stages), we obtain first by lemma 128 that instruction i is not rolled back

$$\forall l. \ rbr_l \quad \rightarrow \quad I_R > i$$

and since the instruction i is by assumption committed in the next cycle

$$c(i)'$$

we conclude by lemma 117 that it was already committed in the current cycle

$$c(i) \tag{38}$$

With lemma 148 we obtain further from $lb(i)'$ that instructions before i are live

$$lb(i) \tag{39}$$

We can thus use the induction hypothesis for t (eq. (32)) in the current (implicit) cycle t and obtain

$$t \sim_p i$$

From the induction hypothesis of previous instructions for future cycles (eq. (36)) with $u := t$ we obtain also for all $j < i$

$$t \sim_p j$$

Combining both we get for $j \leq i$ that the pipeline in the current cycle simulates j, and unfolding the simulation relation we obtain that all registers that are coupled with instruction $j \leq i$ are correct

$$\forall k, R. \ I_k = j \leq i \wedge (R \in reg(k) \wedge vis(R)$$
$$\vee \ R \in reg(k-1) \wedge /vis(R) \wedge rfull_{k-1} \wedge used[R]^j)$$
$$\rightarrow \quad R_\pi = R_\sigma^j \tag{40}$$

We call this the *induction hypothesis for the current cycle*.

For the other part we distinguish as before between update enable and no update enable. In the latter case, as in the previous machines, nothing happens: the real full bit and register contents all stay the same, and the claim is solved immediately by the induction hypothesis. However, unlike in previous machines, the case distinction is no longer a case split on k. Instead we must now consider all stages k with $I_k' = i$ (of which there may be many) and treat there 1) updated invisible registers in stage $k-1$ and 2) updated visible registers in stage k. While the invisible registers in stage $k-1$ are updated by instruction i on ue_{k-1}, visible registers in stage k are updated by instruction $i-1$ on ue_k (and only in the proof for $i > 0$).

Both cases can be treated for the most part uniformly by considering instruction $j \in \{i, i-1\}$ which updates any stage l

$$j \in \{i, i-1\} \wedge I_l = j \wedge ue_l$$

and proving that all outputs of circuit stage l, which are used, are correct. For $j := i$ and $l := k-1$ this deals with invisible registers, and for $j := i-1$ and $l := k$ this deals with visible registers.

To show that outputs of that stage, which are used, are correct, it suffices by lemma 92 to show that inputs of that instruction j, which are used, are correct. Some of these inputs are provided by earlier instructions, which only provide correct data in case they are not misspeculating.

We begin by showing that these earlier instructions g between i and some earlier instruction I_n are in the pipeline, and then show that they are not misspeculating in ISA (i.e., neither $jisr_\sigma^g$ nor $eret_\sigma^g$ holds). The following lemma resembles closely lemma lemma 112, but $I_{\hat{k}}$ is replaced by I_k' and thus the new lemma talks about a later cycle.

Lemma 153. *Let g be an instruction between the instruction I_n in some stage n and instruction $i = I_k'$*

$$g \in [I_n : I_k')$$

Then instruction g is in the pipeline in some stage $m \leq n$

$$I_m = g \wedge rfull_{m-1} \wedge n \geq m$$

Proof. From well-formedness and lemma 105 we get

$$I'_k = I_k + ue_k \leq I_k + 1$$

Since $g < i$ we conclude successively

$$g < I_k + 1,\ g \leq I_k$$

and we split cases on whether $g < I_k$. If $g < I_k$ the claim is lemma 112 with $k := n$ and $\hat{k} := k$.

If $g = I_k$ we have also (from well-formedness and lemma 105)

$$I_k = g < I'_k = I_k + ue_k$$

and we conclude that the stage must have been updated

$$ue_k$$

With eq. (20) we get that the stage had a true full bit

$$rfull_{k-1}$$

From $g \in [I_n : I'_k)$ we conclude
$$I_n \leq g = I_k$$

and with lemma 110 with $k := n$ and $\hat{k} := k$ we get

$$n \geq k$$

The claim follows with $m := k$.   □

In case $n = M$, these instructions g are not interrupted.

Lemma 154. *Let g be an instruction between I_M and $i = I'_k$*

$$g \in [I_M : i)$$

Then instruction g is not interrupted in ISA

$$/jisr^g_\sigma$$

Proof. By lemma 153 instruction g must be in the pipeline in some stage m above stage M

$$I_m = g \ \wedge \ rfull_{m-1} \ \wedge \ M \geq m$$

We add the implicit t and have by eq. (39) that instructions before i are live

$$lb(i)^t$$

and hence by definition of lb instruction $g = I^t_m$ which is before i is live

$$live(I_m^t)^t$$

Thus with lemma 146 and the fact that in the absence of rbr_k instruction $i > I_m^t$ is already committed in cycle t (eq. (38)) we obtain that instruction I_m^t will be in the memory stage in some possibly future cycle $u \geq t$ and will not misspeculate

$$I_M^u = I_m^t \wedge rfull_{M-1}^u \wedge /misspec_{M-1}^u.$$

Thus by definition of $misspec_{M-1} = misspec_3$ we have no interrupt signal from full stage $M-1 = 3$ in hardware in cycle u

$$/(jisr.3^u \wedge full_3^u)$$

and since the stage is really full (and thus also full), we have no interrupt signal

$$/jisr.3^u$$

By assumption $g < i$ and thus $i > 0$, so we can apply the induction hypothesis of previous instructions and all cycles cycles (eq. (36)) and obtain that we also have no interrupt signal in ISA

$$/jisr_\sigma^g$$

which is the claim.   □

In a completely analogous way and again relying on the induction hypothesis for all cycles we obtain that instructions between the decoder and i are not $eret$ instructions.

Lemma 155. *Let g be an instruction between I_{ID} and $i = I_k'$*

$$g \in [I_{ID} : i)$$

Then instruction g is not an eret instruction

$$/eret_\sigma^g$$

Recall that we are actually considering instruction $j \in \{i, i-1\}$ in stage l with ue_l. Since $eret$ drains the pipe, we can obtain a stronger claim also for $eret$, provided we are only interested in instructions earlier than $j \in \{i, i-1\}$ (and thus below stage l).

Lemma 156. *For $i = I_k'$ let g be an instruction between I_M and the instruction $I_l = j \in \{i, i-1\}$ in updated stage l*

$$g \in [I_M : I_l) \wedge ue_l$$

Then instruction g is not an eret instruction

$$/eret_\sigma^g$$

Proof. By lemma 112 with $k := M$ and $\hat{k} := l$ instruction g must be in the pipeline in some stage m between stages M and l

$$I_m = g \wedge rfull_{m-1} \wedge M \geq m > l$$

We split cases on m. For stages $m \leq ID$ we have from lemma 109

$$g = I_m \geq I_{ID}$$

in which case the claim is lemma 155 and we are done. We now consider the case

$$m > ID = stage(eret)$$

in which there is an invisible register $eret.(m-1)$.
    We split cases on l.

- $l = IF$: In this case we conclude from ue_l successively

$$/haz_l, \ /drain, \ /eret(m), \ /eret.(m-1)$$

Hence from the induction hypothesis for the current cycle (eq. (40))

$$/eret_\sigma^g$$

which is the claim.

- $l > IF$: In this case from ue_l we conclude with eq. (20)

$$rfull_{l-1}$$

We want to use lemma 136 with $k := m-1$ and $j := l-1$ and so we need to check that

$$m - 1 \in [2:3] \quad \text{and} \quad l - 1 \in [1:(m-1)-1]$$

We rewrite this as

$$m \in [3:4] \quad \text{and} \quad l \in [2:(m-1)]$$

which can be rewritten further as

$$m \in [EX:M] \quad \text{and} \quad l \in [ID:m)$$

The first part follows from $m \leq M$ and $m > ID$. The second part follows from $m > l$ and $l > IF$.
Now by contraposition of lemma 136 with $k := m-1$ and $j := l-1$ we get that the instruction in stage l is no eret

$$/eret.(m-1)$$

Hence from the induction hypothesis for the current cycle (eq. (40))

$$/eret_\sigma^g$$

which is the claim.

□

We now prove that inputs of instruction $j \in \{i, i-1\}$, which are used and update stage l, are correct.

Lemma 157. *Let $j \in \{i, i-1\}$ be one of the two instructions that updates registers coupled in the next cycle with instruction i*

$$j \in \{i, i-1\} \wedge j = I_l \wedge ue_l$$

Then all used inputs to circuit stage l are correct.

$$\forall X \in cir(l).in. \ used[X]^i \quad \rightarrow \quad X_\pi = X_\sigma^i$$

Proof. By the induction hypothesis for the current cycle (eq. (40)) all invisible registers in stage $l-1$, which are used, and all visible registers in stage l have the correct values in the current cycle, and only the other inputs, which are used, remain. The output of memory in the memory stage is proven exactly as before. This leaves (in order of stage):

- $ia \in cir(IF).in$: we have to show

$$ia_\pi = ia_\sigma^j$$

with $j = I_{IF}$.
The old proof goes through until we use the dpc semantics in case $rfull_{IF}$

$$
ia_\pi = \begin{cases} dpc_\pi & /rfull_{IF} \\ pc_\pi & rfull_{IF} \end{cases}
$$

$$
= \begin{cases} dpc_\sigma^{I_{ID}} & /rfull_{IF} \\ pc_\sigma^{I_{ID}} & rfull_{IF} \end{cases} \qquad \text{IH}
$$

In the old proof we could in the case $full_{IF}$ immediately conclude $pc_\sigma^{I_{ID}} = dpc_\sigma^{I_{ID}+1}$. Again we would like to conclude

$$rfull_{IF} \quad \rightarrow \quad pc_\sigma^{I_{ID}} = dpc_\sigma^{I_{ID}+1} = dpc_\sigma^{I_{IF}}$$

Since the dpc semantics have now changed in case *jisr* and *eret*, we now have in general:

$$
dpc_\sigma^{i+1} = \begin{cases} 0_{32} & jisr_\sigma^i \\ edpc_\sigma^i & eret_\sigma^i \\ pc_\sigma^i & \text{o.w.} \end{cases}
$$

With $i = I_{ID}$ and $rfull_{IF}$ this translates to

$$
dpc_\sigma^{I_{IF}} = dpc_\sigma^{I_{ID}+1} = \begin{cases} 0_{32} & jisr_\sigma^{I_{ID}} \\ edpc_\sigma^{I_{ID}} & eret_\sigma^{I_{ID}} \\ pc_\sigma^{I_{ID}} & \text{o.w.} \end{cases}
$$

We show that the first two cases can not occur. Since $rfull_{IF}$ we have $I_{IF} > 0$ and thus are in the case of the proof for $i > 0$. We obtain by lemma 156 that the instruction $g := I_{ID}$ in the decoder must not be an *eret* instruction

$$/eret_\sigma^{I_{ID}}$$

By lemma 154 it is also not interrupted

$$/jisr_\sigma^{I_{ID}}$$

Thus

$$dpc_\sigma^{I_{IF}} = pc_\sigma^{I_{ID}}$$

and we conclude the proof as before:

$$ia_\pi = dpc_\sigma^{I_{IF}} = ia_\sigma^{I_{IF}}$$

- *imout* $\in cir(IF).in$: the proof of this input only differs from that in section 6.3.6 in that we now use the software condition SC_{eret} from section 7.6.1, which requires a pipe drain by *eret* between the write of an instruction and a fetch of that instruction. We have $i = I_{IF} \geq I_M$ and thus we can (as in section 7.8.3) argue about the cache memory system like we did before to conclude that there is an ISA step $y \in \{I_M, I'_M\}$ with

$$imout_\pi = \ell(m_\sigma^y)(iacc_\sigma^{I_{IF}}.a)$$

By definition I'_M was before scheduled in stage M or EX

$$I'_M \in \{I_M, I_{EX}\}$$

and since scheduling functions are monotonic (lemma 109) is thus at most I_{IF}

$$I'_M \leq I_{IF}$$

Therefore ISA step y is between I_M and I_{IF}

$$I_M \leq y \leq I'_M \leq I_{IF}$$

We have to show that in ISA the memory at that address does not change between steps y and I_{IF}

$$imout_\pi = \ell(m_\sigma^y)(iacc_\sigma^{I_{IF}}.a) \overset{!}{=} \ell(m_\sigma^{I_{IF}})(iacc_\sigma^{I_{IF}}.a) = imout_\sigma^{I_{IF}}$$

Assume for the sake of contradiction that it does change

$$\ell(m_\sigma^y)(iacc_\sigma^{I_{IF}}.a) \neq \ell(m_\sigma^{I_{IF}})(iacc_\sigma^{I_{IF}}.a)$$

From the memory semantics we conclude that there must be an instruction g between y and I_{IF} changing that address

$$I_M \leq y \leq g < I_{IF} \wedge write_\sigma^g \wedge ea_\sigma^g.l = iacc_\sigma^{I_{IF}}.a = ia_\sigma^{I_{IF}}.l$$

From the software condition SC_{eret} (with $i := I_{IF}$) we immediately conclude that there must be an *eret* instruction in some step h between g and I_{IF}

$$I_M \leq g < h < I_{IF} = j \wedge eret_\sigma^h$$

which contradicts lemma 156 with $g := h$.

- $epcf_{ID}, edpcf_{ID} \in cir(ID).in$: We show the slightly more general claim that the forwarded epcs in each stage $k \in [ID : M]$ match the epcs in that stage

$$X \in \{epc, edpc\} \quad \rightarrow \quad Xf_k = X_\sigma^{I_k}$$

which solves the claim with $k := ID$. The claim is shown for each k separately from bottom to top. We only show the proofs for stages $k = M$ and $k = EX$ as the stage $k = ID$ is analogous.

For $k = M$ the claim follows immediately from the induction hypothesis for the current cycle (eq. (40)) for the instruction $j := I_M$

$$epcf_M = spr.dout[3] = spr_\pi(3_5) \stackrel{E\ 40}{=} spr_\sigma^{I_M}(3_5) = epc_\sigma^{I_M}$$

For $k = EX$ we distinguish between three cases: either there was a hit, or no hit because the stage was empty, or no hit because the stage was full but the instruction does not write to the *epc*.

- $hit_{epc}[EX]$: by definition the stage has a true full bit and the instruction is writing to the *epc*

$$rfull_{EX} \wedge sprw.EX \wedge xad.EX = 3_5$$

From the induction hypothesis for the current cycle (eq. (40)) for the instruction $j := I_M$ in the memory stage we conclude

$$sprw_\sigma^{I_M} \wedge xad_\sigma^{I_M} = 3_5$$

From the semantics of the ISA and the circuit stage correctness lemma (lemma 92) we conclude

$$
\begin{aligned}
epc_\sigma^{I_{EX}} &= spr_\sigma^{I_{EX}}(3_5) \\
&= spr_\sigma^{I_M+1}(3_5) && \text{L 104} \\
&= C_\sigma^{I_M} && \text{defn. ISA} \\
&= C.M.in && \text{L 92} \\
&= epcf_{EX} && \text{construction}
\end{aligned}
$$

which is the claim.

– $/hit_{epc}[EX] \wedge /rfull_{EX}$: in this case the scheduling function does not change and the claim follows from the claim for $epcf_M$

$$
\begin{aligned}
epc_\sigma^{I_{EX}} &= epc_\sigma^{I_M} && \text{L 104} \\
&= epcf_M \\
&= epcf_{EX} && \text{construction}
\end{aligned}
$$

– $/hit_{epc}[EX] \wedge rfull_{EX}$: in this case we conclude from $/hit_{epc}[EX]$ that the instruction is not writing to the epc

$$/(sprw.EX \wedge xad.EX = 3_5)$$

From the induction hypothesis for the current cycle (eq. (40)) for the instruction $j := I_M$ in the memory stage we conclude

$$/(sprw_\sigma^{I_M} \wedge xad_\sigma^{I_M} = 3_5)$$

From the semantics of the ISA and the circuit stage correctness lemma (lemma 92) we conclude

$$
\begin{aligned}
epc_\sigma^{I_{EX}} &= spr_\sigma^{I_{EX}}(3_5) \\
&= spr_\sigma^{I_M+1}(3_5) && \text{L 104} \\
&= spr_\sigma^{I_M}(3_5) && \text{defn. ISA} \\
&= epc_\sigma^{I_M} \\
&= epcf_M \\
&= epcf_{EX} && \text{construction}
\end{aligned}
$$

which is the claim.

• $A, B, S \in cir(ID).in$: nothing changes except in two regards. Firstly instead of the induction hypothesis we now use the induction hypothesis for the current cycle (eq. (40)). With this the proof goes through almost literally except in two lines, where we argue that the inputs to the pipelined C register/the gpr from which an instruction in a lower stage $l > ID$ would forward are correct

$$C.(l+1).in \overset{!}{=} C_\sigma^{I_l}, \quad gprin_\pi = gprin_\sigma^{I_M}$$

In the induction schema we used before, these were proven as part of the induction step for stage l. In the new induction scheme this is no longer part of the induction step but they can be proven completely analogously from the induction hypothesis for the current cycle (eq. (40)) and the circuit stage correctness lemma (lemma 92).

• $mode \in cir(ID).in$: by the induction hypothesis for the current cycle (eq. (40)) we have

$$mode_\pi = mode_\sigma^{I_M}$$

and we need to show

$$mode_\pi = mode_\sigma^{I_{ID}}$$

We show that the mode can not have been changed by *eret* or *jisr*. We distinguish between the proofs for $i = 0$ and $i > 0$. In the case $i = 0$ the mode can not have changed as no instructions have been executed

$$mode_\sigma^{I_M} = mode_\sigma^0 = mode_\sigma^{I_{ID}}$$

and the claim follows. In the proof for $i > 0$ assume for the sake of contradiction

$$mode_\sigma^{I_M} \neq mode_\sigma^{I_{ID}}$$

Clearly one of the instructions $g \in [I_M : I_{ID})$ must have changed the mode, which by definition of our ISA can only be done by interrupts and *eret* instructions

$$I_M \leq g < I_{ID} = j \wedge (eret_\sigma^g \vee jisr_\sigma^g)$$

This contradicts lemmas 154 and 156.

- $e \in cir(EX).in$: the external input is sampled and thus correct by definition. In explicit t notation:

$$e_\pi^t = e_\pi^{t_i} = e_\sigma^i$$

$\square$

With this the remainder of the proof is *almost* trivial, except for the program counters, which in ISA are updated under control of $jisr_\sigma$ while in hardware *jisr* is ignored during regular update of the program counters.

Assume thus that visible registers pc, dpc are updated by instruction $I_{ID} = i - 1$

$$ue_{ID} \wedge i = I'_{ID} = I_{ID} + 1$$

In hardware, the update of program counters is done as if the instruction in stage ID was not interrupted, which by lemma 154 for $g := I_{ID}$ is exactly the case

$$
(pc, dpc)'_\pi = (pc, dpc).in = \begin{cases} (epcf_{ID}, edpcf_{ID})_\pi & eret(2) \\ (nextpc, pc)_\pi & \text{o.w.} \end{cases}
$$

$$
= \begin{cases} (epc, edpc)_\sigma^{I_{ID}} & eret_\sigma^{I_{ID}} \\ (nextpc, pc)_\sigma^{I_{ID}} & \text{o.w.} \end{cases} \qquad \text{IH, forwading proof pcs}
$$

$$
= \begin{cases} (epc, edpc)_\sigma^{I_{ID}} & eret_\sigma^{I_{ID}} \\ (4_{32}, 0_{32}) & 0 \\ (nextpc, pc)_\sigma^{I_{ID}} & \text{o.w.} \end{cases}
$$

$$
= \begin{cases} (epc, edpc)_\sigma^{I_{ID}} & eret_\sigma^{I_{ID}} \\ (4_{32}, 0_{32}) & jisr_\sigma^{I_{ID}} \\ (nextpc, pc)_\sigma^{I_{ID}} & \text{o.w.} \end{cases} \qquad \text{with L 154}
$$

$$
= (pc, dpc)_\sigma^{I_{ID}+1} = (pc, dpc)_\sigma^i
$$

7.9 Completing the Liveness Proof

We prove that all instructions are live in our machine. We first show that the lowest instruction in the pipeline is committed and live, and will then use lemma 149 to show that all instructions eventually become the lowest instruction in the pipeline.

Lemma 158.

$$rfull_{k-1}^t \wedge I_k^t = I_K^t \quad \rightarrow \quad \exists u \geq t. \; /haz_k^u$$

Proof. By lemma 145 instructions before the lowest stage are live

$$lb(I_K^t)^t$$

By lemma 138 we have no self-rollback and by lemma 129 the instruction in the lowest stage is committed

$$c(I_K^t)^t$$

Since by assumption $I_k^t = I_K^t$ we get that the instruction in stage k is committed and earlier instructions are live

$$lb(I_k^t)^t \wedge c(I_k^t)^t$$

Thus by the correctness theorem (lemma 140) the coupling relation holds, and the pipeline correctly simulates the instruction I_k^t

$$t \sim_p I_k^t \tag{41}$$

The proof now is by case split on k.

- $k = IF = 1$: By definition of the instruction port, the operating conditions of the instruction port (address stability and that at most one of $.(r, w, cas)$ is raised) are satisfied, and we obtain by liveness of the memory system (section 8.5.11 of [KMP14]) that in a (possibly) future cycle $u \geq t$ the memory responds and is not busy

$$/mbusy(IP)^u$$

Let without loss of generality u be the first such cycle

$$\forall w \in [t : u). \; mbusy(IP)^u$$

and by definition of haz_1 we have a hazard until then

$$\forall w \in [t : u). \; haz_1^u$$

Thus by lemma 103 we have no update enable

$$\forall w \in [t : u). \; /ue_1^u$$

By repeated application of lemma 131 we obtain that the instruction is still in stage $k = IF = 1$ in cycle u

$$I_K^t = I_k^t = I_k^u \wedge rfull_{k-1}^u$$

and by lemma 125 all stages below k must be empty

$$\forall l > k. \ /rfull_{l-1}^u$$

The claim now follows as there is neither a hazard from the memory nor from an *eret* in a lower really full stage

$$haz_1^u = mbusy(IP)^u \vee drain^u$$

$$= 0 \vee \bigvee_{l=2}^{4} rfull_{l-1}^u \wedge eret(l)^u$$

$$= \bigvee_{l=2}^{4} 0 \wedge eret(l)^u$$

$$= 0$$

- $k = ID = 2$: By lemma 125 with $u := t$ all stages below k are empty

$$\forall l > k. \ /rfull_{l-1}^t$$

and thus lower stages do not have a hit (which by definition of *hit* requires a true full bit)

$$\forall l > k. \ /hit_X[l-1]^t$$

By definition of the top hit, none of the stages below is the top hit

$$\forall l > k. \ /top_X[l-1]^t$$

and by definition of haz_A and haz_B forwarding hazards are off

$$haz_2^t = haz_A^t \vee haz_B^t = 0$$

The claim follows with $u := t$.
- $k = M = 4$: In the ISA, at most one of the access bits is on

$$1 \geq \sum_i dacc_\sigma^{I_M}.(r,w,cas)_i$$

With the coupling relation (eq. (41)) we conclude that we use the same access in hardware

$$dacc_\pi^t.(r,w,cas) = dacc_\sigma^{I_M}.(r,w,cas)$$

which thus satisfies the operating condition of the memory port

$$1 \geq \sum_i dacc_\pi^t.(r,w,cas)_i$$

By liveness of the memory system (section 8.5.11 of [KMP14]) in a (possibly) future cycle $u \geq t$ the memory responds and is not busy

$$/mbusy(DP)^u$$

and the claim follows

$$haz_M^u = mbusy(DP)^u = 0$$

- $k \in \{3,5\}$: These stages never have a hazard, and the claim follows.

$\square$

The next condition we need to show before we can apply the key liveness theorem (lemma 151) and show liveness is that rollback hazards eventually disappear.

Lemma 159.

$$\forall t, k. \ full_{k-1}^t \quad \rightarrow \quad \exists u \geq t. \ /rhaz_k^u$$

Proof. The only stage with a rollback hazard at all is stage *ID*. Let thus $k = ID$, and we obtain as in lemma 158 that there is a cycle $u \geq t$ in which the memory system is no longer busy

$$/mbusy(IP)^u$$

and the claim follows

$$rhaz_1^u = mbusy(IP)^u = 0$$

$\square$

We now show that all instructions eventually enter the pipeline and are live

Lemma 160.

$$\forall i. \ \exists k,t. \ rfull_{k-1}^t \wedge I_k^t = i \wedge live(i)^t$$

Proof. By lemma 149 with lemma 159 it suffices to show that the instruction in the lowest stage is always live and committed

$$\forall t. \ live(I_K^t)^t \wedge c(I_K^t)^t$$

We now apply lemma 151, which reduces the claim to lemmas 138, 158 and 159.

$\square$

7.10 Proof Summary

Interrupts and *eret* instructions force rollbacks of instructions in the pipeline. With a new stall engine rollback of instructions is achieved in two stages:

- complete the memory accesses of the instruction. During this time the corresponding rollback pending bits rbp_k are turned on.
- do the actual rollback by clearing the $full_k$ bits.

Full bits without pending rollback bit are called a real full bits

$$rfull_k = full_k \wedge /rbp_k$$

The existence of rollbacks caused global changes in the overall proof structure.

- In the main induction hypothesis for pipeline stages we argue about the correctness of invisible registers only when their stage has true full bits; once rollback is pending we only need to argue that they don't change.
- also in the main induction hypothesis we now use a predicate $t \sim_p i$ stating that data in visible or invisible registers for ISA instruction i are correct

$$t \sim_p i \equiv \forall k, R. \ I_k^t = i \wedge (R \in reg(k) \wedge vis(R)$$
$$\vee \ R \in reg(k-1) \wedge /vis(R) \wedge rfull_{k-1}^t \wedge used[R]^i)$$
$$\rightarrow \quad R_\pi^t = R_\sigma^i$$

and a predicate $t \sim_m i$ stating that the memory is correct and operating conditions are satisfied

$$t \sim_m i \equiv i = I_M^t \rightarrow m(h^t) = \ell(m_\sigma^i) \wedge opc^t$$

The correctness statement for the cache memory system is reformulated in the same spirit and the main induction hypothesis turns into

$$t \sim_p i \wedge t \sim_m i$$

- the above rewriting of the main correctness statement is far from a bookkeeping exercise. By focusing on all stages with relevant data for instruction i in cycle t we can now in a very concise way weaken the induction hypothesis to concern only instructions in the pipe which are committed, i.e., which will not be rolled back

$$c(i)^t \quad \rightarrow \quad t \sim_p i \wedge t \sim_m i$$

So we don't show anything about instructions, which are rolled back in cycle t or in the future. This only works because there is no self rollback

$$nsr$$

i.e., instructions are only rolled back by committed instructions further down the pipe, and thus the decision to roll back (or not) can be proven correct.
- For technical reasons related to the liveness proof of the machine we restrict the correctness statement further to situations where all instructions before i are live and obtain as main induction hypothesis

$$lb(i)^t \wedge c(i)^t \quad \rightarrow \quad t \sim_p i \wedge t \sim_m i$$

- the inductions scheme of the correctness proof is changed. Using nested induction we prove the main hypothesis in an outer induction on ISA instructions i and an inner induction for all hardware cycles t. Thus while arguing about correctness of instruction i in cycle $t + 1$ we can use the correctness of earlier instructions $j < i$ in cycle $t + 1$ and future cycles $u > t + 1$.

The liveness proof is split into three parts:

- preliminary results needed to show processor correctness

- the portions of the liveness proof which do not become easier once processor correctness is established
- after completion of the processor correctness proof: the remaining part of the liveness proof

The absence of self rollbacks hinges on the fact that lowest rollback requests rbr_k are triggered by misspeculation signals $misspec_{k+1}$ which in turn can only become active in truly full stages.

   This structure is not going to change in the future. Establishing that the operating conditions of the cache memory system are fulfilled in the presence of rollbacks obviously requires new arguments.

- For the data access nothing changes: instructions in the memory stage are never rolled back and one uses as before the software condition SC_{ROM} that writes don't access the ROM portion of the cache memory system.
- In contrast instruction fetches can be rolled back both due to *eret* and *jisr* signals. Thus one has to argue about pending rollbacks and show that the stabilizer latch does its job in this situation (section 7.5.7). In later chapters the role of the stabilizer latch will be taken over by other hardware, but pending rollbacks during accesses, which have not yet completed will obviously remain an issue.

We proceed to summarize the induction step $(i,t) \to (i,t+1)$ of the inner induction (the case $(i,0)$ being trivial for all i).

- in the induction step new cases arise if $t+1$ is the first cycle, in which instruction i is committed, i.e. if instruction i is rolled back (for the last time) in cycle t. Rollbacks clear full bits. Therefore proof obligations after rollback only concern visible registers above the circuit stage causing the rollback. In a rollback due to an $eret(2)$ signal in stage $cir(ID)$ such registers don't exist. In case of *jisr* one only has to show that pc and dpc are correctly initialized with the start of the interrupt service routine, which is trivial.
- instructions i which are committed in cycle $t+1$ and not rolled back in cycle t were already committed in cycle t. We can use the induction hypothesis for cycle t, and for stages k, which do not get input from lower stages we can complete the proof as before.
- For stages k which get inputs from lower stages we exploit that i and the instructions below i in the pipe are by definition of 'committed' not rolled back in hardware in cycles $u \geq t$, but before we can apply the pipeline stage correctness lemmas we have to show that this absence of rollback is reflected in ISA, i.e., that the previous instructions below instruction $g < i$ in the pipe do not activate $jisr_\sigma^g$ or $eret_\sigma^g$ in ISA (lemmas 154 and 155). This requires arguing about the correctness of previous instructions in future cycles, which is possible with the new induction scheme.

About inputs coming from memory, lower stages or register stage $reg(k)$ into circuit stage $cir(k)$ we argue more or less along known lines.

- $ia \in cir(IF)$. Committed instructions cannot be rolled back by *eret* or *jisr*. In this situation the old proof for the correctness of the instruction address *ia* goes through.
- $imout \in cir(IF)$: as in the previous chapter one couples instruction accesses of hardware during ue_{IF} and instruction accesses of ISA and then uses the correctness of outputs of cache memory system (lemma 78). However due to the new software condition SC_{eret} one must now use the fact that *eret* instructions drain the pipe.
- forwarded signals $epcf_{ID}, edpcf_{ID} \in cir(ID)$ are used in *eret* instructions. Their correctness follows along the known lines and observing that hit signals now only occur for truly full stages.
- signal $mode \in cir(IF)$ comes straight from the special purpose register file and is used in the computation of the illegal interrupt signal *ill*. The mode bit is only changed by *jisr* or *eret* instructions. Because we assume instruction $i = I'_{ID}$ to be committed, this cannot be caused by instructions below instruction i in the pipeline.
- $A, B, S, ien \in cir(EX)$: proof along the known lines observing that hit signals now use true full bits.
- $dmout \in cir(M)$: as in the previous chapter one couples data accesses of hardware during ue_M and data accesses of ISA accesses and then uses the correctness of outputs of cache memory system (lemma 78).

For the update of the program counters in the absence of hardware rollbacks one has again to argue that this is reflected in the absence of ISA interrupts triggered by instructions below instruction $i = I'_{ID}$ in the pipe.

7.11 Exercises

1. Suppose we wish to turn off redundant fetches in case of misalignment interrupts. Should we use for this the instruction address, i.e.,

$$ica.preq = /(ia[1] \vee ia[0])$$

or should we use the stabilized instruction address

$$ica.preq = /(iaL[1] \vee iaL[0])$$

Hint: you have to consider the stability of memory system inputs during rollback.
2. Usually one would mask external interrupts (setting $sr[0] = 0$) during the execution of *eret* instructions.
   a) Suppose we do not do this. Is ISA still correctly simulated by our pipelined hardware or not?
   b) Explain why?
   c) At which place does this concern the formal correctness proof?

3. Forwarding of *epc* and *edpc* for pipe draining instructions was done in order to minimize changes in the correctness proof of the machine, but intuitively it should not be necessary if we wait to update the program counters until the memory stage.
   a) Modify the hardware in this sense by eliminating these forwarding circuits *and* postponing both the rollback request and the update of *pc* and *dpc* for *eret* instructions.
   b) Prove the correctness of this construction in the absence of interrupts.
   c) Now consider interrupts too in the correctness proof.
   This is not an easy exercise.
4. In our key liveness lemmas (lemmas 149 and 151) we assume that all rollback hazards are cleared eventually, and the lowest real full stage will eventually not have a hazard. Prove that it would suffice to assume that the lowest full stage will eventually be rolled back (in case of a pending rollback) or clocked down (in case the stage is really full), i.e., that the following condition implies liveness:

$$full_{k-1}^t \wedge (\forall l > k. \ /full_{l-1}^t) \quad \rightarrow \quad \exists u \geq t. \begin{cases} /rhaz_k^u & rbp_{k-1}^t \\ /haz_k^u & \text{o.w.} \end{cases}$$

5. As interrupts are only detected after the instruction and rolled-back instructions behind it have already fetched from memory, the cache memory system is affected by instructions that never get executed in ISA. Obviously the cache memory system does affect timing of instruction execution, as cache collisions during these fetch operations can evict other instructions from the instruction cache, which then later cause other instructions to be fetched more slowly. In production processors, effects like this cause a serious system vulnerability (known as meltdown), as malicious users can use timing attacks to snoop the addresses of memory accesses (e.g. fetch accesses) of other processes. Is this a risk for the pipelined processor presented here? Explain your answer.
6. In modern processors branch predictors replace the delay slots. In case the branch is mispredicted, the instruction and subsequent instructions are rolled back. How does this affect the following parts of our machinery? Which of them work as-is, which of them need to be modified, and how?
   a) The stall engine with rollback
   b) The arguments about committed instructions
   c) The liveness arguments

8

Self Modification, Instruction Buffer and Nondeterministic ISA

In most situations self modification of code is considered really bad programming style, but in system programming it cannot be avoided altogether. After a page fault on fetch a new page has to be swapped into memory by the operating system and subsequently instructions are fetched from this page by the user program. While neither the operating system nor the user program alone are self modifying, the entire software consisting of operating system and user programs is, and so dealing with self modification is unavoidable.

Two problems have to be solved:

1. obvious: identifying software conditions permitting to show that the hardware simulates the known sequential ISA.
2. not so obvious: specifying what happens if these software conditions are violated. User programs might violate these conditions; still we want to have some kind of specification permitting us to show that when we return to the operating system, the operating system's data structures should be intact, other user programs are unaffected, etc.

The first problem is already solved with the existing software conditions. In this chapter we introduce nondeterministic ISA, which will permit us to solve the second problem. We proceed in three steps:

1. We review the classical ways to specify nondeterministic finite automata and settle for our purposes on the way with oracle inputs (section 8.1.1).
2. We specify the behaviour of our machines with the help of instruction buffers and a nondeterministic fetch in ISA (section 8.1.3). The nondeterministic choices available in each step will be restricted by *guard conditions*: only steps satisfying the guard conditions are executable, and thus ISA programmers must only make their programs work for all runs satisfying the guard conditions. Using machinery from the multi-core processor correctness proof in [KMP14] we subsequently show processor correctness with respect to this extended ISA in section 8.2 . However, in section 8.3, we have to invest some extra work to show,

© Springer Nature Switzerland AG 2020
P. Lutsyk et al. (Eds.): A Pipelined Multi-Core Machine, LNCS 9999, pp. 331–370, 2020.
https://doi.org/10.1007/978-3-030-43243-0_8

that the ISA computation extracted from the hardware computation during the correctness proof satisfies the guard conditions.

3. As a sanity check we show in section 8.4 an *instruction buffer reduction theorem*: if the software conditions for self modification hold, then the instruction buffer becomes invisible and the extended nondeterministic ISA behaves exactly like the old ISA, which was deterministic and has no instruction buffer.

Processor hardware will stay deterministic; indeed the processor implementation stays unchanged in this chapter. ISA now becomes nondeterministic, even for single core machines. As in the nondeterministic model of cache memory systems the purpose of this is to hide implementation details from the programmer. This comfort of ignoring implementation details comes at the usual price, that programs have to work for all possible nondeterministic choices.

8.1 ISA

8.1.1 Nondeterminism, Oracle Inputs and Stepping Functions

So far ISA was modeled as a deterministic finite automaton with set of states $Z = K_{isa}$. From the external input $e \in \mathbb{B}$ we get input alphabet $A = \mathbb{B}$ and instruction execution was specified by a next state function

$$\delta : Z \times A \to Z$$

where

$$\delta(z, e) = z'$$

means: if the machine reads e in state z, then it goes to state z'. The unique *computation* with input sequence (e^n) and start configuration c^0 is defined as a sequence (c^n) of configurations satisfying

$$\delta(c^n, e^n) = c^{n+1} \quad \text{for all} \quad n$$

Nondeterministic computations can be introduced in any of the following ways.

Transition Relation

One uses a transition relation

$$\delta \subseteq (Z \times A) \times Z$$

where

$$((z, e), z') \in \delta$$

means: if the machine reads e in state z, then it *can go* to state z'. A *computation* with input sequence (e^n) and start configuration c^0 is defined as a sequence (c^n) of configurations satisfying

$$((c^n, e^n), c^{n+1}) \in \delta \quad \text{for all} \quad n$$

Sets of States as Values of Transition Functions

The transition function has the power set

$$2^Z = \{S : S \subseteq Z\}$$

of z as codomain, i.e.

$$\delta : Z \times A \to 2^Z$$

where

$$z' \in \delta(z, e)$$

means: if the machine reads e in state z, then it *can go* to state z'. A *computation* with input sequence (e^n) and start configuration c^0 is defined as a sequence (c^n) of configurations satisfying

$$c^{n+1} \in \delta(c^n, e^n) \quad \text{for all} \quad n$$

Oracle Inputs

For each step n an *oracle input* $o^n \in O$ specifies the nondeterministic choice that should be made. One now has again a transition function

$$\delta : Z \times O \times A \to Z$$

where

$$\delta(z, o, e) = z'$$

means: if the machine reads e in state z and the oracle input is o, then the next state is z. The *computation* with input sequence (e^n), sequence of oracle inputs (o^n) and start configuration c^0 is defined as the sequence (c^n) of configurations satisfying

$$\delta(c^n, (o^n, e^n)) = c^{n+1} \quad \text{for all} \quad n$$

Stepping Functions

In order to streamline notation it turns out to be convenient to unify the external inputs e and the oracle inputs o into combined inputs

$$x = (o, e) \, , \, x \in O \times A$$

The set of combined inputs is denoted by

$$\Sigma = O \times A$$

The sequence (o^n, e^n) of combined external and oracle inputs is then specified by a *stepping function*

$$s : \mathbb{N} \to \Sigma$$

We are just massaging the notation for oracle inputs. Thus transition functions are still specified as

$$\delta : Z \times \Sigma \to Z$$

and the computation with start configuration c^0 and stepping function s is the sequence (c^n) of configurations satisfying

$$c^{n+1} = \delta(c^n, s(n))$$

8.1.2 Guard Conditions and Software Conditions

For every configuration c we can restrict the set of oracle inputs o to be used with c by means of so called *guard conditions*. Formally we use predicates

$$\gamma : Z \times \Sigma \to \mathbb{B}$$

and allow only *valid* stepping functions s where the guard condition $\gamma(c^n, s(n))$ is satisfied for all steps n.

$$valid(s) \equiv \forall n.\ \gamma(c^n, s(n))$$

We will model nondeterministic ISA in the spirit of this formalism. As our machines have more structure than general finite automata, we will end up in a natural way with a more structured set Σ. In processor correctness proofs oracle inputs o^n will be extracted from the hardware computation in much the same way, in which we extracted ISA visible external inputs e_σ^i in section 7.4.5. Moreover we will show, that oracle inputs extracted in this way obey the guard conditions. This permits the ISA programmer to worry only about computations with valid stepping functions.

In particular the programmer has to guarantee software conditions only in valid computations; other computations will not be generated by the hardware anyway, as we hope to establish. A subtle issue arises, when we try to prove this, because in the proof for ISA step n we will have to rely on the software conditions for step n to hold. Clearly we would plan to proceed for ISA step n in the following order

1. conclude with the stepping function extracted from the hardware computation, that the guard condition holds for step n (and by induction hypothesis for steps $m < n$)
2. conclude that the software conditions hold for step n
3. use this as in previous proofs to establish the simulation relation for ISA step n and (all cycles t).

With the definitions in place so far however, this won't work. If software conditions are only supposed to hold if guard conditions are satisfied for *all* ISA steps n, we cannot perform step 2, because at this point we have only established that guard conditions hold until ISA step n and not for all n as required for valid stepping functions. We remedy this by restricting the software conditions:

- software conditions for ISA step n are only allowed to depend on the value of stepping functions $s[0 : n]$, i.e. on ISA steps $m \leq n$ up to and including step n.

Thus we define: a stepping function is valid until step n if the guard conditions hold up to and including step n, i.e.,

$$valid(n, s) \leftrightarrow \forall m \leq n.\ \gamma(c^m, s(m))$$

Alternatively we can say that the initial segment of the stepping function is valid until step n. The single software condition we are left with is SC_{ROM}. We will have to write it as $SC_{ROM}(c^n, s(n))$, and it has to hold for step n only if the stepping function is valid until that step

$$(\forall m \leq n.\ \gamma(c^m, s(m))) \to SC_{ROM}(c^n, s(n))$$

8.1.3 Configurations, Instruction Buffer and Guard Conditions

For the sole purpose of modeling a nondeterministic instruction fetch mechanism ISA configurations c now get as an additional component an instruction buffer $c.ib$. Thus they have now the form

$$c = (c.pc, c.dpc, c.gpr, c.spr, c.m, c.ib)$$

If we drop the instruction buffer we obtain the processor portion of the configuration

$$c.p = (c.pc, c.dpc, c.gpr, c.spr, c.m)$$

The ISA programmer 'sees' the instruction buffer as a cache for instructions capable of storing a finite set of instruction buffer entries

$$ibe = (ibe.a, ibe.I)$$

where

- component
$$ibe.a \in \mathbb{B}^{32}$$
  is a memory address and
- component
$$ibe.I \in \mathbb{B}^{32}$$
  is the instruction stored in the entry.

Thus the set of instruction buffer entries is

$$K_{ibe} = \mathbb{B}^{32} \times \mathbb{B}^{32}$$

and the instruction buffer $c.ib$ of an ISA configuration stores at any time a set of such entries:

$$c.ib \subseteq K_{ibe}$$

Initially the instruction buffer is empty

$$c^0.ib = \emptyset$$

Even for the single core machine under consideration ISA now is nondeterministic with two kinds of steps n:

- *Instruction buffer steps* prefetch instructions into the instruction buffer and are generated by inputs $s(n) = x$ of the form

$$x = (ib, a) \quad \text{with} \quad a \in \mathbb{B}^{32}$$

  Their effect is to load the memory word $c^n.m_4(a)$ at address a into the instruction buffer.

$$s(n) = (ib, a) \quad \rightarrow \quad c^{n+1}.ib = c^n.ib \cup \{(a, c^n.m_4(a))\}$$

The instruction access of ISA occurs now in this step. Thus we have to redefine

$$iacc(c,x).a = x.a$$
$$iacc(c,x).r = 1$$

We allow to prefetch any memory word; thus the guard condition for instruction buffer steps is trivial

$$\gamma(c, (ib, a)) = 1$$

- *Processor steps* are generated by inputs $s(n) = x$ of the form

$$x = (p, I, e) = (p, x.I, x.e) \quad \text{with} \quad I \in \mathbb{B}^{32}, \, e \in \mathbb{B}$$

and will have the effect to execute instruction $x.I$ with external input $x.e$. They have to obey for $c = c^n$ the guard condition $\gamma(c,x)$ that the instruction buffer entry $(c.dpc, x.I)$ is in the instruction buffer $c.ib$, provided $c.dpc$ is aligned

$$\gamma(c,x) \quad \equiv \quad ia(c) = 00 \quad \rightarrow \quad (c.dpc, x.I) \in c.ib$$

Thus we get an input alphabet

$$\Sigma = \Sigma_{ib} \cup \Sigma_p$$

with

$$\Sigma_{ib} = \{ib\} \times \mathbb{B}^{32} \quad \text{and} \quad \Sigma_p = \{p\} \times \mathbb{B}^{32} \times \mathbb{B}$$

Instruction buffers are cleared by interrupts and returns from exception. We will formally define this when we define the effect of instruction execution.

8.1.4 Instruction Execution

Let K be the set of ISA configurations (with instruction buffer component $c.ib$). Then the effect of instruction execution is defined by a transition function

$$\delta : K \times \Sigma \rightarrow K$$

Thus we have to define

$$c' = \delta(c,x) \quad \text{with} \quad c \in K, \, x \in \Sigma, \, \gamma(c,x)$$

Misalignment on fetch is discovered as before

$$malf(c) \quad \equiv \quad ia(c)[1:0] \neq 00$$

in which case the instruction component $x.I$ of input x can be arbitrary, because it is not used.

The salient new part of the definition concerns instruction fetch. Rather than fetching an instruction word in the step in which it is executed, the instruction $I(c,x)$ to be executed is given by component $x.I$ of the oracle input

$$I(c,x) = x.I$$

Note that (in the absence of misalignment) due to the guard condition we have

$$(ia(c), x.I) \in c.ib$$

In a computation where

$$c = c^n, \; x = s(n)$$

this instruction buffer entry was loaded into the instruction buffer by some instruction buffer step $u < n$ in the past, which fetched from that address

$$s(u) = (ib, \; ia(c^n))$$

and fetched exactly that instruction word

$$s(n).I \; = \; c^u.m_4(ia(c^n))$$

If code is not self modifying we have

$$s(n).I \; = \; c^u.m_4(ia(c^n)) \; = \; \ldots \; = \; c^n.m_4(ia(c^n))$$

and the new definition coincides with the old one

$$I(c^n, s(n)) \; = \; s(n).I \; = \; c^n.m_4(ia(c^n)) \; = \; I(c^n)$$

This argument will reappear in the instruction buffer reduction theorem of section 8.4.

In general the instruction $I(c,x)$ to be executed now depends on x. As a consequence almost all functions $f_{old}(c)$ like $opc_{old}(c), rs_{old}(c), alures_{old}(c), \ldots$ from the old definition of ISA have to be written as $f(c,x)$ in a completely straight forward way. The only functions from the old definition of ISA that do not depend on I also do not depend on e. These are

$$ia(c), \; ien(c), \; mode(c), \; malf(c)$$

Among the predicates which depend on the instruction we have in particular

$$jisr(c,x) \quad \text{and} \quad eret(c,x)$$

and if one of these predicates holds, the instruction buffer is cleared, otherwise the instruction buffer is not changed by processor instructions

$$c'.ib = \begin{cases} \emptyset & jisr(c,x) \vee eret(c,x) \\ c.ib & \text{otherwise} \end{cases}$$

With the obvious change of notation all components $c'.X$ with $X \neq ib$ of the next configuration are defined as before. We denote the set of configurations of MIPS machines without instruction buffer with K_{old}, the transition function of ordinary MIPS machines with δ_{old}

$$\delta_{old} : K \times \mathbb{B} \to K$$

and we collect a few observations relating the two kinds of semantics into the following lemma

Lemma 161. *Let the processor portion of $c \in K$ coincide with configuration $d \in K_{old}$, let*

$$x = (p,\ x.I,\ x.e)$$

be an input for a processor step of the instruction buffer machine and let the external interrupt e for d coincide with input $x.e$ for the instruction buffer machine

$$c.p = d \wedge x.e = e$$

Then

1. *if the instruction address is aligned and instruction $I(d)$ coincides with $x.I$ then all intermediate signals f of the semantics specification coincide*

$$ia_{old}(d)[1:0] = 00 \wedge I_{old}(d) = x.I$$

   then all intermediate signals f of the semantics specification coincide

$$f_{old}(d) = \begin{cases} f(c) & f \text{ does not depend on } I \\ f(c,x) & o.w. \end{cases}$$

2. *if the instruction address is misaligned or instruction $I_{old}(d)$ coincides with $x.I$*

$$ia_{old}(d)[1:0] \neq 00 \vee I_{old}(d) = x.I$$

   then the interrupt signal and the next configurations coincide

$$jisr_{old}(d,e) = jisr(c,x) \wedge \delta_{old}(d,e) = \delta(c,x)$$

Proof. Part 1 just repeats how the semantics of the instruction buffer machine was constructed from ordinary MIPS semantics. Misalignment interrupts do not depend on inputs. For part 2 we have to split cases on misalignment interrupts. By hypothesis we get

$$malf(c) \equiv ia(c)[1:0] \neq 00 \equiv ia_{old}(d)[1:0] \neq 00 \equiv malf_{old}(d)$$

Thus a misalignment interrupt occurs in no machine or in both.

- $/malf(c)$: in this case the statement follows trivially by construction of the semantics of the instruction buffer machine.

- $mal\,f(c)$: by construction we get in both machines an interrupt

$$jisr_{old}(d,e) = jisr(c,x) = 1$$

The computation of masked event signals 0 through 4 does not depend on the instruction

$$mev_{old}(d,e)[2:0] = 0^3 = mev(c,x)[2:0]$$
$$mev_{old}(d,e)[3] = e \wedge d.sr[0] = x.e \wedge c.sr[0] = mev(c,x)[3]$$
$$mev_{old}(d,e)[4] = mal\,f_{old}(d) = mal\,f(c) = mev(c,x)[4]$$

Thus bits 0 through 4 of the masked cause are the same

$$i \le 4 \quad \rightarrow \quad mca_{old}(d,e)[i] = mev_{old}(d,e)[i] \wedge / \bigvee_{j<i} mev_{old}(d,e)[j]$$
$$= mev(c,x)[i] \wedge / \bigvee_{j<i} mev(c,x)[j]$$
$$= mca(c,x)[i]$$

As we have misalignment, all higher bits of mca are by definition off

$$i > 4 \quad \rightarrow \quad mca_{old}(d,e)[i] = 0 = mca(c,x)[i]$$

Thus we have

$$mca_{old}(d,e) = mca(c,x)$$

and the lemma follows.

$\square$

8.2 Hardware correctness

8.2.1 Inputs for Processor Steps

For the specification of the stepping function we now have to sample the instruction $x.I$ of the oracle input just like we sampled e for the ISA without instruction buffers.

We now distinguish between sampling time $t_i(I)$ for I and $t_i(e)$ for the external event signal. As before the external event signal is sampled in the unique cycle instruction i is committed and leaves the stage above the memory stage

$$t_i(e) = \varepsilon \left\{ t \mid c(I_{M-1}^t) \wedge I_{M-1}^t = i \wedge ue_{M-1}^t \right\}$$

whereas the instruction is sampled in the cycle instruction i is committed and leaves the fetch stage

$$t_i(I) = \varepsilon \left\{ t \mid c(I_{IF}^t) \wedge I_{IF}^t = i \wedge ue_{IF}^t \right\}$$

8.2.2 Stepping Function

The following definitions hinge on the relation between update enable signals and ends of hardware access as stated in section 6.3.3. While we plan to prove that the software condition for ISA eventually implies that the operating condition opc of the cache memory system are fulfilled, we cannot take this for granted yet. For the definition of the stepping function we therefore split cases on the occurrence $vopc$ of a violation of operating conditions

$$vopc^t \equiv \exists i.\, ca(i).preq^t \wedge ca(i).pacc^t.a[28:r] = 0^{29-r} \wedge ca(i).pacc^t.bw \neq 0^8$$

For every cycle t of the hardware computation we construct a numbers ns^t of ISA steps: at most one processor step and at most one load of the instruction buffer. We thus have

$$ns^t \in [0:2]$$

With operating conditions fulfilled the ISA the processor is stepped when the instruction leaves the memory stage. With a violation of operating conditions $vopc$ all is lost and we pull the *emergency brake*: we do not wait for memory accesses to finish and perform the processor step immediately once the memory access violating the condition starts. We also perform no further ISA steps for the cycle in which this is detected (and all later steps would anyway be potentially incorrect). Only in the course of the overall correctness proof will we be able to show that we are never forced to do that. The instruction buffer is stepped when an aligned instruction has been fetched and is clocked into the instruction register $I.IF$.

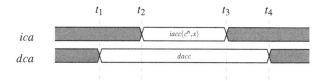

Fig. 147. A data access *dacc* begins manipulating the CMS before an instruction access $iacc(c^n, x)$ of ISA step n begins, but completes after the instruction access. Access *dacc* might violate the operating condition and destroy the memory abstraction for ISA step n.

For the intuition why we *would* pull the emergency brake early is shown in the timing diagram of fig. 147. An instruction access $iacc(c^n, x)$ starts at t_2 and ends at t_3. It is overlapped in time by a data access *dacc*, which may or may not be a data access of an ISA step $dacc(c^m, y)$ starting at t_1 and ending at t_4. Without potential emergency braking the instruction access always ends before the data access, thus ISA step m occurs after ISA step n, i.e. we have $n < m$ independently of violations of the operating conditions. That the instruction is fetched correctly has to be argued for cycle t_3 in the inner induction for step n. This only works if the cache memory system is not compromised since t_1 by a violation of operating conditions by the data access. That ISA step m is executed correctly by the hardware, in particular that $dacc = dacc(c^m, y)$, belongs to the outer induction of ISA step $m > n$, thus we do not know this yet and *cannot yet infer* the operating conditions for the data access from the fact that the ISA program generating $dacc(c^m, y)$ obeys the software condition.

Potential emergency braking changes that. If the data access violates the operating conditions, then ISA step m is already performed when the data access starts, i.e. we have $m < n$ and the outer induction for m is performed first. At cycle t_1 of the inner induction for m we can already conclude $dacc = dacc(c^m, y)$. This however is a contradiction, because $dacc(c^m, y)$ is generated by an ISA program obeying the software condition. Therefore an order with $m < n$ is impossible, and $n < m$ is only possible if the data access does not violate the operating conditions. That the operating conditions are met for all cycles will be shown in lemma 169 along these lines.

In implicit t notation we define formally the number ns of steps generated for cycle t as

$$ns = \begin{cases} ue_M + ue_{IF} & /vopc \\ 1 & vopc \end{cases}$$

We count the total number of ISA steps that have been executed before hardware cycle t in the way familiar to readers of [KMP14] by

$$NS^0 = 0, \quad NS^{t+1} = NS^t + ns^t$$

We define the values

$$s(n) \quad \text{for} \quad n \in [NS^t, NS^{t+1})$$

of the stepping function by four rules.

- for steps n_{ib} triggered by the fetch of an instruction in the absence of an operating condition violation

$$ue^t_{IF} \wedge /vopc^t$$

we load the instruction fetched with store buffer step

$$s(n_{ib}) = (ib, id^t_\pi) \quad \text{for some} \quad n_{ib} \in [NS^t : NS^{t+1})$$

into the instruction buffer of ISA using the instruction address ia_π of the pipelined machine. In ISA the corresponding instruction will only be executed in a later step $v > n_{ib}$. Thus in ISA this amounts to a *prefetch*.

- for steps n_p triggered by the execution of an instruction i in the absence of an operating condition violation, i.e. if

$$ue^t_M \wedge /vopc^t \wedge I^t_M = i$$

holds, we execute in ISA the instruction with inputs sampled for instruction i as defined above.

$$s(n_p) = (p, I^{t_i(I)}_\pi, e^{t_i(e)}_\pi) \quad \text{for some} \quad n_p \in [NS^t : NS^{t+1})$$

- pulling the emergency brake: for steps n_p triggered by the violation of operating conditions, i.e. if

$$vopc^t$$

holds, we execute in ISA the instruction

$$i = I_M^t$$

in the memory stage with inputs sampled for instruction i as defined above.

$$s(n_p) = (p, I_\pi^{t_i(I)}, e_\pi^{t_i(e)}) \quad \text{for some} \quad n_p \in [NS^t : NS^{t+1})$$

In the course of the induction proof we will show, that such steps do not lead to the same ISA instruction being executed twice by establishing $vopc^t = 0$ for all t, i.e. that indeed such steps never occur. As defined above, no other ISA steps are performed for this cycle.
- The order of these steps only matters if access

$$dacc_\pi^t = pacc(1)^t = acc(1,k)$$

to the data cache and access

$$iacc_\pi^t = pacc(0)^t = acc(0,\hat{k})$$

to the instruction cache both end in cycle t, have the same address and the access to the data cache is writing[1]

$$(0,\hat{k}),(1,k) \in E^t \ , \ iacc_\pi^t.a = dacc_\pi^t.a \ , \ dacc_\pi^t.w \vee dacc_\pi^t.cas$$

With the definitions above we end up with indices n_{ib} and n_p such that $s(n_{ib})$ is an instruction buffer step and $s(n_p)$ is a processor core step

$$n_p, n_{ib} \in [NS^t, NS^{t+1}) \ , \ s(n_p) \in \Sigma_p \ , \ s(n_{ib}) \in \Sigma_{ib}$$

In section 6.3 we denoted
  - the k'th (external) access to memory port i by $acc(i,k)$.
  - the cycle when this access ends by $e(i,k)$
  - by $E^t = \{(i,k) \mid e(i,k) = t\} \leq ns^t$ the set of indices such that access $acc(i,k)$ ends in cycle t and by
  - $D^t = \{(1,k) \mid e(1,k) = t\}$ the set of indices of accesses to the data port ending in cycle t

With

$$NE^0 = 0 \ , \ NE^{t+1} = NE^t + \#E^t$$

---

[1] In the memory system we have implemented this can not happen, as no two such accesses can end simultaneously in that implementation. Since we only argue about the specification, we still need to consider this case here.

we counted the accesses NE^t completed before cycle t. We switch to implicit t notation. Indices (i,k) of accesses ending in cycle t received unique sequential numbers of the form

$$seq(i,k) = n_x = NE + x - 1 \quad \text{with local sequential indices} \quad x \in [1 : \#E]$$

and the indices (i,k) belonging to x were denoted by (i_x, k_x):

$$(i_x, k_x) = seq^{-1}(n_x) \quad \text{i.e.} \quad seq(i_x, k_x) = n_x$$

If an access $acc(1,k)$ to the data cache ended in cycle t, i.e. if $(1,k) \in D$, then the local sequential index of that access was denoted by xd

$$seq(1,k) = NE + xd - 1$$

If an access $acc(0,\hat{k})$ to the instruction cache ends at the same cycle, i.e. $(0,\hat{k}) \in E$ it gets a local sequential index x

$$seq(0,\hat{k}) = NE + x - 1$$

Simultaneous processor and instruction buffer steps occur in exactly this situation. We wish to order them (whether there is a conflicting address or not) in the sequential order defined by the cache memory system, i.e. we perform the processor step first, if the data access occurs in the sequential order before the instruction access

$$n_p < n_{ib} \leftrightarrow xd < x$$

Thus if an access to the data port ends in the current cycle

$$ue_M \wedge mop.(M-1) \wedge exec.(M-1)$$

then we consider the local sequential index $\varepsilon\{x \mid i_x = 1\}$ of the access for the CMS and define ISA step n_p with this index as

$$n_p = NS + \varepsilon\{x \mid i_x = 1\} - 1 = NS + xd - 1$$

Similarly if an access to the instruction cache ends in the current cycle

$$ue_{IF}$$

then we consider the local sequential index $\varepsilon\{x \mid i_x = 0\}$ of the access for the CMS and define ISA step n_{ib} with this index as

$$n_{ib} = NS + \varepsilon\{x \mid i_x = 0\} - 1$$

We now can couple local sequential indices $x \in [1 : E]$ of the CMS to the ISA instructions $isa(x)$ which produced them by

$$isa(x) = NS + x - 1$$

and trivially obtain

Lemma 162.

– *Accesses generated by ISA steps are in the same order as the generated accesses*

$$x < y \leftrightarrow isa(x) < isa(y)$$

– *If*

$$i_x = 0 \wedge i_{xd} = 1$$

then

$$(n_{ib} < n_p \leftrightarrow x < xd)$$

– *The access with local sequential index x at the instruction port is generated by the instruction buffer step*

$$i_x = 0 \ \rightarrow \ n_{ib} = isa(x)$$

– *The access with local sequential index x at the data port is generated by the processor step*

$$i_x = 1 \ \rightarrow \ n_p = isa(x)$$

Note that by the rules above processor instructions generating void accesses to the CMS are stepped last. Thus if we count the number of non-void accesses to the cache by

$$nac = ue_{IF} + ue_M \wedge mop.(M-1) \wedge exec.(M-1)$$

then

$$ue_M \wedge /(mop.(M-1) \wedge exec.(M-1)) \ \rightarrow \ n_p \in [NS + nac : NS')$$

8.2.3 Software Condition and Stating Processor Correctness

We need to consider the oracle input in our definition of the software condition and redefine:

$$SC_{ROM}(c,x) \ \equiv \ x \in \Sigma_p \wedge write(c,x) \ \rightarrow \ \langle ea(c,x) \rangle \geq 2^{r+3}$$

The scheduling functions derived from the hardware computation count processor steps. As in [KMP14] we identify the corresponding steps of the ISA computation with

$$pseq(0) = \min \{ n \mid s(n) \in \Sigma_p \}$$
$$pseq(i) = \min \{ n \mid n > pseq(i-1) \wedge s(n) \in \Sigma_p \}$$

Note that in previous machines, all ISA steps were processor steps. Thus we used to have

$$i = pseq(i)$$

and we could use ISA steps and processor steps interchangeably. For each place where we used processor/ISA steps before, now we need to be explicit about whether we mean processor steps or ISA steps.

Similarly, we used to have

$$NS^t = I^t_M$$

and could therefore count the executed ISA steps by counting the instructions that passed the memory stage. Now in contexts in which we argue about ISA steps we will need to use NS instead of I_M to count the number of executed ISA steps.

For registers and signals we used to write R^i_σ for the value of R in step i. We mean instruction i. Thus we adjust notation and identify ISA registers and the instruction buffer $R \in \{pc, dpc, m, gpr, spr, ib\}$ before execution of instruction i by

$$R^i_\sigma = c^{pseq(i)}.R$$

Signals and invisible registers

$$f \in cir(k) \lor f \in reg(k) \land /vis(f)$$

in stage k now depend on the oracle inputs of instruction i, which we define as

$$I^i_\sigma = s(pseq(i)).I \quad , \quad e^i_\sigma = s(pseq(i)).e$$

but not every signal uses each oracle input. For example, signal $malf(c)$ depends only on the configuration. We define

$$f^i_\sigma = \begin{cases} f(c^{pseq(i)}) & f \text{ does not depend on } I \\ f(c^{pseq(i)}, s(pseq(i))) & f \text{ depends on } I \end{cases}$$

For the guard condition γ we introduce a similar shorthand

$$\gamma^i_\sigma = \gamma(c^{pseq(i)}, s(pseq(i)))$$

We proceed to explain the new main induction hypothesis. The new pipeline coupling relation $t \sim_p i$ is between hardware cycles t and instructions i. Thus at the surface nothing changes from the definition in section 7.6.2. Note however that with the updated definitions above, R^i_σ now concerns a signal or register from ISA step $pseq(i)$, not i like before

$$t \sim_p i \equiv \forall k, R. \ I^t_k = i \land (R \in reg(k) \land vis(R)$$
$$\lor R \in reg(k-1) \land /vis(R) \land rfull^t_{k-1} \land used[R]^i)$$
$$\rightarrow R^t_\pi = R^i_\sigma$$

In addition to proving that registers in the pipeline correspond to signals in the ISA, we now also have to prove that the sequence of inputs $s(n)$ defined above is valid, i.e. that the guard conditions hold for all steps. For instruction buffer steps this is trivial because the guard condition is always true. For processor steps, i.e. ISA steps n with $n = pseq(i)$ we will establish the guard condition for instruction i once the instruction has passed the fetch stage

$$i > I^t_{IF} \;\rightarrow\; \gamma^i_\sigma$$

As before this only has to hold in the absence of misspeculation, i.e. if

$$lb(i)^t \wedge c(i)^t$$

Thus the pipeline portion of the induction hypothesis becomes

$$n = pseq(i) \wedge lb(i)^t \wedge c(i)^t \rightarrow t \sim_p i \wedge (i > I^t_{IF} \;\rightarrow\; \gamma^i_\sigma)$$

In contrast to $t \sim_p i$ the new coupling relation $t \sim_m n$ for non pipeline components couples cycles t with ISA steps n. This relation is only stated for ISA steps

$$n = NS^t$$

i.e. it only concerns snapshots c^n of ISA configurations before execution of the first ISA step of cycle t. As before we couple memory by

$$m(h^t) = \ell(m^n_\sigma)$$

We also state, that no writes to the ROM region occurred in any cycle before t, i.e. we include

$$opc^t$$

as defined in section 6.2.3). Finally we summarize, that guard conditions $\gamma(c^{\hat{n}}, s(\hat{n}))$ held for all instructions $\hat{n} < n = NS^t$ in the past.

$$\forall \hat{n} < n.\ \gamma(c^{\hat{n}}, s(\hat{n}))$$

The non pipeline portion of the induction hypothesis thus becomes

$$t \sim_m n$$

with

$$t \sim_m n \;\equiv\; n = NS^t \;\rightarrow\; m(h^t) = \ell(m^n_\sigma) \wedge opc^t \wedge \forall \hat{n} < n.\ \gamma(c^{\hat{n}}, s(\hat{n}))$$

and the main correctness result we want to establish is is

Lemma 163. *There is an initial configuration c^0 satisfying*

$$sim(h^0, c^0)$$

with an empty instruction buffer

$$c^0.ib = \emptyset$$

Furthermore, if the computation (c^n) with stepping function $s(n)$ and initial configuration c^0 satisfies for all n the software condition $SC_{ROM}(c^n, s(n))$ provided the stepping function $s(n)$ has a valid initial segment until n

$$\forall n.\ (\forall m \leq n.\ \gamma(c^m, s(m))) \;\rightarrow\; SC_{ROM}(c^n, s(n))$$

then for all n and t, both of the following hold:

- *If n is the ISA step corresponding to instruction i, instructions before i are live, and instruction i is committed in cycle t*

$$n = pseq(i) \land lb(i)^t \land c(i)^t$$

the hardware in cycle t simulates instruction i, and all instructions below the fetch stage satisfy the guard conditions.

$$t \sim_p i \land (i < I_{IF}^t \to \gamma_\sigma^i)$$

- *The hardware simulates the memory of ISA step n*

$$t \sim_m n$$

Note that the point of the non-deterministic ISA programming model is that the user does not need to know the particular stepping function $s(n)$ extracted from hardware. To use the lemma above, the user therefore needs to prove for all n the software condition $SC_{ROM}(c^n, s(n))$ for *all* stepping functions $s(n)$ which have a valid initial segment until n.

Note also that we make no direct claim about the instruction buffer. This will not cause problems because 1) an instruction buffer abstracted from hardware would contain instructions which are already fetched but not executed, i.e. in pipelined instruction registers $I.k$ of really full stages, and these are already coupled through γ_σ^i with the instruction buffer in ISA 2) instruction buffer steps are always valid.

As before we intend to prove correctness by an outer induction on ISA steps n (which now can be processor or instruction buffer steps) and an inner induction on cycles t. In order to get an idea what we are up to in the induction steps of the inner induction consider figure 148 .

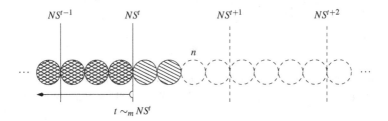

Fig. 148. Proof order in the induction scheme. Correctness is proven for ISA steps from left to right, and for each ISA step for all cycles. In the current machine there are at most two ISA steps per cycle, but this will change as machines get more units.

For the induction step $(n,t) \to (n,t+1)$ of the inner induction we know when $n \in [NS^t : NS^{t+1})$ i) the correctness $t \sim_m NS^t$ of the non pipeline portion at cycle t, i.e. correctness of memory in cycle t, the operating conditions before cycle t and the guard conditions for all ISA steps before NS^t. ii) Correctness of the pipeline portion to the left of n, even for future cycles. This was crucial to establish in lemmas 154 and 156, that instructions committed in hardware are not rolled back by *jisr* or *eret* in ISA. iii) the correct execution of ISA step n until t. However the induction hypothesis makes *no direct statement about any ISA instruction to the right* of n, even if it is stepped later in the same cycle t. In the proof of the induction step we basically have to handle the following situations

- processor steps $n = pseq(i)$ for some i resp $s(n) \in \Sigma_p$. We have to establish

$$t + 1 \sim_p i$$

  This follows known arguments
- also for processor steps we have to establish or maintain the guard condition

$$i < I_{IF}^t \rightarrow \gamma_\sigma^j$$

  It is established in cycles when an instruction is fetched and maintained later because committed instructions are not rolled back
- when $n = NS^{t+1}$ we also have to show the non pipeline portion

$$t + 1 \sim_m n$$

  of the induction hypothesis

There is no explicit proof obligation for instruction buffer steps.

8.2.4 Properties of *pseq*

The processor portion of the configuration is modified only by processor steps, which are identified by *pseq*. We state without proof the following lemma, which corresponds to lemma 9.8 in [KMP14]

Lemma 164.
$$c^{pseq(i+1)}.p = \delta(c^{pseq(i)}, s(pseq(i))).p$$

If instruction i is the last instruction that has not been executed yet, and the processor is stepped in the current cycle, then the instruction i is stepped in the current cycle.

Lemma 165.

$$(i > 0 \rightarrow pseq(i-1) < NS) \wedge NS \leq pseq(i) \wedge (ue_M \vee vopc) \quad \rightarrow \quad NS' > pseq(i)$$

Proof. The processor is by definition of s stepped exactly once

$$\exists n \in [NS : NS'). \, s(n) \in \Sigma_p \wedge \forall u \in [NS : NS'). \, s(u) \in \Sigma_p \rightarrow n = u$$

We now have to split cases on whether $i = 0$. We only treat here the case where $i > 0$ as the other case is analogous. By assumption we have

$$pseq(i-1) < NS \leq pseq(i)$$

and thus n is the first processor step after $pseq(i-1)$. From the definition of $pseq$ we conclude that $pseq(i)$ is n

$$pseq(i) = n$$

The claim follows

$$pseq(i) = n < NS'$$

$\square$

By a straightforward induction over t we prove that in cycle t, instruction $I_M^t - 1$ has already been executed, and instruction I_M^t has not been executed yet

Lemma 166. *Assume opc^t. Then*

$$I_M^t > 0 \quad \rightarrow \quad pseq(I_M^t - 1) < NS^t$$
$$NS^t \leq pseq(I_M^t)$$

Proof. By induction on t. In cycle $t = 0$, we have $I_M^t = I_M^0 = 0$ and the first part of the claim is vacuously true. For the second part we have

$$NS^t = NS^0 = 0 \leq pseq(I_M^0)$$

In the induction step $t \rightarrow t + 1$, we use primed notation. We split cases on ue_M.

- $/ue_M$: in this case we have

$$I_M = I_M'$$

and not much changes. For the first part we have by hypothesis

$$I_M = I_M' > 0$$

and conclude with the induction hypothesis and the monotonicity of NS

$$pseq(I_M' - 1) = pseq(I_M - 1) \overset{IH}{<} NS \leq NS'$$

which proves the claim. For the second part we do not step the processor because the operating condition is not violated

$$/vopc$$

and thus

$$n \in [NS : NS') \rightarrow s(n) \notin \Sigma_p$$

Therefore by definition of $pseq$ none of these steps is equal to $pseq(I_M)$

$$n \in [NS : NS') \rightarrow n \neq pseq(I_M)$$

With the induction hypothesis

$$NS \leq pseq(I_M)$$

we conclude the claim

$$NS' \leq pseq(I_M) = pseq(I_M')$$

- ue_M: In this case we have

$$I'_M = I_M + 1$$

By lemma 165 and the induction hypothesis, instruction I_M is stepped in the current cycle

$$pseq(I'_M - 1) = pseq(I_M) < NS'$$

which is the first part of the claim. For the second part of the claim we know that steps between $pseq(I_M)$ and NS' are not processor steps because the processor is stepped at most once in each cycle, thus

$$pseq(I'_M) \geq NS'$$

$\square$

If the operating conditions hold in the past and an instruction is stepped, it is the instruction in the memory stage which in turn has a really full input stage.

Lemma 167.

$$opc \wedge pseq(i) \in [NS : NS') \rightarrow i = I_M \wedge rfull_{M-1}$$

Proof. We split cases on $i > 0$ or $i = 0$ but only consider the case $i > 0$. By lemma 166 we have

$$pseq(I_M - 1) < NS \leq pseq(I_M)$$

The step with number $pseq(i)$ is by definition of $pseq$ a processor step

$$s(pseq(i)) \in \Sigma_p$$

By definition of the stepping function we conclude that the memory stage is updated or the operating condition is violated

$$ue_M \vee vopc \qquad (42)$$

and by lemma 165 instruction I_M is stepped

$$NS \leq pseq(I_M) < NS'$$

Since the processor is only stepped once in each cycle, we have

$$i = I_M$$

If in eq. (42) ue_M holds we have immediately

$$rfull_{M-1}$$

Otherwise we conclude successively with lemma 134

$$vopc, \; dca.preq, \; full_{M-1}, \; rfull_{M-1}$$

$\square$

8.2.5 Induction Step

Analogous to before we do an outer induction on ISA steps n and then an inner induction on hardware cycles t. We cover here only the interesting case, which is in the induction step $t \rightarrow t+1$ of the inner induction, where we have as outer induction hypothesis for all previous ISA steps $o < n$

$$\forall u.\; u \sim_m o \wedge (o = pseq(j) \wedge c(j)^u \wedge lb(j)^u \rightarrow u \sim_p j \wedge (j < I_{IF}^u \rightarrow \gamma_\sigma^j)) \quad (43)$$

The inner induction hypothesis for t is

$$t \sim_m n \wedge (n = pseq(i) \wedge c(i)^t \wedge lb(i)^t \rightarrow t \sim_p i \wedge (i < I_{IF}^t \rightarrow \gamma_\sigma^j)) \quad (44)$$

Note that these induction hypotheses are not exactly like eq. (33) resp. eq. (32) in section 7.8.1, so the previous proofs will not go through immediately. In the pipeline correctness proof we will later instantiate o as $pseq(j)$ for $j < i$ to return to almost exactly the same statements.

For the sake of convenience, we combine both induction hypotheses into a single equation that works for all $o \le n$ but *only* for cycle t.

$$t \sim_m o \wedge (o = pseq(i) \wedge c(i)^t \wedge lb(i)^t \rightarrow t \sim_p i \wedge (i < I_{IF}^t \rightarrow \gamma_\sigma^j)) \quad (45)$$

We call this equation the induction hypothesis for the current cycle.

We have to show

1. For the memory:

$$t+1 \sim_m n$$

2. For the pipeline:

$$n = pseq(i) \wedge c(i)^{t+1} \wedge lb(i)^{t+1} \rightarrow t+1 \sim_p i \wedge (i < I_{IF}^{t+1} \rightarrow \gamma_\sigma^j)$$

Like before we split the proof between the memory and the pipeline. However, we first show some preliminary lemmas: instead of waiting for n to become equal to NS' before we show that the operating condition opc' is satisfied and that all steps $\hat{n} < NS$ satisfy the guard condition, we begin showing these properties as soon as $n \ge NS$ (the latter one only for $\hat{n} \le n$). This allows us to use these properties already in the proof for the pipeline registers for ISA steps $n \in [NS : NS')$ that end in the current cycle. For example, to show that instruction buffer steps that end in the current cycle read the correct value from memory we already need that the operating conditions are satisfied, as otherwise the cache system might return arbitrary values. Obviously the claims we have to show for opc and γ in the induction step for $n = NS'$ are then just a direct consequence of these lemmas.

The first lemma is just a reformulation of the inner and outer induction hypotheses for the guard condition. The hypothesis has two cases. The first case is used for the straight application of the induction hypothesis, and the second case will be used to complete the induction step for the guard conditions.

Lemma 168. *Let*

$$n \in [NS : NS') \land \hat{n} \leq n$$

or

$$n = NS' \land \hat{n} < n$$

Then

$$\gamma(c^{\hat{n}}, s(\hat{n}))$$

Proof. In what follows we have to refer to the t in the implicit t notation of the statement of the lemma. We split cases on $\hat{n} < NS$ or $\hat{n} \geq NS$.

- $\hat{n} < NS$: in this case we have

$$\hat{n} < NS \leq n$$

We instantiate the outer induction hypothesis (eq. (43)) with $o := NS$ and $u := t$ and obtain after expansion of $t \sim_m NS$

$$\forall \hat{n} < NS.\ \gamma(c^{\hat{n}}, s(\hat{n}))$$

and the claim follows.
- $\hat{n} \geq NS$: We split cases on whether $\hat{n}$ is a processor or instruction buffer step.
    - $s(\hat{n}) \in \Sigma_p$: we have by the induction hypothesis for the current cycle (eq. (45)) with $o := NS \leq n$

$$opc$$

In both cases of the hypothesis of the lemma we have

$$\hat{n} < NS'$$

Thus by lemma 167

$$\hat{n} = pseq(I_M) \land rfull_{M-1}$$

With lemma 108 we conclude

$$I_M < I_{IF} \tag{46}$$

Instruction I_M is committed by construction as there are no rollback requests in the memory stage or below. All instructions below it are live as there are no stall signals below the memory stage.

$$c(I_M) \land lb(I_M) \tag{47}$$

By definition the guard condition for ISA step $\hat{n}$ holds if $\gamma_\sigma^{I_M}$ holds

$$\gamma(c^{\hat{n}}, s(\hat{n})) = \gamma(c^{pseq(I_M)}, s(pseq(I_M))) = \gamma_\sigma^{I_M}$$

and it suffices to show $\gamma_\sigma^{I_M}$. From the induction hypothesis for the current cycle (eq. (45)) with $o := \hat{n} \leq n$ and $i := I_M$ we obtain

$$\hat{n} = pseq(I_M) \land c(I_M) \land lb(I_M) \land I_M < I_{IF} \rightarrow \gamma_\sigma^{I_M}$$

With eqs. (46) and (47) the claim follows

– $s(\hat{n}) \in \Sigma_{ib}$: such steps are always valid and the claim follows

$$\gamma(c^{\hat{n}}, s(\hat{n})) = 1$$

□

The induction step for the operating condition is completed by the following lemma.

Lemma 169.

$$n \geq NS \quad \rightarrow \quad opc'$$

Proof. From the induction hypothesis for the current cycle (eq. (45)) with $o := NS \leq n$ we obtain

$$opc$$

It remains to be shown that in the current cycle there is no violation of the operating condition. Like before in lemma 88 we observe that only the data cache is interesting as the other caches never have write accesses. Assume as before that there is a processor request at the data cache

$$dca.preq$$

and assume for the sake of contradiction that this access violates the operating condition

$$vopc, \quad dca.pacc.a[28:r] = 0^{29-r} \wedge dca.pacc.bw \neq 0^8$$

By lemma 166 instruction I_M has not been stepped before

$$NS \leq pseq(I_M)$$

and by lemma 165 it is stepped in the current cycle as step m

$$m = pseq(I_M) < NS'$$

in fact, by definition of the stepping function this is the only step in this cycle

$$m = pseq(I_M) = NS \leq n \tag{48}$$

We conclude that the stepping function has an initial valid segment until step $pseq(I_M)$ with lemma 168

$$\forall \hat{n} \leq pseq(I_M). \ \gamma(c^{\hat{n}}, s(\hat{n}))$$

From the assumption that valid initial segments imply the software condition SC_{ROM} we conclude

$$SC_{ROM}(c^{pseq(I_M)}, s(pseq(I_M)))$$

and since $s(pseq(I_M)) \in \Sigma_p$ we conclude

$$write_{\sigma}^{I_M} \rightarrow \langle ea_{\sigma}^{I_M} \rangle \geq 2^{r+3}$$

At this point the absence of operating condition violations can be concluded as before in lemma 88, which contradicts the assumption that we have a violation of the operating condition. □

As stated on page 342, we consider like in section 6.3 the set D of external accesses to the data cache ending in the current cycle with cardinality

$$d = \#D \leq 1$$

We define the index of the data access in the sequence of accesses in the current cycle by

$$xd = \varepsilon \{ x \mid n_x \in seq(D) \}$$

and consider the memory M_x before access n_x, which as stated in lemma 85 can be defined as

$$M_x = \Delta_M^{NE+x-1}(m(h^0), lacc)$$

We then prove exactly as before the following two lemmas corresponding to lemmas 86 and 87 in section 6.3:

Lemma 170. *For $x \in [1 : \#E + 1]$:*

$$M_x = \begin{cases} M_1 & d = 0 \vee x \in [1 : xd] \\ \delta_M(M_1, lacc(n_{xd})) & d = 1 \wedge x \in [xd + 1 : \#E + 1] \end{cases}$$

Lemma 171. *Assume opc'.*

$$M_1 = \Delta_M^{NE}(m(h^0), lacc) = m(h)$$
$$M_{\#E+1} = \Delta_M^{NE'}(m(h^0), lacc) = m(h')$$

Memory in ISA also only changes at processor steps which are memory operations. Such steps $o \in [NS : NS' - 1]$ should generate data accesses with local sequential index xd. That this really happens can only be proven if the pipeline correctly implements the instruction i executed by step $o = pseq(i)$: otherwise a memory operation in ISA might be incorrectly implemented as say an ALU operation in hardware. Thus in the lemma below we will need to include the assumption $o \leq n$ from which we can conclude with the induction hypothesis for the current cycle (eq. (45)) that the pipeline correctly implements the instruction.

Lemma 172. *Assume $o \in [NS : NS']$ and $o \leq n$. Then*

$$(d = 0 \vee o \neq isa(xd)) \rightarrow \ell(c^{o+1}.m) = \ell(c^o.m)$$

Proof. For instruction buffer steps and non-writes this is obviously the case. Assume for the purpose of contradiction that step o is a processor step executing some instruction i which is a write

$$s(o) \in \Sigma_p \wedge o = pseq(i) \wedge write_\sigma^i$$

Since the instruction is stepped the memory stage is updated, and there are a real full and full bits above

$$ue_M \wedge rfull_{M-1} \wedge full_{M-1}$$

and thus with the induction hypothesis for the current cycle (eq. (45)) for $o := o$ and $i := i$ we conclude that the operation must be a memory operation in hardware and hence start a data access

$$mop.(M-1), \quad dca.preq$$

Update enable implies an access end with lemma 82

$$\exists k. \, (1,k) \in E$$

and we conclude that there is a data access with local sequential index xd, which is generated by definition of s by a processor step

$$d = 1 \wedge isa(xd) = n_p$$

Since there is only a single processor step in each cycle we have

$$o = n_p = isa(xd)$$

which is a contradiction. □

In completely straightforward fashion one concludes from this the counterpart of lemma 170 in ISA.

Lemma 173. *Let*

$$o \in [NS : NS'] \wedge o \leq n$$

then

$$\ell(c^o.m) = \begin{cases} \ell(c^{NS}.m) & d = 0 \vee o \leq isa(xd) \\ \delta_M(\ell(c^{NS}.m), dacc(c^{isa(xd)}, s(isa(xd)))) & d = 1 \wedge isa(xd) < o \end{cases}$$

Proof. By induction on o. The base case is completely trivial. In the induction step $o \to o+1$, we distinguish whether o is the data access or not.

- $d = 1 \wedge o = isa(xd)$: in this case we have $o + 1 > isa(xd)$ and the claim follows with the induction hypothesis

$$\ell(c^{o+1}.m) = \delta_M(\ell(c^o), dacc(c^o, s(o))) \qquad\qquad \text{L 47}$$
$$= \delta_M(\ell(c^{NS}.m), dacc(c^{isa(xd)}, s(isa(xd)))) \qquad \text{IH}$$

- $d = 0 \vee o \neq isa(xd)$: with lemma 172 we have

$$\ell(c^{o+1}.m) = \ell(c^o.m)$$

and the claim follows with the induction hypothesis

$$\ell(c^{o+1}.m)$$
$$= \ell(c^o.m)$$
$$= \begin{cases} \ell(c^{NS}.m) & d = 0 \vee o \leq isa(xd) \\ \delta_M(\ell(c^{isa(xd)}.m), dacc(c^{isa(xd)}, s(isa(xd)))) & d = 1 \wedge isa(xd) < o \end{cases}$$
$$= \begin{cases} \ell(c^{NS}.m) & d = 0 \vee o+1 \leq isa(xd) \\ \delta_M(\ell(c^{isa(xd)}.m), dacc(c^{isa(xd)}, s(isa(xd)))) & d = 1 \wedge isa(xd) < o+1 \end{cases}$$

□

8.2.6 Correctness of Memory Update

We switch to implicit t notation and unfold the definition of $\sim_m$. Thus the claim becomes

$$n = NS' \;\rightarrow\; m(h') = \ell(m^n_\sigma) \;\wedge\; opc' \;\wedge\; \forall \hat{n} < n.\; \gamma(c^{\hat{n}}, s(\hat{n}))$$

Let thus $n = NS'$. We first conclude from the induction hypothesis for the current cycle (eq. (45)) with $o := NS \le NS' = n$

$$m(h) = \ell(c^{NS}.m) \wedge opc \tag{49}$$

We have

$$n = NS' \ge NS$$

and by lemma 169 the operating condition is satisfied

$$opc'$$

For $\hat{n} < n$ we also have

$$\hat{n} \le n$$

and by lemma 168 the guard condition is satisfied

$$\gamma(c^{\hat{n}}, s(\hat{n}))$$

The proof for the memory has not changed in spirit: we consider at most one data access with local sequential index xd. All ISA steps before or after the data access do not change memory, and also in the sequential memory M_x changes only occur at xd. However, because we now have up to two steps in ISA and correspondingly now count changes to the memory with NS rather than with I_M, there are some technical differences.

We split as usual cases on ue_M.

- $/ue_M$: nothing happens. We have

$$d = 0$$

and only the instruction buffer is stepped, which does not change memory

$$c^{NS}.m = c^{NS'}.m$$

The claim follows

$$
\begin{aligned}
m(h') &= M_{\#E+1} & \text{L 171} \\
&= M_1 & \text{L 170} \\
&= m(h) & \text{L 171, L 169} \\
&= \ell(c^{NS}.m) & \text{E 49} \\
&= \ell(c^{NS'}.m)
\end{aligned}
$$

- ue_M: in this case we have

$$I_M = I'_M - 1$$

and thus by lemma 166 the instruction in the memory stage is stepped in the current cycle

$$pseq(I_M) = pseq(I'_M - 1) \overset{L166}{<} NS'$$

In this case the induction hypothesis for previous ISA steps (eq. (43)) applies for $n := pseq(I_M)$ and $u := t$ and we conclude immediately

$$mop_\sigma^{I_M} = mop.(M-1)$$

Like before we do a case split on $mop.(M-1)$ but consider only the case where the instruction is a memory operation as the other case is trivial

$$mop.(M-1)$$

Like before we prove that a data access ends

$$d = 1$$

and that this access is the same as the access in ISA

$$lacc(n_{xd}) = dacc_\sigma^{I_M}$$

Since all other ISA steps that end in the current cycle are not processor steps and do not change memory, we obtain also

$$c^{NS}.m = c^{pseq(I_M)}.m \wedge c^{pseq(I_M)+1}.m = c^{NS'}.m$$

The claim follows

$$
\begin{aligned}
m(h') &= M_{\#E+1} & \text{L 171} \\
&= \delta_M(M_1, lacc(n_{xd})) & \text{L 170} \\
&= \delta_M(m(h), dacc_\sigma^{I_M}) & \text{L 171, L 169} \\
&= \delta_M(\ell(c^{NS}.m), dacc_\sigma^{I_M}) & \text{E 49} \\
&= \delta_M(\ell(c^{pseq(I_M)}.m), dacc_\sigma^{I_M}) \\
&= \ell(c^{pseq(I_M)+1}.m) \\
&= \ell(c^{NS'}.m)
\end{aligned}
$$

8.2.7 Pipeline Correctness

Let now n be the ISA step executing a committed instruction i such that all previous instructions are live

$$n = pseq(i) \wedge c(i)' \wedge lb(i)'$$

For the proof of the coupling relation $t+1 \sim_p i$ nothing changes except in four places:

- when instruction $i-1$ updates visible register R in the pipeline, we have to prove

$$R'_\pi = R^i_\sigma$$

The proof without instruction buffers relied on the equality

$$R^i_\sigma = d^i.R = \delta_{old}(d^{i-1}, e^{i-1}_\sigma).R$$

which with lemma 93 allowed us to conclude from the correctness of signals of instruction $i-1$ the correctness of the register content for instruction i

$$\delta_{old}(d^{i-1}, e^{i-1}_\sigma).R = R'_\pi$$

As such visible registers R belong to the processor portion $c^{pseq(i)}.p$ of the configuration, lemma 164 shows

$$R^i_\sigma = c^{pseq(i)}.R \overset{L\ 164}{=} \delta(c^{pseq(i-1)}, s(pseq(i-1))).R$$

and with a completely analogous argument to before we can show

$$\delta(c^{pseq(i-1)}, s(pseq(i-1))).R = R'_\pi$$

which proves the claim.
- the notation for the sampling time of the external interrupt has been changed from t_i to $t_i(e)$. Thus the proof for the correctness of e in stage $M-1$ changes to

$$e'_\pi = e^{t_i(e)}_\pi = e^i_\sigma$$

- instruction word I now is sampled. Thus the proof for the correctness of I in stage IF is now (completely analogous to that for e)

$$I'_\pi = I^{t_i(I)}_\pi = I^i_\sigma \tag{50}$$

- the guard condition γ has been introduced, requiring us to prove when instruction i leaves stage IF

$$\gamma^i_\sigma \overset{!}{=} 1$$

This proof is more involved and considered in more detail below; for now we only sketch the proof. With lemma 87 we obtain that the memory from which the instruction is fetched is either $m(h^t)$ or $m(h^{t+1})$, which are coupled with ISA steps I^t_M resp. I^{t+1}_M. By the definition of s we know that the instruction buffer step is in ISA step $n \in \{NS^t, NS^t + 1\}$. Since the instruction buffer step does not change memory we get either

$$\ell(c^n.m) = \ell(c^{NS^t}.m) = m(h^t)$$

or

$$\ell(c^n.m) = \ell(c^{NS^t+1}.m) = \ell(c^{NS^{t+1}}.m) = m(h^{t+1})$$

Thus both in ISA and in hardware the same memory is used to fetch the instruction, and the same instruction is fetched into the instruction buffer. We then obtain using the argument about *jisr* and *eret* instructions in the pipe from section 7.8.5 that instructions between that ISA step u and instruction i are neither *jisr* nor *eret* and thus do not flush the instruction buffer, therefore the instruction is still in the instruction buffer when instruction i intends to use it.

We now turn the argument for the instruction buffer into formal mathematics. We first show that the instruction fetched in hardware (in case its address is aligned) is in the instruction buffer right after the instruction buffer step.

Lemma 174. *Let $l \in [NS : NS')$ be an instruction buffer step simulated in the current hardware cycle*

$$s(l) = (ib, ia_\pi)$$

After that ISA step, provided the instruction address is aligned, the instruction used in hardware is in the instruction buffer

$$ia_\pi[1:0] = 00 \quad \rightarrow \quad (ia_\pi, I_\pi) \in c^{l+1}.ib$$

Proof. The instruction $i = I_{IF}$ in the fetch stage is obviously not stepped in this cycle, thus

$$n = pseq(I_{IF}) \geq NS' \geq NS$$

and analogously to before (eq. (49)) we get with either eq. (43) or eq. (44)

$$m(h) = \ell(c^{NS}.m) \tag{51}$$

Since $n \geq NS$ we obtain that there is no violation of the operating conditions with lemma 169

$$opc'$$

By lemma 167 ISA step $isa(xd)$ (if it exists) executes instruction I_M

$$d = 1 \quad \rightarrow \quad isa(xd) = n_p = pseq(I_M) \tag{52}$$

Since the instruction buffer has been stepped, by definition of s the instruction fetch stage was updated

$$ue_{IF}$$

and hence by lemma 82 a local memory access k ended at the instruction port

$$(0, k) \in E$$

We name the global index of this access n_x with $x \in [1 : \#E]$

$$n_x = seq(0, k)$$

This access by lemma 78 provides a sequentially consistent answer corresponding to the answer in ISA

$ica.pdout$

$$= \Delta_M^{n_x}(m(h^0), lacc)(acc(0,k).a) \hspace{3cm} \text{L 78}$$

$$= M_x(pacc(0).a) \hspace{3cm} (0,k) \in E$$

$$= M_x(ia_\pi.l) \hspace{3cm} \text{Defn.}$$

$$= \begin{cases} \delta_M(M_1, lacc(n_{xd}))(ia_\pi.l) & d = 1 \wedge x > xd \\ M_1(ia_\pi.l) & \text{otherwise} \end{cases} \hspace{1.5cm} \text{L 170}$$

$$= \begin{cases} \delta_M(m(h), lacc(n_{xd}))(ia_\pi.l) & d = 1 \wedge x > xd \\ m(h)(ia_\pi.l) & \text{otherwise} \end{cases} \hspace{1cm} \text{L 171, L 169}$$

$$= \begin{cases} \delta_M(\ell(c^{NS}.m), dacc_\sigma^{I_M})(ia_\pi.l) & d = 1 \wedge x > xd \\ \ell(c^{NS}.m)(ia_\pi.l) & \text{otherwise} \end{cases} \hspace{1.5cm} \text{E 51}$$

$$= \begin{cases} \delta_M(\ell(c^{NS}.m), dacc_\sigma^{I_M})(ia_\pi.l) & d = 1 \wedge isa(x) > isa(xd) \\ \ell(c^{NS}.m)(ia_\pi.l) & \text{otherwise} \end{cases} \hspace{1cm} \text{defn } isa$$

$$= \begin{cases} \delta_M(\ell(c^{NS}.m), \\ \quad dacc(c^{isa(xd)}, s(isa(xd))))(ia_\pi.l) & d = 1 \wedge isa(x) > isa(xd) \\ \ell(c^{NS}.m)(ia_\pi.l) & \text{otherwise} \end{cases} \hspace{0.5cm} \text{E 52}$$

$$= \ell(c^l.m)(ia_\pi.l) \hspace{3cm} \text{L 173}$$

Since the memory address is by assumption aligned we conclude by pure book-keeping with lemma 37

$$I_\pi = \begin{cases} ica.pdout_L & ia_\pi[2] = 0 \\ ica.pdout_H & ia_\pi[2] = 1 \end{cases}$$

$$= \begin{cases} \ell(c^l.m)(ia_\pi.l)_L & ia_\pi[2] = 0 \\ \ell(c^l.m)(ia_\pi.l)_H & ia_\pi[2] = 1 \end{cases}$$

$$= c^l.m_4(ia_\pi) \hspace{3cm} \text{L 37}$$

By the semantics of instruction buffer step l with

$$s(l) = (ib, ia_\pi)$$

we have

$$(ia_\pi, c^l.m_4(ia_\pi)) \in c^{l+1}.ib$$

The claim follows

$$(ia_\pi, I_\pi) \in c^{l+1}.ib$$

$\square$

We now show that the instruction buffer entry is still present in ISA step $pseq(I_{IF})$ in which it will be used.

Lemma 175.

$$c(I_{IF}) \wedge lb(I_{IF}) \wedge ue_{IF} \wedge ia_\pi[1:0] = 00 \quad \rightarrow \quad (ia_\pi, I_\pi) \in ib_\sigma^{l_{IF}}$$

Proof. The instruction in the fetch stage is being clocked down

$$I'_{ID} = I_{IF}$$

Since the instruction fetch stage is updated we are stepping the instruction buffer; for some ISA step $n \in [NS:NS')$ we have

$$s(n) = (ib, ia_\pi)$$

By lemma 174, the instruction buffer entry is inserted

$$(ia_\pi, I_\pi) \in c^{n+1}.ib$$

Because $I_{IF} \geq I_M$ we have by one of the induction hypothesis (depending on whether $I_{IF} = I_M$ or $I_{IF} < I_M$) that the operating condition has so far not been violated

$$opc$$

and with lemma 166 we conclude

$$pseq(I_M - 1) < NS \leq n$$

thus the only processor steps between n and $pseq(I_{IF})$ are those of instructions

$$g \in [I_M : I_{IF})$$

By lemmas 154 and 156 (with $k := ID$, $l := IF$) those instructions are neither *jisr* nor *eret* instructions

$$/jisr_\sigma^g \wedge /eret_\sigma^g$$

We conclude that the instruction buffer is not cleared and the instruction buffer entry is still present in ISA step $pseq(I_{IF})$ when instruction I_{IF} is executed

$$(ia_\pi, I_\pi) \in c^{pseq(I_{IF})}.ib$$

and the claim follows

$$(ia_\pi, I_\pi) \in ib_\sigma^{l_{IF}}$$

$\square$

With this lemma the claim for the guard condition is easily proven.

Lemma 176.

$$i < I'_{IF} \quad \rightarrow \quad \gamma_\sigma^i$$

Proof. We split cases on $i = I_{IF}$.

- $i = I_{IF}$: by lemma 175 in case of aligned fetch the instruction buffer entry (ia_π, I_π) is present when the instruction is executed

$$ia_\pi[1:0] = 00 \quad \rightarrow \quad (ia_\pi, I_\pi) \in ib_\sigma^{I_{IF}}$$

From the coupling and eq. (50) we infer that this is the instruction buffer entry $(ia_\sigma^{I_{IF}}, I_\sigma^{I_{IF}})$

$$ia_\sigma^{I_{IF}}[1:0] = 00 \quad \rightarrow \quad (ia_\sigma^{I_{IF}}, I_\sigma^{I_{IF}}) \in ib_\sigma^{I_{IF}}$$

which is exactly the claim

$$\gamma_\sigma^{I_{IF}}$$

- $i \neq I_{IF}$: as the scheduling function increases at most by one we have

$$i < I'_{IF} \leq I_{IF} + 1$$

From $i \neq I_{IF}$ we conclude

$$i < I_{IF}$$

and the claim is just the inner induction hypothesis for t (eq. (44)).

$\square$

This concludes the changes to the proof of the coupling relation.

8.3 Liveness and Guard condition

As the hardware has not changed liveness is proven like before with only cosmetic changes. We leave the proof as a simple exercise.

Lemma 177.

$$\forall i. \ \exists k, t. \ rfull_{k-1}^t \wedge I_k^t = i \wedge live(i)^t$$

A trivial consequence of liveness is that the number of executed ISA steps becomes arbitrarily large, i.e., every ISA step ends in some cycle.

Lemma 178.

$$\forall n. \ \exists t. \ NS^t \geq n$$

From the main induction hypothesis we know that all steps which end in some cycle satisfy the guard condition. We immediately conclude that all steps satisfy the guard condition

Lemma 179.

$$\forall n. \ \gamma(c^n, s(n))$$

8.4 A Simple Instruction Buffer Reduction Theorem

We show now that the behavior of any ordinary MIPS program which obeys software condition SC_{eret} from section 7.6.1 is unchanged when it is run in the MIPS ISA with instruction buffers. Recall that software condition SC_{eret} states that between the instruction g which writes an instruction and instruction i which executes it, there must be an *eret* instruction h.

$$g < i \, \wedge \, write_{old}(d^g) \, \wedge \, ea_{old}(d^g).l = ia_{old}(d^i).l \;\rightarrow\; \exists h. \; g < h < i \, \wedge \, eret_{old}(d^h)$$

This discipline is in particular satisfied for page fault handlers and their user programs: the handler swaps new code in with instruction g, returns to the user program with an *eret* instruction h and subsequently the user can access the code with instruction i.

The proof that programs that obey this discipline in the ordinary MIPS machine do not have any changed behaviors when executed on the MIPS machine with instruction buffers is not hard, but it requires some notation. Recall that from configurations c of the instruction buffer machine we can drop the instruction buffer and thereby obtain an ordinary MIPS processor configuration $c.p$

$$c.p = (c.pc, c.dpc, c.gpr, c.spr, c.m)$$

We now consider computation (c^n) of the instruction buffer machine with inputs x^n with a transition function δ satisfying

$$c^{u+1} = \delta(c^u, x^u)$$

and the guard condition

$$x^u \in \Sigma_p \, \wedge \, ia(c^u)[1:0] \neq 00 \rightarrow (ia(c^u), x^u) \in c^u.ib$$

We recall that $pseq(i)$ is the step of the entire computation when instruction i is stepped. Obviously prefetches into the instruction buffer do not change the processor configuration

$$x \in \Sigma_{ib} \rightarrow \delta(c, x).p = c.p$$

and this of course also holds for sequences of consecutive instruction buffer steps. A trivial induction on j then gives

Lemma 180.

- $j \in [0 : pseq(0)] \;\rightarrow\; c^j.p = c^0.p$
- $j \in [pseq(i) + 1 : pseq(i+1)] \;\rightarrow\; c^j.p = c^{pseq(i)+1}.p$

We wish to show that instruction buffer machine computations (c^n) simulate MIPS computations (d^i) with external inputs e^i and transition function δ_{old} satisfying

$$d^{i+1} = \delta_{old}(d^i, e^i)$$

provided the MIPS computation started in $c^0.p$ satisfies the software discipline for all possible external input sequences (e^i). We abstract a sequence (d^i) of MIPS configurations and its externals inputs (e^i) from the instruction buffer machine computation in a straight forward way by

$$d^i = c^{pseq(i)}.p$$
$$e^i = x^{pseq(i)}.e$$

and show (with a somewhat technical lemma) that this is indeed a MIPS computation.

Lemma 181. *Suppose the ordinary MIPS machine started in configuration $c^0.p$ obeys for all sequences (e^i) of external inputs software condition SC_{eret}. Then for all i*

1. *if the instruction address is aligned, the fetched instruction $I_{old}(d^{i-1})$ which resulted in ISA configuration d^i coincides with the oracle input $x^{pseq(i-1)}.I$*

$$i > 0 \wedge ia_{old}(d^{i-1})[1:0] = 00 \rightarrow I_{old}(d^{i-1}) = x^{pseq(i-1)}.I$$

2. *the sequence (d^i) with the particular sequence of inputs (e^i) defined above is a MIPS computation*

$$d^i = \begin{cases} c^0.p & i = 0 \\ \delta_{old}(d^{i-1}, e^{i-1}) & i > 0 \end{cases}$$

Proof. Obviously by induction on i. For $i = 0$ lemma 180 immediately gives

$$d^0 = c^{pseq(0)}.p = c^0.p$$

and we are done. For the induction step $i \rightarrow i+1$ we have by definition

$$d^i = c^{pseq(i)}.p \quad \text{and} \quad x^{pseq(i)} \in \Sigma_p$$

If $ia_{old}(d^i)$ is misaligned there is nothing to show for part 1. Both machines perform an interrupt, which is possibly external and part 2 follows. Thus assume address

$$a = ia_{old}(d^i) \in \mathbb{B}^{30} \circ \{00\}$$

to be aligned. Then by the guard condition entry

$$ibe = (a, x^{pseq(i)}.I)$$

must be present in the instruction buffer:

$$ibe \in c^{pseq(i)}.ib$$

We split cases

- no portion of the instruction fetched was ever overwritten in the MIPS computation before step i.

$$g < i \; \rightarrow \; ea_{old}(d^g).l \neq ia_{old}(d^i).l$$

In the MIPS computation the bytes fetched by instruction i were never changed, and we have

$$g \leq i \; \rightarrow \; I_{old}(d^i) = d^g.m_4(a) = d^0.m_4(a)$$

In particular

$$I_{old}(d^i) = d^0.m_4(a)$$

Let

$$k < pseq(i)$$

be any instruction buffer machine step which prefetched an instruction at word address a into the instruction buffer:

$$x^k = (ib, a)$$

By the semantics of instruction buffer steps it prefetches from the current memory content of the instruction buffer machine entry

$$ibe = (a, c^k.m_4(a))$$

Let g be the first instruction such that

$$k < pseq(g)$$

By lemma 180 we get

$$\begin{aligned}
c^k.m_4(a) &= c^{pseq(g)}.m_4(a) \qquad\qquad \text{L 180}\\
&= d^g.m_4(a)\\
&= d^0.m_4(a)\\
&= I_{old}(d^i)
\end{aligned}$$

Thus the instruction buffer entry ibe guaranteed by the guard condition to be in the instruction buffer must satisfy

$$ibe.I = x^{pseq(i)}.I = I_{old}(d^i)$$

and claim 1 of the induction step follows. By the semantics of the instruction buffer machine identical processor configurations, identical instructions and identical external inputs lead to identical next processor configurations:

$$c = d \wedge x.I = I_{old}(d) \wedge x.e = e \; \rightarrow \; \delta(c,x).p = \delta_{old}(d,e)$$

Together with lemma 180 we conclude

$$\delta_{old}(d^i, e^i) = \delta(c^{pseq(i)}.p, x^{pseq(i)}).p$$
$$= c^{pseq(i)+1}.p$$
$$= c^{pseq(i+1)}.p \qquad\qquad \text{L 180}$$
$$= d^{i+1}$$

and claim 2 of the induction step follows.

- The instruction fetched at address a was modified in the MIPS computation. In this case we consider the last step g of the MIPS computation before step i, which modified the line with address $ia_{old}(d^i).l$ from which instruction i fetched

$$g = \max\{y < i \mid ea_{old}(d^g).l = ia_{old}(d^i).l = a.l\}$$

Since that point it was not changed. Thus

$$v \in [g+1:i] \quad \rightarrow \quad d^{g+1}.m_4(a) = d^v.m_4(a) = d^i.m_4(a)$$

By the induction hypothesis part 2, (d^j) with input sequence (e^j) is a MIPS computation until i and thus by assumption software condition SC_{eret} must be satisfied. Therefore there was an intermediate step h of the MIPS computation which performed an *eret* instruction

$$eret_{old}(d^h)$$

By induction hypothesis part 1 and lemma 161 this also holds in the instruction buffer machine computation.

$$eret(c^{pseq(h)}, x^{pseq(h)})$$

and therefore the instruction buffer was cleared by step $pseq(h)$.

$$c^{pseq(h)+1}.ib = \emptyset$$

Now we can proceed along the lines of the first case. Instruction buffer entry *ibe* must have been prefetched by a step u after $pseq(h)$ of the instruction buffer machine

$$u > pseq(h) \wedge x^{pseq(i)}.I = c^u.m_4(a)$$

Let

$$pseq(h) \le pseq(v-1) < u < pseq(v) \le pseq(i)$$

By monotonicity of function $pseq$ we have

$$h < v \le i$$

With lemma 180 we conclude

$$x^{pseq(i)}.I = c^u.m_4(a)$$
$$= c^{pseq(v)}.m_4(a) \qquad\qquad \text{L 180}$$
$$= d^v.m_4(a)$$
$$= d^i.m_4(a)$$

and complete the proof as above.   □

8.5 Summary

8.5.1 ISA

With instruction buffers a new component $c.ib$ has been added to ISA configurations. Moreover ISA has become nondeterministic. Nondeterministic choice *and* possibly external input e in ISA step n was modeled by a stepping function

$$s(n) \in \Sigma$$

Instruction buffer steps ere executed with pure oracle inputs

$$s(n) = x \, , \, x = (ib, x.a)$$

and fetch $c.m_4(x.a)$ into the store buffer if a is aligned. Processor steps are executed with combined oracle and external inputs

$$s(n) = x \, , \, x = (p, x.I, x.e)$$

where $x.I$ specifies the instruction to be executed and $x.e$ the external input visible in ISA.

ISA signals f now depend on the current configuration c and input x and thus have with very few exceptions the form $f(c,x)$. The instruction access now occurs with instruction buffer steps, i.e.

$$s(n) = x \, , \, x = (ib, x.a)$$

and we get

$$iacc(c,x).a = x.a \, , \, iacc(c,x).r = 1$$

Nondeterministic choices, i.e. the values of $s(n)$ are restricted by guard conditions $\gamma(c,x)$. For processor steps, i.e.

$$s(n) = x \, , \, x = (p, x.I, x.e)$$

component $x.I$ chooses an instruction to be fetched, but only among instructions for $c.dpc$ already present in the instruction buffer.

$$\gamma(c,x) \equiv ia(c) = 00 \; \rightarrow \; (c.dpc, x.I) \in c.ib$$

8.5.2 Specifying Processor Correctness

The crucial definition of functions *pseq* couples step numbers n of the stepping function with local step numbers i of the processor:

$$pseq(i) = \min\{n \mid n > pseq(i-1) \wedge s(n) \in \Sigma_p\}$$

Redefining for $R \in \{pc, dpc, m, gpr, spr, ib\}$ and *local* step numbers i

$$R^i_\sigma = c^{pseq(i)}.R$$

With this new meaning of R^i_σ the old coupling relation $t \sim_p i$ between hardware cycles t and now local instructions i is formulated exactly as before. In contrast, the simulation relation for the memory needs to be reformulated in terms of global ISA steps, and we add that all earlier ISA steps satisfy the guard condition

$$t \sim_m n \equiv n = NS^t \rightarrow m(h^t) = \ell(m^n_\sigma) \wedge opc^t \wedge \forall \hat{n} < n. \; \gamma(c^{\hat{n}}, s(\hat{n}))$$

Similarly, the main induction hypothesis is reformulated in terms of global steps n:

1. $t \sim_m n$
2. $n = pseq(i) \wedge c(i)^t \wedge lb(i)^t \quad \rightarrow \quad t \sim_p i \wedge (i < I^t_{IF} \rightarrow \gamma^i_\sigma)$

The stepping function $s(n)$ was extracted from the hardware computation cycle by cycle. The order of global ISA steps for the same cycle was deduced from the sequential order of the corresponding accesses as defined by the cache memory system. In normal operation the instruction buffer was stepped with ue_{IF} and the processor core with ue_M. In this context we coupled local sequential indices x of non-void CMS accesses to the global ISA steps

$$isa^t(x) = NS^t + x - 1$$

that generate them. Moreover we provided an emergency brake: once the violation $vopc$ of the operating conditions of the CMS is discovered at the start of a data access, the processor is stepped immediately.

8.5.3 Correctness Proof

In the proof several things have changed.

- We now do the outer induction on the sequence of global ISA steps n rather than the now local instructions i.
- Redefining X^i_σ to $c^{pseq(i)}.X$ allowed to literally copy most of the previous definitions and proofs, with the small technical exception that one needs to show

$$R^i_\sigma = \delta(c^{pseq(i-1)}, s(pseq(i-1))).R$$

- As part of the correctness proof one obviously has to prove that the guard conditions for the instruction buffer hold. This proof has two parts. By bookkeeping resp. the construction of input $x.I$ of the stepping function one shows that an instruction, which is fetched in cycle t also enters the ISA instruction buffer. That it stays there follows from the fact, that instructions committed in hardware are not rolled back in ISA.
- Establishing the operating conditions opc hinged on the possibility of emergency braking: a violation $vopc$ would lead to an early stepping of the instruction involved due to emergency braking. At the cycle when that occurs one can already establish the correctness of the data access and that the guard conditions hold.

Hence the software conditions hold in ISA, but these imply that the (correct) data access of hardware obeys the operating conditions. With this contradiction we were able to exclude stepping functions with emergency braking and thus to exclude *vopc*.

8.6 Exercises

1. Prove lemma 177.
2. Introduce a barrier instruction which empties the instruction buffer. Implement support for that instruction in hardware. Prove that your extended hardware implements the new ISA. Extend the software condition of the instruction buffer reduction theorem to include the new instruction. Reprove the instruction buffer reduction theorem for the new machine with the extended condition. Hint: to implement the instruction in pipeline, make it drain the pipeline, e.g., in the same way that *jisr* or *eret* instructions do.
3. Observe that our definition of the instruction buffer allows multiple entries with the same instruction address. Define the semantics of an ISA where new instruction buffer steps replace old entries with the same instruction address. Does our processor implement this ISA? Prove your answer.
4. Intel processors detect self-modification in the pipeline and roll back modified instructions. Construct hardware to do that and add it to your processor, then prove that your modified processor implements the ordinary MIPS ISA without instruction buffers (without requiring any software condition for self-modifying code).
5. Our instruction buffer reduction theorem (lemma 181) does not fit perfectly to our processor correctness theorem (lemma 163). The problem is that essentially one wants to conclude the precondition of our processor correctness theorem, that valid initial segments of the stepping function imply the software condition

$$(\forall m \leq n.\ \gamma(c^m, s(m))) \rightarrow SC_{ROM}(c^n, s(n))$$

from the software condition SC_{ROMold} of the machine without instruction buffers

$$SC_{ROMold}(d^i)$$

Ideally one would conclude this from the instruction buffer reduction theorem by showing that the ISA computation without instruction buffers extracted from computation (c^n) satisfies the software condition. However our instruction buffer reduction theorem can not be applied to such a computation (c^n) because it can only be applied to computations which are completely valid. Show a variant of the instruction buffer reduction theorem which can be applied if only the initial segment until step $pseq(j)$ in which some instruction j is executed is valid, i.e., assume only

$$\forall u \leq pseq(j).\ x^u \in \Sigma_p \wedge ia(c^u)[1:0] \neq 00 \rightarrow (ia(c^u), x^u) \in c^u.ib$$

and prove only that the sequence (d^i) is a computation until instruction j:

$$i \leq j \rightarrow d^i = \delta_{old}(d^{i-1}, e^{i-1})$$

6. Combine exercise 5 and lemma 163 to show: if every computation (d^i) of the ISA without instruction buffer satisfies SC_{ROMold} and $SC_{eretold}$, then the machine simulates the ISA without instruction buffer. Do this by using first lemma 163. To prove the precondition of this lemma, that valid initial segments of the stepping function imply the software condition

$$(\forall m \leq n. \ \gamma(c^m, s(m))) \rightarrow SC_{ROM}(c^n, s(n))$$

use (for processor steps $n = pseq(j)$) the instruction buffer reduction theorem from exercise 5 to show that there is an ISA computation (d^i) without instruction buffers with

$$c^n.p = d^j \quad \text{and} \quad s(n).I = I(d^j)$$

and use $SC_{ROMold}(d^j)$ to conclude $SC_{ROM}(c^n, s(n))$. Then use the old instruction buffer reduction theorem (lemma 181) on the ISA computation (c^n) produced by lemma 163 to conclude that there is also an ISA computation (d^i) which is simulated by the hardware machine.

9

Memory Management Units

In a nutshell an operating system running on a machine with ISA M like $M = MIPS$ serves two purposes:

- Simulation of *virtual machines* with ISA M for user processes. As long as a user process u does not communicate, it sees its own virtual processor V_u, where it can execute instructions legal in user mode and possibly with a smaller address space $A_u \subset \mathbb{B}^{32}$. Scheduling of user processes is part of the simulation.
- Providing services to user processes. Typical services are communication between users and access to devices.

The key to virtualization is *address translation* as provided by memory management units (MMUs). In user mode virtual addresses

$$va = ia \quad \text{or} \quad va = ea$$

of user u are translated into physical addresses $trans(u, va)$. Therefore the MMUs redirect for user u addresses ia and ea to address $trans(u, ia)$, where the instruction of virtual machine V_u is fetched and to $trans(u, ea)$, where the data access of virtual machine V_u is performed. Users cannot access each others (simulated) memories if their address spaces are translated to disjoint regions of physical memory

$$u \neq v \rightarrow trans(u, A_u) \cap trans(v, A_v) = \emptyset$$

The region

$$A_{OS} \subset \mathbb{B}^{32}$$

of physical addresses used by the operating system and its data structures, should also not be accessible to the user processes. This is easily achieved with translations satisfying

$$trans(u, A_U) \cap A_{OS} = \emptyset$$

Protection of registers of the OS and user processes is achieved by a process called *context switch*, which comes in two flavors:

© Springer Nature Switzerland AG 2020
P. Lutsyk et al. (Eds.): A Pipelined Multi-Core Machine, LNCS 9999, pp. 371–431, 2020.
https://doi.org/10.1007/978-3-030-43243-0_9

- to run user process u: this is performed in system mode. The operating system (OS) saves its own registers into its own *process control block PCB(OS)* and loads the registers of the users virtual machine from the process control block *PCB(u)* of u into the processor. Then it starts running the user process with an *eret* instruction. In general the user process to be run next is computed by the scheduler
- to save user process u: this is initiated by an interrupt in user mode. The OS saves the user registers into *PCB(u)* and restores its own registers from *PCB(OS)*.

The translation to be performed by the MMUs is defined by the *page tables*, a data structure in physical memory controlled by the operating system. Basically, the page tables form a directed graph, and translated addresses $trans(u, va)$ are computed by a graph traversal directed by portions of va. This graph traversal is also called *page table walking*. Different translations for different users u are simply achieved by giving each user its own starting point of the graph search, which we might call the page table origin $pto(u)$ of user u. While the user process is running, $pto(u)$ is stored in the physical page table origin register $spr[pto]$, otherwise it is stored in the users process control block *PCB(u)*. For details of this mechanism including a complete implementation[1] and a correctness proof see [PBLS16].

Page table walking involves several memory accesses and thus is time consuming. Thus it makes sense to store known translations in a dedicated cache for that purpose, which is called *translation look aside buffer* or short TLB. As the operating system is free to store page tables anywhere in its memory, it would be extremely hard to track in hardware what is currently a page table[2] and even harder to determine on the fly when a modification of a page table makes a translation in the TLB invalid. Therefore *TLBs are held consistent by software*, and it is the responsibility of the OS to invalidate *stale* TLB entries (using the *invlpg* instruction) when page tables are changed. It turns out, that in order to optimize performance, operating systems don't always do this immediately, and we have to model these stale translations in ISA.

As in the case of violated software conditions for code modification, this results in nondeterminism seen by the user. Suppose i) address va was translated resulting in a translation $trans_1(u, va)$ in the hardware TLB. ii) a page table used for this translation was changed but the now stale translation $trans_1(u, va)$ was not invalidated (*invlpg*-ed) by the OS. iii) the user uses again virtual address va. Then one of two things can happen:

- the stale translation was evicted in the mean time from the finite hardware TLB in order to make space for a different translation. Then the hardware MMU will walk the updated page tables with va, produce a new and current translation $trans_2(u, va)$ and store it in the hardware TLB. The user sees the new and current translation.

---

[1] On a machine with a very simple address translation mechanism

[2] Something like a page reachable by walking starting from a known *pto*

- the stale translation is still in the hardware TLB. The hardware, which is unaware of the change of page tables has no reason to trigger a new page table walk and 'happily' presents the user with the stale translation $trans_1(u, va)$.

The formalization of page table walking and ISA in sections 9.1 and 9.2 follows a suggestion of Ernie Cohen and was developed for the Verisoft-XT project [ACH$^+$10]. The key concepts are

- *walks*, which correspond to paths from a page table origin to a page table, i.e. to intermediate or complete results of the process of address translation. The start of translations is nondeterministic and can occur any time. This also happens to cover speculative translation by the hardware, although our MMUs will not do this.
- an ISA TLB *c.tlb of unlimited size* including *all translations* encountered so far in ISA and not explicitly invalidated or flushed.
- oracle inputs to choose between (possibly several) stale translations in the TLB and current translations obtained by page table walking for the same virtual address.

Section 9.3 contains specifications, constructions and correctness proofs of a hardware TLB and a hardware MMU. In section 9.4 we construct a machine with

- two extra pipeline stages: one for the translation of instruction address and one for the translation of effective addresses
- two MMUs: one for each of the new pipeline stages. Note that this results in two hardware TLBs.
- two new caches: one for each of the two MMUs. We freely admit that this is brute force and that our primary motivation was to save construction and correctness proof of an arbitration mechanism between the MMUs and the old parts of the pipeline if we stick to the existing two caches. However, dedicated translation caches *do* exist in real machines albeit not at the first level.

It turns out that the new hardware units can be connected to the existing pipeline and stall engine in a straight forward way. This is also reflected in the correctness proof for the entire machine in section 9.5. Obviously some new arguments have to hinge on the specification of the hardware MMUs, and the fact that the cache memory system has now four ports requires some bookkeeping. Finally there are new guard conditions due to the existence of the MMUs, and we obviously have to prove that these conditions hold for the ISA computation extracted from the hardware computation. No further new arguments are needed.

9.1 Walks and ISA MMU

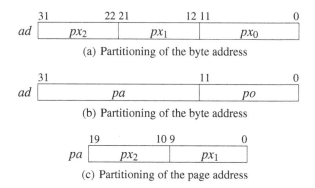

(a) Partitioning of the byte address

(b) Partitioning of the byte address

(c) Partitioning of the page address

Fig. 149. Address partitioning

Pages have $4096 = 4K$ bytes resp. $1024 = K$ words. For $i \in [0:2]$, byte addresses $ad \in \mathbb{B}^{32}$ are partitioned into level i page indices $ad.px_i$ as illustrated in Fig. 149(a) by

$$ad.px_0 = ad[11:0]$$
$$ad.px_1 = ad[21:12]$$
$$ad.px_2 = ad[31:22].$$

Alternatively, we partition addresses just into a page address

$$ad.pa = ad.px_2 \circ ad.px_1$$

and a page offset

$$ad.po = ad.px_0$$

as illustrated in Fig. 149(b). Similarly, page addresses $pa \in \mathbb{B}^{20}$ are decomposed into level 1 and level 2 page indices as illustrated in Fig. 149(c) by

$$pa.px_1 = pa[9:0]$$
$$pa.px_2 = pa[19:10].$$

9.1.1 Page Tables

Fig. 150. Partitioning of page table entries

Page table entries $pte \in \mathbb{B}^{32}$ are one word long, thus K of them fit on a single page. A page whose words are used as page table entries is called a *page table*. Page table entries are partitioned into base address $pte.ba \in B^{20}$, present bit $pte.p \in B$ and rights bits $pte.r \in \mathbb{B}^3$ as indicated in Fig. 150 by

$$pte.ba = pte[31:12]$$
$$pte.p = pte[11]$$
$$pte.r = pte[10:8].$$

The bits $r[2:0]$ of a rights vector for a page will be interpreted in the following way:

- $r[0] = r.w$: write permission,
- $r[1] = r.u$: permission to access as a user, and
- $r[2] = r.ex$: permission to fetch as an instruction and execute.

9.1.2 Walks

Intuitively, multi-level level (here: 2-level) address translation is achieved by walking a graph of page tables, whose edges are defined by the base address fields of the page table entries. In each level i of translation, the edge to follow from a page table is determined by the level i page index $a.px_i$ of the page address a which is translated. The central concept for formalizing this are walks w, which have the following components:

- $w.a \in \mathbb{B}^{20}$: the page address to be translated,
- $w.l \in \{001, 010, 100\}$: coding of the number of walk extensions still required,
- $w.ba \in \mathbb{B}^{20}$: the page address of the page table from which the walking is to be continued,
- $w.r \in \mathbb{B}^3$: the rights still remaining, and
- $w.f \in \mathbb{B}$: the fault bit indicating that the page table entry, from which the walk was extended, was not present.

The set of all walks is denoted by

$$K_{walk} \subseteq \mathbb{B}^{47}$$

and the set of all non-faulting walks is denoted by

$$K_{walk}^+ = \{w \in K_{walk} \mid w.f = 0\}.$$

Walks can be created and extended. For the initiation of a walk one needs a page address $a \in B^{20}$ to be translated and a page table origin $pto \in B^{32}$, which will come from the special purpose register file. The initial walk

$$w = initw(a, pto)$$

has the following components:

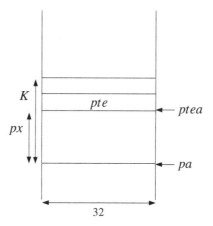

Fig. 151. Page table entry address

- $w.a = a$. The page address to be translated.
- $w.l = 100$. All levels of translation still need to be performed.
- $w.ba = pto.pa$. Translation starts at the page table with page address $pto.pa$.
- $w.r = 111$. Rights have not yet been restricted.
- $w.f = 0$. No missing page table entry and no rights violation has been found, because no page table entry has yet been accessed.

We assume that the page table origin pto is page aligned, i.e. that

$$pto.po = 0_{12}.$$

For a page address $pa \in \mathbb{B}^{20}$ and a page index $px \in \mathbb{B}^{10}$ we define the page table entry address $ptea(pa, px)$, i.e. the address of the page table entry on page pa with index px, as

$$ptea(pa, px) = pa \circ 0^{12} +_{32} 0^{20} \circ px \circ 00$$
$$= pa \circ px \circ 00.$$

This is illustrated in Fig. 151. Overloading notation we define the page table entry address accessed for extending walk w as

$$ptea(w) = ptea(w.ba, w.a.px_{level(w)}).$$

Thus the page table entry address is determined by the base address $w.ba$ of the walk, and the page index $w.a.px_i$ of the address under translation, where $i = level(w)$ is the level of the walk, which determines the number of walk extensions still required.

$$level(w) = \begin{cases} 0 & w.l = 001 \\ 1 & w.l = 010 \\ 2 & w.l = 100 \end{cases}$$

Walks that reach level 0 are called *zero-level* walks. Faulty or zero-level walks cannot be further extended, and therefore are called *complete*.

$$complete(w) \equiv w.f \vee (level(w) = 0)$$

For walk extension with a byte-addressable memory m one looks up the page table entry $pte(w,m)$ in memory m at address $ptea(w)$, i.e.

$$pte(w,m) = m_4(ptea(w)).$$

The extension

$$w' = extw(w, pte)$$

of incomplete walk w with memory m is defined as follows:

$$w'.a = w.a$$
$$w'.l = \begin{cases} 0 \circ w.l[2:1] & pte.p \\ w.l & \text{otherwise} \end{cases}$$
$$w'.ba = pte.ba$$
$$w'.r = pte.r \wedge w.r$$
$$w'.f \equiv pte.p = 0$$

The process of address translation by repeated walk extension is illustrated in Fig. 152.

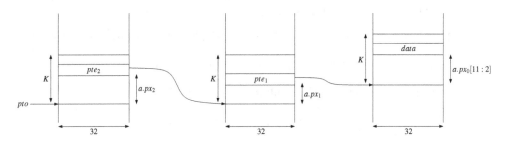

Fig. 152. Process of address translation

A few simple properties of walks are listed in the following lemma.

Lemma 182.

- *Non-faulting walk extension decreases the level.*

$$/w'.f \to level(w') = level(w) - 1$$

- *Zero-level walks are not faulting.*

$$level(w') = 0 \to /w'.f$$

For virtual (byte) addresses $va \in \mathbb{B}^{32}$ and zero-level walks w with address

$$w.a = va.pa$$

we define the translated memory address $tma(va, w)$ obtained by translating va with walk w:

$$(level(w) = 0) \wedge (w.a = va.pa) \ \rightarrow \ tma(va, w) = w.ba \circ va.po.$$

9.1.3 TLBs

A translation look-aside buffer (TLB) is a cache for translations. Formally we simply define it as a set of walks. Thus, if K_{walk} is the set of configurations of walks, then the set K_{tlb} of TLB configurations is

$$K_{tlb} = 2^{K_{walk}}.$$

The model allows the presence of different translations for the same page address in the TLB.

9.1.4 Translation Requests

A translation request trq has two components:

- $trq.a \in \mathbb{B}^{20}$: the page address to be translated, and
- $trq.r \in \mathbb{B}^{3}$: the access rights requested.

A walk w matches an address $a \in \mathbb{B}^{20}$ if w is complete and its address $w.a$ equals a.

$$match(a, w) \equiv complete(w) \wedge (a = w.a)$$

A matching walk leads to a page fault for the request if it is faulting

$$pfault(trq, w) \equiv match(trq.a, w) \wedge w.f.$$

It leads to a general-protection fault if it is not faulting but the rights are insufficient.[3]

$$gfault(trq, w) \equiv match(trq.a, w) \wedge /w.f \wedge /(trq.r \leq w.r)$$

A matching walk provides a translation for the request if the walk is not faulting and provides at least the rights requested.

$$trans(trq, w) \equiv match(trq.a, w) \wedge /w.f \wedge (trq.r \leq w.r)$$

---

[3] Recall, that for bit strings x and y of equal length one defines

$$x \leq y \ \equiv \ \forall i : x_i \leq y_i.$$

9.2 ISA

In addition to the non-deterministic mechanisms introduced in Chap. 8 to model the instruction buffer, ISA for MIPS with TLB is nondeterministic in four more respects:

- the interleaving of processor steps (also called core steps) and TLB steps,
- the (speculative) choice of initial walks to be placed in the TLB,
- the choice of a walk in the TLB that is to be extended, and
- the choice of walks w_I for the translation of instruction addresses and w_E for the translation of effective addresses among the possibly multiple matching walks in the TLB.

Nondeterminism is formalized by a transition function

$$\delta : K \times \Sigma \to K$$

mapping configurations c as well as combined oracle and external inputs x and into a next configuration

$$c' = \delta(c,x).$$

Inputs x, coming from the input alphabet Σ, must among other things specify types of steps to be performed. There are three major cases: TLB steps, instruction buffer steps, and core steps. For core steps, we have to process the external event signal e and we have among other things to deal with the new instructions $flusht$ and $invlpg$ from Table 7 in chapter 4.1.1 . Here we do not deal with tagged TLBs and thus we ignore ASIDs specified in the rs field of the $invlpg$ instruction. For a treatment of machines with ASIDs and nested address translation see [Thesis Petro].

Formally, the input alphabet Σ for transition function δ is the disjoint union of alphabets Σ_p, Σ_{ib}, and Σ_{tlb} resp. for processor core, instruction buffer, and TLB steps.

$$\Sigma = \Sigma_p \dot\cup \Sigma_{ib} \dot\cup \Sigma_{tlb}$$

The alphabets above are (re)defined in the following subsections.

9.2.1 Configuration

Configurations $c \in K$ are now tuples with the components:

- $c.core = (c.pc, c.dpc, c.ddpc, c.gpr, c.spr)$: processor core,
- $c.ib \in K_{ib}$: instruction buffer,
- $c.tlb \in K_{tlb}$: TLB, containing the walks currently available for address translation or extension, and
- $c.m : \mathbb{B}^{32} \to \mathbb{B}^8$: a byte addressable memory.

Due to address translation the instruction fetch stage will be preceded in the pipelined implementation by a stage for the translation of the instruction address. This gives rise to a second delay slot. Thus we need three program counters: pc, dpc, and $ddpc$, and their counter parts epc, $edpc$, and $eddpc$ in the special purpose register file. The new instruction address

$$ia(c) = c.ddpc$$

will subsequently be translated or not depending on the current mode $mode(c)$.

Initialization

The initial ISA configuration c^0 is defined as follows:

- program counters pc, dpc, and $ddpc$ are initialized with 8_{32}, 4_{32}, and 0_{32} resp. pointing at the third, second, and the first instruction of the interrupt service routine (ISR), residing in the memory at byte address $sisr = 0_{32}$.

$$c^0.(pc, dpc, ddpc) = (8_{32}, 4_{32}, 0_{32})$$

- the first general purpose register is always with zero.

$$c.gpr(0_5) = 0_{32}$$

- the external interrupts are masked in the SPR; the exception cause is set to indicate a configuration after the *reset*; the address translation is switched off.

$$c^0.sr[0] = 0_{32}$$
$$c^0.eca = 1_{32}$$
$$c^0.mode[0] = 0_{32}$$

- both the instruction buffer and the translation look-aside buffer are empty.

$$c^0.ib = \emptyset$$
$$c^0.tlb = \emptyset$$

9.2.2 TLB Steps

In system mode no address translation takes place; in particular the ISA TLB does not walk. Thus TLB steps are only allowed in user mode, i.e. when $mode(c) = 1$. They can initialize walks or extend walks, which are already in the TLB.

Walk Initialization

Walk initialization steps are generated by inputs $s(n) = x$ of the form

$$x = (tlb, winit, a) \quad \text{with page address} \quad a \in \mathbb{B}^{20}$$

The only guard condition for such steps is, that the machine is in user mode

$$\gamma(c, (tlb, winit, a)) \equiv mode(c)$$

This step has the effect of placing an initial walk for a and page table origin

$$c.pto = c.spr(pto)$$

into the TLB. The configurations of processor core, instruction buffer, and memory are not affected.

$$c'.tlb = c.tlb \cup \{initw(a, c.pto)\}$$
$$X \in \{core, ib, m\} \rightarrow c'.X = c.X$$

Walk Extension

Walk extension steps are generated by inputs $s(n) = x$ of the form

$$x = (tlb, wext, w) \quad \text{with walk} \quad w \in K_{walk}$$

These steps are only allowed in user mode and for incomplete walks which are already in the TLB.

$$\gamma(c, (tlb, wext, w)) \equiv mode(c) \wedge /complete(w) \wedge w \in c.tlb$$

For such walks w the extension of w with page table entry $pte(w, c.m)$ is included into the TLB. As with initialization steps, the remaining configuration components stay unaffected.

$$c'.tlb = c.tlb \cup \{extw(w, pte(w, c.m))\}$$
$$X \in \{core, ib, m\} \rightarrow c'.X = c.X$$

The input alphabet for TLB steps is

$$\Sigma_{tlb} = \{tlb\} \times \{winit\} \times \mathbb{B}^{20} \cup \{tlb\} \times \{wext\} \times K_{walk}$$

9.2.3 Instruction Buffer Steps

Nothing changes compared to the previous chapter. Instruction buffer steps are generated by inputs $s(n) = x$ of the form

$$x = (ib, a) \quad \text{with} \quad a \in \mathbb{B}^{32}$$

Thus

$$\Sigma_{ib} = \{ib\} \times \mathbb{B}^{32}$$

Such steps prefetch the memory word $c^n.m_4(a)$ at address a into the instruction buffer.

$$s(n) = (ib, a) \quad \rightarrow \quad c^{n+1}.ib = c^n.ib \cup \{(a, c^n.m_4(a))\}$$

The instruction access of ISA occurs in this step. Thus we have

$$iacc(c, x).a = x.a$$
$$iacc(c, x).r = 1$$

Prefetch of any memory word is allowed; thus the guard condition for instruction buffer steps stays trivial

$$\gamma(c, (ib, a)) = 1$$

9.2.4 Processor Steps

In Chap. 8 processor core steps had the form $s(n) = x$:

$$x = (p, I, e) \quad \text{with instruction} \quad I \in \mathbb{B}^{32} \quad \text{and external input} \quad e \in \mathbb{B}$$

With address translation we may need to translate both the instruction address ia and the effective address ea with the help of matching walks. As more than one matching walk might be present in the TLB we have to disambiguate the possible choices with two additional oracle inputs w_I and w_E. On the other hand none of these walks is used in system mode, and in user mode walk w_E is only used in memory operations. There is no point to specify walks, that are not used; thus we allow oracle inputs $w = \bot$ for undefined walks. With

$$K_{walk}^{\bot} = K_{walk} \cup \{\bot\}$$

inputs for core steps now have the form $s(n) = x$ where

$$x = (p, I, e, w_I, w_E) \quad \text{with walks} \quad w_I, w_E \in K_{walk}^{\bot}$$

Consequently the new input alphabet for processor steps is

$$\Sigma_p = \{p\} \times \mathbb{B}^{32} \times \mathbb{B} \times K_{walk}^{\bot} \times K_{walk}^{\bot}$$

In translated mode, walk w_I is used for the translation of the instruction address and walk w_E is used for the translation of the effective address in load, store or CAS operations. Walks which are used are required to be in the TLB and match the corresponding addresses. In order to formalize the latter requirements as guard conditions (analogous to Sect. 8.1.3), we must specify when the walk inputs are used.

$$used[w_I](c, x) \equiv mode(c) \wedge il(c, x) > 4$$
$$used[w_E](c, x) \equiv mode(c) \wedge il(c, x) > 10 \wedge mop(c, x)$$

Thus, walk w_I is used whenever the machine runs in translated mode and the interrupts registered (if any) are of the interrupt level 5 or higher. Similarly, walk w_E is used whenever the machine runs in translated mode, the interrupt registered (if any) are of the interrupt level 11 or higher, and a memory operation is executed. The guard conditions imposing restrictions on walks w_I and w_E (indexed by tlb_I and tlb_E resp.) are given below.

$$\gamma_{wI}(c, x) \equiv used[w_I](c, x) \rightarrow match(ia(c), w_I) \wedge x.w_I \in c.tlb$$
$$\gamma_{wE}(c, x) \equiv used[w_E](c, x) \rightarrow match(ea(c, x), w_E) \wedge x.w_E \in c.tlb$$

In Chap. 8 we introduced a guard condition imposing restrictions on the instruction word input $(x.I)$ for configurations with aligned instruction address $(ia(c))$.

$$\gamma(c, x) \equiv ia(c)[1:0] = 0_2 \rightarrow (ia(c), x.I) \in c.ib$$

This condition must be updated because the instruction to be executed is not always addressed any more by the instruction address $ia(c)$. In translated mode the instruction address must be first translated with walk w_I. We define the *physical memory address* of the instruction to be executed (using translated memory address *tma* from Sect. 9.1.2) as

$$pmaI(c,x) = \begin{cases} tma(ia(c),w_I) & mode(c) \\ ia(c) & \text{otherwise} \end{cases}$$

In the same way we define the physical memory address for data memory access: in system mode it is the effective address $ea(c,x)$; in translated mode it is the effective address translated with walk w_E.

$$pmaE(c,x) = \begin{cases} tma(ea(c,x),w_E) & mode(c) \\ ea(c,x) & \text{otherwise} \end{cases}$$

Moreover, with address translation, the instruction word input is used only if the interrupts registered (if any) are of the interrupt level 7 or higher.

$$used[x.I](c,x) \equiv il(c,x) > 6$$

Now we can substitute guard condition γ with

$$\gamma_I(c,x) \equiv used[x.I](c,x) \rightarrow (pmaI(c,x),x.I) \in c.ib$$

The guard condition for processor steps is now simply the combination of the individual guard conditions for the instruction buffer entry and the walks used by the step:

$$\gamma(c,x) = \gamma_I(c,x) \wedge \gamma_{wI}(c,x) \wedge \gamma_{wE}(c,x)$$

For processor core steps the formal definition of c' is necessarily somewhat lengthy, because we have to adapt the definition of internal interrupt event signals to the case where the machine might be running in translated mode.

Interrupt Signals

The interesting part of the definitions concerns of course the case when the machine is running in translated mode, i.e. if

$$mode(c) = mode(c.core) = 1.$$

- misalignment on fetch. This is not affected by address translation.

$$malf(c) = malf(c.core)$$

- faults on fetch. The translation request for instruction fetch is

$$trqI(c) = (ia(c).pa, 110).$$

We get a page fault or general-protection fault on fetch if translation of this request with the chosen walk w_I produces the corresponding fault.

$$pff(c,x) \equiv mode(c) \wedge pfault(trqI(c), w_I)$$
$$gff(c,x) \equiv mode(c) \wedge gfault(trqI(c), w_I)$$

- illegal interrupt. In translated mode instructions *flusht* and *invlpg* are also illegal.

$$ill(c,x) \equiv undefined(c,x) \vee$$
$$mode(c) \wedge eret(c,x) \vee$$
$$mode(c) \wedge (flusht(c,x) \vee invlpg(c,x)) \vee$$
$$mode(c) \wedge move(c,x) \wedge /(movg2s(c,x) \wedge rd(c,x) = 10_5)$$

- overflow and misalignment on load/store or CAS.

$$ovf(c,x) \equiv alu(c,x) \wedge ovfalu(lop(c,x), rop(c,x), af(c,x), itype(c,x))$$
$$malls(c,x) \equiv mop(c,x) \wedge d(c,x) \nmid \langle pma_E(c,x) \rangle$$
$$\equiv mop(c,x) \wedge d(c,x) \nmid \langle ea(c,x) \rangle$$

- faults on load/store or CAS. The translation request for the effective address is

$$trqE(c,x) = (ea(c,x).pa, 01 \circ write(c,x)).$$

We get a page fault or general-protection fault on load/store or CAS if translation of this request with the chosen walk w_E produces the corresponding fault.

$$pfls(c,x) \equiv mode(c) \wedge pfault(trqE(c,x), w_E)$$
$$gfls(c,x) \equiv mode(c) \wedge gfault(trqE(c,x), w_E)$$

Instruction Execution without Flush or invlpg

The instruction word passed within the combined input x is only executed in the absence of misalignment and — in translated mode — the absence of page fault and general-protection fault on fetch. Nothing else changes compared to Chap. 8: the instruction to be executed is taken directly from the oracle input.

$$I(c,x) = x.I$$
$$used[I](c,x) = used[x.I](c,x)$$

Note, according to guard condition $\gamma_i(c,x)$, the instruction to be executed is present in the instruction buffer in the entry associated with address $pmaI(c,x)$.

$$(pmaI(c,x), I(c,x)) \in c.ib$$

Execution of a memory operation is only possible in the absence of misalignment and — in translated mode — any fault on load/store or CAS. Thus, in the following three cases (resp. for load, store, and CAS) we assume that a memory operation is executed uninterrupted.

$$mop(c,x) \wedge /jisr(c,x)$$

- For loads ($l(c,x)$) we then get

$$fill(c,x) = \begin{cases} 0 & u(c,x) \\ c.m_{d(c,x)}(pmaE(c,x))[8 \cdot d(c,x) - 1] & \text{otherwise} \end{cases}$$

$$lres(c,x) = fill(c,x)^{32-8 \cdot d(c,x)} \circ c.m_{d(c,x)}(pmaE(c,x))$$

$$c'.gpr(y) = \begin{cases} lres(c,x) & y = rt(c,x) \wedge y \neq 0_5 \\ c.gpr(y) & \text{otherwise.} \end{cases}$$

- For stores ($s(c,x)$) we get

$$c'.m(y) = \begin{cases} byte(i, B(c,x)) & y = pmaE(c,x) +_{32} i_{32} \wedge i < d(c,x) \\ c.m(y) & \text{otherwise.} \end{cases}$$

where $B(c,x)$ is gpr register $rt(c,x)$

$$B(c,x) = c.gpr(rt(c,x))$$

- Finally, for CAS ($cas(c,x)$) we get

$$c'.gpr(y) = \begin{cases} c.m_4(pmaE(c,x)) & y = rd(c,x) \wedge y \neq 0_5 \\ c.gpr(y) & \text{otherwise} \end{cases}$$

$$c'.m(y) = \begin{cases} byte(i, B(c,x)) & castest(c,x) \wedge y = pmaE(c,x) +_{32} i_{32} \wedge i < 4 \\ c.m(y) & \text{otherwise.} \end{cases}$$

In the absence of $flusht$ and $invlpg$ instructions, configuration of the TLB component does not change on processor core steps.

$$/flusht(c,x) \wedge /invlpg(c,x) \rightarrow c'.tlb = c.tlb$$

The semantics for the program counters is adjusted in the obvious way.

$$c'.pc = \begin{cases} 8_{32} & jisr(c,x) \\ c.epc & eret(c,x) \wedge /jisr(c,x) \\ nextpc(c) & \text{otherwise} \end{cases}$$

$$c'.dpc = \begin{cases} 4_{32} & jisr(c,x) \\ c.edpc & eret(c,x) \wedge /jisr(c,x) \\ c.pc & \text{otherwise} \end{cases}$$

$$c'.ddpc = \begin{cases} 0_{32} & jisr(c,x) \\ c.eddpc & eret(c,x) \wedge /jisr(c,x) \\ c.dpc & \text{otherwise} \end{cases}$$

Flush or invlpg

We use a single address space and no address space identifiers (ASIDs). Execution of a *flusht* instruction in system mode flushes the TLB.

$$flusht(c,x) \wedge /jisr(c,x) \rightarrow c'.tlb = \emptyset$$

Execution of an *invlpg* instruction in system mode removes from the TLB the walks translating page address given by the GPR register $rt(c,x)$ (abbreviated by $B(c,x)$) from the TLB. Also, it keeps only the zero-level walks.

$$invlpg(c,x) \wedge /jisr(c,x) \rightarrow c'.tlb = \{\, w \in c.tlb \mid w.a \neq B(c,x).pa \wedge level(w) = 0 \,\}$$

The definition of intermediate result C is extended: in case of *invlpg* instructions we include $B(c,x).pa$ in the lower bits of the intermediate result C. This is the page address whose translation in the TLB will be invalidated by the instruction [4]

$$C(c,x) = \begin{cases} S(c,x) & movs2g(c,x) \\ B(c,x) & movg2s(c,x) \\ 0_{12} \circ B(c,x).pa & invlpg(c,x) \\ linkad(c,x) & jal(c,x) \vee jalr(c,x) \\ su.res(c,x) & su(c,x) \\ alu.res(c,x) & \text{otherwise} \end{cases}$$

In both cases the register files, instruction buffer, and the memory are not changed and the program counters are updated.

$$X \in \{gpr, spr, ib, m\} \rightarrow c'.X = c.X$$
$$c'.pc = c.pc +_{32} 4_{32}$$
$$c'.dpc = c.pc$$
$$c'.ddpc = c.dpc$$

9.3 MMU Construction

We describe the construction of a simple memory management unit (MMU). It consists of two subunits: i) a translation look aside buffer (TLB) and ii) a walking unit.

9.3.1 TLB

The TLB is implemented as a content addressable cache. The TLB construction we present is very basic and can be optimized in many ways. As shown in Fig. 153, our construction has the following inputs:

---

[4] If we would use ASIDs, we could store them in the upper 12 bits of C.

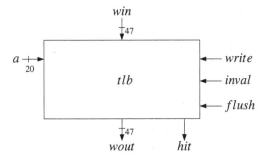

Fig. 153. Symbol for a basic TLB

- $a \in \mathbb{B}^{20}$: the virtual page address to be translated/invalidated on signal *inval*,
- $win \in \mathbb{B}^{47}$: the input walk in case a new walk is written into the TLB,
- *write* $\in \mathbb{B}$: control signal to write the input walk (*win*) into the TLB,
- *inval* $\in \mathbb{B}$: control signal to invalidate walks w with page address $w.a = a$, and
- *flush* $\in \mathbb{B}$: control signal to invalidate all walks in the TLB.

The output signals are as follows:

- *wout* $\in \mathbb{B}^{47}$: a walk providing a translation for page address a in case of a *hit*,
- *hit* $\in \mathbb{B}$: indicates whether a walk providing a translation for page address a is present in the cache.

We require that in the absence of an active *reset* signal at most one of the signals *write*, *inval*, or *flush* is active at any time.

$$/reset \; \rightarrow \; write + inval + flush \leq 1 \tag{53}$$

A construction is partially illustrated in Fig. 154. Registers $R(i)$ in the TLB are treated as walks; to each such register we add an additional valid bit $v(i)$. The hardware TLB $tlb(h)$ of a TLB hardware configuration $h \in K_{tlb}$ then contains the walks stored in registers whose valid bits are set.

$$tlb(h) = \{ h.R(i) \mid h.v(i) \}$$

In the construction we will maintain the following invariant.

Invariant 1. *For any page address a, at most one translation is stored in the cache.*

$$w, w' \in tlb(h) \wedge w.a = w'.a \; \rightarrow \; w = w'$$

Formally, operations of the TLB are specified as follows:

- signal *hit* indicates the existence of a translation for a in the cache.

$$hit \; \leftrightarrow \; \exists w \in tlb(h). \; w.a = a$$

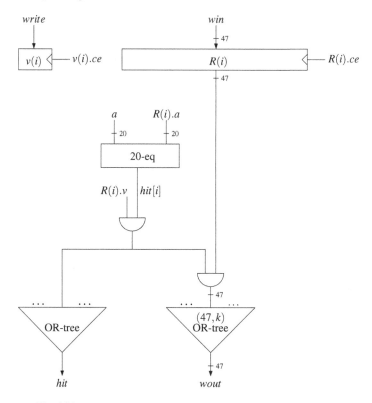

Fig. 154. TLB construction as a content addressable cache

- in case of a hit, output *wout* provides a translation for *a* from the TLB.

$$hit \; \rightarrow \; wout \in tlb(h) \land wout.a = a$$

This translation is unique by invariant 1.
- activation of *flush* empties the TLB.

$$flush \; \rightarrow \; tlb(h') = \emptyset$$

- if the write signal is activated, the input walk is included into the TLB, possibly at the expense of a victim walk.

$$write \; \rightarrow \; win \in tlb(h') \land tlb(h') \subseteq tlb(h) \cup \{win\} \land \#tlb(h') \geq \#tlb(h)$$

- activation of the *inval* signal makes the TLB drop all translations for *a* and all walks with level other than zero.

$$inval \; \land \; (w.a = a \lor level(w) \neq 0) \; \rightarrow \; w \notin tlb(h')$$

Correctness of the hit signal computation is obvious. Output *wout* is computed correctly if we succeed to maintain invariant 1. For that we need to provide input *a* every

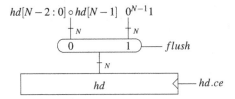

$$hd[N-2:0] \circ hd[N-1] \quad 0^{N-1}1$$

Fig. 155. *hd* register

time we add a new walk into the TLB. We require this input to be equal to the virtual address of the walk which is added. Therefore, we impose the following simple operating condition.

$$write \; \rightarrow \; a = win.a \tag{54}$$

Now suppose the number of registers $R(i)$ together with their valid bits $v(i)$ is N, thus

$$i \in [0 : N-1].$$

We control the writing of new walks into the TLB by an N bit register

$$hd[N-1:0] \in \mathbb{B}^N.$$

In this register always a single bit will be set to 1. As shown in Fig. 155, at the activation of the *flush* signal (which will be activated at *reset*), the register is initialized with $0^{N-1}1$. Thus, the first write after the *flush* goes to register $R(0)$. Subsequent writes go to the next register modulo N. This results in a FIFO eviction strategy. The intuition is as follows:

- if $hd[i] = 1$, then in the absence of a *hit* the next write will go to register $R(i)$, possibly overwriting the previous content of this register.
- in case $hit[i] = 1$, register $R(i)$ is overwritten. This preserves invariant 1.

Register hd is clocked at flushes and at writes, unless the write occurs together with a hit.

$$hd.ce \; \equiv \; flush \lor write \land /hit$$

The valid bit of register i is set only if we write and the hd is pointing to this line. Any other write operation on a line invalidates it. In this way we define register inputs

$$v(i).in = write$$
$$R(i).in = win$$

and the clock enable signals.

$$v(i).ce \equiv \begin{cases} hd[i] \land /hit & write \\ hit[i] \lor /R(i).l[0] & inval \\ 1 & flush \end{cases}$$

$$R(i).ce \equiv write \land (hd[i] \land /hit \lor hit[i])$$

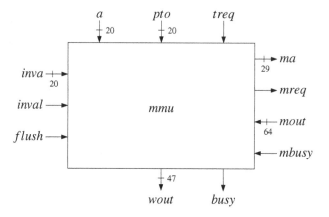

Fig. 156. Memory management unit symbol

Note that with this construction valid walks might be overwritten, even though there are unoccupied cache lines due to previous invalidations. This replacement policy can be changed, for example to LRU (least recently used), where invalid addresses are written first, as long as the invariants for the TLB hold.

9.3.2 Walking Unit and MMU

We complete the construction of MMU by adding to the TLB a walking unit, s.t. a TLB *mmu.tlb* plus a walking unit form a memory management unit *mmu*. In our designs, MMUs interface to two other units:

  i) a processor, providing translation requests, and
 ii) a memory, where page table entries are looked up.

This leads to the following set of inputs and outputs of the MMU (see Fig. 156):

- the processor side for address translation:
    - input $a \in \mathbb{B}^{20}$: the page address to be translated,
    - input $pto \in \mathbb{B}^{20}$: a page address used as a page table origin,
    - input $treq \in \mathbb{B}$: signaling to the MMU a request for address translation,
    - output $wout \in \mathbb{B}^{47}$: the walk to be used by the processor core, and
    - output $busy \in \mathbb{B}$: signaling to the processor, that the translation is not ready.
- the memory system side:
    - output $ma \in \mathbb{B}^{29}$: a cache line address for a read request,
    - output $mreq \in \mathbb{B}$: signaling a (read) request to the memory system,
    - input $mout \in \mathbb{B}^{64}$: a data line returned by the memory system in response to a (read) request, and
    - input $mbusy \in \mathbb{B}$: signaling to the walking unit, that the memory system is not ready.
- the processor side for "instruction execution" (*invlpg* and *flusht*):

- input $inva \in \mathbb{B}^{20}$: a page address to be invalidated on an invalidation request (*inval*),
- input $inval \in \mathbb{B}$: signaling to the MMU a request to invalidate a TLB entry,
- input $flush \in \mathbb{B}$: signaling to the MMU a request to invalidate all TLB entries.

The protocol for *treq* and *busy* is similar to the one for *mreq* and *mbusy* but not identical. The interface of the cache memory system requires memory accesses that have started to complete; moreover, inputs to the cache memory system have to stay stable during an access. In contrast, after interrupts we will *abort* page table walking, possibly in the middle of a translation. In a nutshell, this is due to the fact that interrupts change the mode to system mode, where the ISA TLB does not make steps.

We say that a translation *starts* in cycle t when the MMU is busy in cycle $t-1$ and the request signal is on in cycle t.

$$t\text{-}start(t) \equiv /busy^{t-1} \wedge treq^t$$

A translation *ends* in cycle t if the MMU is not busy anymore while the translation request is on.

$$t\text{-}end(t) \equiv treq^t \wedge /busy^t$$

A translation is *aborted* in cycle t when the translation request is lowered although the MMU is still busy.

$$t\text{-}abort(t) \equiv treq^{t-1} \wedge busy^{t-1} \wedge /treq^t$$

For intervals of cycles $[t : t']$ we define a predicate stating that the translation request stays on during the entire interval.

$$treq[t : t'] \equiv \forall u \in [t : t'] : treq^u$$

The MMU is *live* if the *busy* signal eventually goes away after a translation has started.

$$t\text{-}start(t) \rightarrow \exists t' \geq t : /busy^{t'}$$

We require the following operating conditions:

i) control signals *treq*, *inval*, and *flush* are mutually exclusive.

$$treq + inval + flush \leq 1 \tag{55}$$

ii) a translation request cannot be turned on while the MMU is busy. (This will prevent the use of intermediate results of aborted translations.)

$$/treq \wedge busy \rightarrow /treq' \tag{56}$$

iii) while a translation proceeds regularly, i.e., without being aborted, the MMU address a should not change. This will help us to show that regular translations eventually produce walks matching the requested address.

$$treq \wedge busy \wedge treq' \rightarrow a = a' \tag{57}$$

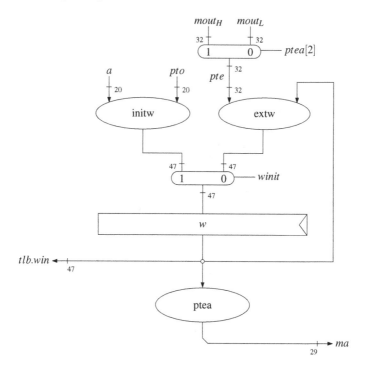

Fig. 157. Walking unit data paths

As MMUs interface to the cache memory system, the termination of translation requests will obviously hinge on the liveness of the cache memory system (section 6.2.7). Overall, our construction consists of three parts:

i) data paths of the walking unit,
ii) an interface to the TLB, and
iii) a control automaton.

Walking Unit Data Paths

A design is shown in Fig. 157. Initial walks *initw* are constructed in the obvious way.

$$initw.a = a$$
$$initw.l = 100$$
$$initw.ba = pto$$
$$initw.r = 111$$
$$initw.f = 0$$

Initial walks or results *extw* of walk extension are clocked into the walk register *mmu.w*.

$$mmu.w.in = \begin{cases} initw & winit \\ extw & \text{otherwise} \end{cases}$$

The page table entry address *ptea* for walk extension and the memory address *ma* are computed resp. as follows.

$$ptea = w.ba \circ (w.a.px_2 \wedge w.l[2] \vee w.a.px_1 \wedge w.l[1]) \circ 00$$
$$ma = ptea.l = ptea[31:3]$$

That this computes the correct page table entry address is stated in

Lemma 183. *Assume that there is a subunit mmu : MMU. Then*

$$mmu.ptea = ptea(mmu.w)$$

The page table entry *pte* to be used for walk extension is constructed from the memory output *mout* in the usual way.

$$pte = \begin{cases} mout_H & ptea[2] = 1 \\ mout_L & ptea[2] = 0 \end{cases}$$

The extended walk *extw* is again constructed from walk

$$w = mmu.w$$

in the obvious way.

$$extw.a = w.a$$
$$extw.l = \begin{cases} 0 \circ w.l[2:1] & pte.p = 1 \\ w.l & pte.p = 0 \end{cases}$$
$$extw.ba = pte.ba$$
$$extw.r = pte.r \wedge w.r$$
$$extw.f = \overline{pte.p}$$

TLB Interface

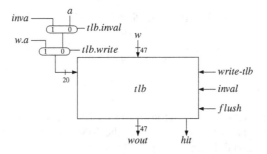

Fig. 158. Wiring of TLB

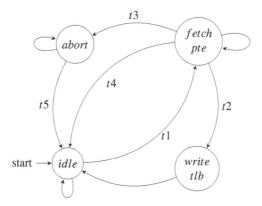

Fig. 159. MMU control automaton

As illustrated in fig. 158, walks from the walk register are written into the TLB, thus

$$tlb.win = w.$$

Control signal *tlb.write* is coming from the control automaton of the walking unit (see the next paragraph). Control signals *tlb.inval* and *tlb.flush* are forwarded from the MMU interface without changes.

$$tlb.inval = inval$$
$$tlb.flush = flush$$

Before the walking unit starts working, one looks for walk matching address a in the TLB. Moreover, on invalidation requests the invalidation address *inva* is provided to the TLB through its address port, but when we write to the TLB, the address comes from the walk register.

$$tlb.a = \begin{cases} inva & tlb.inval \\ w.a & tlb.write \\ a & \text{otherwise} \end{cases}$$

This guarantees that the corresponding operating condition of the TLB (equation 54) is always respected. The walk output (to the processor) always comes from the TLB.

$$wout = tlb.wout$$

Control Automaton

We use the simple control automaton from Fig. 159. Initial state (and the state after the *reset*) is *idle*. The *idle* state is left if the MMU receives a translation request which cannot be served directly from the TLB.

$$(t1) \equiv treq \wedge /hit \wedge /reset$$

In state *fetch-pte* a page table entry is fetched from the memory at address *ptea*. While the *mbusy* signal is on, one has to wait; if in the meantime the *treq* signal was lost, the translation is aborted. If this happens exactly at the end of the memory access the automaton returns immediately to the *idle* state ($t4$), otherwise it waits in state *abort* for completion of the access. The fetch is repeated if the walk extension with the fetched *pte* is not a complete walk (and the translation was not aborted); otherwise the automaton goes to state *write,tlb*, where a complete resulting walk is to be written into the TLB ($t2$).

$$(t2) \equiv treq \wedge /mbusy \wedge complete(extw) \wedge /reset$$
$$(t3) \equiv /treq \wedge mbusy \wedge /reset$$
$$(t4) \equiv /treq \wedge /mbusy \vee reset$$

In state *abort* the automaton simply waits for the memory system to lower the *mbusy* signal. Once the memory is no longer busy, the automaton returns to state *idle*.

$$(t5) \equiv /mbusy \vee reset$$

The memory request signal is active in states *fetch-pte* and *abort*.

$$mreq = fetch\text{-}pte \vee abort$$

The complete walk from register *mmu.w* is written into the TLB in state *write-tlb* (unless the translation request was lost).

$$tlb.write = write\text{-}tlb \wedge treq$$

The multiplexer in Fig. 157 above the walk register is controlled by signal

$$winit \equiv idle \wedge (t1).$$

The walk register is clocked i) if an initial walk is created or ii) if the memory is not busy in state *fetch-pte* and the translation is not aborted.

$$w.ce \equiv winit \vee fetch\text{-}pte \wedge treq \wedge /mbusy$$

The *busy* signal is only off if the automaton is in state *idle* and stays there.

$$busy \equiv /idle \vee (t1)$$

This completes the construction of a simple MMU. An obvious optimization would be to output walks to the processor already from the walk register.

9.3.3 Correctness

As usual we assume that the reset signal is off.

$$reset = 0$$

We show that the operating condition of the TLB is satisfied

Lemma 184.

$$tlb.inval + tlb.flush + tlb.write \leq 1$$

Proof. A TLB write by construction only happens during a translation request. We get

$$tlb.inval + tlb.flush + tlb.write \leq inval + flush + treq \overset{E\,55}{\leq} 1$$

□

The construction maintains the invariant that in state *fetch-pte*, the walk in the walk register is not complete

Invariant 2.

$$fetch\text{-}pte \rightarrow /complete(w)$$

The behavior of the MMU can now be described by a series of very simple lemmas.

Lemma 185.

$$/idle \wedge /inval \rightarrow /hit$$

Proof. The MMU only leaves the idle state when there is no hit (with transition $(t1)$), and does not add a new entry to the TLB until it returns to the idle state (in state *write-tlb*). □

Lemma 186. *When the idle state is left, the initial walk for the current address and the page table origin is clocked into the walk register.*

$$idle \wedge (t1) \rightarrow w' = initw(a, pto)$$

This walk is of level 2 and its address equals a.

$$level(w') = 2 \wedge w.a' = a$$

Proof. The claim follows from the correctness of circuit "initw" (in Fig. 157). □

Lemma 187. *When state fetch-pte is repeated while the memory is busy, the page table entry address stays constant and the walks stored in the TLB stay the same.*

$$mbusy \wedge fetch\text{-}pte \wedge fetch\text{-}pte' \rightarrow ptea = ptea' \wedge tlb(mmu.tlb) = tlb(mmu'.tlb)$$

Proof. That the page table entry address stays constant follows from the fact that the walk register is not clocked when the memory is busy. Formally we conclude successively

$$/w.ce\,,\quad ptea = ptea'$$

Since state *fetch-pte* is repeated, we conclude that the *treq* signal is on and hence by operating condition 55 the *inval* and *flush* signals of the MMU and the TLB are off. Moreover, new walks are written only in state *write-tlb*. Hence walks in the TLB are neither added nor dropped. Formally we conclude successively

$$treq,\ /inval \wedge /flush\,,\ /tlb.write\,,\ tlb(mmu.tlb) = tlb(mmu'.tlb)$$

□

Lemma 188. *When state abort is entered or repeated, the page table entry address stays constant and the walks stored in the TLB stay the same.*

$$(\text{fetch-pte} \vee \text{abort}) \wedge \text{abort}' \ \rightarrow \ \text{ptea} = \text{ptea}' \ \wedge \ \text{tlb}(\text{mmu.tlb}) = \text{tlb}(\text{mmu}'.\text{tlb})$$

Proof. Transitions to state *abort* only occur when the memory is busy. So we conclude as in the previous proof

$$/w.ce \ , \quad \text{ptea} = \text{ptea}'$$

The argument about the TLB stays the same.   □

When the MMU is connected to a cache memory system, the above lemmas imply that inputs to the caches stay constant during an access.

Lemma 189. *When the memory is busy, the page table entry address stays constant*

$$\text{mbusy} \rightarrow \text{ptea} = \text{ptea}'$$

Proof. Because the memory is busy the memory request signal busy be on, which is only the case in states *fetch-pte* and abort.

$$\text{mreq} \ , \ \text{fetch-pte} \vee \text{abort}$$

In state *fetch-pte* and with an active *mbusy* signal the automaton stays in state *fetch-pte* or proceeds to state *abort*

$$\text{fetch-pte}' \vee \text{abort}'$$

In state *abort* and with an active *mbusy* signal the automaton stays in state *abort*

$$\text{abort}'$$

The lemma now follows immediately from lemmas 187 and 188   □

Lemma 190. *In state abort i) the memory busy signal eventually goes away*

$$\text{abort}^t \ \rightarrow \ \exists u \geq t. \ /\text{mbusy}^u$$

and ii) the translation request signal stays low.

$$\text{abort} \rightarrow /\text{treq}$$

Proof. The first part follows from the liveness of the memory interface (lemma 80). The second part can be easily shown by induction on the number of hardware cycles (using operating condition 56).   □

Lemma 191. *In state fetch-pte the memory busy signal eventually goes away.*

$$\text{fetch-pte}^t \ \rightarrow \ \exists u \geq t. \ /\text{mbusy}^u$$

If up to the first such cycle u the translation was not aborted, then the walk in the walk register is extended.

$$\text{fetch-pte}^t \wedge u = \min\{u \geq t \mid /\text{mbusy}^u\} \wedge \text{treq}[t:u] \ \rightarrow \ w^{u+1} = \text{extw}(w^u, \text{pte}^u)$$

Proof. The first part follows either from the liveness of the memory interface (lemma 80) — if the translation was not aborted — or from lemma 190.

The second part follows from the correctness of circuit "extw" (in Fig. 157).   □

Lemma 192. *When state fetch-pte is entered after the start of a translation, then the state is eventually left.*

$$idle^t \wedge fetch\text{-}pte^{t+1} \ \rightarrow \ \exists u > t+1. \ /fetch\text{-}pte^u$$

If the translation request signal stays active while the automaton stays in state fetch-pte

$$idle^t \wedge fetch\text{-}pte^{t+1} \wedge u = \min\{u > t+1 \mid /fetch\text{-}pte^u\} \wedge treq[t:u-1]$$

then the walk in register w in cycle u matches a^t.

$$match(a^t, w^u)$$

Proof. By lemma 186 the walk register in cycle $t+1$ contains a level 2 walk with address component a^t.

$$level(w^{t+1}) = 2 \ \wedge \ w^{t+1}.a = a^t$$

Consider the first cycle $t_1 \geq t+1$, when the memory is not busy.

$$t_1 = \min\{u \geq t+1 \mid /mbusy^u\}$$

This cycle exists by lemma 191. While the memory is busy, the walk register is not clocked, thus

$$w^{t_1} = w^{t+1}.$$

We split cases on $treq[t:t_1]$:

- $/treq[t:t_1]$. The translation is aborted in some cycle $e \in [t+1:t_1]$ with $/treq^e$. In case $e = t_1$, from the construction of the control automaton we conclude that transition $t4$ is taken, and therefore we have $idle^{e+1}$. If $e < t_1$, we conclude that transition $t3$ is taken, and therefore we have $abort^{e+1}$. In both cases the claim follows for $u = e+1$.
- $treq[t:t_1]$. By lemma 191 the walk register in cycle $t_1 + 1$ contains the extended walk.

$$w^{t_1+1} = extw(w^{t_1}, pte^{t_1})$$

Because walk extension does not change the address component we have

$$w^{t_1+1}.a = w^{t_1}.a = w^{t+1}.a = a^t$$

If the present bit in the page table entry used (pte^{t_1}) is off, then the resulting walk w^{t_1+1} is faulting. We get successively

$$/pte^{t_1}.p \;,\; w^{t_1+1}.f \;,\; complete(w^{t_1+1}) \;,\; write\text{-}tlb^{t_1+1}$$

and the claim follows for $u = t_1 + 1$.

If the present bit is on, the control automaton stays in state *fetch-pte*. By lemma 182 the level of the walk in register w decreases in this case, and we conclude successively

$$pte^{t_1}.p \;,\; /w^{t_1+1}.f \;,\; /complete(w^{t_1+1}) \;,\; fetch\text{-}pte^{t_1+1} \wedge level(w^{t_1+1}) = 1.$$

We perform a second memory access which ends in cycle

$$t_2 = \min\{u \geq t_1 + 1 \mid /mbusy^u\}$$

and we split subcases on $treq[t_1 + 1 : t_2]$:

- $/treq[t_1 + 1 : t_2]$. The translation is aborted in some cycle $e \in [t_1 + 2 : t_2]$ during the second memory access. As above we conclude

$$/treq^e \;\rightarrow\; idle^{e+1} \vee abort^{e+1} \;\rightarrow\; u = e + 1.$$

- $treq[t_1 + 1 : t_2]$. Analogous to the case above: by lemma 191 the walk register in cycle $t_2 + 1$ contains walk

$$w^{t_2+1} = extw(w^{t_2}, pte^{t_2})$$

and because walk extension does not change the address component we have

$$w^{t_2+1}.a = w^{t_2}.a = w^{t_1+1}.a = a^t$$

In case the present bit in the page table entry used (pte^{t_2}) is off, then the resulting walk (w^{t_2+1}) is faulting.

$$/pte^{t_2}.p \;\rightarrow\; w^{t_2+1}.f$$

Otherwise, by lemma 182 the walk register in cycle $t_2 + 1$ contains a zero-level walk.

$$pte^{t_2}.p \;\rightarrow\; level(w^{t_2+1}) = 0$$

In both cases the resulting walk is complete, and from the construction of the control automaton we conclude that transition $t2$ is taken, and therefore we have *write-tlb*$^{t_2+1}$. The claim follows for $u = t_2 + 1$. □

Because new walks enter the TLB is only in state *write-tlb*, this state is only reached after state *fetch-pte*, and the walk register in this state contains only complete walks, we can prove the following lemma by induction on the number of hardware cycles.

Lemma 193.
$$w \in tlb(mmu.tlb) \;\rightarrow\; complete(w)$$

We finally can show the main correctness result for the MMU.

Lemma 194.

1. *The MMU is live.*

$$t\text{-}start(t) \;\to\; \exists u \geq t : /busy^u$$

2. *If u is the first such cycle and translation is regular, i.e.,*

$$u = \min\{u \geq t \mid /busy^u\} \wedge treq[t:u]$$

then in cycle u the MMU outputs a walk matching the current MMU address a^u.

$$match(a^u, wout^u)$$

Proof. From $t\text{-}start(t)$ we conclude $/busy^{t-1}$, and therefore $idle^t$, using definitions. Thus translation always starts in the idle state. We split cases on whether transition $t1$ is taken in cycle t:

- $/(t1)^t$. The translation finishes in a single cycle due to a TLB hit.

$$tlb.hit^t$$

From the specification of the hit signal we get

$$tlb.wout^t \in tlb(mmu^t.tlb)$$

and for the output of the MMU we obtain:

$$\begin{aligned} wout^t.a &= tlb.wout^t.a \\ &= tlb.a^t \\ &= a^t. \end{aligned}$$

The output walk, which is a walk from the TLB, is complete by lemma 193.

$$complete(wout^t)$$

Hence we have

$$match(a^t, wout^t)$$

and the claim follows for $u = t$.

- $(t1)^t$. The translation enters state *fetch-pte*. By lemma 192, it enters a different state in some cycle $e > t+1$. Let e be the first such cycle; below we split subcases on the next control state:
  - $idle^e$. The translation was aborted while the automaton was in state *fetch-pte* but the memory was not busy. For the last cycle in state *fetch-pte* we have

$$busy^{e-1} \wedge /treq^{e-1}$$

By operating condition 56, the translation request signal stays off in cycle e. Using definitions, we conclude successively:

$$idle^e \wedge /treq^e \;,\; idle^e \wedge /(t1)^e \;,\; /busy^e$$

which gives the claim for $u = e$.

– $abort^e$. The translation was aborted while the automaton was in state *fetch-pte* and the memory was busy. In state *abort* the MMU remains busy until the memory access finishes in some cycle $e_2 > e + 1$. By lemma 190 such a cycle exists; moreover, from lemma 190 we know that the translation request signal is low in cycle e_2.

$$busy^{e_2} \wedge /treq^{e_2}$$

From the construction, in cycle $e_2 + 1$ the control automaton returns to the idle state. As above we conclude from operating condition 56 and definitions successively

$$idle^{e_2+1} \wedge /treq^{e_2+1} , /busy^{e_2+1}$$

and the claim follows for $u = e_2 + 1$.

– $write\text{-}tlb^e$. The translation was not aborted while the automaton was in state *fetch-pte*. If the translation is aborted in state *write-tlb*, in cycle e we have

$$busy^e \wedge /treq^e$$

which analogous to the cases above yields

$$/busy^{e+1}$$

and gives the claim for $u = e + 1$.

If the translation is not aborted in state *write-tlb*, then it is not aborted at all, i.e., we have

$$treq[t : e + 1]$$

and with operating condition 57 we conclude that MMU address a was kept constant during the translation.

$$a^{e+1} = a^e = a^t$$

By lemma 192, the walk register, written into the TLB in cycle e, satisfies

$$match(a^t, w^e).$$

From the specification of the TLB and operating condition 55, we argue that in cycle $e + 1$ the walk from the walk register is stored in the TLB.

$$w^e \in tlb(mmu^{e+1}.tlb)$$

Therefore we get a TLB hit in cycle $e + 1$ and the MMU busy signal is turned off.

$$idle^{e+1} \wedge tlb.hit^{e+1} , idle^{e+1} \wedge /(t1)^{e+1} , /busy^{e+1}$$

As in the case $/(t1)^t$ we now argue

$$match(a^{e+1}, wout^{e+1})$$

which completes the proof with $u = e + 1$. □

The set of walks stored in an MMU with configuration

$$mmu$$

are defined as the walks stored in the TLB together with the walk in the walk register in case the MMU is not idle.

$$walks(mmu) = tlb(mmu.tlb) \cup \begin{cases} \{mmu.w\} & /mmu.idle \wedge /mmu.abort \\ \emptyset & \text{otherwise} \end{cases}$$

The development of $walks(mmu)$ while the MMU is busy and invalidation requests are off is described in the following lemma.

Lemma 195. *Assume busy, /inval, and /flush and let $w = mmu.w$. Depending on the state of the control automaton*

- *if /(write-tlb ∧ treq):*

$$walks(mmu') = \begin{cases} walks(mmu) \cup \{initw(a, pto)\} & winit \\ walks(mmu) \setminus \{w\} \cup \{extw(w, pte)\} & /winit \wedge w.ce \\ walks(mmu) \setminus \{w\} & /treq \vee (t4) \\ walks(mmu) & abort \end{cases}$$

- *if write-tlb ∧ treq:*

$$walks(mmu') \subseteq walks(mmu) \wedge \#tlb(mmu'.tlb) \geq \#tlb(mmu.tlb)$$

Proof. A busy MMU writes the TLB only in state *write-tlb*, and by the assumption no walks are dropped from the TLB due to *inval* or *flush*. Thus

$$/inval \wedge /flush \wedge /write\text{-}tlb \;\rightarrow\; tlb(mmu'.tlb) = tlb(mmu.tlb).$$

Now the lemma is shown by a simple case split.

- $(t1)$: the claim follows from lemma 186.
- $(t2) \vee /(t1) \wedge w.ce$: the claim follows from lemma 191.
- $/treq \vee (t4)$: the next state is idle or abort

$$idle' \vee abort'$$

and the walk w in the walk register is dropped from the walks stored. Because of lemma 185 there is no hit

$$/hit$$

and because of the specification of the hit signal of the TLB, the walk w is not in the TLB. The claim follows.

- *abort*: w is not considered in $walks(mmu)$ and since the state in the next cycle is

$$idle' \lor abort'$$

the walk w is also not considered in $walks(mmu')$. Nothing else changes and the claim follows.
- *mbusy*: the walk register is not clocked.

$$w' = w$$

- *write-tlb*: walk w in the walk register is stored in the TLB, possibly at the expense of a single victim walk q. without a victim walk q we have

$$walks(mmu') = tlb(mmu'.tlb)$$
$$= tlb(mmu.tlb) \cup \{w\}$$
$$= walks(mmu)$$
$$\#tlb(mmu'.tlb) = \#tlb(mmu.tlb) + 1$$

With a victim walk we have

$$walks(mmu') = tlb(mmu'.tlb)$$
$$= tlb(mmu.tlb) \cup \{w\} \setminus \{q\}$$
$$\subseteq walks(mmu)$$
$$\#tlb(mmu') = \#tlb(mmu) \qquad \Box$$

After invalidation/flush requests walks are correctly removed from the MMU. While no walks are added, then walks are correctly removed after invalidation/flush requests, and nothing happens if no requests are active.

Lemma 196. *Depending on the control signals*

- *if flush:*

$$walks(mmu') = \emptyset$$

- *if inval:*

$$walks(mmu') \subseteq walks(mmu) \setminus \{w \in K_{walk} \mid w.a = inva \lor level(w) > 0\}$$

- *if /treq $\land$ /flush $\land$ /inval:*

$$walks(mmu') \subseteq walks(mmu)$$

Proof. In each case we have /treq and thus the MMU is in state *idle* or *abort* in the next cycle

$$abort' \lor idle'$$

Thus $walks(mmu')$ includes only walks from the TLB, to which nothing is added in the current cycle

$$walks(mmu') = tlb(mmu'.tlb) \subseteq tlb(mmu.tlb)$$

and the lemma follows directly from the TLB specification. $\qquad \Box$

9.4 Pipelined Processor with MMUs

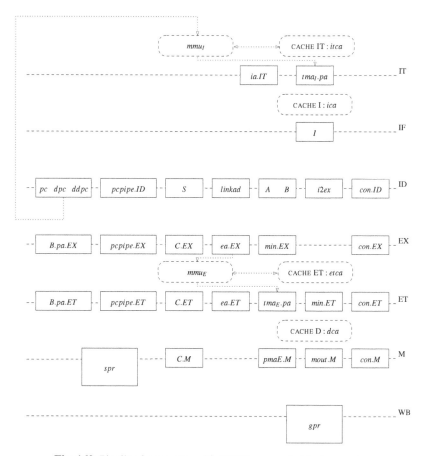

Fig. 160. Pipelined processor with MMUs connected to four caches

Integration of the memory management units into the pipelined processor from Chap. 8 requires a moderate number of fairly straight forward adjustments. For the overall structure (visualized in figure 160):

- Two additional pipeline stages, *IT* (instruction translate) and *ET* (effective address translate) accessing MMUs *mmu$_I$* and *mmu$_E$* for instruction and effective address translation are introduced. In the resulting *seven-stage* pipeline, translation stages *IT* and *ET* are located above the stages where the corresponding memory access are performed, resp. the instruction fetch (*IF*) and memory (*M*) stage. The new numbering of pipeline stages is given in Table 16.

k	pipeline stage
1	IT
2	IF
3	ID
4	EX
5	ET
6	M
7	WB

Table 16. Numbering of pipeline stages in the seven-stage pipeline

- Since the number of pipeline stages above the instruction decode (*ID*) stage, and therefore the number of delay slots, has increased to two, a second delayed PC (*ddpc*) must be introduced: this 32-bit register is added to stage $ID = 3$, next to the other two program counters (*pc* and *dpc*), and one more special purpose register is used to store the exception *ddpc*, which we naturally call the *eddpc*. For this purpose we have already reserved register number 5 of the SPR.

$$eddpc = spr.dout[5] = spr(5_5)$$

- Also, in the seven-stage pipeline the MMUs, accessed in stages $IT = 1$ and $ET = 5$, must be connected to caches. For that purpose we introduce in a some-what brute force way a private instruction translation cache *itca* as well as a private effective address translation cache *etca*. Thus the processor pipeline is now connected to a sequentially consistent cache memory system with four caches:

$$itca = h.ca(0)$$
$$ica = h.ca(1)$$
$$etca = h.ca(2)$$
$$dca = h.ca(3)$$

- the invalidation address $B.pa$ of *invlpg* instructions must be pipelined in a B-pipe $B.pa[4:5]$ in the obvious way.

For the data paths:

- computation of the instruction address, where the third program counter (*ddpc*) must be taken into account,
- forwarding mechanism, where the most recent value of the new *eddpc* register must be provided to stage $ID = 3$ for *eret* instructions

For the control logic:

- interrupt signals from the two MMUs must be hooked into the cause pipeline
- the stall engine must be interconnected with the two new caches and two MMUs.

We elaborate on these modifications in the sections below. The material presented is partially taken from the relevant sections of [Lut18].

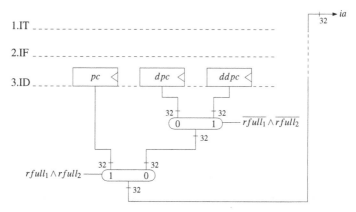

Fig. 161. Instruction address computation

9.4.1 Instruction Address

The instruction address in the seven-stage pipelined machine is taken from the pc, dpc, or $ddpc$, depending on the number of real full stages above the ID stage. Thus, in case there are no real full stages, the instruction address is taken from the $ddpc$. If only one stage has a real full bit, we use the dpc to fetch an instruction. Finally, if both stages have real full bits, we use the pc. Formally, we specify the instruction address as follows.

$$ia = \begin{cases} ddpc_\pi & \overline{rfull_1} \wedge \overline{rfull_2} \\ dpc_\pi & rfull_1 \oplus rfull_2 \\ pc_\pi & rfull_1 \wedge rfull_2 \end{cases}$$

The selection of the instruction address ($\in cir(1)$) from the three program counters ($\in reg(3)$) is illustrated in Fig. 161.

9.4.2 Connecting MMUs to the Pipeline

The following inputs are identical for both memory management units mmu_Y. Recall that both TLB invalidating instructions are allowed only in system mode.

$$mmu_Y.pto = pto$$
$$mmu_Y.inva = B.pa.ET$$
$$mmu_Y.inval = /jisr \wedge rfull_5 \wedge invlpg.5$$
$$mmu_Y.flush = /jisr \wedge rfull_5 \wedge flusht.5$$

Translation requests on both MMUs are raised only in translated mode, in the absence of $jisr$, and only for really full input stages. Translation request on mmu_E stays low in case no memory operation is performed.

$$mmu_I.treq = mode \wedge /jisr \wedge rfull_0$$
$$mmu_E.treq = mode \wedge /jisr \wedge rfull_4 \wedge mop.4$$

Intuitively, translation requests occur in user mode, whereas invalidation requests occur only in system mode. Hence in every cycle t at most one such request is active and operating condition 55 holds. We will only be able to prove this later.

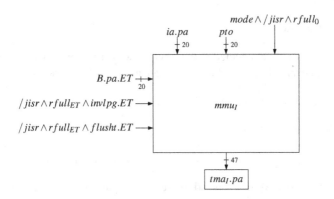

Fig. 162. Connection between mmu_I and processor

As illustrated in fig. 162 the remaining I/O buses of mmu_I are connected as follows.

$$mmu_I.a = ia.pa$$
$$tma_I.pa.in = mmu_I.wout.a$$

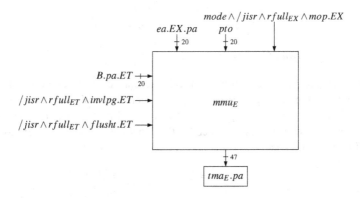

Fig. 163. Connection between mmu_E and processor

As illustrated in fig. 163 the respective buses of mmu_E are connected in an analogous way.

$$mmu_E.a = ea.4.pa$$
$$tma_E.pa.in = mmu_E.wout.a$$

9.4.3 Caches

Translation Caches

Translation caches are connected in the obvious way. They provide instruction translate access *itacc* and effective address translate access *etacc* to their respective caches

$$itca.pacc = itacc \ , \ etca.pacc = etacc$$

Translate accesses only read.

$$itacc.(pr, pw, pcas) = etacc(pr, pw, pcas) = 100$$

On the processor side of the cache addresses and requests are provided by the MMUs

$$itacc.a = mmu_I.ma.l$$
$$etacc.a = mmu_E.ma.l$$
$$itca_\pi.preq = mmu_I.mreq$$
$$etca_\pi.preq = mmu_E.mreq$$

Data outputs and busy signals on the processor side of the caches go to the MMUs.

$$mmu_I.mout = itca.pdout$$
$$mmu_E.mout = etca.pdout$$
$$mmu_I.mbusy = itca.mbusy$$
$$mmu_E.mbusy = etca.mbusy$$

Instruction and Data Caches

Connections to the instruction (*ica*) and the data cache (*dca*) remain almost unchanged: compared to a five-stage pipeline there is an obvious index shift and the physical memory addresses pma_Y used (translated or not) depends on the mode of the machine. The accesses provided by the pipelines to the caches are as before denoted by *iacc* and *eacc*.

$$ica.acc = iacc \ , \ dca.acc = dacc$$

As illustrated in fig. 164 we pipeline the instruction address in register $ia.1$

$$ia.1.in = ia$$

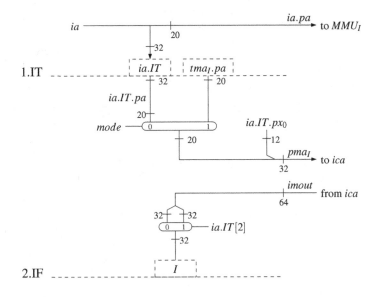

Fig. 164. Adjusting the pipeline for the instruction MMU

Depending on *mode* the page address of the physical memory address pma_I is the taken either from the pipelined instruction address $ia.1$ or from walk w_I

$$pma_I.pa = \begin{cases} ia.1.pa & /mode \\ tma_I.pa & mode \end{cases}$$

The physical memory address obtained by appending the page offset taken from $ia.1$

$$pma_I = pma_I.pa \circ ia.1.px_0$$

The line address of pma_I is used to address the instruction cache on the processor side

$$iacc.a = pma_I.l$$

As illustrated in fig. 165 we proceed for the effective address in a completely analogous way

$$pma_E.pa = \begin{cases} ea.5.pa & /mode \\ tma_E.a & mode \end{cases}$$

$$pma_E = pma_E.pa \circ ea.5.px_0$$

$$dacc.a = pma_E.l$$

Since the instruction fetch and the memory stage shift down in the pipeline, the corresponding control registers are used to provide the access types

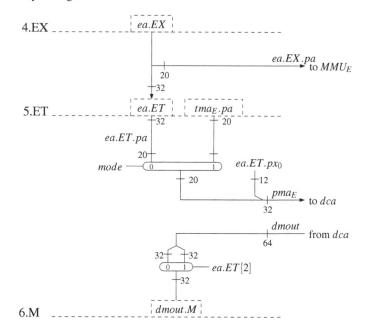

Fig. 165. Adjusting the pipeline for the data MMU

$$iacc.(pr, pw, pcas) = 100$$
$$dacc.(pr, pw, pcas) = (l.5, s.5, cas.5)$$

and activate the processor requests.

$$ica.preq = rfull_1$$
$$dca.preq = rfull_5 \wedge mop.5 \wedge exec.5$$

where $exec.5$ comes from the modified cause pipe that we will present in section 9.4.6.

Data for the memory access are obviously taken from the memory input stage (stage 5) as well. The processor compare-data are connected as specified in Chap. 7, directly to one of the SPR outputs (in contrast to [KMP14], where they were coming from the GPR).

$$dacc.bw = bw.5$$
$$dacc.din = min.5$$
$$dacc.cdata = spr[cdata]$$

9.4.4 Forwarding

The old circuits for $A, B, S, epc, edpc$ are modified in an obvious way, because now they are required to cover more stages and end in a later stage. Signal ien is now forwarded from stage 6 to stage 5. We leave details as an easy exercise.

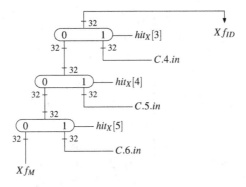

Fig. 166. 3-stage forwarding circuit for $X = eddpc$

The newly added program counter ($ddpc$) is forwarded to $cir(ID) = cir(3)$ by the circuit in figure 166 with

$$X f_M = eddpc$$
$$hit_{eddpc}[k] = rfull_k \wedge sprw.k \wedge xad.k = 5_5$$

9.4.5 PC Environment

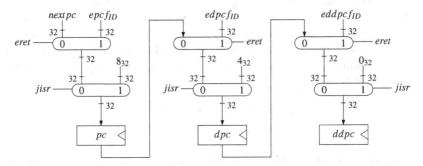

Fig. 167. PC environment

Computation of the next configuration PCs from Chap. 7 is extended in the obvious way to support updates of the $ddpc$. The implementation in Fig. 167 literally follows the specification from Sect. 9.2.4. Formally, for the pipelined machine we specify:

$$pc_\pi.in = \begin{cases} 8_{32} & jisr \\ epcf_{ID} & eret \wedge /jisr \\ nextpc & otherwise \end{cases}$$

$$dpc_\pi.in = \begin{cases} 4_{32} & jisr \\ edpcf_{ID} & eret \wedge /jisr \\ pc_\pi & otherwise \end{cases}$$

$$ddpc_\pi.in = \begin{cases} 0_{32} & jisr \\ eddpcf_{ID} & eret \wedge /jisr \\ dpc_\pi & otherwise \end{cases}$$

where the forwarded exception PCs epc, $edpc$, and $eddpc$ are forwarded from the memory stage (see Sect. 9.4.4). Update of the program counters is performed on both ue_3 and $jisr$.

$$X \in \{pc, dpc, ddpc\} \rightarrow X.ce = ue_3 \vee jisr$$

Note, there is no need to stabilize the PCs in our seven-stage pipeline. The instruction cache is accessed via the physical memory address register, which effectively acts as a latch for the instruction cache address in the five-stage pipeline from Chap. 5.

9.4.6 Interrupts and Cause Pipe

In Chap. 7, where the cause processing hardware was specified and constructed (see Fig. 134), we have deliberately left zeros at the places of the two page fault and two general-protection fault interrupts. As the memory management units are being integrated, we will use the reserved buses to provide most missing event signals. The only remaining event signals are for INIT and SIPI interrupts, which will be introduced in chapter 12.

$$iev[4:3] = gff \circ pff$$
$$iev[10:9] = gfls \circ pfls$$

From now on, by mmu_I we refer to the MMU for the instruction address translation and by mmu_E — to the MMU for the effective address translation. A page fault is generated if the MMU outputs a faulting walk while its translation request is on.

$$pff = mmu_I.treq \wedge mmu_I.wout.f$$
$$pfls = mmu_E.treq \wedge mmu_E.wout.f$$

A general-protection fault is generated if the MMU outputs a non-faulting walk with insufficient rights while its translation request is on.

$$gff = mmu_I.treq \wedge /mmu_I.wout.f \wedge \neg(mmu_I.wout.r \geq 011)$$
$$gfls = mmu_E.treq \wedge /mmu_E.wout.f \wedge \neg(mmu_E.wout.r \geq (write.4) \circ 10)$$

The integration of these signals into the cause pipe is shown in fig. 168.

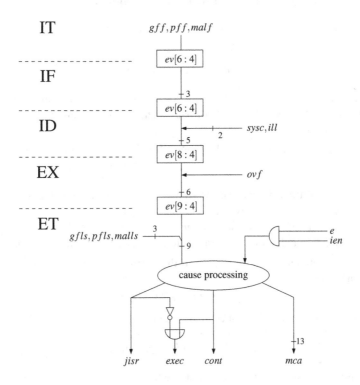

Fig. 168. Seven stage cause pipe with page faults.

Also, according to the specification from Sect. 9.2.4, the TLB invalidating instructions are allowed only in system mode. Therefore, we adjust the data paths in the obvious way to generate an illegal interrupt each time an invalidating instruction is decoded in translated mode.

$$mode \wedge rfull_2 \wedge (invlpg(3) \vee flusht(3)) \rightarrow ill$$

9.4.7 Stall Engine

This subsection is spent to interconnect the new stall engine, which now spans across seven pipeline stages. The ordinary hazard signals, haz_1 and haz_5 below, make sure that in translated mode the translation stages are not updated while the corresponding MMUs are requested.

$$haz_1 = mmu_I.treq \wedge mmu_I.busy \vee drain$$
$$haz_5 = mmu_E.treq \wedge mmu_E.busy$$

Note, the pipeline is drained as specified in Chap. 7, starting from the topmost stage, now $IT = 1$. The remaining hazard signals are as follows.

$$haz_2 = ica_\pi.mbusy$$
$$haz_3 = haz_A \vee haz_B$$
$$haz_6 = dca_\pi.mbusy$$

The rollback hazard signals for the rollback engine stay as in Chap. 7, where they were first introduced. Still the only rollback hazard signal is raised in stage $IF = 2$.

$$rhaz_k = \begin{cases} ica_\pi.mbusy & k = 2 \\ 0 & \text{otherwise} \end{cases}$$

In the absence of the rollback hazard signals for the translation stages, in case of a rollback, the translation requests will simply be lowered and no pending bits will be set for the corresponding translation stages. The latter is possible because the MMUs were designed to handle aborts of translations internally (see Sect. 9.3.2).

The program counters are restored (from the corresponding exception registers) on activation of signal

$$eret = rfull_2 \wedge eret(3).$$

For convenience, we also introduce a shorthand

$$jisr = rfull_5 \wedge jisr.5.$$

No new misspeculation signals are introduced.

$$misspec_2 = eret$$
$$misspec_5 = jisr$$

9.5 Correctness

We proceed in the known order and begin with bookkeeping, that becomes necessary, because we now have 4 caches instead of two. In section 9.5.1 we establish the stability of accesses to the caches, in section 9.5.2 we adjust the definition of local sequential indices of accesses to the cache memory system, and in section 9.5.3 we relate ends of accesses to the instruction and data caches to update enable signals of stages IF and M. All this just requires to adjust in previous arguments indices of caches in a trivial way. Inputs x for processor steps of the stepping function now have walk components w_I and w_E. In section 9.5.4 we specify how these components are extracted from the hardware computation. No new ideas are needed there either: when instruction i is committed we extract w_I when the instruction leaves stage IT stage and walk w_E when it leaves the stage ET. In section 9.5.5 the stepping function is defined such that steps performed for a hardware cycle t are interleaved in the sequential order of the accesses to the cache memory system, that they produce. Moreover MMUs can perform steps during cycles t when the instruction executed/leaving the memory stage triggers an interrupt. For such cycles t the MMU steps should be performed before the instruction execution. The main induction hypothesis presented in section 9.5.6 necessarily contains several new parts:

- a coupling relation for the TLBs stating that the walks in the hardware TLBs should be a subset of the ISA TLB.
- MMU steps of the ISA computation obey the guard conditions: they occur only in user mode and extend only incomplete walks which are already in the ISA TLB.
- processor steps obey the guard conditions related to walks w_I and W_E: they must be present in ISA TLB and match the translated page address.

Section 9.5.7 contains the induction step for the components of the machine outside of the pipeline, i.e. CMS, instruction buffer and MMUs, and section 9.5.8 contains the induction step for registers and register files of the pipeline.

9.5.1 Stability of Inputs of Accesses

With the register stage $reg(IT)$ above the instruction fetch stage this becomes trivial for instruction and data caches

Lemma 197.

- *For the instruction cache:*

$$ica.mbusy \quad \rightarrow \quad /ue_{IT}$$

- *For the data cache:*

$$dca.preq \wedge dca.mbusy \quad \rightarrow \quad /ue_{M-1}$$

The corresponding lemma for the translation caches follows immediately from lemma 189.

Lemma 198.

- *For the instruction translation cache:*

$$itca.mbusy \quad \rightarrow mmu_I.pte = mmu_I.pte'$$

- *For the effective address translation cache:*

$$etca.mbusy \quad \rightarrow mmu_E.pte = mmu_E.pte'$$

9.5.2 Sequential Order and Local Sequential Index of CMS steps

Adapting notation from 6.3 to a cache memory system with four ports we denote

- the k'th (external) access to memory port i by $acc(i,k)$.
- the cycle when this access ends by $e(i,k)$
- by $E^t = \{(i,k) \mid e(i,k) = t\}$ the set of indices such that access $acc(i,k)$ ends in cycle t and
- by $D^t = \{(3,k) \mid e(1,k) = t\}$ the possibly empty set of indices of accesses to the data port ending in cycle t

As before we count with

$$NE^0 = 0 \,,\; NE^{t+1} = NE^t + \#E^t$$

the accesses NE^t completed before cycle t. Indices (i,k) of accesses ending in cycle t received sequential numbers of the form

$$seq(i,k) = NE^t + x - 1 \quad \text{with local sequential indices} \quad x \in [1 : \#E^t]$$

If an access $acc(3,u)$ to the data cache ended in cycle t, i.e. if $(3,u) \in D^t$, then the local sequential index of that access is denoted by xd

$$seq(3,u) = NE^t + xd - 1$$

9.5.3 Relating Update Enable Signals and Ends of Accesses

In a 2 port CMS instruction and data caches had indices 0 and 1. With 4 ports they have now indices 1 and 3. That ending external accesses to the caches correspond exactly to update enable signals of stages IF and M was stated for 2 port CMS in lemmas 82 and 83 of section 6.3.3.

Lemma 199.

 1. An active update enable signal in stage IF signals the end of read accesses to the instruction cache.

$$ue^t_{IF} \quad \rightarrow \quad \exists k.\; e(1,k) = t \wedge acc(1,k).r$$

 2. An active update enable signal in stage 4 together with an active processor request signals the end of an external access.

$$ue^t_M \wedge dca.preq^t \quad \rightarrow \quad \exists k.\; e(3,k) = t$$

Lemma 200. *When a read, write or CAS access ends in cycle t, then the corresponding stage is updated unless it is stalled from the stage below.*

 1. For the instruction cache:

$$e(1,k) = t \wedge /stall^t_{ID} \quad \rightarrow \quad ue^t_{IF}$$

 2. For the data cache:

$$e(3,k) = t \quad \rightarrow \quad ue^t_M$$

9.5.4 Inputs for Processor Steps

For the specification of processor steps $x = (p, I, e, w_I, w_E)$ of the stepping function we now have to sample 4 signals of instructions i. As usual we sample them in a unique way during cycles t, when the instruction is committed.

- Instructions I are sampled when they are clocked into instruction register $I.IF$

$$t_i(I) = \varepsilon\{t \mid c(I_{IF}^t) \wedge I_{IF}^t = i \wedge ue_{IF}^t\}$$

- walks w_I for instruction translation are sampled when they are (partially) clocked into register $tmaI.IT$

$$t_i(w_I) = \varepsilon\{t \mid c(I_{IT}^t) \wedge I_{IT}^t = i \wedge ue_{IT}^t\}$$

- walks w_I for instruction translation are sampled when they are (partially) clocked into register $tmaE.ET$

$$t_i(w_E) = \varepsilon\{t \mid c(I_{ET}^t) \wedge I_{ET}^t = i \wedge ue_{ET}^t\}$$

- similarly external interrupts are sampled when instructions are clocked into the stage $M - 1 = ET$ above the memory stage

$$t_i(e) = \varepsilon\{t \mid c(I_{M-1}^t) \wedge I_{M-1}^t = i \wedge ue_{M-1}^t\}$$

9.5.5 Stepping Function

Definitions hinge on the relation between update enable signals and ends of hardware accesses as actualized in section 9.5.3. For every hardware cycle t of the hardware computation we construct numbers ns^t of ISA steps: at most one processor step, at most one load of the instruction buffer, and at most two MMU steps. We thus have

$$ns^t \in [0:4]$$

If operating conditions are violated, as before we use possible emergency braking. In that case in cycle t we step the processor and only the processor. Otherwise the ISA core is stepped when the memory stage is updated, the store buffer is stepped when the instruction register below the instruction fetch stage is clocked, and the ISA TLB is stepped whenever a walk registers is clocked. Thus

$$ns^t = \begin{cases} 1 & vopc^t \\ ue_M^t + ue_{IF}^t + mmu_I.w.ce^t + mmu_E.w.ce^t & \text{o.w.} \end{cases}$$

The total number NS^t of ISA steps that have been executed before hardware cycle t is

$$NS^0 = 0, \; NS^{t+1} = NS^t + ns^t$$

We define the values

$$s(n) \quad \text{for} \quad n \in [NS^t, NS^{t+1})$$

of the stepping function by seven rules. As before we interleave steps in the sequential order of the memory accesses as implemented by the CMS.

- for steps n_{ib} triggered by the fetch of an instruction in the absence of a violation of the operating condition

$$ue_{IF}^t \wedge /vopc^t$$

we load the instruction fetched with instruction buffer step

$$s(n_{ib}) = (ib, ia_\pi^t) \quad \text{for some} \quad n_{ib} \in [NS^t : NS^{t+1})$$

into the instruction buffer of ISA using the instruction address ia_π of the pipelined machine.

- in case of emergency breaking or execution of an instruction i, i.e. if

$$(ue_M^t \vee vopc^t) \wedge I_M^t = i$$

holds, we execute in ISA the instruction with inputs sampled for instruction i as defined in section 9.5.4 above. Thus for some $n_p \in [NS^t : NS^{t+1})$

$$s(n_p) = (p, I_\pi^{t_i(I)}, e_\pi^{t_i(e)}, mmu_I.wout^{t_i(w_I)}, mmu_E.wout^{t_i(w_E)})$$

- for steps n_{mmuI} triggered by the instruction MMU

$$/vopc^t \wedge mmu_I.w.ce^t$$

we set

$$s(n_{mmuI}) = \begin{cases} (tlb, winit, ia_\pi^t.pa) & winit_I^t \\ (tlb, wext, mmu_I.w^t) & \text{otherwise} \end{cases}$$

- for steps n_{mmuE} triggered by the data MMU

$$/vopc^t \wedge mmu_E.w.ce^t$$

we set

$$s(n_{mmuE}) = \begin{cases} (tlb, winit, ea.3^t.pa) & winit_E^t \\ (tlb, wext, mmu_E.w^t) & \text{otherwise} \end{cases}$$

- Instruction buffer steps do not change TLBs. The only core steps which change TLBs are *flusht*, *invlpg*, *eret* and interrupts. The first three are only legal in system mode, whereas walk registers and updates of the TLBs under control of the MMUs occur only in user mode. Therefore we do not worry here about simultaneous updates of the ISA TLB by MMUs and core. We *do* however have to worry about i) memory updates by the core to addresses which are simultaneously accessed in instruction buffer or walk extension steps and ii) MMU steps occurring simultaneously with interrupts, because we have to be able to infer as in the ISA specification that MMU steps are performed in user mode.

As in the previous chapter we step all units that generate accesses to the cache memory system together and before other steps. This allows us again to define for each local sequential index x the ISA step $isa^t(x)$ that generates the corresponding access by

$$isa^t(x) = NS^t + x - 1$$

Recall that the port i_x of the access with local sequential index x is defined by

$$seq(k_x^t, i_x^t) = n_x^t$$

With this port we can define the order of the steps that generate memory accesses easily with the following equations. If a memory operation leaves the pipeline the processor generates the access at the data port

$$ue_M^t \wedge mop.(M-1)^t \; \rightarrow \; n_p = NS^t + \varepsilon \left\{ x \mid i_x^t = 3 \right\} - 1 = isa^t(xd)$$

When a MMU clocks the walk register and does not perform a walk initialization, it generates the access at its port

$$mmu_I.w.ce^t \wedge /winit_I^t \; \rightarrow \; n_{tlbI} = NS^t + \varepsilon \left\{ x \mid i_x^t = 0 \right\} - 1$$
$$mmu_E.w.ce^t \wedge /winit_E^t \; \rightarrow \; n_{tlbE} = NS^t + \varepsilon \left\{ x \mid i_x^t = 2 \right\} - 1$$

Finally, if the instruction fetch stage is updated (ue_{IF}^t) the instruction buffer generates the access at the instruction port

$$n_{ib} = NS^t + \varepsilon \left\{ x \mid i_x^t = 1 \right\} - 1$$

- In the presence of an interrupt the mode bit must be set to OS mode *after* a possible MMU step. Thus with interrupts we step the processor always last

$$jisr.(M-1)^t \rightarrow n < n_p$$

- Void accesses are stepped last. This concerns processor steps without memory operations *and* walk-init steps of the MMU. We count the number of non-void accesses to the cache memory system by

$$nac^t = ue_{IF}^t + ue_M^t \wedge mop.(M-1)^t \wedge exec.(M-1)^t$$
$$+ mmu_I.w.ce^t \wedge /mmu_I.winit^t + mmu_E.w.ce^t \wedge /mmu_E.winit^t$$
$$= \#E^t$$

We step all of these steps first:

$$ue_{IF}^t \; \rightarrow \; n_{ib} \in [NS^t : NS^t + nac^t)$$
$$ue_M^t \wedge mop.(M-1)^t \wedge exec.(M-1)^t \; \rightarrow \; n_p \in [NS^t : NS^t + nac^t)$$
$$mmu_I.w.ce^t \wedge /mmu_I.winit^t \; \rightarrow \; n_{mmuI} \in [NS^t : NS^t + nac^t)$$
$$mmu_E.w.ce^t \wedge /mmu_E.winit^t \; \rightarrow \; n_{mmuE} \in [NS^t : NS^t + nac^t)$$

For the non-void accesses we can define as before:

$$isa^t(x) = NS^t + x - 1$$

9.5.6 Induction Hypothesis

For the induction hypothesis two things change:

1. We need to maintain that all walks in TLBs in hardware are also in the software TLB, because we may reuse such translations in later steps. In that case we need to argue that the translations we use in those later steps are in the software TLB. In contrast we never reuse instructions from the instruction buffer, and hence do not need to maintain any properties about the instruction buffer.
2. We need to add the guard conditions for TLBs for instructions that pass the appropriate stages.

We redefine $t \sim_m n$ to include the TLBs:

$$t \sim_m n \quad \equiv \quad n = NS^t \rightarrow m(h^t) = \ell(c^n.m) \wedge opc^t$$
$$\wedge \ walks(mmu_I^t) \cup walks(mmu_E^t) \subseteq c^n.tlb$$
$$\wedge \ \forall \hat{n} < n. \ \gamma(c^{\hat{n}}, s(\hat{n}))$$

The simulation relation for the processor core stays unchanged:

$$t \sim_p i \quad \equiv \quad \forall k, R. \ I_k^t = i \wedge (R \in reg(k) \wedge vis(R)$$
$$\vee \ R \in reg(k-1) \wedge /vis(R) \wedge rfull_{k-1}^t \wedge used[R]^i)$$
$$\rightarrow \quad R_\pi^t = R_\sigma^i$$

Although the relation $t \sim_n m$ includes already a statement about the guard conditions, we also have to track that guard conditions for the execution of processor instructions become valid as the instruction passes through the pipeline. The main induction hypothesis then becomes:

Lemma 201. *There is an initial configuration c^0 satisfying*

$$sim(h^0, c^0)$$

and instruction buffer and TLB are empty

$$c^0.ib = c^0.tlb = \emptyset$$

Furthermore: if for the computation (c^n) with stepping function $s(n)$ extracted from hardware and initial configuration c^0 satisfies for all n the software condition $SC_{ROM}(c^n, s(n))$ provided the stepping function $s(n)$ has a valid initial segment until n

$$\forall n. \ (\forall m \le n. \ \gamma(c^m, s(m))) \ \rightarrow \ SC_{ROM}(c^n, s(n))$$

then for all n and t:

- *The components outside the pipeline of ISA step n are simulated correctly*

$$t \sim_m n$$

- *When n is the global index of a committed instruction i such that all previous instructions are live*

$$n = pseq(i) \wedge c(i)^t \wedge lb(i)^t$$

then the pipeline simulates instruction i, and parts of the guard condition become satisfied as the instruction passes the relevant stages

$$t \sim_p i \wedge (i < I_{IT}^t \to \gamma_{wI\sigma}^i) \wedge (i < I_{IF}^t \to \gamma_{I\sigma}^i) \wedge (i < I_{ET}^t \to \gamma_{wE\sigma}^i)$$

In the induction step, the outer induction hypothesis states therefore for all $o < n$

$$\forall u. \ u \sim_m o \wedge (o = pseq(j) \wedge c(j)^u \wedge lb(j)^u$$
$$\to u \sim_p j \wedge (j < I_{IT}^t \to \gamma_{wI\sigma}^j) \wedge (j < I_{IF}^u \to \gamma_{I\sigma}^j) \wedge (j < I_{ET}^u \to \gamma_{wE\sigma}^j)) \tag{58}$$

and the inner induction hypothesis states

$$t \sim_m n \wedge (n = pseq(i) \wedge c(i)^t \wedge lb(i)^t$$
$$\to t \sim_p i \wedge (i < I_{IT}^t \to \gamma_{wI\sigma}^i) \wedge (i < I_{IF}^t \to \gamma_{I\sigma}^i) \wedge (i < I_{ET}^t \to \gamma_{wE\sigma}^i)) \tag{59}$$

Combining both in a straightforward fashion we obtain for all $o \leq n$ and *only* cycle t

$$t \sim_m o \wedge (o = pseq(i) \wedge c(i)^t \wedge lb(i)^t$$
$$\to t \sim_p i \wedge (i < I_{IT}^t \to \gamma_{wI\sigma}^i) \wedge (i < I_{IF}^t \to \gamma_{I\sigma}^i) \wedge (i < I_{ET}^t \to \gamma_{wE\sigma}^i)) \tag{60}$$

which we call the induction hypothesis for the current cycle.

9.5.7 Correctness for Components Outside the Pipeline

We switch to implicit t notation and unfold the definition of $\sim_m$. Thus the claim becomes

$$n = NS' \to m(h') = \ell(c^n.m) \wedge opc'$$
$$\wedge \ walks(mmu_I') \cup walks(mmu_E') \subseteq c^n.tlb$$
$$\wedge \ \forall \hat{n} < n. \ \gamma(c^{\hat{n}}, s(\hat{n}))$$

The proofs for opc' and the memory are literally the same as in chapter 8.

For the TLBs, we split cases on whether an uninterrupted *invlpg* or *flusht* instruction is affecting the TLB in the current cycle:

- $rfull_{M-1} \wedge /jisr \wedge (invlpg.5 \vee flusht.5)$: such instructions are never memory operations

$$/mop.5$$

and hence there is no memory request and the stage is not stalled

$$/stall_M$$

We conclude that it is updated

$$ue_M$$

Thus by lemmas 165 and 166 the instruction I_M is stepped in the current cycle

$$pseq(I_M) < NS' = n$$

and thus the instruction in the memory stage is executed in a previous ISA step. We conclude with the outer induction hypothesis:

$$/jisr_\sigma^{I_M} \wedge (invlpg_\sigma^{I_M} \vee flusht_\sigma^{I_M})$$

Since $invlpg$ and $flusht$ are illegal in user mode (and would cause an interrupt), the instruction is not in user mode

$$/mode_\sigma^{I_M}$$

and hence by the outer induction hypothesis, the machine is not in user mode

$$/mode_\pi$$

We conclude that there is no translation request in the current cycle at either MMU $X \in \{I, E\}$

$$/mmu_X.treq$$

Note that this means that the operating condition (eq. (55)) of the TLB on page 391 is satisfied:

$$mmu_X.treq + mmu_X.inval + mmu_X.flush \leq 1$$

We now need to do a case distinction on whether the instruction is $flusht$ or $invlpg$, but we only show the latter case as the other one is much simpler. Let thus the instruction be an $invlpg$ instruction, and we conclude successively with the outer induction hypothesis for $\hat{n} := pseq(I_M)$

$$invlpg.5,\ mmu_X.inval,\ invlpg_\sigma^{I_M},\ mmu_X.inva = B.pa.5 = B_\sigma^{I_M}.pa$$

Since translation requests are off, the MMU is not making any steps; thus the TLB is changed only by the processor step

$$c^{NS}.tlb = c^{pseq(I_M)}.tlb \text{ and } c^{pseq(I_M)+1}.tlb = c^{NS'}.tlb$$

With lemma 196 and the induction hypothesis we obtain

$$walks(mmu'_X)$$

$$\subseteq walks(mmu_X) \setminus \{ w \in K_{walk} \mid w.a = mmu_X.inva \vee level(w) > 0 \} \qquad \text{L 196}$$

$$= walks(mmu_X) \setminus \left\{ w \in K_{walk} \;\middle|\; w.a = B_\sigma^{IM}.pa \vee level(w) > 0 \right\}$$

$$\subseteq c^{NS}.tlb \setminus \left\{ w \in K_{walk} \;\middle|\; w.a = B_\sigma^{IM}.pa \vee level(w) > 0 \right\} \qquad \text{IH}$$

$$= c^{pseq(I_M)}.tlb \setminus \left\{ w \in K_{walk} \;\middle|\; w.a = B_\sigma^{IM}.pa \vee level(w) > 0 \right\}$$

$$= c^{pseq(I_M)+1}.tlb \qquad \text{defn. ISA}$$

$$= c^{NS'}.tlb$$

- $/(rfull_{M-1} \wedge /jisr \wedge (invlpg.5 \vee flusht.5))$: in this case the operating condition (eq. (55)) is trivially satisfied. Furthermore, stage $M-1$ is either not really full or it is really full but has no invalidation/flush request. We only treat the latter case, which is more difficult. Let thus

$$rfull_{M-1} \wedge /invlpg.5 \wedge /flusht.5$$

Because no $invlpg$ or $flusht$ instruction is executed in the current cycle, the ISA TLB can only grow

$$c^{NS}.tlb \subseteq c^{NS'}.tlb$$

In hardware, the only walk that is added to MMU $X \in \{I, E\}$ is the initial walk or the extended walk. For the sake of brevity we define the set of new walks nw_X of MMU X as

$$nw_X = \begin{cases} \{initw(mmu_X.a, mmu_X.pto)\} & mmu_X.winit \\ \{extw(mmu_X.w, mmu_X.pte)\} & /mmu_X.winit \wedge mmu_X.w.ce \\ \emptyset & \text{o.w.} \end{cases}$$

With lemmas 195 and 196 we obtain

$$walks(mmu'_X) \subseteq walks(mmu_X) \cup nw_X$$
$$\subseteq c^{NS}.tlb \cup nw_X$$
$$\subseteq c^{NS'}.tlb \cup nw_X$$

Thus it suffices to show that the new walks nw_X are also added in ISA

$$nw_X \overset{!}{\subseteq} c^{NS'}.tlb$$

The proof is by case distinction on the three cases of the definition of nw_X and we show only the proof for the case of a walk extension. Let thus

$$/mmu_X.winit \wedge mmu_X.w.ce$$

We conclude that an MMU step $l \in [NS : NS')$ is made with oracle input

$$s(l) = s(n_{mmuX}) = (tlb, wext, mmu_X.w)$$

This adds the walk

$$extw(mmu_X.w, pte(mmu_X.w, c^l.m))$$

to the ISA TLB

$$extw(mmu_X.w, pte(mmu_X.w, c^l.m)) \in c^{l+1}.tlb$$

By lemma 183 both ISA and hardware use the same page table entry address

$$mmu_X.ptea = ptea(mmu_X.w)$$

Completely analogous to how we conclude in lemma 174 that instruction buffer steps fetch the same entry in ISA and in hardware, one can conclude that the same page table entry is fetched. We omit the details of the proof and just conclude

$$mmu_X.pte = pte(mmu_X.w, c^l.m)$$

and the claim follows as the walk added in ISA is exactly the new walk, which stays in the TLB at least until all steps that end in the current cycle (which neither flush nor invalidate the TLB) are executed

$$
\begin{aligned}
nw_X &= \{extw(mmu_X.w, mmu_X.pte)\} \\
&= \{extw(mmu_X.w, pte(mmu_X.w, c^l.m))\} \\
&\subseteq c^{l+1}.tlb \\
&\subseteq c^{NS'}.tlb
\end{aligned}
$$

For the guard conditions, we only need to consider steps $l \in [NS : NS')$ that end in the current cycle. This concerns only the processor step of the instruction in the memory stage, and MMU steps. For MMU steps we need to reason about the content of the spr, in particular about $mode$ and pto registers. These are used in MMU steps $l \in [NS : NS')$ but are with the induction hypothesis only coupled with ISA step $pseq(I_M)$ which may possibly lie in the future. Thus the induction hypothesis might not give us anything about the spr directly.

We use a small detour. The current configuration of the spr has been computed by instruction $I_M - 1$ which has already been executed. We can use the outer induction hypothesis for that instruction in the cycle in which it was executed to prove that the ISA spr is the same as the hardware spr.

This means that we need to argue about several hardware cycles. We switch briefly to explicit t notation, and argue about the cycle u in which instruction $I_M - 1$ was executed. Since there was no emergency braking so far, this is obviously the last cycle in which the memory stage was clocked. Since then, the spr has not changed. This is stated in the following trivial lemma.

Lemma 202.

$$u = \max\{u < t \mid ue_M^u\} \rightarrow spr_\pi^{u+1} = spr_\pi^t$$

From the outer induction hypothesis for this cycle u and instruction $I_M - 1$, we concluded as part of the induction step for that instruction that it updates the *spr* correctly. This is restated in the following lemma.

Lemma 203.

$$u = \max \{ u < t \mid ue_M^u \} \;\rightarrow\; spr_\pi^{u+1} = spr_\sigma^{I_M^{t}}$$

We immediately conclude that the *spr* is still equal to the *spr* of instruction I_M. Switching again to implicit t notation:

Lemma 204.

$$spr_\pi = spr_\sigma^{I_M}$$

Since only processor steps change the *spr*, we conclude in ISA that steps $m \in (pseq(I_M - 1) : pseq(I_M)]$ all see the same *spr*. This is stated in the following lemma.

Lemma 205.

$$m \in (pseq(I_M - 1) : pseq(I_M)] \;\rightarrow\; c^m.spr = spr_\sigma^{I_M}$$

This holds in particular for $m = NS$. Combined with lemma 204 we immediately obtain the crucial result:

Lemma 206.

$$spr_\pi = c^{NS}.spr$$

This ends the detour, and we go back to showing that the guard conditions are satisfied in ISA step $l \in [NS : NS')$. We distinguish between three cases:

- $s(l) \in \Sigma_{ib}$: the claim is trivially satisfied because these guard conditions are always true

$$\gamma(c^l, s(l)) = 1$$

- $l = pseq(I_M)$: since the step ends in the current cycle (and the operating conditions are satisfied) we have

$$ue_M \quad \text{and} \quad rfull_{M-1}$$

Thus by lemma 108 the instruction has passed all stages relevant for the guard conditions

$$I_M < I_{IF}, \quad I_M < I_{ET}, \quad I_M < I_{IT}$$

and thus by the outer induction hypothesis for the pipeline with $o := l$ all parts of the guard condition are satisfied in ISA

$$\gamma_{I\sigma}^{I_M}, \quad \gamma_{wE\sigma}^{I_M}, \quad \gamma_{wI\sigma}^{I_M}$$

Since these are all the parts of the guard condition of ISA step $l = pseq(I_M)$, the claim follows

$$\gamma(c^l, s(l))$$

- $s(l) \in \Sigma_{tlb}$: The guard conditions are slightly different depending on whether the step is initializing or extending a walk, but either way we need to establish that the translation only occurs in user mode

$$c^l.mode$$

so we establish that first. From the fact that the MMU was stepped we obtain that for some MMU $X \in \{I, E\}$ the walk register was clocked

$$mmu_X.w.ce$$

which is only the case if there is a translation request

$$mmu_X.treq$$

from which we conclude that the machine was in user mode at the beginning of the cycle

$$mode_\pi$$

By lemma 206 this is the mode in ISA configuration after NS steps

$$c^{NS}.mode$$

Since by definition of s we never step an MMU after a processor step that switches to user mode, we have

$$c^l.mode = c^{NS}.mode = 1$$

which is the claim.

For walk init steps we are immediately done as this is all that has to be shown. Let thus step l be a walk extension step

$$s(l) = (tlb, wext, mmu_X.w)$$

We need to show that the walk is incomplete and in the TLB.

Since the walk register is clocked and we are not initializing a walk, we must be in state *fetch-pte*

$$mmu_X.w.ce \wedge /mmu_X.winit, \quad fetch\text{-}pte$$

and thus by Invariant 2 on page 396 the walk is incomplete

$$/complete(mmu_X.w)$$

By definition the walk is in the set of walks of the MMU

$$mmu_X.w \in walks(mmu_X)$$

and hence by the outer induction hypothesis for the components outside the pipeline with $o := NS$ it is in the ISA TLB after NS steps

$$mmu_X.w \in c^{NS}.tlb$$

Since walks are not removed by flush or invalidation in the current cycle, the walk is still there before ISA step l

$$mmu_X.w \in c^l.tlb$$

which completes the proof.

9.5.8 Correctness for Pipeline Registers

Let n be the step of instruction i which is committed and where previous instructions are live

$$n = pseq(i) \wedge c(i)' \wedge lb(i)'$$

In case of rollback one repeats the previous arguments (from section 7.8.4) with updated indices for the old visible registers and for the newly introduced $ddpc$ register. We do not show those proofs here again.

For the pipeline registers themselves, in the absence of rollback we argue for the pipelined registers as before only about used inputs of the circuit stages and conclude everything else from updated circuit stage correctness lemmas. For the old inputs of the circuit stages the arguments are exactly as before and we do not repeat them here. In particular with the induction hypothesis for previous ISA steps one can prove just like in chapter 7 the following two lemmas which state that there is no *eret* or *jisr* below in the pipe:

Lemma 207. *Let g be an instruction between I_M and $i = I'_k$*

$$g \in [I_M : i)$$

Then instruction g is not interrupted in ISA

$$/jisr^g_\sigma$$

Lemma 208. *For $i = I'_k$ let g be an instruction between I_M and the instruction $I_l = j \in \{i, i-1\}$ in updated stage l*

$$g \in [I_M : I_l) \wedge ue_l$$

Then instruction g is not an eret instruction

$$/eret^g_\sigma$$

For the new inputs, the arguments are also extremely simple. The new inputs are:

- the walks from the MMUs, which are correct because they are sampled (just like e and I in chapter 8): for $X \in \{E, I\}$ we have

$$t = t_i(w_X), \quad mmu_X.wout^t_\pi = mmu_X.wout^{t_i(w_X)}_\pi = w_X{}^i_\sigma \qquad (61)$$

- The *mode* bit in stages *IF* and *M* (to drive the address multiplexers that distinguish between translated and untranslated addresses). From the induction hypothesis for the instruction in stage *M* we obtain

$$mode_\pi = mode_\sigma^{I_M}$$

which is the claim for the memory stage. In stage *IF* one uses lemmas 207 and 208 to conclude just like in previous chapters that the mode is not changed by any instruction below

$$mode_\sigma^{I_M} = mode_\sigma^{I_{IF}}$$

and the claim follows.

It remains to show that the guard conditions for processor steps are satisfied for the various stages. We have to show that if the sampled instruction is used, it is in the ISA instruction buffer, and if a sampled walk is used it is in the ISA TLB and matches the translated address. For the guard condition γ_I in the fetch stage nothing changes. This leaves the guard conditions for the walks. We show only the guard condition for the data MMU as the proof for the other MMU is completely analogous. Let thus the instruction *i* have passed in the next cycle the effective address translation stage

$$i < I'_{ET}$$

As with the old guard condition γ_I we split cases on whether this is the first cycle in which instruction *i* has passed the stage and consider in detail only the case where it is, i.e.,

$$i = I_{ET}$$

In this case the stage is updated in the current cycle

$$ue_{ET}$$

We need to show γ_{wE}. Thus assume that the instruction I_{ET} in stage *ET* is using walk w_E

$$used[w_E]_\sigma^{I_{ET}}$$

and thus the instruction is in user mode

$$mode_\sigma^{I_{ET}}$$

We have that instruction I_M is stepped no later than instruction I_{ET}, which is stepped in ISA step *n*

$$pseq(I_M) \le pseq(I_{ET}) = n$$

With lemmas 207 and 208 and eq. (60) we conclude that the hardware is also in user mode

$$
\begin{aligned}
mode_\pi &= mode_\sigma^{I_M} & \text{E 60 with } o := pseq(I_M) \\
&= mode_\sigma^{I_{ET}} & \text{L 207, 208} \\
&= 1
\end{aligned}
$$

Furthermore the instruction is a memory operation in ISA and hence by the inner induction hypothesis also in hardware

$$mop_\sigma^{I_{ET}}, \quad mop.(ET-1)$$

Since the hardware is in user mode and the instruction in the memory stage performs a memory operation, there is a translation request

$$mmu_E.treq$$

and since the stage is updated, the MMU is not busy

$$/mmu_E.busy$$

From lemma 194 we obtain that the walk presented by the MMU is matching the effective address

$$match(ea.(ET-1), mmu_E.wout)$$

By eq. (61) with $X := E$ we obtain that the walk output of the MMU is the walk used in ISA

$$mmu_E.wout = w_{E\sigma}^{I_{ET}} \tag{62}$$

Using the inner induction hypothesis for the effective address we conclude

$$match(ea_\sigma^{I_{ET}}, w_{E\sigma}^{I_{ET}}) \tag{63}$$

Furthermore by lemma 193 the walk output is in the set of walks $tlb(mmu_E.tlb)$ abstracted from the hardware TLB

$$mmu_E.wout = mmu_E.tlb.wout \in tlb(mmu_E.tlb)$$

Since instruction I_{ET} has not been executed yet we have

$$NS \leq pseq(I_{ET}) = n$$

By definition the set of walks $tlb(mmu_E.tlb)$ is contained in the set of walks $walks(mmu_E)$ and hence by the induction hypothesis for the current cycle (eq. (60)) with $o := NS$ (for the components outside the pipeline) also in the ISA TLB after NS instructions were executed

$$tlb(mmu_E.tlb) \subseteq walks(mmu_E) \subseteq c^{NS}.tlb$$

Completely analogous to the proof that the instruction buffer is not flushed by instructions $g \in [I_M : I_{IF})$ in lemma 175, we now show that the instructions $g \in [I_M : I_{ET})$ do not drop the walk from the TLB. Assume for the sake of contradiction that such an instruction g executes a $flusht$ or $invlpg$ instruction

$$flusht_\sigma^g \lor invlpg_\sigma^g$$

By lemmas 207 and 208 none of the instructions between I_M and g change the mode (since they can not be *jisr* or *eret*, and other instructions do not change the mode), thus

$$mode_\sigma^g = mode_\sigma^{I_M} = 1$$

Thus instruction g is performing an illegal instruction and is interrupted

$$ill_\sigma^g, \quad jisr_\sigma^g$$

which contradicts lemma 207. We conclude that the instructions $g \in [I_M : I_{ET})$ do not remove any walks from the TLB, and neither do any non-processor steps. Thus

$$c^{NS}.tlb \subseteq c^{I_{ET}}.tlb$$

We conclude

$$mmu_E.wout \in c^{I_{ET}}.tlb$$

and with eq. (62) we obtain

$$w_{E\sigma}^{I_{ET}} \in c^{I_{ET}}.tlb$$

By eq. (63) the walk is matching and hence the claim follows

$$\gamma_{wE\sigma}^{I_{ET}}$$

9.5.9 Proof Summary

Overall the proof followed the established lines. The presence of four caches necessitated some obvious bookkeeping. The salient new features of the correctness proof are

- in the definition of a stepping function simultaneous MMU steps and interrupted processor steps had to be ordered such that the MMU steps are performed first.
- there now is an explicit coupling relation between hardware MMUs and ISA MMU: walks in the hardware MMUs are contained in the ISA TLB. That this holds for *invlpg* and *flusht* instructions in system mode as well as for walk initialization and walk extension in user mode is follows from the correctness of the hardware MMUs in a fairly straight forward way.
- guard conditions for MMU steps n require the ISA machine to stay in user mode. This required to refer to the correctness of the special purpose register file $spr \in reg(M)$ in ISA step $pseq(I_M)$. From the induction hypothesis we only could get the required statement for $pseq(I_M - 1)$. Thus we were forced to argue in lemmas 202 to 206 that the mode register was 0 in ISA step $pseq(I_M - 1) + 1$ and subsequently was not changed before ISA step n.
- guard conditions for the walks w_I, w_E used in processor steps (they should be in the ISA TLB) are shown almost exactly as the guard conditions for the instruction I (it should be in the ISA instruction buffer): that a hardware walk is in the ISA TLB in the cycle it is delivered from an MMU follows from the coupling relation for TLBs and the definition of walk component $x.w_I$ and $x.w_E$ of input x.

That it stays there until it is used follows from the facts that i) *invlpg* and *flusht* instructions are illegal in user mode and ii) instructions committed in hardware are not rolled back in ISA, thus the mode cannot switch to system mode by an interrupt.

Store Buffers

In modern processors memory capacity has scaled with processor clock speed. With the logarithmic gate delay of typical designs this seems at first not to be a problem. However, if one considers wire delay, it turns out that memory latency scales in $O(\sqrt{n})$ with capacity n. Thus memory latency has not kept up with processor clock speed.

To alleviate this problem caches and cache hierarchies were introduced, with cache sizes especially close to the processor growing at a much slower rate than overall memory capacity. Obviously in the not too rare event of a shared cache line or a cache miss, accesses are still very slow.

A second problem arises in multi-processor systems, where multiple processors attempting to access shared memory would need to wait for each other; maximal wait time is obviously proportional to the number of processors.

In the sequential execution of instructions, this means that a slow memory instruction can block execution of subsequent ALU instructions even if the latter did not depend on the memory instruction.

Therefore, processor designers introduced various forms of buffering and reordering, both within the processor (out of order pipelines, store and load buffers, load speculation), and within the cache system (incoherent cache systems). These units allow execution of instructions, which do not depend on previous memory operations, before the memory operations are executed. While in a single-core processor these units are usually invisible to the programmer, in a multi-core system they change the programming model. One speaks of *weak memory models* or *weak memory consistency models*. In contrast the machines we have constructed so far as well as the machine of [KMP14] implement *strong memory consistency* or *sequential consistency*.

In this chapter we study store buffers. This are FIFO queues between each processor and the cache memory system, not unlike a to-do list of store operations for each processor. Whenever a processor has to execute a store instruction, the store operation goes into its store buffer rather than to the cache memory system, and the processor can immediately continue executing subsequent instructions. The store

© Springer Nature Switzerland AG 2020
P. Lutsyk et al. (Eds.): A Pipelined Multi-Core Machine, LNCS 9999, pp. 433–487, 2020.
https://doi.org/10.1007/978-3-030-43243-0_10

buffer is then responsible for raising the memory request signals and accessing memory in the background, while the processor continues executing instructions.

To make store buffers invisible to a single processor, one implements store to load forwarding, which means that loads from each processor can be served by data from the store buffer.

To see how this changes the programming model, consider the following analogy. All the engineers in an office floor share a single bathroom with only one toilet. One summer, the lock of the bathroom door breaks, and it is no longer possible to lock the door. The engineers quickly develop a solution: they put a chalk board in front of the bathroom, and write "occupied" on the chalk board before they enter the bathroom, erasing it again after they leave. One day one of the engineers enters the bathroom in a hurry — having no time to write "occupied" on the chalk board, he instead simply puts it on the mental to-do list. Obviously this is not guaranteed to work.

The pattern described above is a kind of exclusion lock, in which each processor q indicates that it wants to enter the critical section by writing to a shared variable x; then, before entering the critical section, it checks that no other processors $\hat{q}$ have written to the shared variable x. For the engineers this works because at most one engineer can read and write to the chalk board at the same time, i.e., the read-modify-write operation is atomic. Compare-and-swap instructions were introduced to instruction set architectures exactly for this purpose. However, as our example explains, writes of *cas* instructions should not end up in store buffers.

Thus in general there are situations where the store buffers have to be emptied, and instructions that explicitly drain the store buffer are added to instruction set. These instructions block execution of instructions until the store buffer has committed all buffered stores to the memory. In ISA this will be expressed as a guard condition, in hardware this is implemented as a hazard signal. These instructions are 1) compare-and-swap instructions (or more generally interlocked read-modify-write operations), 2) a newly introduced memory fence instruction

$$fence$$

Moreover, store buffers are drained on *jisr* and *eret*.

All of these instructions only drain the store buffer of the processor that executes them. Obviously they partially consume the performance improvements of store buffers, which raises the question of how to use them economically. It has been shown that store buffers are invisible if one executes such an instruction between every racing store instruction and later racing read instruction on the same thread [Obe17]. In particular programs where the only racing read instructions are CAS instructions — as is the case, e.g., in a program where all shared variables are protected with spinlocks — do not need any additional memory fences. Details go far beyond the scope of this book.

As a final remark we point out that the memory consistency model of x86 and x64 processors stems from their usage of store buffers. This memory consistency model is also known as TSO (total store ordering). In a global comparison, TSO is a rather conservative memory consistency model: all other major processor architectures such as ARM, RISCV, or POWER have much more aggressive memory consistency models.

We specify store buffers in section 10.1. In section 10.2 we extend ISA with visible store buffers. Hardware store buffers are constructed in section 10.3 and integrated in the entire machine in section 10.4. We proceed to show processor correctness in section 10.5. In section 10.6 we prove a simple *store buffer reduction theorem*. We consider a programming discipline which forbids to fetch instructions or read page table entries which are modified by writes in the current store buffer. It turns out that i) such a discipline can be formulated for an ISA without store buffers and ii) operating systems usually obey it. Moreover if we run such a program on our machine with store buffers, then it behaves as if the store buffers were not present.

10.1 Specification of Store Buffers

We distinguish between the store buffer structure in hardware, which is obviously of a fixed size, and abstract store buffers in ISA. Such an abstract store buffer is a sequence of store buffer entries

$$sbe = (sbe.a, sbe.data, sbe.bw) \in K_{sbe}$$

which have the following components:

- $sbe.a \in \mathbb{B}^{29}$. The line address of the access.
- $sbe.data \in \mathbb{B}^{64}$. The data to be written under control of the byte-write signals.
- $sbe.bw \in \mathbb{B}^{8}$. The byte-write signals.

Abstract store buffer configurations $sb \in K_{sb}$ are then simply sequences of store buffer entries $sb[i] \in K_{sbe}$, thus

$$K_{sb} = K_{sbe}^{*}$$

We number the entries of store buffers from right to left starting with 0 and ending with $\#sb - 1$, where $\#sb$ is the length of the store buffer:

$$sb = sb[\#sb - 1 : 0].$$

Empty store buffers $sb = []$ are permitted and their length is 0. The head of the queue is $sb[0]$ and the back of the queue is $sb[\#sb - 1]$.

Processor steps performing store accesses will push this store as the new tail of the store buffer. Store buffer steps will pop the head of the store buffer and move it with a write access into the memory system. CAS accesses will never enter store buffers. They can only be performed with empty store buffers. The results of load accesses can often be forwarded from the store buffer. We proceed to specify formally the forwarding of load results from the store buffer.

We define the footprint of a memory operation as a pair

$$fp = (fp.a, fp.ba)$$

where $fp.a \in \mathbb{B}^{29}$ is a line address and $fp.ba \in \mathbb{B}^8$ is a sequence of byte-access signals, which will serve as a search pattern in the byte-write signals $sbe.bw$ of store buffer entries. With the usual decomposition of addresses

$$z = z.l \circ z.o$$

into line addresses $z.l \in \mathbb{B}^{29}$ and offsets $z.o \in \mathbb{B}^3$ and widths of memory accesses $d \in \{1,2,4\}$ the byte-access signals are given by

$$ba(z,d)[i] = 1 \leftrightarrow i \in [\langle z.o \rangle : \langle z.o \rangle + (d-1)]$$

The byte-access signals $ba(z,d)$ constructed in this way simply form a mask for the bytes accessed by the memory access. For bit strings u and v of equal length we have defined on page 21

$$u \leq v \equiv (\forall i.\ u_i \leq v_i)$$

i.e., every raised bit in u is also raised in v. With byte-write/access signals we can thus find whether all bytes accessed by a load operation are also written by another operation. For store buffer entries sbe and footprints fp (of load operations) we have a store buffer entry hit if the line addresses match and the byte-write signals $sbe.bw$ and the byte-access signals $fp.ba$ of the footprint overlap.

$$sbehit(sbe, fp) \equiv sbe.a = fp.a \wedge (sbe.bw \wedge fp.ba) \neq 0^8$$

The hit is complete if all byte-access signals of the footprint are covered by the byte-write signals of the store buffer entry.

$$sbechit(sbe, fp) \equiv sbe.a = fp.a \wedge fp.ba \leq sbe.bw$$

Examples:

$$sbe.bw = 0000\ 1111$$
$$fp_1.ba = 0000\ 1111$$
$$fp_2.ba = 0000\ 1000$$
$$fp_3.ba = 1111\ 0000$$

Assume

$$sbe.a = fp_k.a \quad \text{for all } k$$

Then we have:

$$sbechit(sbe, fp_1)$$
$$sbehit(sbe, fp_2)$$
$$/sbehit(sbe, fp_3)$$

A store buffer hit occurs if there is a hit in some entry[1].

---

[1] A word of warning about notation to lecturers: resist the temptation to save time by dropping the b in $sbhit$.

$$sbhit(sb, fp) \equiv \exists j.\ sbehit(sb[j], fp)$$

Forwarding from a store buffer can only be done from the last (in time: the most recent) entry which produces a hit.

$$maxhit(sb, fp) = \begin{cases} \max\{i \mid sbehit(sb[i], fp)\} & sbhit(sb[i], fp) \\ \bot & \text{otherwise} \end{cases}$$

The data from this hit can only be forwarded if the hit is complete

$$sbf(sb, fp) \equiv maxhit(sb, fp) \neq \bot \land sbechit(sb[maxhit(sb, fp)], fp)$$

In other situations the store buffer will need to be drained until no hit remains. This forwarding discipline appears quite strict. In comparison, in the specification of x86/x64, store to load forwarding is allowed byte-wise, i.e., different bytes can be forwarded from different stores. In theory this is supposed to increase performance by requiring fewer store buffer drains. In practice it is extremely rare that a load has only a partial overlap with an earlier store, and byte-wise forwarding has a large cost in hardware (as forwarding hardware has to be copied once for each byte that needs to be forwarded). Consequently there is currently no x86 or x64 processor on the market that actually applies byte-wise forwarding. The data from the store buffer entry with this index is forwarded.

$$sbf(sb, fp) \quad \rightarrow \quad sbfout(sb, fp) = sb[maxhit(sb, fp)].data$$

Higher indices are prioritized during forwarding. Thus if one splits a store buffer $sb = sbH \circ sbL$ into a part sbH with higher indices and a part sbL with lower indices, forwarding for a single byte from the whole store buffer $sbH \circ sbL$ is the same as forwarding from sbH if one can forward from sbH, or from sbL if one can not forward from sbH. This is stated in the following lemma:

Lemma 209. *Let fp be a footprint with a single byte*

$$\sum_i fp.ba_i = 1$$

Then:

- *One can forward from a store buffer $sb = sbH \circ sbL$ if one can forward from sbH or from sbL*

$$sbf(sbH \circ sbL, fp) \leftrightarrow sbf(sbH, fp) \lor sbf(sbL, fp)$$

- *If one can forward from the store buffer*

$$sbf(sbH \circ sbL, fp)$$

then the forwarded data from the complete store buffer comes the portion sbH with higher indices if possible

$$sbfout(sbH \circ sbL, fp) = \begin{cases} sbfout(sbH, fp) & sbf(sbH, fp) \\ sbfout(sbL, fp) & o.w. \end{cases}$$

From a byte-addressable memory m and a store buffer sb we define a byte-addressable forwarding memory system. Given a byte address z, determine if there is a hit in the store buffer for the single byte addressed by z with the footprint $(z.l, ba(z, 1))$, i.e., compute

$$sbf(sb, (z.l, ba(z, 1)))$$

In that case access the store buffer entry

$$sbfout(sb, (z.l, ba(z, 1)))$$

with the last hit and forward byte $z.o$ of that entry. In all other cases access the memory.

$$fms(m, sb)(z) = \begin{cases} byte(\langle z.o \rangle, sbfout(sb, (z.l, ba(z, 1)))) & sbf(sb, (z.l, ba(z, 1))) \\ m(z) & \text{otherwise} \end{cases}$$

In later constructions we will implement this memory with a more coarse grained forwarding mechanism: hardware will only forward from complete hits, and for incomplete hits we will simply drain the store buffer and then answer from memory.

10.2 Extending ISA

ISA configurations c get an abstract store buffer $c.sb \in K_{sb}$ as a new component. We include a new symbol sb for steps popping the head of the store buffer and committing it to memory into the input alphabet Σ of the transition relation

$$\{sb\} = \Sigma_{sb} \subset \Sigma$$

An ISA configuration without store buffers is extracted from an ISA configuration c with store buffers with

$$c_{old} = c.(core, m, ib, tlb)$$

and as usual we denote all predicates and functions f of the ISA without store buffers by

$$f_{old}$$

For all functions and predicates f of the old ISA which we do not update explicitly below, we use the old definition

$$f(c, x) = f_{old}(c_{old}, x)$$

10.2.1 Processor Steps

We first consider how the presence of store buffers changes processor steps

$$x \in \Sigma_p$$

A new instruction $fence$ is added to the instruction set. We do not care about the encoding and simply take some previously unused instruction code. We assume that there is a predicate

$$fence(c,x)$$

which holds iff the instruction $x.I$ is a memory fence. This instruction is also a legal instruction for programs written in user mode, and is not a branch/jump instruction or gpr write etc.

Intuitively, this instruction empties the store buffer. We define that it is not a branch/jump instruction, and hence its only direct effect is to increment the program counter and update dpc, $ddpc$.

Draining the store buffer is done indirectly through the guard condition, which states that a fence instruction can only be executed while the store buffer is empty. This means that the store buffer will be drained by store buffer steps first, and the fence instruction will block the execution of instructions and therefore prevent further stores from being added into the store buffer. The same holds for cas, $jisr$, and $eret$. Thus we will add to the guard condition:

$$fence(c,x) \lor cas(c,x) \lor jisr(c,x) \lor eret(c,x) \;\rightarrow\; \#c.sb = 0$$

Load instructions drain the store buffer while there is a hit from which the load can not forward. We define the footprint of memory operations as

$$fp(c,x) = (pmaE(c,x).l, ba(pmaE(c,x), d(c,x)))$$

and require that a load is only executed if there is a miss or a hit from which the load can forward

$$l(c,x) \;\rightarrow\; /sbhit(c.sb, fp(c,x)) \lor sbf(c.sb, fp(c,x))$$

We collect both conditions into a guard condition for store buffers

$$\gamma_{sb}(c,x) = (fence(c,x) \lor cas(c,x) \lor jisr(c,x) \lor eret(c,x) \;\rightarrow\; \#c.sb = 0)$$
$$\land (l(c,x) \;\rightarrow\; /sbhit(c.sb, fp(c,x)) \lor sbf(c.sb, fp(c,x)))$$

which we add to the main guard condition

$$\gamma(c,x) = \gamma_{old}(c_{old},x) \land \gamma_{sb}(c,x)$$

Loads now use the forwarded memory system instead of loading directly from the memory

$$lres(c,x) = fill(c,x)^{32-8 \cdot d(c,x)} \circ fms(c.m, c.sb)_{d(c,x)}(pmaE(c,x))$$

Stores now no longer change memory during the processor step. This causes a small inconvenience with the old memory update lemma, which states

$$\delta_M(\ell(m_\sigma^i), dacc_\sigma^i) = \ell(m_\sigma^{i+1})$$

Obviously $dacc_\sigma^i$ so far includes stores. As we do not wish to modify old proofs, we change the definition of $dacc$ slightly so that this lemma still holds: we replace data accesses produced by stores with void accesses. To make this formal we first rename the old definition of the data access into $idacc$, for intermediate data access

$$idacc(c, x) = dacc_{old}(c_{old}, x)$$

If the intermediate data access is a store, it is replaced with a void access

$$dacc(c, x) = \begin{cases} idacc(c, x) & /idacc(c, x).w \\ (0 \ldots 0) & \text{o.w.} \end{cases}$$

Instead of updating memory, stores enter the store buffer. Recall that the store buffer is numbered from right to left, and that the newer store buffer entries have larger numbers. Thus we need to add the new store to the left of the store buffer

$$c'.sb = \begin{cases} c.sb & /s(c, x) \\ idacc(c, x).(a, data, bw) \circ c.sb & \text{o.w.} \end{cases}$$

Other than this nothing changes for processor steps. Note that reading operations use as footprint the address of the intermediate access and the byte-read signals as defined in section 4.2.6.

Lemma 210.

$$read(c, x) \;\rightarrow\; fp(c, x) = (idacc(c, x).a, br(c, x))$$

10.2.2 Store Buffer Steps

Store buffer steps are steps with oracle input

$$x = sb$$

These steps are allowed only when the store buffer is not empty

$$\gamma(c, x) = \#c.sb > 0$$

We construct from the head of the store buffer a memory access $dacc(c, x)$ in the obvious way:

$$dacc(c, x).a = c.sb[0].a$$
$$dacc(c, x).data = c.sb[0].data$$
$$dacc(c, x).bw = c.sb[0].bw$$
$$dacc(c, x).(w, r, cas) = (1, 0, 0)$$

The ISA memory system is updated with this access

$$\ell(c'.m) = \delta_M(\ell(c.m), dacc(c,x))$$

and the head of the store buffer is dropped

$$c'.sb = c.sb[\#c.sb - 1 : 1] = tail(c.sb)$$

10.2.3 Instruction Buffer and MMU Steps

For these steps nothing changes. In particular, the instruction access still loads directly from the memory, ignoring the store buffer.

10.3 Store Buffer Construction

Store buffers are essentially queues with forwarding logic. We construct first a basic, straightforward queue with forwarding logic. This basic queue is correct, but when used in front of the memory system, it adds unacceptable delay which would essentially double cycle time. Thus we also construct an improved queue, which uses the basic queue as a building block but reduces delay by buffering the head of the queue in a special register.

10.3.1 Basic Queue with Forwarding

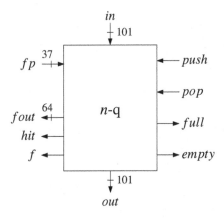

Fig. 169. Symbol of the 2^n-entry basic queue n-q

As shown in fig. 169, an 2^n-entry basic queue has the following inputs and outputs:

- data input and output $in, out \in K_{sbe}$ with $K_{sbe} = \mathbb{B}^{101}$

- two control inputs $push, pop \in \mathbb{B}$
- two control outputs $full, empty \in \mathbb{B}$
- a footprint input $fp \in \mathbb{B}^{37}$ for selecting an entry for forwarding
- hit output signal $hit \in \mathbb{B}$ signalling whether there is a (possibly partial) hit of the footprint in the queue
- signal $f \in \mathbb{B}$ signalling that the last entry with a hit for the footprint has a complete hit, and thus one can forward from the store buffer
- a forwarding output $fout \in \mathbb{B}^{64}$, meaningless when f is zero

Internally, the 2^n-entry basic queue has $N = 2^n$ store buffer entries, which are stored in an $(n, 101)$-R-RW-SPR RAM M (as constructed in section 3.3.10)

$$M : (n, 101)\text{-R-RW-SPR RAM}$$

The reason for using an SPR RAM rather than a regular RAM is that an SPR RAM allows us to read from all individual registers in parallel, which we need to do in order to do forwarding.

Note that the interface of the queue can be split into inputs and outputs that are solely used for forwarding (fp, f, hit, $fout$), and inputs and outputs that are solely used for the functionality of the queue itself (in, out, $push$, pop, $full$, $empty$).

The construction of the queue can be split along similar lines. We first construct the queue itself, and then add the forwarding logic.

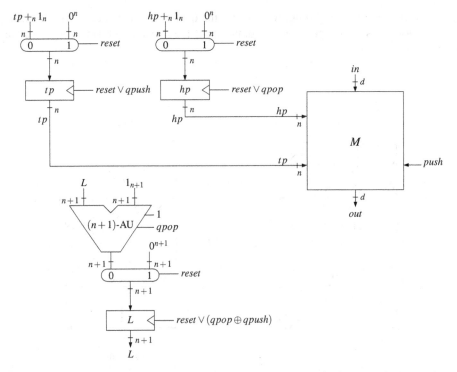

Fig. 170. Construction of the queue. Special inputs and outputs of the SPR RAM M are only used for forwarding and omitted in this figure.

The standard construction of hardware queues is illustrated in fig. 170. Head and tail pointers (hp and tp resp.) point to the first occupied and the first free address in the RAM.

$$hp, tp \in \mathbb{B}^n$$

Pushes store to address tp and increase tp modulo N. Pops read from address hp and increase hp modulo N. The length of the queue, i.e., the number of occupied registers of the RAM, is maintained in a register (L) in binary.

$$L \in \mathbb{B}^{n+1}$$

From a hardware queue configuration q with these components we can reconstruct an abstract queue $aq(q)$ as follows:

$$i \in [0 : \langle q.L \rangle - 1] \rightarrow aq(q)[i] = q.M(q.hp +_n i_n).$$

It is crucial to recall that binary addition $+_n$ is performed modulo 2^n. We say that the queue is full if its length is N and that it is empty if its length is 0.

$$empty \equiv L = 0^{n+1}$$
$$full \equiv L = 10^n$$

For later use with forwarding, we say that the queue is wrapped and write W if the head pointer is larger than the tail pointer or of the queue is full (in which case the pointers are equal).

$$W \equiv \langle hp \rangle > \langle tp \rangle \vee full$$

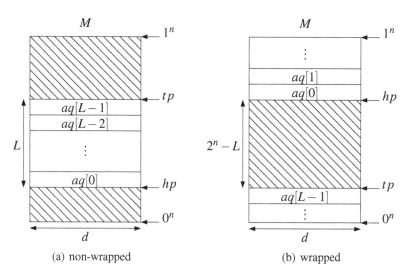

Fig. 171. Mapping hardware queue to abstract queue

Non-wrapped and wrapped queues resp. are illustrated in figs. 171(a) and 171(b).

Operating conditions require:

• one cannot pop from an empty queue

$$empty \rightarrow /pop$$

• one cannot push into a full queue, unless one simultaneously pops from it.

$$full \wedge /pop \rightarrow /push$$

The remaining construction details of the queue are now straight forward. The pointers are implemented by counters

$$hp' = hp +_n pop_n$$
$$tp' = tp +_n push_n$$

and the length is maintained by a counter

$$L' = \begin{cases} L -_{n+1} (pop \oplus push)_{n+1} & pop \\ L +_{n+1} (pop \oplus push)_{n+1} & \text{otherwise.} \end{cases}$$

All counters are initialized with zeros on *reset*.

$$hp^0 = 0^n$$
$$tp^0 = 0^n$$
$$L^0 = 0^{n+1}$$

Due to the operating conditions we have

$$full \leftrightarrow L[n+1].$$

RAM M is an $(n, 101)$-R-RW-SPR RAM as specified and constructed in section 3.3.10. The read address $M.a$ is tied to hp, the write address $M.b$ is tied to tp and the write signal $M.w$ to *push*.

$$M.a = hp$$
$$M.b = tp$$
$$M.w = push$$

Other data inputs of M are not used and we tie them to zero

$$M.ce[i] = 0 \, , \, M.din[i] = 0_{101}$$

The connection of data inputs and outputs is obvious.

$$M.in = q.in$$
$$q.out = M.out$$

One shows in a straightforward fashion for the abstracted queues

Lemma 211.

- $$aq(q^0) = []$$

- $$aq(q') = \begin{cases} in \circ tail(aq(q)) & push \wedge pop \\ tail(aq(q)) & \overline{push} \wedge pop \\ in \circ aq(q) & push \wedge \overline{pop} \\ aq(q) & \overline{push} \wedge \overline{pop} \end{cases}$$

- $$/empty \rightarrow out = aq(q)[0]$$

We now construct the forwarding logic. For this we consider the special outputs $M.dout[i]$ of the SPR RAM which contain store buffer entries from which to forward. As usual we abbreviate

$$dout[i] = M.dout[i]$$

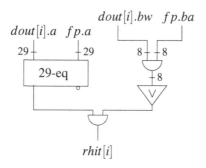

Fig. 172. Computation of the hardware hit signal *rhit*

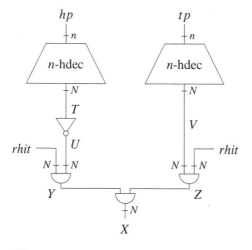

Fig. 173. Computation of the forwarding masks Y,Z and X

For each such special output a register hit signal $rhit[i]$ is computed as illustrated in fig. 172 by

$$rhit[i] \equiv sbehit(dout[i], fp)$$

To compute which special outputs $M.dout[i]$ currently contain store buffer entries, we need to deal with the possibility of a wrapped queue. As illustrated in fig. 173, we first create two mask vectors U and V by feeding the head and tail pointers hp and tp into half decoders and inverting the result T of the half decoder for the head pointer. From the specification of half decoders we get

$$T[i] = 1 \equiv i < \langle hp \rangle$$
$$U[i] = 1 \equiv i \geq \langle hp \rangle$$
$$V[i] = 1 \equiv i < \langle tp \rangle$$

These masks are illustrated in figures 174(a) and 174(b) resp. for non-wrapped and wrapped queues. We identify the indices of hits covered by these masks by ANDing

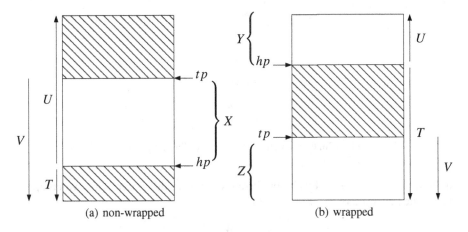

Fig. 174. Masks T, U, V and masked hits X, Y, Z in the store buffer

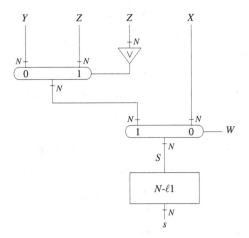

Fig. 175. Computation of forwarding masks S and s

them with the vector of register hit signals. We compute the following vectors of indices of hits:

$$Y = U \wedge hit$$
$$Z = V \wedge hit$$
$$X = Y \wedge Z$$

Possibly non-zero portions of these vectors are also illustrated in figures 174(a) and 174(b). We now compute the region S in which the most recently added hit can be found. In case of the non-wrapped queue, the most recently added entry with the hit has to be in the region X. In case of a wrapped queue it must be either in the region Z or the region Y; and entries in the region Z have been added more recently than those

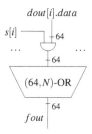

Fig. 176. Computation of the forwarding output $fout$

in the region Y and must thus be preferred. Following this observation we compute S with the hardware of fig. 175 as follows

$$S = \begin{cases} X & /W \\ Z & W \wedge Z \neq 0^N \\ Y & \text{otherwise} \end{cases}$$

The most recent entry can now be found by turning off all raised bits in S except the one with the largest index.

$$s = \ell 1(S)$$

That this identifies the candidate for forwarding in the store buffer from q is stated in

Lemma 212.

$$q.s[i] = 1 \quad \rightarrow \quad maxhit(aq(q), q.fp) = i$$

Thus as illustrated in fig. 176 the candidate for forwarding from a basic queue is

$$fout = \bigvee_i dout[i].data \wedge s[i]$$

There is a hit if there is any register hit

$$hit = \bigvee_i rhit[i]$$

but computation of the forwarding signal f is slightly more involved. The byte-write signals of the last store buffer entry with a hit are

$$fbw = \bigvee_i dout[i].bw \wedge s[i]$$

This entry has a complete hit only if all accessed bytes in the footprint are also written to by the forwarded store buffer entry

$$f = \bigwedge_j (fbw[j] \vee /fp.ba[j])$$

This completes the construction of the basic queue. That the forwarding logic is correct is stated in

Lemma 213.

$$q.hit \quad \equiv \quad sbhit(aq(q),q.fp)$$
$$q.f \quad \equiv \quad sbf(aq(q),q.fp)$$
$$q.f \quad \rightarrow \quad q.fout = sbfout(aq(q),q.fp)$$

10.3.2 Improved Queue Design

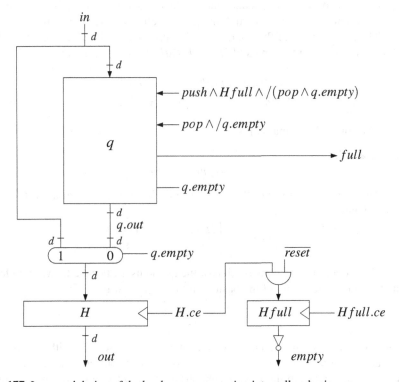

Fig. 177. Improved design of the hardware queue, using internally a basic queue q

Later the store buffer output will serve as an input to the RAMs of the cache systems. Tying the output of a RAM to the input of a second RAM is not good for cycle time (say in the model of [MP00]). We therefore construct an improved queue where the output of the modified queue Q comes directly out of a register (H), while maintaining the behaviour of the basic queue.

The idea is to store the head element in a register

$$H : reg(101)$$

and using a basic queue

$$q : n\text{-}q$$

to store only all elements *behind* the head element. Whether register H currently has data is stored in an additional 1-bit register $Hfull$

$$Hfull : \rho$$

For this purpose, we do two things: 1) we forward the new element into the head register when pushing while the complete queue is empty, and 2) we move the head element of the basic queue into register H when we pop. Note that this improved queue can store $2^n + 1$ elements, whereas the basic queue only stores 2^n elements.

Like before we first construct the queue itself, then the forwarding logic.

The construction of the queue itself is illustrated in fig. 177, except for the definition of clock enable signals of H and $Hfull$. These are computed as

$$H.ce = push \wedge /Hfull \vee q.pop$$
$$Hfull.ce = pop \wedge q.empty \vee H.ce \vee reset.$$

The construction maintains

Invariant 3.

$$/Hfull \rightarrow q.empty$$

This permits to abstract the queue from a hardware configuration Q of the improved queue:

$$aq(Q) = \begin{cases} H \circ aq(Q.q) & Hfull \\ [] & \text{otherwise} \end{cases}$$

This concludes the construction of the queue itself. For the forwarding logic, we first define the footprint of the basic q in the obvious way

$$q.fp = fp$$

The forwarding output can now come from one of two sources: either from the basic queue (through $q.fout$), or from the head of the store buffer in register H. Since we have to forward from the most recent store buffer entry, forwarding from the basic queue has priority. The corresponding hardware is shown in fig. 178.

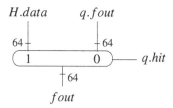

Fig. 178. Computation of the forwarding output $fout$ for the improved queue

The complete queue has a hit if q has a hit or if the head entry is a hit

$$hit = q.hit \lor sbehit(H, fp)$$

The head entry has a complete hit if all bytes read by the forwarding footprint are also written by the head entry

$$Hc = \bigwedge_j (H.bw[j] \lor /fp.ba[j])$$

The last store buffer entry with a hit has a complete hit if either the last store buffer entry in the basic queue has a complete hit, or the head has a complete hit and there is no hit in the basic queue

$$f = q.f \lor /q.hit \land Hc$$

This completes the construction of the improved queue. That the forwarding logic is correct is stated in

Lemma 214.

$$Q.hit \equiv sbhit(aq(Q), Q.fp)$$
$$Q.f \equiv sbf(aq(Q), Q.fp)$$
$$Q.f \rightarrow Q.fout = sbfout(aq(Q), Q.fp)$$

and that the improved queue implements a queue is stated in the following lemma which corresponds to lemma 211

Lemma 215.

- $$aq(Q^0) = []$$

- $$aq(Q') = \begin{cases} in \circ tail(aq(Q)) & push \land pop \\ tail(aq(Q)) & \overline{push} \land pop \\ in \circ aq(Q) & push \land \overline{pop} \\ aq(Q) & \overline{push} \land \overline{pop} \end{cases}$$

- $$/empty \rightarrow out = aq(Q)[0]$$

10.4 Pipelined Processor with Store Buffer

The improved store buffer queue constructed in section 10.3 is now placed as a sub-unit

$$sb : n\text{-}Q$$

between data cache and processor. Thus processor request, busy signals, etc. now are computed by the store buffer under consideration of the signals of processor and data cache. For the most part changes only concern the connection between these components, except that additional hardware needs to be added to the processor for instructions that drain the store buffer. In particular such instructions need to be detected in the decoder, the result needs to be pipelined to the memory stage (using control signals *con.k*), and the processor needs to communicate the store buffer drain to the store buffer through an additional signal

$$drain \in \mathbb{B}$$

which is raised by the processor when a store buffer draining instruction is in the memory stage. Execution of subsequent instructions is then stalled by the store buffer by raising the busy signal.

In fact, the busy signal $busy_M$ for the processor is now raised only in case the processor executes one of the following instructions:

- a store while the store buffer is (and stays) full
- a load which cannot be forwarded from the store buffer during a cache miss
- a compare and swap during a cache miss
- a store buffer draining instruction while the store buffer is not empty

In practice this greatly decreases the number of cycles that the processor has to be stalled because the data cache is busy.

We also rename the data access *dacc* of the processor into

$$idacc$$

to keep in sync with the updated notation in ISA.

10.4.1 Draining Instructions

Decoding hardware for the fence instruction is added in a straightforward fashion. Details are omitted here, important to us is only that there is a hardware signal $fence_\pi$ which corresponds to the fence instruction in ISA. This signal is pipelined as described in section 7.4.4 and used as an input in the memory stage. Thus in particular we have a register

$$fence.ET$$

for which the coupling relation (in case the instruction is committed etc.) will later give us

$$fence_\sigma^{I_M} = fence.ET$$

From these signals we compute the drain signal following the guard condition as

$$drain = full_{ET} \wedge (fence.ET \vee cas.ET \vee jisr \vee eret.ET)$$

10.4.2 Arbitration and Control

Inputs to the data cache *dca* can come from the intermediate data access of the processor, or from the output of the store buffer. Indeed, access to the cache between these two sides is arbitrated by a control automaton with the states *core*, *SB* and *idle*, where in state *core* the access right is given to the processor core, and in state *SB* to the store buffer. However for performance reasons accesses are already started when the automaton is still in state *idle*, in which case the access right is given to the processor if both units request access. Like in the fact that the automaton is in state $X \in \{core, SB, idle\}$ is indicated by a hardware signal of the same name.

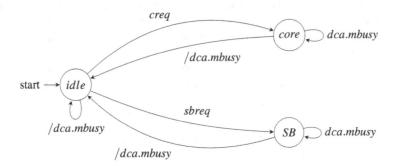

Fig. 179. Control automaton for the memory stage

The control automaton is shown in fig. 179. We proceed to specify the transitions. Usually (whatever this means) the store buffer is accessing the caches. The processor core only requests access to the caches in two situations:

- to perform a load for which no hit is in the store buffer
- to execute a CAS instruction, after the store buffer has been drained

This is indicated by signal

$$cacc = full_{M-1} \wedge exec.(M-1) \wedge (idacc.cas \wedge sb.empty \vee idacc.r \wedge /sb.hit)$$

These requests are only granted while the automaton is in state *idle*. If this request is granted and the access is completed immediately by the cache the automaton remains in state *idle*[2]. Otherwise it goes to state *core* to indicate an ongoing access. This transition is made under control of signal

$$creq = cacc \wedge dca.mbusy$$

---

[2] In the cache memory system constructed in [KMP14] this does not happen: even with a cache hit in an exclusive state a local write takes two cycles. This however will change, when we consider memory mapped I/O. The IO-ports will be realized as registers or register files, which can be written in a single cycle.

The store buffer in turn requests access to the caches when it is not empty, but only if the core is not attempting to access the caches. This is indicated by signal

$$sacc = /sb.empty \land /cacc$$

If this request is granted and the access is completed immediately, the automaton remains in state $idle$. Otherwise it goes to state SB to indicate an ongoing access. This transition is made under control of signal

$$sbreq = sbacc \land dca.mbusy$$

The automaton remains in states $core$ resp. SB until the access completes, and then returns to state $idle$. This ensures that 1) memory accesses of the store buffer are completed even if the processor in the middle of the store buffer access requests access to the cache, and 2) that no cycles are wasted, as the next access can be started right away from state $idle$.

It remains to specify the push and the pop signals of the store buffer. Data are popped from the store buffer if it controls the cache and its access finishes.

$$sb.pop = (sacc \lor SB) \land /dca.mbusy$$

Data are pushed into the store buffer on stores. But this can only be done if the store buffer is not full, or if it is full, but it can pop in the current cycle.

$$sb.push = full_{ET} \land idacc.w \land (/sb.full \lor sb.pop)$$

The request signal $dca.preq$ which is now the joint request signal for requests coming from the store buffer or the processor is active if either core or store buffer want to perform an access

$$dca.preq = cacc \lor sacc$$

A trivial induction shows that the $core$ state is only active when a CAS instruction is executed and the store buffer is empty, or a load instruction is executed and there is no hit

Invariant 4.

$$core \quad \rightarrow \quad cacc$$

Proof. We only sketch the proof. To go into state $core$, signal $cacc$ must be raised by definition of $creq$

$$/core \land core' \rightarrow cacc$$

While we stay in state $core$, $cacc$ is stable because the instruction in the memory stage is a cas or load which does not put any new stores in the store buffer, and it stays in the memory stage until we leave state $core$

$$cacc \land core' \rightarrow cacc'$$

$\square$

Similarly state SB is only active when the store buffer is not empty

Invariant 5.

$$SB \quad \rightarrow \quad /sb.empty$$

Proof. We only sketch the proof. To get into state SB signals $sbreq$ and $sbacc$ must be on and hence the store buffer is not empty. Furthermore the data cache must be busy and hence the store buffer head is not popped

$$/SB \wedge SB' \rightarrow /sb.empty, \, dca.mbusy, \, /sb.pop$$

Thus the store buffer remains not empty

$$/SB \wedge SB' \rightarrow /sb.empty'$$

To stay in state SB, we have a busy data cache and again the head entry is not popped and the store buffer remains not empty

$$SB \wedge SB' \wedge /sbreq \rightarrow dca.mbusy, \, /sb.pop, \, /sb.empty'$$

$\square$

Hence a store buffer pop is only performed when the store buffer is not empty

Lemma 216.

$$sb.pop \rightarrow /sb.empty$$

10.4.3 Connecting the Data Paths

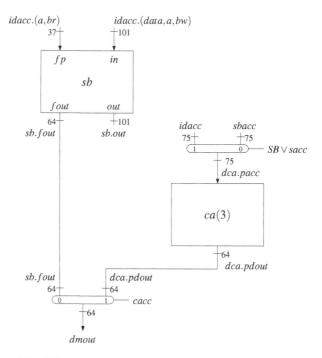

Fig. 180. Data path for the machine with the store buffer

The data paths are illustrated in fig. 180.

The data input *sb.in* of the store buffer comes from the intermediate data access, i.e., the old data access

$$sb.in = idacc.(data, a, bw)$$

Note that the value of this input is irrelevant unless we actually push it into the store buffer. Intuitively this is done exactly if the data access is a store access, but because we must not exceed the capacity of the store buffer, the precise definition of the push signal is slightly more involved and best delayed until we have defined the pop signal.

Analogous to lemma 210 the footprint *sb.fp* — used for forwarding of the load results — is defined using the old data access and the byte-read signals *br* as

$$sb.fp.a = idacc.a$$
$$sb.fp.ba = br.5$$

The access produced by the store buffer is defined by

$$sbacc.(a, data, bw) = sb.out \ , \ sbacc.(w, r, cas) = (1, 0, 0)$$

The data access used in hardware is

$$dacc = \begin{cases} sbacc & SB \lor sacc \\ idacc & \text{o.w.} \end{cases}$$

That this is correct hinges on the fact that the access right is never given to the processor core during store accesses.

The memory output $dmout$ to be used by the processor comes from the forwarded output $sb.fout$ if forwarding for a load is possible, and from cache output $dca.pdout$ otherwise. In the first case the processor core must have access to the cache.

$$dmout = \begin{cases} dca.pdout & cacc \\ sb.fout & \text{otherwise} \end{cases}$$

We also adjust the definition of $dmout$ in ISA using the footprint $fp(c,x)$. The memory output is either the old data output in case there is no forwarding result, or the output of the store buffer

$$dmout(c,x) = \begin{cases} dmout_{old}(c_{old}, x) & /sbf(c.sb, fp(c,x)) \\ sbfout(c.sb, fp(c,x)) & sbf(c.sb, fp(c,x)) \end{cases}$$

We show the following lemma, which connects the load result with the data memory output:

Lemma 217. *If during a read there is no partial hit, i.e., either a complete hit for forwarding or no hit at all*

$$read(c,x) \land (sbf(c.sb, fp(c,x)) \lor /sbhit(c.sb, fp(c,x)))$$

the data memory output determines the load result:

$$byte(i, lres(c,x)) = \begin{cases} fill(c,x)^8 & i \geq d(c,x) \\ byte(i + \langle pmaE(c,x).o \rangle, dmout(c,x)) & i < d(c,x) \end{cases}$$

Proof. We only show the proof for $i < d(c,x)$. Let z be the byte address of byte i

$$z = pmaE(c,x) +_{32} i$$

The i-th byte of the load result comes from the forwarded memory system

$$byte(i, lres(c,x))$$
$$= fms(c.m, c.sb)(pmaE(c,x) +_{32} i)$$
$$= fms(c.m, c.sb)(z)$$
$$= \begin{cases} byte(\langle z.o \rangle, sbfout(c.sb, (z.l, ba(z,1)))) & sbf(sb, (z.l, ba(z,1))) \\ c.m(z) & \text{o.w.} \end{cases} \tag{64}$$

We now distinguish whether we have no hit at all, or whether we have a complete hit for forwarding.

- /$sbhit(c.sb, fp(c,x))$: due to alignment and $i < d(c,x)$, by lemma 34 the line address of this byte address is the same as the address of the intermediate data access, and the offset is equal to the offset of the physical memory address plus i

$$z.l = pmaE(c,x).l = idacc(c,x).a \quad \text{and} \quad \langle z.o \rangle = \langle pmaE(c,x).o \rangle + i \quad (65)$$

Since we are considering a read we have by lemma 210

$$fp(c,x) = (idacc(c,x).a, br(c,x)) = (z.l, br(c,x))$$

and obtain from the assumption that there is no hit for the footprint that there is also no hit for $z.l$ and the byte-read signals

$$/sbhit(c.sb, (z.l, br(c,x))) \qquad (66)$$

Analogous to eq. (12) on page 167 we conclude from eq. (65) that the byte-read signal of byte i is raised

$$br(c,x)[\langle z.o \rangle] = 1$$

Thus the byte-access signals of accessing byte z with width 1 are a subset of the byte-read signals

$$ba(z,1)[i] \leftrightarrow i \in [\langle z.o \rangle : \langle z.o \rangle + (1-1)] \qquad \text{(defn } ba)$$
$$\leftrightarrow i = \langle z.o \rangle$$
$$\rightarrow br(c,x)[i],$$
$$ba(z,1) \leq br(c,x) = fp(c,x).ba \qquad (67)$$

and every store buffer entry hit for these access signals is also a store buffer entry hit for the byte-read signals

$$\forall k. \ sbehit(c.sb[k], ba(z,1)) \rightarrow sbehit(c.sb[k], br(c,x)) \qquad (68)$$

We conclude with eqs. (65) and (66)

$$/sbhit(c.sb, (z.l, ba(z,1)))$$

The claim now follows with eq. (64) and lemma 35 as both load result and *dmout* come from the memory

$$byte(i, lres(c,x)) = c.m(z)$$
$$= byte(i + \langle pmaE(c,x).o \rangle, \ell(c.m)(z.l))$$
$$= byte(i + \langle pmaE(c,x).o \rangle, dmout(c,x))$$

- $sbf(c.sb, fp(c,x))$: Completely analogous to the previous case we infer eqs. (65), (67) and (68) and conclude that the maximum hit j with the byte-read signals can not be before the maximum hit with the accessed signals

$$j = maxhit(c.sb, fp(c,x)) \geq maxhit(c.sb, (z.l, (ba(z,1)))) \qquad (69)$$

Since we can forward, the hit is complete

$$sbechit(c.sb[j], fp(c,x))$$

Thus the hit must include every byte, in particular the accessed byte

$$ba(z,1) \leq br(c,x) = fp(c,x).ba \leq c.sb[j].bw$$

and is thus also a hit for the accessed byte

$$sbehit(c.sb[j], (z.l, ba(z,1)))$$

Since by eq. (69) the maximum hit for the accessed byte can not be later than the maximum hit for the footprint, it must be the same

$$j = maxhit(c.sb, (z.l, (ba(z,1))))$$

and we conclude that both accesses forward from the same entry, which is the memory output

$$sbfout(c.sb, (z.l, (ba(z,1)))) = sbfout(c.sb, fp(c,x))$$
$$= dmout(c,x)$$

and the claim follows with eqs. (64) and (65) as both forwarded memory system and $dmout$ forward from that store buffer entry

$$byte(i, lres(c,x)) = byte(\langle z.o \rangle, sbfout(c.sb, (z.l, ba(z,1))))$$
$$= byte(\langle pmaE(c,x).o \rangle + i, dmout(c,x))$$

□

10.4.4 Computing the Busy Signal

We first study the conditions under which the new memory stage with cache and store buffer cannot complete the instruction currently processed by the memory stage. The execution of the instruction needs to be stalled if:

- for a draining instruction the store buffer is not yet drained

$$busy_{drain} = drain \wedge /sb.empty$$

- for a CAS access the cache is not ready

$$busy_{cas} = idacc.cas \wedge dca.mbusy$$

- for a store instruction the store buffer is full and cannot pop (and simultaneously push) in the current cycle

$$busy_s = idacc.w \wedge sb.full \wedge dca.mbusy$$

- for a load instruction the result can not be forwarded from the store buffer, and we have not received the load result from the cache yet. This can be either because the cache is currently completing a store buffer access (in state SB) or because the memory access of the load has not been completed by the cache ($dca.mbusy$)

$$busy_l = idacc.r \wedge /sb.f \wedge (sacc \vee SB \vee dca.mbusy)$$

We collect these as the hazard signal of the memory stage

$$haz_M = busy_{drain} \vee busy_{cas} \vee busy_s \vee busy_l$$

10.4.5 Stability of Inputs

Since the data cache is now sometimes driven by the store buffers we need to adjust the proofs for the stability of inputs of the data cache. We only state the following two lemmas which jointly imply stability of inputs at the data cache.

Lemma 218.

$$(idle \wedge sacc \vee SB) \wedge dca.mbusy \rightarrow SB' \wedge dacc = dacc'$$

Lemma 219.

$$(idle \wedge cacc \vee core) \wedge dca.mbusy \rightarrow core' \wedge /ue_{M-1} \wedge dacc = dacc'$$

10.5 Correctness

10.5.1 Definition of Stepping Function

In previous chapters we have in the absence of emergency braking always executed steps in two phases: first all steps that have non-void accesses to the caches, then the remaining steps. Recall that this allowed us to define the ISA step generating the access with local sequential index x by the simple equation

$$isa^t(x) = NS^t + x - 1$$

We could continue to do this in this chapter, but the fact that loads can forward from a store buffer in the same cycle in which the store buffer is stepped would make this difficult. In particular, if the load is actually forwarding from the head of the store buffer, which is committed to memory by the store buffer step. Note that in such a situation, the load in hardware does not generate an access to the caches as the access can be answered by the store buffer. If we would step in ISA the store buffer before the load, however, then the load in ISA would not be able to forward and would access the memory. For a machine with a single-core processor this still works because the store buffer step does not change the forwarded memory system of that processor. Thus whether we load before or after executing the store buffer step is irrelevant.

But in a multi-core machine, other processors might overwrite the memory location in the same cycle (recall that the specification of our cache memory system does not prohibit executing conflicting writes in the same cycle). In this case, executing in ISA the load after all the non-void accesses to caches will have a load result coming from one of these other processors. In hardware, however, the load result will always come from the forwarded store in the store buffer.

We avoid this complication by stepping loads which forward from the store buffer before the non-void accesses to the caches. This means that there are now three phases, as shown in fig. 181.

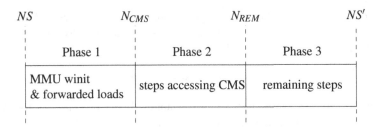

Fig. 181. Three phases of steps that end in the current cycle

For technical reasons we also step walk initialization steps in the first phase (which immediately implies the right order between MMU steps and interrupted processor steps). We denote the number of such steps by nfi (number of forwarding and initialization steps) defined by

$$nfi^t = mmu_I.winit^t + mmu_E.winit^t + ue_M^t \wedge exec.(M-1)^t \wedge l.(M-1)^t \wedge sb.f^t$$

The first ISA step after executing all steps in the first phase is

$$N_{CMS}^t = NS^t + nfi^t$$

In the second phase we step non-void accesses to the cache memory system. These include i) processor instructions which execute a non-forwarding load or a *cas* instruction, but not store instructions ii) walk extensions of the MMUs iii) instruction buffer fetches and iv) store buffer pops. The number of such accesses is given by

$$\begin{aligned} nac^t &= ue_M^t \wedge exec.(M-1)^t \wedge (l.(M-1)^t \wedge /sb.f^t \vee cas.(M-1))^t \\ &\quad + mmu_I.w.ce^t \wedge /mmu_I.winit^t + mmu_E.w.ce^t \wedge /mmu_E.winit^t \\ &\quad + ue_{IF}^t \\ &\quad + sb.pop^t \\ &= \#E^t \end{aligned}$$

The ISA step generating the access with local sequential index x is now defined easily as

$$isa^t(x) = N^t_{CMS} + x - 1$$

The first ISA step after executing all steps of the first two phases is

$$N^t_{REM} = N^t_{CMS} + nac^t$$

In the third phase, we do the possibly remaining processor step. Such a processor step does not execute loads or *cas* instructions. Thus interrupts, store instructions, fences, ALU operations, and so on, are executed here. The number of these steps is

$$nrem^t = ue^t_M \wedge /(exec.(M-1)^t \wedge (l.(M-1)^t \vee cas.(M-1)^t)) \leq 1$$

For the oracle inputs used by each type of step nothing changes with the exception of store buffer steps which are new. These store buffer steps n_{sb} are triggered whenever the store buffer is popped

$$sb.pop^t \rightarrow s(n_{sb}) = sb$$

However the order of these steps slightly changes. If the processor is forwarding from the store buffer, it is stepped in the first phase

$$ue^t_M \wedge exec.(M-1)^t \wedge l.(M-1)^t \wedge sb.f^t \rightarrow n_p \in [NS^t : N^t_{CMS})$$

Similarly walk initialization is only done in the first phase. Let n_{tlbX} be the step of MMU $X \in \{I, E\}$. We have

$$mmu_X.winit^t \rightarrow n_{tlbX} \in [NS^t : N^t_{CMS})$$

The order of these steps does not matter. For the second phase we step the remaining MMU steps

$$/mmu_X.winit^t \rightarrow n_{tlbX} \in [N^t_{CMS} : N^t_{REM})$$

processor steps that access the CMS

$$ue^t_M \wedge exec.(M-1)^t \wedge (l.(M-1)^t \wedge /sb.f^t \vee cas.(M-1))^t \rightarrow n_p \in [N^t_{CMS} : N^t_{REM})$$

instruction buffer steps

$$ue^t_{IF} \rightarrow n_{ib} \in [N^t_{CMS} : N^t_{REM})$$

and store buffer steps

$$sb.pop^t \rightarrow n_{sb} \in [N^t_{CMS} : N^t_{REM})$$

As in previous chapters the order of these steps is determined by the sequential order of the cache accesses. The only difference to the previous chapter is that the access at the data cache may be generated either by the processor *or* by the store buffer, in case we have $sb.pop^t$. Recall that the port i_x of the access with local sequential index x is defined by

$$seq(k_x^t, i_x^t) = n_x^t$$

With this port we can define the order of the steps that generate memory accesses easily with the following equations. If a *cas* or a load which can not forward from the store buffer leaves the pipeline the processor generates the access at the data port

$$ue_M^t \wedge exec.(M-1)^t \wedge (cas.(M-1)^t \vee l.(M-1)^t \wedge /sb.hit^t)$$
$$\rightarrow n_p = NS^t + \varepsilon\left\{x \mid i_x^t = 3\right\} - 1 = isa^t(xd)$$

If on the other hand the store buffer pops, the store buffer generates this access

$$sb.pop^t \rightarrow n_{sb} = NS^t + \varepsilon\left\{x \mid i_x^t = 3\right\} - 1 = isa^t(xd)$$

When a MMU clocks the walk register and does not perform a walk initialization, it generates the access at its port

$$mmu_I.w.ce^t \wedge /winit_I^t \rightarrow n_{tlbI} = NS^t + \varepsilon\left\{x \mid i_x^t = 0\right\} - 1$$
$$mmu_E.w.ce^t \wedge /winit_E^t \rightarrow n_{tlbE} = NS^t + \varepsilon\left\{x \mid i_x^t = 2\right\} - 1$$

Finally, if the instruction fetch stage is updated (ue_{IF}^t) the instruction buffer generates the access at the instruction port

$$n_{ib} = NS^t + \varepsilon\left\{x \mid i_x^t = 1\right\} - 1$$

For the third phase we step the processor in case it has not been stepped in one of the previous phases.

$$(ue_M^t \wedge /(exec.(M-1)^t \wedge (l.(M-1)^t \vee cas.(M-1)^t))) \rightarrow n_p = N_{REM}^t$$

10.5.2 Simulation Relation

The only thing that changes in the coupling relation is that we need to establish the obvious simulation relation between the store buffers of hardware and ISA. The queue $aq(sb_\pi^t)$ abstracted from the hardware store buffer in cycle t equals the ISA store buffer $c^n.sb$

$$aq(sb_\pi^t) = c^n.sb$$

We collect the simulation of memory, store buffer, and TLB in a single simulation relation

$$t \sim_m n \quad \equiv \quad n = NS^t \rightarrow m(h^t) = \ell(c^n.m) \wedge opc^t$$
$$\wedge\ walks(mmu_I^t) \cup walks(mmu_E^t) \subseteq c^n.tlb$$
$$\wedge\ aq(sb_\pi^t) = c^n.sb$$
$$\wedge\ \forall \hat{n} < n.\ \gamma(c^{\hat{n}}, s(\hat{n}))$$

The main correctness theorem states:

Lemma 220. *There is an initial configuration c^0 satisfying*

$$sim(h^0, c^0)$$

in which instruction buffer and TLB are empty

$$c^0.ib = c^0.tlb = \emptyset$$

and the store buffer is also empty

$$c^0.sb = \varepsilon$$

Furthermore: if for the computation (c^n) with stepping function $s(n)$ extracted from hardware and initial configuration c^0 satisfies for all n the software condition $SC_{ROM}(c^n, s(n))$ provided the stepping function $s(n)$ has a valid initial segment until n

$$\forall n. \ (\forall m \le n. \ \gamma(c^m, s(m))) \ \rightarrow \ SC_{ROM}(c^n, s(n))$$

then for all n and t:

- *If n is a processor step executing instruction i, which is committed and only has live instructions before it*

$$n = pseq(i) \ \wedge \ c(i)^t \ \wedge \ lb(i)^t$$

then hardware in cycle t simulates instruction i

$$t \sim_p i$$

and each part of the guard condition holds if instruction i passed the corresponding stage

$$(i < I_{IF}^t \rightarrow \gamma_I^i) \ \wedge \ (i < I_{IT}^t \rightarrow \gamma_{wI}^i) \ \wedge \ (i < I_{ET}^t \rightarrow \gamma_{wE}^i)$$

- *Hardware simulates in cycle t the non-pipelined components of ISA step n*

$$t \sim_m n$$

10.5.3 Managing the Induction Step

We have now with the store buffer for the first time a component which is updated in a non-trivial way by two units in a single hardware cycle. Such components can be a bookkeeping challenge because the effect of multiple steps in ISA is applied in a single hardware cycle, and any data obtained from the components (e.g., during forwarding) in hardware need to match the data obtained in the ISA step, possibly after some changes have been made in ISA by other units.

To tackle this challenge we reuse a simple bookkeeping tool that we already know from hardware: timing diagrams. Recall that timing diagrams visually illustrate how signals change over the range of several hardware cycles. We use a similar tool that visually illustrates how and when the value of ISA components change over the range of several ISA steps. We call them stepping diagrams, and we will use them to relate the state of ISA components to hardware components and (ghost) signals before and after each phase of the stepping function, i.e., after executing $n \in \{NS, N_{CMS}, N_{REM}, NS'\}$ steps.

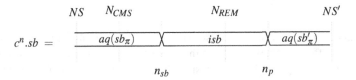

Fig. 182. Stepping diagram for the machine with store buffers

For the ISA configurations after executing NS and NS' steps, our stepping diagrams will always relate each ISA component according to the simulation relation $\sim_m$. For example, in the stepping diagram for the machine with store buffers shown in fig. 182, we relate $c^{NS}.sb$ to $aq(sb_\pi)$ and $c^{NS'}.sb$ to $aq(sb'_\pi)$.

For the configurations between these phases, we observe that steps $n \in [NS : N_{CMS})$ in the first phase of the stepping do not change the store buffer, thus we relate the ISA store buffer after N_{CMS} steps to the store buffer $aq(sb_\pi)$ from the beginning of the cycle. Steps $n \in [N_{CMS} : N_{REM})$ in the second phase only change the store buffer in case they are store buffer steps, in which case they pop the first entry of the store buffer. Obviously there is no store buffer configuration in hardware that corresponds to this intermediary state. We simply define such an intermediary (ghost) store buffer isb, which one obtains from $aq(sb_\pi)$ by considering only pop operations

$$isb = \begin{cases} tail(aq(sb_\pi)) & sb.pop \\ aq(sb_\pi) & \overline{sb.pop} \end{cases}$$

The stepping diagram corresponds in straightforward fashion to a series of formal statements which relate the store buffer in hardware and in ISA. These can be summarized as follows:

$$c^{NS}.sb = aq(sb_\pi)$$
$$c^{N_{CMS}}.sb = aq(sb_\pi)$$
$$c^{N_{REM}}.sb = isb$$
$$c^{NS'}.sb = aq(sb'_\pi)$$

Note that the first of these statements immediately comes out of the coupling relation $t \sim_m NS^t$, and that the last of these statements implies the corresponding portion of the coupling relation $t + 1 \sim_m NS^{t+1}$. Furthermore, each of these statements follows somewhat easily from the previous one by simply executing the steps in ISA, and showing that the effect of the instructions in each phase is also applied on the hardware-side (ghost) store buffer. For example, from lemma 215 one concludes trivially

Lemma 221.

$$aq(sb'_\pi) = \begin{cases} idacc.(data,a,bw) \circ isb & sb.push \\ isb & o.w. \end{cases}$$

which matches the effect of a processor step on the store buffer in ISA, provided we can relate the effect of steps of ISA to the signals in hardware. Due to our induction scheme, that is only possible for ISA steps $o \leq n$. Thus the statements can only be proven if n is sufficiently large. We will therefore prove the following statements:

$$n \geq NS \rightarrow c^{NS}.sb = aq(sb_\pi)$$
$$n \geq N_{CMS} \rightarrow c^{N_{CMS}}.sb = aq(sb_\pi)$$
$$n \geq N_{REM} \rightarrow c^{N_{REM}}.sb = isb$$
$$n \geq NS' \rightarrow c^{NS'}.sb = aq(sb'_\pi)$$

10.5.4 Induction Step

The proof follows the induction scheme and outline from previous chapters. As usual we often only show the parts which are new or have changed.

We begin by repeating the induction hypotheses. The outer induction hypothesis is

$$\forall u.\ u \sim_m o \wedge (o = pseq(j) \wedge c(j)^u \wedge lb(j)^u$$
$$\rightarrow u \sim_p j \wedge (j < I^u_{IT} \rightarrow \gamma^j_{wI\sigma}) \wedge (j < I^u_{IF} \rightarrow \gamma^j_{I\sigma}) \wedge (j < I^u_{ET} \rightarrow \gamma^j_{wE\sigma}))$$
$$(70)$$

and the inner induction hypothesis states

$$t \sim_m n \wedge (n = pseq(i) \wedge c(i)^t \wedge lb(i)^t$$
$$\rightarrow t \sim_p i \wedge (i < I^t_{IT} \rightarrow \gamma^i_{wI\sigma}) \wedge (i < I^t_{IF} \rightarrow \gamma^i_{I\sigma}) \wedge (i < I^t_{ET} \rightarrow \gamma^i_{wE\sigma}))$$
$$(71)$$

Combining both in a straightforward fashion we obtain for all $o \leq n$ and *only* cycle t

$$t \sim_m o \wedge (o = pseq(i) \wedge c(i)^t \wedge lb(i)^t$$
$$\rightarrow t \sim_p i \wedge (i < I^t_{IT} \rightarrow \gamma^i_{wI\sigma}) \wedge (i < I^t_{IF} \rightarrow \gamma^i_{I\sigma}) \wedge (i < I^t_{ET} \rightarrow \gamma^i_{wE\sigma}))$$
$$(72)$$

which we call the *induction hypothesis for the current cycle*.

10.5.5 Preparations

We begin by showing the correctness of the stepping diagram.

Lemma 222.
$$n \geq NS \rightarrow c^{NS}.sb = aq(sb_\pi)$$

Proof. The claim is the induction hypothesis for the current cycle (eq. (72)) with $o := NS \leq n$

$$aq(sb_\pi) = c^{NS}.sb$$

$\square$

Lemma 223.
$$n \geq N_{CMS} \rightarrow c^{N_{CMS}}.sb = aq(sb_\pi)$$

Proof. We have
$$n \geq N_{CMS} \geq NS$$

and thus by lemma 222
$$c^{NS}.sb = aq(sb_\pi)$$

The claim follows as steps $\hat{n} \in [NS : N_{CMS})$ in the first phase do not change the store buffer. Formally, they are either MMU steps which never change the store buffer, or they are processor steps which in hardware are load instructions

$$\hat{n} = pseq(I_M) \wedge l.5$$

Since $\hat{n} < N_{CMS} \leq n$ we can use the outer induction hypothesis to show that they are also load instructions in ISA
$$l_\sigma^{I_M}$$

and the claim follows

$$aq(sb_\pi) \overset{L\,222}{=} c^{NS}.sb = c^{N_{CMS}}.sb \ .$$

$\square$

Lemma 224.
$$n \geq N_{REM} \rightarrow c^{N_{REM}}.sb = isb$$

Proof. We have
$$n \geq N_{REM} \geq N_{CMS}$$

and thus by lemma 223
$$c^{N_{CMS}}.sb = aq(sb_\pi)$$

We couple now with the intermediate store buffer *isb* and split cases on *sb.pop*.

- $sb.pop$: in this case we step the store buffer in step $\hat{n} \in [N_{CMS} : N_{REM})$

$$s(\hat{n}) = sb$$

and there are no other steps in the phase that change the store buffer; as in lemma 223 we can show that all processor steps are loads and CAS operations which do not change the store buffer. Thus

$$c^{\hat{n}}.sb = c^{N_{CMS}}.sb \overset{L\,223}{=} aq(sb_\pi) \quad \text{and} \quad c^{\hat{n}+1}.sb = c^{N_{REM}}.sb$$

By definition of store buffer semantics the step pops a store buffer entry and the claim follows

$$c^{N_{REM}}.sb = c^{\hat{n}+1}.sb = tail(c^{\hat{n}}.sb) = tail(aq(sb_\pi)) = isb$$

- $/sb.pop$: in this case there is no store buffer step, and analogous to above we also obtain that no other steps change the store buffer. The claim follows

$$c^{N_{REM}}.sb = c^{N_{CMS}}.sb = aq(sb_\pi) = isb$$

$\square$

Lemma 225.
$$n \geq NS' \;\rightarrow\; c^{NS'}.sb = aq(sb'_\pi)$$

Proof. We have

$$n \geq NS' \geq N_{REM}$$

and thus by lemma 224

$$c^{N_{REM}}.sb = isb$$

We couple now with the store buffer $aq(sb'_\pi)$ after the hardware cycle and split cases on $sb.push$, and in case $/sb.push$ a nested case split on whether the memory stage is clocked and hence an instruction is stepped.

- $sb.push$: by definition of the push signal, we have that the effective address translate stage ET is full, there is a write access, and the store buffer either has room or is popped and hence getting room in the current cycle

$$full_{ET} \wedge idacc_\pi.w \wedge (/sb.full \vee sb.pop)$$

Since $sb.pop$ is only raised when the data cache is not busy, we obtain

$$/sb.full \vee /dca.mbusy$$

and hence there is no busy signal for store

$$/busy_s$$

The other busy signals are also off because write accesses do not drain or cause other accesses and thus there is no hazard, the memory stage is updated

$$/haz_M, \quad ue_M$$

By lemma 165 the instruction in the memory stage is stepped

$$pseq(I_M) < NS'$$

and hence we can use the outer induction hypothesis for $\hat{n} := pseq(I_M)$ and obtain that the intermediate data accesses in ISA and hardware are equivalent

$$idacc_\pi \equiv idacc_\sigma^{I_M}$$

We successively conclude

$$idacc_\sigma^{I_M}.w, \quad s_\sigma^i, \quad c^{pseq(I_M)+1}.sb = idacc_\sigma^{I_M}.(a,data,bw) \circ c^{pseq(I_M)}.sb$$

There are no other steps in this third phase and the claim follows

$$
\begin{aligned}
c^{NS'}.sb &= c^{pseq(I_M)+1}.sb \\
&= idacc_\sigma^{I_M}.(a,data,bw) \circ c^{pseq(I_M)}.sb \\
&= idacc_\pi.(a,data,bw) \circ c^{NREM}.sb \\
&= idacc_\pi.(a,data,bw) \circ isb \qquad\qquad \text{L 224} \\
&= aq(sb'_\pi) \qquad\qquad\qquad\qquad \text{L 221, } sb.push
\end{aligned}
$$

- $/sb.push \wedge ue_M$: the memory stage is only clocked if there is an instruction in the effective address translate stage and that instruction is not stalled. We infer successively

$$full_{ET}, \quad /haz_M, \quad /busy_s$$

We will now show that the intermediate data access is not a write access by contradiction and some bookkeeping. Assume thus for the sake of contradiction

$$idacc_\pi.w$$

With the definition of $sb.push$ we obtain from $/sb.push$ and $idacc_\pi.w$ and $full_{ET}$ that the store buffer is full and not popped

$$sb.full \wedge /sb.pop$$

With the definition of $busy_s$ we conclude from $/busy_s$ and $idacc_\pi.w$ and $sb.full$ that the data cache is idle

$$/dca.mbusy$$

With the definition of $sb.pop$ we conclude from $/sb.pop$ and $/dca.mbusy$ that the automation is not in state SB and is not attempting to go there

$$/SB \wedge /sacc$$

However, since the store buffer is full it can not be empty

$$/sb.empty$$

and thus by definition of $sacc$ we conclude from $/sacc$ that the processor must attempt to access the cache

$$cacc$$

But since the data access is a write and not a load or CAS, this is obviously not the case

$$/cacc$$

which is a contradiction.

Thus we have that the access is not a write access

$$/idacc_\pi.w$$

Since the memory stage is clocked the instruction is by lemma 165 stepped in the current cycle

$$pseq(I_M) < NS'$$

and the outer induction hypothesis applies for $\hat{n} := pseq(I_M)$. In particular from $full_{ET}$ and $/idacc_\pi.w$ we conclude successively

$$/s_\sigma^{I_M}, \quad c^{pseq(I_M)+1}.sb = c^{pseq(I_M)}.sb$$

The claim follows

$$
\begin{aligned}
c^{NS'}.sb &= c^{pseq(I_M)+1}.sb \\
&= c^{pseq(I_M)}.sb \\
&= c^{NREM}.sb \\
&= isb & \text{L 224} \\
&= aq(sb_\pi') & \text{L 221, } /sb.push
\end{aligned}
$$

- $/sb.push \wedge /ue_M$: In ISA the store buffer does not change, and the claim follows

$$
\begin{aligned}
c^{NS'}.sb &= c^{NREM}.sb \\
&= isb & \text{L 224} \\
&= aq(sb_\pi') & \text{L 221, } /sb.push
\end{aligned}
$$

□

Next we show that steps up to n which end in the current cycle or before satisfy the guard conditions. This corresponds to lemma 168 in chapter 8.

Lemma 226. *Let*

$$n \in [NS : NS') \wedge \hat{n} \leq n$$

or

$$n = NS' \wedge \hat{n} < n$$

Then

$$\gamma(c^{\hat{n}}, s(\hat{n}))$$

Proof. Like before we split cases on $\hat{n} < NS$ but show only the case

$$\hat{n} \geq NS$$

We do a case split on the type of step $\hat{n}$ is.

- $s(\hat{n}) \in \Sigma_{ib} \cup \Sigma_{tlb}$: for these steps the claim is proven as before
- $s(\hat{n}) \in \Sigma_{sb}$: in this case we we need to show that the store buffer is non-empty. We have by definition of the stepping function a store buffer pop in hardware

$$sb.pop$$

and conclude with lemma 216 that the store buffer is not empty, and thus the abstract queue at the beginning of the cycle is non-empty

$$/sb.empty, \quad sb.Hfull, \quad aq(sb_\pi) \neq []$$

Store buffer steps are executed in the second phase and from lemma 223 we conclude

$$c^{NCMS}.sb = aq(sb_\pi) \neq []$$

Since steps between N_{CMS} and the store buffer step $\hat{n}$ do not change the store buffer, the claim follows

$$\#c^{\hat{n}}.sb = \#c^{NCMS}.sb > 0$$

- $s(\hat{n}) \in \Sigma_p$: since $\hat{n} \in [NS : NS')$ we have

$$\hat{n} = n_p = pseq(I_M) \wedge ue_M$$

All old parts of the guard condition are proven like before. The new parts γ_{sb} of the guard condition — which are related to the store buffer — are shown by case distinction on the type of operation. We have to show that store buffer draining instructions are only executed when the store buffer is empty, and that loads are only executed if there is forwarding or no store buffer hit.

 - $fence_\sigma^{I_M} \vee cas_\sigma^{I_M} \vee jisr_\sigma^{I_M} \vee eret_\sigma^{I_M}$: by the induction hypothesis for the current cycle (eq. (72)) with $o := \hat{n} \leq n$ we obtain

$$fence.(M{-}1) \vee cas.(M{-}1) \vee jisr.(M{-}1) \vee eret.(M{-}1)$$

and conclude that the store buffer drain signal is active

$$drain$$

From ue_M we conclude successively

$$/haz_M, \quad /busy_{drain}, \quad sb.empty, \quad /sb.Hfull$$

By definition of aq we have

$$aq(sb_\pi) = []$$

Since the store buffer is empty there is by contraposition of lemma 216 no pop

$$/sb.pop$$

and we obtain

$$isb = aq(sb_\pi) = []$$

Independently of the phase in which ISA step $\hat{n}$ is executed, we have by lemmas 223 and 224 that the store buffer of step $\hat{n}$ is either equal to the abstract queue at the beginning of the hardware cycle, or to the intermediate store buffer

$$c^{\hat{n}}.sb \in \{isb, aq(sb_\pi)\}$$

Since both of these are empty, the store buffer $c^{\hat{n}}.sb$ must also be empty, which is the claim

$$\#sb_\sigma^{I_M} = \#c^{\hat{n}}.sb = \#[] = 0$$

- $l_\sigma^{I_M} \wedge /jisr_\sigma^{I_M}$: by the induction hypothesis for the current cycle (eq. (72)) with $o := \hat{n} \leq n$ we obtain

$$l.(M{-}1) \wedge exec.(M{-}1)$$

and conclude from ue_M successively

$$/haz_M, \quad /busy_l, \quad sb.f \vee (/SB \wedge /sacc \vee /dca.mbusy)$$

We distinguish whether $sb.f$ holds or not. If $sb.f$ holds, we will show that the load forwards in ISA. If $sb.f$ does not hold, we will show that in ISA there is no store buffer hit.

· $sb.f$: by lemma 214 part 2 we have

$$sbf(aq(sb_\pi), sb.fp))$$

With lemma 210 and the induction hypothesis for the current cycle (eq. (72)) with $o := \hat{n} \leq n$ we obtain

$$sb.fp = (idacc_\pi.a, br.5) \stackrel{\text{IH}}{=} (idacc_\sigma^{I_M}.a, br_\sigma^{I_M}) \stackrel{\text{L 210}}{=} fp_\sigma^{I_M}$$

The step is executed in the first phase. Since steps in this phase never change the store buffer we have by lemma 222

$$aq(sb_\pi) = c^{NS}.sb = c^{pseq(I_M)}.sb = sb_\sigma^{I_M}$$

Hence there is a forwarding hit also in ISA

$$sbf(sb_\sigma^{I_M}, fp_\sigma^{I_M})$$

and the claim follows.

· $/sb.f$: the cache is idle and the store buffer is not accessing the cache

$$/SB \wedge /sacc \wedge /dca.mbusy$$

Since the store buffer is not attempting to access the cache ($/sacc$), it must be empty or the processor must be accessing the cache

$$sb.empty \vee cacc$$

If the store buffer is empty there is no hit. And a read only accesses the cache if there is no hit. In either case we obtain that there is no hit

$$/sb.hit$$

By lemma 214 part 1 there is no store buffer hit in the abstract queue $aq(sb_\pi)$

$$/sbhit(aq(sb_\pi), sb.fp)$$

Analogous to the previous case we obtain that the footprint matches the ISA footprint

$$sb.fp = fp_\sigma^{I_M}$$

Since the store buffer is not accessing the cache, the head of the store buffer is not popped, and the store buffer is not stepped

$$/sacc \wedge /SB, \quad /sb.pop, \quad \forall \hat{n} \in [NS : NS').s(\hat{n}) \neq sb$$

We conclude that the store buffer has not been changed yet by any steps that end in the current cycle but before I_M

$$sb_\sigma^{I_M} = c^{pseq(I_M)}.sb = c^{NS}.sb \overset{L\,222}{=} aq(sb_\pi)$$

Thus there is no hit also in ISA and the claim follows

$$/sbhit(sb_\sigma^{I_M}, fp_\sigma^{I_M})$$

$\square$

In order to prove that the operating conditions are satisfied, we need to prove something about store buffer steps. Our software condition SC_{ROM} only directly states that processor steps do not write into the ROM region, but all store buffer entries are created by processor steps. Thus a simple induction shows that all store buffer entries do not write into the ROM

Lemma 227.

$$(\forall \hat{n} < o.\ \gamma(c^{\hat{n}}, s(\hat{n}))) \quad \rightarrow \quad \forall e \in c^o.sb.\ \langle e.a \rangle \geq 2^{r+3}$$

Since by the induction hypothesis for the current cycle (eq. (72)) the guard condition is satisfied for all steps before $o = NS$, we conclude:

Lemma 228.

$$n \geq NS \quad \rightarrow \quad \forall e \in c^{NS}.sb. \langle e.a \rangle \geq 2^{r+3}$$

Lemma 229.

$$n \geq NS \quad \rightarrow \quad opc'$$

Proof. We distinguish whether the data access comes from the processor or the store buffer by case analysis on the state of the automaton. In case the data access comes from the processor the proof is completely analogous to the proof in previous chapters, so we show here only the proof in case the data access came from the store buffer.

We conclude with lemma 228 that the store buffer does not contain any writes to the ROM region in ISA

$$\forall e \in c^{NS}.sb. \langle e.a \rangle \geq 2^{r+3}$$

and hence not in hardware

$$\forall e \in aq(sb_\pi). \langle e.a \rangle \geq 2^{r+3}$$

Thus in particular the store buffer output

$$dca.pacc = dacc_\pi = sb.out \in aq(sb_\pi)$$

is not writing into the ROM

$$\langle dca.pacc.a \rangle \geq 2^{r+3}$$

which proves the claim

$$/vopc, \quad opc'$$

$\square$

For the memory we will need to consider both processor steps *and* store buffer steps, which can both change the memory. However, at most one of these occurs between NS and NS'. Thus for the auxiliary lemmas at the surface nothing changes.

As in lemma 172 we show that only steps that generate data accesses modify memory. As usual this requires proving that instructions executed by ISA step o raise the same signals in hardware and in ISA. Thus one must rely on the induction hypothesis for the current cycle for $o := o$. This is only possible if $o \leq n$.

Lemma 230. *Assume $o \in [NS : NS']$ and $o \leq n$. Then*

$$(d = 0 \vee o \neq isa(xd)) \quad \rightarrow \quad \ell(c^{o+1}.m) = \ell(c^o.m)$$

Proof. For instruction buffer and MMU steps the claim obviously holds. Assume for the sake of contradiction that it is a processor or store buffer step. However, store buffer steps always generate data accesses, i.e., a step o is only a store buffer step if we have $o = n_{sb} = isa(xd)$. Thus we consider like in the proof of lemma 172 only the proof for processor steps; but now only for a compare-and-swap instruction, as stores no longer modify memory either.

$$o \in \Sigma_p \land o = pseq(i) \land cas_\sigma^i$$

Since the instruction is stepped in the current cycle we obtain that the memory stage is updated and there are real full and full bits above

$$ue_M, \quad rfull_{M-1} \land full_{M-1}$$

Thus by the induction hypothesis for the current cycle (eq. (72)) with $o := o$ and $i := i$ we obtain that it is a memory operation and a compare-and-swap in hardware

$$mop.(M-1), \ cas.(M-1)$$

Since the stage is updated there is no stall, no hazard, and in particular neither a hazard due to drain or due to the memory access of the cas

$$/stall_M, \ /haz_M, \ /busy_{drain} \land /busy_{cas}$$

From the lack of the busy drain signal and the fact that cas instructions drain the store buffer we conclude the store buffer must be empty. By contraposition of Invariant 5 on page 455 we conclude that the control automaton is not giving control of the data port to the store buffer, and by definition of $sbacc$ we conclude that the store buffer is not attempting to gain control

$$sb.empty, \ /SB \land /sbacc$$

Thus the store buffer is not being popped

$$/sb.pop$$

However the processor is performing a memory access, and since the $busy_{cas}$ signal is off the data cache must be idle

$$dca.preq, \ /dca.mbusy$$

We conclude that the access to the data cache is ending

$$\exists k. \ (3,k) \in E$$

thus there is a data access

$$d = 1$$

Since the store buffer is not being popped, the data access generates a processor step. Since there is at most one processor step, that step must be step o

$$isa(xd) = n_p = o$$

which is a contradiction. $\square$

The updated version of lemma 173 follows from this lemma exactly like lemma 173 followed from lemma 172.

Lemma 231. *Let*

$$o \in [NS : NS'] \wedge o \leq n$$

then

$$\ell(c^o.m) = \begin{cases} \ell(c^{NS}.m) & d = 0 \vee o \leq isa(xd) \\ \delta_M(\ell(c^{NS}.m), dacc(c^{isa(xd)}, s(isa(xd)))) & d = 1 \wedge isa(xd) < o \end{cases}$$

10.5.6 Correctness for Components Outside the Pipeline

We have to show

$$n = NS' \rightarrow m(h') = \ell(c^n.m) \tag{73}$$
$$\wedge \ opc' \tag{74}$$
$$\wedge \ walks(mmu'_I) \cup walks(mmu'_E) \subseteq c^n.tlb \tag{75}$$
$$\wedge \ aq(sb'_\pi) = c^n.sb \tag{76}$$
$$\wedge \ \forall \hat{n} < n. \ \gamma(c^{\hat{n}}, s(\hat{n})) \tag{77}$$

The proofs for eqs. (74), (75) and (77) are exactly as before. Equation (76) is just lemma 225. It remains to show the claim for the memory.

Just as before one proves

Lemma 232. *For $x \in [1 : \#E + 1]$:*

$$M_x = \begin{cases} M_1 & d = 0 \ \vee \ x \in [1 : xd] \\ \delta_M(M_1, lacc(n_{xd})) & d = 1 \ \wedge \ x \in [xd + 1 : \#E + 1] \end{cases}$$

Lemma 233.

$$M_1 = \Delta_M^{NE}(m(h^0), lacc) = m(h)$$
$$M_{\#E+1} = \Delta_M^{NE'}(m(h^0), lacc) = m(h')$$

The proof of

$$m(h') = \ell(c^{NS'}.m)$$

i.e., of eq. (73) is now almost the same as before, with the exception that the data access might come from the store buffer. We show with the following lemma that the access in hardware nevertheless is equal to the access in ISA. As usual this can only be shown if n is sufficiently large: if $isa(xd)$ is a processor step $isa(xd) = pseq(i)$, we need the induction hypothesis for the current cycle with $o = pseq(i)$ to conclude

$$t \sim_p i, \quad idacc^i_\sigma = idacc_\pi$$

Obviously we can apply this induction hypothesis only for $o = isa(xd) \leq n$.

Lemma 234.

$$n \geq isa(xd) \wedge d = 1 \; \to \; dacc(c^{isa(xd)}, s(isa(xd))) = lacc(n_{xd})$$

Proof. We split cases on the source of the data access.

- $/SB \wedge /sacc$: We only sketch this case. The access comes from the processor, because we have $/SB \wedge /sacc$. Thus we know that step $isa(xd)$ is a processor step executing instruction I_M

$$isa(xd) = n_p = pseq(I_M)$$

We obtain with the induction hypothesis for the current cycle for $o := isa(xd) \leq n$ that the hardware simulates the instruction and thus the data accesses are the same

$$t \sim_p i, \quad idacc_\sigma^i = idacc_\pi$$

and the claim follows because the instruction must be a *cas* or *load* and for these *idacc* and *dacc* are the same

$$lacc(n_{xd}) = idacc_\pi = idacc_\sigma^i = dacc(c^{isa(xd)})$$

- $SB \vee sacc$: Since there is a data access ending in the current cycle $(d = 1)$, the data cache is not busy, which with $SB \vee sacc$ implies a store buffer pop

$$/dca.mbusy, \quad sb.pop$$

We conclude by definition of n_{sb} that the ISA step is a store buffer step

$$isa(xd) = n_{sb}, \quad s(isa(xd)) \in \Sigma_{sb}$$

Thus the data access in ISA is the head of the store buffer in ISA

$$dacc(c^{isa(xd)}, s(isa(xd))).(a, data, bw) = hd(c^{isa(xd)}.sb)$$

Since there are no store buffer steps or store instructions between ISA steps NS and $isa(xd)$, the store buffer remains unchanged

$$c^{isa(xd)}.sb = c^{NS}.sb$$

By lemma 222 we conclude that this is the store buffer abstracted from hardware

$$c^{NS}.sb = aq(sb_\pi)$$

In hardware, the head of the store buffer is by lemma 215 used as the store buffer output *sb.out*, which in state SB is the access *sbacc* at the data port

$$sbacc = sb.out = hd(aq(sb_\pi))$$

The claim follows:

$$lacc(n_{xd}) = sbacc$$
$$= hd(aq(sb_\pi))$$
$$= hd(c^{isa(xd)}.sb)$$
$$= dacc(c^{isa(xd)}, s(isa(xd)))$$

$\square$

The main claim from eq. (73) follows:

$$m(h')$$

$$= M_{\#E+1} \qquad\qquad\qquad\qquad\qquad\qquad \text{L 233}$$

$$= \begin{cases} \delta_M(M_1, lacc(n_{xd})) & d = 1 \land \#E + 1 > xd \\ M_1 & \text{o.w.} \end{cases} \qquad \text{L 232}$$

$$= \begin{cases} \delta_M(m(h), lacc(n_{xd})) & d = 1 \land \#E + 1 > xd \\ m(h) & \text{o.w.} \end{cases} \qquad \text{L 233}$$

$$= \begin{cases} \delta_M(\ell(c^{NS}.m), dacc(c^{isa(xd)}, s(isa(xd)))) & d = 1 \land \#E + 1 > xd \\ \ell(c^{NS}.m) & \text{o.w.} \end{cases} \quad \text{IH, L 234}$$

$$= \begin{cases} \delta_M(\ell(c^{NS}.m), dacc(c^{isa(xd)}, s(isa(xd)))) & d = 1 \land NS' > isa(xd) \\ \ell(c^{NS}.m) & \text{o.w.} \end{cases} \quad \text{defn } isa$$

$$= \ell(c^{NS'}.m) \qquad\qquad\qquad\qquad\qquad\qquad \text{L 231}$$

10.5.7 Correctness for Pipeline Registers

The only thing that changes (other than using updated versions of lemmas) in this proof is the correctness of the memory output, which may now come from the store buffer. Let thus $i = I_M$ be the instruction in the memory stage which is executed in ISA step n and is committed and all previous instructions are live

$$i = I_M \land n = pseq(i) \land c(i)' \land lb(i)'$$

and which uses the memory output and is clocked

$$used[dmout]_\sigma^i \land ue_M$$

We need to show

$$dmout_\sigma^i \overset{!}{=} dmout_\pi$$

Since the memory output is used, the instruction must be a load or CAS which is allowed to execute

$$(l_\sigma^i \lor cas_\sigma^i) \land exec_\sigma^i$$

We now make the same case distinction we have done for the stepping function: either the instruction in hardware is a load which forwards from memory, or it is something else.

- $1.5 \wedge sb.f$: In this case the instruction is stepped in the first phase

$$pseq(I_M) \in [NS : N_{CMS})$$

Since steps in this phase never change the store buffer we have from the induction hypothesis for previous ISA step $\hat{n} := NS$

$$aq(sb_\pi) = c^{NS}.sb = c^{pseq(I_M)}.sb = sb_\sigma^{I_M}$$

We have with lemma 214 a forwarding hit

$$sbf(aq(sb_\pi), sb.fp)$$

The store buffer footprint is the footprint of the intermediate data access, which by the induction hypothesis is the same as that in ISA, which by lemma 210 is the ISA footprint

$$sb.fp = (idacc_\pi.a, br.5) = (idacc_\sigma^i.a, br_\sigma^i) = fp_\sigma^i$$

Thus we also have a forwarding hit in ISA

$$sbf(sb_\sigma^{I_M}, fp_\sigma^i)$$

With Invariant 4 from page 454 we obtain that the automaton is not in state *core*

$$/core$$

The claim follows with lemma 214

$$\begin{aligned} dmout_\sigma^{I_M} &= sbfout(sb_\sigma^{I_M}, fp_\sigma^i) \\ &= sbfout(aq(sb_\pi), sb.fp) \\ &= sb.fout && \text{L }214 \\ &= dmout_\pi && /core \end{aligned}$$

- $1.5 \wedge /sb.f \vee cas.5$: since the instruction is clocked we have no busy signal

$$/busy_l \wedge /busy_{cas}$$

By construction of the intermediate data access we have

$$idacc_\pi.r \vee idacc_\pi.cas$$

and conclude by definition of $busy_l$ and $busy_{cas}$ that the automaton is in state *core*

$$core$$

Therefore the automaton is not in state *SB*, the head of the store buffer is not popped, and the store buffer is not stepped

$$/SB, \quad /sb.pop, \quad \forall \hat{n} \in [NS:NS'). \, s(\hat{n}) \neq sb$$

We conclude that the store buffer has not been changed yet

$$sb_\sigma^i = c^{pseq(I_M)}.sb = c^{NS}.sb = aq(sb_\pi)$$

Like before we conclude that the store buffer footprint is the ISA footprint

$$sb.fp = fp_\sigma^i$$

but unlike before this now implies that there is no forwarding hit in ISA in case the instruction is a load

$$l_\sigma^i \wedge /sbf(sb_\sigma^i, fp_\sigma^i) \vee cas_\sigma^i$$

Since the compare-and-swap drains the store buffer, we know that the store buffer is empty in case of a cas

$$l_\sigma^i \wedge /sbf(sb_\sigma^i, fp_\sigma^i) \vee cas_\sigma^i \wedge sb_\sigma^i = \varepsilon$$

Thus there is no store buffer forwarding hit in either case

$$/sbf(sb_\sigma^i, fp_\sigma^i)$$

Completely analogous to previous chapters we obtain that the data cache output is equal to the old data memory output, and the claim follows

$$\begin{aligned} dmout_\sigma^{I_M} &= dmout_{old\sigma}^{I_M} \\ &= dca.pdout && \text{(old proof)} \\ &= dmout_\pi && core \end{aligned}$$

10.5.8 Proof Summary

Again (and fortunately) the processor correctness proof followed the established lines. Salient new features are:

- stepping function (sec. 10.5.1): basically the head of the store buffer and the data cache form a pipeline. If in a single cycle t a register of a pipeline is read (like a forwarding hit from the head of the store buffer) and *then (!)* at the end of the cycle the register content is advanced to the next pipeline stage, this detailed order of the hardware semantics has to be reflected in the local order of the ISA steps for cycle t: the ISA step belonging to the read has to be scheduled *before* the step advancing the pipeline. As before the order was technically defined by placing ISA steps in different *phases*.
- coupling relation (sec. 10.5.2): obviously it had to be extended to cover store buffers in hardware and ISA. Proving that they are maintained required tracing the evolution of the ISA over the various phases (sec. 10.5.5). This leads to intermediate store buffer contents $c.sb$ which do not have a direct counter part in hardware. In the detailed induction proofs we coupled these contents to a *ghost* signal $isb(h,e)$ of the hardware (sec 10.5.3).

- guard conditions: execution of certain instructions is only allowed with empty store buffers. This gives rise to new guard conditions. With the use of hazard signals this was completely easy to implement and the corresponding correctness proofs are straight forward (lemma 226).
- operating conditions: writes to the CMS now come from the store buffer. From previous proofs one knows that software condition SC_{ROM} implies the operating conditions for the old accesses (now called intermediate accesses). From this one infers the operating conditions for the accesses in the store buffer, simply because they are just copies of the old accesses (lemma 229).
- arbitration of access to the data cache: this requires to show certain invariants for the control automaton of the memory stage (sec 10.4.2).

10.6 A Simple Store Buffer Reduction Theorem

Obviously the programming model with store buffers is more complicated than that without. Luckily, in the absence of multi-core processing, store buffers are almost invisible due to forwarding and draining on partial hits. We will now prove a simple store buffer reduction theorem, which proves that for certain programs store buffers are completely invisible. That is, for every valid stepping function s of the ISA with store buffers, there is also a valid stepping function of an ISA without store buffers which reaches the same state[3].

In our single-processor design, they are always invisible during processor steps, as these steps forward from the store buffer; but they may be visible during instruction buffer steps and walk extension, as these steps bypass the store buffer.

In these cases, from the perspective of the processor, the stores in the store buffer have already been executed, but from the perspective of the other unit they have not. Thus if there is a write in the store buffer that writes to an address which is accessed by the instruction buffer or the MMU, the instruction buffer and the MMU will see values that are inconsistent with the view of the processor.

Therefore we will mitigate such situations by an extremely simple policy: we designate in each step n of the ISA computation a region $PTR_\uparrow(n)$ of memory as page tables and a region $CR_\uparrow(n)$ as code. MMUs are only allowed to fetch page table entries from the page table region, processors are only allowed to execute instructions from the code region. Writing to either $CR_\uparrow(n)$ or $PTR_\uparrow(n)$ is forbidden in step n. This still allows swapping of page tables and modification of code (including for loading code pages): these regions can be rearranged, but only when the store buffer is empty. Thus one can remove a set of addresses from the code region on *jisr*, then overwrite these addresses in the interrupt service routine, and add them back into the code region on *eret*. Similarly, in system mode the page table region $PTR_\uparrow(n)$ is usually empty, which allows the page fault handler to modify page tables of users.

Recall that the goal of this exercise is to make store buffers invisible. Thus if the conditions of the store buffer reduction theorem require us to prove something about

---

[3] As a matter of fact, in our ISA store buffers are invisible for all programs. Proving this fact is beyond the scope of this book and left as a difficult exercise.

the machine with store buffers — e.g., that the store buffers are empty at certain points in the program (where we change, e.g., the code region), we have not made store buffers invisible; we have merely shrunk the area where arguments about store buffers are visible to the conditions of the theorem. To make store buffers fully invisible, we need to formulate the conditions in terms of an ISA without store buffers.

In this ISA, asking whether store buffers are empty directly is meaningless, as there is no store buffer. Obviously store buffers are empty when executing a store buffer draining instruction, so that is the condition we will use to state (indirectly) the software conditions.

With the formalisms we have at our disposal the ISA without store buffers is quickly defined. In order to distinguish the ISA with store buffers from the ISA without store buffers, we use an up-arrow ($\uparrow$) as an index of every definition belonging to the ISA without store buffers, e.g.,

$$c_\uparrow^n, \quad pseq_\uparrow(i), \quad s_\uparrow(n), \quad eret_\uparrow^i$$

Essentially it is the ISA of chapter 9, with a single difference: the inclusion of the *fence* instruction. The conditions are now easily formulated. We assume that for every stepping function $s_\uparrow(n)$ of the machine without store buffers:

- There is a sequence $(PTR_\uparrow(n))$ of *page table regions*, which are sets of line addresses

$$PTR_\uparrow(n) \subseteq \mathbb{B}^{29}$$

such that MMUs only walk these page table addresses

$$s_\uparrow(n) = (tlb, wext, w) \rightarrow ptea(w).l \in PTR_\uparrow(n)$$

- There is a sequence $(CR_\uparrow(n))$ of *code regions*, which are sets of line addresses

$$CR_\uparrow(n) \subseteq \mathbb{B}^{29}$$

such that the processor only executes code from this region

$$n = pseq_\uparrow(i) \rightarrow ia_\uparrow^i.l \in CR_\uparrow(n)$$

- Processor steps do not write into either code or page table regions

$$n = pseq_\uparrow(i) \wedge write_\uparrow^i \rightarrow ea_\uparrow^i.l \notin CR_\uparrow(n) \cup PTR_\uparrow(n)$$

- Page table regions are only allowed to change during a store buffer draining instruction

$$PTR_\uparrow(n) \neq PTR_\uparrow(n+1) \rightarrow \exists i.\, n = pseq_\uparrow(i) \wedge (fence_\uparrow^i \vee jisr_\uparrow^i \vee eret_\uparrow^i \vee cas_\uparrow^i)$$

- Code regions are only allowed to change during an instruction that both drains the store buffer and flushes the instruction buffer

$$CR_\uparrow(n) \neq CR_\uparrow(n+1) \rightarrow \exists i.\, n = pseq_\uparrow(i) \wedge (jisr_\uparrow^i \vee eret_\uparrow^i)$$

With these conditions the store buffer reduction theorem is almost trivial. We run the ISA with store buffers and the ISA without store buffers in parallel using the same stepping order. We maintain the following invariants:

1. the store buffer of the ISA with store buffers can never include stores to the code or page table regions
2. memory of the ISA without store buffers stays consistent with forwarded memory of the ISA with store buffers
3. memory of the ISA without store buffers stays consistent with the memory of the ISA with store buffers on code and page table regions
4. spr, gpr, program counters, and the entire TLB are kept consistent between the two ISAs
5. instruction buffer entries from the code region are kept consistent between the two ISAs. Other instruction buffer entries may not be consistent but this does not harm us since they are never used.

There is only one minor technical detail: the ISA with store buffers has store buffer steps and the ISA without them does not. Thus for each ISA step n of the ISA with store buffers we define a corresponding ISA step $n_\uparrow$ obtained by simply subtracting the number of previous store buffer steps

$$n_\uparrow = n - \#\{m < n \mid s(m) \in \Sigma_{sb}\}$$

Note that this is monotonically increasing and that it increases at the non-store buffer steps:

Lemma 235.

- $n_\uparrow \leq (n+1)_\uparrow$
- $s(n) \notin \Sigma_{sb} \rightarrow (n+1)_\uparrow = n_\uparrow + 1$

Thus we can define a stepping function $s_\uparrow(n)$ obtained by stepping all components except for the store buffer in the same order as in $s(n)$ as follows:

$$s(n) \notin \Sigma_{sb} \quad \rightarrow \quad s_\uparrow(n_\uparrow) = s(n)$$

With these definitions we can easily state and prove the store buffer reduction theorem with the invariants mentioned above.

Lemma 236. *Let n be some ISA step of the ISA with store buffers. Then step $n_\uparrow$ is valid*

$$\gamma_\uparrow(c_\uparrow^{n_\uparrow}, s_\uparrow(n_\uparrow))$$

and all of the following invariants hold:

1. $sbe \in c^n.sb \rightarrow sbe.a \notin CR_\uparrow(n_\uparrow) \cup PTR_\uparrow(n_\uparrow)$
2. $c_\uparrow^{n_\uparrow}.m = fms(c^n.m, c^n.sb)$
3. $\forall a \in CR_\uparrow(n_\uparrow) \cup PTR_\uparrow(n_\uparrow) \quad \rightarrow \quad c_\uparrow^{n_\uparrow}.m(a) = c^n.m(a)$
4. $c_\uparrow^{n_\uparrow}.(spr, gpr, pc, dpc, ddpc, tlb) = c^n.(spr, gpr, pc, dpc, ddpc, tlb)$

5. $ibe \in c^n.ib \wedge ibe.a.l \in CR_\uparrow(n_\uparrow) \rightarrow ibe \in c_\uparrow^{n_\uparrow}.ib$

Proof. The proofs are almost completely straightforward, by joint induction on n. The base case is completely trivial. In the induction step $n \rightarrow n+1$, most claims follow simply from the software conditions and the fact that all components/memory addresses used in a step are coupled by the induction hypothesis. We only consider one example here, which is in the proof that step $n_\uparrow$ is valid if it is a processor step

$$s_\uparrow(n_\uparrow) \in \Sigma_p$$

the part that the instruction buffer entry used by the step exists in the instruction buffer. We obtain first that the instruction addresses used by the ISAs is the same with part 4 of the induction hypothesis

$$ia_\uparrow(c_\uparrow^{n_\uparrow}, s_\uparrow(n_\uparrow)) = c_\uparrow^{n_\uparrow}.ddpc = c^n.ddpc = ia(c^n, s(n))$$

Thus by the software conditions the instruction address (used by either ISA) is in the code region

$$ia(c^n, s(n)).l \in CR_\uparrow(n_\uparrow)$$

Since the stepping function s is valid, it obeys the guard condition and there is a matching instruction buffer entry

$$(ia(c^n, s(n)), s(n).I) \in c^n.ib$$

This instruction buffer entry is from the code region and by part 5 of the induction hypothesis must also exist in the instruction buffer of the ISA without store buffers

$$(ia(c^n, s(n)), s(n).I) \in c_\uparrow^{n_\uparrow}.ib$$

We conclude with the fact that both ISAs use the same instruction address and the definition of $s_\uparrow$ that this is the instruction buffer entry used in the ISA without store buffers

$$(ia(c^n, s(n)), s(n).I) = (ia_\uparrow(c_\uparrow^{n_\uparrow}, s_\uparrow(n_\uparrow)), s_\uparrow(n_\uparrow).I)$$

The claim follows

$$(ia_\uparrow(c_\uparrow^{n_\uparrow}, s_\uparrow(n_\uparrow)), s_\uparrow(n_\uparrow).I) \in c_\uparrow^{n_\uparrow}.ib$$

Most parts of the claim can be proven in a similar manner, except part 2. For this part of the claim there is a slightly technical case which is completely trivial for the other parts: the case where step $s(n)$ is a store buffer step

$$s(n) \in \Sigma_{sb}$$

and hence

$$n_\uparrow = (n+1)_\uparrow$$

In this case with part 2 of the induction hypothesis we reduce the claim to showing that the forwarded memory system does not change during store buffer steps

$$fms(c^{n+1}.m, c^{n+1}.sb) \overset{!}{=} fms(c^n.m, c^n.sb) \overset{IH}{=} c^n_\uparrow.m = c^{(n+1)}_\uparrow.m$$

We prove that the two forwarded memory configurations are the same by proving that they assign the same value to each byte address

$$z \in \mathbb{B}^{32}$$

We define for the sake of brevity

$$\hat{z} = (z.l, ba(z, 1)) \quad \text{and} \quad da = dacc(c^n, s(n))$$

Note that address, data, and byte-write signals of the data access come from the head of the store buffer

$$da.(a, data, bw) = c^n.sb[0] \tag{78}$$

We abbreviate

$$F = fms(c^{n+1}.m, c^{n+1}.sb)(z)$$

By the definition of fms this is equal to

$$F = \begin{cases} byte(\langle z.o \rangle, sbfout(c^{n+1}.sb, \hat{z})) & sbf(c^{n+1}.sb, \hat{z}) \\ c^{n+1}.m(z) & \text{otherwise} \end{cases}$$

By definition of δ the memory $c^{n+1}.m$ after ISA step n is obtained by performing the data access da of ISA step n

$$F = \begin{cases} byte(\langle z.o \rangle, sbfout(c^{n+1}.sb, \hat{z})) & sbf(c^{n+1}.sb, \hat{z}) \\ byte(\langle z.o \rangle, da.data) & z.l = da.a \wedge da.bw_{\langle z.o \rangle} \\ & \wedge /sbf(c^{n+1}.sb, \hat{z}) \\ c^n.m(z) & \text{o.w.} \end{cases}$$

By definition of δ the store buffer $c^{n+1}.sb$ after a store buffer step is the tail of the store buffer $c^n.sb$ before the step. Also, by the definition of $sbechit$ for the footprint $\hat{z}$ which accesses a single byte, the hit $z.l = da.a \wedge da.bw_{\langle z.o \rangle}$ is equivalent to a complete hit

$$F = \begin{cases} byte(\langle z.o \rangle, sbfout(tail(c^n.sb), \hat{z})) & sbf(tail(c^n.sb), \hat{z}) \\ byte(\langle z.o \rangle, da.data) & sbechit(da.(a, data, bw), \hat{z}) \\ & \wedge /sbf(c^{n+1}.sb, \hat{z}) \\ c^n.m(z) & \text{o.w.} \end{cases}$$

With eq. (78) we obtain that the complete hit in da is a complete hit in the head entry of the store buffer. Furthermore, in case there is a complete hit, the data of the data access/head store buffer entry is also the forwarding output one would obtain by forwarding the footprint $\hat{z}$ from the store buffer with the single entry $c^n.sb[0]$

$$sbechit(c^n.sb[0], \hat{z}) \rightarrow sbfout(c^n.sb[0], \hat{z}) = c^n.sb[0].data = da.data$$

Therefore

$$
F = \begin{cases} byte(\langle z.o \rangle, sbfout(tail(c^n.sb), \hat{z})) & sbf(tail(c^n.sb), \hat{z}) \\ byte(\langle z.o \rangle, sbfout(c^n.sb[0], \hat{z})) & sbechit(c^n.sb[0], \hat{z}) \\ & \wedge \, /sbf(c^{n+1}.sb, \hat{z}) \\ c^n.m(z) & \text{o.w.} \end{cases}
$$

With lemma 209 we can now combine the two cases with forwarding from parts of the store buffer into a single case forwarding from the complete store buffer

$$
F = \begin{cases} byte(\langle z.o \rangle, sbfout(tail(c^n.sb) \circ c^n.sb[0], \hat{z})) & sbf(tail(c^n.sb) \circ c^n.sb[0], \hat{z}) \\ c^n.m(z) & \text{o.w.} \end{cases}
$$

The claim follows with the definition of fms

$$
F = \begin{cases} byte(\langle z.o \rangle, sbfout(c^n.sb, \hat{z})) & sbf(c^n.sb, \hat{z}) \\ c^n.m(z) & \text{o.w.} \end{cases}
$$
$$
= fms(c^n.m, c^n.sb)(z)
$$

$\square$

10.7 Exercises

- The state *core* of the control automaton is redundant. Remove it and prove the correctness of the new design.
- Reconstruct the machine without using the improved store buffer, and analyse the delay of the machine.
- Optimize the basic store buffer. Hints: Replace first the length by a single bit register, indicating whether the queue is full. Then replace the head pointer and tail pointer by their unary encoding to get rid of the decoders in the RAM, and of the incrementers. Prove that your optimization is still correct and analyze its cost and delay.
- Prove that with the software conditions of section 10.6, instruction buffers are also invisible.
- One can prove that store buffers are always invisible, i.e., without any software conditions. Complete the following proof outline. This is not an easy exercise.
  - Distinguish between issued writes (which change the forwarded memory system) and executed writes (which change the memory) by defining predicates
$$
iw(n) \quad \text{and} \quad ew(n)
$$
for these writes

– Define a step number $p(n) \in \mathbb{N}$ which maps each step number n to an earlier step number in which the number of issued writes is equal to the number of executed writes

$$\#\{\, i < n \mid ew(i)\,\} = \#\{\, j < p(n) \mid iw(j)\,\}$$

– Prove that the forwarded memory system before ISA step $p(n)$ is the same as the actual memory before ISA step n

$$fms(c^{p(n)}.m, c^{p(n)}.sb) = c^n.m$$

– Define a reordered stepping function

$$r(n)$$

from the stepping function s in which every instruction buffer step and MMU step n has been reordered to position $p(n)$.
– Show that the stepping function $r_\uparrow(n)$ obtained by removing all store buffer steps from the stepping function r creates a computation $(c_\uparrow^m)$ of the ISA without store buffers which is equivalent to the original computation (c^n).

11

Multi-Core Processors

This section contains a moderately renovated proof of the main result of [KMP14] establishing the correctness of a multi-core processor with pipelined processor cores. The definition of multi-core ISA in section 11.1 is straight forward. The coupling of global ISA steps n with local processor steps via functions ic and $pseq$ is parameterized with processor indices q (section 11.2). Hooking a number P of processors into a cache memory system with $4q$ ports is completely straight forward (section 11.3). The correctness proof (section 11.4) follows established lines. In the definition of stepping functions, we have to interleave as before reading and writing memory accesses in the order provided by the sequentially consistent cache memory system. In contrast to previous machines the number d of writing memory accesses completed in any cycle t can now be anywhere between 0 and P. Thus we need some extra notation to specify the interleaving of d writing accesses with up to $P - d$ reading accesses in the same cycle (section 11.4.7).

11.1 Defining Basic Multi-Core ISA

As shown in [KMP14] this is amazingly straight forward. ISA configurations for single processors c are split into processor and memory part:

$$c = (c.p, c.m) \quad \text{with} \quad c.p = (c.p.(pc, dpc, ddpc, gpr, spr, tlb, sb))$$

The set of single core ISA configurations is denoted by K_{old}, the set of processor configurations by K_p and the set of memory configurations by K_m. From the sequential transition function δ_{old} with the set Σ_{old} of oracle inputs we extract functions

$$\delta_p : K_{old} \times \Sigma_{old} \to K_p \quad \text{and} \quad \delta_m : K_{old} \times \Sigma_{old} \to K_m$$

updating core and memory separately:

$$\delta_{old}(c, y) = (\delta_p(c, y), \delta_m(c, y))$$

A configuration c for a *multi-core* processor with P cores has components

© Springer Nature Switzerland AG 2020
P. Lutsyk et al. (Eds.): A Pipelined Multi-Core Machine, LNCS 9999, pp. 489–504, 2020.
https://doi.org/10.1007/978-3-030-43243-0_11

- $c.p : [0 : P-1] \rightarrow K_p$: the sequence of configurations of the processor cores.
- $c.m \in K_m$: the shared memory.

Now units of each processor are stepped non-deterministically. Thus we need to add to the old oracle inputs Σ_{old} the index of the processor that makes the step. Formally, the set of oracle inputs Σ now consists of inputs $x \in \Sigma$ of the following forms:

- for $x \in \Sigma_{p,q}$, i.e., core steps of processor q:

$$x = (p,q,I,e,w_I,w_E)$$

- for $x \in \Sigma_{tlb,q}$, i.e., for TLB steps of the MMU of processor q:

$$x = (tlb,q,winit,a) \quad \text{and} \quad x = (tlb,q,wext,w)$$

- for $x \in \Sigma_{ib,q}$, i.e., IB steps of processor q:

$$x = (ib,q,a)$$

- for $x \in \Sigma_{sb,q}$, i.e., for SB steps of processor q:

$$x = (sb,q)$$

In the obvious fashion we define for each of these oracle inputs $x \in \Sigma$ the processor

$$x.q = q \in [0 : P-1]$$

making the step and the old portion of the oracle input

$$x_{old} \in \Sigma_{old}$$

Multi-core computation are sequences (c^n) of multi-core configurations with the following two properties.

- Initially we require for all cores q

$$c^0.p(q).(ddpc,dpc,pc) = (0_{32}, 4_{32}, 8_{32})$$

- There is a stepping function

$$s : \mathbb{N} \rightarrow \Sigma$$

indicating the order in which units are stepped. Configuration $n+1$ is reached by stepping the unit indicated by oracle input $s(n)$. This affects the memory and the processor configuration of the processor $s(n).q$ to which the unit belongs. Other processor configurations are unaffected.

$$q = s(n).q \rightarrow c^{n+1}.(p(q),m) = \delta_{old}(c^n.(p(q),m),s(n)_{old})$$
$$q \neq s(n).q \rightarrow c^{n+1}.p(q) = c^n.p(q)$$

or, equivalently

$$c^{n+1}.p(q) = \begin{cases} \delta_p(c^n.(p(q),m),s(n)_{old}) & q = s(n).q \\ c^n.p(q) & q \neq s(n).q \end{cases}$$
$$c^{n+1}.m = \delta_m(c^n.(p(s(n).q),m),s(n)_{old})$$

As in previous chapters the exact stepping function s stemming from the implementation details of the system is hidden from the user. This stepping function is again constructed from the order seq of interleaving of the external cache memory system accesses. The only new difficulty in this chapter will be that this order may now include multiple data accesses $xd(1),\dots,xd(n)$ which modify memory in the same cycle.

11.2 Local ISA Configurations and Computations

We need to update the definition of $pseq$, which must now count processor steps of each processor individually. We add a parameter q and define

$$pseq(q,0) = \min\{n \mid s(n).q = q\}$$
$$pseq(q,i) = \min\{n \mid n > pseq(q,i-1) \wedge s(n).q = q\}$$

Thus, multi-core ISA configuration $c^{pseq(q,i)}$ is the configuration immediately before local step i. For global step numbers n we also count the number $ic(q,n)$ of instructions completed on processor q before global step n. This is the same as the number of times processor q was stepped locally before global step n.

$$ic(q,0) = 0$$
$$ic(q,n+1) = \begin{cases} ic(q,n)+1 & s(n).q = q \\ ic(q,n) & \text{otherwise} \end{cases}$$

Properties of these functions are stated in the following two lemmas (corresponding to lemmas 9.6 and 9.7 of [KMP14]).

Lemma 237.
$$ic(q,n) = \#\{j \mid j < n \wedge s(j).q = q\}$$

Lemma 238.

$$ic(q,n) = i \wedge s(n).q = q \quad \rightarrow \quad pseq(q,i) = n$$

To reuse predicates and functions $f(c_{old},x_{old})$ from the previous chapter, we overload notation and define the shorthand

$$f(c,x) = f(c.(p(x.q),m),x_{old})$$

For example, for the effective address we have

$$ea(c,x) = ea(c.(p(x.q),m),x_{old})$$

The local ISA configuration $c^{q,i}$ of processor q before local step i is defined as

$$c^{q,i} = c^{pseq(q,i)}.(p(q),m)$$

This replaces the definition of local hardware configurations $h^{q,i}$ of the sequential reference machine in Sect. 9.2.4 of [KMP14]. For signals, registers or register files X we now redefine as for single core pipelines

$$X_\sigma^{q,i} = \begin{cases} c^{q,i}.X & X \text{ is a component of configuration} \\ X(c^{pseq(q,i)}, s(pseq(q,i))) & X \text{ is a signal} \end{cases}$$

We get from the definition of $dmout(c,x)$ and lemma 47:

Lemma 239.

1. $$\ell(c^{pseq(q,i)+1}.m) = \delta_M(\ell(c^{pseq(q,i)}).m, dacc_\sigma^{q,i})$$
2. $$dacc_\sigma^{q,i}.(r, cas) \neq 00 \rightarrow dmout_\sigma^{q,i} = \ell(c^{pseq(q,i)}.m)(dacc_\sigma^{q,i}.a)$$

For ISA steps n we also abbreviate the data access executed in that step by

$$dacc_\sigma^n = dacc(c^n, s(n))$$

For this data access one easily shows:

Lemma 240.

$$\ell(c^{n+1}.m) = \delta_M(\ell(c^n.m), dacc_\sigma^n)$$

11.3 Hardware

11.3.1 Connecting Processors to the Cache Memory System

We use P pipelined processor cores with configurations $h.p(q)$, store buffers with configurations $h.sb(q)$, data resp. instruction MMUs with configurations $h.mmu_E(q)$ resp. $h.mmu_I(q)$, where $q \in [0 : P-1]$, and a cache memory system with $C = 4P$ ports and configuration $h.cms$. For signals, registers, ghost registers (scheduling functions) and register files X of processor numbers q and cycles t we use double indices q,t referring to the value of X during cycle t

$$X_\pi^{q,t} = \begin{cases} h^t.p(q).X & X \text{ is a register or register file} \\ h.p(q).X^t & X \text{ is a signal} \end{cases}$$

Analogously we abbreviate signals of store buffers and MMUs.

As usual we drop indices t in equations which hold for all cycles, for instance in equations defining connections of hardware signals. Each processor is now associated with its own four caches: for processor number q, these are

- instruction translate cache

$$itca(q) = ca(4q)$$

- instruction cache

$$ica(q) = ca(4q+1)$$

- effective address translate cache

$$etca(q) = ca(4q + 2)$$

- data cache

$$dca(q) = ca(4q + 3)$$

Connection of processor q with its caches is completely analogous to the sequential case. For the sake of illustration we show here only the connections of the data and instruction cache. For the instruction cache $ica(q)$ we connect:

$$ica(q).pacc = iacc_\pi^q$$
$$imout_\pi^q = ica(q).pdout$$
$$haz_2^q = ica(q).mbusy$$

For the data cache $dca(q)$ we connect:

$$dca(q).pacc = dacc_\pi^q$$
$$dmout.in_\pi^q = \begin{cases} dca(q).pdout & core^q \\ sb(q).fout \end{cases}$$
$$haz_6^q = dca(q).mbusy$$

11.4 Correctness

11.4.1 Straight Forward Generalizations of Arguments for Single Core Processors

Fortunately, the generalization of many parts of the correctness proof for pipelined single core machines is a simple bookkeeping exercise, where one just has to keep track with an extra index q what happens to which processor. Just as in pipelined single core machines, inputs to caches remain stable during accesses, and ending external accesses to the caches correspond exactly to update enable signals of stages IF and M. This is stated in the following three lemmas, which are the obvious counter parts of lemmas 81, 82 and 83 for multi-core machines:

Lemma 241.

- *For the instruction caches:*

$$ica(q).mbusy \to ia_\pi^q = ia_\pi^{q\prime}$$

- *For the data caches:*

$$dca(q).preq \land dca(q).mbusy \to /ue_{M-1}^q$$

Lemma 242.

1. *An active update enable signal in stage IF of processor q signals the end of read accesses to the instruction cache ica(q).*

$$ue_{IF}^{q,t} \quad \rightarrow \quad \exists k.\ e(4q+1,k) = t \wedge acc(4q+1,k).r$$

2. *An active update enable signal in stage M of processor q signals the end of an external accesses to the data cache dca(q).*

$$ue_M^{q,t} \wedge dca(q).preq^t \rightarrow \exists k.\ e(4q+3,k) = t$$

Lemma 243. *When a read, write or CAS access ends in cycle t, then the corresponding stage is updated unless it is stalled from the stage below.*

1. *For the instruction cache:*

$$e(4q+1,k) = t \wedge /stall_{ID}^{q,t} \quad \rightarrow \quad ue_{IF}^{q,t}$$

2. *For the data cache:*

$$e(4q+3,k) = t \quad \rightarrow \quad ue_M^{q,t}$$

For the translation caches the counter part of lemma 197 is

Lemma 244.

• *For the instruction translation cache:*

$$itca(q).mbusy \quad \rightarrow \quad mmu_I(q).pte = mmu_I(q).pte'$$

• *For the effective address translation cache:*

$$dtca(q).mbusy \quad \rightarrow \quad mmu_E(q).pte = mmu_E(q).pteq'$$

In order to state processor correctness for multi-core machines we use local scheduling functions $I(q,k,t)$ for the instruction in stage k of processor q in cycle t. In terms of local ghost registers I_k^q these scheduling functions are already defined. Thus we simply set

$$I(q,k,t) = I_k^{q,t}$$

Similarly the ghost predicate $wf^{q,t}$ for well-formedness of the local pipelines is already defined and we have

Lemma 245. *The pipelines of all processors are always well formed.*

$$\forall q.\ wf^{q,t}$$

Proof. For every processor q the definition of the new scheduling functions I_k^q depends only on the full bits and update enable bits for this processor. Thus, in order to prove $wf^{q,t}$ simply rename

$$I_k^{q,t} = I_k^t,\ ue_k^{q,t} = ue_k^t,\ full_k^{q,t} = full_k^t$$

and apply lemma 73 to conclude wf^t for all t. Then rename again.   □

11.4.2 Liveness and Committed

We need to add indices q to the definitions of $c(i)$, $live(i)$, and $lb(i)$ in the obvious way:

$$
\begin{aligned}
c(i)^{q,t} &= \forall u \geq t,\, k.\ rbr_k^{q,u} \rightarrow I_R^{q,u} > i \\
live(j)^{q,t} &\equiv \forall u \geq t,\, k.\ rfull_{k-1}^{q,u} \wedge I_k^{q,u} = j \quad \rightarrow \quad \exists v \geq u.\ I_k^{q,v} = j \wedge ue_k^{q,v} \\
lb(i)^{q,t} &= \forall j < i.\ live(i)^{q,t}
\end{aligned}
$$

11.4.3 Sampling Signals from Outside the Pipeline

We need to add indices q also to the sampling times of signals e, I, w_I, w_E in straightforward fashion:

$$
\begin{aligned}
t_i^q(e) &= \varepsilon\left\{ t \mid c^{q,t}(I_{M-1}^{q,t}) \wedge I_{M-1}^{q,t} = i \wedge ue_{M-1}^{q,t} \right\} \\
t_i^q(w_I) &= \varepsilon\left\{ t \mid c^{q,t}(I_{IT}^{q,t}) \wedge I_{IT}^{q,t} = i \wedge ue_{IT}^{q,t} \right\} \\
t_i^q(w_E) &= \varepsilon\left\{ t \mid c^{q,t}(I_{ET}^{q,t}) \wedge I_{ET}^{q,t} = i \wedge ue_{ET}^{q,t} \right\} \\
t_i^q(I) &= \varepsilon\left\{ t \mid c^{q,t}(I_{IF}^{q,t}) \wedge I_{IF}^{q,t} = i \wedge ue_{IF}^{q,t} \right\}
\end{aligned}
$$

11.4.4 Ordering Instructions by the Cycle they Pass The Memory Stage

We run the hardware computation (h^t) and the ISA computation (c^i) of the multi-core machine in parallel. From the hardware computation (h^t) we construct cycle by cycle a stepping function s for multi-core ISA. In the presence of a violation of the operating condition, we now need to deal during emergency braking with the fact that multiple processors might be violating the operating condition. As before it will be easy to show that the operating condition is not violated by the access generated by ISA step NS^t, but of course only one of the processors can be stepped in the single step NS^t.

From all the processors which are generating an access that violates the operating conditions, we simply step the processor with the lowest index q. We will later show by contradiction that this processor with index q does not violate the operating conditions. Clearly that will imply that no processor can violate the operating conditions.

Thus in the presence of an operating condition violation we define

$$
vopc^t \rightarrow ns^t = 1 \wedge s(NS^t) = (p, q, I_\pi^{q,t_i^q(I)}, e_\pi^{q,t_i^q(e)},
$$
$$
mmu_I(q).wout^{t_i^q(w_I)}, mmu_E(q).wout^{t_i^q(w_E)})
$$

where q is the lowest index of a processor violating the operating conditions:

$$
q = \min\left\{ q \mid dca(q).preq^t \wedge dca(q).pacc^t.a[28:r] = 0^{29-r} \right.
$$
$$
\left. \wedge\, dca(q).pacc^t.bw \neq 0^8 \right\}
$$

In the absence of a violation of the operating conditions, we split as in chapter 10 each cycle into three phases. Completely analogous to before we can define step counts

$$nfi^{q,t}, \quad nac^{q,t}, \quad nrem^{q,t}$$

for each processor q. The total step counts are then the sum of these step counts:

$$nfi^t = \sum_q nfi^{q,t}, \quad \dots$$

The boundaries between the phases are then defined completely analogous to before as

$$N^t_{CMS} = NS^t + nfi^t, \quad N^t_{REM} = N^t_{CMS} + nac^t, \quad NS^{t+1} = N^t_{REM} + nrem^t$$

The definition of steps in each phase is also completely analogous to before. Instead of step numbers $n_p, n_{tlbI}, n_{tlbE}, \dots$ we now have step numbers

$$n^q_p, \quad n^q_{tlbI}, \quad n^q_{tlbE}, \quad \dots$$

with processor indices. Each of these step numbers n^q_X is in the phase we defined for the corresponding step number n_X for the single-core processor in chapter 10

$$
\begin{aligned}
ue^{q,t}_M \wedge exec.(M-1)^{q,t} \wedge l.(M-1)^{q,t} \wedge sb(q).f^t & \rightarrow & n^q_p \in [NS^t : N^t_{CMS}) \\
mmu_X(q).winit^t & \rightarrow & n^q_{tlbX} \in [NS^t : N^t_{CMS}) \\
ue^{q,t}_M \wedge exec.(M-1)^{q,t} \wedge (l.(M-1)^{q,t} & & \\
\wedge /sb(q).f^t \vee cas.(M-1)^{q,t}) & \rightarrow & n^q_p \in [N^t_{CMS} : N^t_{REM}) \\
mmu_X(q).w.ce^t \wedge /mmu_X(q).winit^t & \rightarrow & n^q_{tlbX} \in [N^t_{CMS} : N^t_{REM}) \\
ue^{q,t}_{IF} & \rightarrow & n^q_{ib} \in [N^t_{CMS} : N^t_{REM}) \\
sb(q).pop^t & \rightarrow & n^q_{sb} \in [N^t_{CMS} : N^t_{REM}) \\
ue^{q,t}_M \wedge /(exec.(M-1)^{q,t} \wedge & & \\
(l.(M-1)^{q,t} \vee cas.(M-1)^{q,t})) & \rightarrow & n^q_p \in [N^t_{REM} : NS^{t+1})
\end{aligned}
$$

As before we define

$$isa^t(x) = N^t_{CMS} + x - 1$$

Note that local sequential indices x now include accesses of multiple processors. The access (i^t_x, k^t_x) with local sequential index x accesses port

$$i^t_x \in [0 : 4P)$$

From this port we can easily derive the processor q to which the access belongs by dividing by four. If a cas or a load which can not forward from the store buffer leaves the pipeline processor q generates the access at the data port $4q + 3$

$$
\begin{aligned}
& ue^{q,t}_M \wedge exec.(M-1)^{q,t} \wedge (cas.(M-1)^{q,t} \vee l.(M-1)^{q,t} \wedge /sb(q).hit^t) \\
& \rightarrow n^q_p = NS^t + \varepsilon \left\{ x \mid i^t_x = 4q + 3 \right\} - 1
\end{aligned}
$$

If on the other hand the store buffer pops, the store buffer generates this access

$$sb(q).pop^t \rightarrow n^q_{sb} = NS^t + \varepsilon\left\{x \mid i^t_x = 4q+3\right\} - 1 = isa^t(xd)$$

When a MMU of processor q clocks the walk register and does not perform a walk initialization, it generates the access at its port

$$mmu_I(q).w.ce^t \wedge /mmu_I(q).winit^t \rightarrow n^q_{tlbI} = NS^t + \varepsilon\left\{x \mid i^t_x = 4q+0\right\} - 1$$
$$mmu_E(q).w.ce^t \wedge /mmu_E(q).winit^t \rightarrow n^q_{tlbE} = NS^t + \varepsilon\left\{x \mid i^t_x = 4q+2\right\} - 1$$

Finally, if the instruction fetch stage of processor q is updated ($ue^{q,t}_{IF}$) the instruction buffer generates the access at the instruction port of processor q

$$n^q_{ib} = NS^t + \varepsilon\left\{x \mid i^t_x = 4q+1\right\} - 1$$

The oracle inputs used for these steps are also defined analogously to before

$$ue^{q,t}_M \quad \rightarrow \quad s(n^q_p) = (p, q, I^{q,t^q_i(I)}_\pi, e^{q,t^q_i(e)}_\pi,$$
$$mmu_I(q).wout^{t_i(w_I)}, mmu_E(q).wout^{t_i(w_E)})$$

$$mmu_I(q).w.ce^t \quad \rightarrow \quad s(n^q_{tlbI}) = \begin{cases} (tlb, q, winit, ia^{q,t}_\pi.pa) & mmu_I(q).winit^t \\ (tlb, wext, mmu_I(q).w^t) & \text{o.w.} \end{cases}$$

$$mmu_E(q).w.ce^t \quad \rightarrow \quad s(n^q_{tlbE}) = \begin{cases} (tlb, q, winit, ea^{q,t}_\pi.pa) & mmu_E(q).winit^t \\ (tlb, wext, mmu_E(q).w^t) & \text{o.w.} \end{cases}$$

$$ue^{q,t}_{IF} \quad \rightarrow \quad s(n^q_{ib}) = (ib, q, ia^{q,t}_\pi)$$
$$sb(q).pop^t \quad \rightarrow \quad s(n^q_{sb}) = (sb, q)$$

11.4.5 Software Conditions and Correctness Statement

As in the chapters 8 to 10 the only software condition is SC_{ROM}, which states that there must be no writes to the ROM region. Here we need to extract in steps triggered by an oracle input $x \in \Sigma_p$ of processor $x.q$ the configuration

$$c.(p(x.q), m) \in K_{old}$$

used by the transition of processor $x.q$ and require that it does not write into the ROM region

$$SC_{ROM}(c, x) \leftrightarrow x \in \Sigma_p \wedge write(c.(p(x.q), m), x) \rightarrow ea(c.(p(x.q), m), x) \geq 2^{r+3}$$

In the correctness statement indices need to be added for the processor simulation relation and several other places where $pseq$, lb, etc, are used.

$$t \sim^q_p i \equiv \forall k, R. \ I^{q,t}_k = i \wedge (R \in reg(k) \wedge vis(R)$$
$$\vee \ R \in reg(k-1) \wedge /vis(R) \wedge rfull^{q,t}_{k-1} \wedge used[R]^i)$$
$$\rightarrow \ R^{q,t}_\pi = R^i_\sigma$$

For the simulation relation for components outside the pipeline, indices only need to be added to the portions about the TLBs and store buffers

$$
\begin{aligned}
t \sim_m n \quad \equiv \quad & n = NS^t \rightarrow m(h^t) = \ell(c^n.m) \wedge opc^t \\
& \wedge \ aq(sb(q)_\pi^t) = c^n.p(q).sb \\
& \wedge \ walks(mmu_I(q)^t) \cup walks(mmu_E(q)^t) \subseteq c^n.tlb(q) \\
& \wedge \ \forall \hat{n} < n.\ \gamma(c^{\hat{n}}, s(\hat{n}))
\end{aligned}
$$

The correctness statement is then:

Lemma 246. *There is an initial configuration c^0 satisfying*

$$
sim(h^0.(p(q),m), c^0.(p(q),m)) \quad \text{for all } q \in P
$$

in which instruction buffers and TLBs are empty

$$
c^0.ib(q) = c^0.tlb(q) = \emptyset
$$

and the store buffers are also empty

$$
c^0.p(q).sb = \varepsilon
$$

Furthermore: if for the computation (c^n) with stepping function $s(n)$ extracted from hardware and initial configuration c^0 satisfies for all n the software condition $SC_{ROM}(c^n, s(n))$ provided the stepping function $s(n)$ has a valid initial segment until n

$$
\forall n.\ (\forall m \leq n.\ \gamma(c^m, s(m))) \ \rightarrow \ SC_{ROM}(c^n, s(n))
$$

then for all n and t:

- *If n is a step of processor q executing instructions i which is committed and only has live instructions before it*

$$
n = pseq(q,i) \wedge c(i)^{q,t} \wedge lb(i)^{q,t}
$$

then hardware in cycle t simulates instruction i

$$
t \sim_p^q i
$$

and each part of the guard condition holds if instruction i passed the corresponding stage

$$
(i < I_{IF}^{q,t} \rightarrow \gamma_I^{q,i}) \wedge (i < I_{IT}^{q,t} \rightarrow \gamma_{wI}^{q,i}) \wedge (i < I_{ET}^{q,t} \rightarrow \gamma_{wE}^{q,i})
$$

- *Hardware simulates in cycle t the non-pipelined components of ISA step n*

$$
t \sim_m n
$$

11.4.6 Induction Step

In almost all proofs nothing changes apart from the inclusion of processor indices. The only difference beyond that concerns the CMS, where due to the additional data ports multiple data accesses can end in the same cycle. Thus one needs to show 1) answers produced by the memory system are still consistent with ISA and 2) the final memory abstraction $m(h')$ is equal to the line-addressable memory $\ell(c^{NS'}.m)$.

In these proofs we only need the induction hypothesis for the current cycle, which states for all $o \leq n$:

$$t \sim_m o \,\wedge\, (o = pseq(q,i) \wedge c(i)^{q,t} \wedge lb(i)^{q,t}$$
$$\to t \sim_p i \wedge (i > I_{IF}^{q,t} \to \gamma_I^{q,t}) \wedge (i > I_{IT}^{q,t} \to \gamma_{wI}^{q,t}) \wedge (i > I_{ET} \to \gamma_{wE}^{q,t})) \tag{79}$$

11.4.7 Numbering Accesses to Data Ports

With the inclusion of multiple data ports of course more than one access can modify memory in each hardware cycle. The data port of processor q has index $4q + 3$. Thus the set of accesses to a data port is defined by

$$D = \{\, (i,k) \in E \mid \exists q.\ i = 4q + 3 \,\}$$

The number of such accesses is

$$d = \#D \leq P$$

Recall that in the notation of chapter 6 the port accessed by the access with local sequential index $x \in [1 : \#E]$ is denoted by i_x. Thus we can enumerate the local sequential indices of these accesses in the sequential order given by the cache memory system by

$$xd(1) = \min\{\, x \mid \exists q.\ i_x = 4q + 3 \,\}$$
$$xd(i+1) = \min\{\, x > xd(i) \mid \exists q.\ i_x = 4q + 3 \,\}$$

Furthermore we defined a sequence (M_x) of memories obtained by performing all accesses in the linear order before the access with global index $NE + x - 1$

$$M_x = \Delta_M^{NE+x-1}(m(h^0), lacc)$$

Recall that for local sequential indices $x \in [1 : \#E]$ we have defined

$$n_x = NE + x - 1$$

to be that global index. The definition above however also works for $x = \#E + 1$, which is not the local sequential index of an access but rather identifies the global index of the memory configuration $M_{\#E+1}$ which is obtained by performing all accesses that complete in the current cycle. That the sequence (M_x) of memories changes only at the data accesses $xd(i)$ is proven in the following lemma, which is a trivial extension of lemma 87.

Lemma 247.

$$M_x = \begin{cases} M_1 & d = 0 \vee x \leq xd(1) \\ \delta_M(M_{xd(i)}, lacc(n_{xd(i)})) & d \geq i \wedge i = \max\{i \mid xd(i) < x\} \end{cases}$$

Proof. By a straightforward induction on x. The base case $x = 1$ is trivial. In the induction step $x \to x+1$ we have from the definition of M_{x+1}

$$M_{x+1} = \delta_M(M_x, lacc(n_x))$$

We split cases on whether x is a data access.

- $\forall q.\ i_x \neq 4q + 3$: then the access is not attempting to modify memory and x is not some $xd(i)$

$$lacc(n_x).(w, cas) = (0,0) \quad \text{and} \quad \forall i.\ xd(i) \neq x$$

  The access does not change memory and the claim follows with the induction hypothesis

$$M_{x+1} = M_x$$

$$= \begin{cases} M_1 & d = 0 \vee x \leq xd(1) \\ \delta_M(M_{xd(i)}, lacc(n_{xd(i)})) & d \geq i \wedge i = \max\{i \mid xd(i) < x\} \end{cases} \quad \text{IH}$$

$$= \begin{cases} M_1 & d = 0 \vee x+1 \leq xd(1) \\ \delta_M(M_{xd(i)}, lacc(n_{xd(i)})) & d \geq i \wedge i = \max\{i \mid xd(i) < x+1\} \end{cases}$$

- $i_x = 4q + 3$: then the access is some data access

$$x = xd(i) \wedge i \leq d$$

  Obviously i is the index of the last data access before $x + 1$

$$i = \max\{i \mid xd(i) < x+1\}$$

  The claim follows

$$M_{x+1} = \delta_M(M_x, lacc(n_x))$$
$$= \delta_M(M_{xd(i)}, lacc(n_{xd(i)}))$$

$\square$

That also in ISA only data accesses change memory is stated in the straightforward extension of lemma 230.

Lemma 248. *Assume $o \in [NS : NS']$ and $o \leq n$. Then*

$$(\forall i.\ o \neq isa(xd(i))) \to \ell(c^{o+1}.m) = \ell(c^o.m)$$

The proof follows the lines of the previous proof, with the only differences being the processor and access indices. We omit this proof. From this lemma one concludes in a straightforward way:

Lemma 249. *Assume* $o \in [NS : NS']$ *and* $o \leq n$. *Then*

$$\ell(c^o.m) = \begin{cases} \ell(c^{NS}.m) & d = 0 \vee o \leq isa(xd(1)) \\ \delta_M(\ell(c^{isa(xd(i))}.m), dacc_\sigma^{isa(xd(i))}) & d \geq i \wedge i = \max\{i \mid isa(xd(i)) < o\} \end{cases}$$

The proof is omitted. The straightforward extension of lemma 234 is stated in

Lemma 250.

$$n \geq isa(xd(i)) \wedge d \geq i \rightarrow dacc_\sigma^{isa(xd(i))} = lacc(n_{xd(i)})$$

and a straightforward induction on i shows:

Lemma 251.
$$n \geq xd(i) \wedge d \geq i \rightarrow \ell(c^{isa(xd(i))}.m) = M_{xd(i)}$$

With this lemma the remaining two parts of the correctness proof can be shown as before. We show in detail only two claims: first we show that the memory abstraction $m(h')$ after the cycle completes is equal to the line addressable memory $\ell(c^{NS}.m)$ in ISA after we have executed $n = NS'$ steps.

$$
\begin{aligned}
&m(h') \\
&= M_{\#E+1} &\text{L 233} \\
&= \begin{cases} M_1 & d = 0 \vee \#E + 1 \leq xd(1) \\ \delta_M(M_{xd(i)}, lacc(n_{xd(i)})) & d \geq i \wedge i = \max\{i \mid xd(i) < \#E + 1\} \end{cases} &\text{L 247} \\
&= \begin{cases} \ell(c^{NS}.m) & d = 0 \vee NS' \leq isa(xd(1)) \\ \delta_M(\ell(c^{isa(xd(i))}.m), & d \geq i \\ \quad dacc_\sigma^{isa(xd(i))}) & \wedge i = \max\{i \mid isa(xd(i)) < NS'\} \end{cases} &\begin{array}{l}\text{IH,} \\ \text{L 251, 250}\end{array} \\
&= \ell(c^{NS'}.m) &\text{L 249}
\end{aligned}
$$

Next we show that the reads from the memory are correct. Steps that read from the memory are instruction buffer steps, processor steps executing loads that do not forward from the store buffer, and MMU steps that perform walk extensions. For all of these the proof is nearly the same. We show the proof only for instruction buffer steps. Assume

$$s(n) \in \Sigma_{ib,q}$$

The instruction buffer step fetches from the line with address $ia_\pi^q.l$

$$s(n) = (ib, q, ia_\pi^q)$$

This step generates an access

$$(4q+1,k) \in E$$

at the instruction cache (with port index $4q+1$) which ends in the current cycle. This access has some local index x and by definition of isa this access is generated by ISA step n

$$isa(x) = n_{ib}^q = n \tag{80}$$

This access uses the line address of the instruction address

$$acc(4q+1,k).a = pacc(4q+1).a = ia_\pi^q.l$$

The data from the instruction cache is the data in the memory in ISA configuration c^n at that address

$$
\begin{aligned}
&ica.pdout \\
&= \Delta_M^{n_x}(m(h^0), lacc)(acc(4q+1,k).a) &&\text{L 78}\\
&= M_x(ia_\pi.l)
\end{aligned}
$$

$$
= \begin{cases} \delta_M(M_{xd(i)}, lacc(n_{xd(i)}))(ia_\pi.l) & d \ge i \wedge i = \max\{i \mid x > xd(i)\} \\ M_1(ia_\pi.l) & \text{otherwise} \end{cases} \qquad \text{L 247}
$$

$$
= \begin{cases} \delta_M(\ell(c^{isa(xd(i))}.m), & d \ge i \wedge i = \max\{i \mid x > xd(i)\} \\ \quad lacc(n_{xd(i)}))(ia_\pi.l) \\ \ell(c^{NS}.m)(ia_\pi.l) & \text{otherwise} \end{cases} \qquad \text{L 251}
$$

$$
= \begin{cases} \delta_M(\ell(c^{isa(xd(i))}.m), & d \ge i \wedge i = \max\{i \mid x > xd(i)\} \\ \quad dacc_\sigma^{isa(xd(i))})(ia_\pi.l) \\ \ell(c^{NS}.m)(ia_\pi.l) & \text{otherwise} \end{cases} \qquad \text{L 250}
$$

$$
= \begin{cases} \delta_M(\ell(c^{isa(xd(i))}.m), & d \ge i \wedge i = \max\{i \mid isa(x) > isa(xd(i))\} \\ \quad dacc_\sigma^{isa(xd(i))})(ia_\pi.l) \\ \ell(c^{NS}.m)(ia_\pi.l) & \text{otherwise} \end{cases} \qquad \text{defn } isa
$$

$$
= \begin{cases} \delta_M(\ell(c^{isa(xd(i))}.m), & d \ge i \wedge i = \max\{i \mid n > isa(xd(i))\} \\ \quad dacc_\sigma^{isa(xd(i))})(ia_\pi.l) \\ \ell(c^{NS}.m)(ia_\pi.l) & \text{otherwise} \end{cases} \qquad \text{E 80}
$$

$$
= \ell(c^n.m)(ia_\pi.l) \qquad \text{L 249}
$$

11.5 Instruction Buffer Reduction

Recall that instruction buffers can become invisible under certain conditions. For a single core machine, instruction buffers are invisible if one fetches from an instruction address that has been modified only if there is an *eret* step between the modification and the fetching (cf. section 8.4). This ensures that the stale copy of the instruction, which has been overwritten, is not in the instruction buffer. The only instruction that can be in the instruction buffer must be the up-to-date one.

This condition can be easily extended to multi-core processors: instruction buffers are invisible if one fetches from an instruction address that has been modified only if there is an *eret* step *of the fetching processor* between the modification and the fetching. As before this ensures that the fetching processor must fetch the up-to-date version of the instruction and can not have a stale buffered copy in its instruction buffer.

Stating this condition formally and proving the instruction buffer reduction theorem is an easy exercise. Programming such that this condition is satisfied, would currently be incredibly cumbersome. Clearly we have to synchronize processors when shared code is updated, and this could currently only be done by polling shared variables, i.e., if the computation of processors would proceed in rounds separated by synchronization points. It would be much preferable if the updating processor could send an interrupt to the processor which will later fetch the updated instruction, and thereby cause it to empty its instruction buffer. In the next chapter we will introduce advanced programmable interrupt controllers (APICs) that address this gap. With APICs, processors can send interrupts to other processors. With these APICs, it is not hard to write programs that satisfy the condition stated above. Some subtlety remains, as the interrupts sent with the APIC are not taken immediately. Interrupted processors need to confirm that they took the interrupt with a protocol built on top of shared variables. The details on how to do this go beyond the scope of this book.

We now state the condition formally: let ISA step n (potentially) modify an address which is fetched from by instruction i of processor q in a later global step

$$dacc_\sigma^n.(w,cas) \neq 00 \land dacc_\sigma^n.a = ia_\sigma^{q,j}.l \land n < pseq(q,j)$$

Then there must be an instruction j of processor q that empties the instruction buffer (by executing an *eret*) and which has a global step number between the writing and fetching steps

$$\exists j.\ eret_\sigma^{q,j} \land pseq(q,j) \in [n : pseq(q,i))$$

With this condition, the instruction buffer reduction can be proven just like before.

11.6 Exercises

1. Prove an instruction buffer reduction theorem for the multi-core processor. Hint: consider for each processor q the code region $CR(q,n)$ consisting of all addresses from which the processor will fetch between step n and its next *eret* instruction

$$CR(q,n) = \{ ia_\sigma^{q,i} \mid pseq(q,i) \geq n$$
$$\land (\forall j.\ pseq(q,j) \in [n : pseq(q,i)) \rightarrow \neg eret_\sigma^{q,j}) \}$$

and show for all n: 1) step n does not modify addresses in this code region and 2) the instruction buffer has the most up-to-date data for all addresses in the code region, i.e.,

$$(ia, I) \in c^n.p(q).ib \land ia \in CR(q, n) \;\rightarrow\; I = c^n.m_4(ia)$$

Conclude from this that the instruction buffer is invisible, i.e., that fetching from memory would yield the same instruction as using the instruction buffer entry.

12

Advanced Programmable Interrupt Controllers (APICs)

So far external interrupts were treated as external signals of the machine, which were simply turned on in the ISA computation based on the signal sampled in hardware. We now add an advanced programmable interrupt controller (APIC) to each processor, which controls the external event signal of that processor. In hardware, the external event signals are no longer an external signal coming from outside of the machine, but are now computed inside the machine by the APIC. In ISA, the external event remains an input of the transition function, but it is now controlled by the APIC through guard conditions.

The local APICs adds the following crucial features to our ISA:

- 256 distinct external interrupts. The APIC records in an interrupt request register (IRR) which interrupts are currently being requested, and in an in-service register (ISR) which interrupts are already being serviced by the processor. As with the internal interrupts, each of these interrupts is assigned a priority based on its number (lower numbers have higher priority), and the APIC raises the external event signal only if an interrupt is requested which has a higher priority than any interrupt that is currently being serviced.

  In ISA this is expressed as a guard condition stating that the external event can only be turned on while such an interrupt exists.

  When the interrupt is taken (i.e., on *jisr*), it is as a side effect removed from the IRR and added to the ISR. However the interrupt is not removed from the ISR as a side effect of executing the *eret* instruction; instead it has to be cleared explicitly by the processor by writing to a fixed memory location called the end-of-interrupt (EOI) port.

- soft resets. In addition to the normal 256 external interrupts, two new types of interrupts are added to facilitate soft reset: INIT and SIPI interrupts. INIT interrupts are executed *by the processor* and turn the processor off, SIPI interrupts are executed *by the APIC* (as the processor is turned off) to turn it back on.

  Thus INIT/SIPI usually come in pairs, and between INIT and SIPI the interrupted processor can not make any steps. A request for INIT/SIPI is stored in registers *initrr* resp. *sipirr* of the APIC. Analogous to the external event *e* we in-

P. Lutsyk et al. (Eds.): A Pipelined Multi-Core Machine, LNCS 9999, pp. 505–563, 2020.
https://doi.org/10.1007/978-3-030-43243-0_12

troduce a new input *init* of the transition function coming from the APIC which causes the INIT interrupt to be taken. In addition to turning the processor off, this interrupt also causes a regular *jisr* and hence initializes the processor by clearing the mode bit, setting the program counters to the start of the interrupt service routine, and raising the exception cause bit for the INIT interrupt. The SIPI step of the APIC only restarts the processor and does not change any internal registers. Consequently the exception cause is still the same as after the INIT step, and the interrupt service routine can tell that it was restarted by inspecting the bit for the INIT interrupt.

Interrupts other than INIT and SIPI are called *fixed interrupts* because they jump to the fixed address 0_{32}, whereas INIT/SIPI interrupts normally (e.g., in x86) jump to an address determined by the interrupt. For the sake of simplicity we jump to the fixed address 0_{32} also for INIT interrupts.

- sending interrupts to other processors. These interrupts are controlled through a fixed memory location called the interrupt command register (ICR), which determines the target(s) and the interrupt to be sent. In ISA sending an interrupt consists of two separate steps: 1) a step of the processor issuing the command by writing into the ICR and 2) a non-deterministic step of the APIC which executes the command and sends the interrupt. We do not guarantee any bounds on the number of ISA steps between issuing the command and executing the command, only that each command is eventually executed.

  Through this mechanism the boot processor — which is the only processor turned on at startup — can turn on the remaining processors once it has completed the initialization, by sending a SIPI to all other processors. Note that after reset the exception cause of all processors has a raised first bit (indicating reset), and SIPI does not affect the exception cause; thus non-boot processors can distinguish between a soft reset and a hard reset by inspecting the exception cause.

The full specification of an ISA with interrupt controllers is given in section 12.1. The salient features are

- a simple mechanism for mapping memory addresses to registers of the local APIC. This is also known as memory mapped I/O. Thus processors q now see a memory system with i) the cache memory system CMS, ii) the local store buffer $sb(q)$ and iii) the local APIC $APIC(q)$.
- the delivery of an inter-processor interrupt to one or more other interrupt controllers $APIC(q)$ is a separate *IPI delivery step* of the ISA. The subsequent external interrupt due to the activation of signal $e(q)$ by $APIC(q)$ then happens in a later processor step.
- the processors command their APICs to send IPIs by writing to an interrupt command register *ICR* of the APIC. Writes to the APIC can either come from the local store buffer or – in case of CAS instructions, which drain the store buffer – directly from the local processor. The request to deliver an IPI is activated by setting the delivery status bit *ICR.ds* to 1. A new software condition SC_{APIC} forbids writes to the APIC while this bit is on *in the local forwarded memory system*. i.e. write instructions to the APIC are forbidden both i) if the local delivery status is

1 in the APIC itself or ii) if an entry which will turn it on has been delivered to the local store buffer.

For the hardware constructed in section 12.2 , the following changes are necessary.

- construction of local APICs
- a simple mechanism for mapping memory addresses to registers of the local APIC. This is also known as memory mapped I/O. Because APIC registers have different lengths and addressing within the APIC is by words, this involves some fiddling with bits.
- addition of an interrupt bus for delivery of interprocessor interrupts (IPI), through which APICs are connected to each other. We use –for the first time – the construction from section 3.5. Not surprisingly we use the delivery status bits $ICR.ds$ as request signals to the bus arbiter.
- connection of APICs to the processor core. In particular we have to i) drain memory stage and store buffer before delivering an interrupt, i.e. by rising the external event signal ii) prevent the processor core from executing instructions when it should not be running. With the use of hazard signals of the stall engine this is easy enough.

The construction of the pipelined processor core itself does not change. Neither does the strategy and methodology of the machines correctness proof in section 12.3. New guard conditions of the ISA introduced by the new units have of course to be tracked in the main induction hypothesis. Also due to the new units the definition of the stepping function has to cover more cases. As a consequence the stepping diagrams introduced in section section 10.5.3 get a few extra lines.

Finally the main induction hypothesis has also to cover the operating conditions $opc\text{-}cb$ of the controlled tri-state bus. These operating conditions forbid to clear a request $req = ICR.ds$ before it has been granted, and the new software condition SC_{APIC} has been introduced to prevent this from happening. Proving that this works is somewhat subtle, but having dealt with the operating conditions opc of the cache memory system, we already know the necessary machinery. For bus operation in cycle t we have — from the outer induction hypothesis — guard conditions for ISA steps $o < n$ stepped before cycle t. Hence the ISA program interpreted by the hardware obeys software condition SC_{APIC}. This allows to establish that operating condition $opc\text{-}cb^t$ (which concerns cycles $u < t$) of the bus control is not violated until cycle t. By lemma 31 this suffices to guarantee proper bus operation in cycle t.

12.1 Specification

For each processor q we add a component

$$c.p(q).apic$$

representing the state of the local APIC. The local APIC has subcomponents

$$c.p(q).apic.ports : \mathbb{B}^7 \to \mathbb{B}^8$$
$$c.p(q).apic.sipirr \in \mathbb{B}$$
$$c.p(q).apic.initrr \in \mathbb{B}$$
$$c.p(q).apic.running \in \mathbb{B}$$

Table 17. Structure of the I/O ports

name	length (words)	offset from $base_{APIC}$		description
		words	bytes	
ID	1	0	0	ID Register
ICR	2	1	4	Instruction Command Register
EOI	1	3	12	End-of-Interrupt Register
ISR	8	4	16	In-Service Register
IRR	8	12	48	Interrupt Request Register

Component $c.p(q).apic.running$ records whether processor q is running. The processor is only allowed to make processor steps while it is running. We will express this as a guard condition of processor steps. Processor steps which execute an INIT interrupt will lower the running flag and SIPI interrupts (executed by the APIC while the processor is not running) will raise the flag.

Components $c.p(q).apic.sipirr$ and $c.p(q).apic.initrr$ record whether a SIPI or INIT interrupt is being requested. As illustrated in fig. 183, the I/O ports

$$c.p(q).apic.ports$$

include the ICR, ISR, IRR, EOI, and an additional port containing the ID of the APIC (initialized to q). The ports are *memory mapped*, meaning that they can be accessed using regular write and read operations to a specific memory region. However, we will restrict such accesses to the ports by software conditions: the processor will only be allowed to write to the ICR and EOI ports. For each processor we only map that processor's local APIC to memory, so processors can not access each other's APICs. This results for each processor q in a distinct memory system

$$ms_q(c) : \mathbb{B}^{32} \to \mathbb{B}^8$$

where the first $2^7 = 128$ bytes starting from the (page aligned) APIC base address

$$base_{APIC} = 1^{20}0^{12}$$

are taken from the APIC ports, and the remaining bytes are taken from the memory $c.m$. This concerns addresses in the set

$$\mathcal{A} = \{\, base_{APIC} +_{32} i_{32} \mid i \in [0 : 127]\,\}$$

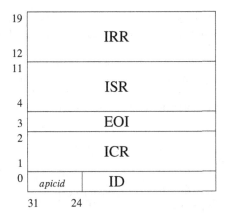

Fig. 183. Layout of the APIC

and the memory system of processor q can be defined as

$$ms_q(c)(a) = \begin{cases} c.p(q).apic.ports(a -_{32} base_{APIC}[6:0]) & a \in \mathcal{A} \\ c.m(a) & \text{otherwise.} \end{cases}$$

Thus in memory system ms_q the processor sees as before for most addresses the cache memory system, but addresses in $\mathcal{A}$ are masked by the local APIC. In accordance with fig. 183 and table 17 we define shorthands

$$c.p(q).apic.ID = c.p(q).apic.ports_4(0_7)$$
$$c.p(q).apic.ICR = c.p(q).apic.ports_8(4_7)$$
$$c.p(q).apic.EOI = c.p(q).apic.ports_4(12_7)$$
$$c.p(q).apic.ISR = c.p(q).apic.ports_{32}(16_7)$$
$$c.p(q).apic.IRR = c.p(q).apic.ports_{32}(48_7)$$

The ID of the APIC is stored in the fourth byte of the **ID** field

$$apicid_q(c) = c.p(q).apic.ID[31:24]$$

Obviously this limits the number of processors to

$$P \leq 2^8 = 256$$

The structure of the interrupt command register is shown in fig. 184 and table 18. The ISR and IRR both consists of 256 bits; bit number $i \in [0:255]$ corresponds to interrupt i, thus bit i of the IRR is raised iff interrupt i is currently being requested, and bit i of the ISR is raised iff interrupt i is currently being serviced by the processor.

Table 18. Structure of the Instruction Command Register (ICR). Bits 18–19 of the ICR are used to specify recipients of inter-processor interrupts. In order to send an interrupt to a single processor, the destination shorthand should be set to *target*; the destination field is used to specify the destination processor. Other values of the destination shorthands can be used to address the sending processor (*self*), all other processors (*all but self*), or simply all processors. Various delivery modes are supported: *Fixed* for regular-IPIs, *INIT* for initialization requests, and *SIPI* for start-up requests. The start-up IPI vector can be specified in the first eight bits of the ICR. Finally, bit number 12 serves as the delivery status (*ds*).

name	bits	description
dest	63-56	destination field
dsh	19-18	destination shorthand: target (00b), self (01b), all (10b), all but self (11b)
ds	12	delivery status: idle (0b), send pending (1b)
dm	10-8	delivery mode: Fixed (000b), INIT (101b), Startup (110b)
vect	7-0	vector

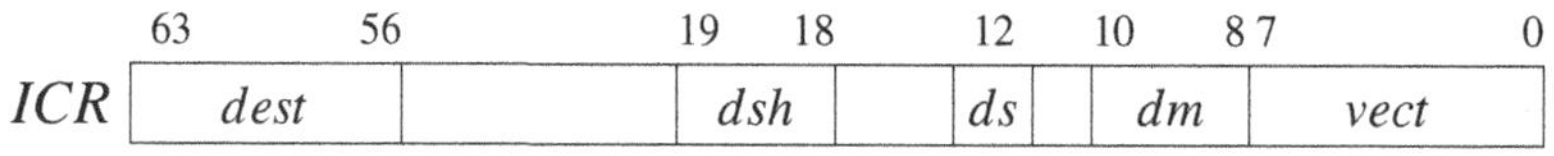

$$
\begin{array}{c|c|c|c|c|c|c}
 & 63 \quad\quad 56 & & 19 \;\; 18 & 12 & 10 \;\; 8\,7 & 0 \\
ICR & dest & & dsh & ds & dm & vect
\end{array}
$$

Fig. 184. Fields of the ICR

12.1.1 Processor Steps

We now consider the specification of processor steps, which are controlled in addition to the old oracle/external inputs also with an additional external input $init \in \mathbb{B}$

$$x = (p, q, I, e, w_I, w_E, init)$$

In addition to the old guard condition, we add the following requirements:

- the processor may only make a step when the running bit is raised
- the external event e must only be raised if there is a fixed interrupt in the IRR with a higher priority than the highest priority interrupt currently in the ISR
- the init signal *init* must only be raised if there is an INIT interrupt request

Thus we define using the old guard condition γ_{old}

$$
\begin{aligned}
\gamma(c,x) = \; & \gamma_{old}(c,x) \\
& \wedge c.p(q).apic.running \\
& \wedge (x.e \; \rightarrow \; \exists i. \, c.p(q).apic.IRR[i] \; \wedge \forall j < i. \, /c.p(q).apic.ISR[j]) \\
& \wedge (x.init \; \rightarrow \; c.p(q).apic.initrr)
\end{aligned}
$$

Apart from this, differences concern only three parts: the memory system, which replaces the memory; external interrupts which affect both IRR and ISR, and INIT interrupts which need to be considered in the event vector ev and which clear the running flag and the INIT request. Note that we left out writes to the EOI port of the local APIC. Processor steps can only modify memory with CAS instructions and we will forbid these on the memory mapped memory regions through a software condition. Consequently processor steps never modify the EOI port and the side effect of writing to the EOI port can be ignored here. We will need to look at these side effects when we define the semantics of store buffer steps.

We define the next configuration c'

$$c' = \delta(c,x)$$

using the old transition function δ_{old} and signals f_{old} without APICs. For this we define the old input x_{old} to the transition function without the new $init$ signal

$$x_{old} = (p,q,I,e,w_I,w_E)$$

After INIT interrupts, we clear the running flag and the INIT request

$$x.init \quad \rightarrow \quad c'.p(q).apic.running = 0 \wedge c'.p(q).apic.initrr = 0$$

The event vector now uses the init interrupt

$$ev(c,x)[2] = x.init$$

For the remaining bits nothing changes

$$i \neq 2 \quad \rightarrow \quad ev(c,x)[i] = ev_{old}(c,x_{old})$$

With this updated definition of ev the other definitions (such as mca, $jisr$, il, etc.) can be taken literally from previous chapters and we do not repeat them here. In particular the external event signal is in position three of the event vector

$$ev(c,x)[3] = x.e$$

Thus masked cause bit three is raised if and only if: 1) there is an external event, 2) the event is not masked, and 3) there is no INIT interrupt.

Loads are now serviced by the memory system $ms_q(c)$ instead of the memory $c.m$

$$lres(c,x) = fill(c,x)^{32-8\cdot d(c,x)} \circ fms(ms_q(c),c.p(q).sb)_{d(c,x)}(pmaE(c,x))$$

With these changes the memory system behaves exactly like memory. For the sake of brevity we specify this using ℓ and δ_M

$$\ell(ms_q(c')) = \delta_M(\ell(ms_q(c)),dacc(c,x))$$

Note that this does not specify what happens to the main memory in the APIC region. Since that region is usually not accessed that does not really matter from the programmer's point of view. However, for the purpose of proving a simulation between the cache memory system and the ISA main memory it makes sense to specify that this memory region never changes.

$$a \in \mathcal{A} \;\rightarrow\; c'.m(a) = c.m(a)$$

It remains to define the effect of *jisr* in a processor step on the *IRR* and *ISR* registers of the local APIC. This concerns only external events. Thus assume

$$mca(c,x)[3] = 1$$

Let i be the highest priority requested interrupt, i.e., the interrupt with the lowest index in the IRR

$$i = \min\{\, n \mid c.p(q).apic.IRR[n] = 1 \,\}$$

Then this interrupt is cleared in the IRR

$$c'.p(q).apic.IRR[i] = 0$$

and raised in the ISR

$$c'.p(q).apic.ISR[i] = 1$$

Other bits in the IRR and ISR do not change.

12.1.2 Store Buffer Steps

For steps of the store buffer of processor q

$$x \in \Sigma_{sb,q}$$

we need to consider writes to the EOI port. We identify such cases using predicate

$$eoiw(c,x) \equiv dacc(c,x).a = (base_{APIC} +_{32} 12_{32}).l \;\wedge\; \bigvee_{i\in[4:7]} dacc(c,x).bw[i]$$

The memory system behaves like normal memory except on such a write

$$/eoiw(c,x) \quad\rightarrow\quad \ell(ms_q(c')) = \delta_M(\ell(ms_q(c)), dacc(c,x))$$

If there is such a write, then only the ISR changes; the value stored to the *EOI* port is discarded. In the ISR the bit corresponding to the highest priority interrupt i in the ISR

$$i = \min\{\, n \mid c.p(q).apic.ISR[n] = 1 \,\}$$

is cleared in the ISR

$$eoiw(c,x) \quad\rightarrow\quad c'.p(q).apic.ISR[i] = 0$$

Other bits and the remainder of the memory system are not changed by steps that write to the *EOI* port.

12.1.3 MMU and Instruction Buffer Steps

For steps of the MMU and instruction buffer of processor q

$$x \in \Sigma_{tlb,q} \cup \Sigma_{ib,q}$$

we add as a guard condition that the running flag of processor q must be set

$$\gamma(c,x) = \gamma_{old}(c,x) \wedge c.p(q).apic.running$$

Other than that nothing changes. In particular MMU and IB steps do not use the memory system but rather continue to access memory directly.

12.1.4 SIPI Steps

SIPI steps are controlled by oracle inputs of the form

$$x = (SIPI, q) \in \Sigma_{apic,q}$$

They can only be made while a SIPI request is active and the processor is not running

$$\gamma(c,x) = c.p(q).apic.sipirr \wedge /c.p(q).apic.running$$

and flip the two bits

$$c'.p(q).apic.sipirr = 0, \quad c'.p(q).apic.running = 1$$

Thus after a SIPI step the SIPI is no longer requested and the processor is now running. These steps do nothing else.

12.1.5 IPI Delivery Steps

Sending of interrupts from one APIC is controlled by oracle inputs of the form

$$x = (IPI, q) \in \Sigma_{apic,q}$$

indicating that the APIC of processor q is executing the command stored earlier into its command and status register. Such steps can only be made while there is a pending command, i.e., with delivery status 1

$$\gamma(c,x) = c.p(q).apic.ICR.ds$$

We first make some auxiliary definitions. We distinguish between three delivery modes, corresponding to the three types of interrupts. Delivery mode *Fixed* for fixed interrupts

$$Fixed(c,x) \equiv c.p(q).apic.ICR.dm = 000$$

Delivery mode *INIT* for INIT interrupts

$$INIT(c,x) \equiv c.p(q).apic.ICR.dm = 101$$

and delivery mode *SIPI* for SIPI interrupts

$$SIPI(c,x) \equiv c.p(q).apic.ICR.dm = 110$$

The set of APIC ids which are targets of the interrupt is specified by the destination shorthand

$$dsh = c.p(q).apic.ICR.dsh$$

If the destination shorthand is 00, all APICs with the ID specified by the destination field of the interrupt command register

$$dest = c.p(q).apic.ICR.dest$$

are targeted. Due to the initialization and the software conditions which forbid writing to the ID register, only one such APIC will exist. If the destination shorthand is 01, only the sending APIC will be a target; if the destination shorthand is 10, all APICs are targets; and if the destination shorthand is 11, all other APICs are targets. Formally we collect all targets in the set

$$itargets(c,x) \subseteq [0:P-1]$$

of processors as follows

$$itargets(c,x) = \begin{cases} \{\,\hat{q} \mid apicid_{\hat{q}}(c) = dest\,\} & dsh = 00 \\ \{q\} & dsh = 01 \text{ (self)} \\ [0:P-1] & dsh = 10 \text{ (all)} \\ [0:P-1]\setminus\{q\} & dsh = 11 \text{ (all but self)} \end{cases}$$

With these definitions we proceed to define the semantics of IPI delivery steps. The step lowers the delivery status bit in the APIC of processor q

$$c'.apic(q).ICR.ds = 0$$

and modifies each target APIC of a processor

$$\hat{q} \in itargets(c,x)$$

depending on the delivery mode:

- *Fixed(c,x)*: the step takes the interrupt i in the vector field of the ICR

$$i = \langle c.p(q).apic.ICR.vect \rangle$$

  and raises the corresponding bit of the interrupt request register of the targets

$$c'.p(\hat{q}).apic.IRR[i] = 1$$

- *SIPI(c,x)*: the step raises the SIPI request register bit

$$c'.p(\hat{q}).apic.sipirr = 1$$

- *INIT(c,x)*: the step raises the INIT request register bit

$$c'.p(\hat{q}).apic.initrr = 1$$

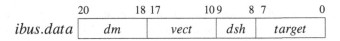

Fig. 185. Fields of the interrupt bus data

12.1.6 Initial Configuration

We specify here the initial configuration c^0, which is reached by the machine after reset. In addition to the specification of components of previous machines, which remain unchanged, we need to specify the state of the running bits and the local APICs.

For the running bit, the *boot processor* 0 is initialized as running

$$c^0.p(0).apic.running = 1$$

and all other processors are not running

$$q \neq 0 \quad \rightarrow \quad c^0.p(q).apic.running = 0$$

The APICs are zero initialized except for the highest-order byte of the APIC id (byte 3 of the overall APIC), which is initialized with a binary representation of the processor index q

$$x \neq 3_5 \quad \rightarrow \quad c^0.p(q).apic.ports(x) = 0_8$$
$$c^0.p(q).apic.ports(3_5) = q_8$$

12.2 Construction

We now give a construction of a local APIC and connect it to the processor. Connection between APICs is done through an extra bus called the *interrupt bus* which transmits all data necessary for the other APICs to determine both whether they are a target and how to react to the interrupt. Control of this bus is managed with the simple bus arbiter described in section 3.5.3. As the pins of the APIC that we will connect to the interrupt bus only make sense after we know the structure of the interrupt bus, we will first specify the interrupt bus in section 12.2.1, then construct the local APIC in section 12.2.2. Afterwards we connect the APICs to the processors and to the interrupt bus.

12.2.1 Interrupt Bus

We call the bus connecting the APICs which is used for transmission of interrupts and — in later machines — other signals the *interrupt bus*. For this we use a controlled tri-state bus

$$ibus : (P, 21)\text{-controlled bus}$$

from section 3.5.4. As illustrated in fig. 185 we introduce the following shorthands for the data output *ibus.data*:

- *ibus.dm* $\in \mathbb{B}^3$ for the delivery mode. For now this is restricted to *fixed*, *SIPI*, or *INIT* modes. In later designs, new components called I/O APICs add two additional modes, so the APICs we construct here will need to work also in the presence of other modes.

$$ibus.dm = ibus.data[20:18]$$

- *ibus.vect* $\in \mathbb{B}^8$ for the binary representation of the interrupt to be sent, in case it is a fixed interrupt. Ignored if the delivery mode is not *fixed*[1].

$$ibus.vect = ibus.data[17:10]$$

- *ibus.dsh* $\in \mathbb{B}^2$ for the delivery shorthand (*target*, *self*, *all*, *all−but−self*).

$$ibus.dsh = ibus.data[9:8]$$

- *ibus.target* $\in \mathbb{B}^8$ for the APIC ID of the interrupt target, in case the delivery shorthand is *target*. Ignored if the delivery mode is anything else.

$$ibus.target = ibus.data[7:0]$$

Recall that this bus also provides a signal *ibus.bhot* which indicates whether an APIC is currently putting a message on the bus. The data on the bus is meaningful only in case *ibus.bhot* is raised, and needs to be ignored otherwise.

12.2.2 Interface of Local APIC

We describe the interface of the local APIC. Since the initialization of the APIC — both in terms of the running flag and the state of the ID port — depends on its processor number q, we make the processor number a parameter of the unit.

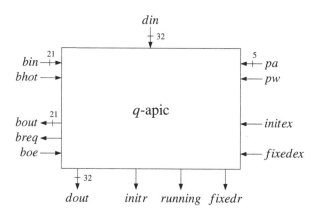

Fig. 186. Symbol of local APIC of processor q

---

[1] The name *vect* stems from the fact that for non-fixed interrupts, one would normally use this line to send the vector of the interrupt, i.e., the address of the start of the interrupt service routine of that interrupt. As mentioned before we have omitted this capability for the sake of simplicity

The symbol for the local APIC of processor q is shown in fig. 186. The local APIC is connected on one side to the processor and on the other side to the interrupt bus and arbiter. The signals of the interfaces are as follows.

$p \rightarrow apic$:

Signals from processor to its local APIC:

- $pw \in \mathbb{B}$ — processor write signal indicating that data should be written
- $din \in \mathbb{B}^{32}$ — data input, to be written into the ports, meaningless if $pw = 0$
- $pa \in \mathbb{B}^5$ — processor address specifying either the word to modify (in case $pw = 1$) or the word to read out (in case $pw = 0$)
- $initex, fixedex \in \mathbb{B}$ — control signals indicating that an INIT or fixed interrupt is being executed on the processor side in the current cycle, and thus $initrr$ etc. need to be adjusted

$apic \rightarrow p$:

Signals from local APIC to its processor:

- $dout \in \mathbb{B}^{32}$ — data output from the port addressed by input pa,
- $fixedr \in \mathbb{B}$ — external interrupt signals for the processor indicating that a fixed interrupt is being requested. This is an intermediate signal from the APIC indicating that an external interrupt e is to be generated once the memory stage is empty, as requested in section 7.4.5. For the implementation of this mechanism see section 12.2.5.
- $initr \in \mathbb{B}$ — external interrupt signal for the processor indicating that an INIT interrupt is being requested. Like the $fixedr$ signal this is only an intermediate signal.
- $running \in \mathbb{B}$ — indicating whether the processor is running

$apic \rightarrow ibus$:

Signals from local APIC to controlled interrupt bus:

- $breq \in \mathbb{B}$ — bus request signal to the arbiter requesting control of the bus,
- $bout \in \mathbb{B}^{21}$ — data to be put on the bus, meaningless if $breq = 0$

$ibus \rightarrow apic$:

Signals from controlled interrupt bus to the local APIC:

- $bin \in \mathbb{B}^{21}$ — bus input from the bus
- $bhot \in \mathbb{B}$ — control signal from the arbiter indicating that the bus is hot, i.e., that some APIC (possibly this one) is putting data on the bus
- $boe \in \mathbb{B}$ — control signal from the arbiter indicating that the APIC has received an output enable signal for the bus

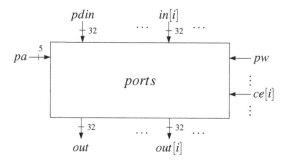

Fig. 187. Implementation of I/O ports

12.2.3 Construction of Local APIC

The construction closely parallels the ISA definition presented in section 12.1. Intuitively we would like to use set-clear flip-flops for the running bit. However, our construction of set-clear flip-flops (which is taken from [KMP14]) is always cleared on reset. For all APICs except that of the bootstrap processor 0 this works. However for the bootstrap processor, we need to initialized the running bit as one. Thus we use set-clear flip-flops for all processors except processor 0.

$$running : \begin{cases} \rho & q = 0 \\ \text{set-clear} & q \neq 0 \end{cases}$$

In either case, we can treat signal *running* as a simple bus (i.e., a bus with a single line) in the construction.

As shown in fig. 187, hardware ports are implemented as an **SPR RAM** (from section 3.3)

$$ports : (32,5){-}SPR$$

Data and address inputs for the ports come from the data and processor address inputs of the local APIC

$$ports.in = din \quad , \quad ports.a = pa$$

but for the write signal we need to consider the fact that writes to the end-of-interrupt ports do not change the content of the EOI port and only change the ISR as a side effect. Such writes are detected with signal

$$eoiw \equiv pw \wedge pa = 3_5$$

and the write signal for the ports is

$$ports.w = pw \wedge /eoiw$$

The data output of the APIC (for reads from the processor side) is taken from the ports

$$dout = ports.out$$

For the special inputs of the ports we need to detect incoming interrupts. Whether the APIC is hit by an interrupt depends on the destination shorthand of the message on the bus, the APIC id of this APIC (in case the destination shorthand is 'target'), and the *boe* signal which indicates whether it is this APIC that is sending the interrupt or another APIC (for shorthands 'self' and 'all-but-self'). We collect this in signal *bhit*

$$bhit \equiv bhot \wedge \begin{cases} ports.dout\,[0][31:24] = bin.dest & bin.dsh = 00 \\ boe & bin.dsh = 01 \\ 1 & bin.dsh = 10 \\ /boe & bin.dsh = 11 \end{cases}$$

The delivery mode of the message on the bus is defined in hardware as

$$Fixed \equiv bin.dm = 000$$
$$INIT \equiv bin.dm = 101$$
$$SIPI \equiv bin.dm = 110$$

Running Bit and Request Registers for INIT/SIPI

Implementation of the request registers for INIT and SIPI is straightforward using set-clear flip-flops of width one. Recall that set-clear flip-flops are initialized with zero after reset. In hardware the INIT request register is raised when we receive an INIT request from the bus. It is cleared when we execute an INIT request.

$$initrr.set = INIT \wedge bhot \wedge bhit$$
$$initrr.clr = initex$$

Note that in the same cycle both signals can be on. This occurs if an INIT interrupt is executed by the processor in the same cycle that an INIT interrupt is delivered to the APIC from the bus. Due to the semantics of set-clear flip-flops, after a cycle in which both set and clear signals are active, the set-clear flip-flop is *set*. Intuitively this means that in ISA, the step that sets the request register must be stepped *after* the step that clears it. Thus we will later step processor steps that execute INIT interrupts (which clear the register) *before* IPI-delivery steps (which might raise the register). The INIT request is passed to the core through output *initr*

$$initr = intitrr$$

The SIPI request register is controlled completely analogously. It is set when a SIPI interrupt comes from the bus. It is cleared when the SIPI request is executed. The SIPI is executed when the running bit is low. For this we introduce a signal

$$sipiex = /running \wedge sipirr$$

With these signals the control of the sipirr is defined straightforwardly as

$$sipirr.set = SIPI \wedge bhot \wedge bhit$$
$$sipirr.clr = sipiex$$

Recall that the running bit of the bootstrap processor needs to be initialized as one and thus is not implemented with a set-clear flip-flop. Thus for the control of the running bit we have to distinguish between $q = 0$ for the APIC of the bootstrap processor, and $q \neq 0$ for the other APICs.

- $q = 0$: the running bit is modified when an INIT or SIPI request is executed, and during reset

$$running.ce = sipiex \vee initex \vee reset$$

The running bit is raised after reset and SIPI interrupts

$$running.in = sipiex \vee reset$$

- $q \neq 0$: the running bit is a set-clear flip-flop which is raised on SIPI interrupts and lowered on INIT interrupts

$$running.set = sipiex$$
$$running.clr = initex$$

I/O Ports

Following the specification (see fig. 183) we give names to the groups of registers within the hardware ports:

$$\mathbf{ID} = ports.dout[0]$$
$$\mathbf{ICR} = ports.dout[2] \circ ports.dout[1]$$
$$\mathbf{EOI} = ports.dout[3]$$
$$\mathbf{ISR} = ports.dout[11] \circ \ldots \circ ports.dout[4]$$
$$\mathbf{IRR} = ports.dout[19] \circ \ldots \circ ports.dout[12]$$

These groups are called the *port registers*. Special inputs of the port registers are named accordingly. For registers consisting of 32 bit we define simply

$$\mathbf{ID}.in = ports.din[0]$$
$$\mathbf{EOI}.in = ports.din[3]$$

For larger registers we map each 32-bit chunk individually to the corresponding special data input

$$\mathbf{ICR}.in[32 \cdot (i+1) - 1 : 32 \cdot i] = ports.din[1+i] \qquad \text{for } i \in [0:1]$$
$$\mathbf{ISR}.in[32 \cdot (i+1) - 1 : 32 \cdot i] = ports.din[4+i] \qquad \text{for } i \in [0:7]$$
$$\mathbf{IRR}.in[32 \cdot (i+1) - 1 : 32 \cdot i] = ports.din[12+i] \qquad \text{for } i \in [0:7]$$

Shorthands for special clock enable registers are defined similarly

$$\mathbf{ID}.ce = ports.ce[0]$$
$$\mathbf{EOI}.ce = ports.ce[3]$$
$$\mathbf{ICR}.ce = ports.ce[1+i] \qquad \text{for } i \in [0:1]$$
$$\mathbf{ISR}.ce = ports.ce[4+i] \qquad \text{for } i \in [0:7]$$
$$\mathbf{IRR}.ce = ports.ce[12+i] \qquad \text{for } i \in [0:7]$$

From these registers one defines in straightforward fashion the message to be put on the bus

$$bout = \mathbf{ID}[7:0] \circ \mathbf{ICR}.(dest, dsh, dm, vect)$$

The request to broadcast is taken from the delivery status bit of the interrupt command register.

$$breq = \mathbf{ICR}.ds$$

A request for a fixed interrupt is sent to the processor iff there is any interrupt request with a higher priority than the highest-priority interrupt which is currently being serviced. This is computed with the help of a parallel-prefix circuit using as input the in-service register

$$256\text{-}PP_\vee(\mathbf{ISR})$$

The resulting mask has a raised bit at position i iff any interrupt with an index $j \leq i$ and hence at least the same priority as the interrupt with index i is currently being serviced. Its inverse therefore has a raised bit at position i iff all interrupts that are currently being serviced have a lower priority, i.e., if the interrupt with index i has a higher priority than the highest-priority interrupt which is currently being serviced. Thus the fixed interrupt request can be computed as

$$fixedr = \bigvee_i (\mathbf{IRR} \wedge /256\text{-}PP_\vee(\mathbf{ISR}))[i]$$

Wiring of Port Registers

Wiring of the ID register varies depending on the processor index q which is a parameter of the APIC. At *reset* the eight most significant bits of the ID register are updated with the processor index represented in binary and the remaining bits are cleared. In the APIC parametrized with index q we have:

$$\mathbf{ID}.in = q_8 \circ 0_{24}$$
$$\mathbf{ID}.ce \equiv reset$$

Thus, throughout the entire execution the content of the ID register could only change through writes to the ID port. Recall that these will be forbidden by a software condition.

Writes to the end-of-interrupt register are signaled by

$$eoiw \equiv pw \wedge (pa = 3_5)$$

According to the specification, such writes have a side-effect of clearing the least significant non-zero bit in the ISR register. Special inputs of the EOI register are used only for initialization on reset:

$$\textbf{EOI}.in = 0_{32}$$
$$\textbf{EOI}.ce \equiv reset$$

The interrupt command register is cleared on hardware reset, and the delivery status bit is cleared when the bus arbiter grants access to the APIC

$$\textbf{ICR}.ce \equiv reset \vee boe$$
$$\textbf{ICR}.in = \begin{cases} 0_{64} & reset \\ \textbf{ICR} \wedge 1^{51}01^{12} & \text{otherwise} \end{cases}$$

The ISR is modified through its special input in three cases: 1) it is cleared on reset. 2) when the processor executes a fixed interrupt, the corresponding bit is set. This bit can be found with the help of a find-first-one circuit as

$$irrmin = \text{f1}(\textbf{IRR})$$

3) when the processor ends servicing the interrupt and writes to the EOI port, the corresponding bit is cleared. This bit can be found with the help of a find-first-one circuit as

$$isrmin = \text{f1}(\textbf{ISR})$$

With these signals, and the input $fixedex$ to be generated by the processor, the construction of the inputs of the ISR is straightforward:

$$\textbf{ISR}.ce \equiv reset \vee fixedex \vee eoiw$$
$$\textbf{ISR}.in = \begin{cases} 0_{256} & reset \\ \textbf{ISR} \vee irrmin & fixedex \wedge /reset \\ \textbf{ISR} \wedge /isrmin & \text{o.w.} \end{cases}$$

We will later make sure that a write to the end-of-interrupt register and the execution of a fixed interrupt will not occur at the same time. Similarly, the IRR is updated on reset and when a fixed interrupt is executed. In the latter case we clear the bit corresponding to that interrupt. However, it is also updated in case an interrupt request for the fixed interrupt with index $\langle bin.vect \rangle$ is received from the bus. A bitmask for this interrupt is obtained by decoding this vector. In case this APIC is not a target of a fixed interrupt, the bitmask is zeroed out. The resulting bitmask is computed by

$$iindex = \text{Dec}(bin.vect) \wedge bhot \wedge bhit \wedge Fixed$$

Note that both reception of interrupt requests from the bus side and execution of an interrupt from the processor side can occur in the same cycle. Both of these steps modify the IRR, and these modifications need to be combined in hardware.

Execution of an interrupt lowers the highest-priority interrupt bit from the IRR, and receiving an IPI raises the corresponding bit. If the same bit is lowered and delivered, the order in which these operations are performed is visible in the next state of the IRR. We can either lower first and then raise

$$\mathbf{IRR}' = iindex \vee (\mathbf{IRR} \wedge /irrmin)$$

or we can first raise and then lower

$$\mathbf{IRR}' = /irrmin \wedge (\mathbf{IRR} \vee iindex)$$

Obviously the final result must be consistent with the order of *jisr* and IPI-delivery steps in ISA, which we will define later by the stepping function. In this order, *jisr* steps must go first because in hardware we compute the interrupt bit (i.e., *irrmin*) based on the state of the IRR *before* the delivery of the interrupt. Consequently we must apply the two operations in the corresponding order and lower first, then raise.

$$\mathbf{IRR}.ce \equiv reset \vee fixedex \vee bhot \wedge bhit \wedge Fixed$$

$$\mathbf{IRR}.in = iindex \vee \begin{cases} 0_{256} & reset \\ \mathbf{IRR} \wedge /irrmin & fixedex \wedge /reset \\ \mathbf{IRR} & o.w. \end{cases}$$

12.2.4 Placing the APICs on the Interrupt Bus

We will place P copies of the APIC into our machine. Each of these APICs receives a unique parameter for its ID. Thus APIC q is placed as

$$apic(q) : q\text{-APIC}$$

This APIC is connected to the interrupt bus in the obvious way. Recall that for the (n,d)-controlled bus which we use here, the input $ibus.a^q$ is for the data that the APIC q wants to put on the bus.

$$ibus.req[q] = apic(q).breq$$
$$ibus.a^q = apic(q).bout$$
$$apic(q).boe = ibus.oe[q]$$
$$apic(q).bin = ibus.data$$
$$apic(q).bhot = ibus.bhot$$

12.2.5 Cause Pipe and Stalling

We now need to connect processor q to its APIC. We begin with the running flag, which is supposed to control whether the pipeline executes instructions or not. To implement this we stall the top stage while the processor is not running:

$$haz_1^q = haz_{old}^q \vee /apic(q).running$$

Next we consider external interrupts, which are now controlled by the APIC, and the new INIT interrupts. As hinted in section 7.4.5, for these the memory stage needs to be drained through a new hazard signal for the stage above the memory stage. This should drain the memory stage when the APIC requests an interrupt

$$haz_{M-1}^q = haz_{M-1\ old}^q \vee (apic(q).fixedr \vee apic(q).initr) \wedge full_{M-1}^q$$

The external event signal is now connected to the fixed interrupt request signal of the APIC, but the signal is masked until the drain completes. This is the case when the full bit of the memory stage is cleared.

$$e^q = apic(q).fixedr \wedge /full_{M-1}^q$$

The request is executed as soon as an instruction with the appropriate event signal is clocked into the memory register stage

$$apic(q).fixedex = ue_M^q \wedge mca.(M-1)^q[3]$$

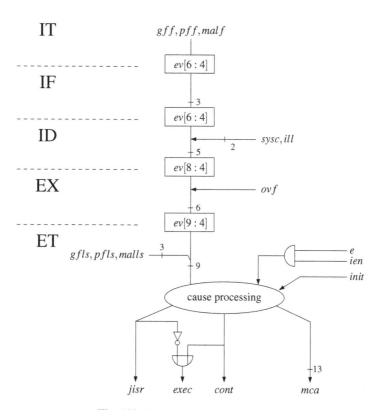

Fig. 188. Cause Pipeline with APIC

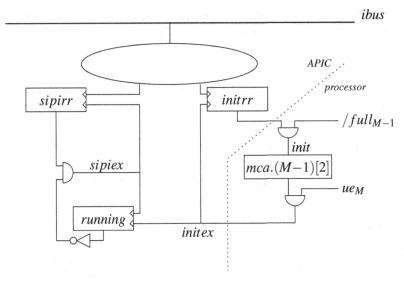

Fig. 189. Interconnect between INIT/SIPI request registers and the processor

As illustrated in fig. 188 we introduce a new signal $init^q$ into the cause pipe. This signal is computed analogously to the external event from the APIC INIT request $apic(q).initr$ and the full bit.

$$init^q = apic(q).initr \wedge / full^q_{M-1}$$

The init request is executed when the instruction is clocked into the memory register stage

$$apic(q).initex = ue^q_M \wedge mca.(M-1)^q[2]$$

This results in the interconnect between INIT/SIPI request registers and the pipeline shown in fig. 189.

12.2.6 Memory Operations to the APIC

Recall that programming of the local APIC is performed by writing to the I/O ports. These I/O ports do not support *cas* instructions and must be programmed with store instructions. Recall that store instructions use the store buffer. This means that accesses from the store buffer and accesses from the processor can go to the I/O ports. Luckily we can simply reuse the existing control automaton to resolve attempts of both units to access the APIC.

We need to change only two things in the connection between the processor/store buffer and the cache memory system: 1) accesses are now only requested if the operation is not going to the APIC. Recall that the APIC occupies 128 bytes starting from byte address $base_{APIC}$. These 128 bytes are $32 = 2^5$ cache lines. Thus accesses to the APIC can be detected by comparing all except the last 5 bits of the data line address $dacc^q.a$ to the base address of the APIC

$$acc^q_{APIC} \equiv dacc^q.a[29:5] = base_{APIC}[31:7]$$

The processor request at the data cache is only raised if the access is not going to the APIC

$$dca(q).preq = dca(q).preq_{old} \wedge /acc^q_{APIC}$$

2) the load result may now come from the APIC

$$lres.M^q.in = \begin{cases} lres.M^q.in_{old} & /acc^q_{APIC} \\ apic(q).dout \end{cases}$$

Accesses to the APIC use a 5-bit word address, whereas the data access uses a line address. To convert the line address into a word address we take the last 4 bits of the line address and append one additional bit ws^q to select the word inside the line that shall be accessed. This bit is raised if we access the upper half of the line and low if we access the lower half of the line. Computing ws^q turns out to be slightly technical. For write operations, which come from the store buffer, we can determine the word using the byte-write signals. We will later only allow aligned, word accesses to the APIC. Thus the fifth byte-write signal $bw[5]$ is raised if and only if the (complete) upper word in the line is written, and can be used for computing ws^q. For load operations, which come from the processor, we need to use bit 2 of the effective address. Compare-and-swap operations are not permitted.

$$ws^q = \begin{cases} dacc^q.bw[4] & dacc^q.w \\ ea.(M-1)^q[2] & \text{o.w.} \end{cases}$$

With this we can define the port address for the APIC by

$$apic(q).pa = dacc^q.a[3:0] \circ ws^q$$

APIC ports are written when the store buffer pops a write to the APIC

$$apic(q).pw = acc^q_{APIC} \wedge sb(q).pop$$

and the data written is constructed in straightforward fashion from either the lower or higher half of the data of the access. Whether this concerns the upper or lower half needs to be reconstructed from the byte-write signals of the access. Recall that only full store operations are supported. This means we only need to check a single byte-write signal of either half to figure out which half is being written, as all other byte-write signals in that half need to be the same as that byte-write signal.

$$apic(q).din = \begin{cases} dacc^q.data_H & dacc^q.bw[4] \\ dacc^q.data_L & \text{o.w.} \end{cases}$$

12.3 Correctness

12.3.1 Stepping Function

Like before we use potential emergency braking. The only difference is that oracle inputs of processor steps now include the INIT flag, which we sample in the same cycle $t_i^q(e)$ in which we sample the external event. Thus in the presence of an operating condition violation we define

$$vopc^t \; \to \; ns^t = 1 \wedge s(NS^t) = (p, q, I_\pi^{q, t_i^q(I)}, e_\pi^{q, t_i^q(e)}, init_\pi^{q, t_i^q(e)},$$
$$mmu_I(q).wout^{t_i^q(w_I)}, mmu_E(q).wout^{t_i^q(w_E)})$$

where q is the lowest index of a processor violating the operating conditions:

$$q = \min\{q \mid dca(q).preq^t \wedge dca(q).pacc^t.a[28:r] = 0^{29-r}$$
$$\wedge dca(q).pacc^t.bw \neq 0^8\}$$

In the absence of a violation of the operating condition

$$/vopc^t$$

we need to deal with two new things: 1) APIC steps on the interrupt bus and 2) memory operations accessing the APIC ports. Both of these steps access the APIC registers and thus their order needs to be consistent with the results obtained from hardware. Furthermore, memory operations accessing the APIC ports do not generate accesses on the cache memory system and thus can not be stepped together with the non-void accesses to the cache memory system. We observe:

- if the processor loads from an APIC port and the APIC makes a step in the same cycle, the processor sees the value of the port at the beginning of the cycle. Thus in such cases the processor needs to be stepped first.
- if the store buffer stores to an APIC port, it must store to the EOI port or (only if the APIC is idle) the ICR port. If the APIC makes a step in the same cycle, the changes of the units affect different ports. The order of these steps does not matter.
- if the store buffer stores to the EOI port and the processor makes a step in the same cycle, the external event signal of the processor is computed based on the old ISR. Furthermore, the processor is not interrupted since the store buffer is not empty. However, it is possible that the processor would be interrupted based on the ISR after the write completes. Thus in such cases we need to step the processor first.
- if the processor executes an interrupted instruction and the APIC receives an interrupt (possibly with a high priority) from the bus, the processor step will be interrupted based on the IRR at the beginning of the cycle and ignores the new interrupt. Furthermore we have constructed the inputs to the IRR in such a way that the effect of taking the interrupt is applied before the effect of receiving the new interrupt. Thus in such cases we step the processor first.

We observe that we must always step the processor before both APIC steps and store buffer steps that access the APIC. On the other hand the order of store buffer and APIC steps is for now not constrained. This will change once we introduce I/O APICs and EOIp registers in chapter 14. In that chapter we will need to step the store buffer after the APIC step if it writes to the EOI port. To reduce complications in that chapter, we already follow this stepping order here.

Furthermore, we need to order SIPI steps with IPI delivery steps in case the latter delivers a SIPI. Since in our construction the SIPI request register will be raised after a cycle in which a SIPI is executed while a new SIPI is delivered, we will perform the SIPI step first.

Like before we define the order between steps by breaking the steps performed in cycle t up into multiple phases. In addition to the three phases from before we add three additional phases for up to one APIC step triggered on the interrupt bus (when the bus is hot), SIPI steps of each processor, and store buffer steps that write to the APIC.

We switch to implicit t notation.

1. In the first phase, consisting of walk initialization steps and processor loads that forward from the store buffer, nothing changes. Using the number nfi^q of forwarding and initialization steps of processor q, we define just like before

$$N_{CMS} = NS + \sum_q nfi^q$$

2. In the second phase, store buffer steps and (non-forwarding) loads that access the APIC are no longer stepped, since they do not have a local sequential index x in the access sequence. We define for processor q the number of accesses to the cache memory system as

$$
\begin{aligned}
nac^q = {}& ue_M^q \wedge exec.(M-1)^q \wedge (l.(M-1)^q \wedge /sb.f^q \vee cas.(M-1)^q) \wedge /acc_{APIC}^q \\
&+ mmu_I.w.ce^q \wedge /mmu_I(q).winit + mmu_E(q).w.ce \wedge /mmu_E(q).winit \\
&+ ue_{IF}^q \\
&+ sb(q).pop \wedge /acc_{APIC}^q
\end{aligned}
$$

The sum of all of these steps of all processors q is the number of accesses to the memory system that end in the current cycle

$$\sum_q nac^q = \#E$$

3. The third phase begins after all these steps have been completed

$$N_{REM} = N_{CMS} + \sum_q nac^q$$

In this phase, all remaining processor steps are completed. This now includes steps which load from the APIC ports, except if they forward from the store buffer

Phase	Steps	Description
1	$[NS : N_{CMS})$	walk initialization, read from store buffer
2	$[N_{CMS} : N_{REM})$	memory accesses (NOT to APIC)
3	$[N_{REM} : N_{SIPI})$	remaining processor steps (includes external and INIT interrupts)
4	$[N_{SIPI} : N_{IBUS})$	SIPI steps of APICs
5	$[N_{IBUS} : N_{APICW})$	IPI delivery steps of APICs
6	$[N_{APICW} : NS')$	stores to the APIC ports

Table 19. Phases of stepping function with APIC

$$nrem^q = ue_M^q \wedge /(exec.(M-1)^q \wedge$$
$$(l.(M-1)^q \wedge sb(q).f \vee (l.(M-1)^q \vee cas.(M-1)^q) \wedge /acc_{APIC}^q))$$

4. The fourth phase begins after all remaining processor steps are completed.

$$N_{SIPI} = N_{REM} + \sum_q nrem^q$$

It consists of all SIPI steps. Such a step is triggered when the processor is not running and has a recorded SIPI request. Recall that this is denoted by $apic(q).sipiex$.

5. The fifth phase, in which APIC steps triggered by the interrupt bus are stepped, begins after all these steps have completed

$$N_{IBUS} = N_{SIPI} + \sum_q apic(q).sipiex$$

There is at most one such APIC step, and it occurs iff the bus is hot.

6. Afterwards, we step all store buffers that write to the APIC

$$N_{APICW} = N_{IBUS} + bhot$$

This happens at most once per processor, in case the store buffer is popped during an access to the APIC

$$apicw^q = sb(q).pop \wedge acc_{APIC}^q$$

These are the last steps to be completed in the cycle

$$NS' = N_{APICW} + \sum_q apicw^q$$

This defines the phases of the stepping function. We have summarized them in table 19.

Next we define the oracle inputs. Processors are stepped when the memory stage is clocked, i.e., on ue_M^q. In this case there is a processor step

$$n_p^q \in [NS : NS' - 1]$$

with

$$s(n_p^q) = (p, q, I_\pi^{q,t_i^q(I)}, e_\pi^{q,t_i^q(e)}, init_\pi^{q,t_i^q(e)},$$
$$mmu_I(q).wout^{t_i^q(w_I)}, mmu_E(q).wout^{t_i^q(w_E)})$$

Oracle inputs for instruction buffer, MMU, and store buffer steps are defined like before and not repeated here. For APIC steps, we have to consider the transmission of interrupts. In case an interrupt is delivered over the interrupt bus, step N_{IBUS} is an APIC step of the APIC q which receives the grant

$$q = \varepsilon\{q \mid apic(q).boe\}$$

Thus

$$ibus.bhot \rightarrow s(N_{IBUS}) = (IPI, q)$$

If processor q executes a SIPI in the current cycle, i.e., $apic(q).sipiex$, then there is some step

$$n_{sipi}^q \in [N_{SIPI} : N_{IBUS} - 1]$$

satisfying

$$s(n_{sipi}^q) = (SIPI, q)$$

Memory operations that access the APIC are no longer stepped together with other memory operations. For processor steps this means we define

$$ue_M^q \wedge exec.(M-1)^q \wedge (l.(M-1)^q \wedge /sb(q).f \wedge /acc_{APIC}^q \vee cas.(M-1)^q)$$
$$\rightarrow n_p^q \in [N_{CMS} : N_{REM})$$

and for store buffer steps we define

$$sb(q).pop \wedge /acc_{APIC}^q \rightarrow n_{sb}^q \in [N_{CMS} : N_{REM})$$

Processor steps accessing the APIC are stepped together with the remaining processor steps

$$ue_M^q \wedge exec.(M-q)^q \wedge l.(M-1)^q \wedge /sb(q).f \wedge acc_{APIC}^q \rightarrow n_p^q \in [N_{REM} : N_{SIPI})$$

Store buffer steps accessing the APIC are stepped in the last phase

$$sb(q).pop \wedge acc_{APIC}^q \rightarrow n_{sb}^q \in [N_{APICW} : NS')$$

The order of steps in the phase consisting of accesses to the CMS is defined exactly as in chapter 11. If a *cas* or a load which can not forward from the store buffer and is not accessing the APIC leaves the pipeline processor q generates the access at the data port $4q + 3$

$$ue_M^q \wedge exec.(M-1)^q \wedge (cas.(M-1)^q \vee l.(M-1)^q \wedge /sb(q).hit \wedge /acc_{APIC}^q)$$
$$\rightarrow n_p^q = NS + \varepsilon\{x \mid i_x = 4q + 3\} - 1$$

If on the other hand the store buffer pops and the access does not go to the APIC, the store buffer generates this access

$$sb(q).pop \wedge /acc^q_{APIC} \ \rightarrow \ n^q_{sb} = NS + \varepsilon \{ x \mid i_x = 4q+3 \} - 1$$

When a MMU of processor q clocks the walk register and does not perform a walk initialization, it generates the access at its port

$$mmu_I(q).w.ce \wedge /mmu_I(q).winit \ \rightarrow \ n^q_{tlbI} = NS + \varepsilon \{ x \mid i_x = 4q+0 \} - 1$$
$$mmu_E(q).w.ce \wedge /mmu_E(q).winit \ \rightarrow \ n^q_{tlbE} = NS + \varepsilon \{ x \mid i_x = 4q+2 \} - 1$$

12.3.2 Software Conditions

We require that the APIC is only accessed by loads and stores, and only by (aligned) word accesses. For processor steps, this can be stated as

$$x \in \Sigma_{p,q} \wedge mop(c,x) \wedge ea(c,x) \in \mathcal{A} \ \rightarrow \ (l(c,x) \vee s(c,x)) \wedge d(c,x) = 4$$

Note that this already implies that store buffers never contain sub-word stores to the APIC. We also forbid the processor from writing any port except the ICR and the EOI ports. As described by table 17 these are words one through three of the APIC.

$$x \in \Sigma_{p,q} \wedge s(c,x) \wedge ea(c,x) \in \mathcal{A} \ \rightarrow \ \langle ea(c,x)[6:2] \rangle \in \{1,2,3\}$$

Furthermore, writing to the ICR is forbidden while an IPI has been issued by the processor, but not yet been delivered by the APIC. Naively one might formally define such situations this by looking at the delivery status bit of the ICR. This does not work, because the store with which the processor has issued the IPI may be in the store buffer for a while. During that time, the delivery status bit in the ICR is still zero, even though the processor has already issued the IPI and must be forbidden from starting other writes to the APIC. Such writes would reach the APIC after the write that raises the delivery status bit. To avoid this problem, we look at the delivery status bit in the *forwarded memory system* of the processor q which is writing. As described by tables 17 and 18 this is bit 12 of the first word of the ICR, which starts at an offset of 4 bytes from the APIC base address $base_{APIC}$. Thus if a processor step issues a store to ports 1 or 2 of the APIC (i.e., the ICR) which start at an offset of 4 resp. 8 bytes

$$x \in \Sigma_{p,q} \wedge s(c,x) \wedge ea(c,x) \in \{ base_{APIC} +_{32} 4_{32}, base_{APIC} +_{32} 8_{32} \}$$

the forwarded memory system must have a lowered delivery status bit for the ICR

$$fms(ms_q(c),c.p(q).sb)(base_{APIC} +_{32} 4_{32})[12] = 0$$

We collect these condition into a software condition for the APIC:

$$SC_{APIC}(c,x) \equiv$$
$$(x \in \Sigma_{p,q} \wedge mop(c,x) \wedge ea(c,x) \in \mathcal{A} \rightarrow (l(c,x) \vee s(c,x)) \wedge d(c,x) = 4)$$
$$\wedge (x \in \Sigma_{p,q} \wedge s(c,x) \wedge ea(c,x) \in \mathcal{A} \rightarrow \langle ea(c,x)[6:2] \rangle \in \{1,2,3\})$$
$$\wedge (x \in \Sigma_{p,q} \wedge s(c,x) \wedge ea(c,x) \in \{base_{APIC} +_{32} 4_{32}, base_{APIC} +_{32} 8_{32}\}$$
$$\rightarrow fms(ms_q(c), c.p(q).sb)(base_{APIC} +_{32} 4_{32})[12] = 0)$$

Note that we do not require that MMUs and instruction buffers do not access the APIC. This is for the simple reason that MMUs and instruction buffers ignore the APIC both in hardware and in ISA. They directly access the main memory/-cache memory system instead. Since in ISA main memory in the APIC region is by definition constant, this means that a careless programmer who points the MMU to the APIC region will interpret whatever data happens to be present in memory after start-up as page table entries. With the non-deterministic instruction buffer it may also happen that the instruction buffer has meaningless entries from that region of memory, but this does not matter as long as the processor never executes an instruction from these addresses.

As in previous chapters we require also that there are no writes to the ROM region. Recall that this is stated by

$$SC_{ROM}(c,x) \leftrightarrow x \in \Sigma_p \wedge write(c.(p(x.q),m),x) \rightarrow ea(c.(p(x.q),m),x) \geq 2^{r+3}$$

12.3.3 Induction Hypothesis

For the induction hypothesis we simply couple the state of the APICs in the obvious way. We also add the operating condition $opc\text{-}cb^t$ from section 3.5.4 which states that the operating conditions of the controlled bus have been satisfied in all cycles $u < t$. Everything else is coupled as before.

$$t \sim_m n \quad \equiv \quad n = NS^t \rightarrow m(h^t) = \ell(c^n.m) \wedge opc^t$$
$$\wedge aq(sb(q)^t_\pi) = c^n.p(q).sb$$
$$\wedge walks(mmu_I(q)^t) \cup walks(mmu_E(q)^t) \subseteq c^n.tlb(q)$$
$$\wedge apic(q)^t = c^n.p(q).apic \wedge opc\text{-}cb^t$$
$$\wedge \forall \hat{n} < n. \; \gamma(c^{\hat{n}}, s(\hat{n}))$$

In the correctness statement we need to add the new software condition, and for processor steps include guard conditions for external interrupts (e and $INIT$) and the running flag. For this we define shorthands

$$\gamma_r(c,x) \equiv x \in \Sigma_{p,q} \rightarrow c.p(q).apic.running$$
$$\gamma_e(c,x) \equiv x \in \Sigma_{p,q} \wedge x.e \rightarrow \exists i. \; c.p(q).apic.IRR[i] \wedge \forall j < i. \; /c.p(q).apic.ISR[j]$$
$$\gamma_{INIT}(c,x) \equiv x \in \Sigma_{p,q} \wedge x.init \rightarrow c.p(q).apic.initrr$$

Like other parts (γ_{wI}, γ_I, ...) of the guard condition, these parts are shown in certain pipeline stages. For the running flag this is the topmost stage, which is stalled while the running flag is zero. For the external interrupts this is the stage above the memory stage, where the external interrupts are sampled.

Lemma 252. *There is an initial configuration c^0 satisfying*

$$sim(h^0.(p(q),m),c^0.(p(q),m)) \quad for\ all\ q \in P$$

in which instruction buffers and TLBs are empty

$$c^0.ib(q) = c^0.tlb(q) = \emptyset$$

and the store buffers are also empty

$$c^0.p(q).sb = \varepsilon$$

Furthermore: if for the computation (c^n) with stepping function $s(n)$ extracted from hardware and initial configuration c^0 satisfies for all n the software conditions $SC_{ROM}(c^n,s(n))$ and $SC_{APIC}(c^n,s(n))$ provided the stepping function $s(n)$ has a valid initial segment until n

$$\forall n.\ (\forall m \leq n.\ \gamma(c^m,s(m))) \ \rightarrow \ SC_{ROM}(c^n,s(n)) \wedge SC_{APIC}(c^n,s(n))$$

then for all n and t:

- *If n is a step of processor q executing instructions i which is committed and only has live instructions before it*

$$n = pseq(q,i) \ \wedge \ c(i)^{q,t} \ \wedge \ lb(i)^{q,t}$$

then hardware in cycle t simulates instruction i

$$t \sim_p^q i$$

and each part of the guard condition holds if instruction i passed the corresponding stage

$$(i < I_{IF}^{q,t} \rightarrow \gamma_I^{q,i})$$
$$\wedge\,(i < I_{IT}^{q,t} \rightarrow \gamma_{wI}^{q,i})$$
$$\wedge\,(i < I_{ET}^{q,t} \rightarrow \gamma_{wE}^{q,i})$$
$$\wedge\,(i < I_1^{q,t} \rightarrow \gamma_r^{q,i})$$
$$\wedge\,(i < I_{M-1}^{q,t} \rightarrow \gamma_e^{q,i})$$
$$\wedge\,(i < I_{M-1}^{q,t} \rightarrow \gamma_{INIT}^{q,i})$$

- *Hardware simulates in cycle t the non-pipelined components of ISA step n*

$$t \sim_m n$$

12.3.4 Scheduling Diagram for APIC

Most APIC components can be modified in two different phases.

- IRR and INITrr are modified when the processor executes the interrupt, and when a new interrupt is received on the bus. Both can occur in the same cycle.
- The ICR is modified when an IPI is delivered or when the processor programs the APIC. Recall that software conditions forbid programming the APIC while the APIC is waiting to deliver an interrupt. Consequently, both modifications can not occur in the same cycle.
- The SIPIrr is modified when the SIPI is received and when it is subsequently executed. If the processor is not running, this happens in the same cycle.
- The ISR is modified when an IPI is taken (to indicate that the interrupt is being serviced) and when the store buffer completes a write to the EOI port. Recall that interrupts drain the store buffer. Thus the interrupt is only taken when the store buffer is already empty at the beginning of the cycle. This makes the situation where both events occur in the same cycle impossible.
- Finally the running flag is modified when an INIT interrupt is taken and raised by SIPI steps. Both can occur in the same cycle.

As we did for the store buffer before, we define intermediate (ghost) states for each of those registers obtained after executing the earlier of the two steps. With the order of phases defined in section 12.3.1, this results in the scheduling diagram in fig. 190.

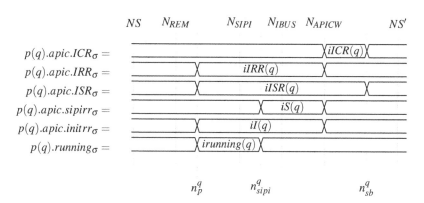

Fig. 190. Stepping diagram with APICs

The intermediate values are defined as follows. For the ICR, we apply the delivery of an interrupt

$$iICR(q) = \begin{cases} apic(q).\mathbf{ICR} \wedge 1^{51}01^{12} & apic(q).boe \\ apic(q).\mathbf{ICR} & \text{o.w.} \end{cases}$$

For the IRR, ISR, INITrr, and the running flag, we apply the *jisr* step.

$$iIRR(q) = \begin{cases} apic(q).\textbf{IRR} \wedge /apic(q).irrmin & apic(q).fixedex \\ apic(q).\textbf{IRR} & \text{o.w.} \end{cases}$$

$$iISR(q) = \begin{cases} apic(q).\textbf{ISR} \vee apic(q).irrmin & apic(q).fixedex \\ apic(q).\textbf{ISR} & \text{o.w.} \end{cases}$$

$$iI(q) = \begin{cases} 0 & apic(q).initex \\ apic(q).initrr & \text{o.w.} \end{cases}$$

$$irunning(q) = \begin{cases} 0 & apic(q).initex \\ apic(q).running & \text{o.w.} \end{cases}$$

For the SIPIrr we apply the step of executing the SIPI

$$iS(q) = \begin{cases} 0 & apic(q).sipiex \\ apic(q).sipirr & \text{o.w.} \end{cases}$$

12.3.5 Induction Step

In the induction step $t \to t+1$ we show only some of the new proofs for APIC components, and that loads from the APIC obtain the correct results. In these proofs we need, just like in chapter 11, only the combined induction hypothesis for the current cycle. This induction hypothesis states for all $o \le n$ and cycle t that the simulation relation holds and, in case o is the global step number of instruction i of processor q, that the registers are correct and the partial guard conditions γ_I etc. hold provided instruction i has passed the relevant stages

$$t \sim_m o \wedge (o = pseq(q,i) \wedge c(i)^{q,t} \wedge lb(i)^{q,t}$$
$$\to t \sim_p i \wedge (i > I_{IF}^{q,t} \to \gamma_I^{q,t}) \wedge (i > I_{IT}^{q,t} \to \gamma_{wI}^{q,t}) \wedge (i > I_{ET} \to \gamma_{wE}^{q,t})) \tag{81}$$

Analogous to how we showed that store buffer entries do not write into the ROM region in lemma 228, we show that store buffer entries satisfy the conditions of section 12.3.2. For two of these conditions — that the accesses must by word-accesses and that they must only write to the ICR and the EOI ports — the proof of this is completely trivial and omitted here. Stating it is slightly technical, because the software conditions are written using byte addresses, while the store buffer entries use line addresses. Furthermore, the ICR port is not line-aligned. The store is allowed to write either a) to the upper half of the first line of the APIC, where the lower half of the ICR resides, or b) to either half of the second line of the APIC, where the upper half of the ICR and the EOI port reside.

Lemma 253. *Let $n \ge NS$ and w be store buffer entry number k of processor q in ISA configuration c^{NS}, and let w write to the APIC*

$$w = c^{NS}.p(q).sb[k] \wedge w.a \in \mathcal{A}$$

Then w must be a word access and write to either the ICR or EOI ports

$$w.bw = 1^4 0^4 \wedge w.a = base_{APIC}[31:3]$$
$$\vee \; w.bw \in \{1^4 0^4, 0^4 1^4\} \wedge w.a = base_{APIC}[31:3] +_{29} 1_{29}$$

For the third condition, that the processor must not issue stores to the ICR while the delivery status is raised in the forwarded memory system, we need to work slightly harder. Observe that while the delivery status is raised in the forwarded memory system, there can be stores in the store buffer that write to the ICR. This is in fact typically the case when the store which raises the delivery status is still in the store buffer. Instead of showing that there are no such stores in the store buffer at all, we will show that *behind* a store which raises the delivery status, there are no newer stores to the ICR. More precisely, if the store in the store buffer entry k goes to the ICR, then the forwarded memory system using only the first k stores (i.e., stores 0 through $k-1$) must not have a raised delivery status bit in the ICR. This can be stated as follows.

Lemma 254. *Let $n \geq NS$ and w be store buffer entry number k of processor q in ISA configuration c^{NS}*

$$w = c^{NS}.p(q).sb[k]$$

and let w write to the ICR

$$w.bw = 1^4 0^4 \wedge w.a = base_{APIC}[31:3] \vee w.bw = 0^4 1^4 \wedge w.a = base_{APIC}[31:3] +_{29} 1_{29}$$

Then the forwarding memory system from the first k stores has a low delivery status bit

$$fms(ms_q(c^{NS}), c^{NS}.p(q).sb[k-1:0])(base_{APIC} +_{32} 4_{32})[12] = 0$$

Proof. We show instead a more general claim for all valid initial segments of the scheduling function. We show for all o satisfying

$$\forall \hat{n} < o. \; \gamma(c^{\hat{n}}, s(\hat{n}))$$

that if store buffer entry w at position k of processor q in ISA configuration c^o

$$w = c^o.p(q).sb[k]$$

writes to the ICR

$$w.bw = 1^4 0^4 \wedge w.a = base_{APIC}[31:3] \vee w.bw = 0^4 1^4 \wedge w.a = base_{APIC}[31:3] +_{29} 1_{29}$$

then the forwarding memory system from the first k stores has a low delivery status bit

$$fms(ms_q(c^o), c^o.p(q).sb[k-1:0])(base_{APIC} +_{32} 4_{32})[12] = 0$$

The original claim is then the special case for $o := NS$, which satisfies the guard conditions by the induction hypothesis for the current cycle (eq. (81)).

The proof of this generalized claim is by induction on o. The base case is trivial as store buffers are originally empty. The induction step $o \rightarrow o+1$ is proven by case analysis on the ISA step o. We treat here only two cases: the case where step o is a step of processor q which creates a new store buffer entry that modifies the ICR, and the case where step o is a step of the store buffer of processor q.

- $s(o) \in \Sigma_{sb,q}$: recall that we have shown as part of lemma 236 that store buffer steps do not change the forwarded memory system. If the number of stores in the store buffer before the store buffer step was l, it is now $l-1$, since the oldest store has been committed to memory. Thus that the forwarded memory system has not changed could be stated as

$$fms(ms_q(c^o), c^o.p(q).sb[l-1:0]) = fms(ms_q(c^{o+1}), c^{o+1}.p(q).sb[l-2:0])$$

This equality actually holds for all l less or equal to the length of the store buffer. The proof of this more general result is along the lines of the proof in lemma 236 and omitted here. In particular with $l := k$ we conclude that the step has not changed the forwarded memory system

$$fms(ms_q(c^o), c^o.p(q).sb[k-1:0]) = fms(ms_q(c^{o+1}), c^{o+1}.p(q).sb[k-2:0])$$

By assumption there is a store buffer entry w which had index k in configuration c^o and which has now index $k-1$ in configuration c^{o+1}

$$w = c^o.p(q).sb[k] = c^{o+1}.p(q).sb[k-1]$$

and this store modifies the ICR

$$w.bw = 1^4 0^4 \wedge w.a = base_{APIC}[31:3] \vee w.bw = 0^4 1^4 \wedge w.a = base_{APIC}[31:3] +_{29} 1_{29}$$

We can conclude with the induction hypothesis that the forwarded memory system had a low delivery status bit

$$fms(ms_q(c^o), c^o.p(q).sb[k-1:0])(base_{APIC} +_{32} 4_{32})[12] = 0$$

Since the store buffer step does not change the forwarded memory system, the same is true after the store buffer step

$$fms(ms_q(c^{o+1}), c^{o+1}.p(q).sb[k-2:0])(base_{APIC} +_{32} 4_{32})[12] = 0$$

This is the claim.
- $s(o) \in \Sigma_{p,q}$: assume that the step executes instruction i of processor q which is a store instruction

$$o = pseq(q,i) \wedge s_\sigma^{q,i}$$

and that the resulting store buffer entry w which is now the last entry in the store buffer

$$w = c^{o+1}.p(q).sb[k] \ \wedge \ k = \#c^o.p(q).sb$$

writes to the ICR

$$w.bw = 1^4 0^4 \wedge w.a = base_{APIC}[31:3] \vee w.bw = 0^4 1^4 \wedge w.a = base_{APIC}[31:3] +_{29} 1_{29}$$

With the semantics of ISA we conclude that the store which created this store buffer entry must write to the ICR. This store has the word address $ea_\sigma^{q,i}$ which goes to word 1 or 2 of the APIC (where the ICR resides)

$$ea_\sigma^{q,i} = base_{APIC} +_{32} i \quad \text{with} \quad i \in \{1,2\}$$

We conclude with the software condition SC_{APIC}: the forwarded memory system must have a low delivery status bit

$$fms(ms_q(c^o),c^o.p(q).sb)(base_{APIC} +_{32} 1_{32})[12] = 0$$

The memory system is obviously not affected by this processor step (among processor steps, only CAS operations and interrupted instructions change the memory system)

$$ms_q(c^o) = ms_q(c^{o+1})$$

The first k entries of the store buffer in ISA configuration c^{o+1} consist exactly of the entries of the store buffer in ISA configuration c^o

$$c^{o+1}.p(q).sb[k-1:0] = c^o.p(q).sb$$

The claim follows

$$fms(ms_q(c^{o+1}),c^{o+1}.p(q).sb[k-1:0])(base_{APIC} +_{32} 1_{32})[12] = 0$$

$\square$

In the next sections we will prove the correctness of the APIC components. We will use the stepping diagram as a visual aid for formulating correctness lemmas. We do not show all proofs of these lemmas as they are very similar to each other. Furthermore, we need to establish the correctness of the store buffer and that initial segment $s[0:n-1]$ of the stepping function is valid.

12.3.6 Correctness of Store Buffers

For the correctness of store buffers we rely for the most part on the arguments of chapter 10. However, store buffer steps that access the interrupt command registers are stepped last. In the same cycle the processor may still push a new store into the store buffer. This inverts the order of steps shown in the old stepping diagram for store buffers (fig. 182). Thus we split cases on whether we use the old stepping order — i.e., the store buffer step accesses the CMS and any processor steps that push new stores are stepped after that — or the new stepping order — i.e., the store buffer step accesses the APIC, and any processor steps that push new stores are stepped before that. Situations in which the stepping order is inverted are detected with predicate

$$sbinv^q \equiv sb(q).pop \wedge acc^q_{APIC}$$

The proof for the store buffer of processor q is now by case split on $sbinv^q$. In case $sbinv^q = 0$ we use the old stepping order and the old proofs just go through. We therefore focus here on the case

$$sbinv^q = 1$$

in which the new stepping order is used. This yields the new stepping diagram in fig. 191.

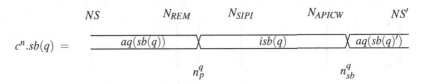

Fig. 191. Stepping diagram for store buffers during a write to the APIC

The proof for this stepping order can be done completely analogously to the previous case with slightly modified definitions and lemmas. We only state these definitions and lemmas but do not show full proofs. The intermediate store buffer is now constructed by pushing, not popping

$$isb(q) = \begin{cases} idacc^q.(data,a,bw) \circ aq(sb(q)) & ue^q_M \wedge exec.(M{-}1)^q \wedge s.(M{-}1)^q \\ aq(sb(q)) & \text{o.w.} \end{cases}$$

That the final store buffer can be obtained by popping from this intermediate store buffer (the counterpart to lemma 221) is shown in

Lemma 255.

$$aq(sb(q)') = \begin{cases} tail(isb(q)) & sb(q).pop \\ isb(q) & sb(q) \end{cases}$$

From this we conclude that the store buffer in ISA before certain steps o is equal to its (possibly ghost) counterpart in hardware, as indicated by the stepping diagram in fig. 191. As in chapter 10 these lemmas rely on the induction hypothesis for the current cycle (eq. (81)) and therefore only work in case $o \leq n$.

Lemma 256.

$$n \geq N_{REM} \rightarrow c^{N_{REM}}.p(q).sb = aq(sb(q))$$
$$n \geq N_{APICW} \rightarrow c^{N_{APICW}}.p(q).sb = isb(q)$$
$$n \geq NS' \rightarrow c^{NS'}.p(q).sb = aq(sb(q)')$$

12.3.7 Validity

We show that steps up to n which end in the current cycle or before satisfy the guard conditions. This corresponds to lemma 226 in chapter 10.

Lemma 257. *Let*

$$n \in [NS : NS') \wedge \hat{n} \leq n$$

or

$$n = NS' \wedge \hat{n} < n$$

Then

$$\gamma(c^{\hat{n}}, s(\hat{n}))$$

Proof. For $\hat{n} < NS$ the claim follows from the induction hypothesis for the current cycle (eq. (88)). For $\hat{n} \in [NS : NS')$, assume that all steps before $\hat{n}$ are valid. The proof for step $\hat{n}$ is by case distinction on the type of step $\hat{n}$. For store buffer, TLB, and instruction buffer steps nothing changes. For processor steps we need to consider the new portions γ_e, γ_{INIT}, and γ_r of the guard condition, but the proof is completely analogous to before and omitted here. This leaves SIPI and IPI delivery steps.

- $s(\hat{n}) = (SIPI, q)$: these steps can only be made while the processor is not running and a SIPI request is active

$$\gamma(c^{\hat{n}}, s(\hat{n})) = /c^{\hat{n}}.p(q).apic.running \wedge c^{\hat{n}}.p(q).apic.sipirr$$

A SIPI step is only generated if that is the case in hardware

$$/apic(q).running \wedge apic(q).sipirr$$

and with the induction hypothesis for the current cycle (eq. (81)) we obtain

$$/c^{NS}.p(q).apic.running \wedge c^{NS}.p(q).apic.sipirr$$

By construction of the stepping function, there is at most one SIPI step in each cycle. Thus none of the steps until $\hat{n}$ are SIPI steps of processor q

$$\forall o \in [NS : \hat{n}).\ s(o) \neq (SIPI, q)$$

But only SIPI steps raise the running bit or lower the SIPI request register. We conclude that the running bit stays low and the SIPI request bit stays high, which is the claim

$$/c^{\hat{n}}.p(q).apic.running \wedge c^{\hat{n}}.p(q).apic.sipirr$$

- $s(\hat{n}) = (IPI, q)$: IPI delivery steps can only be made while the delivery status bit in the ICR is high. Recall that this is bit number 12

$$\gamma(c^{\hat{n}}, s(\hat{n})) = c^{\hat{n}}.p(q).apic.ICR[12]$$

An IPI delivery step is only triggered when the APIC has an output enable bit

$$apic(q).boe, \quad ibus.oe[q]$$

By the induction hypothesis for the current cycle (eq. (81)) the operating conditions of the controlled bus are satisfied so far

$$opc\text{-}cb$$

By the correctness of the controlled bus (lemma 31) the APIC is taking a request, and thus the delivery status bit is high in hardware

$$apic(q).breq, \quad apic(q).ICR[12]$$

With the induction hypothesis for the current cycle (eq. (81)) we obtain that the bit was raised before step NS

$$c^{NS}.p(q).apic.ICR[12]$$

We show that the bit is not changed until step $\hat{n}$. The bit is changed only by three types of steps: 1) store buffer steps writing to the ICR, 2) processor steps executing a CAS instruction to the ICR, and 3) IPI delivery steps. Since there is by definition of the stepping function at most one IPI delivery step in each cycle, we know that no IPI delivery steps may have occurred.

$$\forall o \in [NS : \hat{n}). \ s(o) \neq (IPI, q)$$

Furthermore, the head of the store buffer does not include any writes to the APIC while the delivery status bit is high (this is shown with lemma 253) and hence no store buffer steps write to the ICR either. Finally, all steps before $\hat{n}$ are by assumption valid and hence obey the software conditions. Software condition SC_{APIC} precludes CAS operations to the ICR. We conclude: no steps $o \in [NS : \hat{n})$ lower the delivery status bit of the APIC of processor q

$$c^{\hat{n}}.p(q).apic.ICR[12] = c^{NS}.p(q).apic.ICR[12] = 1$$

and hence the step $\hat{n}$ is valid. That is the claim.

$\square$

12.3.8 Correctness of ICR

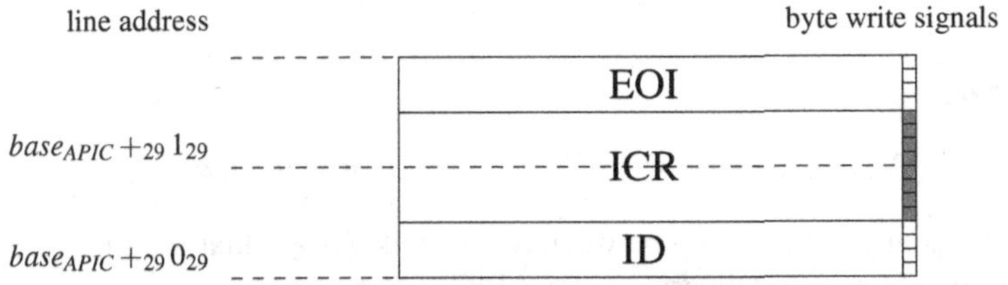

Fig. 192. Line-addressable embedding of the write-able APIC ports

For the correctness proof of the ICR we first show a series of trivial bookkeeping lemmas which relate ISA ICRs in configurations c^o for $o \in [NS : NS']$ to either the ICR at the beginning of the cycle, the intermediate ICR, or the ICR at the end of the cycle. The lemmas follow the stepping diagram in fig. 190. We only state the lemmas and sketch proofs. The first lemma is proven for $o = N_{IBUS}$, i.e., before any of the steps on the interrupt bus that might deliver interrupts. At this point the ICR in ISA has not changed yet.

Lemma 258.

$$N_{IBUS} \leq n \;\rightarrow\; c^{N_{IBUS}}.p(q).apic.ICR = apic(q).ICR$$

Proof. In ISA, store buffer steps that access the ICR, IPI delivery steps, and processor steps performing CAS instructions to the ICR modify the ICR. We show that these steps do not occur before step N_{IBUS}. There can not be any store buffer steps that access the APIC, because these are stepped after N_{IBUS} by definition of the stepping function. IPI delivery steps also do not appear before N_{IBUS} due to the definition of the stepping function. For processor steps performing CAS instructions we have by lemma 257 that all steps until N_{IBUS} are valid

$$\forall \hat{n} < N_{IBUS}. \; \gamma(c^{\hat{n}}, s(\hat{n}))$$

They thus also obey the software conditions, in particular the software conditions for the APIC

$$\forall q, \; i.pseq(q,i) < N_{IBUS} \;\rightarrow\; SC_{APIC}(c^{pseq(q,i)}, s(pseq(q,i)))$$

These software conditions preclude processor steps that execute CAS instructions that modify the ICR. We conclude that between NS and N_{IBUS} there are no changes to the ICR. With the induction hypothesis for the current cycle (eq. (81)) for $o := NS$ the claim follows

$$
\begin{aligned}
c^{N_{IBUS}}.p(q).apic.ICR &= c^{NS}.p(q).apic.ICR & \text{no changes} \\
&= apic(q).ICR & \text{IH}
\end{aligned}
$$

$\square$

After the potential delivery of interrupts, the APIC now has reached the intermediate state $iICR(q)$. Since the execution of SIPI steps does not change the ICR, it remains in this state until $o = N_{APICW}$, i.e., right before the writes to the ICR are executed.

Lemma 259.

$$N_{APICW} \leq n \;\rightarrow\; c^{N_{APICW}}.p(q).apic.ICR = iICR(q)$$

Proof. There is at most one step between N_{IBUS} and N_{APICW} that modifies the ICR in ISA, and that is an IPI delivery step of APIC q. Per construction of the stepping function this step exists if and only if APIC q has an output enable signal for the bus

$$apic(q).boe \leftrightarrow \exists o \in [N_{IBUS} : N_{APICW}). \ s(o) \in \Sigma_{apic,q}$$

The proof is now by case analysis on whether the APIC receives the output enable signal.

- $/apic(q).boe$: nothing changes in ISA (since no IPI delivery step of APIC q occurs) or in hardware (since the $iICR$ is defined to be equal to the ICR in this case). The claim follows with lemma 258

$$c^{N_{IBUS}}.p(q).apic.ICR = c^{N_{APICW}}.p(q).apic.ICR \overset{L \ 258}{=} apic(q).ICR = iICR(q)$$

- $apic(q).boe$: in this case step N_{IBUS} is an IPI delivery step of the APIC of processor q

$$s(N_{IBUS}) \in \Sigma_{apic,q}$$

which lowers the delivery status bit in the ICR. The same happens in the intermediate ICR and we conclude with lemma 258 that the intermediate ICR and the ICR in ISA after step N_{IBUS}

$$\begin{aligned} c^{N_{IBUS}+1}.p(q).apic.ICR &= c^{N_{IBUS}}.p(q).apic.ICR \wedge 1^{51}01^{12} \\ &= apic(q).ICR \wedge 1^{51}01^{12} && \text{L 258} \\ &= iICR(q) \end{aligned}$$

By definition of the stepping function we have

$$N_{APICW} = N_{IBUS} + 1$$

and the claim follows

$$c^{N_{APICW}}.p(q).apic.ICR = c^{N_{IBUS}+1}.p(q).apic.ICR = iICR(q)$$

$\square$

Recall that in chapter 10 we have shown lemma 221 which states that the final store buffer $aq(sb'_\pi)$ can be derived from the intermediate store buffer by considering only push operations. We now show a similar lemma which states that the hardware ICR at the end of the cycle can be computed from the intermediate (ghost) ICR $iICR(q)$ by applying any potential stores to the ICR in the last phase of the stepping function. Since the ICR is not line-aligned, we need to take the upper half of the store data in case the store goes to the lower half of the ICR, and the lower half of the store data if the store goes to the upper half of the ICR. This is illustrated in fig. 192. The proof of lemma 221 was completely trivial as it followed directly from the specification of the store buffer. The corresponding lemma for the ICR is not trivial: it relies on the fact that in a single cycle, the ICR can be modified either by the delivering an interrupt or by a store from the store buffer, but not both.

Lemma 260. *Assume*

$$n \geq NS'$$

Then

$$apic(q)'.ICR_L = \begin{cases} sb(q).out.data_H & sb(q).pop \wedge acc^q_{APIC} \\ & \wedge apic(q).pa = 1_5 \\ iICR(q)_L & \end{cases}$$

$$apic(q)'.ICR_H = \begin{cases} sb(q).out.data_L & sb(q).pop \wedge acc^q_{APIC} \\ & \wedge apic(q).pa = 2_5 \\ iICR(q)_H & \end{cases}$$

Proof. We elaborate the proof only for the lower half of the ICR. By construction the ICR is updated in case of an output enable signal, in which case the delivery status bit is cleared, or (in the absence of an output enable signal) in case of a write. We distinguish between these cases and the additional case where the ICR is not updated.

- $apic(q).boe$: in case of an output enable signal the delivery status is cleared, as happens in the intermediate ICR

$$apic(q)'.ICR_L = apic(q).ICR_L \wedge 1^{19}01^{12} = iICR(q)_L$$

It suffices to show that the store buffer can not be popping a write to the ICR. Assume for the sake of contradiction that this is the case

$$sb(q).pop \wedge acc^q_{APIC} \wedge apic(q).pa = 1_5$$

We conclude with the induction hypothesis for the current cycle (eq. (81)): this is the head of the store buffer in ISA configuration c^{NS}, which we will denote by w

$$sb(q).out = aq(sb(q)_\pi)[0] \stackrel{IH}{=} c^{NS}.p(q).sb[0] = w$$

Since the port address used by the APIC is the address of the lower half of the ICR, the store buffer entry w writes to the lower half of the ICR

$$w.bw[4] = 1 \wedge w.a = base_{APIC}[31:3]$$

By lemma 253 the access must be a word access

$$w.bw = 1^4 0^4$$

By lemma 254 the forwarded memory system using the first $k := 0$ stores of the store buffer, and hence the actual ICR of processor q, must have a low delivery status bit

$$\begin{aligned} & c^{NS}.p(q).apic.ports(1)[12] \\ &= ms_q(c^{NS})(base_{APIC} +_{32} 4_{32})[12] & \text{defn. } ms \\ &= fms(ms_q(c^{NS}), \varepsilon)(base_{APIC} +_{32} 4_{32})[12] & \text{defn. } fms \\ &= fms(ms_q(c^{NS}), c^{NS}.p(q).sb[-1:0])(base_{APIC} +_{32} 4_{32})[12] \\ &= 0 & \text{L 254} \end{aligned}$$

Again with the induction hypothesis for the current cycle we conclude that the same holds for the ICR in hardware at the beginning of the cycle

$$apic(q).ports(1)[12] = c^{NS}.p(q).apic.ports(1)[12] = 0$$

This means that the APIC of processor q is not requesting a grant. By the induction hypothesis for the current cycle (eq. (81)) the operating conditions of the controlled bus are satisfied so far

$$opc\text{-}cb$$

and hence by lemma 31 processor q does not receive an output enable signal from the controlled bus

$$apic(q).breq = 0, \quad ibus.oe[q] = 0 \quad apic(q).boe = 0$$

which contradicts our assumption that the APIC has an output enable signal.

- $/apic(q).boe \wedge apic(q).pw \wedge apic(q).pa = 1_5$: by construction such a write only comes from a store buffer pop which writes to the APIC

$$sb(q).pop \wedge acc^q_{APIC}$$

By construction in the absence of an output enable signal there is no special clock enable for the ICR

$$apic(q).ICR.ce = 0$$

Furthermore, by construction of the port address, the byte-write signal number 4 is raised

$$dacc^q.bw[4] = sb(q).out.bw[4] = 1$$

By the semantics of the SPR-RAM used for the ports, the new data in the ICR is exactly the data provided by the popped store buffer entry, and the claim follows

$$apic(q)'.ICR_L = dacc^q.data_H = sb(q).out.data_H$$

- No update: since there is no update we have that no store buffer entry was popped that writes to the APIC port number 1

$$\neg(sb(q).pop \wedge acc^q_{APIC} \wedge apic(q).pa = 1_5)$$

and that also no output enable signal was given

$$\neg apic(q).boe$$

The claim follows

$$apic(q)'.ICR_L = apic(q).ICR_L = iICR(q)_L$$

$\square$

It remains to show that the ICR in ISA configuration $c^{NS'}$ reached after completing all steps executed in the current cycle equals the ICR $apic(q)'.ICR$ in hardware at the end of the cycle.

Lemma 261.

$$NS' \leq n \; \rightarrow \; c^{NS'}.p(q).apic.ICR = apic(q)'.ICR$$

Proof. We show the claim only for the lower half of the ICR, the proof for the upper half is analogous. Between steps N_{APICW} and NS', the ICR is in ISA updated only by up to one store buffer write that modifies the ICR. Let w be the store buffer entry that might be popped to the APIC

$$w = c^o.p(q).sb[0]$$

We have

$$c^{NS'}.p(q).apic.ICR_L$$
$$= \begin{cases} w.data_H & o \in [N_{APICW} : NS') \land s(o) \in \Sigma_{sb,q} \\ & \land w.a = base_{APIC}[31:3] \land w.bw[4] \\ c^{N_{APICW}}.p(q).apic.ICR_L \end{cases}$$

With the coupling of store buffer in ISA and in hardware established in section 12.3.6 we obtain that w is also the head of the store buffer in hardware

$$w = c^o.p(q).sb[0] \stackrel{\text{L } 256}{=} aq(sb(q))[0] = sb(q).out$$

and that there is a store buffer step accessing the APIC in ISA iff there is also a store buffer pop accessing the APIC in hardware. Thus

$$c^{NS'}.p(q).apic.ICR_L$$
$$= \begin{cases} w.data_H & sb(q).pop \land acc^q_{APIC} \\ & \land w.a = base_{APIC}[31:3] \land w.bw[4] \\ c^{N_{APICW}}.p(q).apic.ICR_L \end{cases}$$

By construction of the APIC port address $apic(q).pa$ we obtain that in case of a store buffer write with effective address

$$w.a = base_{APIC}[31:3]$$

and byte-write signal

$$w.bw[4] = 1$$

is writing to port 1. We conclude

$$c^{NS'}.p(q).apic.ICR_L$$
$$= \begin{cases} w.data_H & sb(q).pop \land acc^q_{APIC} \\ & \land apic(q).pa = 1 \\ c^{N_{APICW}}.p(q).apic.ICR_L \end{cases}$$

By lemma 259, the ICR before step N_{APICW} in ISA is the intermediate ICR

$$c^{N_{APICW}}.p(q).apic.ICR = iICR(q)$$

and the claim follows with lemma 260.

$$
\begin{aligned}
&c^{NS'}.p(q).apic.ICR_L \\
&= \begin{cases} w.data_H & sb(q).pop \wedge acc^q_{APIC} \\ & \wedge apic(q).pa = 1 \\ c^{N_{APICW}}.p(q).apic.ICR_L \end{cases} \\
&= \begin{cases} w.data_H & sb(q).pop \wedge acc^q_{APIC} \\ & \wedge apic(q).pa = 1 \\ iICR(q)_L \end{cases} \\
&= apic(q)'.ICR_L \qquad\qquad\qquad\qquad \text{L 260}
\end{aligned}
$$

$\qquad\qquad\qquad\qquad\qquad\qquad\qquad\qquad\qquad\qquad\qquad\qquad\qquad\qquad\qquad$ □

This concludes the proof for the ICR. We will show in the following sections that the correctness of the other registers can be established in similar fashion.

12.3.9 Correctness of IRR

The IRR does not change until step N_{REM}.

Lemma 262.

$$N_{REM} \le n \ \rightarrow \ c^{N_{REM}}.p(q).apic.IRR = apic(q).IRR$$

Proof. In these phases, the IRR might only be changed by 1) interrupted processor steps, and 2) processor steps which violate the software conditions and perform CAS operations to the IRR. IPI delivery steps and store buffer steps to the APIC, which might also change the IRR, are trivially excluded in these phases as they are stepped later. We show that also no interrupted processor steps exist between NS and N_{REM} by contradiction. Assume thus that some step o is an interrupted processor step

$$o \in [NS : N_{REM}) \wedge s(o) \in \Sigma_{p,q} \wedge jisr(c^o, s(o))$$

This step executes some instruction i of processor q which is a *jisr*

$$o = pseq(q,i) \wedge jisr^{q,i}_\sigma$$

Only (in hardware) memory operations which are executed are stepped before N_{REM}

$$ue^q_M \wedge mop.(M-1)^q \wedge exec.(M-1)^q$$

and by the induction hypothesis for the current cycle (eq. (81)) the instruction is also an executed memory operation in ISA

$$mop_\sigma^{q,i} \wedge exec_\sigma^{q,i}$$

We observe that the only interrupts that can affect memory operations are of type repeat or abort. Thus from $exec_\sigma^{q,i}$ we conclude that the instruction is not interrupted at all

$$/jisr_\sigma^{q,i}$$

which is a contradiction. Finally we know from lemma 257 that all steps until N_{REM} are valid

$$\forall \hat{n} < N_{REM}.\ \gamma(c^{\hat{n}}, s(\hat{n}))$$

and thus obey the software conditions. We obtain that there are no processor steps executing CAS operations to the IRR either.

We conclude: neither IPI steps nor processor steps modify the IRR before N_{REM}. Thus the IRR is not changed. The claim follows with the induction hypothesis for the current cycle for $o := NS$

$$c^{N_{REM}}.p(q).apic.IRR = c^{NS}.p(q).apic.IRR \overset{IH}{=} apic(q).IRR$$

$\square$

Between steps N_{REM} and N_{IBUS}, the IRR can be changed by a processor step which takes the external interrupt. Recall that the effect of this is to lower the highest-priority interrupt in the IRR. This is also the effect of taking the interrupt in hardware, which has been applied in the intermediate IRR. Hence the IRR in ISA corresponds to the intermediate IRR before step N_{IBUS}.

Lemma 263.

$$N_{IBUS} \leq n \ \rightarrow \ c^{N_{IBUS}}.p(q).apic.IRR = iIRR(q)$$

Proof. We distinguish whether processor q executes an *external* interrupt between steps N_{REM} and N_{IBUS}.

- $o \in [N_{REM} : N_{IBUS}) \wedge o = pseq(q,i) \wedge mca_\sigma^{q,i}[3] = 1$: since processor q is stepped, it must have an update enable in hardware

$$ue_M^q$$

and by the induction hypothesis for the current cycle (eq. (81)) we obtain that it is taking the external interrupt in hardware

$$mca.(M-1)^q[3] = 1$$

By construction the processor executes the fixed request

$$apic(q).fixedex$$

Thus in hardware the intermediate IRR is obtained by turning low the highest-priority interrupt bit.

$$iIRR(q) = apic(q).IRR \wedge /apic(q).irrmin$$

Let i be the index of the highest-priority interrupt

$$i = \min\{\,j \mid apic(q).IRR[j]\,\}$$

By the correctness of the find-first-one circuit used to compute $irrmin$, we have that exactly bit i is raised

$$apic(q).irrmin[j] \leftrightarrow j = i$$

Thus bit j of the intermediate IRR can be rephrased as

$$iIRR(q)[j] = \begin{cases} 0 & j = i \\ apic(q).IRR[j] \end{cases}$$

There is at most one step of processor q in any cycle. Between N_{REM} and N_{IBUS} there are no IPI delivery steps that could modify the IRR. Hence the IRR before step N_{IBUS} is updated at most once (in step o). With lemma 262 which couples the state of the ISA IRR in step N_{IBUS} to the hardware IRR we conclude

$$c^o.apic(q).IRR = c^{N_{REM}}.apic(q).IRR = apic(q).IRR$$

Thus i is also the index of the highest-priority interrupt in the ISA IRR

$$i = \min\{\,j \mid apic(q).IRR[j]\,\}$$

By definition of ISA bit j of the IRR before step $o+1$ is equal to zero if $j = i$ and to the value of bit j of the IRR before step o otherwise

$$c^{o+1}.apic(q).iRR = \begin{cases} 0 & j = i \\ c^o.apic(q).IRR[j] \end{cases}$$

The claim follows with lemma 262 and the observation that there are no other changes to the IRR between N_{REM} and N_{IBUS}

$$
\begin{aligned}
c^{N_{IBUS}}.p(q).apic.IRR[j] &= c^{o+1}.p(q).apic.IRR[j] && \text{no other change} \\
&= \begin{cases} 0 & j = i \\ c^o.apic(q).IRR[j] \end{cases} \\
&= \begin{cases} 0 & j = i \\ c^{N_{REM}}.apic(q).IRR[j] \end{cases} && \text{no other change} \\
&= \begin{cases} 0 & j = i \\ apic(q).IRR[j] \end{cases} && \text{L 262} \\
&= iIRR(q)[j]
\end{aligned}
$$

- No such step: then with the induction hypothesis for the current cycle eq. (81) we conclude that in hardware processor q is not clocking an instruction out of the memory stage which has an external interrupt

$$/(ue_M^q \wedge mca.(M-1)^q[3])$$

Thus a potential fixed request of the APIC is not executed

$$/apic(q).fixedex$$

Thus in hardware the intermediate IRR is unchanged

$$iIRR(q) = apic(q).IRR$$

Furthermore, steps until N_{IBUS} are valid by lemma 257

$$\forall \hat{n} < N_{IBUS}. \; \gamma(c^{\hat{n}}, s(\hat{n}))$$

Thus they obey the software conditions and do not perform CAS operations to the IRR. We conclude that in ISA the IRR is also unchanged. The claim follows with lemma 262

$$c^{N_{IBUS}}.p(q).apic.IRR = c^{N_{REM}}.p(q).apic.IRR \overset{L\,262}{=} apic(q).IRR = iIRR(q)$$

$\square$

Step N_{IBUS} may be an IPI delivery step which raises the bit in the IRR corresponding to the delivered interrupt. Steps after that only include 1) SIPI steps which do not modify the IRR and 2) store buffer steps, which per software condition do not write to the IRR. By bookkeeping one can show that in hardware, the final IRR can also be computed from the intermediate IRR by raising the bit corresponding any potential delivered interrupt.

Lemma 264.

$$apic(q)'.IRR[j] = \begin{cases} 1 & j = \langle apic(q).din.vect \rangle \\ & \wedge apic(q).bhot \wedge apic(q).bhit \wedge apic(q).Fixed \\ iIRR(q)[j] & o.w. \end{cases}$$

Proof. We abbreviate 'receive'

$$rec = apic(q).bhot \wedge apic(q).bhit \wedge apic(q).Fixed$$

By construction the interrupt index *iindex* is the output of the decoder using the vector from the interrupt bus, anded with the *rec* signal

$$apic(q).iindex = \text{Dec}(apic(q).bin.vect) \wedge rec$$

The specification of the decoder states that output bit j of this decoder is raised iff the interrupt vector encodes the number j

$$apic(q).iindex[j] \leftrightarrow j = \langle apic(q).bin.vect \rangle \wedge rec$$

The claim follows from the construction of the interrupt request register

$$apic(q)'.IRR[j]$$

$$\equiv iindex[j] \vee \begin{cases} apic(q).IRR[j] \wedge /apic(q).irrmin[j] & apic(q).fixedex \\ apic(q).IRR[j] & \text{o.w.} \end{cases}$$

$$\equiv iindex[j] \vee iIRR(q)[j]$$

$$\equiv (j = \langle apic(q).bin.vect \rangle \wedge rec) \vee iIRR(q)[j]$$

$$\equiv \begin{cases} 1 & j = \langle apic(q).bin.vect \rangle \wedge rec \\ iIRR(q)[j] & \text{o.w.} \end{cases}$$

$\square$

Lemma 265.

$$NS' \leq n \;\rightarrow\; c^{NS'}.p(q).apic.IRR = apic(q)'.IRR$$

Proof. By lemma 253 store buffers do not contain writes to the IRR. Hence any store buffer steps do not modify the IRR. The only steps between N_{IBUS} and NS' that modify the IRR are IPI delivery steps. By construction of the stepping function there is at most one such step, namely potentially step N_{IBUS}. We abbreviate

$$o = N_{IBUS}$$

This step changes the IRR of processor q if and only if it is delivering a fixed interrupt and processor q is a target of the interrupt. We conclude:

$$c^{NS'}.p(q).apic.IRR[j] = \begin{cases} 1 & \begin{aligned} s(o) &= (IPI, \hat{q}) \\ &\wedge q \in itargets(c^o, s(o)) \\ &\wedge Fixed(c^o, s(o)) \end{aligned} \\ c^o.p(q).apic.IRR[j] & \end{cases}$$

By lemma 258 with $q := \hat{q}$, the ISA ICR before step $o = N_{IBUS}$ is equal to the hardware ICR from the beginning of the cycle

$$c^o.p(\hat{q}).apic.ICR = apic(\hat{q}).ICR$$

We show a few trivial bookkeeping sublemmas which show that hardware and ISA agree on whether processor q is a target of a fixed interrupt.

Lemma 266.

$$s(o) = (IPI, \hat{q}) \;\rightarrow\; apic(q).Fixed = Fixed(c^o, s(o))$$

Proof. By definition of the stepping function, the bus is hot and the APIC of processor $\hat{q}$ has an output enable signal

$$ibus.bhot \land apic(\hat{q}).boe$$

By the induction hypothesis for the current cycle (eq. (81)) the operating conditions of the bus have been satisfied so far

$$opc\text{-}cb$$

and we can use part three of lemma 31 to show that the data on the bus comes from APIC $\hat{q}$. Trivial bookkeeping shows the claim

$$
\begin{aligned}
apic(q).Fixed &\equiv apic(q).bin.dm = 000 \\
&\equiv ibus.data.dm = 000 \\
&\equiv apic(\hat{q}).ICR.dm = 000 \qquad \text{L 31} \\
&\equiv c^o.p(\hat{q}).apic.ICR = 000 \\
&\equiv Fixed(c^o, s(o))
\end{aligned}
$$

$\square$

Lemma 267.

$$s(o) = (IPI, \hat{q}) \;\rightarrow\; apic(q).bhit \equiv q \in itargets(c^o, s(o))$$

Proof. Since the ID port is never changed we have

$$apic(q).ID = apic(q)^0.ID = c^0.p(q).apic.ID = c^o.p(q).apic.ID$$

The construction of *bhit* corresponds directly to the definition of *itargets*. Trivial bookkeeping involving the correctness of the equality testers now shows the claim. We omit the proof. $\square$

Furthermore, step o is the IPI delivery of the APIC of *some* processor $\hat{q}$ if the bus is hot

Lemma 268.

$$s(o) = (IPI, \hat{q}) \;\leftrightarrow\; apic(q).bhot$$

Proof. The bus is hot if the interrupt bus is hot

$$apic(q).bhot = ibus.bhot$$

and an IPI delivery step is generated exactly if the interrupt bus is hot

$$ibus.bhot \leftrightarrow \exists \hat{q}.\, s(o) = (IPI, \hat{q})$$

$\square$

With these lemmas we conclude that bit j in the IRR is raised if processor q receives an IPI *in hardware*. The claim follows with lemmas 263 and 264

$$c^{NS'}.p(q).apic.IRR[j] = \begin{cases} 1 & s(o) = (IPI, \hat{q}) \\ & \wedge\, q \in itargets(c^o, s(o)) \\ & \wedge\, Fixed(c^o, s(o)) \\ c^o.p(q).apic.IRR[j] \end{cases}$$

$$= \begin{cases} 1 & apic(q).bhot \qquad \text{L 266} \\ & \wedge\, apic(q).bhit \qquad \text{L 267} \\ & \wedge\, apic(q).Fixed \quad \text{L 268} \\ c^o.p(q).apic.IRR[j] \end{cases}$$

$$= \begin{cases} 1 & apic(q).bhot \\ & \wedge\, apic(q).bhit \\ & \wedge\, apic(q).Fixed \qquad \text{L 263} \\ iIRR(q)[j] \end{cases}$$

$$= apic(q)'.IRR[j] \qquad\qquad \text{L 264}$$

$\square$

12.3.10 Correctness of ISR

The first part of the proof is completely analogous to the proof for the IRR. We only sketch proofs.

Lemma 269.

$$N_{REM} \le n \;\rightarrow\; c^{N_{REM}}.p(q).apic.ISR = apic(q).ISR$$

Proof. Due to the software conditions and the definition of the stepping functions, steps before N_{REM} do not change the ISR. The claim follows from the induction hypothesis of the current cycle (eq. (81))

$$apic(q).ISR = c^{NS}.p(q).apic.ISR = c^{N_{REM}}.p(q).apic.ISR$$

$\square$

Lemma 270.

$$N_{APICW} \le n \;\rightarrow\; c^{N_{APICW}}.p(q).apic.ISR = iISR(q)$$

Proof. Either both hardware and ISA complete a processor step which executes an external interrupt, or neither does. In case neither does nothing changes and the claim follows with lemma 269. If both do, they both execute the same external interrupt (this is shown with lemma 262)

$$i = \min\{\,j \mid c^{N_{REM}}.p(q).apic.IRR[j]\,\} = \min\{\,j \mid apic(q).IRR[j]\,\}$$

Both in hardware and in ISA, bit number i is raised, and the claim follows with lemma 269

$$c^{N_{APICW}}.p(q).apic.ISR[j] = \begin{cases} 1 & j = i \\ c^{N_{REM}}.p(q).apic.ISR[j] & \text{o.w.} \end{cases}$$

$$= \begin{cases} 1 & j = i \\ apic(q).ISR[j] & \text{o.w.} \end{cases}$$

$$= iISR(q)[j]$$

$\square$

From this point on, proofs differ from those for the IRR, so we consider them in more detail. This is the part of the proof where we consider the effect of store buffer writes to the EOI port of the APIC. In hardware, such writes clear the bit corresponding to the highest-priority interrupt bit in the ISR at the beginning of the cycle. This is bit

$$i = \min\{\,j \mid apic(q).ISR[j]\,\}$$

In ISA, such steps clear the highest-priority interrupt bit in the ISR in configuration N_{APICW}. This is bit

$$\hat{i} = \min\{\,j \mid c^{N_{APICW}}.p(q).apic.ISR[j]\,\}$$

which by lemma 270 comes from the intermediate ISR

$$\hat{i} = \min\{\,j \mid iISR(q)[j]\,\}$$

Note that the intermediate ISR differs from the ISR at the beginning of the cycle in at most one bit, which is raised in the intermediate ISR. If this bit is the index of a higher-priority interrupt than that with index i, we have

$$\hat{i} < i$$

and thus in ISA and hardware, different bits of the ISR would be cleared. However, such a situation with $\hat{i} \neq i$ can only occur if an external interrupt is taken by processor q in the current cycle. Such interrupts drain the store buffer, i.e., are only taken while the store buffer is empty. Thus a write to the EOI port can not occur in cycles where $\hat{i} \neq i$.

This allows us to show the following lemma, which states that when a write to the EOI port occurs, it clears bit $\hat{i}$ in hardware.

Lemma 271.

$$n \geq N_{APICW} \;\rightarrow\; apic(q)'.ISR[j] = \begin{cases} 0 & j = \hat{i} \\ & \land\, apic(q).pw \land apic(q).pa = 3_5 \\ iISR(q)[j] & \text{o.w.} \end{cases}$$

Proof. We split cases on whether there is a write to the EOI port. We omit the case where there is no such write because that case is trivial. Assume thus

$$apic(q).pw \wedge apic(q).pa = 3_5$$

There must be a store buffer pop which writes to the APIC

$$acc_{APIC}^q \wedge sb(q).pop$$

Thus the store buffer must be non-empty

$$/sb(q).empty$$

Since interrupts drain the store buffer, they are due to the hazard signal $busy_{drain}$ only executed (in hardware) when the store buffer is empty. Thus

$$/(ue_M^q \wedge jisr.(M-1)^q)$$

Thus we have in particular no execution of an INIT interrupt

$$/(ue_M^q \wedge mca.(M-1)[2]^q), \quad /apic(q).initex$$

and hence the intermediate ISR is equal to the ISR

$$iISR(q) = apic(q).ISR$$

With lemma 270 we conclude that ISA and hardware use the same ISR for computing the index of the interrupt, and thus $i = \hat{i}$

$$
\begin{aligned}
i &= \min\{\, j \mid apic(q).ISR[j]\,\} \\
&= \min\{\, j \mid iISR(q)[j]\,\} \\
&= \min\{\, j \mid c^{N_{APICW}}.p(q).apic.ISR[j]\,\} \qquad \text{lemma 270} \\
&= \hat{i}
\end{aligned}
$$

The claim follows. $\square$

We finally show that the ISR before step NS' must be again in sync with the ISR in hardware after the current cycle.

Lemma 272.

$$n \geq NS' \;\rightarrow\; c^{NS'}.p(q).apic.ISR = apic(q)'.ISR$$

Proof. We first show a bookkeeping sublemma. If there is a write to the EOI port in hardware, there is also such a write in ISA.

Lemma 273.

$$apic(q).pw \wedge apic(q).pa = 3_5 \;\leftrightarrow\; \exists o \in [N_{APICW} : NS').\, s(o) \in \Sigma_{sb,q} \wedge eoiw(c^o, s(o))$$

Proof. We only show the direction from left to right. Assume thus

$$apic(q).pw \wedge apic(q).pa = 3_5$$

There must be an store buffer pop which writes to the APIC

$$acc^q_{APIC} \wedge sb(q).pop$$

Thus the store buffer must be non-empty

$$/sb(q).empty$$

By definition of the stepping function there must also be a corresponding store buffer step o in the last phase

$$o \in [N_{APICW} : NS') \wedge s(o) \in \Sigma_{sb,q}$$

Note that since we have a store buffer pop, as described in section 12.3.6 the order of the store buffer and processor steps of processor q is inverted

$$sbinv^q$$

The step executes the same store as in hardware. This follows from lemma 256 with the observation that only step o changes the store buffer of processor q in this phase

$$
\begin{aligned}
c^o.p(q).sb[0] &= c^{N_{APICW}}.p(q).sb[0] &&\text{no other changes} \\
&= isb(q)[0] &&\text{L 256} \\
&= \begin{cases} aq(sb(q))[0] & \dots \\ (\dots \circ aq(sb(q)))[0] & \dots \end{cases} &&\text{defn } isb \\
&= aq(sb(q))[0] &&sb(q) \text{ not empty} \\
&= sb(q).out
\end{aligned}
$$

Since the store in hardware is a write to the EOI port, the store in ISA must also write to the EOI port

$$eoiw(c^o, s(o))$$

$\square$

Since no other steps in this phase change the ISR, we conclude that the ISR at the end of the phase, before step NS', has merely cleared bit $\hat{\imath}$. Since that is the same change that happens in hardware (lemma 271), the claim follows with the definition of ISA and lemma 270.

$$apic(q)'.ISR[j]$$

$$= \begin{cases} 0 & j = \hat{i} \wedge apic(q).pw \wedge apic(q).pa = 3_5 \\ iISR(q)[j] & \text{o.w.} \end{cases} \qquad \text{L 271}$$

$$= \begin{cases} 0 & j = \hat{i} \wedge \exists o \in [N_{APICW} : NS'). \\ & s(o) \in \Sigma_{sb,q} \wedge eoiw(c^o, s(o)) \\ iISR(q)[j] & \text{o.w.} \end{cases} \qquad \text{L 273}$$

$$= \begin{cases} 0 & j = \hat{i} \wedge \exists o \in [N_{APICW} : NS'). \\ & s(o) \in \Sigma_{sb,q} \wedge eoiw(c^o, s(o)) \\ c^{N_{APICW}}.p(q).apic.ISR[j] & \text{o.w.} \end{cases} \qquad \text{L 270}$$

$$= \begin{cases} c^{o+1}.p(q).apic.ISR[j] & j = \hat{i} \wedge \exists o \in [N_{APICW} : NS'). \\ & s(o) \in \Sigma_{sb,q} \wedge eoiw(c^o, s(o)) \\ c^{N_{APICW}}.p(q).apic.ISR[j] & \text{o.w.} \end{cases} \qquad \text{defn. ISA}$$

$$= c^{NS'}.p(q).apic.ISR[j] \qquad \text{no other changes}$$

$$\square$$

12.3.11 Remaining Registers

The EOI port by construction never changes (since $ports.w = 0$ when the address is the EOI port). It also never changes in ISA. Thus the proof for this register is trivial.

Lemma 274.

$$n \geq NS' \;\to\; c^{NS'}.p(q).apic.EOI = apic(q)'.EOI$$

The remaining registers (SIPIrr, INITrr, running bit) can be proven correct along similar lines. We only state the lemmas.

Lemma 275.

$$n \geq N_{SIPI} \;\to\; c^{N_{SIPI}}.p(q).apic.sipirr = apic(q).sipirr$$
$$n \geq N_{IBUS} \;\to\; c^{N_{IBUS}}.p(q).apic.sipirr = iS(q)$$
$$n \geq NS' \;\to\; c^{NS'}.p(q).apic.sipirr = apic(q)'.sipirr$$

Lemma 276.

$$n \geq N_{REM} \;\to\; c^{N_{REM}}.p(q).apic.initrr = apic(q).initrr$$
$$n \geq N_{IBUS} \;\to\; c^{N_{IBUS}}.p(q).apic.initrr = iI(q)$$
$$n \geq NS' \;\to\; c^{NS'}.p(q).apic.initrr = apic(q)'.initrr$$

Lemma 277.

$$n \geq N_{REM} \; \rightarrow \; c^{N_{REM}}.p(q).apic.running = apic(q).running$$
$$n \geq N_{SIPI} \; \rightarrow \; c^{N_{SIPI}}.p(q).apic.running = irunning(q)$$
$$n \geq NS' \; \rightarrow \; c^{NS'}.p(q).apic.running = apic(q)'.running$$

12.3.12 Correctness of Components outside the Pipeline

We have to show: if n is the number of steps executed in the current cycle and all previous cycles

$$n = NS'$$

then all components are coupled correctly and steps before NS' are valid:

$$m(h') = \ell(c^n.m) \wedge opc' \tag{82}$$
$$\wedge \; aq(sb(q)'_\pi) = c^n.p(q).sb \tag{83}$$
$$\wedge \; walks(mmu_I(q)') \cup walks(mmu_E(q)') \subseteq c^n.tlb(q) \tag{84}$$
$$\wedge \; apic(q)' = c^n.p(q).apic \wedge opc\text{-}cb' \tag{85}$$
$$\wedge \; \forall \hat{n} < n. \; \gamma(c^{\hat{n}}, s(\hat{n})) \tag{86}$$

The proof of eq. (82) is exactly as before. For the proof of eq. (83) we split cases on whether the order of store buffer steps is inverted or not.

- $/sbinv^q$: proof is exactly as before
- $sbinv^q$: the claim is lemma 256

Correctness of the TLB (eq. (84)) is shown exactly as before. For the correctness of APICs we prove the operating conditions of the controlled bus (from section 3.5.4) and the correctness of the APIC state separately.

- $apic(q)' = c^n.p(q).apic$: this is proven jointly by lemmas 261, 265, 272 and 274 to 277.
- $opc\text{-}cb'$: by the induction hypothesis for the current cycle (eq. (81)) with $o := NS$ we know that the operating condition was satisfied so far

$$opc\text{-}cb$$

Thus it remains to show the conditions for the current cycle. First we show that if any APIC q has a request and no output enable, it keeps the request active

$$ibus.req[q] \wedge /ibus.oe[q] \; \rightarrow \; ibus.req[q]'$$

Assume thus that APIC q has a request and no output enable. By construction we conclude

$$apic(q).ICR.ds = 1 \wedge /apic(q).boe$$

We show that the delivery status bit is still set after the cycle. Since APIC q does not have an active output enable signal, by definition of the stepping function there are no IPI delivery steps of APIC q

$$\forall o \in [NS : NS'].\ s(o) \neq (IPI, q)$$

Thus IPI steps do not change the delivery status in ISA. By lemma 257 all steps until NS' are valid

$$\forall \hat{n} < NS'.\ \gamma(c^{\hat{n}}, s(\hat{n}))$$

and thus obey the software conditions. With SC_{APIC} we conclude that there are no CAS operations in ISA to the APIC

$$\forall o \in [NS : NS'].\ s(o) \in \Sigma_{p,q} \wedge cas(c^o, s(o)) \ \rightarrow\ ea(c^o, s(o)) \notin \mathcal{A}$$

Thus processor steps do not change the delivery status in ISA. This leaves only store buffer steps. By the induction hypothesis for the current cycle the delivery status bit is set in ISA

$$c^{NS}.p(q).apic.ICR.ds = apic(q).ICR.ds = 1$$

Therefore by contraposition of lemma 254 the store buffer does not contain any writes to the ICR. Thus store buffer pops in the current cycle can also not affect the ICR. We conclude:

$$c^{NS'}.p(q).apic.ICR.ds = c^{NS}.p(q).apic.ICR.ds = 1$$

The claim follows with lemma 261

$$ibus.req[q]' = apic(q)'.ICR.ds = c^{NS'}.p(q).APIC.ICR.ds = 1$$

Next we show that if an APIC has an output enable signal, it turns of its request the next cycle

$$ibus.oe[q] \ \rightarrow\ /ibus.req[q]'$$

Assume that the APIC has an output enable signal. Then in this cycle, it clears the delivery status bit.

$$apic(q).boe, \quad apic(q).ICR.ce, \quad apic(q)'.ICR.ds = 0$$

Thus by construction it has no request in the next cycle

$$/apic(q).breq', \quad /ibus.req[q]'$$

which is the claim.

Finally, eq. (86) is proven by lemma 257.

12.3.13 Correctness of Pipeline

Assume in what follows that n is a step of processor q executing instruction i

$$n = pseq(q, i)$$

We have to show that pipeline registers of instruction i are correct after the current cycle. This involves two new parts: 1) reading from the APIC, and 2) the new parts of the guard condition:

$$i > I'_1 \rightarrow \gamma_r^{q,i}$$
$$i > I'_{M-1} \rightarrow \gamma_e^{q,i}$$
$$i > I'_{M-1} \rightarrow \gamma_{INIT}^{q,i}$$

For the reading from the APIC we only show the centerpiece of the correctness argument, that hardware and ISA read from the same APIC configuration. We omit the bit-fiddling details of the proof (e.g., that the correct register is selected and that the read result is constructed correctly from the value loaded from the APIC), which are completely analogous to similar proofs for the cache memory system and store buffer forwarding. Assume that instruction i is in the memory stage and completes a read from the APIC

$$i = I_M^q \wedge l_\sigma^{q,i} \wedge ea_\sigma^{q,i} \in \mathcal{A} \wedge ue_M^q$$

In hardware, the processor obviously reads directly from the APIC ports, i.e., from configuration

$$apic(q).ports$$

at the beginning of the cycle. Thus we need to show that the processor reads from the same configuration in ISA, i.e.,

$$c^n.p(q).apic.ports \overset{!}{=} apic(q).ports$$

Since we have ue_M, step n executing instruction i must be completed in the current cycle

$$n \in [NS : NS')$$

By definition of the stepping function, processors are never stepped after N_{SIPI}. Thus in fact

$$n \in [NS : N_{SIPI})$$

However, none of the steps in the interval $[NS : n)$ modify the APIC of processor q: they are not IPI or SIPI steps or store buffer steps accessing the APIC because those are not stepped before N_{SIPI}. They can also not be processor steps of processor q because there is at most one such step in each cycle, and that step is step n. With the induction hypothesis for the current cycle (eq. (81)) we conclude:

$$c^n.p(q).apic.ports = c^{NS}.p(q).apic.ports \qquad \text{no changes}$$
$$= apic(q).ports \qquad \text{IH}$$

For the new parts of the guard condition, we consider two cases: 1) the instruction is still in the relevant stage in the current cycle, but below it in the next cycle. This is the exciting case where the action happens, as we have to establish that the guard condition will hold in the ISA step $n = pseq(q, i)$ in which the instruction is executed. 2) the instruction is already below the stage in the current cycle, and stays below it. In this case the proof is completely trivial as the induction hypothesis for the current cycle already states that the guard condition holds in the ISA step $n = pseq(q, i)$ in which the instruction is executed. Recall that we have already established that in case 1). We show the proof of case 2) first but only for γ_r. The other parts of the guard condition are proven identically. Assume thus

$$i > I_1^q \wedge i > I_1^{q'}$$

By the induction hypothesis for the current cycle (eq. (81)) we have

$$\gamma_r^{q,i}$$

which is the claim.

We now treat the more interesting case 1). We show each part of the guard condition separately. Consider first the guard condition for the running bit, which is sampled in the first stage. Assume thus

$$i = I_1^q \wedge ue_1^q$$

From ue_1^q we conclude that there is no hazard, and thus the running bit is on

$$/haz_1^q, \quad apic(q).running$$

Thus by the induction hypothesis for the current cycle, the running bit is on in ISA configuration NS

$$c^{NS}.p(q).apic.running$$

We show that the running bit is not turned off until step n by contradiction. The running bit is only turned off by an INIT interrupt. Assume for the sake of contradiction that some step o executes such an interrupt, or more generally, any interrupt at all

$$o \in [NS : n) \wedge o = pseq(q, g) \wedge jisr_o^{q,g}$$

Instruction g has not been executed yet, and is executed before instruction i. The first instruction that has not been executed yet is the instruction in the memory stage. Thus

$$I_M^q \leq g < i$$

Analogous to lemma 154 we can show that there is no such interrupt

Lemma 278. *Let g be an instruction between I_M and $i = I_1'$*

$$g \in [I_M : i)$$

Then instruction g is not interrupted in ISA

$$/jisr_o^g$$

This is a contradiction. We conclude that the running bit is not changed

$$c^n.p(q).apic.running = c^{NS}.p(q).apic.running = 1$$

which is the claim.

Consider now the other two guard conditions for INIT and external interrupts. These are sampled in the stage above memory. Assume thus

$$i = I^q_{M-1} \wedge ue^q_{M-1}$$

We only show the proof for the external interrupt, as the INIT interrupt can be shown completely analogously. We need to show

$$e^{q,i}_\sigma \xrightarrow{!} \exists h.\ c^n.p(q).apic.IRR[h] \wedge \forall j < h.\ /c^n.p(q).apic.ISR[j]$$

Assume $e^{q,i}_\sigma$. By definition of $e^{q,i}_\sigma$ we know that there must be an external event signal e^q in hardware in the current cycle. Thus the memory stage is empty and there is a request from the APIC

$$\begin{aligned}
1 &= e^{q,i}_\sigma \\
&= e^q \\
&= apic(q).fixedr \wedge /full^q_{M-1}
\end{aligned}$$

Because there is a request for an interrupt, there must be an interrupt h which in hardware is being requested and where no higher-priority interrupts is being serviced

$$\exists h.\ apic(q).IRR[h] \wedge \forall j < h.\ /apic(q).ISR[j]$$

From the induction hypothesis for the current cycle (eq. (81)) we conclude that the same holds for ISA step NS.

$$\exists h.\ c^{NS}.p(q).apic.IRR[h] \wedge \forall j < h.\ /c^{NS}.p(q).apic.ISR[j] \tag{87}$$

Because the memory stage is not full, the instruction in the stage above is the next instruction to be executed by processor q

$$I^q_M = I^q_{M-1} = i$$

Thus between ISA step NS and ISA step n, no other processor steps of processor q can modify the APIC or insert new entries into the store buffer.

$$\forall o \in [NS:n).\ s(o) \notin \Sigma_{p,q} \wedge \forall e \in c^o.p(q).sb.\ e \in c^{NS}.p(q).sb$$

By lemma 253, store buffer entries which have entered in configuration c^{NS} do not write to the IRR or ISR. Thus the IRR and ISR are only modified by 1) IPI delivery steps and 2) store buffer steps writing to the EOI port. The former only raise bits in the IRR. Thus every bit that is currently active in the IRR will still be active when processor q executes instruction i

$$c^n.p(q).apic.IRR \geq c^{NS}.p(q).apic.IRR$$

The latter only lower bits in the ISR. Thus every bit that is currently low in the ISR will still be low when processor q executes instruction i

$$c^n.p(q).apic.ISR \leq c^{NS}.p(q).apic.ISR$$

From eq. (87) we conclude that there is still a valid interrupt bit in configuration c^n

$$\exists h.\ c^n.p(q).apic.IRR[h] \wedge \forall j < h.\ /c^n.p(q).apic.ISR[j]$$

which is the claim.

12.3.14 Summary

12.4 Exercises

1. If the head of the store buffer goes to the APIC ports, it is not competing with the processor for access to the caches. The same is true for loads from the processor to the APIC, which do not compete with store buffer accesses. Optimize the hardware by allowing simultaneous completion of such memory accesses. Keep in mind that this means that $dca(q).mbusy$ will no longer be a valid signal for detecting store buffer pops, as a load instruction to memory can raise $dca(q).mbusy$ in the same cycle a store buffer write to the APIC completes.

13

Adding a Disk

The addition of I/O-devices to the hardware and ISA models of processors needs no motivation. Using nondeterministic hardware and ISA it turns out to be easy enough to do. In this chapter we demonstrate this with a hard disk, that can be accessed by all processors. Deviating from the usual order we introduce disks first as a new hardware unit (section 13.1). Using an arbitrated device bus and a few address decoders we integrate the hardware disk into the overall hardware (section 13.2). Then we define the ISA model (section 13.3). No new proof techniques are needed in the correctness proof of section 13.4. Due to the new hardware units there is an extra phase in the definition of the stepping function. Simulation relations, guard conditions and operating conditions have to be extended to cover the disk. As usual new operating conditions $opc\text{-}d$ for disks can only be guaranteed after one has shown the guard conditions of the ISA computation extracted from the hardware computation, because only then can one conclude, that this computation obeys new software conditions SC_{DISK} for the disk, which then establish that the operating conditions in hardware hold.

Note that disks not only serve to store user programs and their permanent data. After reset a boot loader residing in the ROM portion of memory loads the operating system from the disk. Also the memory management units of chapter chapter 9 support *demand paging*, where disk memory is used to virtualize the memory of user processes such that the total size of virtual user memories is much larger than the physical memory of the machine. Obviously in an ISA without disks one cannot possibly prove the correctness of a boot loader or of page fault handlers. On the other hand the ISA model introduced and justified by the hardware correctness proofs so far is clearly adequate for such a task. For a correctness proof of a boot loader and of demand paging on a single core machine see chapter 15 of [PBLS16].

Our disk model provides also an interrupt line, which signals the end of a disk operation. For the time being we ignore this signal, thus the end of disk operations can only be found out by polling, but in the next chapter we will connect the disks interrupt signal to an I/O APIC.

© Springer Nature Switzerland AG 2020
P. Lutsyk et al. (Eds.): A Pipelined Multi-Core Machine, LNCS 9999, pp. 565–589, 2020.
https://doi.org/10.1007/978-3-030-43243-0_13

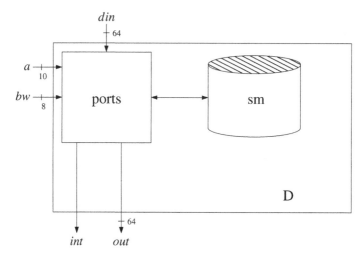

Fig. 193. Swap memory interface

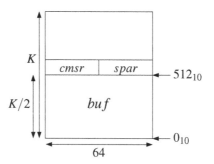

Fig. 194. Ports local memory map

13.1 Hardware Disk as a Basic Unit

We introduce disks as a new basic unit D without worrying about how to implement one. The configuration of such a disk has two parts: the configuration of its ports, which can be accessed by processors with store and load instructions, and the configuration of the swap memory. The ports consist of $K = 1024$ lines of memory. The swap memory consists of 2^{28} many pages (with K words resp. $32K$ bits each). As shown in fig. 193 the ports include:

- a page-sized buffer buf, which is used to transfer pages to and from the disk.
- a command and status register $cmsr$, with which the processor commands the disk to either copy a page from swap memory into the buffer (read command) or to copy the buffer into one of the pages of swap memory (write command). These commands take multiple cycles to complete. The exact number of cycles is unknown to the programmer. We will model this with a non-deterministic

disk step which atomically completes the operation. That this disk step is really perceived as atomic will depend on operating conditions which forbid accessing the buffer while a command is going on. For now, the processor is not notified that the command has completed. Instead, it must poll the command register, which is updated by the disk in the cycle in which the command completes. For later use, the command register also includes an interrupt flag. In the next chapter we introduce I/O APICs, which will use this interrupt flag to notify processors when the disk completes a command.

- a swap page address register spa, which contains the address of the page in swap memory which shall be accessed by the command

Formally, a configuration $h \in K_D$ of a disk has components

$$h.ports : \mathbb{B}^{10} \to \mathbb{B}^{64}$$
$$h.sm : \mathbb{B}^{28} \to \mathbb{B}^{32K}$$

A local memory map of the ports is shown in Fig. 194. As a page with K words occupies $K/2 = 512$ double words, we have

$$buf = ports_{512}(0_{10}).$$

Command and status register together with swap page address are packed into the single double word with local address 512_{10}:

$$cmsr = ports(512_{10})[63 : 32]$$
$$spar = ports(512_{10})[31 : 0]$$

Only the last 28 bits of the swap page address register are actually used for the address. We introduce the shorthand

$$spa = spar[27 : 0]$$

Bit 0 of the $cmsr$ indicates an ongoing read request, and bit 1 an ongoing write request. Read and write predicates for the disk are thus defined as

$$hdr = cmsr[0]$$
$$hdw = cmsr[1]$$

The disk is busy if one of these bits is on an idle otherwise

$$hdbusy = cmsr[1 : 0] \neq 00$$
$$hdidle = /hdbusy$$

Bit 2 of the $cmsr$ is the interrupt flag, indicating that the disk wants to notify the processor about a completed command. For now this bit is ignored, but we will return to it in chapter 14, where it will be connected to the APIC.

As illustrated in Fig. 193 the disk has

- data input $din \in \mathbb{B}^{64}$,
- data output $out \in \mathbb{B}^{64}$,
- address input $a \in \mathbb{B}^{10}$,
- byte-write signals $bw[7:0] \in \mathbb{B}^8$, and
- interrupt output signal $int \in \mathbb{B}$

Operating conditions forbid simultaneous read and write commands and forbid writes to the ports of a busy disk.

$$a = 512_{10} \wedge bw[4] \rightarrow din[33:32] \neq 11$$
$$hdbusy \rightarrow bw = 0^8$$

We collect these conditions in a single operating condition $opc\text{-}d$.

$$opc\text{-}d^t \leftrightarrow \forall u < t. \, (a^u = 512_{10} \wedge bw^u[4] \rightarrow din^u[33:32] \neq 11)$$
$$\wedge \, (hdbusy^u \rightarrow bw^u = 0^8)$$

We define now the semantics of the disk under the assumption that the operating conditions are satisfied in all cycles $u \leq t$, i.e., under the assumption

$$opc\text{-}d^t$$

If this is the case, in idle disks the ports behave like memory and the swap memory does not change.

$$idle \rightarrow$$
$$out = ports(a)$$
$$ports'(x) = \begin{cases} modify(ports(a), din, bw) & x = a \\ ports(x) & \text{otherwise} \end{cases}$$
$$sm' = sm$$

The question what happens when such a write is performed simultaneously with the end of an access has not to be answered, because this write would violate the operating conditions. In non-idle disks, only the command and status register/page swap address register can be read out

$$/idle \wedge a = 512_{10} \rightarrow out = ports(a)$$

For other ports nothing is specified. The interrupt output signal produces the state of bit number 2 of the command and status register, which has the interrupt bit

$$int = cmsr[2]$$

Disks are live, i.e., a disk which is busy in cycle t with some read or write operation involving swap memory will become idle in some later cycle u.

$$hdbusy^t \rightarrow \exists u > t. \, hdidle^u$$

A swap disk access interval or short *sm-interval* is an interval $[u:t]$ satisfying

$$sm\text{-}int(u,t) \equiv hdidle^{u-1} \wedge hdidle^{t+1} \wedge \forall y \in [u:t].\, hdbusy^y$$

The last cycle of an sm-interval is identified by predicate $hdend^t$:

$$hdend^t \equiv hdbusy^t \wedge hdidle^{t+1}$$

During such intervals *cmsr* and *spar* do not change.

$$sm\text{-}int(u,t) \wedge y \in [u:t] \wedge X \in \{cmsr, spar\} \; \rightarrow \; X^y = X^u$$

That an sm-interval is over is signalled by clearing bits 1 and 0 of the *cmsr*, and raising bit 2 (for the interrupt)

$$sm\text{-}int(u,t) \rightarrow cmsr^{t+1}[2:0] = 100$$

The semantics of disk writes and disk reads are defined with the help of sm-intervals $[u:t]$.

- $sm\text{-}int(u,t) \wedge hdw^u$: disk write. The buffer does not change

$$y \in [u:t+1] \rightarrow buf^y = buf^u$$

The buffer is copied to page *spa* of the swap memory. Other pages of the swap memory do not change

$$sma(x)^{t+1} = \begin{cases} buf^u & x = spa^u \\ sma(x)^u & \text{otherwise} \end{cases}$$

- $sm\text{-}int(u,t) \wedge hdr^u$: disk read. Page *spa* of the swap memory is copied to the buffer, and the swap memory does not change.

$$buf^{t+1} = sm^u(spa^u)$$
$$sm^{t+1} = sm^u$$

Note that for $y \in [u+1,t]$ we did not specify in all cases the buffer buf^y and the swap memory sm^y. Leaving their state unspecified makes sense, since this allows the disk to modify these ports in any way it wishes. However, for purely technical reasons, leaving their state unspecified would later cause difficulties. Recall the operating condition which forbids reading from the buffer while the disk is busy. Due to this software condition, the actual state of the buffer and swap memory while the disk is busy is completely irrelevant. Speaking from a purely technical point of view, we can specify these states any way we wish. To simplify future technical arguments, we specify here: *all* ports and swap memory are unchanged while the disk is busy

$$sm\text{-}int(u,t) \wedge y \in [u:t] \; \rightarrow \; ports^y = ports^u \wedge sm^y = sm^u$$

A trivial induction shows:

Lemma 279.

$$opc\text{-}d \; \rightarrow \; cmsr[1:0] \neq 11$$

13.2 Connecting the Disk with the Processors

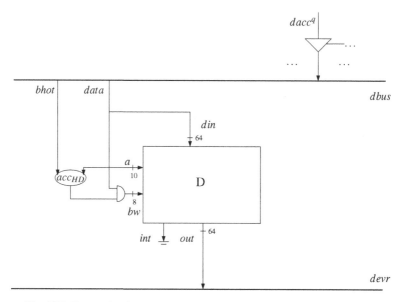

Fig. 195. Connection between disk and data accesses via a controlled bus.

Like accesses to the local APIC, accesses to the disk bypass the cache memory system. Unlike local APICs, the disk is shared between all processors. This means we need some arbitration to prevent simultaneous access of processors to the bus. For this purpose we use an (n, d)-controlled bus from section 3.5.4. This bus is used to transmit data accesses to the disk. The connection between the data accesses and the disk is illustrated in fig. 195. Later we will also place the I/O APIC on this bus, which we call the *device bus*.

We forbid CAS operations on the device bus. Thus compare data

$$dacc^q.cdata$$

is irrelevant and does not need to be transmitted. Nevertheless, for the sake of simplicity in the formal bookkeeping, we transmit all 136 bits of the data access (including the compare data) over the device bus. This avoids having to argue about parts of the data access. We place the device bus as a subunit

$$dbus : (P, 136)\text{-controlled bus}$$

which connects processors and the devices (for now only the disk). This bus ensures that only one processor can read or write to device ports at the same time. It does not ensure the operating condition, that disk ports must only be modified if the disk is idle. Processor q places its access on the bus through input a^i of the device bus

$$dbus.a^q = dacc^q$$

Thus while the bus is hot, the data on the bus is an access

$$dbus.data \in K_{acc}$$

from one of the processors (for load instructions) or store buffers (for store instructions). CAS operations will be forbidden. For the disk and other devices we reserve a region B of memory starting at a 16-page aligned *device base address*

$$base_{dev} \in \mathbb{B}^{32} \quad \text{with} \quad base_{dev}[15:0] = 0^{16}$$

We allocate 16 pages of memory for this region, of which we only three will be used in the course of this book

$$B = \{ base_{dev} +_{32} i_{32} \mid i \in [0:16 \cdot 4K) \}$$

We require that the APIC region A and this region are disjoint

$$A \cap B = \emptyset$$

and that the ROM region is disjoint from B. Recall that an address y is in the ROM region if predicate $romsel(y)$ (defined in section 3.3.7) holds

$$\{ y \mid romsel(y) \} \cap B = \emptyset$$

Computing whether an accesses goes to region B is easily done with an equality tester comparing the upper part of the address of the access to the upper part of the device base address

$$acc^q_{dev} \equiv dacc^q.a[28:13] = base_{dev}[31:16]$$

and accesses to this region bypass the cache memory system. Thus such accesses do not start accesses at the cache

$$dca(q).preq = dca(q).preq_{old} \wedge /acc^q_{dev}$$

and instead request access to the device bus

$$dbus.req[q] = acc^q_{dev} \wedge dca(q).preq_{old}$$

Accesses from store buffer and memory operations of the processor may no access the data cache *or* the devices. Thus we can not simply use the busy signal of the data cache to test whether such an access has completed. We define a combined busy signal *mbusy* which during accesses to the cache comes from the data cache, and during accesses to the devices comes from the device bus. For the latter case, we consider an access completed as soon as the access is broadcast on the bus, i.e., once we have an output enable signal from the bus. Note that this means in particular for load operations that the answer from the device is received in the same cycle as the access is first placed on the bus. This may create unacceptable cycle times. Dealing with this issue is left as a simple exercise (ex. 3).

In the latter case, the busy signal is active while the store buffer resp. processor does not receive an output enable signal from the bus.

$$mbusy^q = dca(q).mbusy \wedge dca(q).preq \vee /dbus.oe[q] \wedge dbus.req[q]$$

In all places that previously referenced the busy signal of the data cache, we must now use the new busy signal:

- For going to states *SB* resp. *core* in the control automaton of the store buffer:

$$sbreq^q = sbacc^q \wedge mbusy^q$$
$$creq^q = cacc^q \wedge mbusy^q$$

- For store buffer pops:

$$sb(q).pop = (sacc^q \vee SB^q) \wedge /mbusy^q$$

- For stalls due to the busy signal[1]:

$$busy^q_{cas} = idacc.cas^q \wedge mbusy^q$$
$$busy^q_s = idacc.w^q \wedge sb(q).full \wedge mbusy^q$$
$$busy^q_l = idacc.r^q \wedge /sb(q).f \wedge (sacc^q \vee SB^q \vee mbusy^q)$$

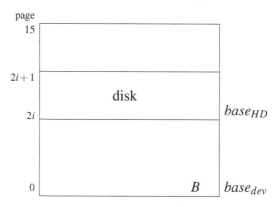

Fig. 196. Embedding of disk in device region $\mathcal{B}$.

As illustrated in fig. 196, the disk is placed into the region $\mathcal{B}$ starting from disk base address

---

[1] Note that due to the software condition which forbids CAS operations to the device region, it is not really necessary to change the busy signal for CAS. We still do it for the sake of uniformity

$$base_{HD} \in \mathcal{B}$$

We require that this base address is double-page aligned

$$base_{HD}[12:0] = 0^{13}$$

We define a signal acc_{HD} which identifies accesses to the disk. This can be computed using the address of the data access $dbus.data$ from the device bus: if the address $dbus.data.a$ of this data access has the same double-page address as the disk base address $base_{HD}$ and the device bus is hot, the access is a disk access. Since all double pages in the region $\mathcal{B}$ share the same first 16 bits of the address, these bits do not need to be compared. Thus it suffices to compare the remaining bits $[13:10]$ of the line address of the data access to bits $[16:13]$ of the byte address of the disk base address.

$$acc_{HD} \equiv dbus.hot \wedge dbus.data.a[13:10] = base_{HD}[16:13]$$

The inputs of the disk are taken from the access on the device bus. However byte-write signals are masked if the access is not a write access to the disk

$$D.din = dbus.data.data$$
$$D.a = dbus.data.a[9:0]$$
$$D.bw = dbus.data.bw \wedge dbus.data.w \wedge acc_{HD}$$

The response of the disk is put on a separate bus for the device response. For now only the disk can output data on this bus

$$devr = D.out$$

Later we will use multiplexers to select between disk output and I/O APIC output.

Processors that execute loads select between the device response and the cache memory system depending on whether they have an access to the device

$$dmout^q = \begin{cases} dmout^q_{old} & /acc^q_{dev} \\ devr & \text{o.w.} \end{cases}$$

This completes the connection between disks and processors. For now, the interrupt output of the disk is ignored. In chapter 14 we will connect the interrupt output of the disk to the I/O APIC over the interrupt bus.

13.2.1 Operating Conditions of the Device Bus

Obviously we need to prove the operating conditions of the device bus. Unlike for the interrupt bus, where the operating conditions relied on software conditions (in particular, that interrupt commands are never withdrawn by software), the operating conditions for the device bus follow in trivial fashion from pipeline control. The proof is completely analogous to proofs for the stability of inputs of the cache memory system and is omitted here.

Lemma 280.

$$\forall t.\, opc\text{-}cb(dbus)^t$$

13.3 ISA

For ISA, the byte addressable disk model from [PBLS16] is maintained. This model
has disk ports

$$c.disk.ports : \mathbb{B}^{13} \to \mathbb{B}^8$$

and swap memory

$$c.disk.sm : \mathbb{B}^{28} \to \mathbb{B}^{32K}$$

We introduce the obvious shorthands

$$buf(c) = c.disk.ports_{4096}(0_{13})$$
$$spar(c) = c.disk.ports_4(4096_{13})$$
$$cmsr(c) = c.disk.ports_4((4096+4)_{13})$$

for the buffer, swap page address register, and command and status register in ISA.
The memory system $ms_q(c)$ is now constructed from $c.m$, APIC ports, *and* the disk
ports. For addresses outside range $\mathcal{B}$ this

$$ms_q(c)(x) = \begin{cases} ms_{q\ old}(c)(x) & x \notin \mathcal{B} \\ c.disk.ports(x[12:0]) & \exists i \in [0:2^{13}).\ x = base_{HD} +_{32} i_{32} \end{cases}$$

Note that this memory system is undefined for addresses $x \in \mathcal{B}$ in the device region $\mathcal{B}$
which are outside the disk. We will forbid processors from accessing such addresses
through a software condition. We now consider the oracle inputs. In addition to the
existing oracle inputs for processor, store buffer, MMU, instruction buffer, and APIC
steps, we now introduce oracle input d for disk steps. The set of disk oracle inputs is

$$\{d\} = \Sigma_d$$

and the set of all oracle inputs is the union of the set of all oracle inputs from the
previous chapter, and the new set of disk oracle inputs

$$\Sigma = \Sigma_{old} \cup \Sigma_d$$

We now define the guard condition γ and transition function δ for this new oracle
input. Let thus

$$c' = \delta(c,x)$$

The single new oracle input

$$x = d$$

indicates the completion of a disk command. Such a step with oracle input $x = d$ can
only be performed if the disk is busy

$$\gamma(c,x) \equiv cmsr(c)[1:0] \neq 00$$

Their effect is to change the command and status register in the next configuration to
idle, and to raise the interrupt bit (which for now has no special effect)

Phase	Steps	Description
1	$[NS : N_{CMS})$	walk initialization, read from store buffer
2	$[N_{CMS} : N_{REM})$	memory accesses (NOT to Devices)
3	$[N_{REM} : N_{SIPI})$	remaining processor steps (includes external and INIT interrupts)
4	$[N_{SIPI} : N_{IBUS})$	SIPI steps of APICs
5	$[N_{IBUS} : N_{DISK})$	IPI delivery steps of APICs
6	$[N_{DISK} : N_{DEVW})$	disk step
7	$[N_{DEVW} : NS')$	stores to device ports

Table 20. Phases of stepping function with APIC

$$cmsr(c')[2 : 0] = 100$$

Furthermore, depending on whether the command was a write command or read command, it copies a page from the buffer to the swap memory or vice versa. Recall that reads are indicated by bit 0 and writes by bit 1 of the command and status register.

$$buf(c') = \begin{cases} c.disk.sm(spar(c)[28 : 0]) & csmr(c)[0] \\ buf(c) & \text{o.w.} \end{cases}$$

$$c'.sm(a) = \begin{cases} buf(c) & a = spar(c)[28 : 0] \wedge csmr(c)[1] \\ c.disk.sm(a) & \text{o.w.} \end{cases}$$

For other steps, only one thing changes. Steps that access the memory system use now the updated memory system $ms_q(c)$ with device region $\mathcal{B}$.

13.4 Correctness

13.4.1 Stepping Function

We proceed to define the stepping function. Except for the inclusion of disk steps very little changes. Due to the software condition, disk steps only conflict with processor steps reading from disk ports. These will always see the old state of the disk port and must be stepped first. Thus disk steps need to be performed after the processor steps which currently occur in phase 3 ($[N_{REM} : N_{SIPI})$). For now this is the only requirement, but in chapter 14 the I/O APIC will read from the disk ports as well in phase 5 (step N_{IBUS}). With this future constraint in mind we step the disk directly after phase 5, i.e., in phase 6. Former phase 6 (stores to APIC) becomes phase 7. Furthermore, store buffer steps that write to the device region $\mathcal{B}$ do not modify the cache memory system any more and can no longer be stepped in phase 2. We step them in phase 7 together with stores to the APIC. Thus phase 7 is now more generally the phase of stores to *devices*, i.e., APIC *or* disk. This results in the seven phases shown in table 20.

Formally the changes are slightly more involved. Since processor resp. store buffer steps that access the APIC or the devices are always stepped together (in phases 3 or 7), we introduce a shorthand

$$acc^q_{CMS} \equiv /acc^q_{APIC} \wedge /acc^q_{dev}$$

for accesses to the cache memory system. In the number of accesses of processor q to the cache memory system (nac^q), we only consider such accesses

$$\begin{aligned}
nac^q = \; & ue^q_M \wedge exec.(M{-}1)^q \wedge (l.(M{-}1)^q \wedge /sb.f^q \vee cas.(M{-}1)^q) \wedge acc^q_{CMS} \\
& + mmu_I.w.ce^q \wedge /mmu_I(q).winit + mmu_E(q).w.ce \wedge /mmu_E(q).winit \\
& + ue^q_{IF} \\
& + sb(q).pop \wedge /acc^q_{APIC} \wedge /acc^q_{dev}
\end{aligned}$$

Phase 6 now begins with step N_{DISK}

$$N_{DISK} = N_{IBUS} + ibus.bhot$$

and the number of steps in this phase is 1 if the disk completes a command, and 0 otherwise. Recall that completion of a command is indicated by signal $hdend$. Phase 7 now begins with step N_{DEVW} right after that up to one step

$$N_{DEVW} = N_{DISK} + hdend$$

This phase includes all accesses that do not target the cache memory system

$$devw^q = sb(q).pop \wedge /acc^q_{CMS}$$

These are the last steps to be completed in the cycle

$$NS' = N_{DEVW} + \sum_q devw^q$$

We also need to adjust the equations that define which steps are made when. Processor steps and store buffer steps which access the cache memory system go in phase 2

$$ue^q_M \wedge exec.(M{-}1)^q \wedge (l.(M{-}1)^q \wedge /sb(q).f \vee cas.(M-1)^q) \wedge acc^q_{CMS}$$
$$\rightarrow n^q_p \in [N_{CMS} : N_{REM})$$
$$sb(q).pop \wedge acc^q_{CMS} \rightarrow n^q_{sb} \in [N_{CMS} : N_{REM})$$

Processor steps not accessing the CMS are stepped together with the remaining processor steps

$$ue^q_M \wedge exec.(M{-}q)^q \wedge (l.(M{-}1)^q \wedge /sb(q).f \vee cas.(M{-}1)^q) \wedge /acc^q_{CMS} \rightarrow n^q_p \in [N_{REM} : N_{SIPI})$$

Store buffer steps not accessing the CMS are stepped in the last phase

$$sb(q).pop \land /acc^q_{CMS} \to n^q_{sb} \in [N_{DEVW} : NS'])$$

The order of steps in the phase consisting of accesses to the CMS is defined exactly as in chapter 11. We do not repeat the definitions here. Finally we specify that phase 6 consists of a disk step in case the disk completes a command

$$hdend \to s(N_{DISK}) = d$$

Note that we do not need to change potential emergency braking despite the new operating conditions of the disk: the pathological case of the cache memory system, in which an access has started that violates the operating condition but is not completed yet, can not occur with the devices. With the devices, the access only matters in the single cycle in which the processor has an output enable signal, i.e., in which the access is completed. Thus accesses that have only been requested but not completed yet can not violate the operating conditions.

13.4.2 Software Condition for Disk

Obviously the operating condition of the disk is not satisfied by all programs. Analogous to the software conditions for APICs which forbid overwriting the command register after a command has been issued, we need to forbid certain accesses to the disk after a command was issued. Like before this is defined with the help of the forwarded memory system. The only accesses that are permitted while the lowest two bits of the command and status register in the forwarded memory system are unequal to zero

$$fms(ms_q(c), c.p(q).sb)(base_{HD} +_{32} 5163_2)[1 : 0] \neq 00$$

are load operations to the command and status register

$$x \in \Sigma_{p,q} \land mop(c,x) \land (\exists i \in [0 : 2^{13}).\ ea(c,x) = base_{HD} +_{32} i_{32})$$
$$\to fms(ms_q(c), c.p(q).sb)(base_{HD} +_{32} 5163_2)[1 : 0] = 00$$
$$\lor l(c,x) \land ea(c,x) = base_{HD} +_{32} 5163_2$$

Furthermore we need to forbid stores that issue simultaneously read and write commands. For this we consider the last two bits of the data

$$B(c,x)$$

to be written to the memory in case the effective address is equal to the byte address of the command and status register

$$x \in \Sigma_{p,q} \land mop(c,x) \land ea(c,x) = base_{HD} +_{32} 5163_2 \land s(c,x)$$
$$\to B(c,x)[1 : 0] \neq 11$$

Combining these in a single software condition SC_{DISK} for the disk yields

$$SC_{DISK}(c,x) \equiv$$

$$(x \in \Sigma_{p,q} \wedge mop(c,x) \wedge (\exists i \in [0:2^{13}). \; ea(c,x) = base_{HD} +_{32} i32)$$
$$\rightarrow fms(ms_q(c),c.p(q).sb)(base_{HD} +_{32} 516_{32})[1:0] = 00$$
$$\vee l(c,x) \wedge ea(c,x) = base_{HD} +_{32} 516_{32})$$
$$\wedge (x \in \Sigma_{p,q} \wedge mop(c,x) \wedge ea(c,x) = base_{HD} +_{32} 516_{32} \wedge s(c,x)$$
$$\rightarrow B(c,x)[1:0] \neq 11)$$

Finally we forbid CAS operations to the device region $\mathcal{B}$, and any memory operations in the device region that do not go to a device. For now the only device is the disk, thus we forbid all memory accesses outside the disk.

$$SC_{DEV}(c,x) \equiv x \in \Sigma_{p,q} \wedge mop(c,x) \wedge ea(c,x) \in \mathcal{B}$$
$$\rightarrow (l(c,x) \vee s(c,x)) \wedge \exists i \in [0:2^{13}). \; ea(c,x) = base_{HD} +_{32} i32$$

13.4.3 Induction Hypothesis

We add the obvious coupling for the disk:

$$t \sim_m n \quad \equiv \quad n = NS^t \rightarrow m(h^t) = \ell(c^n.m) \wedge opc^t$$
$$\wedge aq(sb(q)^t_\pi) = c^n.p(q).sb$$
$$\wedge walks(mmu_I(q)^t) \cup walks(mmu_E(q)^t) \subseteq c^n.tlb(q)$$
$$\wedge apic(q)^t = c^n.p(q).apic \wedge opc\text{-}cb(ibus)^t$$
$$\wedge D^t = c^n.disk \wedge opc\text{-}d^t$$
$$\wedge \forall \hat{n} < n. \; \gamma(c^{\hat{n}}, s(\hat{n}))$$

The coupling relation for pipelined registers is not changed. The main correctness lemma states:

Lemma 281. *There is an initial configuration c^0 satisfying*

$$sim(h^0.(p(q),m),c^0.(p(q),m)) \quad \text{for all } q \in P$$

in which instruction buffers and TLBs are empty

$$c^0.ib(q) = c^0.tlb(q) = \emptyset$$

and the store buffers are also empty

$$c^0.p(q).sb = \varepsilon$$

Furthermore: if for the computation (c^n) with stepping function $s(n)$ extracted from hardware and initial configuration c^0 satisfies for all n the software conditions $SC_{ROM}(c^n,s(n))$, $SC_{APIC}(c^n,s(n))$, and $SC_{DISK}(c^n,s(n))$ provided the stepping function $s(n)$ has a valid initial segment until n

$$\forall n. \; (\forall m \leq n. \; \gamma(c^m,s(m))) \rightarrow SC_{ROM}(c^n,s(n)) \wedge SC_{APIC}(c^n,s(n)) \wedge SC_{DISK}(c^n,s(n))$$

then for all n and t:

- *If n is a step of processor q executing instructions i which is committed and only has live instructions before it*

$$n = pseq(q,i) \wedge c(i)^{q,t} \wedge lb(i)^{q,t}$$

then hardware in cycle t simulates instruction i

$$t \sim_p^q i$$

and each part of the guard condition holds if instruction i passed the corresponding stage

$$(i < I_{IF}^{q,t} \rightarrow \gamma_I^{A,i})$$
$$\wedge (i < I_{IT}^{q,t} \rightarrow \gamma_{wI}^{A,i})$$
$$\wedge (i < I_{ET}^{q,t} \rightarrow \gamma_{wE}^{A,i})$$
$$\wedge (i < I_1^{q,t} \rightarrow \gamma_r^{A,i})$$
$$\wedge (i < I_{M-1}^{q,t} \rightarrow \gamma_e^{A,i})$$
$$\wedge (i < I_{M-1}^{q,t} \rightarrow \gamma_{INIT}^{A,i})$$

- *Hardware simulates in cycle t the non-pipelined components of ISA step n*

$$t \sim_m n$$

13.4.4 Induction Step

With the usual induction scheme we obtain the following induction hypothesis for the current cycle:

$$t \sim_m o \wedge (o = pseq(q,i) \wedge c(i)^{q,t} \wedge lb(i)^{q,t}$$
$$\rightarrow t \sim_p i \wedge (i > I_{IF}^{q,t} \rightarrow \gamma_I^{A,t}) \wedge (i > I_{IT}^{q,t} \rightarrow \gamma_{wI}^{A,t}) \wedge (i > I_{ET} \rightarrow \gamma_{wE}^{A,t}))$$
$$\tag{88}$$

With the software conditions we obtain lemmas corresponding to lemmas 253 and 254 for the devices.

Lemma 282. *Let $n \geq NS$ and w be store buffer entry number k of processor q in ISA configuration c^{NS}, and let w write to the device region*

$$w = c^{NS}.p(q).sb[k] \wedge w.a \in \mathcal{B}$$

Then w must access the disk

$$\exists i \in [0 : 2^{10}). \ w.a = base_{HD}[31:3] +_{29} i_{29}$$

Lemma 283. *Let $n \geq NS$ and w be store buffer entry number k of processor q in ISA configuration c^{NS}*

$$w = c^{NS}.p(q).sb[k]$$

and let w write to the disk

$$\exists i \in [0 : 2^{10}). \; w.a = base_{HD}[31 : 3] +_{29} i_{29}$$

Then the forwarding memory system from the first k stores has an idle command and status register

$$fms(ms_q(c^{NS}), c^{NS}.p(q).sb[k-1:0])(base_{HD} +_{32} 516_{32})[1:0] = 00$$

Proofs are completely analogous to the proofs of lemmas 253 and 254 and we omit them here.

13.4.5 Validity

We prove the lemma corresponding to lemma 257

Lemma 284. *Let*

$$n \in [NS : NS') \wedge \hat{n} \leq n$$

or

$$n = NS' \wedge \hat{n} < n$$

Then

$$\gamma(c^{\hat{n}}, s(\hat{n}))$$

Proof. For $\hat{n} < NS$ the claim follows from the induction hypothesis for the current cycle (eq. (88)). For $\hat{n} \in [NS : NS')$, assume that all steps before $\hat{n}$ are valid. The proof for step $\hat{n}$ is by case distinction on the type of step $\hat{n}$. For all steps except disk steps the proof is literally as before. We do not repeat these proofs here. For disk steps we know step $\hat{n}$ must be step N_{DISK} and the disk makes a step in hardware

$$s(\hat{n}) = d \wedge \hat{n} = N_{DISK} \wedge hdend$$

By definition of $hdend$ we conclude that the disk is busy in this cycle, i.e., the command and status register is not equal to zeroes

$$hdbusy, \quad cmsr[1:0] \neq 00$$

With the induction hypothesis for the current cycle (eq. (88)) for $o := NS$ we obtain that the state of the disk is the same in ISA before step NS

$$c^{NS}.disk = D$$

and hence the command and status register has the same state

$$csmr(c^{NS})[1:0] = cmsr[1:0] \neq 00$$

It suffices now to show that the command and status register is not set to zeroes between steps NS and $\hat{n}$

$$\gamma(c^{\hat{n}}, s(\hat{n})) \equiv cmsr(c^{\hat{n}})[1:0] \neq 00$$

Observe that the only steps that might change the command and status register are 1) stores to the CMSR, which by lemma 283 can not occur while the disk is busy. 2) disk steps, of which there is at most one in each cycle and hence none of the steps $[NS : \hat{n})$ can be disk steps. And 3) processor steps $o \in [NS : \hat{n})$ performing a CAS to the disk. Assume thus for the sake of contradiction that such a step o exists

$$o \in [NS : \hat{n}) \wedge s(o) \in \Sigma_p \wedge cas(c^o, s(o)) \wedge ea(c^o, s(o)) \in \mathcal{B}$$

By assumption all steps before $\hat{n}$ are valid. This includes all steps until o. We can thus use the software conditions to conclude that step o is not a CAS to the device region $\mathcal{B}$, which is a contradiction. It follows that none of the steps $o \in [NS : \hat{n})$ changed the command and status register, which is therefore still not idle

$$cmsr(c^{\hat{n}})[1:0] = cmsr(c^{NS})[1:0] \neq 00$$

The claim follows

$$\gamma(c^{\hat{n}}, s(\hat{n}))$$

$\square$

13.4.6 Operating Condition of Disk

We establish the operating condition for the disk

$$opc\text{-}d'$$

since that is required for the disk to give correct responses and get updated correctly. Store buffers can never violate the operating conditions of the disk because they are by lemma 283 not allowed to operate on the disk while it is busy. The only way to violate the operating condition of the disk is by a processor step which reads the wrong port or writes while the disk is busy.

Thus, if a step $n \in [NS : NS')$ reads from the disk or updates it, or if $n = NS'$ and we want to show that the disk is correct (to establish the simulation relation $\sim_m$ for the next cycle), we must show that in hardware no access from the processor is violating the operating condition of the disk. If a processor is reading from the disk, it obviously has unique access to the disk (due to the arbitration on the device bus) and hence no such access can occur. If the disk is updated by a disk step, then this occurs in phase 6, and $n = NS'$ occurs after phase 7. If in the same cycle a processor would start an access that would violate the operating conditions, that access would also complete in the same cycle. The processor (and its access to the disk) would be stepped as some processor step o in phase 3, i.e., before the updating step in phase 6 or the end of phase 7:

$$o < n$$

In this case we can use the induction hypothesis for the current cycle to show that the processor access is not violating the operating condition after all.

Lemma 285. *Let* $n \in [NS : NS')$ *either be a processor step accessing the disk, or a disk step*

$$n = pseq(q,i) \wedge mop_\sigma^{q,i} \wedge (\exists i \in [0:2^{13}). \; ea_\sigma^{q,i} = base_{HD} +_{32} i_{32}) \vee s(n) = d \vee n = NS'$$

Then the disk satisfies its operating conditions

$$opc\text{-}d'$$

Proof. By the induction hypothesis for the current cycle (eq. (88)) we have that the operating conditions were satisfied in previous cycles

$$opc\text{-}d$$

Assume for the sake of contradiction that there the operating condition of the disk is violated in the current cycle, i.e., either a store to the command and status register that raises both bits for read and write commands, or a write to the disk while the disk is busy. We treat here only the latter case, the other case can be treated analogously. Assume thus

$$hdbusy \wedge D.bw \neq 0^8$$

By construction a byte-write to the disk occurs only while the device bus is hot and the access on the bus is a writing access to the disk

$$acc_{HD} \wedge dbus.bhot \wedge dbus.data.bw \neq 0^8$$

By lemma 280 the operating conditions of the device bus are satisfied. With lemma 31 we conclude: the data on the bus is the data access of some processor q which is requesting access

$$dbus.req[q] \wedge dbus.oe[q] \wedge dbus.data = dacc^q$$

Since the access is granted in the current cycle, the *mbusy* signal is off

$$/mbusy^q$$

Since the processor is requesting the bus, it is executing an access to the devices

$$acc_{dev}^q$$

With *hdbusy* and the induction hypothesis for the current cycle (eq. (88)) we conclude that the disk is busy in ISA

$$cmsr(c^{NS})[1:0] = cmsr[1:0] \neq 00$$

and hence by contraposition of lemma 283 the store buffer does not contain any stores to the disk in ISA

$$\forall w \in c^{NS}.p(q).sb, \ i \in [0:2^{10}). \ w.a \neq base_{HD}[31:3] +_{29} i_{29}$$

By the induction hypothesis for the current cycle (eq. (88)) the same holds in hardware

$$\forall w \in sb(q), \ i \in [0:2^{10}). \ w.a \neq base_{HD}[31:3] +_{29} i_{29}$$

By assumption the access on the bus is going to the disk (acc_{HD}), and thus

$$\exists i \in [0:2^{10}). \ dacc^q.a = base_{HD}[31:3] +_{29} i_{29}$$

Therefore the access can not come from the store buffer. It must come from the core, from the instruction in circuit stage M

$$cacc^q$$

Trivial bookkeeping shows: the instruction is not stalled, and is clocked into the memory stage

$$ue_M^q$$

This access generates a processor step o in the third phase

$$o \in [N_{REM} : N_{SIPI}) \wedge o = pseq(q, I_M^q)$$

We first show

$$o \overset{!}{\leq} n$$

by a case split.

- $n = pseq(\hat{q}, i) \wedge mop_\sigma^{q,i} \wedge (\exists i \in [0:2^{13}). \ ea_\sigma^{q,i} = base_{HD} +_{32} i_{32})$: if such a step was generated, then by the induction hypothesis for the current cycle (eq. (88)) a corresponding access must have been generated in hardware

$$ue_M^{\hat{q}} \wedge idacc^{\hat{q}}.a = ea_\sigma^{q,i}[31:3] \wedge mop.(M-1)^{\hat{q}}$$

and the update enable signal would only be active if signal $mbusy^{\hat{q}}$ was low

$$/mbusy^{\hat{q}}$$

Obviously this access would go to the devices, in which case the $mbusy$ signal is only low while the processor has the output enable signal on the bus

$$acc_{dev}^{\hat{q}}, \quad dbus.oe[\hat{q}]$$

Since the operating conditions of the device bus are always maintained (lemma 280) we conclude with lemma 31:

$$\hat{q} = q$$

As each processor is only stepped once per cycle, the claim follows

$$i = I_M^q \wedge o = pseq(q, i) = n$$

- $s(n) = d \lor n = NS'$: in either case we have immediately the claim

$$o < N_{SIPI} \leq n$$

Because $o \leq n$ we can use the induction hypothesis for the current cycle (eq. (88)) to conclude that the access in hardware is the same access as that of instruction o

$$idacc_\sigma^{q,I_M^q} \equiv idacc^q = dacc^q$$

Since all steps in the current cycle are valid (lemma 284), we can use the software condition SC_{DISK} to conclude: the step is not executing a CAS instruction

$$/dacc^q.cas$$

It is of course also not executing a store instruction, because store instructions of the core never access the memory bus (they go to the store buffer instead)

$$/dacc^q.s$$

Since it is neither a store nor a CAS it must have no byte-write signals

$$dacc^q.bw = 0^8$$

which is a contradiction.   □

13.4.7 Disk Correctness

The disk is updated by at most one step in each cycle: either by the one processor/-store buffer that is granted the output enable signal in hardware, or by a disk step. That both can not occur in the same cycle has already been shown in lemma 285. This makes a stepping diagram unnecessary. We simply show:

Lemma 286.
$$n = NS' \;\rightarrow\; c^{NS'}.disk = D'$$

Proof. By case split on what changes the disk.

- $hdend$: in this case the disk is busy

$$hdbusy$$

and by lemma 285 the operating conditions are satisfied

$$opc\text{-}d'$$

These require that for a busy disk byte-write signals are low

$$D.bw = 0^8$$

We conclude using the induction hypothesis for the current cycle (eq. (88)) that no processor or store buffer steps are generated in the current cycle that would change the disk. Thus:

$$c^{N_{DISK}}.disk = c^{NS}.disk \quad \text{and} \quad c^{N_{DISK}+1}.disk = c^{NS'}.disk$$

By the induction hypothesis for the current cycle the disk was correct at the beginning of the cycle

$$c^{N_{DISK}}.disk = c^{NS}.disk = D$$

and obviously the semantics of the disk in ISA match perfectly the semantics of the disk in hardware. With

$$s(N_{DISK}) = d$$

we conclude the claim

$$c^{NS'}.disk = c^{N_{DISK}+1}.disk = D'$$

- $/hdend \wedge D.bw \neq 0^8$: by lemma 285 the disk is not busy

$$hdidle$$

and the ports behave like memory. The ports also behave like memory in ISA. Since the disk does not make a step in the current cycle and at most one processor or store buffer can be granted access to the device bus in the current cycle, there is only a single step $o \in [NS : NS')$ which modifies the disk

$$c^o.disk = c^{NS}.disk \quad \text{and} \quad c^{o+1}.disk = c^{NS'}.disk$$

This step o is a store buffer step in the last phase

$$o \in [N_{DEVW} : NS') \wedge s(o) \in \Sigma_{sb,q}$$

and since the store buffer is maintained correctly it executes the same access in hardware and in ISA

$$\begin{aligned}
dacc(c^o, s(o)).(a, data, bw) &= c^o.p(q).sb[0] \\
&= aq(sb(q))[0] \\
&= sb(q).out \\
&= dacc^q.(a, data, bw)
\end{aligned}$$

By lemma 280 the operating conditions of the device bus are maintained and by lemma 31 the data on the device bus comes from this data access

$$dbus.data = dacc^q$$

This is the access executed on the disk both in ISA and in hardware. Thus the disk is updated in the same fashion and the claim follows

$$c^{NS'}.disk = c^{o+1}.disk = D'$$

- neither: in this case nothing changes in hardware

$$D = D'$$

and also in ISA no steps are generated that would change the disk

$$c^{NS'}.disk = c^{NS}.disk$$

The claim follows with the induction hypothesis for the current cycle

$$c^{NS'}.disk = c^{NS}.disk = D = D'$$

$\square$

13.4.8 Correctness of Non-Pipelined Components

Assume $n = NS'$. We have to show:

$$m(h') = \ell(c^n.m) \wedge opc'$$
$$\wedge \ aq(sb(q)'_\pi) = c^n.p(q).sb$$
$$\wedge \ walks(mmu_I(q)') \cup walks(mmu_E(q)') \subseteq c^n.tlb(q)$$
$$\wedge \ apic(q)' = c^n.p(q).apic \wedge opc\text{-}cb'$$
$$\wedge \ D' = c^n.disk \wedge opc\text{-}d'$$
$$\wedge \ \forall \hat{n} < n. \ \gamma(c^{\hat{n}}, s(\hat{n}))$$

The claim for the disk is lemma 286. The claim for the operating conditions of the disk is lemma 285. All other claims are proven as before.

13.4.9 Correctness of the Pipeline

In this proof only the correctness of the memory output *dmout* is affected. The memory output may now come from the disk rather than the CMS or the APIC. However the proof for the result from the disk is mostly like that from the APIC. Only two things change: 1) if a processor completes a load from the disk in the current cycle, one needs to use lemma 285 to establish the operating conditions of the disk. Otherwise the disk will not provide a correct result. 2) if the disk is busy, correct results are only guaranteed for the command and status register. One has to use the software condition SC_{DISK}, which states that only that register is read while the disk is busy.

Assume that the instruction in the memory stage has global step number n and is clocked down and thus stepped in the current cycle

$$n = pseq(q, I_M^q) \wedge ue_M^q \wedge n \in [NS : NS')$$

Assume that the data memory output is used

$$used[dmout]_\sigma^{q, I_M^q}$$

We need to show that the data memory output is correct, i.e.,

$$dmout^q = dmout_\sigma^{q,r_M^q}$$

If the access does not go to the device region $\mathcal{B}$ the proof is just as before and we only cover the remaining case. Assume thus

$$acc_{dev}^q$$

By lemma 285 the operating conditions of the disk are satisfied

$$opc\text{-}d'$$

and since by lemma 284 all steps until n are valid, we can use the software condition SC_{DISK} to conclude: the instruction is not a CAS operation

$$/cas_\sigma^{q,r_M^q}$$

Since the load result is used, the instruction must be a load operation

$$l_\sigma^{q,r_M^q}$$

We do a case split on whether the memory output is forwarded from the store buffer or comes from the disk. However the forwarding case can be treated exactly as before, so we assume that the memory output comes from the disk

$$/sbhit(c^n.p(q).sb, fp(c^n, s(n)))$$

We do a case split on whether the disk is idle.

- $hdidle$: in this case ports behave like memory and we have

$$dmout^q = devr = D.ports(dbus.data.a[9:0])$$

As usual we conclude with lemmas 31 and 280 that the data on the bus comes from the access of processor q, which by the induction hypothesis for the current cycle (eq. (88)) it also executes in ISA

$$dbus.data.a = dacc^q.a = dacc_\sigma^{q,r_M^q}.a$$

Since at most one processor can access the disk, we know that the disk is not changed between steps NS and n. With the induction hypothesis for the current cycle (eq. (88)) we conclude that the disk in ISA has the same configuration as in hardware

$$c^n.disk = c^{NS}.disk = D$$

Furthermore, by the software condition SC_{DEV} the access must go to the disk

$$\exists i \in [0:2^{10}). \; dacc_\sigma^{q,r_M^q}.a = base_{HD}[31:3] +_{29} i_{29}$$

The claim follows since we do not forward from the store buffer

$$dmout_{\sigma}^{q,I_M^q} = \ell(ms_q(c^n))(dacc_{\sigma}^{q,I_M^q}.a)$$
$$= c^n.disk.ports(dbus.data.a[9:0])$$
$$= D.ports(dbus.data.a[9:0])$$
$$= dmout^q$$

- *hdbusy*: step n is a processor step and must thus occur before the potential disk step that might change the disk. No other steps change the disk in this cycle and thus

$$c^n.disk = c^{NS}.disk = D$$

We conclude in the usual way that the disk must also be busy in ISA

$$cmsr(c^n)[1:0] \neq 00$$

All steps until n are valid by lemma 284 and thus we can use the software condition SC_{DISK}. While the disk is busy, the processor is allowed only to load from the command and status register

$$ea_{\sigma}^{q,I_M^q} = base_{HD} +_{32} 5163_2$$

With the induction hypothesis for the current cycle we conclude that the data access in hardware is using this effective address

$$dbus.data.a = dacc^q.a = dacc_{\sigma}^{q,I_M^q}.a = ea_{\sigma}^{q,I_M^q}[31:3]$$

Thus the data access reads from the combined command and status register/swap page address register

$$dbus.data.a[9:0] = 512_{10}$$

For this register even in a busy disk, the ports behave like memory

$$dmout^q = devr = D.ports(dbus.data.a[9:0])$$

and the proof can be completed as before.

13.5 Exercises

1. Come up with the specification of a second device (e.g., a keyboard). Define a basic unit for the device and place it on the device bus.
2. During read accesses to the devices, the data *acc.data* of the access is ignored. This means that we can use those same lines for transmitting the data from the device. This reduces the number of lines on the device bus from 200 to 136.
   - Why can we not use the (n,d)-controlled bus for this optimization?
   - Construct an alternative tri-state bus which can be used for this optimization

3. In our construction, the device needs to respond to read accesses in the same cycle in which the access is first broadcast on the bus. This involves 1) the access reaching the device over the bus, 2) the address decoders at the device ports, and 3) the response travelling back over the bus to the processor. This may create an unacceptable cycle time. Extend the construction in such a way that the response of the device is allowed to arrive as late as the next cycle, without modifying the controlled bus. Prove the correctness of your construction. Hints: 1) the output enable signal of the read access is turned off in the cycle in which the response should be sent. In that cycle, the access has been taken off the device bus. Stabilize the access using a latch on the device side, which is transparent while the bus is hot. 2) during reads from a device, activate the busy signal for one additional cycle. Do this by introducing a simple set-clear flip-flop which is raised when the processor receives an output enable signal and turns itself off in the next cycle.

4. We have avoided doing the proof with potential emergency braking since it was not strictly necessary. However, using potential emergency braking to prove the operating conditions of the disk would have simplified some parts of the proof. Use potential emergency braking to show the operating conditions of the disk:
   - define a violation of the operating conditions of the disk (cf. *vopc* for the operating conditions of the CMS).

$$vopc\text{-}d = \ldots$$

   - define the stepping function by case analysis on *vopc-d* and define that a processor which violates the operating condition is stepped immediately
   - prove by contradiction that the operating condition *opc-d'* of the disk is satisfied as long as $n \geq NS$

14

I/O APIC

In the previous chapter we introduced a disk, which was operated via the command and status register. After the programmer sent a command, she had to poll the command and status register until the command had been completed by the disk. Obviously we would prefer to use the cycles used for polling for something else, while still reacting to the disk as quickly as possible. Rather than polling the device status and wasting precious computational cycles, we will rely on the disk to notify the program when the command has completed through a device interrupt. The life cycle of a device interrupt is as follows:

- The device requests the interrupt by raising its interrupt request flag $D.int$, which we have introduced in the previous chapter. This interrupt request will stay active until the programmer turns it off by software.
- The interrupt request flag is sampled by a new hardware unit that we introduce for this purpose, the so called input/output (I/O) APIC.
- The interrupt is delivered to the local APIC, where it raises a bit in the interrupt request register. Note that at this point, the interrupt request flag in the device is still active. To prevent the I/O APIC from sampling the interrupt a second time (and subsequently delivering it again), the I/O APIC records the fact that the interrupt has been delivered to a remote interrupt request register in the aptly named remote interrupt request register (rirr). As long as the rirr is raised, the I/O APIC will not sample the device interrupt again.
- The processor reacts to the interrupt by jumping to the interrupt service routine. During the interrupt service routine, the processor 1) turns of the interrupt request in the device, and 2) commands the local APIC to send an end-of-interrupt (EOI) message to the I/O APIC.
- The local APIC transmits an EOI message to the I/O APIC, which turns off the rirr bit. Consequently, the I/O APIC is now ready to sample the next device interrupt.

Due to the design of the interrupt life cycle, the processor can (after turning off the previous interrupt request) already issue a new command to the device before the

© Springer Nature Switzerland AG 2020
P. Lutsyk et al. (Eds.): A Pipelined Multi-Core Machine, LNCS 9999, pp. 591–625, 2020.
https://doi.org/10.1007/978-3-030-43243-0_14

interrupt service routine is complete or the EOI message has been sent to the I/O APIC, without the risk of losing or repeating interrupt requests.

In section 14.1, we formally specify this mechanism by adding the I/O APIC and the EOI mechanism to the ISA. In sections 14.2 and 14.3 will then design and verify an implementation of these features.

14.1 Specification of I/O APIC

In a general design, the I/O APIC would use a small interrupt redirection table with one row per device to store the destination and interrupt vector used by that device. Since we have only a single device, our redirection table has only a single row. We call this row the redirection register. As described in table 21, this register is structured almost as the APIC interrupt command register described in table 18, except

- it does not have a delivery mode (the I/O APIC will only send fixed interrupts)
- it does not have a destination shorthand (the I/O APIC will only send single-target interrupts)
- it has a remote interrupt request register (rirr) bit at position 10
- it has a mask bit at position 16

name	bits	description
dest	63-56	destination field
mask	16	interrupt mask
ds	12	delivery status: idle (0), send pending (1)
rirr	10	remote interrupt request bit
vect	7-0	vector

Table 21. The layout of the redirection register of the I/O APIC.

If either the rirr or mask bits are raised, the I/O APIC will not sample active interrupt requests of the disk. The key difference between these two bits is that the rirr is managed by hardware — raised by the I/O APIC upon delivery of the interrupt, and lowered upon receiving the EOI message — for the sole purpose of ensuring that each interrupt is delivered exactly once. The mask bit on the other hand is a software-controlled means of turning off device interrupts, for example if the device driver wants to poll the status bit rather than relying on interrupts.

We now add the state of the I/O APIC to ISA configurations c. The state of the I/O APIC is completely encapsulated in its redirection register

$$c.rr \in \mathbb{B}^{64}$$

Just as the disk ports, this register is addressable by all processors through a memory-mapped I/O port in the device region $\mathcal{B}$. We place this register on some page-aligned base address

$$base_{IO} \in \mathcal{B} \quad \text{with} \quad base_{IO}[11:0] = 0_{12}$$

This address must not be inside the double page used by the disk

$$base_{IO}[31:13] \neq base_{HD}[31:13]$$

We encapsulate the redirection register in the memory system abstraction $ms_q(c)$ in the obvious way using the memory system abstraction $ms_{q\ old}(c)$ of the ISA without I/O APICs:

$$ms_q(c)(a) = \begin{cases} ms_{q\ old}(c)(a) & a.l \neq base_{IO}.l \\ byte(\langle a.o \rangle, c.rr) & a.l = base_{IO}.l \end{cases}$$

The redirection register behaves as memory. Thus the memory system $ms_q(c')$ in configuration c' after a processor step

$$c' = \delta(c, (p, q, \ldots))$$

is exactly the memory one obtains after the data access, provided the line address of the access is the same as the line address of the redirection register

$$dacc(c,x).a = base_{IO}.l \ \rightarrow \ \ell(ms_q(c')) = \delta_M(\ell(ms_q(c)), dacc(c,x))$$

14.1.1 I/O APIC Steps

We proceed to define the effect of I/O APIC steps in ISA. These steps are triggered by oracle inputs of the I/O APIC. The set of all such oracle inputs is denoted by

$$\Sigma_{IO}$$

and as usually we define

$$c' = \delta(c, x)$$

by case split on $x \in \Sigma_{IO}$.

Delivery of interrupts via the I/O APIC proceeds in two ISA steps, defined by the following oracle inputs

- $x = sample \in \Sigma_{IO}$: samples the device interrupt and sets the delivery status bit to 1 (pending). Enabled when the interrupt is not masked, the interrupt is not currently being served remotely, and the device is requesting the interrupt

$$\gamma(c,x) \ = \ /c.rr.mask \ \wedge \ /c.rr.rirr \ \wedge \ cmsr(c)[2]$$

and the effect is to raise the delivery status bit

$$c'.rr.ds = 1$$

Nothing else is affected.

- $x = deliver \in \Sigma_{IO}$: delivers the interrupt to the target processor. The semantics is similar to a normal APIC IPI delivery. The step is enabled if there is a pending interrupt

$$\gamma(c,x) = c.rr.ds$$

The step sends the fixed vector from the *vect* field of the redirection register

$$IPI(c,x) = (FIXED, c.rr.vect)$$

and delivers it to the destination specified by the *dest* field

$$itargets(c,x) = \{ q \mid c.p(q).apic.id = c.rr.dest \}$$

The APICs which are targets are affected and undergo the APIC transition

$$q \in itargets(c,x) \quad \rightarrow \quad c'.p(q).apic = \delta_{APIC}(c.p(q).apic, IPI(c,x))$$

In the I/O APIC, the delivery status bit is lowered

$$c'.rr.ds = 0$$

and the remote interrupt request bit is raised

$$c'.rr.rirr = 1$$

14.1.2 EOI Mechanism and the Local APIC

After delivery of an interrupt from a device the remote interrupt request bit is raised, which prevents further sampling and delivery of interrupts from that device. After the interrupt handler has dealt with the interrupt and lowered the interrupt bit in the command and status register of the device, it must also lower the rirr bit to receive more interrupts from the device; however, it does not do this manually by overwriting the rirr bit, but by instruction the local APIC to send an EOI message to the I/O APIC.

For this we repurpose the EOI port of the local APIC, which as defined in section 12.1 upon a write has the side effect of lowering the bit corresponding to the highest priority interrupt i in the ISR. Rather than only lowering the bit, we now move this bit into an internal register which we call the EOI pending (EOIp) register

$$c.p(q).apic.EOIp \in \mathbb{B}^{256}$$

Thus if x is a store buffer step of processor q (recall that processor steps do not modify ports of the local APIC)

$$x = (sb, q)$$

which executes a write to the EOI port

$$eoiw(c,x)$$

then the bit corresponding to the highest priority interrupt i in the ISR

$$i = \min\{\, n \mid c.p(q).apic.ISR[n] = 1 \,\}$$

is cleared in the ISR and raised in the EOIp

$$c'.p(q).apic.ISR[i] = 0 \,\wedge\, c'.p(q).apic.EOIp[i] = 1$$

In a separate ISA step of the local APIC, the pending end-of-interrupt message for the highest priority interrupt vector in the EOIp register of processor q is delivered to the I/O APIC. This clears the remote interrupt request bit if i is also the interrupt described in the *vect* field of the redirection register. The step is controlled by oracle inputs x of the form

$$x = (EOI, q) \in \Sigma_{apic,q}$$

which are enabled if there are any pending EOI messages

$$\gamma(c,x) = c.p(q).apic.EOIp \neq 0_{256}$$

The vector of the highest priority interrupt vector v in the EOIp register is defined by

$$\langle v \rangle = \min\{\, n \mid c.p(q).apic.EOIp[n] = 1 \,\}$$

The step clears the pending EOI bit of this vector

$$c'.p(q).apic.EOIp[\langle v \rangle] = 0$$

and clears the rirr bit of the redirection register if the *vect* field equals v

$$c.rr.vect = v \quad \rightarrow \quad c'.rr.rirr = 0$$

This completes the specification of the I/O APIC.

14.2 Construction

Construction of the I/O APIC is similar to the local APIC. For delivery of interrupts, the I/O APIC uses the interrupt bus of the local APICs. Similarly, the local APICs send EOI messages via the interrupt bus to the I/O APIC. Interrupts are sampled via a direct connection between the disk and the I/O APIC.

To distinguish IPIs from EOI messages, we introduce one new delivery mode in hardware:

$$\mathbf{EOI} = 001$$

Obviously local APICs must treat these messages properly: they must ignore them. Fortunately our construction of local APICs already ignores these messages[1]

---

[1] In crucial places, when deciding to receive an interrupt, the local APICs compute signals of the form *Fixed* $\wedge \ldots$, *INIT* $\wedge \ldots$, or *SIPI* $\wedge \ldots$, but not *EOI* $\wedge \ldots$.

so nothing has to be changed on the receiving side. We still need to make minor changes to allow local APICs to send EOI messages to the I/O APIC; we do so in section 14.2.1.

While each processor is connected to its own local APIC in a straight forward way, the I/O APIC is connected to all processors via the device bus, next to the disk. This means we will need to multiplex responses from disk and I/O APIC when the processor is reading from the device bus.

14.2.1 Local APIC Revisited

We revisit the simple local APIC from section 12.2.2 and add the capability to send EOI messages. For this we add for each local APIC a second driver on the interrupt bus purely for delivering EOI messages. This ensures fair arbitration between EOI messages and IPIs. However, since for every received IPI an EOI response is sent, this takes up half of the bandwidth of the interrupt bus. Obviously there are more efficient designs. For example, rather than requiring that processors send EOI messages over the bus by writing to the EOI port of the local APIC, one can introduce EOI registers for I/O APICs and require that the processor clears the RIRR flag by writing to this register. In the intel architecture, this mechanism is known as *directed EOI*.

In order to control the additional driver, the local APIC receives new input and output buses

$$boutb \in \mathbb{B}^{32}$$
$$breqb \in \mathbb{B}$$
$$boeb \in \mathbb{B}$$

This is illustrated in fig. 197 below.

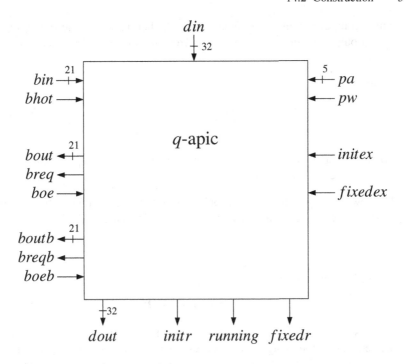

Fig. 197. Symbol of the local APIC with second interrupt bus driver

We make the following changes:

- We implement the EOIp register from the specification in the obvious way with a 256 bit register

$$EOIp : reg(256)$$

- When any EOI message is pending (i.e., any bit in the EOIp is raised), the local APIC is ready to send an EOI message. We can find out both whether there is any pending EOI message and what interrupt vector among the pending EOI messages has the highest priority by using a find-first-one circuit followed by the 8-bit encoder from page 96

$$eoienc : 8\text{-}enc$$

on the output of the EOIp register. Using the find-first-one circuit we compute the minimum index

$$EOIpmin = 256\text{-}f1(EOIp)$$

of a raised bit in the EOIp register. We pass this index into the 8-bit encoder

$$eoienc.in = EOIpmin$$

which computes with output *eoienc.any* whether any bit in the EOIp is raised, and in output *eoienc.out* the vector corresponding to the lowest bit (if any is raised)

Lemma 287.

$$eoienc.any \equiv \exists v. \, EOIp[i] = 1$$
$$eoienc.any \to \langle eoienc.out \rangle = \min\{\, i \mid EOIp[i] = 1 \,\}$$

Proof. Trivial bookkeeping with lemmas 27 and 29 and the specification of find-first-one circuits.   □

• The new connection to the interrupt bus is for the most part wired in the obvious way: the vector put on the bus is the output of the EOI encoder

$$boutb.vect = eoienc.out$$

The delivery mode is always EOI

$$boutb.dm = \textbf{EOI}$$

The bus is requested if there is any pending EOI, except if the local APIC just delivered an EOI message. This is necessary to satisfy the operating condition of the controlled bus, that requests are taken away after receiving the output enable signal. For this purpose we add a one bit register which buffers the output enable signal for the EOI messages for one cycle

$$oebuf : \rho, \quad oebuf' = boeb$$

and mask the request if we have a buffered output enable signal

$$breqb = eoienc.any \wedge /oebuf$$

For future use we collect that an EOI message is delivered by this APIC in the current cycle in signal

$$eoidelivery = boeb$$

That this signal really corresponds to delivery of an EOI message is not obvious only from looking at the construction of the local APIC alone. In the complete machine which includes all the interrupt bus connections, recall that the bus output enable signal *boe* comes from a controlled bus (cf. section 3.5.4) which only gives an output enable signal for the bus if it is requested. Thus in such a machine we will have

$$boeb \quad \to \quad breqb$$

We conclude from the definition of *breqb* that a bus output enable signal will in such a machine be given only in case we have a pending EOI

$$boeb \quad \to \quad eoienc.any$$

- The EOIp register is initialized as all zeroes. It is then (in ISA) only changed by processor steps that write to the EOI port, and by EOI delivery steps. In hardware we thus clock the register in case of reset for initialization, and in case we deliver an EOI message or there is a write to the EOI port (for the latter we reuse the signal *eoiw* from section 12.2.3 which has already been defined for the purpose of updating the ISR):

$$EOIp.ce \equiv reset \lor eoidelivery \lor eoiw$$

Both EOI delivery and write to the EOI port can occur in the same cycle in hardware, e.g., if a store buffer entry writing to the EOI register is committed and the interrupt bus becomes available in the same cycle. Thus construction of the input *EOIp.in* of the EOI pending register is not completely trivial. We need to take a brief look at how the induction step of the coupling relation for this register will work. We need to 1) plan the intended order of the two steps in ISA and 2) simulate the sequential execution of these steps in a single, combined update. Since the EOI message on the bus in hardware comes from the state of EOIp register at the beginning of the cycle, which simulates the EOIp register in ISA before the processor step, we must step the EOI delivery before the write. Thus in case there is both a write request to the EOI register and a bus grant from the bus arbiter, we must first apply the effect of delivery the EOI message, then of writing to the EOI port. This results in the up to three distinct EOIp configurations shown in fig. 198 below.

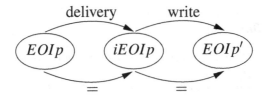

Fig. 198. Up to three states of EOIp in ISA for steps simulated in a single hardware cycle. ISA begins in a state *EOIp* corresponding to hardware *EOIp* at the beginning of the cycle. If an EOI is delivered, ISA then reaches a distinct intermediary EOIp state *iEOIp*; if no EOI is delivered, *iEOIp = EOIp*. Then if a write to **EOI** port is observed, we reach a distinct state *EOIp′*. If no write is observed, *EOIp′ = iEOIp*. After completion of the hardware cycle, the hardware *EOIp* must equal *EOIp′*.

We implement these three possible configurations in a straightforward fashion in hardware by adding a signal *iEOIp* corresponding directly to the intermediate state of the EOIp register in ISA: in case of an EOI delivery we compute the effect of the EOI delivery by lowering the first index of a raised bit in the *EOIp* register, and otherwise we have *iEOIp = EOIp*

$$iEOIp = \begin{cases} EOIp \wedge /EOIpmin & eoidelivery \\ EOIp & \text{o.w.} \end{cases}$$

Note that unlike previous intermediate states, this is *not* a ghost signal.

Using this intermediary state the inputs $EOIp.in$ of the $EOIp$ register can be computed in a completely analogous and straightforward fashion by applying the effect of a write to the EOI register (raising the bit corresponding to the highest priority interrupt in the ISR) in case such a write occurs, and simply taking the intermediate EOI pending state ($iEOIp$) otherwise.

$$EOIp.in = \begin{cases} 0_{256} & reset \\ iEOIp \vee isrmin & eoiw \\ iEOIp & \text{o.w.} \end{cases}$$

This concludes the changes to the construction of the local APIC.

That the changes done in ISA to the EOIp register can be done in hardware using 'find first one' circuits as described above is stated in the following lemma. The proof is a completely trivial bookkeeping exercise and omitted here.

Lemma 288. *Let $c' = \delta(c,x)$. Then both of the following are true:*

- *if the step is an EOI delivery*

$$x = (\boldsymbol{EOI}, q)$$

the next state of the EOIp register can be computed by turning off the first raised bit from the EOIp register

$$c'.p(q).apic.EOIp = c.p(q).apic.EOIp \wedge /f1(c.p(q).apic.EOIp)$$

- *if the step is a store buffer step that writes to the EOI port*

$$x = (sb,q) \wedge eoiw(c,x)$$

the next state of the EOIp register can be computed by turning on the first raised bit from the ISR

$$c'.p(q).apic.EOIp = c.p(q).apic.EOIp \vee f1(c.p(q).apic.ISR)$$

14.2.2 I/O APIC

Figure 199 shows the input and output buses of the I/O APIC. In particular, the I/O APIC has an interface to the device bus consisting of

- input $din \in \mathbb{B}^{64}$ for data to be written to the redirection register
- input $bw \in \mathbb{B}^8$ for byte-write signals
- output $dout \in \mathbb{B}^{64}$ for the content of the redirection register

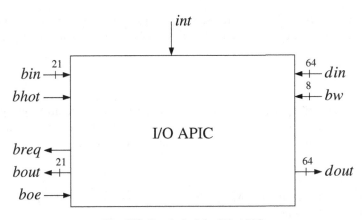

Fig. 199. Symbol of the I/O APIC

It further has the same interface to the interrupt bus as the local APIC, consisting of

- input $bin \in \mathbb{B}^{29}$ for the message currently on the interrupt bus
- input $bhot \in \mathbb{B}$ from the controlled bus signaling that there is currently a message on the interrupt bus
- output $breq \in \mathbb{B}$ to the controlled bus signaling that the I/O APIC is requesting control of the bus
- output $bout \in \mathbb{B}^{29}$ for the message to be put on the bus
- input $boe \in \mathbb{B}$ from the controlled bus signaling that the I/O APIC is broadcasting on the bus in the current cycle

Finally it has an additional input bus *int* coming from the disk. This bus is used for sampling the interrupt from the disk

$$int \in \mathbb{B}$$

Internally, we use an array of eight 8-bit registers for the redirection register, which we call the redirection register banks

$$rrb : \mathrm{reg}(8)([0:7])$$

which can be controlled individually by the byte-write signals.

We use the shorthand *rr* (for redirection register) for the concatenation of the eight banks

$$rr = rrb(7) \circ \ldots \circ rrb(0)$$

from which we will select individual fields such as *dest* and *vect*.

The data output is simply the current content of the redirection register

$$dout = rr$$

All banks of the redirection register except bank 1 (where delivery status and remote interrupt requests are located) are controlled by the byte-write signal and data input

$$i \neq 1 \quad \rightarrow \quad rrb(i).ce = bw[i] \wedge rrb(i).in = din[8 \cdot i + 7 : 8 \cdot i]$$

Similar to the EOIp register of the local APIC, bank 1 of the redirection register is accessed from both the processor side and the interrupt bus (when sending interrupts or receiving EOI messages). Writes to the bank 1 by the processor are detected by signal

$$bw[1]$$

An interrupt is sent by the I/O APIC when the output enable signal is granted by the bus control, i.e., if signal

$$boe$$

is high. Additionally the I/O APIC can sample interrupts from the disk, which will also modify the redirection register (by raising the ds bit). We consider now how the APIC can detect these situations. Writes from the processor side are detected through byte-write signals. Delivery of an IPI is indicated by the bus output enable signal coming from the interrupt bus. EOI messages are received when the interrupt bus is hot and carries a message with the new delivery mode **EOI**, but these messages only have an effect if the vector transmitted on the interrupt bus is also the vector of the interrupt in the redirection register. For later use we define a signal *eoi* which identifies this situation

$$eoi \equiv bhot \wedge (bin.dm = \textbf{EOI}) \wedge (bin.vect = rr.vect)$$

Finally, the I/O APIC samples the disk interrupt when there is an interrupt (as indicated by *int*), and the interrupt is neither masked, nor already delivered (as indicated by the remote interrupt request register bit *rirr*), nor already sampled but not delivered (in which case the delivery status bit would be high)

$$sample \equiv int \wedge /rr.mask \wedge /rr.rirr \wedge /rr.ds$$

Bank 1 of the redirection register is updated if any of these situations arise.

$$rrb(1).ce = bw[1] \vee boe \vee eoi \vee sample$$

Keeping with our stepping order from the previous chapter, we will step store buffer steps that modify devices (including now the I/O APIC) last. Consequently writes triggered by byte-write signals must overrule any changes made to the redirection register by messages from the interrupt bus or the disk. We specify the input to this register bank bitwise. Bits 4 (delivery status) and 2 (remote interrupt request register) receive special treatment as they are updated by sampling/delivering interrupts and delivering interrupts/receiving EOI messages, respectively.

$$rrb(1).in[i] = \begin{cases} 0_8 & reset \\ din[8+i] & bw[1] \wedge /reset \\ (rrb(1)[i] \vee sample) \wedge /boe & i = 4 \wedge /bw[1] \wedge /reset \\ (rrb(1)[i] \vee boe) \wedge /eoi & i = 2 \wedge /bw[1] \wedge /reset \\ rrb(1)[i] & o.w. \end{cases}$$

This appears to imply a particular stepping order between sample and IPI delivery, and between IPI delivery and EOI reception. However in the complete construction only sampling and EOI reception can occur in the same cycle, meaning that there is never a conflict. Sampling requires that the delivery status is low, while IPI delivery requires that the delivery status is high. IPI delivery and EOI reception both require access to the bus, and are therefore mutually exclusive (provided we satisfy the operating conditions of the controlled bus).

The I/O APIC requests the interrupt bus while that register has a raised delivery status

$$breq = rr.ds$$

The message put on the interrupt bus by the I/O APIC consists of the destination and vector from the intermediate redirection register

$$bout.(dest, vect) = irr.(dest, vect)$$

and of the delivery mode and destination shorthand required by the specification

$$bout.(dm, dsh) = (FIXED, TARGET)$$

This concludes the construction of the I/O APIC. For configurations h of the I/O APIC we introduce the shorthand

$$rr(h) = h.rrb(7) \circ \ldots \circ h.rrb(0)$$

denoting the complete content of the redirection register. Since we will only place a single copy

$$ioapic$$

of the I/O APIC in our complete design, we abbreviate further

$$rr^t = rr(h^t.ioapic)$$

for the single redirection register of that I/O apic. We use this redirection register with implicit t notation, i.e., we write

$$rr \text{ for } rr^t \quad \text{and} \quad rr' \text{ for } rr^{t+1}$$

when appropriate.

Obviously the output of the I/O APIC to the memory bus is the value of its redirection register

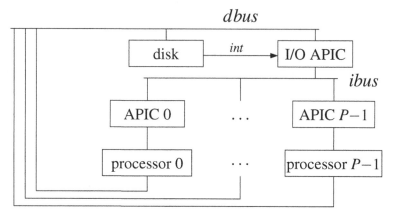

Fig. 200. Overview of the connection between processors, APICs (including the I/O APIC), and the disk. Connections to cache memory system not shown. Recall that *ibus* and *dbus* are controlled buses and include tri-state drivers which are not shown in this figure.

Lemma 289.

$$dout = rr$$

The data put on the interrupt bus is obviously computed based on this state.

Lemma 290.

$$bout.(dest, vect, dm, dsh) = (rr.dest, rr.vect, FIXED, TARGET)$$

14.2.3 Connecting Everything

We now connect everything to the interrupt and device buses. This results in the machine shown in fig. 200.

For this we first place an instance

$$ioapic$$

of the I/O APIC into our machine. The disk is connected directly to the I/O APIC to deliver interrupts

$$ioapic.int = D.int$$

We then add a tri-state driver for the I/O APIC to the interrupt bus, as well as P drivers for the EOI messages of local APICs. Thus we have now for P processors subunit

$$ibus : (2P+1, 21)\text{-controlled bus}$$

The local APIC of processor q is connected to tri-state drivers number $2q$ and $2q+1$ in the obvious way

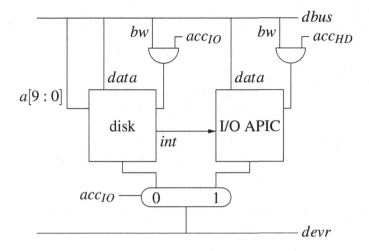

Fig. 201. Multiplexing of responses of disk and I/O APIC

$$q < P \quad \rightarrow \quad ibus.a^{2q} = apic(q).bout$$
$$\wedge\, ibus.req[2q] = apic(q).breq$$
$$\wedge\, ibus.a^{2q+1} = apic(q).boutb$$
$$\wedge\, ibus.req[2q+1] = apic(q).breqb$$

and the I/O APIC is now connected to tri-state driver number $2P$

$$ibus.a^{2P} = ioapic.bout$$
$$ibus.req[2P] = ioapic.breq$$

The bus input, bus hot, and bus output enable signals of all APICs are connected in the obvious way

$$apic(q).bin = ioapic.bin = ibus.data$$
$$apic(q).bhot = ioapic.bhot = ibus.bhot$$
$$apic(q).boe = ibus.boe[2q]$$
$$apic(q).boeb = ibus.boeb[2q+1]$$
$$ioapic.boe = ibus.boe[2P]$$

We also need to connect the I/O APIC to the device bus. As address ranges of disk ports and the redirection register are disjoint, it suffices to give any request to the unit that is responsible for that request based on the address, and use a multiplexer to select the response. This is shown in fig. 201.

The I/O APIC is responsible if the access is going to the redirection register. We compute this with signal

$$acc_{IO} \equiv dbus.data.a = base_{IO}$$

Phase	Steps	Description
1	$[NS : N_{CMS})$	walk initialization, read from store buffer
2	$[N_{CMS} : N_{REM})$	memory accesses (NOT to Devices)
3	$[N_{REM} : N_{SIPI})$	remaining processor steps (includes external and INIT interrupts)
4	$[N_{SIPI} : N_{IBUS})$	SIPI steps of APICs
5	$[N_{IBUS} : N_{SAMPLE})$	IPI and EOI delivery steps of APICs
6	$[N_{SAMPLE} : N_{DISK})$	sampling device interrupts by I/O APIC
7	$[N_{DISK} : N_{DEVW})$	disk step
8	$[N_{DEVW} : NS')$	stores to device ports

Table 22. Phases of stepping function with I/O APIC

In case acc_{IO} is raised, the response for the memory request is taken from the I/O APIC, otherwise from the disk

$$devr = \begin{cases} ioapic.dout & acc_{IO} \\ disk.dout & \text{o.w.} \end{cases}$$

The byte-write signals are forwarded to the I/O APIC only in case acc_{IO} is raised

$$ioapic.bw = dbus.data.bw \wedge acc_{IO}$$

The data input if the I/O APIC is taken from the access in the obvious fashion

$$ioapic.din = dbus.data.data$$

Recall that the I/O APIC only has a single cache line consisting of a double word of data. Thus there is no need to provide an address to the I/O APIC.

14.3 Correctness Proof

14.3.1 Stepping Function

We proceed to define the stepping function. Besides the addition of I/O APIC steps and EOI delivery steps nothing changes. Both the IPI delivery and EOI delivery steps are triggered by the interrupt bus, and are hence performed in phase 5. For sampling from the disk we insert a new phase behind phase 5. The resulting phases of the stepping function are illustrated in table 22.

The definition of the stepping function in case of emergency braking is completely unchanged. In the absence of emergency braking, the definitions of N_{CMS}, N_{REM}, N_{SIPI}, N_{IBUS} are unchanged. N_{SAMPLE} is defined analogously to the previous N_{DISK} by

$$N_{SAMPLE} = N_{IBUS} + ibus.bhot$$

Note that signal *bhot* can now also be activated by EOI messages, or when the I/O APIC takes control of the bus. Consequently the oracle input

$$s(N_{IBUS})$$

of the step triggered by the interrupt bus needs to be redefined. Let i be the index of the participant which has an output enable signal

$$i = \varepsilon \{ i \mid ibus.oe[i] \}$$

If this index is lower than $2P$, it triggers a step of a local APIC. Whether that step is an EOI delivery or IPI delivery step depends on whether i is odd or even:

$$ibus.bhot \wedge i < 2P \; \rightarrow \; s(N_{IBUS}) = \begin{cases} (IPI, q) & i = 2q \\ (EOI, q) & i = 2q + 1 \end{cases}$$

If the index is equal to $2P$, the interrupt bus is controlled by the I/O APIC which performs an IPI delivery step

$$ibus.bhot \wedge i = 2P \; \rightarrow \; s(N_{IBUS}) = deliver$$

The I/O APIC samples a new interrupt when its *sample* signal is high

$$N_{DISK} = N_{SAMPLE} + ioapic.sample$$

The oracle input of such a step is defined in the obvious way by

$$ioapic.sample \; \rightarrow \; s(N_{SAMPLE}) = sample$$

For the remaining steps, nothing changes.

14.3.2 Software Conditions

We need to add a software condition for the I/O APIC which forbids overwriting the delivery status or remote interrupt request bits. We define $SC_{IO}(c,x)$ to be that software condition

$$\begin{aligned} SC_{IO}(c,x) \; \equiv \; & x \in \Sigma_{p,q} \wedge s(c,x) \wedge exec(c,x) \\ & \rightarrow \quad \nexists i < d(c,x). \; ea(c,x) +_{32} i_{32} = base_{IO} +_{32} 1_{32} \end{aligned}$$

The software condition which forbids CAS instructions to the redirection register is already covered by SC_{DEV}. However, SC_{DEV} is slightly too strict right now as it forbids writing to the redirection register (only writing to the disk is permitted). We adjust the condition as follows:

$$\begin{aligned} SC_{DEV}(c,x) \equiv \; & x \in \Sigma_{p,q} \wedge mop(c,x) \wedge ea(c,x) \in \mathcal{B} \\ & \rightarrow \; (l(c,x) \vee s(c,x)) \\ & \quad \wedge ((\exists i \in [0 : 2^4). \; ea(c,x) = base_{IO} +_{32} i_{32}) \\ & \quad \quad \vee (\exists i \in [0 : 2^{13}). \; ea(c,x) = base_{HD} +_{32} i_{32})) \end{aligned}$$

The software condition SC_{APIC} for the local APIC must also be adjusted slightly. If the delivery mode of a local APIC was set to EOI and the interrupt was delivered over the interrupt bus, triggering a step with oracle input

$$(IPI, q)$$

then this step would have no effect on the I/O APIC in ISA but would be considered a valid EOI message in hardware. To avoid this situation we forbid using the delivery mode EOI for IPIs. More precisely, if the processor issues a write to the lower half of the ICR (where the delivery mode is stored in bits 10-8, cf. fig. 184 on page 510)

$$SC_{APIC}(c,x) \equiv$$
$$SC_{APIC\ old}(c,x)$$
$$\wedge\, (x \in \Sigma_{p.q} \wedge s(c,x) \wedge ea(c,x) = base_{APIC} +_{32} 432 \wedge exec(c,x)$$
$$\rightarrow\ B(c,x)[10:8] \neq \mathbf{EOI})$$

The remaining software conditions SC_{DISK} and SC_{ROM} remain unchanged.

14.3.3 Induction Hypothesis

We add the obvious coupling for the redirection register:

$$t \sim_m n\ \ \equiv\ \ n = NS^t \rightarrow m(h^t) = \ell(c^n.m) \wedge opc^t$$
$$\wedge\ aq(sb(q)^t_\pi) = c^n.p(q).sb$$
$$\wedge\ walks(mmu_I(q)^t) \cup walks(mmu_E(q)^t) \subseteq c^n.tlb(q)$$
$$\wedge\ apic(q)^t = c^n.p(q).apic \wedge opc\text{-}cb(ibus)^t$$
$$\wedge\ D^t = c^n.disk \wedge opc\text{-}d^t$$
$$\wedge\ rr^t_\pi = c^n.rr$$
$$\wedge\ \forall \hat{n} < n.\ \gamma(c^{\hat{n}}, s(\hat{n}))$$

Note that as usual, the guard condition γ now includes additional cases for the new types of steps (I/O APIC steps and EOI delivery steps).

Lemma 291. *There is an initial configuration c^0 satisfying*

$$sim(h^0.(p(q),m), c^0.(p(q),m))\quad for\ all\ q \in P$$

in which instruction buffers and TLBs are empty

$$c^0.ib(q) = c^0.tlb(q) = \emptyset$$

and the store buffers are also empty

$$c^0.p(q).sb = \varepsilon$$

Furthermore: if for the computation (c^n) with stepping function $s(n)$ extracted from hardware and initial configuration c^0 satisfies for all n the software conditions $SC_{ROM}(c^n, s(n))$, $SC_{APIC}(c^n, s(n))$, $SC_{IO}(c^n, s(n))$ and $SC_{DISK}(c^n, s(n))$ provided the stepping function $s(n)$ has a valid initial segment until n

$$\forall n.\ (\forall m \le n.\ \gamma(c^m, s(m))) \ \rightarrow\ SC_{ROM}(c^n, s(n)) \wedge SC_{APIC}(c^n, s(n))$$
$$\wedge\, SC_{DISK}(c^n, s(n)) \wedge SC_{IO}(c^n, s(n))$$

then for all n and t:

- *If n is a step of processor q executing instructions i which is committed and only has live instructions before it*

$$n = pseq(q, i) \ \wedge\ c(i)^{q,t} \ \wedge\ lb(i)^{q,t}$$

then hardware in cycle t simulates instruction i

$$t \sim_p^q i$$

and each part of the guard condition holds if instruction i passed the corresponding stage

$$(i < I_{IF}^{q,t} \rightarrow \gamma_I^{A,i})$$
$$\wedge\, (i < I_{IT}^{q,t} \rightarrow \gamma_{wI}^{A,i})$$
$$\wedge\, (i < I_{ET}^{q,t} \rightarrow \gamma_{wE}^{A,i})$$
$$\wedge\, (i < I_1^{q,t} \rightarrow \gamma_r^{A,i})$$
$$\wedge\, (i < I_{M-1}^{q,t} \rightarrow \gamma_e^{A,i})$$
$$\wedge\, (i < I_{M-1}^{q,t} \rightarrow \gamma_{INIT}^{A,i})$$

- *Hardware simulates in cycle t the non-pipelined components of ISA step n*

$$t \sim_m n$$

14.3.4 Induction Step

As before the only interesting case is the induction step $t \rightarrow t+1$ for $n > 0$ and we only show the proof for that case. In this case we have as an induction hypothesis for the current cycle

$$t \sim_m o \ \wedge\ (o = pseq(q, i) \wedge c(i)^{q,t} \wedge lb(i)^{q,t}$$
$$\rightarrow t \sim_p i \wedge (i > I_{IF}^{q,t} \rightarrow \gamma_I^{A,t}) \wedge (i > I_{IT}^{q,t} \rightarrow \gamma_{wI}^{A,t}) \wedge (i > I_{ET} \rightarrow \gamma_{wE}^{A,t})) \tag{89}$$

We show as before invariants that can be concluded from the software conditions. As usual we only show those lemmas that are used in the changed parts of the proofs. Accesses to the device region $\mathcal{B}$ in the store buffer must go either to the disk *or* to the redirection register.

Lemma 292. *Let $n \geq NS$ and w be store buffer entry number k of processor q in ISA configuration c^{NS}, and let w write to the device region*

$$w = c^{NS}.p(q).sb[k] \wedge w.a \in \mathcal{B}$$

Then w must access the disk or the redirection register

$$\exists i \in [0 : 2^{10}). \ w.a = base_{HD}[31 : 3] +_{29} i_{29}$$
$$\vee \ w.a = base_{IO}[31 : 3]$$

Furthermore, store buffer entries that access the redirection register do not write to redirection register bank 1, where the delivery status and remote interrupt request registers are.

Lemma 293. *Let $n \geq NS$ and w be store buffer entry number k of processor q in ISA configuration c^{NS}, and let w write to the redirection register*

$$w = c^{NS}.p(q).sb[k] \wedge w.a = base_{IO}[31 : 3]$$

Then byte-write signal $w.bw[1]$ must be low

$$\overline{w.bw[1]}$$

Finally, the delivery mode of local APICs is never **EOI**

Lemma 294. *Let $n \geq NS$ and q some processor. The delivery mode of the local APIC of processor q in configuration c^{NS} is not **EOI***

$$c^{NS}.p(q).apic.ICR.dm \neq \textbf{EOI}$$

Proofs of these lemmas are completely analogous to proofs of lemmas 253 and 254 and are omitted here.

14.3.5 Validity

We prove the lemma corresponding to lemma 284

Lemma 295. *Let*

$$n \in [NS : NS') \ \wedge \ \hat{n} \leq n$$

or

$$n = NS' \ \wedge \ \hat{n} < n$$

Then

$$\gamma(c^{\hat{n}}, s(\hat{n}))$$

Proof. For $\hat{n} < NS$ the claim follows from the induction hypothesis for the current cycle (eq. (89)). For $\hat{n} \in [NS : NS')$, assume that all steps before $\hat{n}$ are valid. The proof for step $\hat{n}$ is by case split on the type of step $\hat{n}$. For all steps except 1) I/O APIC steps and 2) EOI delivery steps the proof is literally as before. We do not repeat these proofs here. We split cases on these types of steps. For I/O APIC steps we split further between sampling and IPI delivery.

- $s(\hat{n}) = sample$: we have to show that in configuration $c^{\hat{n}}$ mask bit and remote interrupt request register are low, and that the disk has an interrupt. In hardware we know that this is true because we would not sample an interrupt otherwise, i.e., we have

$$sample, \quad ioapic.int \wedge /rr.mask \wedge /rr.rirr, \quad D.int, \quad cmsr[2]$$

With the induction hypothesis for the current cycle (eq. (89)) we conclude that the same holds in configuration c^{NS}

$$cmsr(c^{NS})[2] \wedge /c^{NS}.rr.mask \wedge /c^{NS}.rr.rirr$$

By definition of the stepping function, sampling only occurs in phase 6, before stores to device ports and before disk steps. By the software condition, CAS instructions to disk or I/O APIC are forbidden. For the disk, which is only affected by memory operations and disk steps, it immediately follows that there are no changes between steps NS and $\hat{n}$

$$cmsr(c^{\hat{n}})[2] = cmsr(c^{NS})[2] = 1$$

and thus the interrupt flag is raised in configuration $c^{\hat{n}}$. For the mask bit of the I/O APIC we conclude in the same way

$$c^{\hat{n}}.rr.mask = c^{NS}.rr.mask = 0$$

It remains to show that the remote interrupt request register stays low. For this we must also consider potential IPI delivery steps of the I/O APIC in phase 5, which would raise the remote interrupt request register. However, by construction, we only sample device interrupts if the delivery status of the I/O APIC is low, i.e., from $sample$ we conclude

$$/rr.ds$$

Since the delivery status is low, the I/O APIC is not requesting the interrupt bus. Recall that the I/O APIC is connected to tri-state driver number $2P$ on the interrupt bus.

$$/ibus.req[2P]$$

By the induction hypothesis for the current cycle (eq. (89)) the operating conditions of the interrupt bus are maintained

$$opc\text{-}cb(ibus)$$

and by lemma 31 the I/O APIC can not receive an output enable signal in the absence of a request

$$/ibus.oe[2P]$$

By definition of the stepping function, the I/O APIC is not delivering an interrupt in this cycle

$$\forall o \in [NS : NS'). \ s(o) \neq deliver$$

Thus the remote interrupt request register is not raised by such a step between steps NS and $\hat{n}$, and stays low

$$c^{\hat{n}}.rr.rirr = c^{NS}.rr.rirr = 0$$

The claim follows

$$\gamma(c^{\hat{n}}, s(\hat{n}))$$

- $s(\hat{n}) = deliver$: we need to show that the delivery status bit is raised in configuration $c^{\hat{n}}$. By definition of the stepping function an IPI delivery step is only triggered if tri-state driver number $2P$ (which is controlled by the I/O APIC) is driving the bus

$$ibus.oe[2P]$$

By the induction hypothesis for the current cycle (eq. (89)) the operating conditions of the interrupt bus are maintained

$$opc\text{-}cb(ibus)$$

and thus by lemma 31 there is no output enable signal without a request. We conclude successively

$$ibus.req[2P], \quad ioapic.breq, \quad rr.ds$$

Thus the delivery status is raised in hardware. By the induction hypothesis for the current cycle (eq. (89)) it is also raised in ISA configuration c^{NS} and as in the case $s(\hat{n}) = sample$ we conclude that it must also be raised in ISA configuration $c^{\hat{n}}$

$$c^{\hat{n}}.rr.ds = c^{NS}.rr.ds = rr.ds = 1$$

which is the claim

$$\gamma(c^{\hat{n}}, s(\hat{n}))$$

- $s(\hat{n}) = (EOI, q)$: we need to show that some bit in the EOI pending register is raised in ISA configuration $c^{\hat{n}}$. Completely analogously to how we concluded in the proof for the case $s(\hat{n}) = deliver$ that tri-state driver number $2P$ must have a request, we conclude that there is a request on the tri-state driver number $2q + 1$ which handles EOI messages for the APIC of processor q. We conclude successively

$$ibus.req[2q+1], \quad apic(q).breqb, \quad apic(q).eoienc.any$$

By the specification of the encoder (lemma 27) we conclude that some bit in the input of the encoder must be raised. The input is by construction the EOIp register, which must therefore have a raised bit

$$apic(q).EOIp \neq 0_{256}$$

With the induction hypothesis for the current cycle (eq. (89)) we obtain that the same holds in configuration c^{NS}

$$c^{NS}.p(q).apic.EOIp = apic(q).EOIp \neq 0_{256}$$

The EOI pending register is only modified by EOI delivery messages and store buffer steps which write to the EOI port (i.e., not the CMS). By construction of the stepping function, steps $o \in [NS : \hat{n})$ are neither, and thus do not modify the EOI pending register

$$c^{\hat{n}}.p(q).apic.EOIp = c^{NS}.p(q).apic.EOIp \neq 0_{256}$$

and the claim follows

$$\gamma(c^{\hat{n}}, s(\hat{n}))$$

$\square$

14.3.6 Correctness of the EOI Pending Register

The correctness proof of the EOI pending register is completely analogous to existing proofs and only summarized here. We use the (non-ghost) intermediate state of the EOI pending register $iEOIp$ in a stepping diagram. As shown in fig. 202, the EOIp in ISA changes twice: once after potential delivery of the EOI message, and once after a potential write to the EOI port coming from the store buffer in the last phase.

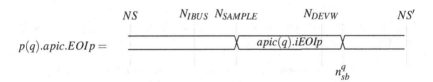

Fig. 202. Stepping diagram for the EOI pending register

Simple bookkeeping shows that 1) the EOIp register is not changed until step N_{IBUS}, 2) after the potential step from the interrupt bus, the EOIp in ISA is equal to the intermediate EOIp, and 3) after completing all steps from the current cycle, the EOIp in ISA is equal to the next EOIp in hardware.

Lemma 296.

$$n \geq N_{IBUS} \rightarrow c^{N_{IBUS}}.p(q).apic.EOIp = apic(q).EOIp$$
$$n \geq N_{SAMPLE} \rightarrow c^{N_{SAMPLE}}.p(q).apic.EOIp = apic(q).iEOIp$$
$$n \geq NS' \rightarrow c^{NS'}.p(q).apic.EOIp = apic(q)'.EOIp$$

Proof. The claim can be shown in the usual way using the software condition SC_{APIC} which forbids CAS instructions to the EOI register. Details are omitted. For the second claim we split cases on whether the local APIC delivers an EOI message or not.

- $ibus.oe[2q+1]$: the local APIC delivers an EOI message. We conclude succesively from the hardware construction

$$apic(q).boeb, \quad apic(q).eoidelivery$$

It immediately follows that the intermediate EOIp is obtained by turning off in the EOIp all bits masked by $apic(q).EOIpmin$:

$$apic(q).iEOIp = apic(q).EOIp \wedge /apic(q).EOIpmin$$

From the induction hypothesis for the current cycle (eq. (89)) we obtain that the operating conditions of the interrupt bus are maintained

$$opc\text{-}cb(ibus)$$

and by the correctness of the controlled bus (lemma 31) the bus is only granted to a participant that requests it. We conclude successively

$$ibus.req[2q+1], \quad apic(q).breqb, \quad apic(q).eoienc.any$$

By the correctness of the encoder (lemma 27), a bit in the input of the EOI-encoder must be raised. This input is the EOIp register

$$apic(q).EOIp \neq 0_{256}$$

Thus the find-first one circuit which computes the mask $apic(q).EOIpmin$ from the EOIp register finds the lowest index of such a raised bit

$$apic(q).EOIpmin[i] \equiv i = \min\{\, j \mid apic(q).EOIp[j] = 1 \,\}$$

By construction of the controlled bus, since a participant is granted an output enable signal, the bus is hot

$$ibus.bhot$$

and a step is triggered from the interrupt bus. By definition of the stepping function, this step is an EOI delivery step

$$s(N_{IBUS}) = (EOI, q)$$

The effect of this step on the EOI register is to clear the bit corresponding to the vector v of the highest-priority interrupt currently in the EOIp register

$$\langle v \rangle = \min\{\, j \mid c^{N_{IBUS}}.p(q).apic.EOIp[j] = 1 \,\}$$

By the first claim, the EOIp in ISA in that configuration is equal to the hardware EOIp. Thus

$$\langle v \rangle = \min\{\, j \mid apic(q).EOIp[j] = 1 \,\}$$

We conclude: the mask $apic(q).EOIpmin$ lowers the bit corresponding to vector v

$$apic(q).EOIpmin[i] \equiv i = \langle v \rangle$$

and a bitwise analysis of the intermediate EOIp yields

$$apic(q).iEOIp[i] = \begin{cases} 0 & i = \langle v \rangle \\ apic(q).EOIp[i] & \text{o.w.} \end{cases}$$

From the first claim we conclude that the EOIp in hardware is equal to the EOIp in ISA in configuration $c^{N_{IBUS}}$, and the claim follows

$$apic(q).iEOIp[i] = \begin{cases} 0 & i = \langle v \rangle \\ c^{N_{IBUS}}.p(q).apic.EOIp[i] & \text{o.w.} \end{cases}$$
$$= c^{N_{SAMPLE}}.p(q).apic.EOIp[i]$$

- $/ibus.oe[2q+1]$: the local APIC does not deliver an EOI message. We conclude successively from the hardware construction

$$/apic(q).boeb, \quad /apic(q).eoidelivery, \quad apic(q).iEOIp = apic(q).EOIp$$

By definition of the stepping function, no EOI delivery step is triggered. The other potential steps made between N_{IBUS} and N_{SAMPLE} — IPI delivery steps of the I/O APIC or local APICs — do not change the EOIp register in ISA. The claim follows from the first claim

$$apic(q).iEOIp = apic(q).EOIp$$
$$= c^{N_{IBUS}}.p(q).apic.EOIp$$
$$= c^{N_{SAMPLE}}.p(q).apic.EOIp$$

The third claim can be proven completely analogously to lemma 272. The details are omitted. □

14.3.7 Correctness of the Redirection Register

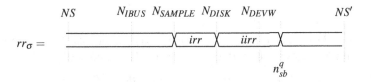

Fig. 203. Stepping diagram for the redirection register

We show that the redirection register is simulated correctly. As usual we use a stepping diagram and intermediate ghost states. However, unlike other components which are changed in only two phases, the redirection register can be changed in up to three phases. Thus we introduce not only one intermediate redirection register, but two: *irr* and *iirr*, to be defined later. The resulting stepping diagram is shown in fig. 203. Until step N_{IBUS} nothing changes

Lemma 297.

$$n \geq N_{IBUS} \ \rightarrow \ c^{N_{IBUS}}.rr = rr$$

The proof of this lemma is completely analogous to the proof of lemma 258, and omitted here. The first intermediate redirection register, *irr*, is obtained after a potential step is triggered on the interrupt bus. This step may either be an IPI delivery step of the I/O APIC, which would clear the delivery status bit and raise the remote interrupt request register, or it may be an EOI delivery step of some local APIC which lowers the remote interrupt request register. As described in table 21 these are bits 12 and 10, respectively. Thus the state of the intermediate request register is defined bitwise by

$$irr[j] = \begin{cases} 0 & j = 12 \land ioapic.boe \\ 1 & j = 10 \land ioapic.boe \\ 0 & j = 10 \land ioapic.eoi \\ rr[j] & \text{o.w.} \end{cases}$$

That this is indeed a definition relies on the fact that the I/O APIC can not in the same cycle deliver an IPI and receive an EOI message. This is shown in the following lemma.

Lemma 298.

$$n \geq NS \ \rightarrow \ \neg(ioapic.boe \land ioapic.eoi)$$

Proof. Assume for the sake of contradiction that the I/O APIC delivers an IPI and receives an EOI message

$$ioapic.boe \land ioapic.eoi$$

By construction, an EOI message is received if the bus is hot and has an EOI message on it

$$ibus.bhot \land ibus.data.dm = \textbf{EOI}$$

By the induction hypothesis for the current cycle (eq. (89)) the operating condition of the interrupt bus has been maintained

$$opc\text{-}cb(ibus)$$

and by lemma 31 the controlled bus is giving a bus output enable signal to the I/O APIC only if it requests it. Furthermore the data on the bus comes from the I/O APIC

$$ibus.oe[2P], \quad ibus.req[2P], \quad ibus.data = ibus.a^{2P} = ioapic.bout$$

However the I/O APIC only sends fixed messages

$$ibus.data.dm = ioapic.bout.dm = Fixed \neq \textbf{EOI}$$

which contradicts the assumption that the message on the bus is an EOI message. $\square$

We show:

Lemma 299.
$$n \geq N_{SAMPLE} \;\rightarrow\; c^{N_{SAMPLE}}.rr = irr$$

Proof. By case split along the lines of the definition of N_{SAMPLE} and $s(N_{IBUS})$.

- $/ibus.bhot$: in this case nothing is stepped

$$N_{SAMPLE} = N_{IBUS}$$

Thus with lemma 297 it suffices to show that the intermediate redirection register is also equal to the redirection register:

$$
\begin{aligned}
c^{N_{SAMPLE}}.rr &= c^{N_{IBUS}}.rr \\
&= rr \qquad\qquad \text{L 297} \\
&\overset{!}{=} irr
\end{aligned}
$$

It obviously suffices to show that the I/O APIC neither delivers an IPI nor receives an EOI message. Since the bus is not hot, by definition the I/O APIC is not receiving an EOI message

$$/ioapic.bhot, \quad /ioapic.eoi$$

By construction, the bus is hot if any participant has an output enable signal. Since the bus is not hot, no participant, in particular not the I/O APIC (with index $2P$), has an output enable signal

$$/ibus.oe[2P], \quad /ioapic.boe$$

The claim follows

$$rr = irr$$

- $ibus.bhot \wedge ibus.oe[2q]$: a local APIC is broadcasting an IPI on the interrupt bus. In ISA this triggers an IPI delivery step of the local APIC

$$s(N_{IBUS}) = (IPI, q)$$

and such steps do not change the redirection register. As in the previous case it suffices to show that the intermediate redirection register is equal to the redirection register:

$$
\begin{aligned}
c^{N_{SAMPLE}}.rr &= c^{N_{IBUS}}.rr \\
&= rr \qquad\qquad \text{L 297} \\
&\overset{!}{=} irr
\end{aligned}
$$

That the message on the bus is not an EOI message can be shown with lemma 294, which states that the local APIC of processor q does not have delivery mode **EOI**

$$c^{NS}.p(q).apic.ICR.dm \neq \textbf{EOI}$$

Straightforward bookkeeping using 1) the correctness of the controlled bus (lemma 31), 2) that the operating conditions of the interrupt bus are maintained (eq. (89)), 3) that the APICs in hardware at the beginning of the cycle have the same state as in configuration c^{NS} (also eq. (89)), and 4) the construction shows: the message on the bus is not an EOI message

$$
\begin{aligned}
ibus.data.dm &= ibus.a^{2q}.dm &\qquad \text{L 31, E 89}\\
&= apic(q).bout.dm \\
&= apic(q).ICR.dm \\
&= c^{NS}.p(q).apic.ICR.dm &\qquad \text{E 89}\\
&\neq \textbf{EOI}
\end{aligned}
$$

From the construction it quickly follows that the I/O APIC is not receiving an EOI message

$$ioapic.bin.dm \neq \textbf{EOI}, \quad /ioapic.eoi$$

Using again the correctness of the controlled bus (lemma 31) and that the operating conditions of the interrupt bus have been maintained (eq. (89)) we obtain also that only one participant has an output enable signal, and that is not the I/O APIC (with index $2P$). Hence the I/O APIC is not delivering an IPI in this cycle

$$/ibus.oe[2P], \quad /ioapic.boe$$

and the claim follows

$$irr = rr$$

- $ibus.bhot \wedge ibus.oe[2q+1]$: a local APIC is broadcasting an EOI message on the interrupt bus. In ISA this triggers an EOI delivery step of the local APIC

$$s(N_{IBUS}) = (EOI, q)$$

which lowers the remote interrupt request bit in the I/O APIC iff the vector of the redirection register is equal to the vector of the EOI. All other bits of the redirection register are left unchanged. We show here only the proof of the remote interrupt request bit and omit the proofs for the other bits. As described in table 21 this is bit 10. Let v be the vector of the EOI message, defined by

$$\langle v \rangle = \min \left\{ i \mid c^{N_{IBUS}}.p(q).apic.EOIp[i] = 1 \right\}$$

By lemma 296 the EOIp of this APIC in configuration $c^{N_{IBUS}}$ is equal to its counterpart in hardware

$$c^{N_{IBUS}}.p(q).apic.EOIp = apic(q).EOIp$$

Thus index $\langle v \rangle$ is also the index of the highest-priority interrupt in the EOIp in hardware

$$\langle v \rangle = \min \{ i \mid apic(q).EOIp[i] = 1 \}$$

By the correctness of the encoder, vector v is the output of the EOI-encoder, which is the vector put on the bus

$$apic(q).boutb.vect = eoienc.out = v$$

Since the operating conditions of the interrupt bus are maintained (eq. (89)) we obtain with lemma 31 that this is also the vector received by the I/O APIC

$$
\begin{aligned}
ioapic.bin.vect &= ibus.data.vect \\
&= ibus.a^{2q+1}.vect \qquad\qquad \text{L 31, E 89} \\
&= apic(q).boutb.vect \\
&= v
\end{aligned}
$$

Completely analogously we conclude that the message on the bus is an EOI message

$$ioapic.bin.dm = apic(q).boutb.dm = \mathbf{EOI}$$

The remote interrupt request bit is lowered in ISA if the vector $rr.vect$ in the redirection register of the I/O APIC is equal to this vector. By lemma 297 we can use the redirection register of hardware to do this computation

$$
\begin{aligned}
c^{NSAMPLE}.rr.rirr &= \begin{cases} 0 & c^{NIBUS}.rr.vect = v \\ c^{NIBUS}.rr.rirr & \text{o.w.} \end{cases} \\[2mm]
&= \begin{cases} 0 & rr.vect = v \\ rr.rirr & \text{o.w.} \end{cases} \qquad\qquad \text{L 297} \\[2mm]
&= \begin{cases} 0 & rr.vect = ioapic.bin.vect \\ rr.rirr & \text{o.w.} \end{cases}
\end{aligned}
$$

Since the bus is hot and the delivery mode is **EOI**, the I/O APIC receives an EOI message iff the vectors $rr.vect$ of the redirection register and $ioapic.bin.vect$ are equal

$$
\begin{aligned}
ioapic.eoi &\equiv ioapic.bhot \wedge (ioapic.bin.dm = \mathbf{EOI}) \wedge (ioapic.bin.vect = rr.vect) \\
&\equiv ioapic.bin.vect = rr.vect
\end{aligned}
$$

The claim follows

$$
\begin{aligned}
c^{NSAMPLE}.rr.rirr &= \begin{cases} 0 & rr.vect = ioapic.bin.vect \\ rr.rirr & \text{o.w.} \end{cases} \\[2mm]
&= \begin{cases} 0 & ioapic.eoi \\ rr.rirr & \text{o.w.} \end{cases} \\[2mm]
&= irr.rirr
\end{aligned}
$$

- *ibus.bhot* $\wedge$ *ibus.oe*[2P]: the I/O APIC is broadcasting an IPI. In ISA this triggers an IPI delivery step of the I/O APIC

$$s(N_{IBUS}) = deliver$$

By construction the I/O APIC is also delivering the interrupt in hardware

$$ioapic.boe$$

and both in hardware and in ISA, the delivery status bit is lowered and the remote interrupt request bit is raised. The claim follows with lemma 297

$$c^{N_{SAMPLE}}.rr[i] = \begin{cases} 0 & i = 12 \\ 1 & i = 10 \\ c^{N_{IBUS}}.rr[i] & \text{o.w.} \end{cases}$$

$$= \begin{cases} 0 & i = 12 \\ 1 & i = 10 \\ rr[i] & \text{o.w.} \end{cases}$$

$$= irr[i]$$

$\square$

The second intermediate request register, which we denote by *iirr*, is obtained after potentially sampling an interrupt from the disk. This raises the delivery status bit (bit 12) and leaves everything else unchanged

$$iirr[j] = \begin{cases} 1 & j = 12 \wedge ioapic.sample \\ irr[j] & \text{o.w.} \end{cases}$$

We show:

Lemma 300.

$$n \geq N_{DEVW} \;\rightarrow\; c^{N_{DEVW}}.rr = iirr$$

Proof. Of the steps $[N_{SAMPLE} : N_{DEVW})$ at most one step (N_{SAMPLE}) changes the redirection register at all, and it only changes bit 12 (the delivery status). This is also the only bit changed between the *iirr* and the *irr*. Thus for all bits other than bit 12, the claim follows directly with lemma 299, and we only show the proof for bit 12.

We split cases on whether a disk interrupt is sampled or not.

- *ioapic.sample*: if the I/O APIC samples a disk interrupt, a corresponding step is triggered in ISA

$$s(N_{SAMPLE}) = sample$$

Bit 12 is raised both in hardware and in ISA, and the claim follows

$$c^{N_{DEVW}}.rr.ds = 1$$

$$= iirr.ds$$

- /*ioapic.sample*: no steps between N_{SAMPLE} and N_{DEVW} change the redirection register in ISA, and the delivery status is also not changed between *iirr* and *irr* in hardware. The claim follows with lemma 299

$$c^{N_{DEVW}}.rr.ds = irr.ds \qquad\qquad \text{L 299}$$
$$= iirr.ds$$

$\square$

A simple bookkeeping lemma shows: the final configuration rr' of the redirection register can be obtained by applying the incoming data access to the *iirr*. The proof is omitted.

Lemma 301.

$$rr' = modify(iirr, ioapic.din, ioapic.bw)$$

With this lemma we easily conclude that the final configuration of the redirection register is correct. The proof is omitted.

Lemma 302.

$$n \geq NS' \;\rightarrow\; c^{NS'}.rr = rr'$$

14.3.8 Correctness of Non-Pipelined Components

Assume

$$n = NS'$$

We have to show:

$$m(h') = \ell(c^{NS'}.m) \wedge opc'$$
$$\wedge\; aq(sb(q)'_\pi) = c^{NS'}.p(q).sb$$
$$\wedge\; walks(mmu_I(q)') \cup walks(mmu_E(q)') \subseteq c^{NS'}.tlb(q)$$
$$\wedge\; apic(q)' = c^{NS'}.p(q).apic \wedge opc\text{-}cb(ibus)'$$
$$\wedge\; D' = c^{NS'}.disk \wedge opc\text{-}d'$$
$$\wedge\; rr'_\pi = c^{NS'}.rr$$
$$\wedge\; \forall \hat{n} < n.\; \gamma(c^{\hat{n}}, s(\hat{n}))$$

For the most part these proofs proceed along the same lines as before, using the new lemmas lemmas 296 and 302 in a straightforward way. The only thing which is slightly more involved is the proof for the operating conditions of the interrupt bus. Recall that the interrupt bus now includes a driver controlled by the I/O APIC, and drivers for EOI messages. We have to show for every index $i \in [0 : 2P]$:

$$ibus.req[i] \wedge /ibus.oe[i] \;\rightarrow\; ibus.req[i]'$$
$$ibus.oe[i] \;\rightarrow\; /ibus.req[i]'$$

We do a case split on the index i.

- $i = 2q$: drivers with indices $i = 2q$ are controlled by local APICs for the purpose of delivering IPIs. For these drivers one can recycle the proof from section 12.3.12 with changed indices: instead of using q as the index of request and output enable signals on the bus, one has to use index $i = 2q$.
- $i = 2P$: this driver is controlled by the I/O APIC for the purpose of delivering IPIs. Its control is completely analogous to that of the drivers with indices $2q$, and the operating conditions can be concluded in similar fashion. The main difference is in the proof that a request is not withdrawn before the I/O APIC receives an output enable signal. As before, one needs to show that the delivery status bit is not killed by the processor either through CAS instructions or store buffer steps. For the local APICs this was concluded with the software condition SC_{APIC} and the corresponding invariant for store buffer entries shown in lemma 254. For the I/O APIC one concludes the same instead with the software condition SC_{IO} and lemma 293. We leave the details as a simple exercise.
- $i = 2q + 1$: we first show that requests are not withdrawn before output enable is granted:

$$ibus.req[i] \wedge /ibus.oe[i] \rightarrow ibus.req[i]'$$

Since we do not have output enable, there is no EOI delivery

$$/apic(q).boeb, \quad /apic(q).eoidelivery$$

and thus the intermediate EOI pending register is the same as the EOI pending register

$$apic(q).iEOIp = apic(q).EOIp$$

By construction the EOIp in the next configuration is obtained by possibly *raising* bits in the intermediate EOIp

$$apic(q).EOIp' = \begin{cases} apic(q).iEOIp \vee \ldots & apic(q).eoiw \\ apic(q).iEOIp & \text{o.w.} \end{cases}$$
$$\geq apic(q).iEOIp$$
$$= apic(q).EOIp$$

We conclude: if there is any bit raised in the EOIp in this cycle, there must also be a raised bit in the EOIp in the next cycle

$$1 \in apic(q).EOIp \rightarrow 1 \in apic(q).EOIp'$$

Since there is a request in the current cycle, by construction the *any* bit of the EOI-encoder must be high. With the correctness of the EOI-encoder (lemma 27) we conclude successively:

$$apic(q).eoienc.any, \quad 1 \in apic(q).EOIp, \quad 1 \in apic(q).EOIp', \quad apic(q).eoienc.any'$$

Furthermore, since there is a request the output enable buffer must be low

$$/apic(q).oebuf$$

and since we do not have an output enable signal in the current cycle, it stays low

$$/apic(q).oebuf'$$

The claim follows

$$apic(q).breqb, \quad ibus.req[2q+1]$$

We now show the second claim, that after the output enable signal is granted, the request is withdrawn.

$$ibus.oe[i] \ \rightarrow \ /ibus.req[i]'$$

This follows directly from the construction and our use of the output enable buffer. We conclude successively from the output enable signal:

$$apic(q).boeb, \quad apic(q).oebuf', \quad /apic(q).breqb', \quad /ibus.req[i]'$$

14.3.9 Correctness of Pipelined Registers

For the correctness of pipelined registers only the data memory output for loads from the redirection register is changed at all. The correctness of the data memory output can be concluded analogously to the correctness of the data memory output in the disk chapter (section 13.4.9). We only sketch the proof. Consider thus the instruction $i = I_M^q$ of processor q which is executed in global step number

$$n = pseq(q, I_M^q)$$

As in the proof in the disk chapter we consider only accesses to the device region, which by the software condition SC_{DEV} must be a load instruction. Assume thus

$$acc_{dev}^q \quad \text{and} \quad l_\sigma^{q,I_M^q} \wedge exec_\sigma^{q,I_M^q}$$

We split cases on whether the access goes to the disk or to the redirection register by splitting as in the multiplexer in the construction which selects the device response (fig. 201) on acc_{IO}.

- $/acc_{IO}$: in hardware the response comes from the disk. By the adjusted software condition SC_{DEV} the access in ISA must either go to the disk or the redirection register

$$dacc_\sigma^{q,I_M^q}.a = base_{IO}[31:3] \vee \exists i \in [0:2^{10}). \ dacc_\sigma^{q,I_M^q}.a = base_{HD}[31:3] +_{29} i_{29}$$

In the usual way we obtain that in hardware the same access is used, and that that is also the access on the device bus

$$dacc_\sigma^{q,I_M^q} = dacc_\pi^q = dbus.data$$

Since we have $/acc_{IO}$ and the equality tester used to compute this signal is correct, we conclude successively

$$dacc_\sigma^{q,I_M^q}.a \ne base_{IO}[31:3], \quad \exists i \in [0:2^{10}).\ dacc_\sigma^{q,I_M^q}.a = base_{HD}[31:3] +_{29} i_{29}$$

With this statement the proof can be concluded exactly as before.

- acc_{IO}: analogous to the previous case we conclude with the correctness of equality testers from acc_{IO}

$$dacc_\sigma^{q,I_M^q}.a = base_{IO}[31:3]$$

Thus the data output in ISA is the content of the redirection register

$$dmout_\sigma^{q,I_M^q} = c^n.rr$$

Step n must be in phase 3

$$n \in [N_{REM} : N_{IBUS})$$

in which the redirection register has not been changed yet (cf. fig. 203), and still equals the redirection register in hardware (eq. (89))

$$c^n.rr = c^{NS}.rr \overset{IH}{=} rr_\pi$$

By the construction the device response in hardware comes from the redirection register, and hence the data memory output

$$
\begin{aligned}
dmout_\pi^q &= devr \\
&= ioapic.dout \\
&= rr_\pi \\
&= c^n.rr \\
&= dmout_\sigma^{q,I_M^q}
\end{aligned}
$$

This is the claim.

14.4 Exercises

1. It is straightforward to add more than one device. Each device is linked to its own redirection register. Each redirection register samples interrupts from its device and delivers them as specified above. When an EOI message is delivered, all redirection registers with the same vector are affected. Add a second disk and a redirection register for that disk. Adjust both the specification and the hardware construction accordingly.

2. In this chapter we added a second interface to the interrupt bus to the local APIC. One can also add an internal arbiter to the local APIC which multiplexes between requests from the ICR (for delivery of IPIs) and requests from the EOIp (for delivery of EOI messages). Adjust the construction accordingly. Prove that your updated construction still satisfies the operating conditions of the interrupt bus.

3. Specify and implement a *directed EOI* mechanism. With such a mechanism, an EOI message is not delivered by the APIC after writing to the EOI port. It is instead delivered by the program by writing to a special port of the I/O APIC.

   • Add a register called the *spurious interrupt vector register* to the local APIC. Use bit 12 of this register to indicate whether the local APIC should deliver EOI messages or whether the program will deliver the EOI messages directly: while the bit is zero, while the bit is zero, writes to the EOI port raise a bit in the EOIp. While the bit is raised, writes to the EOI port only lower a bit in the ISR but do not modify the EOIp.

   • Add an EOI register to the I/O APIC. Writing to this register has the side effect of clearing the remote interrupt request register in the I/O APIC.

References

ACH⁺10. E. Alkassar, E. Cohen, M. Hillebrand, M. Kovalev, and W. J. Paul. Verifying shadow page table algorithms. In *Formal Methods in Computer Aided Design*, pages 267–270, Oct 2010.

APST10. Eyad Alkassar, Wolfgang J. Paul, Artem Starostin, and Alexandra Tsyban. Pervasive verification of an OS microkernel - inline assembly, memory consumption, concurrent devices. In *Verified Software: Theories, Tools, Experiments, Third International Conference, VSTTE 2010, Edinburgh, UK, August 16-19, 2010. Proceedings*, pages 71–85, 2010.

BD94. Jerry R. Burch and David L. Dill. Automatic verification of pipelined microprocessor control. In *Proceedings of the 6th International Conference on Computer Aided Verification*, CAV '94, pages 68–80, London, UK, UK, 1994. Springer-Verlag.

Bey05. Sven Beyer. *Putting It All Together — Formal Verification of the VAMP*. PhD thesis, Saarland University, Saarbrücken, 2005.

BJK⁺03. Sven Beyer, Christian Jacobi, Daniel Kroening, Dirk Leinenbach, and Wolfgang J. Paul. Instantiating Uninterpreted Functional Units and Memory System: Functional Verification of the VAMP. In Daniel Geist and Enrico Tronci, editors, *Correct Hardware Design and Verification Methods, Proc. 12th IFIP WG 10.5 Advanced Research Working Conference (CHARME'03)*, L'Aquila, Italy, volume 2860 of *LNCS*, pages 51–65. Springer, 2003.

CS10. Ernie Cohen and Bert Schirmer. From Total Store Order to Sequential Consistency: A Practical Reduction Theorem. In Matt Kaufmann and Lawrence C. Paulson, editors, *Proc. Interactive Theorem Proving, First International Conference (ITP'10)*, Edinburgh, UK, volume 6172 of *LNCS*, pages 403–418. Springer, 2010.

DHP05. Iakov Dalinger, Mark A. Hillebrand, and Wolfgang J. Paul. On the Verification of Memory Management Mechanisms. In Dominique Borrione and Wolfgang J. Paul, editors, *Correct Hardware Design and Verification Methods, Proc. 13th IFIP WG 10.5 Advanced Research Working Conference (CHARME'05)*, Saarbrücken, Germany, volume 3725 of *LNCS*, pages 301–316. Springer, 2005.

GHSW14. Dietmar Gross, Werner Hauger, Jörg Schröder, and Wolfgang A. Wall. *Technische Mechanik 2: Elastostatik*. Springer, 2014.

GHSW16. Dietmar Gross, Werner Hauger, Jörg Schröder, and Wolfgang A. Wall. *Technische Mechanik 1: Statik*. Springer, 2016.

© Springer Nature Switzerland AG 2020
P. Lutsyk et al. (Eds.): A Pipelined Multi-Core Machine, LNCS 9999, pp. 627–628, 2020.
https://doi.org/10.1007/978-3-030-43243-0

KMP14.   M. Kovalev, S.M. Müller, and W.J. Paul. *A Pipelined Multi-core MIPS Machine: Hardware Implementation and Correctness Proof*, volume 9000 of *LNCS*. Springer, 2014.

Kri15.   Wolfgang Krings. *Kleine Baustatik: Grundlagen der Statik und Berechnung von Bauteilen*. Springer, 2015.

Krö01.   Daniel Kröning. *Formal Verification of Pipelined Microprocessors*. PhD thesis, Saarland University, 2001. http://www-wjp.cs.uni-saarland.de/publikationen/Kr01.pdf.

LS09.   Dirk Leinenbach and Thomas Santen. Verifying the Microsoft Hyper-V Hypervisor with VCC. In Ana Cavalcanti and Dennis R. Dams, editors, *FM 2009: Formal Methods*, volume 5850 of *LNCS*, pages 806–809. Springer, 2009.

Lut14.   Petro Lutsyk. Pipelined mips processor with a store buffer. Master's thesis, Saarland University, 2014.

Lut18.   Petro Lutsyk. *Correctness of Multi-Core Processors with Operating System Support*. PhD thesis, Saarland University, Saarbrücken, 2018.

MP00.   Silvia M. Müller and Wolfgang J. Paul. *Computer Architecture, Complexity and Correctness*. Springer, 2000.

Obe17.   Jonas Oberhauser. *Justifying The Strong Memory Semantics of Concurrent High-Level Programming Languages for System Programming*. PhD thesis, Saarland University, Saarbrücken, 2017.

PBLS16.   W.J. Paul, C. Baumann, P. Lutsyk, and S. Schmaltz. *System Architecture: An Ordinary Engineering Discipline*. Springer, 2016.

PS98.   W.J. Paul and P.M. Seidel. On the complexity of booth recoding. In *3rd Conference on Real Numbers and Computers (RNC3)*, volume 3, pages 199–218, 1998.

Sch13.   Sabine Schmaltz. *Towards the Pervasive Formal Verification of Multi-Core Operating Systems and Hypervisors Implemented in C*. PhD thesis, Saarland University, Saarbrücken, 2013.

Sch14.   Oliver Schmitt. Design and verification of memory management units for single-core cpus. Bachelor's thesis, Saarland University, 2014.

Sch16.   Konstantin Schwarz. Correctness of Multicore Machines with Non-Pipelined Processors and Inter-Processor Interrupts. Master's thesis, Saarland University, 2016.

SS86.   Paul Sweazey and Alan J. Smith. A class of compatible cache consistency protocols and their support by the IEEE futurebus. *SIGARCH Computer Architecture News*, 14(2):414–423, may 1986.

VCAD15.   Muralidaran Vijayaraghavan, Adam Chlipala, Arvind, and Nirav Dave. Modular deductive verification of multiprocessor hardware designs. In Daniel Kroening and Corina S. Păsăreanu, editors, *Computer Aided Verification: 27th International Conference, CAV 2015, San Francisco, CA, USA, July 18-24, 2015, Proceedings, Part II*, pages 109–127, Cham, 2015. Springer International Publishing.

Printed in the United States
By Bookmasters